OSWAAL BOOKS®

LEARNING MADE SIMPLE

ONE FOR ALL

GENERAL KNOWLEDGE GUIDE

For all Government Job Exams (UPSC, State PSC, PSUs, SSC, Banking, Railways RRB, Defence NDA/CDS, Teaching, State Gov. & more)

Powered by oswaal.ai LEARNING MADE SMARTER

Smart guidance that helps you learn, practise and improve

This Edition: 1st

ISBN: 9789357289047

Disclaimer

This publication has been prepared by qualified subject matter experts with rigorous editorial review. Despite our best efforts, errors may exist. Readers are encouraged to report any by scanning the QR code on the Table of Contents page so corrections can reach all users.

This book is a study aid. Examination results depend on multiple factors including individual preparation and the specific examination conducted. No particular outcome is guaranteed.

Links in this book provide access to supplementary content. Accessibility depends on internet connectivity and device compatibility. Third-party content linked herein was verified at the time of printing; however, the Publisher does not guarantee that such content will remain accurate, available, or appropriate over time.

Views expressed by individual contributors are their own and do not represent the Publisher's position. The Publisher does not endorse personal opinions or political statements contained herein.

All maps, boundaries, and diagrams are artistic representations for educational reference only and are not geographically or politically authoritative.

For details on personal data processing, see our Privacy Policy at www.oswaalbooks.com/privacy. This publication is governed by the laws of India. Disputes shall be subject to the exclusive jurisdiction of courts in Agra, Uttar Pradesh.

Published by: Oswaal Books and Learning Private Limited, Oswaal House, 1/11, Sahitya Kunj, M.G. Road, Agra-282002 (U.P.), India

contact@oswaalbooks.com

+91-562-2857671

Printed at: SRG Traders Pvt. Ltd., Noida

CONTENTS

Contd...

❑❑❑

Stay Informed: Exam & Recent Improvements

Exam Updates

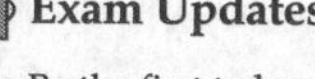

Be the first to know about latest updates and changes! Scan the QR Code to get the latest scoop!

Recent Improvements

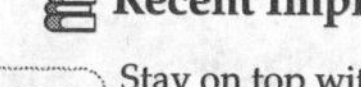

Stay on top with updated materials! Mark important changes in your book. Share feedback to help improve future editions.

Learning is fun when you're always up to date! Keep scanning!

PREFACE

"Knowledge is power and knowledge shared is knowledge multiplied."

In our ever-changing world, staying informed isn't just a plus – it's a must. General Knowledge isn't just data; it's the pulse of wise choices, your ticket to acing exams, and your path to appearing smart wherever you are. Especially in the realm of government exams, where a solid foundation of general knowledge is often the key that unlocks career opportunities, its importance is truly paramount. It serves as the foundation upon which candidates build their expertise, providing them with the insight and confidence needed to excel in competitive examinations, secure coveted government positions, and make a tangible impact in their chosen fields.

Let's explore how this book will add to your knowledge bank:

1. **Keep up with the Latest Trends:** Access up-to-the-minute content covering the most recent developments and trends across diverse subjects.
2. **Organized by Subject:** Easily navigate through subject-specific content with a user-friendly structure.
3. **Dive Deep with Comprehensive Explanations:** Delve into in-depth explainers offering detailed insights into key concepts, terms, and theories.
4. **Visualize Knowledge with Infographics:** Use of graphs, photos, tables makes this book easy to understand.
5. **Historical Milestones at Your Fingertips:** Stay on top of historical events, scientific breakthroughs, and critical timelines.
6. **Government Policies Unveiled:** Explore major government policies, initiatives, and schemes, and understand their objectives and impacts.
7. **Think Globally:** Broaden your horizons with a global perspective, including insights into international relations and geopolitical events.
8. **Notable Figures in the Limelight:** Meet key personalities in politics, science, literature, arts, and other fields.
9. **Exam Oriented Approach:** Important one-liners which makes this book easy to revise in exam time

We owe immense gratitude to our dedicated team of teachers who have worked tirelessly to compile this treasure trove of knowledge.

As you embark on this enriching journey with Oswaal GK Guide, remember that knowledge is power, and it's yours for the taking. So, without further ado, grab your copy today and simplify your learning.

Knowledge is waiting; let's dive in!

Warm regards,

Team Oswaal Books

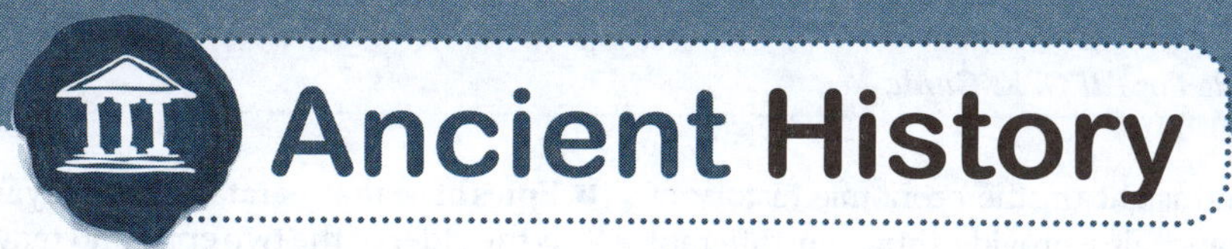

Ancient History

Unit-1: Pre-Historic Times

Introduction

Definition of History

- History is the study of the past in relation to present developments and future hopes.
- History is a chronological record of significant events.
- A branch of knowledge that records and explains past events.
- The word History is derived from the Greek word "historia" originally meant inquiry, the act of seeking knowledge, as well as the knowledge that results from inquiry.
- The German historian "Leopold Von Ranke" is known as The Father of Modern source-based History.
- "Herodotus" was first called the Father of History because he was the first historian to systematically record the events that happened.
- **Voltaire:** "History is nothing but a pack of tricks we play on the dead".
- **John Jacob Anderson:** "History is a narration of the events which have happened among mankind, including an account of the rise and fall of nations, as well as of other great changes which have affected the political and social condition of the human race".
- **James Joyce:** "History, Stephen said, is a nightmare from which I am trying to awake".
- **NCERT:** "History is the scientific study of past happenings in all their aspects, in the life of a social group, in the light of present happenings".
- **Jawaharlal Nehru:** "History is the story of Man's struggle through the ages against Nature and the elements; against wild beasts and the jungle and some of his own kind who have tried to keep him down and to exploit him for their own benefit".

Concept of B.C. and A.D.

- The terms "A.D." and "B.C." basically belong to Christianity.
- "A.D." stands for *anno domini* and it refers specifically to the birth of Jesus Christ (in the year of the Lord).
- "B.C." stands for "before Christ" and refers specifically to before the birth of Jesus Christ.
- In recent years, an alternative form of B.C./A.D. has gained traction. Many publications use "C.E.", or "common era", and "B.C.E.", or "before common era" in order to make non-Christians.

History Glossary

- **Anachronism:** An artifact that belongs to another time.
- **Chronological order:** Listing events in the order that they occurred.
- **Era/period:** A period of time that is joined by historical factors. For example, Industrial era.
- **Year:** A unit of time equal to 12 months.
- **Decade:** A unit of time that is equal to 10 years.
- **Century:** A unit of time that is equal to 100 years.
- **Millennium:** A unit of time that is equal to 1000 years.

Phases of Indian history

- The phases of Indian history are mentioned below:
  - **Ancient History:** Prehistoric to 647 A.D. (From Stone Age to death of Harshavardhana)
  - **Medieval History:** 647 A.D. to 1757 A.D. (Death of Harshavardhana to Battle of Plassey)
  - **Modern History:** 1757 A.D. to 1947 A.D. (Battle of Plassey to Indian independence)

Pre Historic Times

- History (from the Greek word – Historia, meaning "inquiry", knowledge acquired by investigation) is the study of the past. History is an umbrella term that relates to past events as well as the discovery, collection, organisation, presentation and interpretation of information about these events.
- It is divided into prehistory, protohistory and history.

Prehistory, Protohistory and History

Prehistory	Protohistory	History
• Prehistory is the time during the development of human culture before the appearance of the written word. • Information about prehistoric times is collected by archaeologists by excavating and studying the remains. • For instance, the Stone Age	• Protohistory is the time just before the earliest recorded history. • Written records about protohistoric times are few and the script is yet to be decoded. • For instance, the Indus Valley Civilization	• History is a continuos, typically chronological, record of events. • Information about historic time can be collected through various sources- written as well as archeological. • For instance, the Vedic Age

Construction of Ancient Indian History

- The sources which help in reconstructing history are:
  - Non-literary sources - which include coins, material remains, inscriptions etc.
  - Literary sources – which include religious literature & secular literature.

Non-Literary Sources

- **Coins:** Ancient Indian currency came in the form of coins as paper was not in existence. The earliest coins found in India had only a few symbols, punch-marked coins made of silver & copper, but later coins mentioned the names of the kings, gods, dates, etc. The locations where they were discovered show the area in which they circulated. This allowed the history of multiple reigning dynasties to be reconstructed, especially during Indo-Greek rule who came to India from Northern Afghanistan and ruled India in the 2nd and 1st

BCE. Coins provide insight on the economic history of different dynasties and also provide input on different parameters involved such as the script, art, religion of that time. It also assists in understanding the advancements achieved in metallurgy, science, and technology. (The study of coins is called Numismatics).

- **Archaeology/Material remains:** Archaeology is the study that deals with the methodical excavation of old mounds in successive layers in order to establish a concept of the material lives of the people. Material remnants found during excavation and exploration are submitted to a variety of studies. Their dates are fixed according to radiocarbon dating. For example, excavated sites belonging to the Harappan period help us to know about the life of the people who lived in that era. Similarly, the Megaliths (graves in south India) throw light on the life of the people living in the Deccan and South India before 300 BCE. The study of plant remnants, particularly pollen analysis, reveals the history of climate and vegetation.
- **Inscriptions/Prashastis:** (Epigraphy is the study and interpretation of ancient inscriptions.). Engraved writings on hard surfaces such as stone and metals such as copper, which generally record certain achievements, thoughts, royal commands, and choices, aid in comprehending diverse faiths and administrative systems of that era. For example, inscriptions detailing state policy issued by Emperor Ashoka and inscriptions recording the land grants by Satavahanas, Kings of the Deccan.
- **Foreign accounts:** Foreign accounts can enhance indigenous writing. The Greek, Chinese, and Roman travellers to India, whether as explorers or religious converts, left behind a comprehensive record of our history. Some of the notables among them were:
  - Megasthenes, a Greek ambassador, wrote "Indica" and supplied vital information on Mauryan society and governance.
  - "The Periplus of the Erythrean Sea" and "Ptolemy's Geography" both written in Greek, give valuable information about the ports and commodities of trade between India and the Roman Empire.
  - Fa-Hein Faxien (337 CE – 422 CE), a Buddhist traveller, left a vivid account of the age of the Guptas.
  - Hsuan-Tsang, a Buddhist pilgrim, visited India and described India under the reign of King Harshavardhana, as well as the magnificence of the Nalanda University.

Literary Sources

- **Religious Literature:** Religious literature sheds information on the ancient Indian period's social, economic, and cultural situations. Some of the sources are:
  - **The Four Vedas:** The Vedas may be assigned to 1500 – 500 BCE. The Rigveda mainly contains prayers while the later Vedic texts (Samaveda, Yajurveda, Atharvaveda) comprise not only prayers but rituals, magic and mythological stories.
  - **Upanishads:** The philosophical discussions on "Atma" and "Paramatma" are found in the Upanishads (Vedanta).
  - **Epics of Mahabharata and Ramayana:** The Mahabharata is the elder of the two epics and may depict the condition of events from the 10th century BCE to the 4th century CE. It originally had 8800 verses (named the Jaya Samhita). The final compilation increased the number of verses to 100,000, which became known as the Mahabharata or Satasahasri Samhita. It contains narrative, descriptive and didactic material. The Ramayana originally consisted of 12000 verses which were later raised to 24000. This epic also has its didactic portions which were added later.
  - **Sutras:** Sutras include ritual literature such as Shrauta Sutras (which include sacrifices and royal coronation) and Grihya Sutras (which cover household rituals such as birth, name, marriage, death, and so on).
  - **Buddhist religious texts:** The early Buddhist writings were written in Pali and are often referred to as the Tripitaka. (three baskets) – Sutta Pitaka, Vinaya Pitaka, and Abhidhamma Pitaka. These books shed essential information on the era's social and economic situations. They also make allusions to political events from the Buddha's time.
  - **Jaina's religious texts:** The Jain texts, commonly called "angas", were written in the Prakrit language, and contain philosophical concepts of the Jainas. They contain several manuscripts that aid in the reconstruction of Mahavira's political history in eastern Uttar Pradesh and Bihar. The Jain writings make several references to commerce and traders.

Secular Literature

There is also a large body of secular literature such as:

- **Dharmashastras/Law books:** These specify the responsibilities of the several varnas, as well as the monarchs and their officers. They provide the rules for holding, selling, and inheriting property. They also impose penalties on those who commit theft, murder, and other crimes.
- **Arthashastra:** Arthashastra of Kautilya reflects the state of society and economy in the age of the Mauryas.
- **Literary work of Kalidasa:** Kalidasa's works include kavyas and plays, the most notable of which is Abhijnanasakuntalam. They are not only creative creations, but they also provide insight into the social and cultural life of northern and central India during the Gupta era.
- **Rajatarangini:** This is a well-known book written by Kalhana that covers the social and political life of Kashmir in the 12th century CE.
- **Charitas/Biographies:** Charitas are the biographies written by court poets in admiration of their rulers, such as Harshacharita, written by Banabhatta in praise of King Harshavardhana.
- **Sangam literature:** This is the earliest South Indian literature, created by a group of poets (Sangam), and it contains vital information on the social, economic, and political lives of people living in deltaic Tamil Nadu. This Tamil literature contains literary gems such as 'Silappadikaram' and 'Manimekalai'.

Prehistoric Periods in India – According to Tools

Ancient history can be divided into different periods according to the tools used by people then.

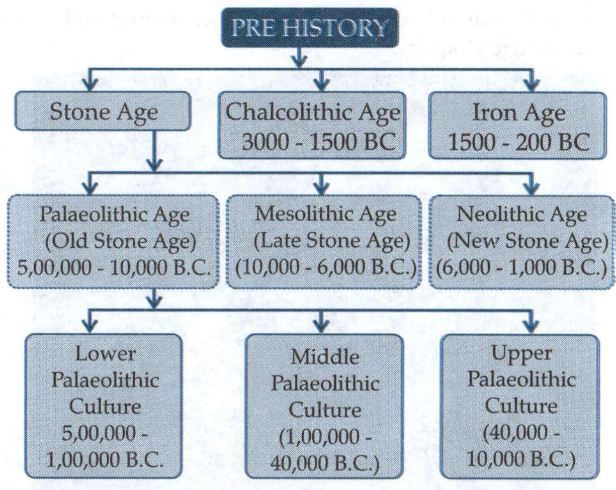

Stone Age

- The Stone Age is the prehistoric period, i.e., the period before the development of the script, therefore, the main source of information for this period is the archaeological excavations. Robert Bruce Foote is the archaeologist who discovered the first Paleolithic tool in India, the Pallavaram handaxe.

Palaeolithic Age (Old Stone Age)

- **The Paleolithic Period** is an ancient cultural stage of human technological development characterized by the creation and use of rudimentary chipped stone tools.
- **The Paleolithic Period** was also characterized by the manufacture of small sculptures (e.g., carved stone statuettes of women, clay figurines of animals, and other bone and ivory carvings) and paintings, incised designs, and reliefs on cave walls.

Main Characteristics of the Paleolithic Age

- Paleolithic humans in India lived in the open air, river valleys, caves, and rock shelters.
- They were foragers, eating wild fruits and vegetables and survived on hunting.
- There was no understanding of homes, pottery, or agriculture. It wasn't until later that they found fire.
- In the upper Paleolithic age, there is evidence of art in the form of paintings.
- Humans used unpolished, rough stones like hand axes, choppers, blades, burins and scrapers.

  Palaeolithic men are also known as 'Quartzite' men in India because their stone tools were composed of quartzite, a hard rock.

Paleolithic Period	Notable Features	Important Sites
Lower Paleolithic	The Lower Paleolithic age in India is characterized by the emergence of early stone tool industries, such as the Soan Culture and the Acheulean industry. These industries represent the earliest known human tool-making techniques. Hominins crafted simple tools, including handaxes and cleavers, for various purposes like hunting, butchering animals, processing plants, and shaping materials.	• **Bhimbetka:** Located in Madhya Pradesh, Bhimbetka is a UNESCO World Heritage Site known for its extensive rock shelters containing rock paintings dating back to the Lower Paleolithic period. • **Attirampakkam:** Situated in Tamil Nadu, Attirampakkam is an important archaeological site revealing Acheulean tools and evidence of early human habitation dating back to around 1.5 million years ago.
Middle Paleolithic	The Middle Paleolithic age in India is associated with the Middle Paleolithic culture, characterized by the presence of Levallois technology and the use of fire by early hominins. Middle Paleolithic India was inhabited by archaic humans and early Homo sapiens.	• **Bhimbetka:** In addition to its Lower Paleolithic significance, Bhimbetka also contains Middle Paleolithic archaeological deposits. • **Jwalapuram:** Situated in Andhra Pradesh, Jwalapuram is an archaeological site with Middle Paleolithic artifacts, including stone tools and fossils.
Upper Paleolithic	The Upper Paleolithic age in India marks significant cultural advancements, including the emergence of advanced stone tool industries. Blade technologies, backed tools, and microliths became prevalent during this period. This period also witnessed the development of symbolic and artistic expressions, as seen in the production of intricate cave art and personal adornments. Homo sapiens became the dominant hominin species during this time.	• **Patne:** Situated in Maharashtra, Patne is an archaeological site revealing Upper Paleolithic stone tools, bone artifacts, and animal remains.

Mesolithic Period (Middle Stone Age)

- Mesolithic is formed from two Greek words:'meso' and 'lithic'. 'Meso' means middle in Greek, while 'lithic' implies stone. As a result, the Mesolithic period of prehistory is often known as the 'Middle Stone Age'.

- The Holocene era includes both the Mesolithic and Neolithic stages. There was an increase in temperature throughout this time period, and the environment got warmer, resulting in the melting of glaciers and changes in flora and fauna.

Characteristic Features of the Mesolithic Era

- Initially, humans of this era subsisted on hunting, fishing, and food collection, but they subsequently tamed animals and cultivated plants, opening the path for agriculture.
- The first animal to be domesticated was the wild ancestor of the dog. Sheep and goats were the most common domesticated animals.
- The Mesolithic people lived in semi-permanent communities as well as caves and open areas.
- The people of this era believed in life after death, and hence, they buried the dead with food items and other goods.
- Microliths were the defining tools of this epoch, being small stone tools formed of crypto-crystalline silica, chalcedony, or chert in both geometrical and nongeometrical forms. They were not only used as tools but were also used to make composite tools, spearheads, arrowheads, and sickles after hafting them on wooden or bone handles. These microliths enabled the Mesolithic man to hunt smaller animals and birds.
- The Mesolithic men started to wear clothes made of animal skin.
- The Mesolithic people were art enthusiasts who pioneered rock art. The subject matter of these paintings was largely wild creatures, although hunting scenes, dance, and food gathering were also shown. These rock drawings provide insight into the evolution of religious practises while also reflecting the gendered distribution of employment.
- The first human colonization of the Ganga Plains happened during this period.

Important Mesolithic Sites

- Bagor in Rajasthan is one of India's largest and best-documented Mesolithic sites. Bagor is located on the Kothari River, where microliths, animal bones, and shells have been discovered.
- Adamgarh in Madhya Pradesh provides the earliest evidence for the domestication of animals.
- There are around 150 Mesolithic rock art sites in India, with a high concentration in Central India, including the Bhimbetka caves in Madhya Pradesh, Kharwar, Jaora, and Kathotia in Madhya Pradesh, Sundargarh and Sambalpur in Odisha, and Ezhuthu Guha in Kerala.
- Microliths have also been found in some valleys of river Tapi, Sabarmati, Narmada, and Mahi.
- Important Mesolithic sites include Langhnaj in Gujarat and Biharanpur in West Bengal. Wild animal bones (rhinoceros, blackbuck, etc.) have been discovered at Langhnaj. These sites have yielded many human skeletons and a considerable quantity of microliths.
- Though pottery is absent at most Mesolithic sites, they have been found in Langhnaj (Gujarat) and in the Kaimur region of Mirzapur (Uttar Pradesh).

Tool Types and Technology

- **Microliths** are the predominant and the most common tool types of this cultural phase.
  - Microliths are described in terms of **geometric and non-geometric shapes**.

- Geometric ones are types such as trapeze, triangle, lunate or crescent. The nongeometric types are named by the nature of blunting of the back, such as partly, fully or obliquely blunted blades or after their functions such as scraper, point, knife, blade, awl, burin and borer.
- These were used as composite tools for plant gathering and harvesting, slicing, grating, plant-fibre processing.
- Another type of tool used by the Mesolithic people is called the Macrolith.
  - These were bigger than Microliths, and were a continuation of the Upper Palaeolithic types such as scrapers.
  - These are considered as heavy-duty tools.
- Bone and antler tools are yet another category of tools used by the Mesolithic people.

Neolithic Period (New Stone Age)

The name Neolithic is derived from the Greek words 'neo' (new) and 'lithic' (stone). As a result, the name "Neolithic Age" alludes to the "New Stone Age". It is also known as the 'Neolithic revolution' because it brought about many significant improvements in man's social and economic existence. Man evolved from a food gatherer to a food producer throughout the Neolithic period.

Characteristic Features of the Neolithic Age

- **Tools and Weapons:** In addition to polished stone tools, the inhabitants employed microlithic blades. Celts were notably essential for grinding and polished hand axes. They also employed bone tools and weaponry like as needles, scrapers, borers, arrowheads, and so on. The adoption of new polished tools improved humans' ability to grow, hunt, and undertake other tasks.
- **Agriculture:** The people of the Neolithic age cultivated land and grew fruits and corn like ragi and horse gram (kulati). They also domesticated cattle, sheep and goats.
- **Pottery:** With the introduction of agriculture, humans were needed to store their food grains in addition to cooking and eating the produce. That is why it is stated that pottery appeared on a wide scale during this period. The pottery of this period was classified under greyware, black-burnished ware, and mat impressed ware. In the initial stages of the Neolithic age, handmade pottery was made but later on, foot wheels were used to make pots.
- **Housing and Settled Life:** The people of the Neolithic age lived in rectangular or circular houses which were

made of mud and reeds. Neolithic man could also build boats and spin cotton, wool, and weave textiles. The Neolithic people lived a more stable life and prepared the groundwork for the emergence of civilization.

- Neolithic communities generally settled near rivers, lakes, fertile valleys, and other areas suitable for agriculture and animal husbandry, since they were fully reliant on stone weapons and tools.

Important Neolithic Sites

- **Koldihwa and Mahagara (lying south of Prayagraj, Uttar Pradesh):** This site has traces of circular huts as well as rudimentary handcrafted ceramics. Koldihwa provides some of the earliest evidence of rice cultivation in the Indian subcontinent.
- **Mehrgarh (Balochistan, Pakistan):** The oldest Neolithic settlement, where people lived in homes made of sun-dried bricks and grew crops such as barely and wheat.
- **Burzahom (Kashmir):** Domestic dogs were buried beside their owners in their tombs; humans lived in pits and utilised polished stone and bone implements.
- **Gufkral (Kashmir):** This neolithic site is known for pit dwelling, stone tools, and house graveyards.
- **Chirand (Bihar):** The Neolithic men used tools and weapons made of bones.
- **Piklihal, Brahmagiri, Maski, Takkalakota, Hallur (Karnataka):** The people were cattle herders. They domesticated sheep and goats. Ash mounds have been found.
- **Belan Valley (which is located on the northern spurs of the Vindhyas and middle part of Narmada valley):** All the three phases i.e., Paleolithic, Mesolithic and Neolithic ages are found in the sequence.

Chalcolithic Age (Stone Copper Age)

The Chalcolithic Age saw the introduction of metal tools alongside stone implements. Copper was the first metal utilised. The Chalcolithic period was generally associated with the pre-Harappan period, but it emerges in many regions of the nation following the end of the bronze Harappan culture.

Characteristics of the Chalcolithic Age

- **Agriculture & cattle rearing:** During the stone-copper period, mankind tamed animals and produced food crops. They raised cattle, sheep, goats, pigs, and buffaloes and hunted deer. It is unclear if they were familiar with the horse or not. The people reared cattle, sheep, goats, pigs, and buffaloes and supplemented agriculture with hunting and fishing. The people of the Chalcolithic phase produced wheat and rice, they also cultivated bajra. They also produced several pulses such as lentil (masur), black gram, green gram, and grass pea. Cotton was grown in the black cotton soil of the Deccan, whereas ragi, bajra, and other millets were grown in the lower Deccan. The people of the stone-copper era in the eastern areas subsisted mostly on fish and rice, which is still a popular diet in that section of the nation.
- **Pottery:** The inhabitants of the stone-copper phase utilised many forms of pottery, one of which is known as black and red pottery and appears to have been commonly used at the time. Also popular was ochre-colored earthenware. The potter's wheel was utilised, and white linear motifs were painted.
- **Rural settlements:** The Stone Age inhabitants were known for their rural communities and were unfamiliar with charred bricks. They resided in mud brick-built thatched homes. This period also saw the emergence of societal inequities, with leaders living in rectangular mansions and commoners in round huts. Their villages consisted of more than 35 houses of different sizes, circular or rectangular in shape. The Chalcolithic economy is considered as a village economy.
- **Art and Craft:** The Chalcolithic people were accomplished coppersmiths. They mastered the trade of copper smelting and were also skilled stone masons. They were well-versed in spinning and weaving, as well as the technique of making fabric. They did not, however, understand the art of writing.
- **Worship:** The chalcolithic sites have yielded little clay representations of earth deities. As a result, they may be said to have honoured the Mother Goddess. Stylized bull terracottas from Malwa and Rajasthan reveal that the bull was used as a sacred cult.
- **Infant mortality:** As evidenced by the burial of a significant number of youngsters in West Maharashtra, infant mortality was high among the Chalcolithic people. Despite being a food-producing economy, infant mortality was quite high. The Chalcolithic social and economic system did not favour lifespan.
- **Jewellery:** The Chalcolithic people loved ornamentation and decorating. The women wore shell and bone decorations and carried delicately crafted combs in their hair. They manufactured beads of semi-precious stones such as carnelian, steatite, and quartz crystal.

Important Chalcolithic Sites

- **Ahar (Banas valley, South Eastern Rajasthan):** This region's residents conducted smelting and metallurgy, and they provided copper implements to other modern societies. Rice was grown in this area.
- **Gilund (Banas valley, Rajasthan):** Stone blade industry was discovered here.
- **Daimabad (Ahmednagar, Maharashtra):** The Godavari Valley's most important Jorwe culture site. It is well-known for recovering bronze items like as bronze rhinoceros, elephants, a two-wheeled chariot with a rider, and a buffalo.
- **Malwa (Madhya Pradesh):** The settlements of Malwa culture are mostly located on the Narmada and its tributaries. It provides evidence of the richest chalcolithic ceramics and also spindle whorls.
- **Kayatha (Madya Pradesh):** Kayatha culture settlements were largely concentrated around the Chambal River and its tributaries. Mud-plastered floors were discovered in houses, as well as pre-Harappan components in pottery and copper artefacts with sharp cutting edges.
- **Chirand, Senuar, Sonpur (Bihar), Mahishdal (West Bengal):** These are the prominent chalcolithic sites in these states.
- **Songaon, Inamgaon and Nasik (Maharashtra):** Large mud houses with ovens and circular pit houses have been discovered here.
- **Navdatoli (on Narmada):** It was one of the largest chalcolithic settlements in the country. It was spread over 10 hectares and cultivated almost all food grains.

- **Nevasa (Jorwe, Maharashtra) and Eran (Madhya Pradesh):** These sites are known for their non-Harappan culture.

Painted Grey Ware (PGW)

- Painted Grey Ware (PGW) is a very fine, smooth, and even-coloured grey pottery, with a thin fabric. It was made out of well-worked, very high-quality clay.
- PGW seems to have been a deluxe ware, forming a very small percentage of the total pottery assemblage at the levels at which these were found.
- The dates of the PGW culture range from 1200–600 BCE, and the sites show a wide geographical distribution, stretching from the Himalayan foothills to the Malwa plateau in central India, and from the Bahawalpur region of Pakistan to Kaushambi near Allahabad in Uttar Pradesh.

  Apart from the plains, it has been found in the hilly regions of Kumaon and Garhwal. Sporadic potsherds were found at a few places like Vaishali in Bihar, Lakhiyopur in Sind and Ujjain in Madhya Pradesh.

Unit-2: Indus Valley Civilization

- Indus Valley Civilization was the first major civilization in South Asia, which spread across a vast area of land in present-day India and Pakistan (around 12 lakh sq.km).
- The time period of the mature Indus Valley Civilization is estimated between B.C. 2600- B.C.1900 i.e. For 700 years. But early Indus Valley Civilization had existed even before BC.2700.
- Around 2,500 B.C., IVC flourished in the western section of South Asia, in what is now Pakistan and Western India.
- The Harappan civilisation covered the largest geographical area among the four great Bronze Age civilisations of Egypt, Mesopotamia, India, and China.
- The Archaeological Department of India conducted excavations in the Indus Valley in the 1920s, unearthing the ruins of two ancient towns, Mohenjodaro and Harappa.
- In 1924, John Marshall, Director-General of the ASI, proclaimed to the world the discovery of a new civilisation in the Indus Valley.

Important sites of Harappa Civilization

Site	Discovered by	Present Location	Findings
Harappa	Daya Ram Sahini in 1921	Located on the banks of the Ravi River in the Montgomery district of Punjab (Pakistan).	The fortified wall, the R-37 cemetery, Quarters for workers, Copper bullock cart specimen, Cubical Limestone Weight Human anatomy sandstone sculptures, coffin burials (discovered only in Harrapa).
Mohenjodaro (Mound of Dead)	R. D. Banerjee in 1922	Situated on the Bank of River Indus in Larkana district of Punjab (Pakistan).	A small fragment of cotton, Bronze dancing girl, Well known for the Great Bath, Unicorn Seals (Most numbers of it in here), Seal of a man with deers, elephants, tiger and rhinos around- Considered to be Pashupati Seal), Steatite statue of beard man, Bronze buffalo.
Sutkagendor	Aurel Stein in 1929	In southwestern Balochistan province, Pakistan on the Dast river	Trade point between Harappa and Babylon situated on natural rock, Flint Blades, Stone Vessels, Stone Arrowheads, Shell Beads, Pottery, Bacteria-Margiana Archaeological Complex (BMAC) associated Copper-Bronze Disc.
Chanhudaro	N. G. Majumdar in 1931	Sindh on the Indus River	A manufacturing site during the Harappan period, Bangle Factory, the footprint of a dog chasing a cat, Cart with a seated driver, Bead makers shop.
Amri	N. G. Majumdar in 1929	On the bank of Indus river	Antelope evidence

Kalibangan	Amlanand Ghose in 1953	Rajasthan on the bank of the Ghaggar River	Mud-brick fortification, Evidence of earliest datable earthquake, Discovery of a plough field, Camel's bone, Fire alters, Furrowed land, Copper Ox, Evidence of an earthquake.
Lothal	R. Rao in 1954	Gujarat on the Bhogva River near the Gulf of Khambhat	• Fire altars • Chess playing • Rice husk • One of the earliest known dockyards in the world. • Dockyard
Surkotada	J. P. Joshi in 1964	Gujarat	• Bones of horses • Beads
Banawali	R. S. Bisht in 1974	Hisar district of Haryana	• Evidence of both pre-Harappan and Harappan culture • Beads • Barley
Dholavira	R. S. Bisht in 1989-90	Gujarat in Rann of Kachchh	• Water harnessing system • Water reservoir

Phases of IVC

- Three phases of IVC are:
  - the Early Harappan Phase from 3300 to 2600 BCE
  - the Mature Harappan Phase from 2600 to 1900 BCE
  - the Late Harappan Phase from 1900 to 1300 BCE
- The Early Harappan Phase is linked to the Hakra Phase, which was discovered in the Ghaggar-Hakra River Valley.
- The Indus script's earliest specimens date back to 3000 BC.This stage is distinguished by centralised power and a more urban quality of life.
- This phase stands characterized by centralized authority and an increasingly urban quality of life.
- Trade networks had been developed, and there is also evidence of agricultural production. Peas, sesame seeds, dates, cotton, and other crops were farmed during the time.
- Kot Diji represents the phase leading up to Mature Harappan Phase.
- By 2600 BC, the Indus Valley Civilization had entered into a mature stage.
- The early Harappan societies, such as Harappa and Mohenjodaro in Pakistan and Lothal in India, were growing into enormous urban centres.
- The traces of the Indus River Valley Civilization's steady decline are said to have begun around 1800 BC, and by 1700 BC, most of the towns had been abandoned.
- However, several features of the Ancient Indus Valley Civilization may be seen in succeeding societies.
- Archaeological data indicates the persistence of the Late Harappan culture till 1000-900 BC.

Institutions

- There have been very few written objects unearthed in the Indus valley, and experts have yet to understand the Indus script.
- As a result, determining the nature of the Indus Valley Civilization's state and institutions is challenging.
- No temples have been discovered at any of the Harappan sites. As a result, the prospect of priests dominating Harappa can be ruled out.
- Harappa was possibly ruled by a class of merchants.
- If we are looking for a centre of authority or images of persons in power, archaeological records do not give immediate answers.
  - Some archaeologists believe that Harappan culture had no rulers and that everyone had equal rank.
  - Another idea contends that there was no single monarch, but rather a collection of rulers who represented each of the metropolitan centres.

Religion

- Numerous clay figures of women have been discovered at Harappa. A plant is represented sprouting out of a woman's embryo in one figure.
  - Terracotta female figurines have been interpreted by some scholars as representations of a fertility or mother goddess.
- The masculine god is shown on a seal with three horned heads, seated in the stance of a yogi.
  - This god is surrounded by elephants, tigers, rhinoceroses, and a buffalo beneath his throne. Two deer emerge at his feet. Pashupati Mahadeva is the name of the deity represented.
- Numerous stone phallus and female sex organ symbols have been discovered.
- The Indus region's inhabitants also revered plants and animals.
- The unicorn is the most common animal depicted on Harappan seals and appears to be a mythical creature.
- Amulets have also been found in large numbers.

Town Planning and Structures

- The Harappan culture was distinguished by its urban planning system.
- Both Harappa and Mohenjodaro had their own citadels or acropolis, which were likely held by members of the governing elite.

- Below the citadel in each city was a lower town with brick buildings occupied by the ordinary people.
- The striking feature about the layout of dwellings in cities is that they adhered to the grid pattern.
- Granaries were a significant feature of Harappan towns.
- The use of burnt bricks in the Harappan cities is remarkable because in the contemporary buildings of Egypt mainly dried bricks were used.
- The drainage system of Mohenjodaro was very impressive.
- Every big or little residence in practically every city has its own courtyard and bathroom.
- In Kalibangan, many houses had their wells.
- At sites such as Dholavira and Lothal (Gujarat), the entire settlement was fortified, and sections within the town were also separated by walls.

Agriculture

- The Harappan communities, which were generally located on the river plains, produced enough food grains.
- There was wheat, barley, rai, peas, sesame, lentil, chickpea, and mustard production. Millets have also been discovered in Gujarat. While rice was used infrequently.
- The Indus people were the earliest people to produce cotton.
- While the prevalence of agriculture is indicated by finds of grain, it is more difficult to reconstruct actual agricultural practices.
- Representations on seals and terracotta art suggest that the bull was known, and archaeologists believe that oxen were also utilised for ploughing.
- Most Harappan sites are in semi-arid areas where irrigation was most likely necessary for cultivation.
- Canal traces have been discovered at the Harappan site of Shortughai in Afghanistan, but not in Punjab or Sindh.
- Although the Harappans conducted agriculture, they also raised animals on a massive scale.
- Evidence of the horse comes from a superficial level of Mohenjodaro and from a doubtful terracotta figurine from Lothal. In any case the Harappan culture was not horse-centred.

Economy

- The presence of numerous seals, regular writing, and controlled weights and measures across a large region attests to the importance of commerce in the life of the Indus people.
- The Harappans carried on considerable trade in stone, metal, shell, etc.
- Metal money was not used and trade was carried by barter system.
- They practised navigation on the coast of the Arabian Sea.
- They had established a commercial colony in northern Afghanistan, which clearly aided commerce with Central Asia.
- They also traded with people living around the Tigris and Euphrates rivers.
- The Harappans carried on long-distance trade in lapis lazuli; which may have contributed to the social prestige of the ruling class.

Crafts

- The Harappans were well-versed in the production and application of bronze.
- Copper was acquired from Rajasthan's Khetri copper mines, while tin was likely transported from Afghanistan.
- Textile imprints have also been discovered on a number of artefacts.
- The massive brick construction suggests that brick-laying was a valuable skill. This also confirms the existence of a mason class.
- The Harappans were skilled at boat-building, bead-making, and seal-making. Terracotta production was also a significant skill.
- The goldsmiths made jewellery of silver, gold and precious stones.
- The potter's wheel was in full swing, and the Harappans created their own distinctive pottery, which was glossy and shining.

Decline of the Indus Valley Civilization

- The IVC died out circa 1800 BCE, although the causes for its death are still contested.
- According to one version, the Indo-European tribe Aryans invaded and subjugated the IVC.
  - Various elements of IVC culture have been identified in succeeding cultures, indicating that the civilisation did not disappear suddenly as a result of invasion.
- On the other hand, many scholars believe natural factors are behind the decline of the IVC.
  - The natural factors could be geological and climatic.
  - It is believed that the Indus Valley region experienced several tectonic disturbances which caused earthquakes. It also changed courses of rivers or dried them up.
  - Another natural reason might be changes in patterns of rainfall.
  - According to a research conducted by IIT Kharagpur and the Archaeological Survey of India, a weaker monsoon may have contributed to the fall of the Indus Valley Civilization.

Unit-3: Vedic Age

- The age of the Vedic Civilization was between 1500 BC and 600 BC. This is the next major civilization after the Indus Valley Civilization. This period is named after the Vedas, which serve as its primary source of knowledge. The Vedic Age started from the time of the Aryans or Indo-Aryans.

The Aryans

- The Aryans fall in the group of semi-nomadic pastoral people.
- The word Aryan is taken from the Sanskrit word "arya" which means noble, not ordinary.

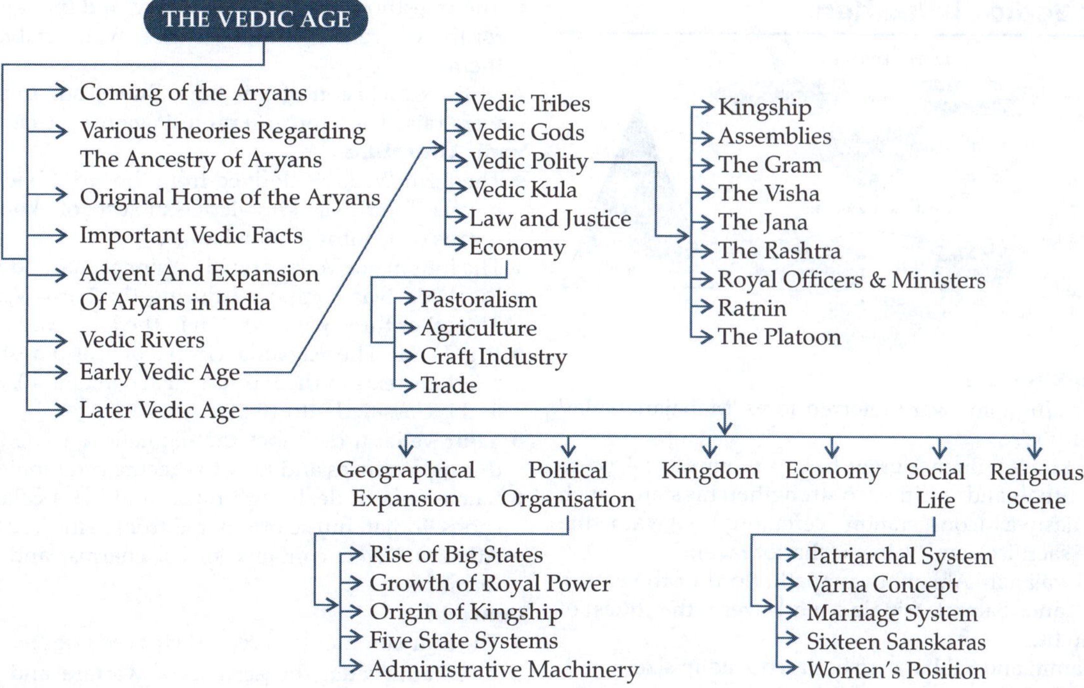

- Different researchers have different ideas on the Aryans' ancestral country. Some claim to be from the Central Asian region near the Caspian Sea. Max Muller proposed this Central Asia idea. Others believe they originated in the Russian Steppes. But Bal Gangadhar Tilak was of the opinion that the Aryans came from the Arctic region following their astronomical calculations.
- Sanskrit, an Indo-European language was their language for communication.
- They lived in rural, semi-nomadic life in contrast to the Indus Valley people who were generally urbanised.
- Many historians believe Indo-Aryan-speaking groups entered northwestern India through passes in the Hindu Kush region, including routes near the Khyber Pass.

Vedic Civilization

- Originally, the Aryans dwelt in the "Sapta Sindhu" (Land of the Seven Rivers). Sindhu (Indus), Vipash (Beas), Vitasta (Jhelum), Parushni (Ravi), Asikni (Chenab), Shutudri (Satluj), and Saraswati were the seven rivers.
- We can divide the timelines of the Vedic Period are given below:
  - Early Vedic Civilization or Rig Vedic Period (1500 BC – 1000 BC)
  - Later Vedic Civilization or Painted Grey Ware Phase (1000 BC – 600 BC)

Early Vedic Civilization or Rig Vedic Period (1500 BC – 1000 BC)

Political Structure:

- The administration is monarchical, with a king known as Rajan.
- **Patriarchal families:** Jana was the largest social unit in Rig Vedic times.
- **Social grouping:** Kula (family) – grama – vish – jana.
- Sabhas and Samitis were tribal assemblies. Tribal kingdoms include the Bharatas, Matsyas, Yadus, and Purus.

Social Structure

- Women held an honourable status. They were permitted to participate in Sabhas and Samitis. There were also female poets (Apala, Lopamudra, Viswavara and Ghosa).
- Cattle, especially cows, became very important.
- Monogamy was practised but polygamy was observed among royalty and noble families.
- There was no child marriage.
- Social distinctions existed but were not rigid and hereditary.

Economic Structure

- They were pastoralists and cattle raisers.
- They worked in agriculture.
- They had horse-drawn chariots.
- Rivers were employed as modes of transportation.
- Spun cotton and woollen cloths were utilised.
- Initially, Trade was largely by barter; nishka (a gold ornament) served as a unit of value, with punch-marked coinage emerging only in the later Vedic period.

Religion

- They worshipped natural forces like as earth, fire, wind, rain, thunder, and so forth by personifying them as deities.
- Indra (thunder) was the most important deity. Other deities were Prithvi (earth), Agni (fire), Varuna (rain) and Vayu (wind).
- Ushas and Aditi were the female goddesses.
- There were no temples or idols to worship.

Later Vedic Civilization

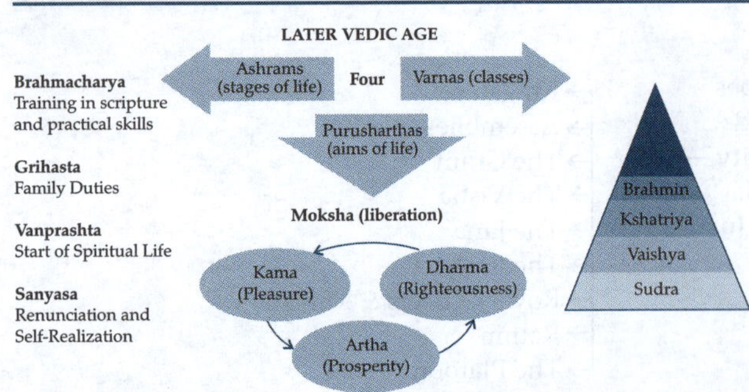

Political Structure

- Larger kingdoms were referred to as 'Mahajanapadas' or 'rashtras'.
- As the king's influence grew, he was required to execute many rituals and sacrifices to strengthen his status, such as Rajasuya (consecration ceremony), Asvamedha (horse sacrifice), and Vajpeyi (chariot race).
- Rajavisvajanan, Ahilabhuvanapathi (lord of the earth), Ekrat, and Samrat (single ruler) were the titles of monarchs.
- The Samiti and Sabha were both reduced in size.

Social structure

- The Varna system grew in importance, and society was split into four groups: Brahmins, Kshatriyas, Vaisyas, and Sudras.
- Brahmins and Kshatriyas had higher positions.
- Occupation was used to separate several sub-castes.
- Women were viewed as inferior and submissive to males, and they were also denied political participation in assemblies.

Economic structure

- More land was treated for cultivation by clearing forests.
- Agriculture became the main occupation of people to grow barley, rice, and wheat.
- Metalwork, leatherwork, carpentry, and pottery progress became significant among industrial activities.
- Internal trade and external trade (Babylon via the sea) expanded as well.
- Hereditary merchants (Vaniya) were a distinct class.
- Vaisyas who engaged in trade and business formed guilds known as 'Shrenis'.
- Gold coins like 'satamana' (besides 'nishka') and silver coins like 'krishnala'–were used as mediums of exchange.

Religion

- Indra and Agni lost their importance and Prajapathi (the creator), Vishnu (the protector) and Rudra (the destroyer) became the main gods.
- Prayers grew less important as rituals got increasingly complex.
- The priesthood became hereditary, and the regulations for these ceremonies and sacrifices were established by them.
- At the conclusion of this time, Buddhism and Jainism were raised as a forceful protest against the clergy.

Vedic Literature

- The term "Veda" is derived from the word "vid", which means "spiritual knowledge/subject of knowledge/ means of acquiring knowledge".
- The four major Vedas are: Rig, Yajur, Sama, and Atharva.
- Rig Veda was composed during the Early Vedic Age. The other three were written in the Later Vedic Age.
- **Rig Veda:** The Rigveda is one of the oldest known religious texts in the world which contains 1028 hymns and is classified into 10 mandalas.
- **Yajur Veda:** It describes the regulations to be followed during sacrifices and how to execute ceremonies.
- **Sama Veda:** It deals with music and has a collection of songs. Indian music originated from Sama Veda.
- **Atharva Veda**: contains spells, charms, and magical formulas.

Upaveda

- The four commonly accepted Upavedas are:
  1. **Dhanurveda:** the science of warfare and military training; associated with the Yajur Veda.
  2. **Gandharvaveda:** deals with music, dance, drama, and other performing arts; associated with the Sama Veda.
  3. **Ayurveda:** the science of health, medicine, and life; associated with the Atharva Veda.
  4. **Sthapatyaveda:** deals with architecture, engineering, construction, and town planning; generally associated with the Yajur Veda.
     (Some traditions include Arthashastra as an Upaveda instead of Sthapatyaveda.)
- Other Important Vedic Texts
- **Brahmanas:** Prose texts that explain Vedic rituals, sacrifices, and the meaning of Vedic hymns.
- **Aranyakas:** Also known as "Forest Texts"; they discuss rituals, meditation, and spiritual ideas.
- **Upanishads (Vedanta):** Philosophical texts that discuss the soul (Atman), ultimate reality (Brahman), karma, rebirth, and liberation (Moksha). Traditionally, 108 Upanishads are recognized.

Epics

- The two great Indian epics are:
- **Mahabharata** – traditionally attributed to Ved Vyasa.
- **Ramayana** – traditionally attributed to Valmiki.
- These epics developed over a long period and are important sources of Indian culture, religion, and history.

Unit-4: Jainism and Buddhism

Jainism

- Jain tradition regards Rishabhanatha as the first Tirthankara, but historians do not consider him the historical founder of Jainism. Historically, Mahavira is the best-attested figure associated with the development of Jainism.
- The 23rd Tirthankara Parshwanath (symbol: snake) was the son of King Ashvasena of Benaras. His main teachings were:
- Non-injury
- Non-lying
- Non-stealing
- Non-possession

- The 24th and the last Tirthankara was Vardhman Mahavira (symbol: lion). He added **celibacy** to his main teachings.

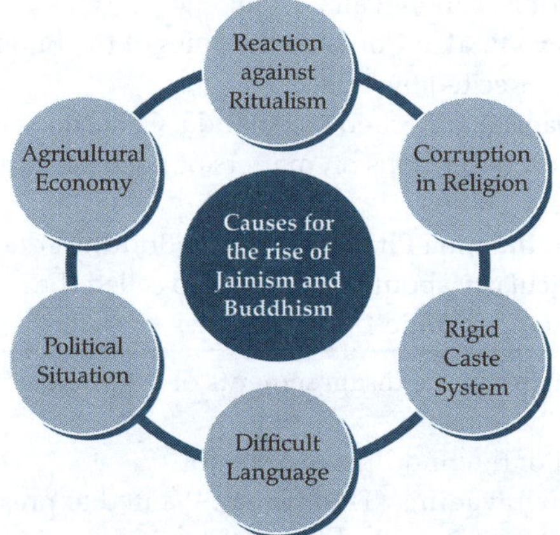

Life of Mahavira

- Born in 540 BC at Kundagrama near Vaisali. (The traditional Jain date for Mahavira's birth is 599 BCE as per Digambara tradition or 615 BCE as per Swetambara tradition).
- Siddhartha was his father: Trisala his mother, Yasoda his wife and his daughter was Priyadarshana married to Jamali.
- Jamali became his first disciple.
- Attained Kaivalya at Jrimbhikagrama in eastern India at the age of 42.
- He got title of Jina, Arihant and Mahavira.
- Died at the age of 72 in 468 BC at Pavapuri near Rajagriha.
- He was called Jina or Jitendriya, Nirgrantha and Mahavira.
- Bimbisara was contemporary of both Mahavira and Buddha. The Jain texts mention that he was a disciple of Lord Mahavira.

Way to Nirvana (Three Ratnas)

- Right faith (Samyak vishwas)
- Right knowledge (Samyak jnan)
- Right conduct (Samyak karma)

The Principles of Jainism as Preached by Mahavira

- Rejected the authority of the Vedas and the Vedic rituals.
- Did not believe in the existence of God.
- Believed in karma and the transmigration of soul.
- Laid great emphasis on equality.
- All action controlled by universal law

Five Main Teachings

- Non-injury (ahimsa)
- Non-lying (satya)
- Non-stealing (asateya)
- Non-possession (aparigraha)
- Observe continence (Brahmacharya)

(The first four principles are of Parsavanath and the fifth Brahmacharya was included by Mahavira).

Jaina Philosophy

- **Syadvada:** All our judgements are necessarily relative, conditional and limited. According to Syadvada (the theory of may be) seven modes of predication (saptabhangi) are possible. Absolute affirmation and absolute negation both are wrong. All judgements are conditional.
- **Anekantavada:** The Jaina metaphysics is a realistic and relativistic pluralism. It is called Anekantavada or the doctrine of the manyness of reality'. Matter (Pudgala) and Spirit (Jiva) are regarded as separate and independent realities.

Literature

The sacred literature of the Svetambaras is written in a form of Prakrit called Ardhamagadhi, and may be classified as follows:

(a) The twelve Angas (b) The twelve Upangas (c) The ten Parikarnas (d) The six Chhedasutras (e) The four Mulasutras.

Jain Councils

First: 300 B.C.

- Place: Patliputra
- Presided: Sthulbhadra
- Result: The compilation of 12 Angas to replace the lost 14 Purvas

Second: 512 A.D.

- Place: Vallabhi
- Presided: Devridhigani
- Result: Final compilation of 12 Angas and 12 Upangas

Split in Jainism

Jainism was split into two parts:

- The Digambar: Naked leader: Bhadrabahu
- The Swetambar: White clothes leader: Sthulabhadra.

Buddhism and Jainism: Differences

Buddhism	Jainism
Did not believe in the soul.	Believed in the soul.
Sangha and monks were given prominence.	Lay followers were given prominence.
Liberal feelings and practical actions.	Extreme Ahimsa was emphasized.
The middle path is a reasonable way to salvation.	Methods of salvation that are far from ordinary (Extreme).
It quickly spread to other countries.	Mostly limited to India.

Buddhism

Buddha's Life

- Gautama, the Buddha also known as Siddhartha, Sakyamuni and Tathagata.
- Born in 563 BC (widely accepted), at Lumbini, near Kapilvastu, capital of the Sakya republic.
- Left home at the age of 29 and attained enlightment at the age of 35 at Bodh Gaya (Uruvela), in Magadha (Bihar) under the Pipal tree.
- Delivered his first sermon at Sarnath.
- He attained Mahaparinirvana at Kusinara in 483 BC.
- His first sermon is called 'Dhammacakkappavattana' or 'Turning of the Wheel of Law'.
- Attained Mahaparinirvana at Kushinagar (identical with village Kasia in Deoria district of U.P.) in 483 B.C. at the age of 80 in the Malla republic.

Council	President	Patron	Venue	Outcome
First Council (483 BC)	Monk Mahakasyapa	King Ajatshatru (Haryanka Dynasty)	Sattapani cave at Rajgriha	• Teachings of Buddha was divided into three Pitakas/ Buddhist canon/ Pali Canon: ▪ **Vinaya Pitaka:** Contains the rules of the Buddhist order. Recited by Upali. ▪ **Suttapitaka:** Recited by Ananda. Collections of Buddha's sermons on matters of doctrine and ethical beliefs. ▪ **Abhidhamma Pitaka:** Elaborate Buddhist doctrines, particularly about the mind, also called the "systematic philosophy" basket.
Second Council (383 B.C)	Sabbakami	Kalasoka (Shisunaga Dynasty)	Vaishali	• **Aim:** Settle the disagreements of different subdivisions. • Split of the Buddhist order into: ▪ **Sthaviravadinis (Theravada):** Wanted to preserve the teachings of Buddha in the original spirit. ▪ **Mahasanghikas (Great Community):** Interpreted the Buddha's teachings more liberally. • Council rejected the Mahasangikas as canonical Buddhist texts.
Third Council (250 BC)	Moggliputta Tissa	King Ashoka (Mauryan Dynasty)	Patliputra	• Made Sthaviravada School as an orthodox school - believed that the past, present, and future are all simultaneous. • **Codification of Abhidhamma Pitaka**, dealing with Buddhist philosophy written in Pali.
Fourth Council (98 AD)	Vasumitra. Ashvaghosa was his deputy	King Kanishka of (Kushan Empire)	Kundalvana, Kashmir.	• According to Si-Yu-Ki, this council was convened to unite the then 18 sects of Buddhism. • This council had brought 18 sects into two schools- **Mahayana (Great Vehicle) and Hinayana (Lesser vehicle/Abandoned Vehicle).** • **"Mahavibhashasastra"**, a Sarvasti-vadin doctrine, was compiled. Elaborate commentaries on Tripitakas viz., Upadesa Sastras, Vibhasa Sastras were prepared. • Deliberations in the council were held in Sanskrit.

Note:
- Sects like Sthaviravadins, Sammatiyas and Sautantrikas came to form-Hinayana led by Sthaviravadins.
- Sarvastivadins, Mahasangikas, Chaityakas, Purvasila, Aparasila etc., were formed into - Mahayana led by Mahasangikas.

Buddhist Philosophy

- **Idealism:** Two sources of valid knowledge: **(a) Perception** and **(b) Inference.**
- **Doctrine of dependent origination (Pratityasamutpada):** Central theory of Buddhist Philosophy. It tells us that in the empirical world dominated by the intellect, everything is relative, conditional dependent, subject to birth and death and therefore impermanent.
- **Theory of momentariness (Kshanabhanga or Impermanence):** It tells that everything in this world is merely a conglomeration of perishable qualities. According to it, Things that can produce effect exist and whatever cannot produce effect has no existence.

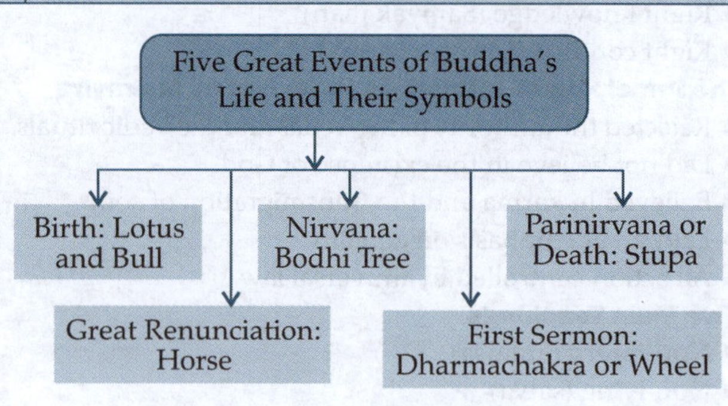

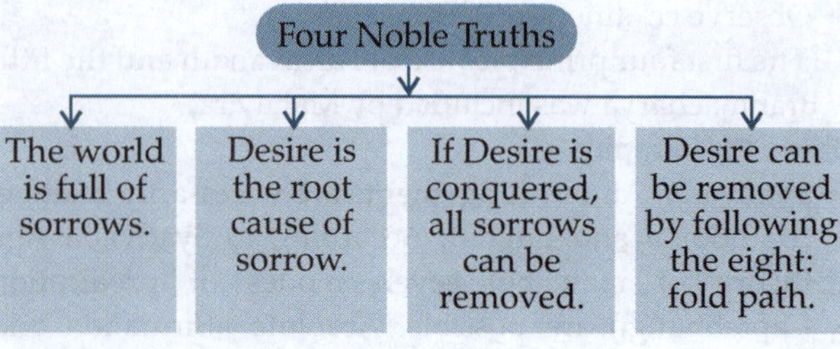

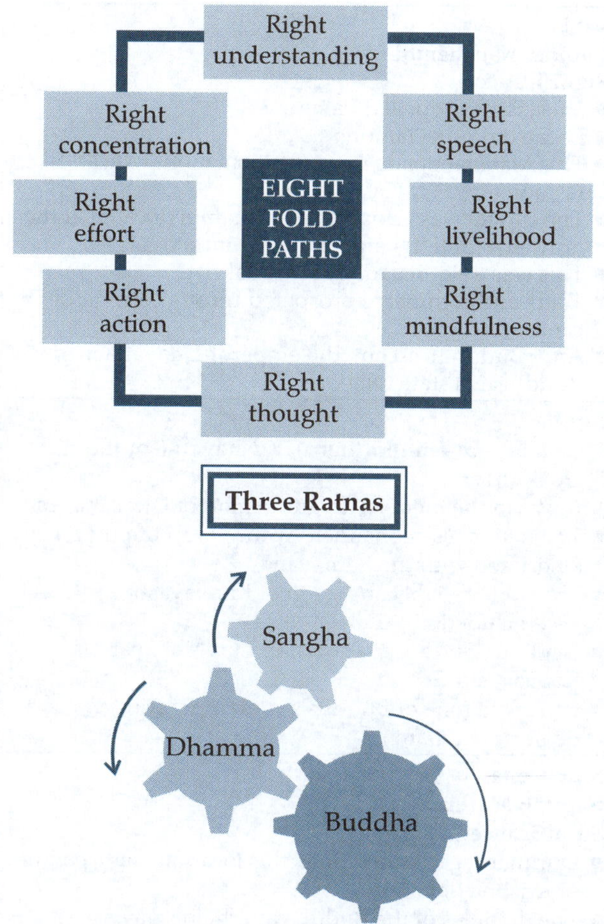

Belief in Ahimsa: One should not cause injury to any living being, animal or man.

Law of Karma: Man reaps the fruits of his past deeds.

The Sangha

- Consists of monks (Bhikshus and Shramanas) and nuns.
- Bhikshus acted as the torch bearer of the Dhamma.
- Apart from Sangha, the worshippers were called Upasakas.

Buddhist Text

- All were written in Pali or Ardhamagadhi.

The Vinaya Pitaka:

- Mainly it deals with rules and regulations which the Buddha promulgated.
- It describes in detail the gradual development of the Sangha.
- An account of the life and leaching of the Buddha is also given.

The Sutta Pitaka:

- Consists chiefly of discourses delivered by Buddha himself on different occasions,
- Few discourses delivered by Sariputta, Ananda. Moggalana and others are also included in it.
- It lays down the principles of Buddhism.

The Abhidhamma Pitaka:

- Contains the profound philosophy of the Buddha's teachings.
- It investigates mind and matter, to help the understanding of things as they truly are.

The Khandhakas: Khandhaka is the second book of Vinay Pitaka. It has two volumes viz. Mahavagga and Cullavagga. Mahavagga deals with the awakening of Buddha and his great disciples. Cullavagga deals with the first and second Buddhist councils and establishments of the community of Buddhist nuns and rules for the Buddhist community.

Important Facts

- The Buddha extended the teaching of two elder contemporaries, Alara Kalama, and Udlaka.
- According to Buddhism, there is no self, no God, no soul and no spirit.
- There is very little theological or philosophical speculation involved.
- Buddhism is scientific in approach, a search for cause and effect relationships and knowledge of reality, as each individual human being experiences it.
- It is psychological in approach, that is, it begins with the human being.
- If women were not admitted into the monasteries, Buddhism would have continued for a thousand years, but because this admission has been granted, it would last only five hundred years-Buddha

Contribution of Buddhism

- The doctrine of Ahimsa—so strongly stressed, devoutly preached and sincerely practiced by the Buddhists & was incorporated in Hinduism of later days.
- The practice of worshipping personal Gods, making their images and erecting temples in their honor became a part of the later day Hinduism.
- Buddhism proved to be one of the greatest civilizing forces, which India gave to the neighboring countries.
- Buddhism broke the isolation of India and helped in establishment of intimate contacts between India and foreign countries.

Causes of Decline of Buddhism

- It succumbed to the Brahminical rituals and ceremonies such as idol worship, etc. which Buddhism had earlier denounced.
- Revival of reformed Hinduism with the preaching of Shankaracharya from the eighth century onwards.
- Use of Sanskrit, the language of intellectuals in place of Pali, the language of the common people.
- Deterioration in the moral standards among the monks living in the Buddhist monasteries.
- Attacks of Huna king Mihirkula in the sixth century and the Turkish invaders in the 12th century A.D. which continued till the 13th century A.D.

Unit-5: Mahajanapadas

- The Janapadas were the main kingdoms of Vedic India. The Aryans were the most powerful tribes of the time, and they were referred to as 'Janas'.
- Janapada means territory where a tribe settles, or rest their feet.
- By the sixth century BCE, there were possibly 16 Mahajanapadas .
- Socioeconomic successes, particularly the use of iron tools in agriculture and warfare, as well as religious and political improvements, led to the formation of the

Mahajanapadas from minor kingdoms known as Janapadas.

- Rather than the tribe or jana, the residents formed a strong connection to the land or Janapada to which they belonged.
- After the Harappan civilisation, this is also called the second urbanisation age.
- During this time, the political centre changed from the west to the east of the Indo-Gangetic plains.
- This was connected to enhanced land fertility as a result of increasing rainfall and rivers. This location was also nearer to iron-producing sites.

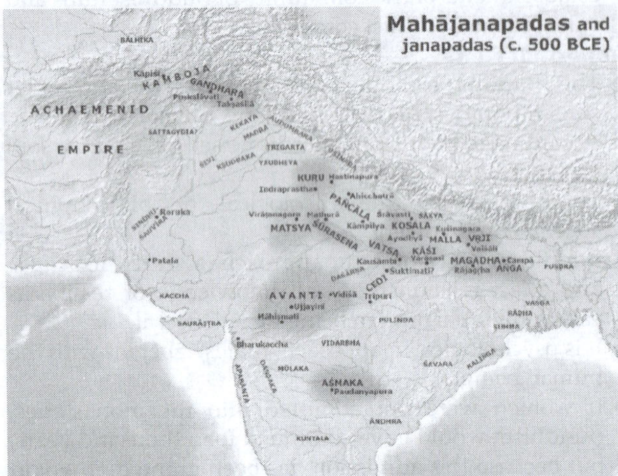

This map is not to scale and is for reference only.

16 Mahajanapadas

Anga
Capital: Champa
Significance:
- Both the Mahabharata and the Atharva Veda mention Anga Mahajanapada.
- It was conquered by the Magadha Empire under the reign of Bimbisara.
- It may be found in contemporary Bihar and West Bengal.
- Its capital, Champa, was located at the confluence of the Ganga and Champa rivers.
- Merchants travelled from here to Suvarnabhumi, since it was a key commercial centre on the trading routes (South East Asia).

Magadha
Capital: Rajagriha
Significance:
- Magadha is mentioned in the Atharva Veda.
- The Champa River separated it from Anga in modern-day Bihar.
- Later, Magadha was converted into a Jain centre, and Rajagriha held the first Buddhist Council.

Kasi
Capital: Kasi
Significance:
- Varanasi was the location.
- According to the Matsya Purana, this city was named after the rivers Varuna and Asi.
- Kosala apprehended Kasi.

Vatsa
Capital: Kaushambi
Significance:
- Vatsa is often spelled Vamsa.
- Located on the Yamuna's banks.
- This Mahajanapada was ruled in a monarchical fashion.
- The capital was Kausambi/Kaushambi (located at the northern (or left) bank of the Yamuna river).
- This was a significant commercial city.
- Trade and commerce prospered throughout the sixth century.
- After Buddha's ascent, the emperor Udayana made Buddhism a state religion.

Kosala
Capital: Shravasti (northern), Kushavati (southern)
Significance:
- It was in the modern Awadh region of Uttar Pradesh.
- The region also contained Ayodhya, an important city associated with the Ramayana.
- The tribal republican region of Kapilavastu's Sakyas is also included in Kosala.
- Gautama Buddha was born in Lumbini near Kapilavastu.
- Prasenajit (one of Buddha's contemporaries) was a powerful monarch.

Shurasena
Capital: Mathura
Significance:
- During Megasthenes' time, this location was a centre of Krishna devotion.
- The disciples of the Buddha also held sway.
- Awantipura is a powerful king (Disciple of Buddha).
- Its capital, Mathura, was situated on the banks of the Yamuna.

Panchala
Capital: Ahichchhatra and Kampilya
Significance:
- Kannauj, the famed city, was located in the Kingdom of Panchala.
- Later, the form of government changed from monarchy to republic.
- Its northern Panchala capital was Ahichchatra (modern Bareilly), while its southern Panchala capital was Kampilya (modern Farrukhabad).

Kuru
Capital: Indraprastha
Significance:
- Kuru Mahajanapada was probably born in the vicinity of Kurukshetra.
- It adopted a republican form of government.
- The Mahabharata, an epic poem, describes a war between two branches of the ruling Kuru clan.

Matsya
Capital: Viratnagar
Significance:
- It was located west of the Panchalas and south of the Kurus.
- Viratanagara (modern Bairat) was the capital.
- It is located in Rajasthan, near Jaipur, Alwar, and Bharatpur.
- Founder – Virata

Chedi
Capital: Sothivathi
Significance:
- The Rigveda makes reference to this.
- The capital was Sothivati/Shuktimati/Sotthivatinagara.
- It is presently in the Bundelkhand region of Central India.
- Shishupala is the King. During the Rajasuya sacrifice of Pandava monarch Yudhishthira, he was murdered by Vasudeva Krishna.

Avanti
Capital: Ujjaini or Mahishmati
Significance:
- Avanti had a significant part in the formation of Buddhism.
- Avanti's capitals were Ujjaini in the north and Mahishmati in the south.
- It was in what is now Malwa and Madhya Pradesh.
- Pradyota was a powerful king.

Gandhara
Capital: Taxila
Significance:
- Taxila was the capital (Takshashila).
- Modern Peshawar and Rawalpindi, Pakistan, as well as the Kashmir valley.
- The Atharva Veda mentions Gandhara.
- The people were skilled in the art of combat.
- It was significant in terms of international trade.
- Pushkarasarin is a formidable ruler.
- Gandhara was captured by the Persians in the late sixth century BCE.

Kamboja
Capital: Poonch
Significance:
- Poonch (Rajapura or Rajapur) was the capital of Kamboja.
- It is located in modern-day Kashmir and the Hindukush.
- Kamboja was a republic, according to several literary sources.
- Kambojas had an exceptional horse breed.

Asmaka
Capital: Potali/Podana/Pratisthan
Significance:
- It was on the banks of the Godavari.
- It was the only Mahajanapada in Dakshinapatha, located south of the Vindhya Range.
- It includes the Pratisthan or Paithan area.

Vajji
Capital: Vaishali
Significance:
- The Vajjis ruled the state north of the Ganga in the Tirhut division.
- The most powerful clans were the Lichchhavis (Capital – Vaishali), Videhans (Capital – Mithila), and Jnatrikas (based in Kundapura).
- Mahavira was a member of the Jnatrikas clan.
- Ajatashatru triumphed over the Vajjis.

Malla
Capital: Kusinara
Significance:
- It is mentioned in Buddhist and Jain scriptures, as well as in the Mahabharata.
- Malla was a democratic republic.
- Its area went all the way to the northern border of the Vajji state.
- The capitals are Kusinara and Pava.
- Both capitals have important Buddhist histories. Before entering Mahaparinirvana in Kusinara, the Buddha ate his farewell meal at Pava.

Magadha: The Most Powerful Mahajanapada

- Magadha faced competition from Avanti, Kosala, and Vatsa for supremacy, however, over the years (600-400 BC), Magadha gained sovereignty and became the most powerful Mahajanapada.

Difference between Janapadas and Mahajanapadas

'Jana' refers to persons in both ways. These individuals represented a tribe, an ethnic community, or a tribal political organisation. As indicated in early Vedic writings, Indo-Aryans used to dwell in semi-nomadic tribal kingdoms. This tribal-state organisation known as 'Jana' evolved into the Janapadas at the end of the Vedic era. Janapadas was a tribe's footing during the time. When the Janapadas began to develop, they turned into Majahanapadas.

Features of Mahajanapadas

- There are seven features or main constituents of a Mahajanapada and they are listed below:
  - The King
  - The Minister
  - The Country
  - Fortified City
  - Treasury
  - Army
  - Ally

Unit-6: Mauryan Empire

Early Mauryan Empire (322 BCE – 185 BCE

- Vacuum created by Alexander's destruction of the tribal republics in Punjab and neighbouring regions gave opportunity to Chandragupta Maurya.
- The Maurya Empire (322 – 185 B.C.E.), ruled by the Mauryan dynasty, was a geographically extensive and powerful political and military empire in ancient India.
- Chandragupta Maurya founded the Empire in 322 B.C.E., after overthrowing Dhanananda of Nanda Dynasty.

Sources	
Literary	Archaeological
• Megasthenes' 'Indica' • Kautilya's 'Arthashastra' • Visakha Datta's 'Mudra Rakshasa' • Dharmashastra texts, Puranas • Buddhist Text (Jataka Stories, Deepvamsa, Mahavamsa, Divyavadana)	• Punch-marked coins, Northern Black Polished Ware (NBPW) • Wooden Palace of Chandragupta Maurya in Pataliputra • Ashokan inscriptions and Edicts

Origin and Expansion

- Following Alexander the Great's death in 323 BCE, Chandragupta Maurya, the founder of the Mauryan dynasty, seized the Punjab area from the southeastern margins of Alexander's old kingdom.
- Now that the western frontier was at peace, Chandragupta could concentrate his military efforts to the east and south.
- His son, Bindusara, continued the empire's expansion well into the Deccan, stopping around the region known today as Karnataka.
- Bindusara's son, Ashoka (reigned 273–232 BCE), added Kalinga to the already vast empire.
  - That addition would be the last, however, as the brutal conquest of that region led Ashoka to abandon military conquest.
  - Rather, he embraced Buddhism and instituted dharma as the state ideology.
- After Ashoka's death, the empire shrank because of invasions, defections by southern princes, and quarrels over ascension.
- Brihadratha, the last emperor, was assassinated in 185 BCE by his Brahman commander-in-chief, Pushyamitra, who established the Shunga dynasty, which reigned in central India for roughly a century.

Chandragupta Maurya (322 BC - 298 BC)

- At the age of twenty-five, Chandragupta Maurya, the founder of the Mauryan empire, overthrew the Nanda throne.
- The historical texts have it that the Brahmana Kautilya was his mentor and guide.

Political Achievements

Victory over Nandas

- With the help of Chanakya (Vishnugupta/ Kautilya), Chandragupta Maurya defeated Dhana Nanda (322 BCE) and founded the Mauryan Dynasty.

Victory over the Greeks

- The Seleucids, a contending dynasty for Alexander's legacy, attempted to advance into India in 305 BCE.
- However, they were defeated and, after the conclusion of a treaty, the Seleucids and the Mauryans maintained friendly relations.

Victory over Southern India

- Chandragupta Maurya's triumph over Southern India is referenced in Ashoka'a inscriptions, Jain writings, and Sangam literature. He took charge of the Northern Karnataka region.
- According to Jain sources, Chandragupta embraced Jainism towards the end of his life and stepped down from the throne in the favour if his son.
- Accompanied by Bhadrabahu, a Jain saint, and several other monks, he is said to have gone to Sravana Belgola in Karnataka.

Bindusara (298 BC – 273 BC)

- Bindusara, known to the Greeks as Amitrochates (Sanskrit, Amitraghata = the slayer of opponents), succeeded Chandragupta. Bindusara is also known as Madrasar and Simhasena.
- Bindusara followed the extreme fatalistic order (religion) 'Ajivika' founded by Makhali Gosala.
- Bindusara maintained good diplomatic relations with Antiochus I, the Seleucid king of Syria. Antiochus sent Deimachus as ambassador to the Bindusara's court.
- Bindusara requested Antiochus to send him some sweet wine, dried figs and a Sophist (philosopher); the last being not meant for export, was not sent.
- Tibetan Buddhist monk Taranatha describes Bindusara as "conqueror of the land between two seas"e., peninsular India.
- The Buddhist biographical history of Mauryan Kings, Divyavadan, recalls an insurrection at Taxila being repressed by Ashoka, the son of Bindusara and viceroy of Ujjain at the time.

Ashoka (273 BC – 232 BC)

- He was the son of Bindusara. Right from his childhood Ashoka showed great promise in the field of administration.
- Bindusara appointed him as governor of Ujjain/Avanti after being pleased by his competence and wisdom.
- After becoming a monarch, Ashoka fought only one combat, the combat of Kalinga. The 13th Major Rock Edict mentions this war.
- Ashoka fought this battle in the 8th year of his reign in 261 BC.
- The bloodshed in this war, had a deep impact on Ashoka which ultimately changed his personality from a warrior, to a saint as a result of which he gave up the policy of Digvajaya and adopted the policy of Dhammavijaya.

Ashoka's Dhamma

- Initially, Ashoka practised the Brahmin faith. However, during the Kalinga conflict, he turned to Buddhism.
- He remained a simple adorer for 2.5 years after converting to Buddhism. Then he joined the Buddhist sangha and became a Bhikshu Gatik (those who have lived in viharas for some time are known as Bhikshu Gatik).
- But he never became a Buddhist monk rather always remained an adorer.
- The definition of Dhamma is produced by Ashoka in his 2nd and 7th pillar edict.

Rock Edicts

- In the 13th Major Rock Edict Ashoka considers Dhammavijaya to be the greatest victory.
- Ashoka was the first ruler in the world history carried out this policy of Dhamma imperialiste victory without violence.
- For the propagation of Dhamma Ashoka appointed a new category of ministers named "Dhammamahamatra".

- In the 13th year of his reign (256 BC), Ashoka addresses the appointment of royal officials in his 5th Major Rock Edict.
- Aside from Dhammamahamatras, additional officials like as Yukta, Rajukka, Pradeshika, and others were tasked with spreading Dhamma ideals.

Mauryan Administration

- The core was the King, who was aided by Mantri Parishad members Yuvraj, Purohita, Senapati, and others.
- Tirthas were the highest ranking officers, and Adhyakshas (superintendents) oversaw 26 departments.

Important Officials:

Name	Function/Post
Mantriparishad Adhyaksha	Head of Council of Minister
Purohita	Chief Priest
Senapati	Commander-In-Chief
Yuvaraj	Crown Prince
Samaharta	Revenue Collector
Shulkadhyaksha	Officer-In-Charge of Royal Income
Gudhapurushas	Spies
Prativedakas	Informers

Local Administration

- Mauryan state also had local and municipal administration; 'Vish' or 'Ahara' (districts) were the units of a province.
- Megasthenese mentioned in his account 6 committees of five members each for administering the municipalities.

Important officers:

Sitadhyaksha	Supervised agriculture
Panyadhyaksha	Superintendent of Commerce
Yukta	Subordinate Revenue Officer
Prasdesika	Chief Revenue Officer
Sthanika	Tax collector (worked under Pradeshika)
Rajuka	Revenue Settlement Officer (Modern day Patwari)
Samsthadhyaksha	Superintendent of market
Pautavadhyaksha	Superintendent of weight & measure
Navadhyaksha	Superintendent of ships
Sulkaadhyaksha	Collector of tolls

Village Level Officers

Gramika	The head of the village.
Gramvrid-dhas	Panchayat consists of Village elders to settle disputes.

- Sudarshan Lake was constructed during the reign of Chandragupta Maurya near the Girnar Hill in Gujarat.
- Tamralipti (Tamlook in Midnapur, WB) in the east and Bharuch/ Broach/Barygaza (Gujarat) in the west were two important ports.
- A large army and navy were maintained, in which all four varnas were permitted to serve.
- Swami (king), Amatya (minister), Janapada (territory), Durga (fort), Kosha (treasury), Danda (army), Mitra (ally).

Decline of the Mauryan Empire

- The major causes of downfall were over-centralisation, onerous bureaucracy, excessive taxes (on nearly every activity), and foreign invasions.
- Neglect of North-West frontier and construction of Great Wall of China.
- Financial Crisis- Ashoka incurred huge expenditure for promotion of his 'Dhamma Mission'.
- Over-tolerant, non-violent attitude killed the fighting spirit of the army.
- Following Ashoka's death in 232 B.C., Mauryan Emperors were inept and tyrannical.
- Pushyamitra Shunga, a Mauryan army commander, killed the last Mauryan emperor Brihadratha and founded Shunga Dynasty in 185 B.C.
- Brahmins annoyed by Ashoka for banning rituals, supported Pushyamitra Shunga who was a Brahmin.
- Pushyamitra shunga overthrew Mauryan king and established the Shunga dynasty.

Post- Mauryan Period (200 BC – 300 AD)

Shungas (187 B.C. – 73 B.C.)

- Capital in Patliputra, with a secondary capital at Vidisha (under the viceroyalty of son Agnimitra).
- Pushyamitra Shunga defended the country (the Gangetic valley) and its culture against foreign invasions (Greeks). Pushyamitra shunga erected Bharhut stupa.
- After Pushyamitra, his son Agnimitra ruled.
- Kalidasa's play 'Malvikagnimitra' is a love story of the King Agnimitra and a handmaiden Malvika.
- Demetrius I of Bactria's substantial attempt to penetrate India was effectively resisted by Vasumitra, son of Agnimitra.
- Performed 'Ashwamedh' sacrifice for revival of Brahmanical order and patronised scholars like Patanjali and Manu.
- After Agnimitra, Vasumitra became the King and was succeeded by 7 more kings of the same dynasty.
- Shunga's empire covered regions of Bihar, Bengal and Uttar Pradesh and northern Madhya Pradesh.
- Devabhuti was the final emperor of the Shunga dynasty. He was assassinated by Vasudeva, who founded the Kanva Dynasty, which reigned over eastern and central India.
- Shungas issued gold and silver coins and they inherited and continued with Mauryan structure of administration.

Kanva Dynasty (73 B.C. – 28 B.C.)

- Vasudeva Kanva killed his King Devabhuti of Shunga and founded Kanva rule with Vidisha and Patliputra as their capital.
- Bhumimitra, Vasudeva's son, and Narayan, Bhumimitra's son, governed for the next 26 years.
- Susarman, the last Kanva monarch, was assassinated by the Satavahana (Andhra) ruler, and the Kanva dynasty of Brahmins perished with him.

Chedi Dynasty

- In the first century B.C., the Kingdom of Chedis or Chetis was established in Kalinga.
- The politics of this time are remembered for the 3rd Chedi monarch of Kalinga, Kharvela.
- Hathgumpha inscription of Udaigiri hills of Orissa describes him as a great conqueror who Magadh, Satavahana and Pandyas of Madurai.
- Kharvela was a Jaina follower who donated caves to Jaina Monks in Udayagiri Hills.
- Chedis are also referred to as Cheta or Chetavamsa, and Mahameghavahana.

Satavahana (60 B.C.- 225 A.D.)

- The Satavahana are known as "Andhras" in the Puranas.
- Simuka established the Satavahana dynasty.
- In the first century B.C., the Satavahanas were documented from the northwestern part of the Deccan, with their principal capital at Pratishthana (modern Paithan in Maharashtra) on the Godavari River and their secondary capital at Amravati.
- Information about history of Satavahana are obtained from Aitreya Brahmana, Puranas, epics, Brihat Katha of Gunadya, Kamasutra of Vatasayana.
- Nanaghat inscription, Nasik Inscription, Hatigumpa inscription of Kharavela, Erragudi inscription of Ashoka provides important information about Shungas.
- Gujrata and Malawa were conquered as per the Nasik inscription of Naganika, his wife.
- Gautamiputra Satkarni was the next major ruler, and his achievements are recounted in the Nasik inscription of his mother, Gautami Balashri.
- Gautamiputra Satkarni (also known as Ekabrahmana) defeated Sakas, Greeks, Parthians and Nahapana (king of western Satrapa)
- Around 150 CE, Rudradaman took advantage of the weak successors of Gautamiputra Satkarni and defeated them.
- 'Amatyas' and 'Mahamatras' were district officers under Satavahana rule; the districts were called 'Ahara'.
- Satavahana supported architectural growth in the highlands of the Western Ghats, where caves were carved in Ajanta, Nasik, Kaule, Bhaja, Kondain, and Kanheri.
- These caves were cut in to make Chaityas (Buddhist cave-temple) and Viharas (Buddhist rest houses).
- Karle Chaitya is the largest cave temple.
- Nagarjunkonda and Amravati were prominent commercial and artistic hubs. Stupas were built here for the first time, and white marble was also used for the first time.

Indo-Greeks (2nd century BC to 1st century AD)

- Indo-Greeks were the Greek people who got settled in India and became localised over a period of time.
- Indo- Greek authority in India had three branches: Bactria (North Afghanistan), Taxila (Takshashila), and Sakal or Sialkot (today in Pakistan).
- An ambassador from the Taxila branch, Heliodorus was sent to court of King of Vidisha.
- Heliodorus got a stone pillar constructed in Greek style (different from Ashokan style) which was dedicated to Lord Vasudeva.
- Demetrious and Menander or Milind are two significant rulers mentioned from Sakal or Sialkot branch of Indo-Greek.
- Menander or Milind (165 BC – 145 BC) adopted Buddhism under Nagasen who wrote "Milindpanho" in Pali. This book is a great source of history of this age.
- The development of metallurgy, medicine, astronomy, stonecutting, and perfume-making are examples of Indo-Greeks' technological advances.
- Patronising both Buddhism and Hinduism, the greatest contribution of Indo-Greeks is witnessed in the development of the Gandhara School of Art.

Parthians (1st Century BC - 1st Century AD)

- Toward the end of the 1st century BCE, rulers with Iranian names — known as Pahlavas or Indo-Parthians — captured parts of northwestern India.
- In the reign of Gondophernes (the most significant of the Indo-Parthians) St. Thomas is said to have come to India for the propagation of Christianity.

Sakas (1st Century BC - 4th Century AD)

- Sakas who were also known as Scythians, were from Western China.
- Maues or Moga (about 80 BC) was the first Shaka ruler, as shown by inscriptions and a set of coins.
- Saka monarchs ruled from Mathura, Ujjain, and Girnar in north India.
- They ruled in capacity of 'Satrapas' i.e., governors and Mahasatrapas.
- With control over western Ganga valley, parts of central India and Gujrat, Sakas were almost always at war with Satavahana and put pressure over Deccan region.
- Rudradaman (130 CE – 150 CE) of Ujjain centre of Sakas is of significance as he finds mention in Junagarh inscription.
- This inscription is in Sanskrit, unlike previous Prakrit inscriptions.
- Rudradaman had the lake Sudarshan restored for improved irrigation (it had been built during the reign of Chandragupta Maurya).
- In 58 CE, the King of Ujjain vanquished Sakas, taking the title 'Vikramaditya' and establishing the Vikram Samvat or period.

Kushanas (1st Century AD - 3rd Century AD)

- Kushanas (or Yueh-Chis) too were from China, they ruled in North-West India with Purushpur (Peshawar) as their capital.
- Kanishka, a Mahayan Buddhist, was the most important Kushana ruler.
- Other significant Kushana monarchs in India included Wem Kadphises, Huviska, and Vasiska.
- During Kanishka's reign, the 4th Buddhist council was convened in Kundalvan Vihar (Kashmir), with Vasumitra as president.
- Ashwaghosh was vice-president of this Mahayan Buddhist council.
- "Buddha Charita" i.e., biography of Buddha, was composed by Ashwaghosh of Patliputra.
- Nagarjuna propounded the Madhyamika Philosophy of Mahayan Buddhism.
- Nagarjuna also discussed the idea of relativity and hence, is sometimes called as Einstein of India.

Unit-7: Gupta Period

- The Gupta Rule for witnessing all-round progress i.e., in spheres of art, architecture, literature, science and technology, metallurgy and philosophy, regarded as the Golden Age of Ancient India.
- Stable polity, profitable trade, secured and peaceful social set up provided the required conducive environment for development of North India.
- Sri Gupta was the first ruler of the dynasty followed by his son.
- Bhitari pillar inscription dating to his reign gives the chronology of Guptas and his conflict with Pushyamitra and Hunas.

Ruler	Related Information
Chandragupta-I (319 CE – 335 CE)	• The first important ruler was Chandragupta-I (319 CE – 335 CE) who is considered the actual founder of the dynasty. • He assumed the title of 'Maharajadhiraj'. • His domain included sections of South Bihar, Jharkhand, and Eastern Uttar Pradesh (Saketa and Prayaga). • His accession in about AD 319-20 marks the beginning of the Gupta Samvat (era). • Chandragupta-I married the Licchavi princess Kumardevi and increased his influence in the North Bihar region (Nepal). • Gold coins depicting Kumardevi and Chandragupta were first minted as Kumardevi Coins.
Samudragupta (335 CE – 380 CE)	• The son of Chandragupta-I, Samudragupta, became the next ruler whose conquests are recorded in Prayaga Prashasti (Eulogy). • Harishena, Samudragupta's court poet, scholar, and minister, wrote these victories Prayaga Prashasti in classical Sanskrit. • According to Prayaga Prashasti, Samuddragupta conquered: Eight kings of Aryavarta – (northern India i.e., Ganga Valley). • Samudragupta captured and reinstated 12 kings of Dakshinapatha (South India). • A large part of the subcontinent succumbed to the power of Samudragupta and paid tribute. • Following these accomplishments, Samudragupta conducted the Ashwamedh Yajna (sacrifice). • He issued Ashwamedh coins, Tiger-slayer coin, Battle-axe coin and Veena-Coin in which he is displayed playing the Veena. • Samudragupta was not only a great conqueror but also a distinguished poet, musician, and patron of learning. • Samudragupta's remarkable conquests earned him the title 'Napoleon of India', as given by historian V. A. Smith. • Allahabad pillar inscriptions called him "Dharma Prachar Bandhu".
Chandragupta-II (380 CE – 414 CE)	• When Chandragupta-II ascended to the throne, he vanquished the Sakas in the western area (Gujarat, Kathiawar, and west Malwa), took the title 'Vikramaditya', and reigned from Ujjain. • Udaigiri Cave Inscription (Vidisha, MP) and Sanchi inscription inform us about this. • He married Kubernaga of the Naga family and had a daughter by her named Prabhavatigupta. • Prabhavatigupta was married to Vakataka Rudrasen 2nd of Central India, after Rudrasen's death, Prabhavatigupta ruled as a regent between 390 CE to 410 CE. • Chandragupta-II was the first Gupta monarch to mint silver coins with lion motifs patterned after Saka coinage. • Mehrauli iron pillar inscription (Delhi's Qutb-minar complex) of Chandragupta-II records that Chandragupta-II defeated Valhikas of Bacteria crossing the Saptsindhu. • His court was a home to Kalidasa and Amarsinha. • Fa-hien, a Chinese Buddhist monk, paid a visit to his court.

Kumargupta I (414 CE – 455 CE)	• The Karamdanda (Fyzabad) inscription refers to King Kumargupta I as ruler of four seas, the Mandsor inscription as ruler of the entire globe, and the Damodarpur copper plate inscription as 'Maharajadhiraj'. • Bilsad (Etah) inscription also mentions Kumargupta I. • Kumargupta I performed Ashwamedha yajna and assumed titles like Ashwamedha-Mahendra and Mahendraditya. • Kumargupta I, himself a Shiva devotee, produced Kartikeya-style coins depicting a peacock. • While the threat of the Hunas crossing Hindukush was building up during Kumargupta I, on the whole, his reign remained peaceful. • During his reign Nalanda University was established.
Skandagupta (455 CE – 467 CE)	• Son of Kumargupta I, Skandgupta, during his lifetime bravely fought and defeated Hunas on the North-Western frontier. • His victory against Pushyamitra is commemorated in the Bhitari Pillar inscription. • Got the Sudarshan Lake repaired (Junagadh inscription). • Skandagupta's death in 467 CE was followed by incompetent successors who could not keep the empire intact.

Decline of Gupta Dynasty

- Feudal lords (recipients of land grants) began asserting themselves and establishing their own dynasties.
- Decentralised bureaucracy and the absence of a big, permanent, and professional army were significant contributors to decline.
- Decline of foreign trade, invasions of Huna, weak successors contributed to their decline
- Vishnugupta (540 CE- 550 CE) was the last recognized Gupta ruler.

Socio-economic condition during Gupta period

Administration	• King was assisted by council of minister. • Bhukti (province) and Vishaya (province division) were administrative units headed by Uparika and Vishayapati respectively. • Vishaya was further subdivided into Vithi, with village being the smallest subdivision. • The bureaucracy was not as refined as that of Maurya. **Important Offices:** • Mahanandanayaka: Justice Delivery • Mahapratihara: Chief of the Guards • Dutakas: Associated with Gifts and Grants • Sandhi–Vigrahika: Minister of Peace and War • Pilupati: Headed Elephants • Asvapati: Headed Horses • Narapti: Headed Foot Soldiers • Ranabhandagrika: In charge of stores • Akshapataladhikrita: Superintendent of Records and Accounts.
Economy	• Agriculture, trade, business, and art and crafts all thrived throughout the Gupta era. • The King's administration facilitated irrigation, ensured measurement and categorization of land into cultivated (Kshetra) and un-cultivated (Khila/ Aprahata) lands. • Landowners (Mahattars, Gramika, and Kutumbika) gained power since land was a valuable asset that could be sold or bestowed. • Craftsmen produced both utility and luxury items; particular craftsmanship became the basis 'jaati'-formation i.e., caste. • Shreni continued to govern the trader's affairs. • Common people traded in cowrie shells. • Issued less pure gold coins than Kushana.
Society and Religion	• Society became clearly feudalistic, Brahmins (Brahmadiyas & Agraharas) and feudal chiefs received land grants. • Women's and Shudras' status improved when they were permitted to listen to the Ramayana and Mahabharata and were urged to adore Krishna. • Sati was first mentioned in Bhanugupta's Airana (Eran) inscription, and child marriage was also practised. • Fahien records almost the absence of crime and death penalty. He describes relatively peaceful conditions.

	• Vishti a kind of forced labour for state/public works. • Chandalas were outcasts, meaning they were excluded from the four-fold varna system and forced to live outside village communities. • Various religious sects coexisted harmoniously. • Vaishnavite or Shaivite Kings got temples constructed for their respective deity. • Religious texts like Puaranas, Mahabharata and Ramayana were expanded in this period. • Bhagvatism centered around Vishnu emerged.
Art and Architecture	• Continued growth of the Ajanta School (Theme: Buddha's life) was accompanied by emergence of Bagh School near Hoshangabad in Madhya Pradesh. In this cave-walls were decorated (painted) in local themes i.e., it related to common people. • Sculpture– making made considerable growth with evidences of various stone images. • Several locations have documented metal and stone images of Buddha (bronze, Bhagalpur), Shiva, and Vishnu. • Images of God appeared first time. • Stupa and cave construction reduced and temple construction (Shikhara) picked up: • Dashavatar Temple: Jhansi, U.P. • Bhitargav Temple (Brick): Kanpur, U.P. • Parvati Temple: Nachnakuthara, M.P. • Vishnu Temple: Jabalpur, M.P. • Bagh Cave Paintings are from this time period.

Literature during Gupta Period

- Development of literature in Gupta period was diverse as it covered from poetry and play, art (dance and music), philosophy, religion to science, mathematics, physiology, astronomy etc.
- In Chandragupta II's court, there were Navaratnas, or Nine Gems, who were experts in certain subjects. Amarsimha, Dhanvantri, Harisena, Kalidasa, Kahapanaka, Sanku, Varahamihira, Vararuchi, and Vetalbhatta were among them.
- Dharmashashtras, Narad Smriti, Vishnu Smriti, Brihaspati Smriti and portion of Ramayana and Mahabharata, Bhasa's 12 plays were also written in this period.
- The majority of the literature is written in the elaborate Sanskrit language.

Administration

- During the Gupta period, monarchy was the prevailing form of government.
- The rulers of the Gupta dynasty had their own councils.
- The council of ministers was known as Mantri Parishad.
- It consisted of high officials like the kumaramatya and the sandhivigrahika.
- The empire was divided into provinces which were known as 'bhuktis'.
- The bhuktis were further divided into 'Vishyas'.
- Each bhukti was under the control of an 'uparika' and the Uparikas were appointed by the king.
- The vishayas were under the control of Vishayapatis who were appointed by the provincial governor or sometimes the king himself.
- The village administration was managed by the headman of the village.
- Unlike the Mauryan times, the administration in the Gupta period seems to have been managed from grassroot levels.

Unit-8: Sangam Period & South Indian Kingdom

Introduction

- Sangam Age is the period from the 3rd century B.C. to the 3rd century A.D. in south India.
- There were 3 Sangams conducted in ancient South India called Muchchangam, Tamil legends say.
- These Sangams prospered under the royal patronage of the Pandya kings of Madurai.
- Three dynasties ruled during the Sangam Age – the Cheras, Cholas and Pandyas.
- The key source of evidence about these kingdoms is outlined from the literary references of the Sangam Period.

Sources of Sangam Age

The following are the sources of Sangam Age:

- **Sangam Literature:** It is a major source that mentions about Sangam Age.
- The Greek Authors including Megasthenes, Pliny etc. mentioned the trade contacts between South India and the West.
- Tamil kingdoms are mentioned in Ashokan edicts.
- Adhichanallur excavations brought to surface articles depicting the life of the Sangam Period.

Introduction to Cheras, Cholas and Pandyas of Sangam Period

Sangam Period Dynasty	Modern-Day State	Ancient Capital	Important Ruler	Important Ports	Emblem
Cheras	Kerala and Tamil Nadu	Vanjji	Cheran Senguttuvan	Musiri, Tondi	Bow and Arrow
Cholas	Tamil Nadu	Uraiyur, Puhar	Karikala	Kaveripattanam	Tiger
Pandyas	Tamil Nadu	Madurai	Neduncheliyan	Korkai, Saliyur	Fish

Sangam Literature: Major source giving details of Sangam Age

The Sangam literature includes Tolkappiyam, Ettutogai, Pattuppattu, Pathinenkilkanakku, and two epics named – Silappathikaram and Manimegalai.

- Tolkappiyam, written by Tolkappiyar, is regarded as the first Tamil literary work. Though it is a treatise on Tamil language, it also gives insights on the time's political and socioeconomic realities.
- Ettutogai (Eight Anthologies) consist of eight works – Aingurunooru, Narrinai, Aganaooru, Purananooru, Kuruntogai, Kalittogai, Paripadal and Padirruppatu.
- The Pattuppattu (Ten Idylls) consists of ten works – Thirumurugarruppadai, Porunararruppadai, Sirupanarruppadai, Perumpanarruppadai, Mullaippattu, Nedunalvadai, Maduraikkanji, Kurinjippattu, Pattinappalai and Malaipadukadam.
- Pathinenkilkanakku is a collection of eighteen writings about ethics and morals. The most notable of these works is Thiruvalluvar's Tirukkural, written by the renowned Tamil poet and philosopher Thiruvalluvar.
- The two epics Silappathikaram is written by Elango Adigal and Manimegalai by Sittalai Sattanar. They also provide valuable details about the Sangam society and polity.

Other Sources that give details about the Sangam Period are:

- Commercial trade ties between the West and South India are mentioned by Greek authors such as Megasthenes, Strabo, Pliny, and Ptolemy.
- The Chera, Chola, and Pandya monarchs to the south of the Mauryan Empire were referenced in the Ashokan inscriptions.
- Hathigumpha inscription of Kharavela of Kalinga also has mention of Tamil kingdoms.

Political History of Sangam Period

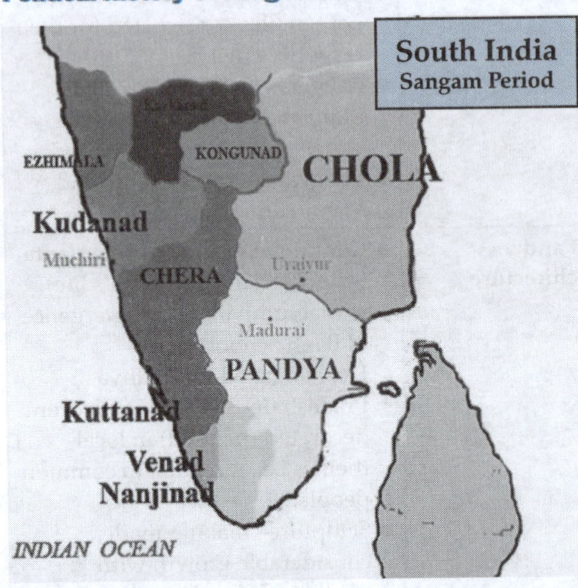

This map is not to scale and is for reference only.

During the Sangam Age, South India was dominated by three dynasties: the Cheras, Cholas, and Pandyas. The Sangam Period literary allusions are the primary source of knowledge about these countries.

Dynasties	Important Notes
Cheras	• The Cheras ruled over large parts of modern-day Kerala. • Vanjji was the Cheras' capital. • During this time, the most prominent seaports were Musiri and Tondi. • The emblem of Cheras is the 'bow and arrow'. • The first-century Pugalur inscriptions references to 3 generations of Chera kings. • Senguttuvan (2nd century CE) was the prominent ruler of the Chera dynasty. • The military achievements of Senguttuvan have been recorded in the epic Silapathikaram, which talks about his Himalayan expedition where he vanquished many rulers from northern India. • Senguttuvan popularised the Pattini religion, or the worship of Kannagi as the ideal bride, in Tamil Nadu. • He was the first to send an ambassador to China from South India.

Cholas	• The Chola monarchy of the Sangam period encompassed modern-day Tiruchirapalli District, Tiruvarur District, Nagapattinam District, Ariyalur District, Perambalur District, Pudukkottai District, and Thanjavur District. • Initially, the capital of the Cholas was Uraiyur. Later it was shifted to Puhar (also called Poompuhar). • King Karikala was a prominent king of the Sangam Chola dynasty. • The insignia/emblem of the Cholas was 'tiger'. • Pattinappalai, a novel authored by Kadiyalur Uruttirangannanar, portrays his life and military exploits. • Several Sangam poems recount the Battle of Venni, in which he beat an alliance of Cheras, Pandyas, and 11 minor chieftains. • Vahaipparandalai was another important battle fought by Karikala. • Trade and commerce prospered during his rule. • He also constructed irrigation tanks near river Kaveri to make available water for reclaimed land from the forest for farming.
Pandyas	• The Pandyas ruled over modern-day Tamil Nadu's southern area. • Madurai was the capital of Pandyas. • Their emblem was the 'Fish'. • King Neduncheliyan was also called Aryappadai Kadantha Neduncheliyan. • According to legend, the curse of Kannagi, Kovalan's wife, burned and destroyed Madurai. • Maduraikkanji, authored by Mangudi Maruthanar, discusses the socioeconomic state of Korkai's ports.

End of Sangam Age

- The Sangam period saw its gradual fall around the end of the third century A.D.
- The Kalabhras inhabited Tamil nation between 300 AD and 600 AD, a time known as an interregnum or 'dark era' by older historians.

Unit-9: Harshavardhana Period

- Harsha, also called Harshavardhana, (born 590 CE—died 647 CE), was a ruler of a large empire in northern India from 606 CE to 647 CE.
- Harsha's reign seemed to mark a transition from the ancient to the medieval period, when decentralized regional empires continually struggled for hegemony.
- He was the last ruler of the Vardhana Empire, one of the great empire in ancient India before the Islamic Invasion.
- After the fall of great Gupta Empire in the middle of the 6th century CE, under whom India saw its own golden age, it was Harshavardhana who unified most of northern India and ruled for four decades from his capital Kanyakubja.

Harsha Ascension

- When Prabhakara Vardhana died, his elder son Rajyavardhana ascended to Thanesar's kingdom.
- Harsha had a sister, Rajyashri, who was married to Kannauj's King Grahavarman. Sasanka, the Gauda monarch, slew Grahavarman and imprisoned Rajyashri.
- This provoked Rajyavardhana to confront Sasanka. However, Sasanka assassinated Rajyavardhana.
- This led the 16-year old Harshavardhana to ascend the throne of Thanesar in 606 AD.
- He vowed to avenge his brother's murder and also rescue his sister.
- He formed an alliance with Bhaskaravarman, the Kamarupa ruler, to accomplish this. Harsha and Bhaskaravarman marched in opposition to Sasanka. Sasanka eventually left for Bengal, and Harsha became king of Kannauj as well.

Empire of King Harshvardhana

- On acquiring Kannauj, Harsha united the two kingdoms of Thanesar and Kannauj.
- He moved his capital to Kannauj.
- After the fall of the Guptas, North India was divided into many small kingdoms.
- Harsha was able to unite many of them under his command. He had under his control of Punjab and central India. After Sasanka's death, he annexed Bengal, Bihar and Odisha.
- In Gujarat, he also vanquished the Vallabhi king. (The Vallabhi monarch and Harsha reached an agreement through a marriage between Harsha's daughter and the Vallabhi king Dhruvabhata).
- However, Harsha's plans to conquer lands to the south were hampered when the Chalukya king, Pulakesin II defeated Harsha in 618-619 A.D. This sealed Harsha's southern territorial limit as the Narmada River.
- Even the feudatories were under the tight command of Harsha. Harsha's reign marked the strengthening of feudalism in India.
- During Harsha's reign, Hiuen Tsang visited India. He has painted a fairly positive picture of King Harsha and his realm. He compliments him on his generosity and justice.
- Harsha was a generous supporter of the arts. He was a skilled writer in his own right. He is known for his Sanskrit writings Ratnavali, Priyadarshika, and Nagananda.

- Banabhatta was his court poet and he composed the Harshacharita which gives an account of Harsha's life and deeds.
- Harsha generously supported the Nalanda University.
- He had an excellent tax structure. A quarter of the taxes collected were spent for charitable and cultural causes.
- Harsha was a capable military conqueror and administrator.

Territories

- Under Harsha, there were two sorts of territories.
- One kind was directly under him, while the other was feudatories.
  - **Direct territories:** Central Provinces, Bengal, Kalinga, Rajputana, Gujarat.
  - **Feudatories:** Jalandhar, Kashmir, Kamarupa, Sind, Nepal.

Society and Religion

- The caste system was widespread among Hindus. They were split into four castes or varna: Brahmana, Vaishya, Kshariya, and Shudra, each with its own subcaste.
- Women's standing has fallen from the liberal age of former times.
- Satipratha (widow immolation) was common, and widow remarriage was not allowed in higher castes.
- Harsha was a worshiper of Shiva in the beginning but later became a Mahayana Buddhist.
- Yet, he was tolerant of other faiths.
- With a view to popularize and propagate the doctrines of Mahayana Buddhism, Harsha arranged at Kanyakubja a great assembly which was presided over by Hiuen Tsang, in 643 CE.

Art and Education

- Harsha supported both art and education. He was also an author, having written three Sanskrit dramas, Nagananda, Ratnavali, and Priyadarshika. One-fourth of his earnings were used to support students.
- Furthermore, Hiuen Tsang describes the prestigious Nalanda University, which was at its peak during Harsha's rule.
- The curriculum included Vedas, Buddhism, philosophy, logic, urban planning, medicine, law, astronomy, etc.
- Also, a famous Indian writer and poet named Banabhatta served as the 'Asthana Kavi' (primary poet of the kingdom) in the court of Harshavardhana.

Death and Legacy

- Harsha's dominion saw the birth of feudalism in India.
- Land was allocated in villages, giving local landowners influence.
- This resulted in the empire's decline and the emergence of local feuds. Harsha had to be constantly on the go to keep everything in order.
- After ruling over most parts of North India for more than 40 years, Harsha died in 647 C.E.
- Since he did not have any heirs his empire collapsed and disintegrated rapidly into small states.
- The demise of King Harshavardhana marked the end of the mighty Vardhana dynasty.

Ancient Travellers to India

- **Deimachus (3rd Century B.C.):** Deimachus was a Greek ambassador sent by the Seleucid king Antiochus I to the court of Bindusara.
- **Megasthenes (302-298 B.C.):** Megasthenes was Seleucus' diplomat who visited India under the reign of Chandragupta Maurya.
- During his tour to India, he authored a book called INDICA about the country. He referred to Chandragupta Mauryan as 'SANDROCOTTUS'.
- **Fa Hein (399–414 A.D.):** He was a Buddhist monk from China who came to India during Chandragupta II's (Vikramaditya) reign. On his tour to India, he visited Lumbini, i.e., Buddha's birthplace. His travelogue was called "Records of Buddhist Kingdom".
- **Hiuen Tsang (630-645 A.D.):** Hiuen Tsang was another Buddhist monk from China who came to India during Harsha Vardhana's reign. He wrote "The Records of Western World", also called Si-Yu-Ki. He was called to King Harshavardhana's court after becoming a guest of the Kamarupa ruler, Bhaskaravarman.
- **I-Tsing (671-695 A.D.):** I-Tsing visited India during the reign of Harshavardhana. He was a Chinese wanderer who journeyed to India to study Buddhism. He published several biographies of Indian monks.
- **Al Masudi (957 A.D.):** Al Masudi was a traveller who visited India from Arabia in the middle of the 10th century A.D. He described his views on India in his book, Muruj-ul-Zehab.
- **Al Beruni (1024-1030 A.D.):** Al Beruni travelled to India with Mahmud of Ghazni. He was a Persian scholar who visited India. His work 'Tahqiqi-e-Hind' discussed India. He has also been dubbed the "Father of Indology" for his contributions.
- **Macro Polo (1292-1294 A.D.):** Macro Polo came during the reign of Rudramma Devi of the Kakatiyas. He was a European scholar who entered India from the South. He wrote "The Book of Sir Marco Polo", which gives an invaluable account of Indian economic history.
- **Ibn Batuta (1333-1347 A.D.):** In the 14th century, under the reign of Mohammed Bin Tughlaq, he journeyed from Morocco to India and penned "RIHLA".
- **Nicolo Conti (1420-1421 A.D.):** Nicolo Conti was a merchant from Italy who came to India while Devaraya I of the Sangam dynasty of the Vijayanagar Empire was ruling.
- **Abdul Razak (1443-1444 A.D.):** He was a Persian scholar. He was also a Persian ambassador. He came during the reign of Deva Raya II of the Vijayanagara Empire.
- **Duarte Barbosa (1500-1516 AD):** Duarte Barbosa was a Portuguese traveller who visited India in the early 16th century. His writings include details about the Vijayanagara Empire's people and government.

Important Literature

Books	Authors
Rajtarangini	Kalhana
Kathasaritsagar	Shaivite Somadeva
Kamasutra	Vatsayana
Prashnottarmalika	Amoghavarsha
Buddha Charita	Asvaghosa
Natyashastra	Bharata Muni

Amarkosa	Amarasimha
Panch tantra	Vishnu Sharma
Indica	Megasthanese
Arthasastra	Kautilya
Charaka Samhita	Charaka
Lilawati	Bhaskara II
Harshacharita, Kadambari	Banabhatta
Nagananda, Ratnavali, Priyadarsika	Harsha
Gathasaptashati	Hala
Astadhyayi	Panini
Mahabhasya	Patanjali
Naishadhacharitra	Sri Harsha
Gitagovinda	Jayadeva
Navratna	Virsena
• Abhigyanshakuntalam • Vikramorvasiyam • Malavikagnimitra • Kum-rasambhava • Raghuvansham • Meghadootam • Ritusamhara • Jyotirvidabharana	Kalidasa
• Nitisara	Kamandaka
• Mudrarakshas • Devichandraguptam	Vishakhadatta
• Brihatkatha	Gunadhya
• Mrichhakatikam	Sudraka
• Panchasiddhantika (5 books, Brihatsamhita most notable)	Varahamihir
• Susrutsamhita on surgery	Susrut
• Ashtanghridaya	Vagabhata
• Ayurveda	Dhanavantari
• Amarkosh	Amar Singh
• Aryabhattiyam	Aryabhata
• Brahmasphutasiddhanta	Brahmagupta
• Svapanavasaydattam	Bhasa

Important Literature

Important Inscription

Inscription	King
Ayodhya	Pushyamitra Sunga
Besnagar Garuda Pillar	Bhagabhadra
Hathigumpha	Kharvela King of Kalinga
Aihole	Pulkeshin (II)
Gwalior	Bhoja
Allahabad	Samudragupta
Junagarh	Rudradaman
Bhitari	Skandagupta
Nanaghat	Satkarni (I)
Nasik	Gautamiputra Satkarni
Mandsaur	Yashodharman

❑❑❑

Medieval History

Unit-1: Early Medieval Kingdoms

- The early mediaeval period of Indian history is defined as the time between AD 750 and AD 1200. Due to frequent conflicts between regional states, it was previously referred to as the 'dark age' of Indian history.
- According to recent research, even though India was politically split, it had exceptional progress in the fields of art, literature, and language.
- During this perizod, Kannauj became more significant and Pataliputra lost its importance as a sign of the sovereignty of India. There was total decentralisation, which resulted in Indian feudalism. The development of various regional powers waging continual conflicts against one other weakened India's political cohesiveness.
- The political development of this period is mainly divided into two phases.

The first phase (750 AD - 1000 AD)

- It saw the development of three major political forces in India: the Gurjara Pratiharas (North India), the Palas (Eastern India), and the Rashtrakutas (South India).

The second phase (1000 AD - 1200 AD)

- It witnessed break-up of these powers.

Tripartite Struggle

- Tripartite Struggle was an armed conflict between Palas of East, Gurjara Pratiharas of North and Rashtrakutas of South India. These powers were fighting with each other to set up their control on the Gangetic region in northern India.
- The main objective of the conflict was to possess the Kannauj city, then a symbol of sovereignty.

Gurjara-Pratihara Empire (Western India): 730-1036 AD

- Pratiharas are known as Gurjara – Pratihara, as they originated from Gurjaras, who were primarily pastoralists and fighters.
- Dynasty was founded by Harichandra, in and around Jodhpur, south western Rajasthan.
- Pratihara were instrumental in containing Arab armies moving east of the Indus River.
- Gurjara-Pratihara are known for their sculptures, carved panels and open pavilion style temples. The greatest influence of their architecture also can be seen at Khajuraho, now a UNESCO World Heritage Site.
- Sanskrit Poet & Dramatist Rajasekhara lived in the court of Mahipala–a grandson of Mihirbhoja.
- Foreign traveller Al-Masudi had visited Pratihara Empire.

Important Rulers

Nagabhatta I (730-760 AD)	The most notable Pratiharas monarchs were noted for containing Arab forces.
Vatsaraja (780-800)	• Made Kannauj in western U.P. as his capital. • Expansionist strategy drove him into confrontation with Dharmapala, the Pala monarch, and Rashtrakuta ruler Dhruv, kicking off the "tripartite struggle" that lasted around 200 years. • 'Vatsaraja defeated Dharmapala (Pala) and was later defeated by Dhruva (Rashtrakuta).
Nagabhata II (805–833)	• He took Kannauj and the Indo-Gangetic Plain as far as Bihar from the Palas, and checked the Muslims in the west once again. • He reconstructed the Shiva temple at Somnath, Gujarat, that had been destroyed by an Arab assault from Sindh.
Bhoja I/ Mihir Bhoja (836-885)	• Greatest ruler of Pratiharas, got victories over Palas and Rashtrakutas. • Capital at Kannauj, which also known as Mahodaya. • Devotee of Vishnu, adopted the title 'Adivaraha'.

The Palas of Bengal: 750-1150 AD

- In 750 AD, Gopala founded the Pala dynasty.
- **Capital:** Muddagiri/ Munger (Bihar)
- Pala kingdom included Bengal and Bihar, which included major cities of Pataliputra, Vikrampura, Monghyr, Tamralipti.
- Palas were followers of Mahayana Buddhism and Tantric schools of Buddhism.

Important Rulers:

Gopala (around 750 AD)	• According to the Khalimpur copper inscription of Dharampala, he established the Pala dynasty, which succeeded the subsequent Guptas of Magadha and Khadga dynasties. • Built famous Odantpuri monastery at Bihar, 2nd largest after Nalanda university.
Dharampala (770-810)	• Defeated by Rashtrakuta king Dhruva and Pratihara king Nagabhata II. • Vikramshila University was founded near Bhagalpur, Bihar, while the Somapuri monastery was erected at Paharpur (present-day Bangladesh). • Revived Nalanda University.
Devapala (810-850)	• Expanded empire in the east and included Assam. • His Inscriptions proclaims his victory over Hunas, Gurjaras and Dravidas. • Vajradatta, the author of Lokesvarasataka and a Buddhist scholar, was his Court poet.

Pala and Pratihara's Administration:

- The regions immediately managed were split into Bhukti (provinces) and Mandala or Visaya (districts).
- Uparika, the governor of Bhukti, was responsible for collecting land income and maintaining peace and order.
- The head of Visaya was Visayapati and had same duties like Uparika within their territories.
- Smaller unit below the Visaya was pattala.
- Bhogapatis or Samantas were small chieftain, dominated villages.

The Rashtrakutas (Deccan): 752-973 CE

- Dantidurg was the founder of the kingdom.
- Rashtrakutas meaning 'the chief of a rashtra', they considered as the feudatory of the Chalukyas.
- **Capital:** Manyakheta or Malkhed near Gulbarga.
- Rashtrakuta was continually at odds with the eastern Chalukyas of Vengi, the Pallavas of Kanchi, and the Pandyas of Madurai.

Important Rulers

Dantidurga (753-756)	• Feudatory of the Chalukyan king, Kirtivarman II. • Founded Rashtrakuta kingdom in 753 AD.
Krishna I (756-774)	• He expanded his dominion to cover present-day Karnataka and Konkan. • Pallavas was dealt the ultimate blow. • During his reign, the rock-cut Kailasanath (Shiva) temple at Ellora caves was created.
Dhruva (780-793)	• He led successful expeditions to Kannauj, defeated the Nagabhatta II (Pratiharas) and Dharmapala (Pala).
Amoghavarsha I (814-878)	• Called as "Ashoka of the South" and also compared to Gupta king Vikramaditya. • Built new capital city at Manyakheta (Modern Malkhed). • Defeated the Eastern Chalukyas while maintaining amicable relations with neighbours. • He wrote Kavirajamarga (Kannada) and the Prashnottara Ratnamalika (Sanskrit). • He was follower of Jainism.

Art and Architecture

- Architecture reached a milestone in the Dravidian style, the finest example of which is seen in the Kailasanatha (Shiva) Temple at Ellora in modern Maharashtra.
- Other important contributions are the Kashivishvanatha temple and the Jain Narayana temple at Pattadakal (significant contributions from the Rashtrakuta dynasty in the 9th century) in modern Karnataka, both of which are UNESCO World Heritage Sites.
- The great Apabhramsha poet Svayambhu and his son lived in Rashtrakuta court.

Literature

Book	Writer
Kavirahasya	Halayudha
Parsvabhudya	Jinasena
Adipurana	Jinasena
Amogavritti	Sakatayana
Ganitasaram	Viracharya
Nalachampu	Trivikrama Bhatta
Vikramarjuna Vijaya	Pampa
Santipurana	Ponna

Administration

- The administrative system throughout these empires was founded on the concepts and practises of the Gupta Empire.
- The King was the head of government as well as the commander in chief of the armed forces. He also served as a judge.
- The king was assisted by number of ministers, generally form leading families and their position was hereditary.
- The empires consisted of areas administered directly and areas ruled by vessels. The latter had autonomy in internal affairs.
- The directly administered territories were divided into: Rashtra (province) and Visaya (Districts) and Bhukti.
- The head of Rashtra was Rashtrapati, and had similar functions as the Uparaika performed in Pala and Pratihara.
- Village was the smallest unit. The village headman carried out duties with the help of Grama-Mahajana or Grama-Mahattara (village elders).
- Villages also had committees in charge of schools, tanks, temples, and so forth.
- Koshtapala or Kotwal was in charge of law and order in the towns and surrounding territories.
- The hereditary revenue officers were known as Nad-Gowdas or Desa-gramakutas.

The Rise of Rajputs

- After Harsha's death (647 A.D.) and disintegration of Pratihara Empire many Rajput states emerged in Rajasthan and Indus plain. The Gahadavalas of Kannuj, Parmars of Malwa, and Chauhans of Ajmer were the prominent Rajput rulers.
- The Rajputs always insisted that they were of the kshatriya caste and they were divided into clans.
- The Rajput kings belonged to ordered family, which connected them with either the sun-family (surya-vanshi) or the moon-family (chandra-vanshi) of ancient Indian kings. However, there were four clans who claimed that they had not descended from either of these two families, but rather from the fire-family (agni-kula).

Rajput Clans

- Four agni-kula clans established their power in western India and parts of central India.

- **Pratiharas:** The Pariharas ruled in the region of Kannauj.
- **Chauhans:** The Chauhans were strong in central Rajasthan.
- **Solankis:** Solanki power rose in the region of Kathiawar and the surrounding areas.

- **Pawars:** The Pawars established themselves in the region of Malwa with their capital at Dhar near Indore.
- Besides, some other minor rulers also became powerful and gradually built small kingdoms in various parts of northern India, for example:
- Nepal
- Kamarupa (in Assam)
- Kashmir
- Utkala (in Odisha)
- Many of the hill states of Punjab also developed during the early phase of medieval period; such as:
- Champaka (Chamba)
- Durgara (Jammu)
- Kuluta (Kulu) in Himachal
- Some other worth noting kingdoms of central India (contemporary to the Rajputs) were:
- The Chandelas in Bundelkhand
- The Guhilas in Mewar to the south of the Chauhans
- The Tomaras in Haryana and the Delhi region
- Over a period of time, the Chauhans defeated the Tomaras and annexed their kingdom.
- Prithviraj III, the prince of Chauhan dynasty, was the most powerful king of that period in northern India. Chandbardai, the Hindi poet of his (Prithviraj's) court had written the famous epic poem 'Prithviraja-raso'.

Important Battles fought by Rajputs:

- The Rajputs led by Prithviraj Chauhan defeated Ghurids, led by Muhammad Ghori in the First Battle of Tarain in 1191.
- In 1192, Muhammad Ghori defeated and killed Prithviraj in the Second Battle of Tarain.
- In the Battle of Chandawar, Jaichand was defeated by Mohammad Ghori (1194).

Causes of Decline of Rajputs

- Feudal system proved fatal for Rajput kingdoms.
- Turkish invasion weakened Rajput states.
- Lack of political unity.
- Rajput states were engaged in constant war against each other for power which led to the wastage of their resources.

Indian Feudalism

Early Pali texts give us a glimpse of such feudal policies as the "Brahmadeya" in Pre Mauryan Periods. The Guptas and the Kushans played a major role in the introduction and practice of feudalism in India.

Feudalism was a dominant social system in the medieval times. In this system the nobility held lands from the Crown in exchange for military service, and vassals were in turn tenants of the nobles, while the peasants were obliged to live on their lord's land and give him homage, labour, and a share of the produce, in exchange for military protection.

Factors for Rise of Feudalism

- In Ancient India feudalisms were largely absent, land grants were usually for Buddhist monks.
- During Gupta Dynasty, feudal lords became supremely independent, and central authority had absolute non-interference in the affairs and functioning of the feudal regimes.
- In the 2nd century AD, hereditary rights and civil jurisdiction powers were also transferred to the feudal.
- Indian Feudalism rose during the advent of the 7th century when in place of cash, land grants intensified and took its final shape during 9th-12th century AD.

Feudal rise was accompanied by various dimensions of distinctions, most importantly being the 4-dimensional zones of Feudal distinction, these are:

- **North-West:** Gurjara-Pratihara
- **Bengal and Bihar:** Pala
- **Deccan:** Rashtrakutas
- Feudatories of **Southern states**

Impact

- Disintegration and balkanization of states gave rise to fall of the central authority.
- Rise of the small authoritarian states.
- Hereditary administrative status.
- Decentralisation: Samanthas were given land instead of salary, and they continued to own the territory, calling themselves vassals of the ruler.

Regressive Taxation System

Manorial System: The landowner grants land to an individual who performs a variety of services, including working on the lord's land, in exchange for the land.

After independence, land reforms in the 1950s-60s and the abolition of privy purses in 1971 ended the feudal system and helped in the upliftment of the weaker section.

Unit-2: Delhi Sultanate

Dynasties of Delhi Sultanate (1206-1526 A.D.)

Early Period and Slave Dynasty

- Sources of Medieval Indian History: Tarikh i Firoze Shahi (Ziauddin barani); Tuzuk-i-Mubarak Shahi (Yahaya bin Ahmed Sirhindi); Futuhat-i-Firoze Shahi (Firoze Shah Tughluq), etc.
- The invasions of Mahmud of Ghazni and Muhammad Ghori introduced a new political chapter in India.
- The campaigns of Muhammad Ghori paved the way for the rule of the Turk; and the Afghans.
- Mahmud of Ghazni targeted the North Indian temple cities for wealth and iconoclastic fervour.
- Muhammad Ghori nominated his trusted and prominent slave, Qutubuddin Aibak as his representative to govern the newly conquered regions in India. It was the beginning of the slave dynasty.
- Delhi became the centre of Turkish and Afghan power.
- The Turkish rule from Delhi came to be known as the Delhi Sultanate.
- The phrase 'Delhi Sultanate' is applied to the history of Northern India, extending from 1206 to 1526.

The Mamluk dynasty or The Slave Dynasty (1206-1290 AD)

Ruler	Period	Events
Qutb-ud-din Aibak	(1206–1210)	Founder of Mamluk Dynasty and Slave of Muhammad Ghori
Aram Shah	(1210–1211)	Eldest son of Qutb-ud-din Aibak
Shams-ud-din Iltutmish	(1211–1236)	Son-in-law of Qutb-ud-din Aibak
Ruknuddin Feruz Shah	(1236)	Son of Iltutmish
Razia Sultana	(1236–1240)	Daughter of Iltutmish and Grand Daughter of Qutb-ud-din Aibak.
Muizuddin Bahram	(1240–1242)	Son of Iltutmish
Alauddin Masud	(1242–1246)	Son of Ruknuddin Feruz Shah
Nasiruddin Mahmud	(1246–1266)	Razia's Brother who was born in 1229
Ghiyas-ud-din Balban	(1266–1286)	Father-in-law of Nasiruddin Mahmud and the most powerful ruler of the Slave Dynasty
Muiz ud din Kaiqubad	(1287–1290)	Grandson of Ghiyasuddin Balban
Kaimur	1290	Son of Muiz-ud-din Kaiqubad

- The word Mamluk is an Arabic word that means "slave/ owned". In fact, three dynasties were established during this period. They were:
- Qutbi dynasty (c. 1206 – 1211 CE) – Its founder was Qutub-ud-din Aibak.
- First Ilbari dynasty (c. 1211- 1266 CE) – Its founder was Iltutmish.
- Second Ilbari dynasty (c. 1266 – 1290 CE) – Its founder was Balban.

Qutub-ud-din Aibak (1206 – 1210 CE)

- Qutub-ud-din Aibak established the Slave dynasty. He was a Turkish slave of Muhammad Ghori.
- Muhammad Ghori made him the governor of his Indian possessions. He raised a standing army and established his hold over north India during the lifetime of Ghori.
- He was referred as "Lakh Baksh" or giver of lakhs because he donated liberally.
- He was titled as "Sultan" and he made Lahore as his capital.
- He also started the construction of the Qutub Minar (first storey only) after the name of the famous Sufi saint Khwaja Qutubuddin Bakhtiyar but it was later completed by Iltutmish.
- He died suddenly while playing Chaugan (horse polo) in 1210 CE.

Aram Shah (1210 CE)

- Qutub-ud-din was succeeded by his son Aram Shah.
- He was incapable as a ruler. He was opposed by the Turkish armies and his rule lasted for only eight months.

Iltutmish (1210 – 1236 CE)

- Iltutmish belonged to the Ilbari tribe and therefore, his dynasty was named the Ilbari dynasty. Iltutmish dethroned Aram Shah and became the Sultan with the name of Shamsuddin in 1211 CE.
- He is regarded as the real consolidator of Turkish rule in India.
- He defeated Yaldauz in the battle of Tarain in 1215 CE.
- When in 1220 CE, Genghis Khan, the leader of the Mongols, started his march towards Central Asia. The diplomatic policy of Iltutmish helped him to save his empire from the wrath of Genghis Khan.
- Iltutmish organised Turkan-i-Chahalgani, a new class of the ruling elite of forty powerful military leaders.
- He brought Bengal and Bihar back into the Delhi Sultanate.
- He suppressed the Rajput revolts and recovered Ranthambore in 1226 CE.
- By 1231 CE, Iltutmish established his control over Bayana, Mandor, Jalore and Gwalior.
- He completed the construction of Qutub Minar in Delhi.
- He introduced the Arabic coinage in India and the silver tanka, weighing 175 grains, became a standard coin in medieval India.
- He patronised many scholars and many Sufi saints came to India during his reign.
- Contemporary scholars during his reign were Minhaj-us-Siraj (author of Tahaqqat-i-Nasuri), Taj-ud-din, Muhammad Junaidi, Fakhrul-Mulk-Isami, Malik Qutub-ud-din Hasan .
- He nominated his daughter as his successor.

Ruknuddin Feruz Shah (1236 CE)

- He was the eldest son of Iltutmish who ascended the throne with the help of nobles.
- When the governor of Multan revolted, Feroz Shah marched to suppress the revolt. Using this opportunity, Iltutmish's daughter Raziya with the help of the Amirs of Delhi seized the throne of the Delhi Sultanate.

Raziya Sultan (1236 – 1240 CE)

- Raziya Sultan was the first and only female ruler of medieval India's Sultanate period.
- Raziya appointed an Abyssinian slave, Malik Jamal-ud-din Yaqut as master of the Royal horses (Amir-i-akhur).
- In 1240 CE, Altunia, the governor of Bhatinda (Sirhaind) revolted against her. Raziya alongside Yaqut marched against Altunia, but on the way, Turkish followers of Altunia murdered Yaqut and took Raziya prisoner. In the meantime, the Turkish nobles put Bahram, another son of Iltutmish on the throne. However, Raziya won over her captor, Altunia and after marrying him, proceeded to Delhi. But she was defeated and killed on the way by Bahram Shah.

Bahram Shah (1240 - 1242 CE)

- After Razia,Iltutmish's third son Bahram Shah was put on the throne by the powerful Turkish council Chalisa.
- He was considered only as de jure ruler, while Naib-e-mamlakat (the regent) was the de facto ruler.
- Bahram Shah lost his life after his failed attempt to assert his authority once on the throne.

Masud Shah (1242 - 1246 CE)

- He was the son of Ruknuddin but was deposed after Balban and Nasiruddin Mahamud's Mother,Malika-e-Jahan,conspired against him and established Nasiruddin Mahamud as the new Sultan.

Nasiruddin Mahamud (1246 - 1266)

- He was the son of Iltutmish and was known as the Darvesi King as he was very pious and noble.He died in 1266.

Balban (1266 – 1286 CE)

- He was one of the Turkish chiefs.
- He laid the foundation for a strong centralised government.
- He sought to increase the prestige and power of the monarchy.
- He stood as a champion of Turkish nobility.
- He broke the power of Chahalgani.
- He administered justice with extreme impartiality.
- Strong centralised army with a network of spies to ensure order.
- Balban adopted a policy of "Blood and Iron", to crush the rebels.
- He insisted on the ceremony of Sijdah (prostration) and paibos (Kissing the monarch's feet).

Important Department

Department	Function
Diwan-i-Risalat (Foreign Minister)	Dealing with diplomatic correspondences
Diwan-i-Ariz	Military department
Diwan-i-Bandagan	Department of slaves
Diwan-i-Qaza-i- Mamalik	Department of justice
Diwan-i-Isthiaq	Department of pensions
Diwan-i-Mustakhraj	Department of arrears
Diwan-i-Khairat	Department of charity
Diwan-i-Kohi	Department of agriculture
Diwan-i-Insha	Department of Correspondence

Important Central Officials

Wazir	The Chief Minister of the State-in Charge of revenue and finances, controlled by other departments
Ariz-i-Mumalik	Head of Military department
Qazi	Legal Officer [dispensed civil law based on Muslim law Shariat)
Wakil-i-dar	Controller of the royal Household
Barid-i-mumalik	Head of the state news agency
Amir-i-majlis	Officer-in-charge of royal feasts, conference and festivals
Majlis-i-am	Council of friends and officers consulted on important affairs of the state
Dahir-i-mumalik	Head of the royal correspondence
Sadr-us-sudur	Dealt with the religious matters and endowments
Sadr-i-jahan	Officers-in-charge of religious and charitable endowment
Amir-i-dad	Public prosecutors
Naib wazir	Deputy Minister
Mushrif-i-mumalik	Accountant General
Amir-i-hazib	Officer-in-charge of the royal court
Kazi-i-mumalik	Chief Justice
Kazi-ul-kazat	Head of the Central Judicial department

There were five types of taxes: (i) Ushra (ii) Kharaj (iii) Khams (iv) Jaziya (v) Zakat.

Khalji Dynasty

The Khaljis (1290-1320 A. D)

Jalaluddin Khalji (1290-96 A.D)

- He founded Khalji dynasty.
- He believed that state should be based on the willing support of the governed.
- He followed a policy of tolerance towards the nobility.

Alauddin Khilji (1296-1316 A.D)

- He was harsh towards nobles and banned festivals, use of wines and intoxicants.
- He weakened the power of nobles.
- He was followed by a Hindu convert Khusrau, who was defeated by Tughlaqs.
- He was the first Delhi Sultan to launch successful military campaigns into the far south of India.
- He introduced Diwan-i-Mustakraj (Revenue ministry).
- Malikafur (Senapati) commander of Alauddin conqured southern kingdoms of Yadava, Kakatiya, Hoysala and Pandya.
- Malik Mohammad Jayasi, sufi poet, wrote "Padmavat", where Rajput women perform 'Jauhar' in order to save their honour.
- He brought in Market reforms, military reforms, reduced the powers of iqtadars, increased central control, collected revenue directly in some regions.

Mubarak Khan (1316-1320)

- Following the death of Kafur, Mubarak khan was freed from prison. He captured the throne at the first opportunity he got,but could rule only for a year as he sank into debauchery and could not give up his dissipated lifestyle.
- He awarded his lover Mubarak Hassan authority over army and palace guards, who soon obtained full control over Sultan's palace. Mabarak Hassan was given the title Khusrau Khan by the Sultan and within months Khusrau killed Mubarak Khan and assumed the title of Nasirudin in mid-1320.

Khusrau Khan: 1320

- Khusrau Khan was killed by Ghazi Malik, governor of Dipalpur, when he tried to oppose a rebellion by Ghazi Malik and his son Fakhruddin Jauna. This brought the end of Khilji dynasty and established the Tughlaq dynasty on the throne of Delhi.

The Tughlaqs (1320-1412 A.D)

- It was founded by Ghazi Malik/Ghiyaz-ud-din Tughlaq (1320-25 A.D).

Ghiyasuddin Tughlaq (1320- 1325)

- Khusrau Khan , the last king of the Khilji dynasty was killed by Ghazi Malik. Ghazi Malik ascended the throne assuming the title Ghiyasuddin Tughlaq.

- He died in an accident and his son Jauna (Ulugh Khan) succeeded him under the title Mohammad-bin-Tughlaq.

Muhammad Bin Tughlaq (1325-1351)

- Muhammad bin Tughlaq was the only Delhi Sultan who had received a comprehensive literary, religious and philosophical education.
- Muhammad bin Tughlaq wanted to make Devagiri his second capital so that he might be able to control South India better.
- In 1327, he made extensive preparations for the transfer of the royal household and the ulemas and Sufis from Delhi to Devagiri, which was renamed as Daulatabad.
- Muhammad bin Tughlaq issued copper coins at par with the value of the silver tanka coins.
- In order to overcome financial difficulties, Muhammad bin Tughlaq increased the land revenue on the farmers of Doab (land between Ganges and Yamuna rivers.
- A severe famine was also ravaging that region at that time. It had resulted in a serious peasant revolt.
- He launched a scheme by which taccavi loans (loans for cultivation) were given to the farmers to buy seed and to extend cultivation.
- A separate department for agriculture, Diwan- i- Kohi was established. Model farm under the state was created in an area of 64 square miles for which the government spent seventy lakh tankas.
- The rebellion of Hasan Shah resulted in the establishment of the Madurai Sultanate. In 1336 the Vijayanagar kingdom was founded. In 1347 Bahmani kingdom was established.
- In Gujarat Taghi rose in revolt against the Sultan who spent nearly three years chasing him. Muhammad bin Tughlaq's health became worse and he died in 1351.

Firoz Tughlaq (1351-1388)

- He appointed Khan-i-Jahan Maqbal, a Telugu Brahmin convert as wazir (prime minister).
- He strictly followed the advice of the ulemas in running the administration. He pleased the nobles and assured hereditary succession to their properties (iqta system).
- As per the Islamic law he levied the taxes. Jiziya was strictly imposed on non-Muslims.
- He was the first Sultan to impose irrigation tax. But at the same time he dug irrigation canals and wells. The longest canal was about 150 kilometres from Sutlej to Hansi.
- The special tax on 28 items was abolished by him since they were against the Islamic law.
- He also developed royal factories called karkhanas in which thousands of slaves were employed.
- About 300 new towns were built during his reign. The famous among them was Firozabad near Red Fort in Delhi, now called Firoz Shah Kotla.
- A new department called Diwan-i-Khairat was created to take care of orphans, widows and for marriage of poor girls.
- Firoz patronized scholars like Barani and Afif.

After Firoz Shah Tughlaq (1388-1414)

- The Tughlaq dynasty could not survive much after Firoz Shah's death.The Malwa,Gujarat and Sharqi-Jaunpur) Kingdoms broke away from the Sultanate.

Timur's Invasion (1398-1399)

- Timur, a Turkish Chief and cruel conqueror from Mangolia and descendant of Genghis Khan,invaded India in 1398 during the reign of Muhammad Shah Tughlaq. Timur's army plundered Delhi mercilessly . Timur returned to Central Asia, leaving a nominee named Khizr Khan to rule to Punjab.

The Sayyid Dynasty (1414-50 AD)

- **Khizr Khan(1414-1421):** Timur's nominee captured Delhi and was proclaimed the new Sultan. He was the first of the Sayyid dynasty which ruled over Delhi and surrounding districts.
- **Mubarak Shah (1421-1434):** He succeeded Khizr Khan at the throne after his successful expeditions against Mewatis, Katehars and the Gangetic Doab area. He was killed by the nobles in his own court.
- **Muhammad Shah (1434-1443):** The nobles put Muhammad Shah on the throne, but he could not survive the in-fighting among the nobles in the court. He was authorised to rule only a meagre area around 30 miles, and rest the of the Sultanate was ruled by nobles.
- **Alam Shah (1443-1451):** The last Sayyid king descended in favour of Bahlol Lodi and retired. Thus began the Lodi dynasty which was confined to Delhi and a few surrounding areas.

The Lodi Dynasty (1451-1526 AD)

Bahlol Lodi (1451- 1488)

- Bahlol Lodi was one of the Afghan Sardars. He established himself in Punjab after the invasion of Timur.
- He established the Lodi dynasty.

Sikandar Lodi

- Sikandar Lodi succeeded Bahalul Lodi in the Delhi Sultanate (1489-1517).
- Sikandar Lodi was considered the greatest ruler of the Lodi dynasty.
- In 1504, Sikandar Lodi constructed the city of Agra and shifted the capital from Delhi to Agra.
- Sikandar Lodi was responsible for the destruction of many Hindu temples and imposed restrictions on Hindus.

Ibrahim Lodi and Decline of Lodi Dynasty

- Ibrahim Lodi, succeeded Sikandar Lodi.
- Ibrahim Lodi faced challenges as an administrator and had conflicts with nobles and governors.
- Allam Khan Lodi and Daulat Khan Lodi, close relatives of Ibrahim Lodi, invited Babar to invade India.
- Rana Sanga, the ruler of Mewar, also invited Babar to invade India.
- Krishnadevraya was the emperor of Vijayanagara in southern India during this period.
- In 1526 AD, Babar defeated and killed Ibrahim Lodi in the first Battle of Panipat.
- Ibrahim Lodi was the last sultan of the Delhi Sultanate.
- The victory at the Battle of Panipat marked the beginning of the Mughal rule in India under Babar.

Causes of the decline of Delhi Sultanate

- The Sultanate of Delhi was autocratic. The Sultans of Delhi ruled as despots. They concentrated all of the

Sultanate's power in their own hands, and the Amirs held the reins of the empire in their own hands.

- The people were denied the right to participate in the affairs of the kingdom.
- Thus, there was a wide gulf between the Sultan and the people, which widened even more during the reigns of the late unsuccessful Sultans, and thus continued to disintegrate with the passage of time.
- The Ulema and orthodox Muslims held a privileged position in the Sultanate and influenced the Sultan's policies.
- Because the majority of Hindus were not treated favourably by the Muslim rulers, they never cooperated with them.
- They amassed a lot of wealth during their invasions and plundered the temples, but they also spent a lot of money organising the army and repelling the Mongol invasion.
- Furthermore, Muhammad Tughluq's ridiculous schemes depleted the royal treasury, and no government could be stable without sound finances.
- The invasion of Babur proved to be the final significant reason for the decline of the Sultanate of Delhi.
- Ibrahim Lodi failed to measure swords with the Mughal army and fell prostrate before it. Babur's well-equipped and disciplined army completely uprooted the Delhi Sultanate.

Unit-3: Administration, Economy & Society under Delhi Sultanate

Adminstration during Delhi Sultanate Period

- With the establishment of the Delhi sultanate a new ruling class emerged in India. This new class introduced a new administrative system.
- During the Sultanate period, the administrative apparatus was headed by the Sultan who was helped by various nobles. There were various other offices along with the office of the Sultan. Theoretically, there was a council of Ministers Majlis-i-Khalwat to assist the Sultan.
- Sultanate administration is called as Turko-Afghan setup in Indian environment.
- The Sultans considered themselves as representatives of the Caliph.
- Iltutmish was the first sultan to receive recognition letter from Caliph.
- Delhi sultanate was neither a theocratic state nor a secular state. It was depended on ruler.
- Mullahs were interpreters of shariyath.
- Qajis were executors of Shariyath.

Sultan
↓
Naib/wali

1. Diwan-i-wazirath (finance minister)
2. Wazir acted as Prime minister
3. Diwan-i-Ariz- defence minister
4. Diwan-i-insha- department of correspondence
5. Diwan-i-rasalath- dealing with diplomatic correspondences
6. Qazi-Judicial department chief

Iqta System

The Iqta system was a one-of-a-kind land distribution and administrative system that was implemented during the reign of Iltutmish. The territories of the Delhi Sultanate were split into various big and small areas called Iqta and distributed to the Sultan's troops, officers, and nobles under the Iqta system.

Territorial Administration:

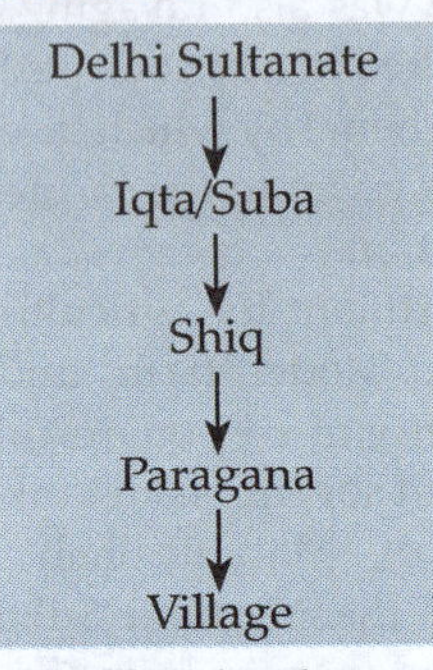

- Shiqs were controlled by shiqdar.
- Paragana were controlled by amil.
- Villages were ruled by village chiefs. He is known as muqaddam, chaudhri, and khut. Patwaries were village bookkeepers.
- The lands were classified into three categories:
  - **Iqta land:** Lands assigned to officials as iqtas instead of payment for their services.
  - **Khalisa land:** The Sultan had direct authority over the land, and the income generated were used to support the royal court and royal family.
  - **Inam land:** Land assigned or granted to religious leaders or religious institutions.

Economy during Delhi Sultanate Period

- Land revenue was a significant source of money for the government.
- The peasantry paid one-third of their output as land income, and occasionally even half.
- Agriculture formed the occupation of the bulk of the people.
- The peasants produced a large variety of food crops, cash crops, fruits, vegetables and spices.
- The Persian wheel was the most advanced water lifting device of this period.
- Cotton textile and silk industry flourished in this period.
- During the reign of the Delhi Sultans, paper-making technology developed by the Chinese and learned by the Arabs was introduced to India.
- These karkhanas were part of the royal establishment.
- In the field of commerce India had trade links with contemporary central Asia, China, South-east Asia and Europe etc.

Literature and Languages during Delhi Sultanate

- Persian became the official language of the Sultanate of Delhi.
- With the works of Amir Khusrau, the development of Persian literature on the subcontinent entered a new phase.
- The court chronicles were an important feature of the literature during the period of the Delhi Sultanate.
- During this time, Ziauddin Barani produced the most significant contribution to Persian literature. His most noteworthy works are the Tarikh-I Firozshahi and the Fatwa-I Jahandari.
- Ziauddin Barani was an outspoken opponent of Muhammad ibn Tughlaq.
- Minhaj-us-Siraj wrote Tabaqat-iNasari, a general history of Muslim dynasties up to 1260.
- Abu Bakr's Chachanamh is the first geographical treatise deals with conquest of sindh.
- During this period there were many works that were translated into Persian. The Tuti Nama (book of the parrot) by Zia Nakshabi was the first Persian translation of Sanskrit stories.

Architecture during Delhi Sultanates

During the medieval period, new architectural forms and styles were introduced in India. The fusion of Indian and Islamic architectural elements resulted in the birth of Indo-Islamic architecture.

- The arch and dome were new architectural additions of the period.
- The use of lime-mortar in the construction of buildings and houses altered the building techniques.
- The development of the true arch was important feature of the architectural style of the period.
- Initially, they transformed temples and other ruined sites into mosques. For example, the Quwwat-ul-Islam mosque near Qutub Minar in Delhi was erected from materials salvaged from the destruction of several Hindu and Jain temples.
- With the arrival of artisans from West Asia the arch and dome began to show up with precision and perfection. Gradually local artisans also acquired the skill. The tomb of Balban has the first real arch, while the Alai Darwaza, erected by Alaud-din Khalji as an entrance to the Quwwatul-Islam Mosque, has the first true dome.
- Ghiyasuddin Tughlaq added Tughlaqabad to Delhi.
- Muhammad bin Tughlaq added Jahanpanha to Delhi.
- Firoz shah Tughlaq added Ferozabad to Delhi.
- Muhammad bin Tughlaq built the tomb of Ghyasuddin on a high platform.
- After Tughlaqs Sikander Lodi constructed Jama masjid in Agra, it is the first structure in middle of garden.

Music during Delhi Sultanate

- The important phase in the development of music during this period belongs to the time of Amir Khusrau.
  - Amir Khusrau was the first to describe Kashmir as Eden on earth.
  - He proclaimed himself as tuti-i-hind or parrot of India.
  - He was contemporary of Jalaluddin Khalji, Alauddin Khalji,Ghiyasuddin Tughlaq.
  - He witnessed rule of eight sultans.
- It is during this period that the qawwali style is said to have developed. He is also credited for the development of many modern ragas like aiman, gora and sanam.
- He is credited with the creation of a new musical instrument, the sitar that was a combination of the Indian vina and the Iranian tambura.
- New musical instruments such as sarangi and rabab were introduced during this period.
- Raja Man Singh of Gwalior was a great lover of music. He encouraged the composition of a great musical work called Man Kautuhal.

Society under Delhi Sultanate

- The civilization of the Delhi Sultanate was split into four basic groups: nobles (Aristocrats), priests, townspeople, and peasants.
- Nobles included Sultan and his relatives, courtiers and holders of Iqta, Hindu and Muslim chieftains, merchants, bankers etc. Almost all the wealth and power was concentrated in this group. They lived in luxury and style.
- Brahmins and Ulemas made up the second group of priests.
- Brahmins and Ulemas were both awarded tax-free land grants, making them wealthy and influential. Throughout much of the Sultanate period (save under Alauddin Khilji), the influence of Ulema was so strong that it frequently impacted the Sultan's policy.
- The town people included urban wealthy merchants, traders and artisans. Since nobles and merchants lived in towns, they gradually became centres of administration and military. Sufi saints' homes become pilgrimage destinations. In metropolitan areas, there was a tendency of artisan communities, with weavers living in a weavers' colony and goldsmiths residing in a goldsmiths' colony. International trade was thriving. The state paid royal Karkhanas to produce things.
- The lowest stratum of the society of Delhi Sultanate was peasants. They lived in villages, paid taxes to state as land revenue. A change in dynasty generally did not brought any change in their lives. There was a rigid caste system. Intercaste marriage and dining got totally prohibited. Hindus and Muslims inspired each other's cultures and practises. Those who converted to Islam maintained their previous traditions, and so India's composite culture was established.

Unit-4: Mughal Empire

- The Mughals were descendants of two great lineages of rulers.
- Babur was the founder of the Mughal Empire in India. He was related to Timur from his father's side and to Genghis Khan through his mother.
- Babur succeeded his father as the ruler of Farghana (Uzbekistan), but soon lost his kingdom.
- Financial difficulties, apprehension of Uzbek attack on Kabul and invitation of Rana Sanga to invade India forced Babur to look towards India.

Babur (1526-1530 AD)

- **First Battle of Panipat (1526):** Babur decisively defeated Ibrahim Lodi. It Replaced the Lodi and established Mughal era in India.

- **Reasons for Babur's victory:** Alternatively resting one wing of Army, Services of two ottoman master gunners – Ustad Ali & Mustafa, Use of Gunpowder, scientific use of cavalry & artillery tactics – tulughma and the araba, effective use of Cannons.
- **Battle of Khanwa (1527):** Babur defeated Rana Sangha and assumed title of Ghazi.
- **Battle of Chanderi (1528):** Medini Rai was defeated and with this resistance across Rajputana was shattered.
- **Battle of Ghagra (1529):** Babur defeated Mahmud Lodi who aspired to the throne of Delhi.

Significance of Babur's advent into India

- Babur Introduced Char-Baghs and symmetrically laid out gardens.
- Built mosques at Panipath and Sambhat in Rohilkhand.
- Babur wrote Tuzuk-I-Baburi (Babarnama) & Masnavi.
- Kabul and Kandhar became integral parts of Mughal Empire.
- Babur popularized the gun powder, cavalry and artillery in India. (Gunpowder used earlier in India, but Babur popularized its use).
- Strengthened India's foreign trade.
- Babur introduced a new mode of warfare in India.
- Defeating Sangha & Lodi he smashed the balance of power and laid the foundation for all India Empire.
- He had assumed title of Padshah.

Humayun (1530-40 AD & 1555-56 AD)

- In 1530, Humayun succeeded Babur. He had to contend with the Afghans' and Gujarat's Bahadur Shah's fast rise to prominence.
- At the battle of Chausa (1539) & battle of Kannauj (1540) Sher Shah, defeated Humayun and forced him to flee India.
- He sought refuge with the Iranian monarch for a spell. After the disintegration of the Suri Empire, he recovered Delhi in 1555.
- Humayun built a new city at Delhi which he named "Dinpanah".
- Mosques: Paid contribution in the construction of Jamali mosque and mosque of Isa Khan at Delhi.
- His widow Hamida Banu Begum built Humayun's tomb (UNESCO site).
- Humayun's sister, Gul Badan Begum, wrote "Humayun-Nama".
- The foundation for the Mughal painting was laid by Humayun when he was staying in Persia.
- He imported two artists to India, Mir Sayyid Ali and Abdal Samad, who became prominent during Akbar's rule.

Akbar (1556-1605)

- He succeeded the throne after his father Humayun's death.
- He defeated Hemu (Suri's wazir) at the second battle of Panipat in 1556.
- Akbar governed under Bairam Khan's regency from 1556 until 1560. Bairam was appointed Wakil of the realm, with the title Khan-i-Khanan.
- Battle of Haldighati (1576): Akbar's general Man Singh defeated Rana Paratap following most of the Rajput rulers accepted Akbar's suzerainty.
- Akbar defeated Gujarat ruler Muzaffar Shah. To commemorate this victory, he built Buland Darwaza at Fatehpur Sikri.
- Akbar gradually enlarged the Mughal Empire to include much of the Indian subcontinent.

Jahangir (1605-1627)

- When Akbar died in 1605, Prince Salim replaced him as Jahangir (World Conqueror). His son Khusrau revolted but was beaten and imprisoned, and his supporter, the fifth Sikh Guru, Guru Arjun Dev, was murdered.
- British Visited Machilipatnam during his reign. Captain Hawkins and Thomas Roe visited his court. Thomas Roe got the Farman for setting up an English factory at Surat.
- His wife Nurjaha had influence over the state affairs.
- Jahangir built Zanjr-i-Adal at Agra for those seeking royal justice.
- Mahtab Khan, his military commander, had revolted against him.
- Autobiography: Tuzuk-i- Jahangiri in Persian.
- Faced tough fight of Malik Amber in his expeditions to Ahmednagar.
- Introduction of the "Du-aspah and Sih-aspah" system. It was modification to Mansabdari. Nobles were allowed to maintain a large number of troops without raising their zat ranks.

Art and Architecture

- Started decorating wall with floral designs made of semi-precious stones (Pietra Durra) during his reign.
- Built Moti Masjid at Lahore. Shalimar and Nishant gardens in Kashmir built during his reign.
- The use of Halo or Divine lights behind king's head started under him.

Shahjahan (1628-1658)

- Inayat Khan's Shah Jahan Nama is a historical chronicle of Shah Jahan's reign. Dara Shikoh, his son, translated the Bhagavat Gita and the Upanishads into Persian.
- In 1628, he succeeded Jahangir and rose to the throne.
- Mumtaj Mahal, his adored wife, died three years after his ascension in 1631.
- In the north-west, the campaign to seize Balkh from the Uzbegs was unsuccessful and Qandahar was lost to the Safavids.
- His Deccan policy was more successful. He defeated the forces of Ahmadnagar and annexed it. Both Bijapur and Golkonda signed a treaty with the emperor.
- The palace, army, and family relocated from Agra to Shahjahanabad, the freshly finished imperial capital.
- It was a new addition to Delhi's historic residential city, along with the Red Fort, Jama Masjid, and Chandni Chowk.
- Under Shah Jahan, the salutation was chahar taslim and zaminbos (kissing the earth).
- During his reign, war of succession among his sons broke out.
- Battle of Dharmat, Battle of Samugarh, Battle of Khajwah, and Battle of Deorai took place and finally, Aurangzeb emerged victorious.

- His court historian Abdul Hameed Lohiri wrote "Padshah-Nama".

Architecture

- In 1632-53, he built the Taj Mahal to honour his wife, Mumtaj Mahal.
- Agra's Moti Masjid (completely made of white marble), Sheesh Mahal, and Mussaman Burj.
- Red Fort with its Rang Mahal, Diwan-i-Am and Diwan-i-Khas at Delhi.
- Jama Masjid in Delhi (red stone), Shalimar Bagh in Lahore and city of Shahjahanabad.
- The pietra dura method was used on a large scale in the Taj Mahal by Shah Jahan.

Aurangzeb (1658-1707)

- Masir – I Alamgiri book written by Mustaid Khan throws light on Aurangzeb's rule.
- He took the title Alamgir, World Conqueror. Also known as Zinda Pir.
- During his rule, the Mughal Empire expanded to encompass practically the whole Indian subcontinent.

Later Mughals and Decline of Mughals

A war of succession broke out among the sons when father Aurangzeb died in 1707. Muazzam emerged victorious after defeating Muhammad Azam Shah in the Battle of Jajau.

Successors of Aurangzeb

Important Rulers	Important Events
Muazzam (Bahadur Shah I) (1707-1712)	Hindus are more accepting. Jizya was never abolished, but it was not properly enforced. Marathas Sardeshmukhi of Deccan was granted, but Chauth was not. Mughal historians such as Khafi Khan bestowed the title Shah-i-Bekhabar on him.
Jahandar Shah (1712-1713)	• Introduced Ijarah (Revenue Farming). • Became emperor with help of Zulfikhar Khan (later became PM) • To foster amicable ties with the Maratha and Rajputs, he abolished Jizya, bestowed the titles of Sardeshmukhi and Chauth of Deccan on Shahu, and bestowed the title of Mirza Raj Sawai on Jai Singh of Ambar and Maharaja on Ajit Singh.
Farruk Siyar (1713-1719)	• Abolished Jizya completely. • Puppet of Sayyed Brothers – Abdula Khan & Hussain Ali (known as kingmakers). • Policy of religious tolerance – abolished Jizya & pilgrimage tax. • Gave Farman to British in 1717. • Dethroned by Sayyed Brothers.
Rafi-ud-Darajat	• Ruled for the shortest period of time among the Mughals.
Muhammad Shah Rangeela (1719-1748)	• Autonomous states emerged under his reign: ■ **Nizam-ul-Mulk**: Deccan ■ **Saadat Khana**: Awadh ■ **Murshid Quli Khan**: Bengal, Bihar and Orissa • Nadir Shah invaded India and plundered the city of Delhi. He also stole the legendary peacock throne, and (reportedly also took the Kohinoor Diamond). • He became king with the assistance of the Sayyed Brothers, and then assassinated them with the assistance of Nizam-ul-Mulk. • Ahmad Shah Abdali also raided Delhi for first time during his reign.
Ahmad Shah (1748-1754)	• Mohd. Shah Rangeela's only son. • Was incompetent ruler; left the state affairs in the hands of Udham Bai. She was given the title of Qibla-i-Alam.
Alamgir II (1754-1759)	• Battle of Plassey (1757) was fought during his reign.
Shah Alam II/Aligauhar (1759-1806)	• During his reign, the third Battle of Panipat was fought between the Marathas and Ahmad Shah Abdali. • Along with Mir Qasim and Shuja-ud-Daula, he took part in the Battle of Buxar (1764) against the British East India Company. Was beaten and compelled to sign the Treaty of Allahabad (1765), which awarded the Company Diwani of Bengal. • Diwani of Bengal, Bihar and Orissa. • Became pensioner of the English.
Akbar II (1806-1837)	• Gave Ram Mohan Roy the title of "Raja". • Introduced Hindu-Muslim unity festival Phool Walon ki Sair.
Bahadur Shah II (1837-1857)	• Last Mughal Emperor • Was an Urdu Poet using Zafar as his pen name. • Participated in the revolt of 1857 after which he was deported to Rangoon and died.

Reasons for Decline of the Mughals

- After Aurangzeb, there was a lack of stability.
- The majority of emperors were puppets in the hands of strong Nobles who frequently administered government on their behalf.
- Weal military and political administration as exposed by Nadir Shah and Ahmad Abdali's invasion.
- Emergence of autonomous states and hence, weakening of central power.
- **Orthodox policy of Aurangzeb:** His attitude towards Marathas, Rajputs and Jats made them his enemy. His religious policies too alienated the Hindus.

Unit-5: Economic & Social Life under Mughals

Mughal relations with other rulers

- The Mughal rulers campaigned constantly against rulers who refused to accept their authority.
- However, when the Mughals grew in power, many other monarchs freely joined them. Rajputs, for example.
- The Mughals were able to expand their influence over numerous kings and chieftains by carefully balancing defeating but not humiliating their opponents [but not with Shivaji by Aurangzeb].

Mansabdars and Jagirdars

- As the empire expanded to encompass different regions, the Mughals recruited diverse bodies of people like Iranians, Indian Muslims, Afghans, Rajputs, Marathas and other groups.
- Those who joined Mughal service were enrolled as mansabdars – an individual who holds a mansab, meaning a position or rank.
- The Mughals utilised it to determine rank, income, and military tasks.
- The mansabdar's military obligations obliged him to have a certain number of sawar or cavalrymen on hand.
- Mansabdars received their salaries as revenue assignments – jagirs which were somewhat like iqtas. But unlike muqtis, mansabdars did not administer jagirs directly; they only had rights to collect revenue (through their agents) while they themselves served in a different part of the empire.
- During Akbar's rule, these jagirs were carefully appraised such that their income were about equivalent to the mansabdar's wage.
- However, throughout Aurangzeb's rule, the number of mansabdars increased dramatically, resulting in a lengthy wait for a jagir.
- Jagirdari Crisis was witnessed and whoever got jagirs they extracted more revenue than allowed.
- Aurangzeb couldn't control this development and the peasantry therefore suffered tremendously.

Zabt and Zamindars

- Mughal kings relied on obtaining taxes from rural products (peasantry) to fund their government.
- Mughals used a single name, zamindars, to characterise all mediators, whether they were village headmen or strong chieftains who collected taxes for kings.
- A careful survey was done to evaluate crop yields.
- On the basis of this data, the tax was fixed.
- Each province was divided into revenue circles with its own schedule of revenue rates for individual crops. This revenue system was known as zabt.
- However, rebellious zamindars were present. They challenged the stability of the Mughal Empire from the end of the 17th century through peasant revolt.

Akbar Nama & Ain-i Akbari

- Akbar Nama, a three-volume history of Akbar's reign, was written by Abul Fazl.
- The first volume focused on Akbar's forefathers.
- The second chronicled occurrences during Akbar's rule.
- The third is the Ain-i Akbari. It deals with Akbar's administration, household, army, the revenues and geography of his empire. It provides rich details about the traditions and culture of the people living in India. It also got statistical details about crops, yields, prices, wages and revenues.

Akbar's Policies

- The empire was split into provinces known as subas, which were administered by a subadar who served both political and military roles.
- Subadar was supported by other officers such as the military paymaster (bakhshi), the minister in charge of religious and charitable patronage (sadr), military commanders (faujdars) and the town police commander (kotwal).
- Each province had a financial officer or diwan.
- Akbar's nobles commanded large armies and had access to large amounts of revenue.
- Akbar's discussions on religion with the ulama, Brahmanas, Jesuit priests who were Roman Catholics, and Zoroastrians took place in the ibadat khana.
- He understood that religious professors who focused on ritual and theology were frequently bigots. Their doctrines caused discord and dissension among his subjects.
- This eventually developed to Akbar's concept of sulh-i kul, or "universal peace".
- Abul Fazl helped Akbar in framing a vision of governance around this idea of sulh-i kul.
- This principle of governance was followed by Jahangir and Shah Jahan as well.

Organization of Trade and Commerce

- The Mughals prioritised roads and sarais, which facilitated communication. At the point of entry into the empire, goods were subject to a uniform tax.
- Rahdari (a transit duty, a toll) or Road cesses was declared illegal, though some local rajas continued to collect it (kings).
- The Mughals introduced high-purity silver rupees, which became a standard coin in India and abroad, aiding in the growth of India's trade.
- Mughals also implemented policies that aided in the commercialization of the economy and the development of a money economy.
- During the Mughal era, the salaries of the standing army and many administrative personnel (except the nobles) were paid in cash. Furthermore, the land revenue was assessed and required to be paid in cash under the zabti system.
- Small townships grew in popularity as rural grain markets expanded (or qasbas). Nobles' demand for all types of luxury goods resulted in the expansion of handicraft production as well as the growth of towns.
- When Ralph Fitch visited India during Akbar's reign, he stated that Agra and Fatehpur Sikri were both larger than London.
- Monserrate stated that Lahore was superior to no other city in Europe or Asia. According to Bernier, Delhi was not much smaller than Paris, and Agra was larger than Delhi.

Standard of Living: Pattern of Village Life and the Masses

- Many European traders and travellers visited India during this time period, and some of them left accounts of the country's social and economic conditions.
- In general, they have emphasised India's wealth and prosperity, as well as the ostentatious lifestyle of the ruling classes, on the one hand, and the grinding poverty of the ordinary people—peasants, artisans, and laborers—on the other.
- The scanty clothing worn by the common people struck Babur. He observed, 'Peasants and people of low standing go about naked'.
- Income and wages ultimately determined one's standard of living. It is difficult to calculate the real income of the vast majority of peasants because money is rarely used in village transactions.
- The social structure of the village was highly unequal. The khudkasht, who claimed to be the village's original settlers, frequently belonged to a single dominant caste or castes.
- Not only did these castes dominate village society, but they also exploited the other or weaker sections. In turn, they were frequently exploited by zamindars.
- A peasant was not evicted from his land in medieval times as long as he paid the land tax.
- He could also sell his land if he could find a buyer and the rest of the neighbourhood did not object. His children inherited his land as a matter of right after his death.
- The pattern of his life was determined partly by the seasons and partly by custom and tradition, which included fairs, pilgrimages, ceremonies, and so on.
- The situation of the landless and some artisans, including the menials, must have been much worse. However, this was not the case for all peasants.
- Resident cultivators (khudkasht) had generally larger lands to cultivate, and a small section of them also had many ploughs and oxen.
- They could also rent out a portion of their land to ordinary farmers (muzarian) on favourable terms.
- These sections and village zamindars could and did invest in agricultural expansion and improvement.

Mughal Administration

- Since Mughals hailed from the-Central Asian, their administrative and political agendas represented the Persian-Arabic style.
- After Babur defeated Lodi successors in the First Battle of Panipat along with the Rajput ruler, Rana Sangha.
- When Akbar ascended the throne, he reorganized this administrative and judicial system in a new manner.
- The head of the revenue department was termed Wazir and he was responsible for managing the Jagirs.
- Mir Bakshi was the title given to the military head.
- Mir Saman was in charge of the imperial households.
- For handling the religious matters, a Qazi was appointed in the Mughal court.
- A wazir or a normal minister from the Mughal court could be assigned as the Wakil whose role was to be the Naib of the empire.
- At the Pargana structure, the two most renowned revenue officers were Amil, Qanungo, Chaudhuri.
- In the Mughal empire, a feudalistic system existed also known as the Mansabdari.
- Despite economic and commercial prosperity inequalities were a glaring fact. Poverty existed side by side with the greatest opulence.
- At the time of Shahjahan's reign, highest ranking mansabdars were nominal and they are the ones who receive maximum salaries than others.
- The scale of revenue collection [tax] left very little for investment [in tools and supplies] in the hands of the primary producers – the peasant and the artisan.

17th century and after

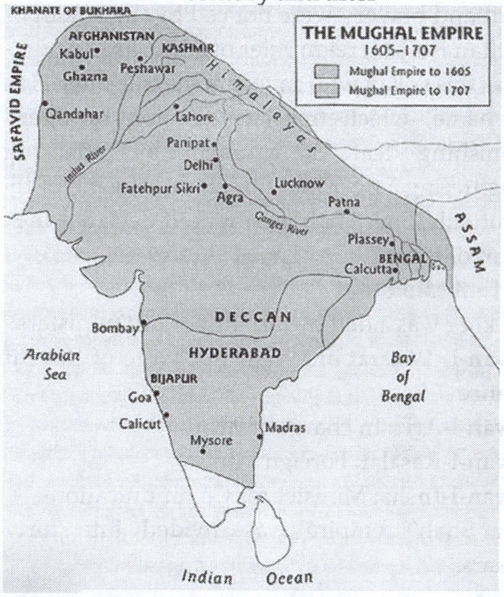

This map is not to scale and is for reference only.

- As the authority of the Mughal emperor slowly declined, his servants emerged as powerful centres of power in the regions. They constituted new dynasties and held command of provinces like Hyderabad and Awadh but still were loyal to Mughals.
- By the 18th century, the provinces of the empire had consolidated their independent political identities.

Unit-6: Sur/Suri Dynasty

- The Suri dynasty was started by Sher Shah Suri, whose birth name was Farid. With great success, he challenged the rule of Mughal emperor Humayun, drove him out of India, and took the throne of Delhi.
- He was the son of an Afghan jagirdar of Sasaram in Bihar, who had been mistreated by his stepmother and father and neglected by his father.
- All of this amply demonstrates his extraordinary hand, head, and heart qualities. Sher Shah restored the Afghan Empire that had been subsumed under Babur.
- Sher Shah Suri's conquests include Bundelkhand, Malwa, Multan, Punjab, and Sind.
- His empire occupied the whole of North India except Assam, Gujarat, Kashmir, and Nepal.

- Though his rule lasted for only 5 years, he has organized an excellent administrative system.

The encounters between Sher Shah and Humayun

The three encounters were as follows:

- The Chunar Fort encounter and Sher Shah's diplomatic capitulation.
- The Battle of Chausa was a notable military engagement between the Mughal emperor, Humayun, and the Afghan, Sher Shah Suri. It was fought on 26 June 1539. Sher Shah was victorious and crowned himself Farid al-Din Sher Shah.
- The Battle of Kannauj took place at Kannauj, Uttar Pradesh, India between Sher Shah Suri and Humayun on 17 May 1540. This battle is also known as the battle of Bilgram, where Humayun was defeated.

Rise to Power

- Unlike other Indian sultans, Sher Shah was not born into a position of great power. He was born one of eight sons of a horse breeder and small landholder. He began his career as a soldier in the army of the governor of Jaunpur but quickly rose through the ranks when his talent and bravery were noticed by the sultan of Bihar. A sultan is a sovereign ruler of a Muslim state.
- It was this sultan who gave him the title Sher. He earned the name, which translates as lion or tiger, in an astonishing feat of courage: by attacking and slaughtering a tiger that threatened the life of the king. Eventually, Sher Shah was himself declared the official sultan of Bihar.

Important Ministers

- The king was aided by four important ministers.
  - **Diwan-i- Wizarat or Wazir:** In charge of Revenue and Finance
  - **Diwan-i-Ariz:** In charge of Army
  - **Diwan-i-Rasalat:** Foreign Minister
  - **Diwan-i-Insha:** Minister for Communications
- Sher Shah's empire was divided into forty-seven Sarkars.

Officers

- Each sarkar was further divided into various Parganas and in charge of various officers.
- **Shiqdar:** Military Officer
- **Amin:** Land Revenue
- **Fotedar:** Treasurer
- **Karkuns:** Accountants

Land Revenue Administration

- Under Sher Shah, the land revenue administration was well organized.
- The land survey was sensibly done.
- All cultivable lands were classified into three classes – good, middle and bad.
- The state's share was one-third of the average production and it was paid in cash or crop.
- Sher Shah introduced
  - Patta → statement of land and revenue demand.
  - Qabuliyat → agreement by cultivator.

Police system

- Police were competently restructured and crime was less during his regime.
- Shah borrowed many ideas like the branding of horses from Alauddin Khalji.
- Sher Shah had also developed the communications by laying four important highways.
  - Sonargaon to Sind
  - Agra to Burhanpur
  - Jodhpur to Chittor
  - Lahore to Multan

Sher Shah built the following buildings

- Sher Shah's Mausoleum in Sasaram, Bihar.
- Rohtasgarh Fort on the banks of the Jhelum River in the north-west.
- Purana Qila at New Delhi
- Mosque in the Purana Qila

Well organised 'dak' system

Dak Chaukis were also made from sarais. Two horses were kept at each Sarai so that the news bearers could acquire fresh horses at regular intervals to keep up with the pace.

Sarais

About 1700 sarais were constructed on both sides of the roads. Each sarai had separate rooms for the Hindus and the Muslims. Each sarai had a well and a mosque. These sarais also functioned as dak Chaukis. Because of their importance, these sarais were dubbed "veritable arteries of the empire".

Promotion of Education

A Maktab was linked to each mosque for the purpose of giving primary education and teaching Arabic and Persian to Muslims. Madrasas were set up for higher education. Endowments and grants were given to educational institutions. Provision was also made for scholarships on the basis of merit.

Currency

Sher Shah introduced the silver Rupiya, weight approximately 178 grains. Sher Shah introduced new copper coins called "Dam".

The exchange rate between the Dam and the rupee was set at 64 to 1. During the Mughal and British eras, the currency was based on the same coin-rupee ratio.

There was no defined ratio among so many coins of various metal alloys previously. He abolished the old and mixed metal currency. He issued fine coins of gold, silver and copper of uniform standard.

Estimate of Sher Shah

- Sher Shah remained a pious Muslim and generally tolerant towards other religions.
- He also employed Hindus in important offices.
- The old fort called Purana Qila and its mosque was built during his period.
- He also built a Mausoleum at Sasaram, which is considered as one of the masterpieces of Indian architecture.
- The famous Hindi work Padmavat by Malik Muhammad Jayasi was written during his reign.
- In 1545, Sher Shah died and his successors ruled till 1555 later when Humayun reconquered India.
- The tomb he built for himself at Sasaram is a master piece of architecture.

Unit-7: Vijayanagar and Bahmani Empire

Vijayanagar Empire (1336 – 1565 AD)

- Vijayanagar kingdom and the city were founded by Harihar and Bukka (sons of Sangama) who were feudatories of Kakatiyas and later became minister in the court of Kampili.
- Vijayanagar kingdom lay in the Deccan, to the south of the Bahmani kingdom.
- This period can be divided into four distinct dynasties viz. Sangama, Saluva, Tuluva and Aravidu.
- Kumarakampana's expedition to Madurai was described in the Maduravijayam. He destroyed the Madurai Sultans and as a result, the Vijayanagar Empire comprised the whole of South India up to Rameswaram.

The Sangama Dynasty (1336 – 1485 AD)

- **Harihara I and Bukka I (1336 – 56):** They laid the foundation of Vijaynagara. Conflict of Vijayanagar – Bahmani began with the foundation of kingdoms.
- **Clash of interests in three areas:** Raichur doab (between Krishna and Tungabhadra), Krishna – Godavari delta and Marathwada.
- **Bukka I (1356 – 79):** He strengthened the city of Vidyanagar and renamed it Vijayanagar. He restored harmony between the warring Vaishnavas and the Jains. Rulers of Malabar, Ceylon and other countries kept ambassadors at his court' or 'Malabar, Ceylon and other countries sent ambassadors to his court.
- **Harihar II (1379 – 1404):** Bukka I was succeeded by his son Harihar II.

Dynasty	Period	Founder
Sangama Dynasty	1336 – 1485	Harihar and Bukka
Saluva Dynasty	1485 – 1505	Saluva Narsimha
Tuluva Dynasty	1505 – 1570	Veer Narsimha
Aravidu Dynasty	1570 – 1650	Tirumala

- **Deva Raya I (1406 – 22):** He was the third son of Harihara II. His greatest achievement was his irrigation works where a dam was built across the Tungabhadra, with canals leading to the city. Nicolo de Conti visited Vijayanagar during his reign.
- **Deva Raya II (1423 – 46):** He was the grandson of Deva Raya I. He began the practice of employing Muslim cavalrymen and archers in the army on large scale (Their induction had begun during Deva Raya I). He was called Praudh Deva Raya. In his inscriptions he has the title of Gajabetekara (the elephant hunter) Sri Lanka paid a regular tribute to him. Dindima was the court poet, whereas Srinatha was given the title of 'Kavisarvabhauma'. Abdur Razzak, the envoy of Shah Rukh visited Vijayanagar during his reign.

The Saluva Dynasty (1486 – 1505 AD)

- Saluva Narsimha founded the Saluva dynasty.
- Tirumal (1491) and Immadi Narasimha (1491 – 1505): Both were minors during the regency of Narsa Nayaka. Vasco Da Gama landed in Calicut during his reign in 1498.

The Tuluva Dynasty (1505 – 70 AD)

Vira Narsimha (1505-09): He was the son of Narsa Nayaka, became the king after the assassination of Immadi Narsimha, the last Saluva ruler.

Krishna Deva Raya (1509 – 29 AD)

- Saluva Timma was the chief minister of Vira Narsimha. He placed Krishna Deva Raya, the brother of Vira Narsimha, on the throne.
- Krishna Deva Raya maintained friendly relations with Albuquerque, the Portuguese governor, whose ambassador Friar Luis resided in Vijayanagar. He won Orissa (Gajapti kingdom) for Vijayanagar and Vijayanagar emerged strongest during his reign.
- He took the titles of Yavanaraja Sthapnachrya (restorer of the Yavana kingdom i.e. Bidar kingdom) and Abhinava Bhoja. He is also known as Andhra Bhoj and Andhra Bhoja.
- He was a gifted scholar in both Telugu and Sanskrit, of which only two works are extant: the Telugu work on polity 'Amuktamalyada' and the Sanskrit drama Jambavati Kalyanam'.
- His court was adorned by the 'Ashtadiggajas' (the eight celebrated poets of Telugu): Peddana ('Manucharitam'), Timmaya ('Parijata Apaharanama'), Bhattamurthi, Dhurati, Mallan, Raju Ramchandra, Surona and Tenali Ramkrishna ('Panduranga Mahatmyamu').
- Krishna Deva Raya, a contemporary of Babur, was the most illustrious ruler of the Vijayanagara.
- Duarte Barbosa and Dominigo Paes, Portuguese travellers, visited Vijaya – nagar during the time of Krishna Deva Raya.
- **Achyuta Deva Raya (1529 – 42):** Krishna Deva Raya nominated his brother Achyuta Deva Raya as the successor. During his reign, Farnao Nunij, a Portugese horse trader, visited Vijayanagar.
- **Venkata I (1542) and Sadashiva Raya (1543 – 76):** Real power was exercised by Rama Raja/Raya and his two brothers. The Battle of Talikota (also called the Battle of RakshasaTangadi) was fought on 23 Jan 1565. Rama Raja was taken prisoner and executed by Hussain Nizam Shah I.

The Aravidu Dynasty (1570 – 1650 AD)

- Tirumala Raya ruled in the name of Sadasiva Raya. On his failure to repopulate Vijayanagar, he shifted the capital to Penugonda. He divided his empire into three practically linguistic sections.
- This empire slowly shrunk and the dynasty ended in 1646.

Administration

- Nayankar System was the feature of provincial administration.
- Ayyangar System was the special feature of village administration.
- The rulers of Vijayanagar issued gold coins called Varahas or Pagodas. The Perta was half a Varaha. The Fanam was one-tenth of Perta. All were of gold mixed with alloy. The Tar was a silver coin. The Jital was a copper coin.

Society

- Vijayanagar was the only empire in Medieval India which employed women in the state services. Women even went to battles and it was the only state that promoted widow remarriage. Status of women improved during this time.

- Viprulu: Brahmins, Rajulu: Kshatriya, Nalavajativaru: Shudras, Vipravinodins: Artisans, Kaikollas: Weavers, Sahagaman: Sati, Besabaga: Forced labour.

Architecture

- The ruins of the Vijaynagar at Hampi were brought to light in 1800 by an engineer of English East India Company named colonel Colin Mackenzie.
- The Vijayanagar rulers produced a new style of architecture.
- Another important feature was the Mandapa or open pavilion with a raised platform, meant for seating deities and Amman Shrine.
- The rulers of Vijayanagar started the practice of inscribing the stories of the Ramayana and the Mahabharata on the walls of the various temples. Vithalswami and Hazara Rama Temple are examples of this type of wall inscription.

Vijayanagar Empire was visited by many foreign travellers:

Traveller	Fact
Nicolo Conti	Venitian traveller, visited during the reign of Devaraya I.
Abdur Razzak	Ambassador of Sultan Shahrukh to the court of Devaraya II.
Domingo Paes	He visited Krishna Devaraya's court.
Ferona Nuniz	A Portuguese who visited during Achyuta Raya's reign.
Durate Barbosa	A Portuguese who visited Krishnadeva Raya's court.
Afanasy Nikitin (1415)	He was a Russian, who visited during Deva Raya I's period He wrote, 'Voyage to India'.

Bahmani Kingdom

- **Alauddin Hasan Bahman Shah (1347-58):** He was also known as Hasan Gangu. He founded the Bahmani kingdom with its capital at Gulbarga.
- **Tajuddin Firoz Shah (1397-1422):** He was determined to make Deccan the cultural centre in India. He inducted large number of Hindus in the administration on large scale. He paid much attention to the ports of his kingdom, Chaul and Dabhol which attracted trade ships from Persian Gulf and Red Sea.
- **Ahmad Shah Wali (1422-35):** He transferred the capital from Gulbarga to Bidar.

Muhammad Gawan

- He was the vakil as well as the wazir of Muhammad Shah III between 1463-81.
- He improved the administration, systematized finances, encouraged public education, reformed the revenue system, disciplined the army and eliminated corruption.
- In 1481 Muhammad Gawan persecuted by the Deccan Muslims who were jealous of him and sentenced to death by Muhammad Shah.
- He introduced the use of gunpowder in the war against the Vijayanagar kings in Belgaum.

Break up of Bahmani Empire into 5 Kingdoms

S. No.	Five Kingdoms	Year	Founder	Dynasty	Annexation (by)
1.	Berar	1484	Fataullah Imad Shah	Imad Shahi	1574 (Ahmadnagar)
2.	Bijapur	1489	Yusuf Adil Shah	Adil Shahi	1686 (Aurangzeb)
3.	Ahmadnagar	1490	Malik Ahmad	Nizam Shahi	1633 (Shahjahan)
4.	Golconda	1518	Quil Qutub Shah	Qutab Shahi	1687 (Aurangzeb)
5.	Bidar	1526 – 27	Amir Ali Barid	Barid Shahi	1610 (Bijapur)

- Gol Gumbaz was built by Muhammad Adil Shah; it is famous for the so – called 'Whispering Gallery'.
- Quli Qutub Shah built the famous Golconda Fort.
- Muhammad Quli Qutub Shah was the greatest ruler of Qutub Shahi dynasty and it was he who founded the city of Hyderabad, originally known as Bhagyanagar after the name of the Sultan's favourite, Bhagyamati and he also built the famous Charminar.

Unit-8: Maratha Empire

Shivaji (1627-1680)

- Shivneri Fort is where he was born. Father Shahaji Bhosle first served Ahmednagar's Nizam monarch. He later joined the Bijapur.
- In 1637, he received the jagir of Poona from his father.
- He took the Torna fort at the age of 16, followed by numerous other forts.
- He created an independent Maratha kingdom with Raigad as its capital.
- He captured Javali from Chandra rao More in 1656. At the Battle of Pratapgarh (1659) he killed Afzal Khan (Adil Shah's general).
- The Battle of Pavankhind (1660) saw a smaller Maratha force headed by Baji Prabhu Deshpande repel a greater opponent, allowing Shivaji to flee.
- Shivaji was defeated by Shaista Khan (sent by Aurangzeb). Later He made a bold attack on Shaista Khan's military camp at Poona in 1663 & wounded him.

Treaty of Purander (1665)

- It was built between Raja Jai Singh (under Aurangzeb) and Shivaji.
- Shivaji relinquished certain forts to the Mughals and travelled to Agra to see Aurangzeb.
- He defeated Mughals in Battle of Salher (1672). He was crowned & assumed the title Maharaja Chhatrapati in 1674 at Raigad fort.
- He died in 1680 at the age of 52.

Shivaji's Administration

- He partitioned the country into three provinces. Provinces were further separated into Prants, which were further subdivided into Parganas or Tarafs.

- Shivaji's army and navy were well-organized. The regular army was known as Paga, while the loose auxiliaries were known as silahdars and were controlled by havildars.
- Salary in cash was paid to the regular soldier, though sometime the chiefs received revenue grants (saranjam).
- He was assisted by a council of ministers called "Ashtapradhan" Mandal. Each minister was directly responsible to Shivaji.

Ashtapradhan Mandal

Peshwa (Mukhya Pradhan)	Finance & general administration. Later became prime minister
Senapati (Sar-i-Naubat)	Military Commander
Majumdar (Amatya)	Accountant General
Waqenavis (Mantri)	Intelligence, posts and household affairs
Sachiv (Surnavis)	Correspondence
Dabir (Sumant)	Foreign minister & Master of ceremonies.
Nyayadhish	Justice
Panditrao (Sadar)	High Priest, managing internal religious matters

Revenue

- Shivaji's income system was modelled on that of Ahmednagar's Malik Amber.
- Kathi, a measuring rod, was used to measure the land.
- Revenue farming has been discouraged.
- Chauth (1/4th of land revenue) paid to Marathas to avoid Maratha raid.
- Sardeshmukhi was additional levy of ten percent, that is 1/10 of standard land revenue on those lands on which the Marathas claimed hereditary rights.
- Reduced the power of existing Deshmukhs and Kulkarnis.
- Appointed own revenue officer called Karkuns.

Sambhaji (1680-1689)

- Sambhaji was Shivaji Maharaj's son and, according to the Treaty of Purandar, a Mughal Mansabdar.
- The continuing conflicts between the Maratha kingdom and the Mughal Empire, as well as other nearby kingdoms such as Siddis, Mysore, and the Portuguese in Goa, impacted his rule significantly.
- In 1687, at the Battle of Wai he defeated Mughal forces.
- In 1689, Sambhaji was captured, tortured and executed by the Mughals.
- He was succeeded by his brother Rajaram I.

Chhattrapati Shahu (1707-1749)

- During Shahu's reign, the Peshwas rose to power, reducing the Bhosale family to the status of mere figureheads.
- By the time of Rajaram II/Ram Raja, the power of Chhatrapati was almost overshadowed by that of Peshwa.

Balaji Vishwanath (1713-1720): First Peshwa

- He started his career as a small revenue official. He was given a title of Sena Karte in 1708 by Shahu.
- He became a Peshwa in 1713 & made the post most important and powerful as well as hereditary.

Maratha Confederacy (1720-1818)

Baji Rao I (1720-40)

- Balaji Vishwanath succeeded. Under him, Maratha strength reached its pinnacle.
- After Shivaji, he was one of the most prominent exponents of guerilla warfare.
- Initiated the system of confederacy. Thus, many families became prominent and established their authority.
- His several expeditions in the north weakened the Mughal and made Marathas supreme power in India.
- He said about Mughal: "Let us strike at the trunk of the withering tree and the branches will fall of themselves".

Kingdoms	Territory
Scindia	Gwalior
Holkar	Indore
Pawar	Dhar
Gaekwad	Baroda
Bhosale	Nagpur
Peshwa	Poona

Balaji Baji Rao I/ Nana Sahib I: (1740-1761)

- Nawab of Bengal Alivardi Khan was defeated in 1751, and the Maratha Empire gained control of one-third of the Indian subcontinent.
- Signed agreement with Ahmad Shah (Mughal emperor) – Peshwas assured to protect the Mughal from internal and external enemies in return for the Chauth of the north-west provinces, total revenue of Agra & Ajmer provinces.
- The defeat of Marathas by Ahmad Shah Durrani in the Third Battle of Panipat in 1761 halted the Marathas' advance and split the empire.
- His son Vishwas Rao were killed at the battle of Panipat.
- Madhav Rao, Narayan Rao, Sawai Madhav Rao, and Baji Rao II succeeded him.

Anglo-Maratha Wars

There were three wars fought between the Maratha Empire and the British East India Company over territory.

First Anglo-Maratha War (1775–1782)	• The First Anglo-Maratha War stemmed from a power struggle between Sawai Madhav Rao and Raghunath Rao, which was supported by the British. • The treaty of Salbai in May, 1782 – British acknowledged Madhavrao as the Peshwa of the Maratha Empire and ended the Anglo-Maratha War.

Second Anglo-Maratha War (1803–05)	• The second war began in 1802 with Peshwa Baji Rao II's defeat by the Holkar (one of the prominent Maratha clans) and his acceptance of a subsidiary alliance (Treaty of Bassein). • Unhappy Maratha confederacy challenged the British power but got defeated.
Third Anglo-Maratha War (1817-1818)	• Pindaris, bands of irregular marauders, began looting surrounding territories due to financial distress even those of corporations. • Lord Hasting (Governor General) charged Marathas with giving shelter to the Pindaris and hence fought war. • Maratha warlords fought separately instead of forming a common front and they surrendered one by one.

End of Maratha Kingdom

- The Maratha Empire was destroyed in the third Anglo-Martha war. The British captured all of the Maratha kingdoms.
- The Peshwa was ultimately apprehended and imprisoned on a tiny estate near Kanpur called Bithur.
- The Maharaja of Satara was restored as the ruler of his territory as a princely state. Most of his territory was annexed and became part of the Bombay Presidency.
- In 1848 this territory was also annexed under the "doctrine of lapse policy" of Lord Dalhousie.

War of Succession: There ensued a war of succession after the death of Shivaji between his sons, Shambaji and Rajaram. Shambaji emerged victorious but later he was captured and executed by the Mughals. Rajaram succeeded the throne but the Mughals made him to flee to the Ginjee fort.

Political structure: Divisions within

- Another factor for the Maratha empire's demise was its own structure. It was a confederacy in which authority was divided among the leaders or sardars (Bhonsle, Holker, etc.).

Weak Revenue Administration

- Marathas depended on the collection of Chauth and Sardeshmukhi and on their exploits from plunder and loot. They failed to create an efficient revenue management system. New regions were captured, but the administration received far less attention. Rulers were mainly interested in raising revenue from peasantry through taxation.

Weak Diplomacy

- Marathas did not bother to investigate what was going on abroad or what their opponents were up to. There was no visionary leadership or good plan. They failed to cultivate alliances with forces around them.

Anglo-Maratha Wars and Subsidiary Alliance

- By accepting the Treaty of Bassein in 1802, Peshwa Baji Rao II accepted a subsidiary alliance. This was the end of the Maratha empire. By 1818, the Maratha authority had been decimated, and the major rulers who represented it in central India had bowed and accepted the East India Company's overlordship.
- Shivaji was really a constructive genius and nation-builder. His rise from jagirdar to Chatrapathi was spectacular. He united the Marathas while being a major foe of the Mughal empire. He was a courageous soldier and an astute administrator. Following his reign, infighting and discord among the Maratha confederacy became a key cause of their demise.

Important Books of Medieval Period

Writer	Books
Hassan Nizami	Tajul Masir
Minhaj Us Siraj	Tabakate Nasiri
Ziauddin Barani	Tarikh-i-Firozshahi, Fatwa-e-Jahandari
Babur	Tuzuk-i-Babri, Diwan, Risal-i-Usaj
Gulbadan Begum	Humayunnama
Abul Fazl	Akbarnama, Ain-i-Akbari
Jahangir	Tuzuk-i- Jahangir
Amir Khusrau	Devalrani Khizr Khan, NuheSipehar, Khazain Ul Fatuh
Alberuni	Tehqeeq-e-Hind
Ibn Battuta	Rehla
Firoz Shah Tughlaq	Futuhat-e – Firoz Shahi
Isami	Futuh-us-Salatin
Yahya bin Sirhindi	Tarikh-e-Mubarakshahi
Abbas Khan Shekhani	Tarikh e Shershahi
Ishwardasnagar	Futuhat e Alamgiri
Ahmad Yadgar	Tarikh e Salatin e Afghan
Abdullah	Tarikh e Dawoodi
Mir Muhammad Masoom	Tarikh-e-Sindh
Al Utbi	Tarikh-e-Yamini
Taimur	Malfuzat-e-Taimuri
Ali Yazdi	Zafarnama
Muhammad Ali Kufi	Chachnama
Firdausi	Shahnama

Mir Hasan Dehlavi	Fawaid-ul-Fawad
Mirza Haider	Tarikh-e-Rashidi
Nizamuddin Ahmad	Tabaqat-e-Akbari
Khafi Khan	Muntakhab-ul-Lubaab
Bhimsen	Nuskha-e-Dilkhusa
Darashikoh	Sirr-e-Akbar, Yogavasistha, Safinat-al-Auliya, Shakinat-al-Auliya
Abul Fazl	Razmanama
Mutamid Khan	Iqbalnama
Ganga Devi	Madurai Victory
Madhvacharya	Narkasurvijay
Krishnadevaraya	Amuktamalyada
Tenliramakrishna	Pandurang Mahatmya
Srinatha	Haravilasamu
Jagannath Pandit	Gangaalhari
Maharana Kumbha	Sangeet Raj, Sangeet Mimamsa
Bhanudutt	Rastarangini
Jai Singh Suri	Hammir Mardan
Tulsidas	Vinaya Patrika, Ramcharitmanas, Barvai Ramayana
Surdas	Sur Sagar, Nal – Damayanti
Kabir	Sakhi, Bijak, Rekhta, Gyan sagar
Malik Muhammad Jayasi	Padmavat
Malukdas	Chitravali
Jagnik	Alhakhand
Narpati Nalh	Bisaldevraso
Sant Dnyaneshwar	Dnyaneshwari
Samarth Ramdas	Dasbodh

Important Monuments

Monument	Founder	Location
Agra Fort	Mughal Emperor Akbar	Agra, Uttar Pradesh
Red Fort	Mughal Emperor Shah Jahan	Delhi
Taj Mahal	Mughal Emperor Shah Jahan	Agra, Uttar Pradesh
Konark Sun Temple	Narasimhadeva I (Eastern Ganga Dynasty)	Konark, Odisha
Fatehpur Sikri	Mughal Emperor Akbar	Agra, UP
Bibi Ka Maqbara	Azam Shah (Son of Aurangzeb)	Aurangabad, Maharashtra
Jama Masjid	Mughal Emperor Shah Jahan	Delhi
Mehrangarh Fort	Rao Jodha	Jodhpur, Rajasthan
Tajmahal	Mughal Emperor Shah Jahan	Agra, Uttar Pradesh
Qutub Minar	Qutubuddin Aibak	Delhi
Makkah Masjid	Muhammad Quli Qutb Shah	Hyderabad, Telangana
Hawa Mahal	Maharaja Sawai Pratap Singh	Jaipur, Rajasthan
Moti Masjid	Mughal Emperor Shah Jahan	Agra, Uttar Pradesh
Moti Masjid	Mughal Emperor Aurangzeb	In Red Fort, Delhi
Humayun's Tomb	Humayun's wife Empress Bega Begum	Delhi
Charminar	Quli Qutub Shah	Hyderabad, Telangana
Elephanta Caves	Not exactly known	Mumbai, Maharashtra
Bara Imambara	Asaf-ud-Daula	Lucknow, Uttar Pradesh
Dilwara Temples	Vastupal-Tejpal	Mount Abu, Rajasthan
Gateway of India	George Wittet	Mumbai, Maharashtra
India Gate	Edwin Lutyens	Delhi
Jantar Mantar	Maharaja Jai Singh	Delhi
Purana Qila (Old Fort)	Shershah Suri	Delhi
Golden Temple	Guru Arjan Dev	Amritsar, Punjab
Group of Hampi Monuments	Vijayanagara Empire	Hampi, Karnataka

Important One Liners (Ancient and Medieval History)

- Mohenjodaro is a prominent Harappan site, being surrounded by flood barriers in order to protect it with the aid of UNESCO funds.
- Upnishads are books on Philosophy.
- During Dhana Nanda's reign, Alexander invaded India (327–325 BCE).

- The Battle of the Hydaspes was fought in 326 BC between Alexander the Great and King Porus of the Paurava kingdom (region between Jhelum and Beas).
- Maurya Period from 322 BCE to 185 BCE.
- Chandragupta was succeeded by his son Bindusara.
- The best known of the Kushanas was Kanishka who was an ardent follower of Mahayana form of Buddhism. Gandhara art developed during his period.
- The Saka Era was founded by Kanishka, the emperor of Kushana Empire from the year 78 A.D.
- Kanishka was the first Indian ruler who had territory outside India.
- Samudragupta organised Ashwamedha Yajna in Gupta Period.
- Kanishka was the first Indian ruler who had territory outside India.
- Chinese Traveller Hiuen Tsang travelled during the reign of Harshvardhana in seventh Century.
- Harshavardhana started the organization of Kumbh fair at Allahabad.
- Harshavardhana shifted his capital from Thanesar to Kannauj.
- Pulakesin II was the greatest ruler of the Chalukyas.
- The capital of the early Chalukyas was Badami.
- Lokesvara temple at Pattadakal in Karnataka built by Chalukya king Vikramaditya II to commemorate his victory over the Pallavas.
- The Uttaramerur inscription provides information on the administration of the Cholas.
- Bahmani dynasty (1347–1527) founded by Ala-ud-Din Hassan Bahman Shah who was also known as Hassan Gangu.
- The capital of Bahmani kingdom was Gulbarga from 1347 AD to 1425 AD. It was moved to Bidar in 1425 AD.
- Sunga Dynasty was from 185 BC to 73 BC
- The period between 1206 AD and 1526 AD in India's history is known as the Delhi Sultanate period. The kingdoms of Delhi Sultanate are as follows:
  - Slave dynasty 1206 - 1290
  - Khilji dynasty 1290 - 1320
  - Tughlaq dynasty 1321 - 1413
  - Sayyid dynasty 1414 - 1450
  - Lodi dynasty 1451 - 1526
- Iltutmish was the first ruler to issue Pure Arabic coin in India.
- The founder of the Lodi Dynasty was Bahlol Lodi.
- Harihara and Bukka is the founder the Vijayanagar empire in 1336 A.D. on the southern banks of Tungabhadra.
- Hampi as the capital city of Vijayanagar empire.
- Krishnadeva Raya from the Tuluva dynasty was the most famous king of the Vijayanagar Empire.
- Vikramashila university was founded by Pala king Dharmapala.
- Mihira Bhoja was a ruler of the Gurjara-Pratihara dynasty.
- Babur entered India in 1526 and defeated Ibrahim Lodi at the First Battle of Panipat in 1526. Babur was the first Mughal emperor In India.
- The leader of the Bhakti movement focusing on Lord Rama was Ramananda.
- The Red Fort of Delhi was constructed during the reign of Shah Jahan.
- In 1799, Sawai Pratap Singh constructed Hawa Mahal in Jaipur.
- Indian Mughal paintings originated during the rule of Mughal Emperor, Humayun.
- Humayun's Tomb is located in Delhi.
- During the Mughal Period the Official and Court language was Persian.
- Gol Gumbaz was designed by Yaqut of Dabul.
- Shah Jahan was imprisoned for the rest of his life by Aurangzeb.
- Buddha, Dhamma and Sangha together are known as Triratna.
- Kamarup is an ancient name of Assam.
- Akbar introduced Mansabdari system in India.
- Battle of Talaikota led to the downfall of the Vijayanagar empire.
- Rana Kumbha has built the Vijay Stambha (Tower of Victory) in Chittorgarh.
- Shah nama written by Ferdowsi.
- Guru Nanak founded Sikhs Religion. His teachings composed in Adi Granth.
- Guru Ramdas was Founder of Amritsar.
- Guru Arjan Dev was the fifth guru of Sikhs.
- Mir Zafar betrayed Siraj-ud-Daulah in the battle of Plassey in 1757.
- Indian Mughal paintings originated during the rule of Mughal Emperor, Humayun.
- During the Mughal Period the Official and Court language was Persian.
- Shah Jahan was imprisoned for the rest of his life by Aurangzeb.
- In 1799 Sawai Pratap Singh constructed Hawa Mahal in Jaipur.
- First battle of Panipat was fought between the army of Babur and Ibrahim Lodi in 1526.
- Multan was named by the Arabs as City of gold.
- Rana Kumbha has built the Vijay Stambha (Tower of Victory) in Chittorgarh.

❑❑❑

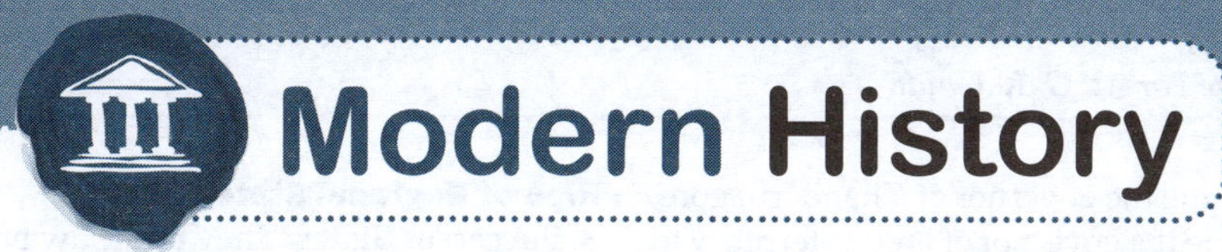

Modern History

Unit-1: Advent of Europeans and Consolidation of British Power in India

Advent of the Europeans in India

Advent of Europeans

Name	Year
Portuguese	1498 AD
English	1600 AD
Dutch	1602 AD
Danish	1616 AD
French	1664 AD
Swedish	1731 AD

Portuguese

- **Vasco Da Gama**
- Vasco da gama arrived at Calicut (modern Kozhikode) in 1498 where he was cordially received by King Zamorin, the ruler of Calicut.
- A Muslim navigator (often identified as Ahmad ibn Majid) guided his fleet from East Africa to the Indian coast.
- By 1502, Vasco's second visit led to the establishment of trading stations at Calicut, Cochin and Cannanore and fortification of the same.
- **Pedro Alvarez Cabral:** He established the first factory at Calicut, in 1500.
- **Francisco de Almeida (1505-09)**
- First governor, appointed by king to protect Portuguese interest, initiated the blue water policy (Cartaze system).
- **Cartaze system:** It was naval trade license issued by authority without which trade was prohibited.
- **Albuquerque (1509-1515):** He secured strategic control of Indian Ocean; captured Goa from Bijapur rulers; received permission from Sri Krishna Deva Rai (1510) of the Vijayanagar; to built a port in Bhatkal banned the practice of sati in his area of influence. He was considered to be the founder of the Portuguese power in India.
- **Significance of the Portuguese**
- Introduced printing press.
- Introduced of cannon on ship.
- Introduced the cultivation of tobacco to India.
- Introduced the art of the goldsmith flourished at Goa.
- The famous Jesuit Saint Francisco Xavier arrived in India with Martin Alfonso de Souza.
- Introduced nut, potato, tomato, chillies, capsicum.
- In 1612 Battle of Swally (also known as Battle of Suvali) was fought between English and Portuguese in which Portuguese were confined to Daman, Diu and Goa.

Dutch

- In 1602, the Dutch East India Company was formed and it received the sanction of their government to trade in East including India.
- They established first factory at Masulipatnam, Andhra Pradesh in 1605.
- Cornelis de Houtman was the first Dutchman to reach Sumatra and Bantam in 1596.
- Dutch Factories in India: Masulipatnam (1605), Pulicat (1610), Surat (1616), Bimlipatnam (1641), Karikal (1645), Chinsurah (1653), Cassimbazar (Kasimbazar). Baranagore, Patna, Balasore, Nagapatnam (1658) and Cochin (1663). (It covered both and western coasts).

Significance of the Dutch

- **Battle of Bedara (1759):** The English defeated the Dutch. Dutch were ousted from India.
- The British agreed to withdraw all their claims on Indonesia and the Dutch retired from India.

English

- In 1600, Elizabeth, the Queen of England granted a charter to the governor and company of Merchants of London to trade with East Indies.
- William Hawkins arrived at Jahangir's court in 1609 but failed to secure permission due to opposition by Portuguese.
- In 1611, Captain Middleton obtained the permission of the Mughal governor of Surat to trade there, also started trade in Masulipatnam.
- In 1613, a factory of East India Company was established at Surat.
- In 1615, Sir Thomas Roe, the ambassador of King James I arrived at Jahangir's court.
- In 1616, the Company established its first factory in the south in Masulipatnam.
- In 1632, the Company got the golden Farman from the Sultan of Golconda which ensured safety and prosperity of their trade.
- In 1633, the Company established its first factory in east India in Hariharpur, Balasore, Odisha.
- Fort St George is the first English fortress in India, founded in 1644 at the coastal city of Madras (Modern day Chennai).
- In 1667, Aurangzeb gave the English a farman for trade in Bengal.
- In 1717, the Mughal emperor Farrukhsiyar issued a farman called Magna Carta of the Company, giving the Company a large number of trade concessions in Bengal, Gujarat and Hyderabad. It included:
- Company's import and export were exempted from duties.
- Permission to issue dastaks for transportation of goods.
- Duty free trade in Hyderabad.
- Company minted coins to act as currency throughout Mughal Empire.

Danes

- Danish East India company was established in 1616 AD.
- Danish East India company established settlement at Tranquebar (Tamil Nadu) in 1620 and Serampore (Bengal) in 1676.
- **Significance of the Danes:** They were the foremost promoters of Christianity in India.

French

- In 1664, Colbert, a minister of Louis XIV, laid the foundations of French East India Company. It was granted 50-year monopoly on French trade in the Indian and Pacific Oceans.
- The French factory was established at Surat by Francois Caron in 1668 and second at Masulipatnam in 1669.

- In 1730, Dupleix became the governor of Chandernagore, and in 1741, he became the governor of French territory in India.
- In 1673 AD, the French obtained a village called Pondicherry from Sher Khan Lodi, the ruler of Bijapur and founded a thriving city on it which later became the main stronghold of the French in India.

Carnatic Wars

- Carnatic was the name given to the Coromandel coast and its hinterland by the Europeans.
- **First Carnatic War (1746-48):** The First Carnatic War is remembered for the Battle of St. Thome (in Madras) fought between the French forces and the forces of Anwar-ud-din, the Nawab of Carnatic supported by British forces.
- English seized French ships, French seized Madras.
- The war was ended with the Treaty of Aix-La-Chapelle (1748). Under this treaty, France agreed to leave the Austrian Netherlands and give back Madras to Britain in return for Louisbourg.

Second Carnatic War (1749-54)

- The French authorities, annoyed at the heavy financial losses that Dupleix's policy involved, decided to recall him in 1754.
- Charles Robert Godeheu succeeded Dupleix as the French Governor-General in India.
- **Treaty of Pondicherry:** Godeheu adopted a policy of negotiations with the English and signed the Treaty of Pondicherry with them under which the English and the French agreed not to interfere in the quarrels of native princes.

Third Carnatic War (1758-63)

- Background of the war was the Seven Years war in Europe (1756-63).
- The Battle of Wandiwash in 1760 was the final blow to the French. General Eyre Coote of the English totally routed the French army under Count de Lally.
- The third war ended with the Treaty of Peace of Paris (1763) under which Pondicherry and Chandannagar were returned to France but they could only have trading activities in them.

Items of Import

- **Persian Gulf Region:** Pearls, raw silk, wool, dates, dried fruits, and rose water;
- **Arabia:** Coffee, gold, drugs, and honey;
- **China:** Tea, sugar, porcelain, and silk;
- **Tibet:** Gold, musk, and woollen cloth;
- **Africa:** Ivory and drugs;
- **Europe:** Woollen cloth, copper, iron, lead and paper.

Items of Export

- Cotton textiles, raw silk and silk fabrics, hardware, indigo, saltpeter, opium, rice, wheat, sugar, pepper and other spices, precious stones and drugs.

India on the Eve of British Conquest

- The first half of the 18th century saw the decline of Mughals. The reign of Aurangzeb (1658-1707) was the beginning of the end of Mughal era in India.
- The misguided policies of Aurangzeb weakened the stability of the state and the decline gained momentum after his death due to wars of succession and weak rulers.

Rise of Regional States

- **Successor States:** They broke away from the empire but did not challenge the sovereignty of the Mughals.
  Examples: Bengal, Awadh, Hyderabad.
- **Independent Kingdoms:** These were established due to destabilization of Mughal control over the provinces.
  Examples: Mysore, Kerala, Rajput.
- **New States:** These were set by rebels against the Mughals.
  Examples: Marathas, Sikhs, Jats.

Name	Founder
Hyderabad	Chin Qilich Khan/Nizam-ul-Mulk
Awadh	Saadat Ali Khan/Burhan-ul-Mulk
Bengal	Murshid Quli Khan
Mysore	Initially ruled by the Wodeyars, later Hyder Ali usurped the power
Kerala	Martanda Varma
The Jats	Churaman and Badan Singh
The Sikhs	Guru Gobind Singh
The Marathas	Shivaji Maharaj
Rohilakhand and Farukhabad	Mohammad Khan Bangash

Expansion and Strengthening of British Power in India

Timeline of the Event

- **1740:** Anglo French struggle began for supremacy in India with First Carnatic War(1740-1748).
- **1757-23rd June 1757:** Battle of Plassey (1757): British forces defeated the Nawab of Bengal at Plassey - The British East India Company (commanded by Robert Clive) against Siraj-ud-Daulah, the Nawab of Bengal, Bihar and Orissa supported by French force.
- It was a decisive victory for the British. Mir Jafar Khan entered Murshidabad with Clive and became Nawab of Bengal, Bihar and Orissa. Mir Jafar Khan was compelled to pay substantial sums of money to the East India Company.
- **1761:** Third Battle of Panipat: Fought between Maratha Empire and a coalition of the King of Afghanistan, Ahmad Shah Durrani, the Rohilla Afghans of the Doab and Shuja-ud-Daula, the Nawab of Oudh. Marathas lost the battle and their prestige. English benefited from this war.
- **1764 - Battle of Buxar:** Fought between British East India Company and Mir Qasim, the Nawab of Bengal, Shuja-ud-Daulah, the Nawab of Awadh and Shah Alam II, the Mughal Emper. British defeated the combined forces of Mir Qasim, Shuja-ud-Daulah, and Shah Alam II.
- **1765 - Treaty of Allahabad:** Battle of Buxar led to the signing of the Treaty of Allahabad. It was signed by Lord Robert Clive with Mughal Emperor Shah Alam II.

Anglo-Mysore Wars

- **First Anglo-Mysore war (1767-69)**
- **Cause:** In 1766, the East India Company joined the Nizam (ruler) of Hyderabad against Hyder Ali in return for the cession of the Northern Circars.

- **Participants:** Britishers along with the Marathas and the Nizam of Hyderabad declared war on Mysore.
- **Result:** Hyder Ali was able to bring the Marathas and the Nizam to his side.
- The Treaty of Madras was signed in 1769 which brought an end to the war.

- **Second Anglo-Mysore War (1780-84)**
- **Cause:** The Marathas attacked Mysore in 1771. But the British refused to honor the Treaty of Madras and did not give support to Hyder Ali.
- **Participants:** Hyder Ali forged an alliance with the Nizam and the Marathas and defeated the British forces in Arcot.
- **Result:** Treaty of Mangalore (1784). Both parties agreed to return the captured territories and prisoners to each other.

- **Third Anglo-Mysore War (1790-92)**
- **Cause:** Tipu Sultan, after Hyder Ali's death, had French help in bettering his military resources. Tipu declared war on Travancore in 1789. Travancore was a friendly state of the British.
- **Participants:** Tipu Sultan and East India Country led by Lord Cornwallis.
- **Result:** The war ended with the Treaty of Seringapatam in 1792. Accounting to which Tipu had to cede half of his kingdom to the English including the areas of Malabar, Dindigul, Coorg and Baramahal.

- **Fourth Anglo-Mysore War (1799)**
- **Cause:** Tipu refused to accept the Subsidiary Alliance of Lord Wellesley. He aligned with the French which British saw as a threat to them.
- **Participants:** Marathas, Nizams and English vs Tipu Sultan.
- **Result:** The British secured a decisive victory at the Battle of Seringapatam in 1799.
- Tipu's territories were divided between the British and the Nizam of Hyderabad.
- The core area around Seringapatam and Mysore was restored to the Wodeyar dynasty who had been ruling Mysore before Hyder Ali became the de-facto ruler.

Anglo-Maratha Wars

- **First Anglo-Maratha War (1775-1782)**
- **Cause:** The Death of Madhav Rao resulted in fighting among the Marathas. English used this for their advantage. Nana Phadnavis went against a treaty signed with the Calcutta Council and granted a port on the west coast to the French in 1777.
- Another cause was increased importance of cotton trade.
- **Participants:** Marathas and East India Company.
- **Results:** A famous battle at Wadgaon was fought in which the Marathas under Mahadji Scindia secured a decisive victory over the English. The English were forced to sign the humiliating Treaty of Wadgaon in 1779. Warren Hastings rejected this treaty. Later, the war concludes by Treaty of Salbai. Scindia was the guarantee of the treaty.
- Treaty of Salbai was signed on 17 May 1782, by representatives of the Maratha Empire and the British East India Company after long negotiations to settle the outcome of the First Anglo-Maratha War. It was signed between Warren Hastings and Mahadaji Scindia.

- **Second Anglo-Maratha War (1803-05)**
- **Cause:** Internal squabbles among Maratha houses. In the Battle of Poona in 1802, Yashwant Rao Holkar, the chief of the Holkars of Indore defeated the Peshwas and the Scindias.
- Baji Rao II sought British help and signed the Treaty of Bassein (subsidiary alliance) with them.
- The Treaty of Bassein was a pact between the English East India Company and Baji Rao II, the Maratha confederacy's Peshwa. It was signed on 31 December 1802 after the Battle of Poona.
- The Scindias and the Bhonsles did not accept this treaty and this caused the second Anglo-Maratha war in central India in 1803.
- **Participants:** Scindias, Bhonsles, Holkars vs the British.
- **Result:** British defeated all the Maratha forces. As a result, large parts of central India came under British control.

- **Third Anglo-Maratha War (1817-18)**
- **Cause:** British conflict with the Pindaris whom the British suspected were being protected by the Marathas.
- **Participants:** The Maratha chiefs Peshwa Bajirao II, Malhar Rao Holkar and Mudhoji II Bhonsle united front against the English.
- **Result:** The British won decisively.
- Battle of Koregaon was fought during this war. In this, an army of mahar (depressed class) led by English officer defeated the army of Peshwa.
- This was the last major war fought and won by the British. With this, the British controlled most parts India directly or indirectly.

Anglo-Sikh Wars

- **First Anglo-Sikh War (1845-46)**
- **Cause:** Immediately after the death of Ranjit Singh, British East India Company had begun increasing its military strength to protect the empire from any Russian invasion from northwest. Growing influence of Sikh Army in the court worried the British. Due to the British provocation, Sikh forces crossed the Sutlej and took offensive positions against the English forces.
- **Participants:** Sikh Army vs British Forces.
- **Result:** British victory at Sobraon led to the signing of the Lahore Treaty in 1846, which ended the war.

- **Second Anglo-Sikh War (1848-49)**
- **Cause:** Murder of few East India civil service officers led to Hostility.
- Dalhoussie and his policy of extension.
- **Participants:** Sikhs vs English.
- **Result:** Final battle was fought at Gujrat near Chenab in 1849 in which British forces won.
- The famous Koh-i-Noor diamond went into British hands.

Important Policies of Britishers

- **Policy of Ring Fence**
- Warren Hastings- 1770s to 1800s
- It can be called the predecessor of subsidiary alliance.
- To protect major provinces, set up subsidiary forces in the surrounding regions. Example- stationing army at Awadh giving some weird, illogical reason. The main agenda was to protect Bengal from any external threat.

- **Policy of Subsidiary Alliance**
- It is a treaty between the British East India Company and the Indian princely states, under which the Indian princely states lost their sovereignty to the English.
- It was framed by Lord Wellesley, the Governor-General of India from 1798 to 1805.

- It was actually used for the first time by the French Governor-General Marquis Dupleix.

- **Features of Subsidiary Alliance**
- Indian ruler entering into Subsidiary Alliance with the British had to dissolve his own armed forces and accept British forces in his territory.
- He had to pay for the British army's maintenance. If he failed so, a portion of his territory would be taken away and ceded to the British.
- British promised non-interference in internal affairs of the Indian state.
- Indian state could not enter into any alliance with any other foreign power.
- He could also not employ any other foreign nationals other than Englishmen in his service.
- The Indian state could also not enter into any political connection with another Indian state without the approval of British.
- A British Resident was stationed in the Court of Indian Rulers.

Doctrine of Lapse

- It was an annexation policy followed by Lord Dalhousie when he was India's Governor-General from 1848 to 1856.
- **Features of the Policy**
- Any princely state under the direct or indirect control of the East India Company who did not have a legal male heir would be annexed by the company, any adopted son of the Indian ruler could not be proclaimed as heir to the kingdom.
- The adopted son would only inherit his foster father's personal property and estates. The adopted son would also not be entitled to any pension that his father had been receiving or to any of his father's titles.
- In 1824, before the time of Dalhousie, the princely state of Kittur was acquired by the East India Company using this doctrine.

Unit-2: Rising Resentment Against Company Rule

People's Resistance Against British Before 1857

- The British expansionist policies, economic exploitation and administrative innovations over years were the cumulative effect that resulted in simmering discontent among all sections which burst in the form of the 1857 revolt.

Causes of the Revolt

Economic causes	• The British economic policies destroyed the traditional economy of the country, as a result, peasants suffered heavy taxation under the new revenue settlement system.
	• The British annexed many Indian States which led to loss of patronage of many artisans. • The traditional industry's destruction. • The land rights of Zamindars were forfeited.
Political causes	• Socio religious affairs of the Indian public were interfered. • The Doctrine of Lapse and Subsidiary alliance forced people for the revolt. • Improper governance system of British. • Certain rights given to Mughal rulers were also denied.
Administrative causes	• Increase in the rate of corruption in the company's administration.
Socio-Religious causes	• The British racial arrogance. • Christian missionaries increased their activities. • Support for widow remarriage, women education and abolition of sati. • The Religious Disabilities Act, 1850, which changed Hindu customs.
Immediate causes	• The introduction of Enfield greased rifles whose cartridges were said to have a greased cover made of beef and pork sparked off the revolt.
Influence of outside event	• The serious losses suffered by the British-the First Afghan War (1838-42), Punjab Wars (1845-49), Crimean Wars (1854-56), Santhal Revolt (1855-57).

The Revolt of 1857

- **The Beginning of the Mutiny**: On 29 March 1857 at Barrackpore near Calcutta, Mangal Pandey, a young Indian Brahmin sepoy from 34th Bengal Native Infantry, refused to use greased cartridge. He attacked British officers including Sergeant-Major Hewson and Lieutenant Baugh. On 10 May 1857 the rebellion started in the form of a mutiny of sepoys of the Company's army in the garrison town of Meerut, which is 40 miles northeast of Delhi. It then brusted in the upper Gangetic plain and central India into other mutinies and civilian rebellions.

Sepoy Mutinies

- **Reasons**
- Discrimination in payment and promotions.
- Mistreatment
- Refusal of the government to pay foreign service allowance while fighting in remote areas.
- Religious objections of the high caste hindu sepoys to Lord Canning's General service Enlistment Act (1856) ordering all recruits to be ready for service both within and outside India.
- **Leaders and their centers**

Leader	Place	British Officials
Bahadur Shah II, General Bakht Khan	Delhi	John Nicholson, William Hudson and James Outram
Begum Hazrat Mahal	Lucknow	Colin Campbell
Tatya tope Nana Sahib	Kanpur	Colin Campbell

Rani Lakshmibai	Jhansi	Hugh Rose
Khan Bahadur	Bareilly	Colin Campbell
Kunwar Singh	Arrah, Bihar	William Taylor
Maulvi Ahmadullah	Faizabad	General Renord
Liaqat Ali	Allahabad	Colonal Neil

Causes for Failure of the Revolt

- Limited territorial and social base.
- All classes did not join.
- Poor Arms and Equipment.
- Uncoordinated and Poorly organized, lack of central leadership.
- No Unified Ideology.

Note: During this revolt, there was widespread unity between Hindus and Muslims at all levels.

Consequences of the Revolt

- Abolition of Company's rule and Crown took over the administration.
- Annexation of Indian states and expansion as a policy were ended by the British.
- Army was thoroughly reorganized by the British based on British military policy "division and counterpoise".
- Increase in racial hatred between the ruled and the ruling class.

White Mutiny

- Because of the cancellation of Bhatta that they used to receive earlier, there was resentment among company forces to transfer their allegiance to the British Army.

Views on Revolt

- According to D. Savarkar it was the first war of Indian independence.
- It was described as "War of Nation's Independence" by Tara Chand.
- According to R.C. Majumdar, revolt of 1857 of independence was neither the first, nor national, nor a war of independence.
- As per Surender Nath Sen it began as a fight for religion and ended as a war of independence.
- **Important sepoy mutinies before 1857 revolt:**
  - Vellore mutiny, 1806
  - Mutiny of 47th Native Infantry Unit, 1824
  - Revolt of Grenadier Company, Assam, 1825
  - Mutiny in Solapur, 1833
  - Mutiny of 34th Native Infantry Unit, 1844
  - Mutiny of 22nd Native Infantry Unit, 1849
  - Mutiny of 66th Native Infantry Unit, 1850
  - Mutiny of 37th Native Infantry Unit, 1852

Unit-3: Reform Movements

Socio-Religious Reform Movements: General Features

Raja Rammohan Roy (1772-1833)

- **Organisations:** Atmiya Sabha (1814), Calcutta Unitarian Committee (1823), Vedanta College (1825), Brahmo Samaj (1828).
- **Significance:** He put his faith in monotheism.
- His famous works include Gift to Monotheists (1809) and translation of the Vedas and the five Upanishads into Bengali.
- In 1814, he set up the Atmiya Sabha (or Society of Friends) in Calcutta to propagate the monotheistic ideals of the Vedanta and to campaign against idolatry.
- He founded the Brahmo Sabha in August 1828. It was later renamed as Brahmo Samaj.
- He launched a movement for the abolition of sati through his journal sambad kaumudi (1821).
- Raja Ram Mohan Roy was the father of Modern India's Renaissance and a tireless social reformer who inaugurated the age of enlightenment and liberal reformist modernisation in India.
- Ram Mohan Roy was given the title of 'Raja' by the Mughal Emperor Akbar II.

Debendra Nath Tagore

- **Organisations:** Tattvabodhini Sabha (founded in 1839). Adi Brahmo Samaj (founded in 1866).
- He joined Bramho Samaj in 1842.
- Tattvabodhini Sabha studied India's past with a rational outlook.
- His famous work include Tattvabodhini Patrika.

Keshab Chandra Sen

- **Organisations:** Brahmo Samaj of India (founded in 1866).
- He joined the Brahmo Samaj in 1858 and became acharya.
- He was a champion of women's rights. His ideology was a mix of religious and social ideas.
- He established the Nava Vidhan in 1881 along with the newspaper "New Dispensation" to disseminate his religious ideas and philosophy.

Ananda Mohan Bose, Shibchandra Deb and Umesh Chandra Datta

- **Organisations:** Sadharan Brahmo Samaj
- **Significance:** It reiterated the Brahmo doctrines of faith in a Supreme being, one God, the belief that no scripture or man is infallible, belief in the dictates of reason, truth and morality.

Atmaram Pandurang

- **Organisations:** Prarthana Samaj in 1867, Bombay with the help of Keshav Chandra Sen.
- **Significance:** It works on a four-point social agenda—
  - Disapproval of caste system.
  - Women's education.
  - Widow remarriage.
  - Raising the age of marriage for both males and females.
- Mahadeo Govind Ranade joined it in 1870 and popularised it.
- Other important leaders include R. G. Bhandarkar, N. G. Chandavarkar, Dhondo Keshav Karve and Vishnu Shastri.

D. K. Karve and M. G. Ranade

- **Movement/ Organisations:** Widow Remarriage Movement and Widow Home Association.
- It provided education and training to widows so that they could support themselves.
- Karve himself married a widow and tied with the example for others to follow.

Henry Vivian Derozio

- **Movement:** Young Bengal Movement.
- He taught at the Hindu College from 1826 to 1831, was the leader and inspirer of this progressive trend.
- They demanded induction of Indians in higher grades of services, protection of ryots from oppressive zamindars, better treatment to Indian labour abroad in British colonies, revision of the Company's charter, freedom of press and trial by jury.

Ishwar Chandra Vidyasagar

- He started a movement in support of widow remarriage.
- He became principal of Sanskrit College and opened it to non-Brahmins to break priestly monopoly. He also served as Secretary of Bethune School, Calcutta which was the pioneer of higher education for women.
- His works include, "Bahuvivah", written in protest of polygamy.

Jyotiba Phule

- **Organisations:** Satyashodhak Samaj in 1873.
- His works include Sarvajanik Satyadharma and Gulamgiri. He dedicated his book Gulamgiri to all those Americans who had fought to free slaves.
- Phule used the symbol of Rajah Bali as opposed to the brahmins' symbol of Rama.
- He with the help of his wife, Savitribai, opened a girls' school at Poona.
- He was a pioneer of widow remarriage movement in Maharashtra and also opened Balhatya Pratibandhak Griha (Home for the Prevention of Infanticide) in Pune in 1863.

Balshastri Jambhekar

- **Organisations:** He founded the Bombay Native General Library and started the native Improvement Society.
- He was a pioneer of social reform through journalism in Bombay.
- He attacked brahmanical orthodoxy and tried to reform popular Hinduism.
- He started the newspaper "Darpan" in 1832. He was also known as the father of Marathi journalism.
- In 1840, he started Digdarshan (1840) which published articles on scientific subjects as well as history.

Dadoba Pandurang, Durgaram Mehtaji

- **Organisation:** Paramahansa Mandali in 1849.
- They were primarily interested in breaking caste rules.

Gopalhari Deshmukh

- He wrote for a weekly Prabhakar under the pen name of Lokahitawadi on social reform issues.
- He started a weekly, Hitechhu, and also played a leading role in finding the periodicals, Gyan Prakash, Indu Prakash and Lokahitawadi.

Gopal Ganesh Agarkar

- He was the co-founder of the New English School, the Deccan Education.
- Society and Fergusson College.
- He was a principal of Fergusson College.
- He was also the first editor of Kesari, the journal started by Lokmanya Tilak.
- He started his own periodical, Sudharak, which spoke against untouchability and the caste system.

Gopal Krishna Gokhale

- **Organisations:** The Servants of India Society in 1905.
- The aim of the society was to train national missionaries for the service of India; to promote, by all constitutional means, the true interests of the Indian people; and to prepare a cadre of selfless workers who were to devote their lives to the cause of the country in a religious spirit.

Narayan Malhar Joshi

- **Organisation:** Social Service League (1911).
- He founded the Social Service League in Bombay with an aim to secure for the masses better and reasonable conditions of life and work
- He was also founded the All India Trade Union Congress (1920) along with Lala Lajpat Rai and others.

Dayananda Saraswati

- **Organisations:** Arya Samaj.
- He established the Arya Samaj at Girgaon, Bombay on 10th April, 1875 and later the headquarter of the Samaj were established at Lahore.
- It was a Hindu revivalist movement. The samaj started a Shuddhi Movement to convert non-Hindus to Hinduism.
- The samaj also established DAV Schools with emphasis on western education.
- He gave the slogan 'back to the Vedas' and said they were infallible. He attacked the Hindu orthodoxy.

Swami Vivekananda

- **Movement:** The Ramakrishna Movement
- It was initiated to spread the message of Vedanta with its headquarters at Belur, Calcutta.
- Swami Vivekananda addressed the famous Parliament of Religions at Chicago in 1893.
- Two objectives of the Ramakrishna movement were:
  - To bring into existence a band of monks dedicated to a life of renunciation and practical spirituality, from among whom teachers and workers would be sent out to spread the universal message of Vedanta as illustrated in the life of Ramakrishna.
  - In conjunction with lay disciples to carry on preaching, philanthropic and charitable works, looking upon all men, women and children, irrespective of caste, creed or colour, as veritable manifestations of the Divine.
- Unlike the Arya Samaj, the Mission recognises the utility and value of image worship in developing spiritual fervour and worship of the eternal omnipotent God, although it emphasises on the essential spirit and not the symbols or rituals.

Behramji M. Malabari

- **Organisations:** Seva Sadan (1908)
  - It worked against child marriage and for widow remarriage among Hindus.
  - He acquired and edited the Indian Spectator.

Radhakant Deb

- **Organisations:** Dharma Sabha (1830) to counter the ongoing social reform movements led by protagonists such as Raja Ram Mohan Roy and Henry Derozio.

- He was the founder president of British India Association in 1851 along with Debendranath Tagore as its secretary.
- It favoured the promotion of Western education even for girls.

Madam Mohan Malviya

- **Organisations:** Bharat Dharma Mahamandal
- An all-India organisation of the orthodox educated Hindus, it stood for a defence of orthodox Hinduism against the teachings of the Arya Samajists, the Theosophists, and the Ramakrishna Mission.

Sree Narayana Guru Swamy

- **Movement:** Narayana Guru Dharma Paripalana Movement and Temple Entry Movements.
- **Aruvippuram movement:** To show that consecration of an idol was not the monopoly of the higher castes. It was started by installing Shivlinga on Shivratri in 1888.

C. N. Mudaliar, T. M. Nair, Tyagaraja

- **Movement:** Justice Movement - It began in Madras in order to secure jobs and representation for non Brahmins.
- In 1917, the Madras Presidency Association- demanded separate representation for the lower castes in the legislature. It came under the leadership of Periyar E. V. Ramaswamy and his Self-Respect Movement.

E. V. Ramaswamy Naicker

- **Movement:** The Self respect Movement was in 1920s.
- He emphasised to undermine the position of brahmin priests by formalising weddings without brahmin priests.

M. G. Ranade and Raghunath Rao

- **Movement:** Indian National Social Conference, 1887
- It met annually from its first session in Madras in 1887 at the same time and venue as the Indian National Congress.
- It advocated inter-caste marriages, opposed polygamy and kulinism.
- It launched the 'Pledge Movement' to inspire people to take a pledge against child marriage.

Islamic Reforms Movement

Sayyid Ahmad

- **Movement:** Wahabi Movement, 1820
- It was an Islam revivalist movement. India was considered to be dar-ul-Harb (land of the kafirs) and it needed to be converted to dar-ul-Islam (land of Islam).

Haji Shariatullah

- **Movement:** Faraizi Movement, 1819
- It emphasised on the Islamic pillars of faith. It aims to eradication of social innovations or un-Islamic practices among the Muslims and ask to perform their duties.

Mirza Ghulam Ahmad

- **Movement:** Ahmadiyya Movement, 1889
- It described itself as the standard-bearer of Mohammedan Renaissance, and based itself, like the Brahmo Samaj, on the principles of universal religion of all humanity, opposing jihad.
- The movement spread Western liberal education among the Indian Muslims.

Sir Syed Ahmed Khan

- **Movement:** Aligarh Movement, 1875
- This movement emerged as a liberal trend in Muslim intelligencia.
- He started Muhammadan Anglo-Oriental College at Aligarh in 1875. It became Aligarh Muslim University in 1920.
- Sir Syed's progressive ideas are propagated through his work Tahdhib-al-Akhlaq.
- He supported woman empowerment and opposed purdah system and Polygamy, condemned the system of piri and muridi.
- He opposed congress on the ground that it will lead to political monopoly of Hindu's.

Mohammad Qasim Nanotavi and Rashid Amhed Gangohi

- **Movement:** Deoband School, 1867
- The school aimed to train religious leaders for Muslim community. It was seen as a revivalist movement organized by the Ulema.
- It welcomed the formation of the Indian National Congress.

Parsi Reform Movements

- **Rahnumai Mazdayasnan Sabha:** It was founded in 1851 by a group of English-educated Parsis for the "regeneration of the social conditions of the Parsis and the restoration of the Zoroastrian religion to its pristine purity".
- The movement was founded by Naoroji Furdonji, Dadabhai Naoroji, K. R. Cama and S.S. Bengalee.
- Its newspaper was Rast Goftar (Truth-Teller).

Sikh Reform Movements

- Singh Sabha Movement was founded at Amritsar in 1873 with objective–
  - to make available modern western education to the Sikhs,
  - to counter the proselytising activities of Christian missionaries as well as the Brahmo Samajists, Arya Samajists and Muslim Maulvis.
- The Akali movement (also known as Gurudwara Reform Movement) was an offshoot of the Singh Sabha Movement.
- It aimed at liberating the Sikh gurudwaras from the control of corrupt Udasi mahants (the post having become hereditary).

Other Important movements

- **Theosophical Movement:** It was led by H. P. Blavatsky and M. S. Olcott in 1875.
- This movement came to be allied with Hindu renaissance. It accepted hindu beliefs such as reincarnation, Upanishads and Vedanta.
- Annie Besant is associated with this movement and was elected as the President of the Theosophical Society in 1907.
- Annie Besant had come to India in 1893. She laid the foundation of the Central Hindu College in Benaras in 1898 where both Hindu religion and Western scientific subjects were taught.
- The college became the Banaras Hindu University in 1916.

Unit-4: The Struggle Begins

Beginning of Modern Nationalism in India

Ilbert Bill Controversy

- Ilbert Bill, was a controversial bill proposed in 1883 which allow senior Indian judges to try European offenders, earlier only European judges could try European offenders.
- The bill was introduced by Viceroy Lord Ripon.
- The bill had to face intense criticism from the Europeans and Britishers because they looked it as a humiliation as it placed Indian judges at par with European Judges.
- It was withdrawn due to opposition in Britain and from British settles in India and was reintroduced in much diluted state.

Indian National Congress: Foundation and the Moderate Phase

- The leaders of this period were Dadabhai Naoroji, Mahadev Govinda Ranade, Gopal Krishna Gokhale, W. C. Banerjee, S. N. Banerjee, Pheroz Shah Mehta etc.
- They raised basic questions regarding the nature and purpose of British rule.
- They did economic critique using following arguments:
  - Drain Theory
  - Critique of Railways
  - De–industrialization of India
- **Some Leaders behind Economic Critique**
  - **Romesh Chandra Dutt:** He was a retired ICS officer, published The Economic History of India at the beginning of the 20th century in which he examined in minute detail the entire economic record of colonial rule since 1757.
  - **Justice M. G. Ranade:** He taught an entire generation of Indians the value of modern industrial development and said that if India is poor today it is because of economic policies of British.
  - **Dadabhai Naoroji:** He was also called the Grand old man of India.
  - Gokhale called him Gladstone of India. He was the main proponent of Drain Theory.
  - He wrote Poverty and un-British Rule in India.
- **Foundation and the Moderate Phase of Indian National Congress**
  - A. O. Hume mobilized the leading intellectuals and organized the first session of INC at Bombay in Dec. 1885.
  - The first session of INC was presided over by W. C. Bannerjee. Other important presidents include Dadabhai Naoroji (was elected 3 times as president), Badruddin Tyabji, Pherozshah Mehta, Sarojini Naidu among others.
  - Safety Valve theory: Hume argued that INC would prove to be a safety valve for releasing the growing discontent of Indian.

Important Sessions of the Congress

Session	Year	President	Place	Important Remarks
First	1885	W. C. Banerjee	Bombay	Attended by 72 members.
Second	1886	Dadabhai Naoroji	Calcutta	Number of delegates increased to 436.
Third	1887	Badruddin Tyabji	Madras	First Muslim President
Fourth	1888	George Yule	Allahabad	First English President
Twelfth	1896	Rahimtulla Sayani	Calcutta	Vande Matram was sung for the first time.
Twentieth	1904	Henry Cotton	Bombay	
Twenty First	1905	Gopal Krishna Gokhale	Varanasi	
Twenty Second	1906	Dadabhai Naoroji	Calcutta	The word Swaraj used for first time by the President.
Twenty Third	1907	Rash Bihari Ghosh	Surat	First split of Congress into Moderates and Extremists.
Twenty Sixth	1911	Bishan Narayan Dhar	Calcutta	Jana-Gana-Mana was sung for the first time.
Twenty Seventh	1912	R. N. Mudholkar	Bankipur/Patna	
Thirty First	1916	Ambika Charan Mazumdar	Lucknow	A pact between Congress and Muslims league.
Thirty Second	1917	Annie Besant	Calcutta	First Woman President of Congress.
Thirty Third	1918	Madan Mohan Malviya	Delhi	Resignation of S. N. Banerjee
Thirty Fourth	1919	Motilal Nehru	Amritsar	
Thirty Fifth	1920	C. Vijayaraghavachariar	Nagpur	Non-cooperation movement resolution passed.
Thirty Sixth	1921	C. R. Das (In prison)	Ahmedabad	Hakim Ajmal Khan (Acting President)
Thirty Seventh	1922	C. R. Das	Gaya	

Thirty Eighth	1923	Maulana Muhammed Ali	Kakinada	
Special Session	1923	Abul Kalam Azad	Delhi	Youngest President (35 years old)
Thirty Ninth	1924	Mahatma Gandhi	Belgaum	
Fortieth	1925	Sarojini Naidu	Kanpur	First Indian Women President.
Fourty First	1926	Srinivas Iyengar	Guwahati	Every Congress person to compulsorily wear khadi.
Fourty Second	1927	M. A. Ansari	Madras	The Congress decided to boycott the forthcoming Simon Commission.
Fourty Third	1928	Motilal Nehru	Calcutta	One-year ultimatum was given to the British to accept dominion status recommendations.
Fourty Fourth	1929	Jawaharlal Nehru	Lahore	Poorna Swaraj Resolution passed.
Fourty Fifth	1931	Vallabhbhai Patel	Karachi	Resolution on Fundamental Rights and National Economic Policy.
Fourty Eighth	1934	Rajendra Prasad	Bombay	Focused on structural reforms to make the party a highly disciplined, the demand for a constituent assembly.
Fiftieth	1937	Jawaharlal Nehru	Faizpur (Maharashtra)	First session to be held in a village.
Fifty First	1938	Subash Chandra Bose	Haripura	National Planning Committee set up under the chairmanship of Jawaharlal Nehru.
Fifty Second	1939	Subash Chandra Bose/ Rajendra Prasad	Tripuri	Resignation of Bose (Rajendra Prasad took over), formation of Forward Bloc.
Fifty Third	1940, 1941-45	Maulana Abul Kalam Azad	Ramgarh	No Session held during 1941-45.
Fifty Fourth	1946	J. B. Kripalani	Meerut	J. B. Kriplani was the President of Congress at the time of independence.
Fifty Fifth	1948	Pattabhi Sitarammaiya	Jaipur	The session began with singing the Vande Mataram and Jana-Gana-Mana.

Unit-5: Era of Mass Nationalism (1919-1949)

Emergence of Gandhi

- Gandhi returned to India from South Africa on January 9, 1915.

Facts about Gandhi	
Birth	October 2, 1869, Porbandar (Gujarat)
Parents	Father: Karamchand Gandhi Mother: Putalibai
Wife	Kasturba (1883)
Political Guru	Gopal Krishna Gokhale
Literary Works	Hind Swaraj (1909), My Experiments with Truth (Autobiography written in Gujarat language).
Journals/ Papers	Indian Opinion, Harijan, Young India, Navjeevan (Gujarati).

- Gandhi first established the Kochrab Ashram in 1915 near Ahmedabad.
- The famous Sabarmati Ashram was established in 1917.
- Gandhi was assassinated on January 30, 1948 at Birla House in Delhi by Nathuram Godse.

Gandhi in South Africa

- In 1893, he proceeded to Natal, South Africa in relation with a case involving his client, Dada Abdullah. On his journey from Durban to Pretoria, he was thrown out of a first -class compartment by a white man.
- Gandhi established Natal Indian Congress in 1894
- He started a paper called Indian Opinion in 1903. In 1904, he established Phoenix Settlement in Natal.
- In 1910, Gandhi established Tolstoy Farm in Johannesburg with support of his German architect friend Kallenbach.

Three Significant Struggles

- During the period of 1917 and early 1918, Gandhiji was involved in three significant struggles.
- **Champaran Satyagraha (1917)**
  - Rajkumar Shukla invited Gandhi to look into the problems of farmers in the context of Indigo planters in Bihar. Peasants were forced to grow indigo on 3/20th part of the land (Tinkathia System).
  - European planters demanded high rents and illegal dues to maximise their profits. A committee was constituted to look into the issue, and Gandhi was a member of the committee.
  - The Tinkathia system was abolished and 25 percent of the compensation was provided. (Not full)

- Other leaders associated were - Rajendra Prasad, Mazhar-ul-Haq, Mahadeo Desai, Narhari Parekh, J. B. Kripalani etc.

- **Ahmedabad Mill Strike (1918)**
- There was a dispute between Gujarat mill owners and their workers over the question of plague bonus.
- Workers demanded for a rise of 50 percent in wages.
- Gandhi demanded for a 35 percent hike and under took a fast unto death.
- Anusuya Sarabhai was a social worker who invited Gandhi to fight for workers.
- Gandhiji's efforts resulted in a 35% wage hike for workers.

- **Kheda Satyagraha (1918)**
- The peasants of Kheda district were in extreme distress due to failure of crops.
- The farmers were entitled to remission according to revenue code when crop production fell below a prescribed level.
- Government was adamant to the demands and ordered seizure of property if taxes were not paid.
- Gandhi asked the farmers not to pay the taxes.
- Other leaders associated with the movement were - Sardar Vallabhai Patel, Narhari Parekh, Shankarlal Parikh Mohanlal Pandya etc.

Rowlatt Act (1919)

- The British Government passed the Rowlatt Act on 18 March 1919. It empowered the British Government to arrest anyone without warrant and imprisoned without trial.
- The act officially called Anarchical and Revolutionary Crimes Act.
- It recommended imprisonment of activists without trial for two years.
- Gandhi called it a "Black Act" and in protest called for a nation-wide satyagraha on 6 April 1919.
- He organized Satyagraha Sabha and roped in youngsters of Home rule leagues and Pan Islamists.
- Form of protest finally chosen included observance of a nationwide hartal accompanied by fasting and prayer and civil disobedience was against specific laws etc.

Jallianwala Bagh Incident (1919)

- On April 10, 1919, Dyer ordered the arrest of two local leaders, Dr. Satyapal and Dr. Kitchlew who were associated with the reception committee for the annual session of Congress to be held in December 1919.
- The protest against their arrest, a peaceful public meeting was held at Jallianwala Bagh in Amritsar on Baisakhi day on April 13, 1919, where Dyer arrived with armoured cars and troops and fired on the crowd without warning while at that time Martial Law was imposed and people were unaware.
- Gandhi surrendered his Kaiser-i-Hind medal and Rabindranath Tagore renounced his knighthood in protest against this incident.

The Khilafat Movement (1919)

- During The First World War, Turkey was an ally of Germany against Britain. The Sultan of Turkey was the Caliph (or Khalifa) of the Islamic world. Turkey was defeated in the First World War. It hurt the sentiments of Indian Muslims who regarded Khalifa as the religious head of the muslim world.
- Maulana Muhammad Ali and Maulana Shaukat Ali started the Khilafat movement.
- A Khilafat Committee was formed under the leadership of Maulana Azad, Hakim Ajmal Khan and Hasrat Mohani.
- All-India Khilafat Conference was held in Delhi on November 23, 1919, which was presided over by Gandhiji.
- **Rand Murder:** On 22 June 1897, the first political murder of the British was committed by the Chapekar brothers – Damodar Hari Chapekar, Balkrishna Hari Chapekar, Vasudeo Hari Chapekar. The Chapekar brothers attacked and murdered W.C.Rand and his military escort Lt. Ayerst was shot accidentally.
- **Alipore Bomb Conspiracy Case:** On 30 April, 1908 Prafulla Chaki and Khudiram Bose made an attempt to kill Douglas Kingford by throwing a bomb at a carriage he was travelling but Unfortunately, Douglas Kingsford was not in the carriage at which the bomb was thrown and instead two British ladies got killed.
- **Assasination of Curzon Wyllie:** In 1909, an Indian Home Rule Society called India House was started by Shyamji Krishnavarma in London. Revolutionaries such as Savarkar, Hardayal became its members. In 1909, one of its members, Madanlal Dhingra assassinated Curzon Wyllie who was a British Indian army officer.
- **Delhi Conspiracy Case:** On 23 December 1912 - Rashbihari Bose and Sachindra Nath Sanyal made an attempt to assassinate the then Viceroy Lord Hardinge by throwing a bomb. Basant Kumar Biswas, Avadh Behari and Amir Chand were convicted for the attempt and were executed. Rashbehari Bose escaped from the arrest.
- **Ghadar Movement:** In 1913, a revolutionary group called Ghadar Party was established by Lala Hardayal at San Francisco. It was established to carry out revolutionary activities against the British.
- The party planned to bring about a revolt in India for which the Komagata Maru incident and outbreak of the First World War paved the way.
- In 1908 - Barrah dacoity took place in order to raise funds for carrying out the revolutionary movements. Pulin Behari Das organised the dacoity.
- In 1909 Anant Lakshman Kanhere who was a member of Abhinav Bharat and killed A.M.T. Jackson, the Collector of Nashik.

Revolutionary Extremities

- HRA Hindustan Republican Association (Later renamed as Hindustan socialist Republic Association) was founded at Kanpur in October 1924, by Sachindra Nath Sanyal, Jogesh Chandra Chatterjee, and Ram Prasad Bismil. Its objective was to organise armed revolution to overthrow colonial rule and establish in place a Federal Republic of the United States of India whose basic principle would be adult franchise.
- On 9 August 1925, the train at Kakori was looted. Ashfaqulla Khan, Ramprasad Bismil, Roshan Singh and Rajendra Lahiri were hanged in this case.
- Saunders Murder - HSRA revolutionaries organised this plan.
- Saunders, police official responsible for the lathi charge in Lahore and for death of Lala Lajpat Rai during anti-Simon commission protest.

- Bhagat Singh, Azad and Rajguru shot dead Saunders.
- Bhagat Singh, Sukhdev and Rajguru were hanged on March 23, 1931 in Lahore Conspiracy Case.
- On 8th April 1929 Bomb in the central legislative assembly was thrown in order to protest against the passage of the Public safety Bill and Trade disputes bill which are restrictive on civil liberties.
  The bombs had been deliberately made harmless and were aimed at making the 'deaf hear'.
- On February 27, 1931, Chandrashekhar Azad was surrounded by the police at Alfred Park, Allahabad, and met a heroic death in the police encounter.
- **Chittagong Armoury (April, 1930):** It was Led by Surya Sen. The plan was to occupy two main armouries in Chittagong to seize and supply arms to revolutionaries.
- The Philosophy of the Bomb was written by Bhagwati Charan Vohra and Bandi Jiwan by Sachindranath Sanyal.

Non-Cooperation Movement (1920-22)

- The non-cooperation movement which was the first mass movement under the leadership of Gandhi, was launched to address three main demands:
  - The Khilafat issue
  - The failure of the British Government to heal up the wounds of Jallianwala Bagh tragedy, and
  - The attainment of Swaraj.
- The movement was started on August 1, 1920.
- A special session of Congress was convened at Calcutta in September 1920, to approve the non-cooperation scheme.
- **The Nagpur Session of the INC (December 1920):** It changed the Constitution and defined its object as the attainment of Swaraj by peaceful and legitimate means. The resolution of non-cooperation was again repeated and adopted at this session. It was C. R. Das who moved the resolution for non-cooperation movement.
- The congress session held in 1921 at Ahmadabad called upon the people not to pay taxes to the Government.
- The Non-Cooperation Movement gained momentum through 1921-22. Thousands of students left government controlled schools and colleges. Many lawyers such as Motilal Nehru, C. R. Das, C. Rajagopalachari and Asaf Ali gave up their practices.

Chauri Chaura Incident

On February 4, 1922, a Congress procession at Chauri Chaura, was fired upon by the police. The angry crowd attacked and burned the police station, causing the death of 22 policeman. On hearing the incident, Gandhiji decided to withdraw the movement. Gandhiji was arrested on March 10, 1922 and was sentenced for 6 years for spreading disaffection against the government.

Swaraj Party (1923)

- At the Gaya session of the Congress, No-changers led by C. Rajagopalachari defeated the pro changers. As a result C. R. Das who presided over the Gaya Congress resigned from the presidentship of the Congress.
- On 1 January 1923, C. R. Das and Motilal Nehru formed the Congress – Khilafat Swaraj Party better known as Swaraj Party. C. R. Das was the President and Motilal was the secretary of the new party. Swaraj Party was to function as a group within the Congress.
- The elections to the legislatures were held in November 1923, under the Government of India Act, 1919. The Swarajists won 42 out of 101 elected seats in the Central Legislative Assembly.

Civil Disobedience Movement and Congress Rule in Province

Simon Commission

- On November 8, 1927, the Secretary of State for India Lord Birkenhead, in London, and the Viceroy Lord Irwin in New Delhi, announced the setting up of an Indian Statutory Commission under John Simon commonly referred to as the Simon Commission, was a group of seven British Members of Parliament under the chairmanship of Sir John Simon.
- The Objective of this commission was to report on India's constitutional progress for introducing constitutional reforms.
- The Commission, in addition to the Chairman, consisted of six members. Party-wise, there were four Conservations, two Labourites and one Liberal. It was an all- white Commission with no Indian representation.
- When Simon Commission landed on February 3, 1928 in Bombay complete hartal was observed in all cities and towns. Processions were taken out with the slogan Go Back Simon.
- The report of the Simon Commission published on May 27, 1930.

Major Recommendations

- It proposed the abolition of dyarchy and the establishment of representative government in the provinces.
- It recommended that separate communal electorates be retained.
- It accepted the idea of federalism but not in the near future.
- It also suggested that the Indian army should be Indianised though British forces must be retained.

Nehru Report (1928)

- When Congress gave a call to boycott the Simon commission, Lord Birkenhead, the Secretary of State for India challenged the Indians to formulate a concrete scheme of constitutional reforms which had the support of wide sections of Indian political opinion.
- An answer to Lord Birkenhead's challenge, prepared by a committee headed by Motilal Nehru, the committee included Tej Bahadur Sapru, Subhash Bose, M. S. Aney, Mangal Singh, Ali Imam, Shuab Qureshi and G. R. Pradhan as its members. Nehru report was submitted in August 1928.
- Some important features of Nehru report were:
  - It defined Dominion status as the form of government desired by India.
  - It rejected the principle of separate communal electorates.
  - It recommended equal rights of women, freedom to form unions and dissociation of the state from religion in any form.

- The Nehru Report was approved by the majority vote at the annual session of Congress held of Calcutta in December 1928.

Jinnah's Fourteen Points

Jinnah did not accept the Nehru Report on the ground that it rejected separate electorates for the muslims. He drew up a list of demands for the muslims in the form of Fourteen Points. These included demands such as separate electorates for Muslims, creation of muslim - majority provinces, reservation of posts for muslims in all services of the State, etc.

Lahore Session of the Congress (1929)

- Lahore session of the Congress in December 1929 was presided by Jawaharlal Nehru. The Lahore session passed a resolution declaring Poorna Swaraj (complete independence) to be the Congress objective.
- On December 31, 1929 the newly adopted tri-colour flag of freedom was hoisted on the banks of river Ravi in Lahore.
- January 26, 1930 was fixed as the first Independence Day (Poorna Swaraj Day). In order to perpetuate the memory of 26th January, our new Constitution was enforced on this day in 1950.

The Civil Disobedience Movement/Salt Satyagraha

The Lahore Congress of 1929 had authorized the Working Committee to launch a programme of civil disobedience including non-payment of taxes.

Dandi March

- The Civil Disobedience Movement was started by Gandhi on March 12, 1930 with his famous Dandi march. Together with 78 chosen followers Gandhi walked nearly 240 miles (nearly 375 km) from Sabarmati Ashram (Ahmedabad) to Dandi (Navsari District, Gujarat), a village on Gujarat sea coast. He reached Dandi on April 5, 1930.
- On April 6, 1930, Gandhi by picking up a handful of salt, broke the salt law as a symbol of the Indian people's refusal to live under British made laws and therefore under British rule.

Satyagraha at different Places

- In Malabar, K. Kelappan, the hero of the Vaikom Satyagraha marched from Calicut to Payannur to break the salt law.
- A band of Satyagrahis walked from Sylhet in Assam to Noakhali on the Bengal coast to make salt.
- C. Rajgopalachari organized a march from Trichinopoly to Vedaranniyam on Tanjore coast to break the salt law in April 1930.
- In Andhra, a number of sibirams (military style camps) were set up in different districts to serve as headquarters of salt satyagraha.
- In the North-West Frontier Province (NWFP) Khan Abdul Gaffar Khan, popularly known as Frontier Gandhi, who formed a band of non - violent revolutionaries, the Khudai Khidmatgars (servants of Gods) popularly known as Red Shirts, played an extremely active role in the civil disobedience movement.
- In the North East, the Manipuris joined the movement and the young Rani Gaidinliu with her Naga followers actively supported the movement.
- Jawaharlal Nehru was arrested on April 14 and Gandhiji was arrested on May 4, 1930. Gandhiji was sent to Yervada jail.
- In east India there was a no - tax campaign i.e. refusal to pay chowkidara tax. In Bengal there was an anti - chowkidara and anti – union board agitation. In U.P. there was a no -revenue, no - rent campaign.

Extent of Participation

- Women and students participated in huge numbers, merchants and traders were enthusiastic, active participation of tribals, workers and peasants whereas muslim participation was nowhere near the 1920-22 level.
- Amidst all these happenings, Viceroy on July 9, 1930 suggested a Round Table conference and reiterated the goal of Dominion status. He also allowed Tej Bahadur Sapru, and M. R. Jayakar should explore the possibilities of peace between the Congress and the Government.
- On January 25, 1931 the Viceroy announced the unconditional release of Gandhiji and invited him for talks which ultimately led to Gandhi Irwin Pact.

First Round Table Conference (12 November 1930 to 19 January 1931)

- The first Round Table Conference was summoned to discuss the Simon report.
- Participants- British representatives-Labour, conservative and Liberal, Muslim league members- Jinnah, Aga Khan, Indian state's representatives.
- British India representatives-Ambedkar, Tej Bahadur Sapru.
- **Important Facts:**
  - All India Federation was accepted.
  - Responsible Government at provinces.
  - INC did not participate.

Gandhi - Irwin Pact (March 5, 1931)

- Gandhi - Irwin Pact in also known as Delhi Pact. It was concluded between Gandhi and Irwin an March 5, 1931. The Government on its part agreed to:
  - Release all political prisoners except those who were involved in violent activities,
  - Return of confiscated property of the concerned individuals,
  - Allowed preparation of salt within a limited territory near the sea - coast,
  - Allow peaceful demonstrations before the shops selling foreign good and liquors.
- The Congress on its part, agreed to:
  - Suspend the civil disobedience movement,
  - Participate in the second Round Table Conference.

Karachi Session of Congress (1931)

- The Congress met at Karachi on March 29, 1931 to endorse Gandhi Irwin Pact.
- The Karachi session became memorable for its resolution on Fundamental Rights and National Economic Programme.

Second Round Table Conference (7 September to 1 December 1931)

- **Participants:** Mahatma Gandhi, representative of INC. Other participants who are involved in the first-round table were present. Sarojini Naidu participated to represent women.

- **Important Facts**
- Gandhi claimed the congress alone represent political India.
- Untouchables and Muslims should not be treated as minorities.
- No separate electorate for minorities.

Resumption of Civil Dis-obedience Movement (1932-34)

- Civil Disobedience was resumed after the failure of the Round Table Conferences, Viceroy Willingdon refused a meeting with Gandhi on December 31. On January 4, 1932, Gandhi was arrested.
- The Congress and its allied organizations were declared illegal and their offices and funds were seized. Almost all Gandhi ashrams were occupied by the police.
- The movement was effectually crushed within a few months. However, the movement continued till early April 1934, when Gandhiji decided to withdraw the movement.

Communal Award (1932)

- The Communal Award was announced by the British Prime Minister, Ramsay MacDonald, on August 16, 1932.
- The Communal Award, allotted to each minority a number of seats in the legislature to be elected on the basis of a separate electorate, that is Muslims would be elected only by Muslims and Sikhs only by Sikhs and so on. Muslims, Sikhs and Christians had already been treated as minorities. The Award declared the Depressed Classes (scheduled castes of today) also to be a minority community entitled to separate electorate and thus separated them from the rest of the Hindu. MacDonald, however, promised to accept any alternative scheme mutually agreed upon by the Hindus and the depressed classes.

Gandhi's Fast unto Death and Poona Pact (1932)

- Gandhiji, was in Yervada jail at that time, reacted very strongly. He demanded that the representatives of the Depressed Classes should be elected by the general electorate. He went on a fast unto death on September 20, 1932 to enforce his demand.
- Various leaders including B. R. Ambedkar, Madan Mohan Malviya and M. C. Rajah finally found out a compromise with Gandhi in the form of Poona pact. Ambedkar signed it on behalf of the depressed classes and Madan Mohan Malviya on behalf of the Upper Caste Hindus as a means to end the fast that Gandhi was undertaking in jail.
- According to the Pact, the idea of separate electorates for the Depressed Classes was abandoned, the seats reserved for the depressed classes were increased from 71 in the Award to 148 and in the central legislature to 18% of the total.

Third Round Table Conference (17 November 1932 to 24 December 1932)

Participants: Labour party and INC refused to attend. Ambedkar attended, Jinnah not attended.

Provincial Elections and Formation of Popular Ministries in Provinces (1937)

- In the elections held in 1937 under the Government of India Act, 1935, Congress got absolute majority in 5 provinces - Madras, United Provinces, Central Provinces, Bihar and Orissa; in Bombay, Assam and North West Frontier Province.
- In Bombay, Assam and North West Frontier Province, it was the largest party and formed Governments. In Bengal, Punjab and Sindh it did not have majority.
- In Punjab, Unionist Party and Muslim League formed a coalition government. In Bengal the coalition of the Krishak Praja Party and Muslim League came to power.

Unit-6: Towards Freedom and Partition (1939-47)

Nationalist Response in the Wake of World War II

- Haripura Session, 1938 of Congress was held under the Presidency Subash Chandra Bose. He was instrumental in setting up National Planning Commission for the economic development of the country through planning.
- **Tripuri Crisis:** Subhash announced his candidature for the 1939 elections of the President of Congress, Dr. Pattabhi Sitaramayya was the candidate supported by Gandhiji.
- The result was declared on January 29, 1939 and Subhash winning by a narrow but clear margin.
- Bose in his presidential speech of Tripuri session spoke of giving 6-month ultimatum to British to grant the independence. If the ultimatum was rejected, he wanted to start a civil disobedience movement.
- Gandhi, on the other hand, was firm in the belief that it was not the right time for such ultimatums as neither the Congress nor the masses were yet ready for struggle.
- Bose wanted an immediate struggle led by Gandhi, whereas Gandhi was firm in his belief that the time was not ripe for struggle.
- Bose resigned from President's post in April 1939. In May, 1939, After resigning from INC, Bose and his followers formed the Forward Bloc as a new party within the Congress.

Second World War and Resignation of Congress Ministries

- The Second World War broke out in September 1939, when Germany invaded Poland. The Government of India declared India to be at war with Germany without consulting the Congress or the elected members of the Central Legislature.
- The Congress Working Committee which met at Wardha on September 14, declared that it could not associate themself in war unless British Government publicly stated that India would be granted political independence after the war. But there were no positive response from the Government, the Congress Ministries resigned after being in the office for 28 months.
- The Muslim League celebrated the Deliverance Day (December 22, 1939), on the day of the resignation of the Congress Ministries in the provinces.

Congress Socialist Party (1934)

In May 1934, Acharya Narendra Dev, Jayaprakash Narayan and Achyut Patwardhan, who were members of Congress

Working Committee, established the Congress Socialist Party.

August 8, 1940 Offer

- After the resignation of Congress Ministries, the annual session of Congress was held at Ramgarh (Bihar) in March 1940. The Congress offered to cooperate with British Government if a Provisional National Government was set up at the Centre.
- In response, on August 8, 1940 the Viceroy Linlithgow, a set of proposals to the Congress, for securing its co operation during the war, which are popularly known as August Offer.
- The August Offer turned down the Congress demand for setting up the Provisional National Government, but it offered the following:
  - An immediate expansion of the Viceroy's Executive Council by inducting into that body a number of representative Indians.
  - Establishment of War Advisory Council comprising representatives of British India;
  - A representative constitution making body would be set up after the war.
- The Congress rejected the August Offer. Jawaharlal Nehru said that the whole idea of Dominion status, on which the offer was based, was as dead as a doornail.

Individual Satyagraha (October 17, 1940)

- Gandhiji gave the call for a limited satyagraha in October, 1940, by a few selected individuals after the Congress Ministries had resigned.
- Individual satyagraha was started on October 17, 1940 from Paynar Ashram in Maharastra. Vinoba Bhave was the first individual satyagrahi on October 17, 1940 and Jawaharlal Nehru was the second one.

Demand for Pakistan

- The ideological and political background of separate independent Muslim state had been prepared by the Aligarh movement, the foundation of the Muslim League and Morley Minto reforms (it introduced separate electorates for the Muslims). However, it was Muhammad Iqbal who first articulated the demand for a separate Muslim state in the Indian continent. He presided over the Allahabad session of the Muslim League in 1930.
- Also during the Round Table Conference, Rahmat Ali (a muslim student in England) conveyed the Muslim delegates, the scheme of a separate muslim nation consisting of Punjab, West Frontier or Afghan North province, Kashmir, Sindh and Baluchistan.
- The proposed separate Muslim state was to be named Pakistan. The name was derived by taking the first letter of the first four provinces and the end of the last name province. Rahmat Ali founded the Pakistan National Movement in 1933 to propagate the idea. He wrote a book Now or Never.
- Muslim League, in March 1940 in its Lahore session declared that the Muslims in India must have a separate independent state. It was presided by M. A. Jinnah. Muslim League adopted a resolution an March 24, 1940 in which, famous Pakistan Resolution, was passed which totally rejected the scheme of Federation given by the Government of India Act, 1935.

Cripps Mission (1942)

- To secure the Indian cooperation, the British Government sent to India on March 11, 1942 a mission headed by a cabinet minister, Stafford Cripps (a left wing Labourite).
- **Main Clauses:**
  - Dominion status to India and permission to opt out of Commonwealth and free to join any international bodies, including UN.
  - After the war, a constituent assembly would be formed to design a new constitution. Members of this parliament would be chosen in part by provincial legislatures using proportional representation and in part by the princes.
- The British government would accept the new constitution subject to two conditions:
  - Any province that does not choose to join the Union may have its own constitution and create its own Union. The new constitution-making body and the British government would draft a treaty to complete the transfer of power and to protect ethnic and religious minorities.
- In the meantime, defence of India would remain in British hands and the governor-general's powers would remain intact.

Quit India Movement (1942)

- The failure of the Cripps Mission to solve the constitutional deadlock exposed Britain's unchanged attitude on constitutional advance.
- The Congress Working Committee meeting held at Wardha on 14 July 1942 and proposed massive Civil Disobedience, if the British did not accede to the demands. On August 8, 1942, All India Congress meeting held at Gowalia Tank, Bombay and the 'Quit india' resolution were passed and Gandhiji gave the slogan of 'Do or die'.
- **The meeting resolved to:**
  - Demand an immediate end to British rule in India.
  - Declare commitment of free India to defend itself against all types of Fascism and imperialism.
  - Form a provisional Government of India after British withdrawal.
  - Sanction a civil disobedience movement against British rule.
- **Gandhi's General Instructions**
  - **For Government Servants:** Do not resign but declare your allegiance to the Congress.
  - **For Soldiers:** Do not leave the Army but do not fire on Compatriots.
  - **For Students:** If confident, leave studies.
  - **For Peasants:** If zamindars are anti-government, pay mutually agreed rent, and if not, do not pay rent.
  - **For Princes:** Support the masses and accept sovereignty of your people.
  - **For Princely states' people:** Support the ruler only if he is anti-government and declare yourselves to be a part of the Indian nation.
- **Parallel Governments**
  - **Ballia:** The first parallel government was proclaimed in Ballia in East U. P. in August 1942, under the leadership of Chittu Pandey.
  - **Jatiya Sarkar:** In Tamluk in the Midnapur district of Bengal, the Jatiya Sarkar came into existence on December 17, 1942 and lasted till September 1944.
  - **Satara:** A parallel government or Prati Sarkar was set up in Satara, Maharastra. Nana Patil, Y. B. Chavan, Achyut Patwardhan were its important leaders. Nyayadan Mandals or people's court were set up and justice dispensed.

- **Gandhiji's Fast and Release from Jail**
  - Gandhiji decided to observe 21 days fast against the violence of the state, He commenced a fast on February 10, 1943 in jail. There was a country wide agitation for his release. But the Viceroy refused to set him free.
  - Three members of the Viceroy's Executive Council - H. P. Modi, N. R. Sarcar and M. S. Aney resigned from their offices in protest.
  - Lord Wavell, who had taken over as the Viceroy of India, in October 1943, released Gandhiji on May 6, 1944 because of his deteriorating health.
- **Indian National Army (Azad Hind Fauz)**
  - The INA was initially organized by Captain Mohan Singh, but it was Rash Behari Bose who provided political leadership. In March, 1942, he convened a conference in Tokyo at which it was decided to form the Indian National Army (INA). The INA was initially organized by Captain Mohan Singh an Indian officer of the British army in Malaya who had surrendered to the Japanese. It passed a resolution to form Azad Hind Fauz or Free India Legion (Indian National Army). On September 1, 1942, the first division of INA was formed with 16300 men.
  - The second phase of the INA began when Subash Chandra Bose was brought to Singapore on July 2, 1943 by the means of German and Japanese submarines. He went to Tokyo and Prime Minister Tojo declared that Japan had no territorial designs on India.
  - Subash Chandra Bose retuned to Singapore and set up the Provisional Government for Free India on October 21, 1943. He set up two INA headquarters, in Rangoon (Barma) and in Singapore and gave his famous call Delhi Chalo.
  - Subash Bose in a broadcast on Azad Hind Radio addressed to Gandhiji as Father of our Nation on July 6, 1944.
  - The INA prisoners were tried in the famous Red Fort trial in Delhi. Shah Nawaz Khan, Gurbaksh Singh Dhillon and P. K. Sehgal etc. were put on trial. The defence of INA prisoners was taken up by the Congress. Bhulabhai Desai, Tej Bahadur Sapru, K. N. Katju, J. L. Nehru and Asaf Ali appeared in court at the historic Red Fort trials.
- **Rajagopalachari Formula (1944):** Muslim League observed the Pakistan Day on March 23, 1943 and declared that Pakistan was the final goal of the Muslims in India. In March, 1944, C. Rajagopalachari evolved a formula which stated that League should cooperate with the Congress in its demand of complete independence and at the end of the war, a plebiscite would be held in the Muslim majority provinces to decide whether or not they should form a separate state. The formula was however rejected by the Muslim League.
- **Desai - Liaquat Pact:** Bhulabhai Desai (leader of the Congress in the Central Legislative Assembly) and Liaquat Ali Khan (deputy leader of the League in the Assembly) proposed that an Interim Government should be formed at the centre consisting of equal number of members nominated by the Congress and the League in the Central Legislature. Muslim League rejected this scheme again.
- **Wavell Plan and Shimla Conference**
  - Lord Wavell announced a plan known as Wavell Plan simultaneously in London and New Delhi on June 14, 1945.
  - It was related to the formation of a provisional interim government at the Centre. It was proposed that the Viceroy's Executive Council would have equal representation of Muslims and Hindus. The new Executive Council at the Centre would have Indian members except the Viceroy and the commander in chief. All portfolios except defence would be held by the Indian members.
  - Lord Wavell convened a conference of 22 political leaders at Shimla to discuss the new proposals on June 25, 1945. But the conference broke down on the issue of reconstitution of the Viceroy's Executive Council and Congress refused to accept the claims of the Muslim League to be the sole representative of the Muslim opinion. Abul Kalam Azad represented the Congress at the Shimla conference.
- **General Elections (1945-46)**
  - In the Central Assembly, the Congress secured 91.3 percent votes in general constituencies, the Muslim League won every Muslim seat. The Muslim League could secure majority only in Bengal and Sindh.
  - In the Provincial Legislature, the Congress won absolute majority in Bombay, Madras, Bihar, Orissa, Central Provinces and United Provinces. In NWFP the Congress won 30 seats while the League got only 17 seats. In Punjab a coalition Government of the Congress, Akalis and the Unionist was formed.
- **Revolt of RIN Ratings (1946)**
  - The famous Royal Indian Navy (RIN) revolt started on February 18, 1946 when 1100 ratings on HMIS Talwar protested against the ill treatment given to them such racial discriminations, unpalatable food etc.
  - The strike had spread to naval bases all over the country by February 22.
- **Cabinet Mission Plan (1946):** The Cabinet Mission composed of three British Cabinet Ministers – Sir Pethick Lawrence, the Secretary of State for India, Sir Stafford Cripps, President of the Board of Trade and A. V. Alexander, First Lord of Admiralty. It arrived in New Delhi on March 24, 1946. It announced following recommendations:
  - There was to be a Union of India comprising both British India and Indian states, with control over foreign affairs, defence and communications.
  - Residuary powers should be left to the Provinces. The provinces could organise themselves to groups.

- India was to be divided into 3 groups of provinces:
  - **Group A:** Madras, Bombay, Central Provinces, United Provinces, Bihar and Orissa.
  - **Group B:** NWFP, Punjab, Sindh and Baluchistan.
  - **Group C:** Bengal and Assam.
- **Direct Action Day:** The Muslim League withdrew its assent to the Cabinet Mission on July 29, 1946 and pledged to resort to direct action to achieve Pakistan. August 16, 1946 fixed as Direct Action Day by the Muslim League, a communal frenzy took place in Calcutta by the battle cry Lekar rahenge Pakistan, "Larke lenge Pakistan".
- **Interim Government**
- The Interim Government was formed with Jawaharlal Nehru as its Vice President, took office on September 2, 1946. Later, Viceroy persuaded Muslim League to join the Government and five Muslim League nominees were added to it on October 26, 1946.
- The Muslim League members of the Interim Government led by Liaqat Ali Khan (Finance Minister) formed a King's Party and embarrassed the Congress members in different ways.
- **Constituent Assembly:** The Constituent Assembly which met on December 9, 1946, was boycotted by the elected members of the Muslim League.
- **Clement Attlee's Declaration (20 February 1947):** June 30, 1948 was the deadline for transfer of power irrespective of any situation in India.

Freedom with Partition

- **Mountbatten Plan (June 3, 1947)**
- Mountbatten Plan, as the 3rd June 1947 plan came to be known, sought to effect on early transfer of power on the basis of Dominion status to two successor states India and Pakistan.
- Mountbatten advanced the date for transfer of power to August 15, 1947.
- The Plan was accepted by both Congress and the Muslim League.
- This became the basis of the India Independence Act which was ratified by the British Parliament and Crown on July 18 and implemented on August 15, 1947. Pakistan gained independence on August 14, 1947 and India on August 15, 1947.
- Jinnah became the first Governor-General of Pakistan and Liaqat Ali was the first Prime Minister whereas Lord Mountbatten was the first Governor General of independent India and Jawaharlal Nehru was the first Prime Minister of India.
- **Boundary Commission (1947):** In order to settle the boundaries of the new dominions of India and Pakistan, two commissions with a common Chairman Cyril Radcliffe were set up.

Unit-7: India Under British Rule: Governance and other Aspects

Constitutional, Administrative and Judicial Developments

Constitutional Development Between 1773 and 1858

Regulating Act 1773

The regulating act was passed in the British parliament in June 1773. It was first parliamentary ratification and authorization defining the power and authority of the East India company (EIC) w.r.t its Indian possessions.

Provisions of the Act

- It introduced the element of centralized administration; it did not take over the power completely, hence regulated.
- As per this, Warren hasting appointed as Governor General of the presidency of fort William.
- The Supreme Court was established at Calcutta. Judges were from England.
- It had civil and criminal jurisdiction over the British subjects and not Indian Natives.
- Governor General has Control over council of Bombay and Madras.

Pitt's India Act, 1784

- This act resulted in dual control of British possession in India by British government and company with final authority resting with the government.
- The Company became a subordinate department of the State.
- It introduced Board of control who in charge of civil, military and revenue affairs, Court of directors to trading activity.

Act of Settlement 1781

Governor General of Bengal presidency was given veto, Madras and Bombay presidencies became sub ordinates.

The Charter Act of 1793

- The act continued company's trade monopoly in India for 20 more years.
- Governor General was given more power to override his council decision.
- The revenue administration was separated from the judiciary functions and this led to disappearing of the Maal Adalats.

The Charter Act of 1813

- This Act renewed the EIC charter for another 20 years.
- It defined for 1st time constitutional position of British Indian territories.
- The company's monopoly with trade ended except for trade in tea and with China.
- The regulations made by the Councils of Madras, Bombay and Calcutta were now required to be laid before the British Parliament.
- This Act allowed Christian missionary to preach their religion.
- It allocated 100,000 rupees for Indian education and allowed Christian missionaries to teach English and their religion.

The Charter Act of 1833

- It was also called GOI act 1833 or Saint Helena act 1833.

- This act made EIC exclusive administrative body.
- Trade link with china was also ended.
- The act legalized the British colonization of the country.
- The position of Governor General of Bengal re-designated as Governor General of India. Lord William Bentinck became the first Governor General of India.
- Slavery was abolished by this act.

The Charter Act of 1853

- This act ended patronage system to civil service.
- This act appointed separated Governor of Bengal presidency from Governor General India.
- The legislative wing came to be known as the Indian Legislative Council.

Government of India Act 1858

- It shifted from company rule to crown rule.
- It changed designation from Governor General to viceroy.
- A new Secretary of State for India in the British Parliament was appointed, assisted by an India Council.
- Lord canning was the first viceroy.

Indian Council Act, 1861

- The portfolio system introduced by Lord Canning laid the foundations of cabinet government in India.
- The Secretary of state for India in Britain could also dissolve any act passed by Governor General council.

Indian Councils Act, 1892

- Indian National Congress (INC) was formed in 1885 and there was growing feeling of nationalism and this led the INC put fourth demand to British authorities, demand was to reform legislative councils.
- It increased non-official members to the council, in 1894 out of 24 only 5 were Indians.
- This act give Right to ask question on budget, but could not ask supplementary question.
- This act empowered Legislative council to make law and repeal old law with permission of Governor General.

Indian Council Act 1909

- It was popularly known as the Morley-Minto Reforms.
- The Act made the first attempt to bring in a representative and popular element in the governance of the country.
- The strength Legislative Council at Centre and provinces was increased.
- Central 16 to 60 members and provincial level 50 members.
- The elected member would be elected indirectly.
- The member could discuss budget and move resolution and ask supplementary question.
- Satyendranath P. Sinha as the first Indian member to viceroy's executive council.
- Governor General had veto power.
- The introduction of separate electorates for Muslims.

Government of India Act 1919

- The act is known as Montagu-Chelmsford reforms.
- The Act provided for increasing Indian participation in every branch of administration with due progressive devolution of responsible government.
- Dyarchy was introduced at provincial level by this act.
- The subjects were divided to reserved and transferred.
- The Indian Legislative Council at the Centre was replaced by a bicameral system.
- The principle of communal representation was extended with separate electorates for Sikhs, Christians and Anglo-Indians, besides Muslims.
- 25% of the budget was subject to vote, rest was non votable.
- The act provides for the first time, to establish of a public service commission in India.

Simon Commission (1928)

- **Recommendation**
  - It abolish dyarchy.
  - It extend responsible government in the provinces.
  - It establishment of a federation of British India and princely states.
  - It advocate for continuation of communal electorate and so on.
  - 'White Paper on Constitutional Reforms.

Government of India act 1935

- The Act, establishment of an All-India Federation in which Governors' Provinces and the Chief Commissioners' Provinces and those Indian states which might accede to be united were to be included.
- Creation of all India federation was done by this act.
- The Provision of division of powers: - Federal list, Provincial list and Concurrent list.
- The viceroy was vested with residual power.
- The provision of provincial autonomy, dyarchy was abolished at the provincial levels, Governor was head of the executive.
- The act advocated for dyarchy at the center, federal public service commission, federal court, central bank.

Indian Independence Act, 1947

- The Indian Independence Act which was based on the Mountbatten Plan was passed on July 5, 1947 the British Parliament and was implemented on August 15, 1947.
- The Act provided for the creation of two independent dominions of India and Pakistan with effect from August 15, 1947.
- Each dominion was to have a Governor General to be responsible for the effective operation of the Act.
- The constituent assembly of each new dominion was to exercise the powers of the legislature of that dominion, and the existing Central Legislative Assembly and the Council of States were to be automatically dissolved.
- As per the provisions of this Act, Pakistan became independent on August 14 while India got its freedom on August 15, 1947. M. A. Jinnah became the first Governor-General of Pakistan.
- India, however, decided to request Lord Mountbatten to continue as the Governor-General of India.

Development of Indian Press

- **1780 - first newspaper:** Bengal Gazette- by James Augustus Hickey
- **1784:** Calcutta Gazette
- **1788:** Madras Courier

- **1789:** Bombay Herald
- **Vernacular Press Act, 1878:** This was enacted by Lord Lytton.
  - District Magistrate was empowered to for search and seizure (of deposits) of any Vernacular press if found publishing anything against government or antipathy between persons of different religions, caste, race through published material.
  - It was termed as "the gagging act" due to discrimination between English and vernacular press, and it had no right of appeal.
- **1882:** Lord Ripon repealed the Act after strong opposition from the nationalists.
- **Newspaper (Incitement to Offences) Act, 1908:** It Aimed against extremist nationalist activity, the act empowered the magistrates to confiscate press property which published objectionable material likely to cause incitement to murder or acts of violence.
- **Indian Press Act, 1910:** This act revived the worst features of the VPA- local government was empowered to demand a security at registration from the printer/ publisher and forfeit/deregister if it was an offending newspaper, and the printer of a newspaper was required to submit two copies of each issue to local government free of charge.
- **Indian Press (Emergency Powers) Act, 1931:** This Act gave sweeping powers to provincial governments to suppress propaganda for CDM.
- **During the Second World War:** Under the Defence of India Rules, pre-censorship was imposed and amendments made in the Press Emergency Act and Official Secrets Act. At one time, publication of all news related to Congress' activity was declared illegal.
- **After Independence**
  - Press Inquiry Committee, 1947- It repealed Act of 1931, modified sections 124A and 153A.
  - Press Commission under Justice G. S. Rajadhyaksha- establishment of All India Press Council, which set proper rules for the future press.

Development of Education

- **1781:** Calcutta Madrasa established by Warren Hastings.
- **1784:** Asiatic society of Bengal was established in 1784. The aim of this society was to foster oriental studies in India. James Prinsep was the founding editor of the Journal of the Asiatic Society of Bengal.
- **1791:** Sanskrit College, established by Jonathan Duncan, resident at Benares.
- **1800:** Fort William College by Wellesley- for the training of civil servants.
- **1813:** Charter Act- sanctioned 1 lakh rupees annually. But it never came to effect till 1823.
- **1817:** Calcutta College- imparting education in English, western humanities and sciences.

Orientalists-Anglicists Conflict

- **1835:** Lord Macaulay's Minute – it was in favor of Anglicists, Government funding was to be devoted to western learning.
  - English was decided to be the medium of instruction.
  - Mass education was neglected. Few English schools and colleges were opened.
  - They applied the Downward Filtration Theory. They believed in educating the upper class and gradually pass on to the masses.
- **1854:** Wood's Despatch - It was also known as the "Magna carta of English education in India".

  Recommended government to take up education of masses. So no downward filtration.
- **Proper hierarchy:** Vernacular primary schools at villages followed by Anglo- Vernacular high schools, Affiliated colleges at district level, Affiliating universities at presidency levels.
  - Laid stress on female education, vocational education, teachers training.
  - Education imparted in government institutions should be secular.
- **1882-83: Hunters Commission**
- It was mainly for primary and secondary education.
- **Recommendation**
  - The State need to pay attention for extension and improvement of primary education.
  - Primary education should be imparted through vernacular.
  - Transfer of control of primary education to newly set up district and municipal boards.
  - Two divisions in Secondary Education-literary and Vocational.
- **1904:** Indian Universities Act (based on Raleigh Commission, 1902)
- Universities should focus more on study and research.
- **1917-19:** Saddler University Commission - For the improvement of university education, improvement of secondary education was a necessary pre-condition:
  - It was set up to study and report problems of Calcutta University, but its recommendations were applicable to other universities as well.
  - It reviewed the whole education system- from school to university level.
- **1929: Hartog Committee**
  - Primary education should be focused upon, but not expanded or made compulsory.
  - Only deserving students should go to high school. Rest should get vocational training after 8th grade Admissions to universities should be restricted for better efficiency.
- **1937: Wardha Scheme of Basic Education**
  - INC organized National Conference on education in Wardha.
  - Based on the resolution, Zakir Hussain Committee formulated a detailed scheme.
  - Overall system based on Gandhi's ideas published in weekly Harijan.
  - Inclusion of basic handicraft in the syllabus.
  - First 7 years of education- free, compulsory and in the mother tongue.

- **1944:** Sergeant Plan of Education (Educational advisor to Government)
- Aimed at making Indian education on par with European education.

Tribal Movements

Year	Tribal Uprising	Features
1776	Chuar Uprising	Midnapore aboriginal tribesmen organised a protest over land revenue demands and economic misery.
1778	Pahariyas' Rebellion	It was headed by Raja Jagganath who led Pahariyas of Raj Mahal Hills against British expansion on their land.
1818-1831 and 1913	Bhil Uprising	Bhil Raj was created in the Western Ghats in opposition to the Company's control. Reorganised under Govind Guru in 1913 to fight for Bhil Raj.
1820–37	Ho and Munda Uprisings	By Ho tribals led by Raja Parahat in Singhbhum and Chottanagpur region against new farming revenue policy. This later became the Munda rebellion.
1822-29	Ramosi Uprising	By the Ramosi tribals of western ghats, under Chittur Singh against Britisher's occupation of the region.
1829	Koli Uprising	In 1829, 1839, and 1844-48, tribals in Gujrat and Maharashtra rose against the Company's authority.
1832	Kol Rebellion	Tribals of Chottanagpur under Buddho Bagat revolted against Britishers and money lenders.
1837-56	Khond Rebellion	Chakra Bisoi led an uprising of hill tribes from Tamil Nadu to Bengal against interference in tribal rituals and the imposition of new levies.
1855-56	Santhal Rebellion	Tribals of Bihar led by Sido and Kanhu against moneylenders and zamindars.
1868	Naikada Movement	Tribals of Madhya Pradesh and Gujrat against the British and caste Hindus to establish Dharma Raj.
1870s	Kharwar Rebellion	Tribals of Bihar led by Bhagrit Majhi against revenue settlement activities.
1867	Bhuyan and Juang Rebellions	Tribes of Keonjhar, Orissa revolted twice in 1867 and 1891.
1899-1900	Munda Rebellion	Tribals in Chotanagpur revolted against the 'Dikus' under the leadership of Birsa Munda.
1879-80	Koya Uprising	Tribals of the eastern Godavari region led by Tomma Sora and Raja Annantyar revolted against the police and moneylenders.
1910	Bastar Revolt	By tribals of Jagdalpur against new feudal and forest levies.
1914-1919	Tana Bhagat Movement	Chottanagpur's tribals, led by Jatra Bhagat and Balram Bhagat, revolted against outsiders' intrusion.
1921-22	Chenchus Uprising	Tribals of Nallamalla Hills led by K. Hanumanthu revolted against the British forest laws.
1922-24	Rampa Rebellion	Led by Alluri Sitaraman Raju of Koyas, Andhra Pradesh against British interference.

North Eastern Frontier Tribal Movement

1828-33	Ahom's Revolt	In Assam, people are protesting the failure of Britishers to keep their pledge to leave their territory after the Burmese war.
1830s	Khasis' Revolt	Led by Tirath Singh in the hills of Jaintia and Garo against the occupation of their region.
1830s	Singphos' Rebellion	In Assam against occupation to their region by Britishers.
1917- 19	Kukis' Revolt	In Manipur, against British policies of recruiting labour during World War.
1920	Zeliangsong Movement	Manipur tribes protested the British inability to protect them during the Kuki uprising.
1905-31	Naga Movement	By tribals of Manipur, led by Jadonang against British rule and to form Naga raj.

Peasant Movements 1857–1947

- **Narkelberia Uprising (1831)**
  - **Location:** 24 parganas (Bengal)
  - Titu Mir inspired the Muslim tenants in West Bengal to rise against the Hindu landlords.

- **Faraizi Revolt (1838-57)**
  - **Leader:** Haji Sharait Allah and Dadu Mian
  - It supported the cause of peasants against zamindars. Also wanted to overthrow the Britishers.
- **Pagal Panthis (1820s-1840s)**
  - **Leader:** Karam Shah and Tipu
  - It was against zamindari oppression, religious and political motives.
  - It captured lot of areas and this area remained disturbed for almost two decades.

Peasant Movement

- **Indigo Revolt (1859-60):** It was directed against British who forced peasants to sign contracts which forced them to grow Indigo even when it was not profitable to them.
  - Rebellion organised under the leadership of Digambar Biswas and Bishnu Biswas of Nadia district.
  - Peasants were supported by the intelligentsia of Bengal. Nildarpan, a play was written by Dinabandhu Mitra based on this agitation.
  - It was the first Satyagraha movement in Modern India.
- **Pabna Revolt:** Zamindar enhanced rent from tenants from acquiring occupancy under act X of 1859. Peasants formed agrarian association to resist the demands of the zamindars.
  - In 1885 Bengal tenancy act was passed, which solved the major issues. This was supported by Bankim Chandra Chatterjee, R. C. Dutt and Surendranath Banerjee.

Rangpur Dhing (1783)

- The Rangpur rebellion occurred in Bengal.
- It is known as the first hard peasant insurrection against the East India Company's control.
- It clearly exposed the horrors associated with the colonial exploitation system, such as the Ijaradari plan.
- It paved the way for formulating a land settlement that would be permanent in nature.
- The rebellion spread over a significant area, including Ranchi, Hazaribagh, Palamau and Manbhum.
- After two years of strong confrontation, they lost to modern weapons of the British.

Mappila Rebellion in Malabar (1841-1920)

- The Mappila insurrection was a series of rebellions by the Mappila Muslims of Kerala's Malabar area.
- The major causes were an increase in land tax, a lack of tenure security, and landlord exploitation of the poor peasantry.
- The revolt goes fell into the trap of Hindu-Muslim riot.
- During this period there was Khilafat movement was raised for the fulfilment of freedom for Muslims.
- The 1921 rebellion was an expression of long-standing agricultural discontent, which was only exacerbated by their religious and ethnic differences, as well as their political estrangement.
- The rebellion was suppressed thoroughly and largely shadowed by that of the other rebellions.

Deccan Uprising (1875)

- The British expanded their foothold outside Bengal with the Permanent Settlement.
- The revenue system implemented in the Bombay Deccan region was Ryotwari Settlement.
- The revolt started in Poona and henceforth it spread to Ahmednagar.
- This uprising also involved a social boycott of the moneylender.

Tebhaga Movement (1946–47)

- In the mid-1940s, the Tebhaga movement emerged in undivided Bengal.
- This movement centers around a demand for tebhaga (two-third shares) by sharecroppers of their produce for themselves, instead of one-half traditionally given to them by the jotedars—a class of intermediary landowners.
- The colonial rulers utilised all available oppressive tactics to bring this movement to a halt, including imposing a reign of terror in rural regions.

Telangana Movement (1946-52)

- Andhra Pradesh's Telangana Movement (1946-52) battled against the authorities' and local landowners' feudal oppression.
- The agrarian social structure of Hyderabad emerged to be very oppressive in the 1920s and thereafter.
- In rural Telangana's political economy, the Jagirdars and Deshmukhs, locally known as Dora, played a dominant role.

The Kisan Sabha Movement

- **United Provinces Kisan Sabha:** It is founded by Gauri Shankar Mishra and Indra Narayan Dwivedi.
- **Awadh Kisan Sabha (1920):** It is founded by Baba Ramchandra.
- **Eka Movement (1921)** - Region of Revolt - Some Northern districts of the United Provinces - Hardoi, Bahraich, Sitapur. Eka Movement involved a symbolic religious ritual in which the assembled peasants took vows that pay only recorded rent, not leave when evicted, refuse to do forced labour, not help criminals, abide by panchayat decisions. This was lead under the leadership by Madaripasi.
- **Mappila Revolt (1921):** Mopalas were muslim cultivators of south Malabar who were generally taken as Jemis or Janmi (Bonded labour) by Namboodri upper caste Hindu Landlords.
- **Poligars:** Dindigul Malabar and North Arcot began revolting against the company land revenue system during 1790. This uprisings continued in Madras presidency upto 1856.
- **Bardoli Satyagraha (1928):** This was lead by Sardar Patel. The women of Bardoli gave Vallabhai Patel the title of "Sardar".

Unit-8: Miscellaneous

Important Personalities and their Work

Bal Gangadhar Tilak (1856-1920)

- He founded the Poona New English School in January 1880.
- He was Associated in the formation of Deccan Educational Society (1884) and foundation of Fergusson College, Poona.
- He started akharas, lathi clubs and Anti- cow-killing societies.
- He celebrated Sivaji and Ganapati festivals to inculcate the spirit of service to the nation.
- He was tried in the Sedition Case (1908) related to Kesari writings supporting revolutionaries (Muzaffarpur case = Khudiram Bose).
- He declared "Swaraj is my birthright and i shall have it".
- He was called as 'Father of Unrest in India' by Britishers.
- He set up Home Rule League at Poona in 1916.
- He started two Newspapers entitled 'The Maharatta' (English) and 'Kesari' (Marathi).
- His work include The Arctic Home of the Vedas and Gita Rahasya.

Bipan Chandra Pal (1858-1932)

- He is known as 'Father of Revolutionary thoughts 'in India.
- He belonged to Lal Bal Pal trio.
- He is a chief exponent of Swadeshi, Boycott and National Movement.
- His famous work are:
- Indian Nationalism.
- Nationality and Empire.
- Swaraj and the present situation.
- The Basis of social reform.
- The soul of India.

Lala Lajpat Rai (1865-1928)

- He was known as Sher-i-Punjab.
- He was associated in the establishment of D.A.V College.
- He was involved in the formation of Swaraj party.
- He cooperated with Malaviya in organizing Hindu Sangathan Movement.
- He edited The Panjabee, The Vande Matram and the English Weekly, The People.

Sri Aurobindo Ghosh (1872-1950)

- He attended the 1906 congress meeting headed by Dadabhai Naoroji.
- He was arrested in 1908 in connection with Alipore Bomb case.
- He converted from politics into spirituality Karmayogin in English and Dharma in Bengali.
- His books are:
- The Life divine.
- The synthesis of yoga.
- Essays on the Gita.
- The secret of the Vedas.

Annie Beasant (1847-1933)

- She is a socialist, theosophist, women's rights activist, writer and supporter of Indian Self-rule.
- In 1907, she became president of theosophical society.
- She launched home rule league in India to campaign for democracy in India and dominion status within British Empire.
- She started a central Hindu School (1898) in Benares and was associated with Malviya in establishing Benares Hindu University in 1917.
- She became the first women president of congress in 1917.

M. N. Roy (1887-1954)

- He was Indian revolutionary, radical activist, political activist, philosopher.
- M.N. Roy helped establish first Communist group in Tashkent (1920).
- He was instrumental in establishment of Radical Democratic Party in the year 1940.
- He developed a philosophy of Radical Humanism.
- Some of his writings:
- Beyond communism.
- Poverty or plenty.
- India's Message.
- A political biography.
- The historical role of Islam.
- Science and Philosophy.
- Radical Humanist.
- Reason, Romanticism and Revolution.

Chronological order of Important Events

- **20 June 1956: Black Hole Tragedy -** It is alleged that Siraj-ud-daulah, Nawab of Bengal, imprisoned 146 Britishers in a room of 18'x14', most of them were found dead the next morning and only 23 survived.
- **23 June 1757: Battle of Plassey -** Sirajuddaula vs Robert Clive (East India Company) English defeated the Nawab of Bengal.
- **1759: Battle of Bidara -** English defeated Dutch.
- **1761: Third Battle of Panipat -** The Marathas were defeated by the combined troops of Ahmad Shah Abdali Baloch Khanate, Oudh state, and Pashtun Rohillas.
- **1764: Battle of Buxar (October 22, 1764) -** This was fought between the English army led by Major Munro and an alliance of Shuja-ud-daulah (Nawab of Awadh), Shah Alam-II (Mughal emperor) and Mir Qasim in which English defeated the alliance led by Shuja-ud-daulah.
- **1765: Treaty of Allahabad -** Grant of the 'Diwani' of Bengal, Bihar, and Orissa to the East India Company by Shah Alam II, under Treaty of Allahabad.
- **1765-72:** Robert Clive introduced Dual Government of Bengal. (company + rights). Warren hasting did away.

- **1766:** Treaty of Hyderabad (English vs Nizam).
- **1767-69:** The First Anglo Mysore War.
- **1769:** Treaty of Madras.
- **1770:** The Great Bengal Famine.
- **1772:** Abolition of Dual Government of Bengal.
- **1773:** The Regulating Act was passed, bringing the company partially under Parliament's control and the Presidencies under Calcutta's control.
- **1773-85:** Warren Hastings Governor-General of Bengal. Establishment of the Supreme Court, Calcutta.
- **1775-82:** The First Anglo-Maratha War & Treaty of Salbai (1782).
- **1776:** Treaty of Purandar.
- **1789:** French revolution started.
- **1780-84:** Second Anglo-Mysore War.
- **1784:** Treaty of Mangalore between Tipu and the English. Pitt's Act passed, Setting up Board of Control for East India Company. Asiatic Society of Bengal was founded by Sir William Jones.
- **1790-92:** Third Anglo-Mysore War.
- **1792:** Treaty of Srirangapatna signed between Tipu Sultan and English.
- **1793-98:** Sir John Shore, Governor-General.
- **1793:** The Permanent Zamindari Settlement of Bengal. introduced by Lord Cornwallis in Bengal, Bihar and Orissa.
- **1798:** Lord Wellesley as Governor-General and brought Subsidiary Alliance.
- **1799:** Fourth Anglo-Mysore War.
  Fall of Srirangapatnam.
  Death of Tipu Sultan.
- **1800:** Establishment of the College of Fort William by Lord Wellesley at Kolkata (objective - train British civilians for administrative purpose in India)
- **1802:** The Treaty of Bassein between Peshwa and English.
- **1803-05:** Second Anglo-Maratha War.
- **1806:** Vellore Mutiny - It was the first scene of a large and violent mutiny by Indian sepoys against the East India Company, preceding the Indian Rebellion of 1857.
- **1809:** Treaty of Amritsar-Ranjit Singh and British sign Treaty of Perpetual Amity.
- **1814-16:** Anglo-Gurkha War.
- **1817-18:** Pindari War-Peshwa defeated at Kirkee.
- **1817:** Paika rebellion.
- **1818-19:** Last Anglo-Maratha War.
- **1820-27:** Sir Thomas Munro introduced Ryotwari settlement in Madras and Bombay.
- **1824-26:** First Burmese War.
- **1828:** Ahom revolt against Britishers led by Gomdhar Konwar.
- **1829:** Prohibition of Sati, by efforts of Lord William Bentinck and Raja Ram Mohan Roy.
- **1833:** Charter Act of 1833.
- **1835:** Macaulay's Education Resolution. English became the official language instead of Persian.
- **1835:** Foundation of Calcutta Medical College.
- **1839:** Death of Ranjit Singh.
- **1839-42:** 1st Anglo-Afghan war.
- **1843:** Slavery was abolished by Lord Ellenborough.
- **1845-46:** First Anglo-Sikh War, and Treaty of Lahore.
- **1848-49:** Second Anglo-Sikh War. Defeat of Sikhs and annexation of the Punjab. Opening of a Hindu Girls' School in Calcutta by Bethune.
- **1848-56:** Introduction of policy of doctrine of lapse by lord Dalhousie.
- **1852:** Second Anglo-Burmese War.
- **1853:** Railway service from Bombay to Thana. Telegraph line from Calcutta to Agra.
- **1854:** Charles Wood's despatch on Education.
- **1855-56:** Santhal rebellion.
- **1856:** Annexation of Awadh.
  Indian University Act.
  Hindu Widow's Remarriage Act passed by Lord Canning.
- **1859-60:** Indigo revolt.
- **1857-58:** Revolt of 1857. Revolt at Meerut begins on May 10, 1857.
- **1858:** British India placed under the direct government of the Crown. Lord Canning (1858-62) became 1st Viceroy of India.
  Edward Henry Stanley became 1st secretary of state for India.
- **1861:** Indian Councils Act.
  Archaeological Survey of India set up.
  Indian Civil Service Act.
  Introduction of the Penal code.
- **1872:** Native Marriage Act, 1872 (Sharda Act) prevent child marriage.
- **1872:** 1st census in India during the British period under Lord Mayo.
- **1873:** Satyashodhak Samaj founded by Jyotiba Phule.
- **1875:** Arya Samaj founded by Swami Dayananda Saraswati. Theosophical Society was founded by Madame Blavatsky and Col. Olcott.
- **1877:** Lord Lytton held Durbar at Delhi where Queen Victoria was proclaimed Empress of India.
- **1878-80:** First Famine Commission (1878-80) under Sir Richard Strachey.
- **1879:** Organisation of Ramosi Peasant Force by Vasudev Balwant Phadke.
- **1880:** Deccan Educational Society established by B. G. Tilak.
- **1880:** Viceroy Lytton appointed Royal Commission of Famine under the presidency of Richard Strachey.
- **1878:** Vernacular Press Act under Lord Lytton.
- **1879:** Theosophical Society was set up at Adayar, Madras.
- **1881:** Factory Act 1881, under Lord Ripon.
- **1882:** Hunter Commission to review educational development appointed by Lord Ripon.
- **1883:** Indian National Conference held in Calcutta.
- **1883-84:** Ilbert Bill controversy.
- **1885:** Formation of INC by A. O. Hume, First session of the Indian National Congress held at Bombay.

- **1889:** Ahmadiya Movement founded by Mirza Ghulam Ahmad.
- **1892:** Indian Councils Act.
- **1896:** Ramakrishna Mission founded.
- **1896:** For the first time National song (Vande Mataram) was sung in the Calcutta session.
- **1898:** Indian Currency Committee or Fowler Committee was a government committee appointed by the British Government.
- **1902:** Establishment of Anushilan Samiti in Midnapur by Jnanendranath Basu and in Calcutta by Promotha Mitter, Jatindranath Banerji and Barindra Kumar Ghosh.
- **1902:** Second Police Commission was set up in 1902 under the chairmanship of Andrew Fraser.
- **1904:** Indian Universities Act, 1904 was enacted based on the recommendation of the Raleigh commission.
- **1905:** INC Banaras session presided by G. K. Gokhale.
- **1905-08:** Swadeshi Movement- The formal proclamation of the Swadeshi Movement was made on 7 August, 1905. On the same day, the famous Boycott Resolution was passed.
- **1905:** Servant of India society was founded by Gokhale.
- **1905:** Partition of Bengal on 16 October under Lord Curzon.
- **1905:** National Council of Education was established in November.
- **1905:** Shyamji Krishna Verma founded the India Home Rule Society in London in 1905, with the object of securing Home Rule for India.
- **1906:** Shimla Deputation- Muslim representative under the leadership of Agha Khan met Viceroy and demanded separate electorate for Muslims at Shimla in October.
- **1906:** 30 December 1906 - All India Muslim League formed at Dacca by Nawab Salimullah Khan and Agha Khan.

  Nawab Waqar- ul - mulk the 1st president of Muslim league.
- **1907:** Surat Split.
- **1908:** Tilak was convicted of sedition.
- **1908:** Alipore Conspiracy Case (Muzaffarpur Conspiracy Case) was a revolutionary conspiracy by Khudiram Bose and Praffula Chaki to kill the Chief Presidency Magistrate D. H. Kingsford of Muzaffarpur.
- **1909:** Curzon Wyllie's Assassination.
- **1909:** Morley-Minto Reforms. Also known as Indian Councils Act 1909 under which provision for separate electorate (for Muslims) was introduced.
- **1911: 12 December 1911-** Capital shifted from Kolkata to Delhi.
- **1911:** Delhi Durbar - Partition of Bengal annulled. Transfer of Capital to Delhi announced.
- **1912:** Delhi Conspiracy Case also known as Delhi-Lahore Conspiracy was headed by Ras Bihari Bose to assassinate the then Viceroy of India, Lord Hardinge.
- **1913:** Establishment of Ghadar party in USA (San Francisco) by Lala Hardayal.
- **1914:** September 29, 1914 - Komagata Maru Incident.
- **1915:** January 1915, Mahatma Gandhi returned India from South Africa.
- **1916:** Lucknow Pact of Indian National Congress and All-India Muslim League. It was presided by A. C. Majumdar. In this session, separate electorate demand of Muslim league was accepted by INC.
- **1916:** Foundation of Women's University at Poona by D. K. Karve.
- **1916:** Home Rule League founded by Annie Besant & Tilak. Tilak's Home Rule League founded in April 1916. Annie Besant's league was founded in Oct 1916.
- **1917:** Saddler Commission (education) was set up to study and report on problems of Calcutta University.
- **1917:** Champaran Satyagraha By Mahatma Gandhi.
- **1918:** Ahmedabad Mill Strikes.
- **1918:** Kheda Satyagrah.
- **1919:** Montagu-Chelmsford Reforms.
- **1919:** Rowlatt Act passed.
- **1919:** On April 13, Massacre at Jallianwala Bagh, Amritsar. Hunter commission was appointed to inquire about the event.
- **1920:** Khilafat Movement and Non Co-operation Movement launched on 1 August, 1920.
- **1920-22:** Non Cooperation Movement was the first mass movement under the leadership of Mahatma Gandhi.
- **1920:** All India Home Rule League changed its name to Swarajya Sabha.
- **1920:** B. R. Ambedkar established All India Depressed Class Federation.
- **1921:** Moplah Rebellion.
- **1922: 5 February 1922-** Chauri Chaura (near Gorakhpur) incident. Gandhiji suspended NCM.
- **1923:** Swaraj Party was formed in 1923 by C. R. Das and Moti Lal Nehru.
- **1924:** Ambedkar founded Depressed Class Institutions.
- **1924:** Lee Commission (civil services) was set up.
- **1924:** Hindustan Republican Association (HRA) was founded at Kanpur in October 1924, by Sachindranath Sanyal, Jogesh Chandra Chatterjee, and Ram Prasad Bismil.
- **1925: August 1925-** Kakori Conspiracy took place under leadership of Ram Prasad Bismil.
- **1925:** Bhagat Singh and his colleagues started a militant youth organisation called the Naujawan Bharat Sabha.
- **1927:** Appointment of Simon Commission (7 member commission without any Indian).
- **1927:** All India Women Conference was held.
- **1928: February 1928-** Simon Commission comes to India.
- **1928: November 1928-** Death of Lala Lajpat Raj during the protest for Simon Commission.
- **1928:** Nehru Report - Moti Lal Nehru was chairman.
- **1928:** Hindustan Socialist Republican Association (HSRA) was formed at Ferozshah Kotla ground in Delhi

on September 9-10, 1928 under the collective leadership of Chandrashekhar Azad, Bhagat Singh, Sukhdev and Bhagwaticharan Vohra.

- **1928:** Bardoli Satyagraha led by Sardar Patel.
- **1929:** Congress at Lahore Session declaring its objective of Poorna Swaraj for India. Jawahar Lal Nehru declared the aim of Congress as Purna Swaraj.
- **1929:** Lahore Conspiracy Case (Saunders Murder Case) - Bhagat Singh and his associates plotted the assassination of James A. Scott, the Superintendent of Police. However, the revolutionaries shot J. P. Saunders.
- **1929: 8 April 1929-** Bhagat Singh and Batukeshwar Dutt drops bombs in the Legislative Assembly against the passage of the Public Safety Bill and Trade Disputes Bill.
- **1929:** Whitley Commission on Labour was set up.
- **1930:** Chittagong Armory Raid led by Surya Sen.
- **1930:** Sarda Act (1930) increased the marriage age to 18 and 14 for boys and girls, respectively.
- **1930 - 12 March 1930-6 April 1930:** Dandi March started by Gandhiji and his 78 companions.
- **1930:** Civil Disobedience Movement.
- **1930-31:** November 1930- January 1931 First Round Table Conference.
- **1931: 5 March 1931-** Gandhi-Irwin Pact/Delhi Pact.
- **1931: 23 March 1931-** Bhagat Singh, Rajguru & Sukhdev were hanged for Lahore-Conspiracy.
- **1931: 26-29 March 1931-** Karachi session of INC (President Sardar Patel).
- **1931: 7 December 1931-** 2nd RTC. Gandhiji participated. Sarojini Naidu represented Indian women at the Second Round Table Conference.
- **1932: August 1932-** Communal Award announced by Ramsay Mcdonald.
- **1932: September 1932-** Gandhiji founded All India Untouchability League from Yervada Jail.
- **1932: September 1932-** Poona Pact was signed between Gandhi and Ambedkar.
- **1932:** Harizan Sewak Sangh established by Gandhiji. 1st president - Ghanshyamdas Birla with Amritlal Takkar as its secretary.
- **1932: November - December 1932-** Third Round Table Conference.
- **1934:** Formation of Congress Socialist Party by Jaiprakash Narayan (loknayak), he was coordinator and Acharya Narendra Dev was president.
- **1935:** Government of India Act, 1935 passed by British Parliament.
- **1936:** All India Kisan Sabha founded in Lucknow in April 1936 with Swami Sahjanand Saraswati as the president.
- **1937: February 1937-** Elections were held in the provincial legislature. Congress emerged as the single largest party.
- **1938:** Haripura session of the Congress. (President - S. C. Bose)
- **1938:** National Planning Committee set up in 1938 under Congress President Subhas Bose.
- **1939: September 1939-** Second World War begins.
- **1939: 22 October 1939-** Congress government of all provinces resigned.
- **1939: March 1939-** Forward Bloc was formed in March 1939, by Subhash Chandra Bose.
- **1940:** Pakistan resolution passed by Muslim League at Lahore. Two nation theory of jinnah was accepted in Lahore session of Muslim League.
- **1940: 8 August 1940 Offer:** The Viceroy Linlithgow, offered from Shimla, a set of proposals to the Congress, for securing its co- operation during the war, which are popularly known as August Offer.
- **1940: October 1940-** After rejecting August offer, INC started Individual satyagraha. Vinoba Bhave was the first satyagrahi. Jawaharlal Nehru was second satyagrahi.
- **1942: March 1942-** Cripps Mission - Cripps comes to India with his proposals. Jawaharlal Nehru & Maulana Azad were official negotiator from Congress.
- **1942: 11 April 1942-** Congress rejects Cripps Proposal. Gandhi termed this deal as post-dated cheque.
- **1942:** On August 8, 1942 "Quit India" resolution passed by Congress. 9 August 1942 - All top leaders arrested
- **1942:** Azad Hind Fauj (Indian National Army) was established in Japanese-occupied Singapore during World War II on 1 September 1942. The army was first formed in 1942 under Captain Mohan Singh by Indian PoWs of the British Indian Army captured by Japan in the Malayan campaign and at Singapore.
  The second phase of the INA began when Subash Chandra Bose was brought to Singapore on July 2, 1943.
- **1944:** C. Rajagopalachari Formula - It stated that League should cooperate with the Congress in its demand of complete independence and at the end of the war, a plebiscite would be held in the Muslim majority provinces to decide whether or not they should form a separate state. The formula was however rejected by the League.
- **1945:** Desai-Liaquat Pact - Bhulabhai Desai (leader of the Congress in the Central Legislative Assembly) and Liaquat Ali Khan(deputy leader of the League in the Assembly) proposed that an Interim Government should be formed at the centre consisting of equal number of members nominated by the Congress and the League in the Central Legislature. The Muslim League rejected this scheme as well.
- **1945: June 14, 1945** – Wavell Plan -It related to the formation of a provisional interim government at the Centre. It was proposed that the Viceroy's Executive Council would have equal representation of Muslims and Hindus.
- **1945: June 25, 1945** – Shimla Conference - Lord Wavell convened a conference of 22 political leaders at Simla to discuss the new proposals. Abul Kalam Azad represented the Congress at the Shimla conference.
- **1945-46:** General Elections In the elections to the Central and Provincial Legislatures held in 1945-46, Congress made its presence at both the Central and Provincial legislatures.

- **1945:** INA trials - INA day was celebrated from November 12, and INA week was celebrated from November(5-11). The first of these was the joint trial of Shah Nawaz Khan, Prem Sahgal and Gurbaksh Singh Dhillon.
- **1946:** Royal Indian Navy (RIN) revolt started on February 18, 1946 .
- **1946:** Cabinet Mission Plan - British Government announced the sending of a Cabinet Mission to India, a day after the RIN Ratings mutiny began. It was composed of three British Cabinet Ministers-Sir Pethick Lawrence, the Secretary of State for India, Sir Stafford Cripps, President of the Board of Trade and A. V Alexander.
- **1946:** On June 29, 1946, the Cabinet Mission left India and the Viceroy formed a caretaker Government comprising nine officials.
- **1946:** The Muslim League withdrew its assent to the Cabinet Mission on July 29, 1946 and pledged to resort to direct action to achieve Pakistan.
- **1946:** Direct Action Day - August 16, 1946 fixed as Direct Action Day by the Muslim League, a communal frenzy took place in Calcutta.
- **1946:** Interim Government - On September 2, 1946 the Interim Government with Jawaharlal Nehru as its Vice President of Executive Council.
- **1946:** On October 26, 1946, Viceroy persuaded Muslim League to join the Government and nominees were five Muslim League added to it.
- **1946:** Constituent Assembly - The Constituent Assembly which met on December 9, 1946, was boycotted by the elected members of the Muslim League.
- **1947:** Climent Attlee's Declaration - February 20, 1947 Attlee made a statement in British parliament, that the date of British withdrawal from India was fixed as June 30, 1948 and the appointment of new Viceroy, Lord Mountbatten was announced.
- **1947:** Mountbatten Plan - On June 3, 1947 Lord Mountbatten was sworn in as the Governor-General on March 24, 1947. The Mountbatten Plan, as the 3rd June 1947 plan came to be known, sought to effect on early transfer of power on the basis of Dominion status to two successor states India and Pakistan. Mountbatten advanced the date for transfer of power to August 15, 1947. The Plan was accepted by both Congress and the Muslim League.
- **1947:** This became the basis of the India Independence Act which was ratified by the British Parliament and Crown on July 18 and implemented on August 15, 1947. Pakistan gained independence on August 14, 1947 and India on August 15, 1947.
- **1947:** Jinnah became the first Governor- General of Pakistan and Liaqat Ali was the first Prime Minister. Lord Mountbatten was the first Governor General of independent India and Jawaharlal Nehru was the first Prime Minister of India. Lockhart was the Commander - in - chief of the Indian army from August 15 to December 31, 1947.
- **1947:** Boundary Commission - To settle the boundaries of the new dominions of India and Pakistan, two commissions with a common Chairman Cyril Radcliffe were set up.
- **1947:** Indian Independence Act - On July, 1947 British Parliament passed the Indian Independence Act. The act was implemented on 15 August, 1947.

Governor-Generals and Viceroys of India

Governer of Bengal

Robert Clive (1757-60 & 1765-67)

- Robert Clive was appointed the first Governor of Bengal by the East India.
- He concluded the treaty of Allahabad (1765) with Nawab Shuja-ud-daulah of Avadh and Mughal Emperor Shah Alam II.

Governor General of Bengal

Warren Hastings (1774-1785)

- He became the first Governor General of Bengal after enactment of regulating Act of 1773.
- The first Anglo - Maratha war and treaty of salbai.
- Rohila War of 1784.
- Pitts India Act of 1784.
- Foundation of Asiatic Society with William Jones in 1784.
- He was the only Governor General against whom impeachment proceedings were initiated in England.

Lord Cornwallis (1786-1793)

- He introduced civil services in India.
- He introduced permanent settlement in Bengal and Bihar in 1793.
- He also introduced the cronwallis code incorporating several judicial reforms and the separation of revenue administration and civil administration.
- Third Mysore war (1790-92) and treaty.

Sir John Shore (1793-1798)

- Famous for his policy of non-intervention.
- Battle of Kharda (1795), between Nizam and Maratha Empire, in which Nizam was badly defeated.

Lord Richard Wellesley (1798-1805)

- Introduced subsidiary Alliance system (1798) to bring Indian states under control of British Power.
- Founded the Fort Williams college at calcutta (1800).

Sir George Barlow (1805-1807)

- Sepoy mutiny at Vellore (1806).

Lord Minto I(1807-1813)

- Signed treaty of Amritsar in 1809 with Maharaja Ranjit Singh.

Lord Fransis Hastings (1813-1823)

- Anglo-Nepal war (1814-16) and the Treaty of Sagauli (1816).
- Military operations to suppress Pindaris.
- Bombay turned into the capital of Bombay Presidency in 1819, after the Maratha rout in the Anglo-Maratha war.

- Establishment of Ryotwari system by Thomas Munro, Governor of Madras, in 1820. Treaty with Scindia 1817.
- Strive with Pindaris.

Lord Amherst (1823-1828)

- First Anglo-Burma war (1824-26).

Governor General of India

Lord William Bentinck (1828-1835)

- By the Charter Act of 1833, the Governor General of Bengal became the Governor General of India. Thus, Bentinck became the first Governor General of India.
- Abolition of Sati (1829), and suppression of Thugi (1830) with the help of Colonel Sleeman.
- He established the first medical College in Calcutta.

Charles Metcalfe (1835-1836)

- He is known as the liberator of Indian press.

Lord Auckland (1836-1842)

- First Anglo- Afghan war (1836-1842).
- Lord Ellenborough (1842-1844).
- Put an end to the slave system in 1843.
- Annexation of Sindh in 1843.

Lord Hardinge I (1844-1848)

- First Anglo- Sikh war and Treaty of Lahore (1846).
- Social reforms including abolition of female infanticide and human sacrifice.

Lord Dalhousie (1848-1856)

- He introduced the doctrine of Lapse. Some states annexed by enforcement of doctrine Lapse were- Satara (1848), Udaipur (1852), Jhansi (1854), Jaitpur and Sambhalpur (1854), and Nagpur (1854).
- Railway minister of 1853 and first rail between Bombay to Thane in 1853.
- Charles wood's despatch of Indian education.
- Shimla became a summer capital of India and permanent head quarter of Army.
- Post office Act, 1854 passed and postage stamps were issued for the first time.
- Public works Department was also established.

Lord Canning (1856-1857)

- Universities of Bombay, Calcutta and Madras were established in 1857.
- The revolt of 1857.

Viceroys (By Government of India Act, 1858)

Lord Canning (1857-1863)

- He was the last Governor - General of India and the first Viceroy of India.
- Proclamation of Queen Victoria and transfer of Indian administration to British crown.
- Indian Penal Code (1860), Code of Criminal Procedure (1861) were introduced.
- Official end of Doctrine of Lapse in 1859.

Lord Elgin I (1862-1863)

- During his reign, the Wahabis revolted on the North - Western Frontiers but were suppressed.

Sir John Lawrence (1864-1869)

- High Courts in Calcutta, Bombay and Madras established in 1865.
- Bhutan war (1865).

Lord Mayo (1869-1872)

- Established Maryo college in Ajmer and Rajkot college in Kathiawar.
- Established statistical Survey of India, Department of Agriculture and Commerce.
- First census in India was conducted in 1872.

Lord Northbrook (1872-1876)

- Kuka movement in Punjab.
- Child marriage prohibited by passing Native Marriage Act, 1872.

Lord Lytton (1876-1880)

- Famine Committee appointed under Sir Richard Strachey.
- Held first Delhi Durbar in 1877 where the Queen was conferred with the title Kaiser-i-Hind.
- Vernacular Press Act Passed in 1878, which was called the Gagging Act.
- Arms Act (1878).
- The maximum age in Indian Civil Services lowered from 21 years to 19 years.

Lord Ripon (1880-1884)

- The first organised census held in 1881.
- First Factory Act in 1881.
- Appointment of Hunter commission on school education in 1882.
- Repealed Vernanular press Act, hence Ripon is Known as the Liberator of Indian press.
- Acts relating to Local Self Government passed.
- Known as father of Local Self Government.
- Ilbert bill controversy (1884).
- He had to resign from his office as a result of Ilbert Bill controversy (1883-84).

Lord Dufferin (1884- 1888)

- Formation of Indian National Congress in 1885.
- Third Burmese war 1885-86.

Lord Lansdowne (1888-1894)

- Durand commission (1893) formed to demarcate boundary between Indian and Afghanistan.
- Factory Act 1891.
- Indian Council Act 1892.

Lord Elgin II (1894- 1899)

- A Famine Committee under Lyall appointed.

Lord Curzon (1899-1905)

- A Famine Commission under sir Anthony Macdonnell, and a Police Commission under Andrew Frazer appointed.
- Appointment of universities commission 1902 and passing of Indian University Act 1904.
- Partition of Bengal on October 16, 1905.
- The Indian coinage and paper Currency Act, 1899 Ancient Monuments preservation Act, 1904 passed.
- An Archaeological Department established.
- Establishment of Department of commerce and industry.

Lord Minto II (1905-1910)

- Morley - Minto reforms (Indian Council Act of 1909).
- Formation of Muslim League.

- Surat Split 1907.
- Swadeshi Movement.

Lord Hardinge (1910-1916)
- Capital of India shifted from Calcutta to Delhi.
- First world war.
- Partition of Bengal reversed in 1911.
- Establishment of Hindu Mahasabha by Madam Mohan Malviya in 1915.
- Ghadar Party formed at San Francisco in 1913.
- Nobel prize in literature for Rabindranath Tagore in 1913.

Lord Chelmsford (1916-1921)
- Lucknow session of congress and Lucknow Pact between Congress and Muslim League (1916).
- Formation of Saddler commission for education in 1917.
- Rowlatt Act 1919.
- Jallianwala Bagh Massacre 1919.
- Launch of non cooperation and khilafat movement.
- Montagu - Chelmsford reforms.

Lord Reading (1921-1926)
- Moplah rebellion in Malabar coast 1921.
- Chauri Chaura incident on 5 February 1922.
- Kakori train robbery 1925.
- Establishment of Swaraj party.
- Formation of communist party of India by M. N. Roy in 1920 in Tashkent.
- Decision to hold civil services simultaneously at London and Delhi with effect from 1923.

Lord Irwin (1926-1931)
- Appointment of Simon commission in 1927.
- Lahore session of Congress 1929; Purna Swaraj resolution.
- Dandi March (12 March 1930).
- Dipawali declaration by lord Irwin in 1929 first Round Table Conference.
- Gandhi - Irwin Pact, 1931.
- Appointment of Harcourt Butler Indian states commission in 1927.

Lord Willingdon (1931-1936)
- Second and third Round Table conference.
- Ramsay Mac-Donald announced the communal Award.
- The Government of India Act, 1935 passed.
- Indian Military Academy established on Dehradun in 1932.
- Burma separated from India in 1935.

Lord Linlithgow (1936-1943)
- Second world war.
- Cripps Mission, 1942.
- Quit India movement, 1942

Lord Wavell (1943-1947)
- C. R. Formula, 1944
- Cabinet Mission, 1946,
- Direct Action Day by Muslim League on August 16, 1946.
- First meeting of constituent Assembly on December 9, 1946 under Sachidanand Sinha.

Lord Mountbatten (1947-48)
- He was the last British viceroy of India and first Governor General of India after independence.
- Announced June 3,1947 plan.
- Appointment of two boundary commissions under the Sir Cyril Radcliffe.
- Partition of India.

C. Rajagopalachari (1948-1950)
- Last Governor - General in India and first Indian Governor General of independent India.
- He remained in office from June 21, 1948 to January 25, 1950.

Agrarian Policy of the British Administration
- **Permanent Settlement:** It was introduced by Lord cornwallis in 1793 in Bengal, Bihar and Orissa. The zamindars who earlier collected land revenue were recognised as landlords. The land revenue was fixed for years in a permanent basis, John Shore was associated with this system.
- **Ryotwari System:** It was connected to Thomas Munro and captain Reed. It was introduced in 1820. The land settlement in Madras and Bombay province was called Ryotwari settlement. In this system rent was directly settled with the ryots.
- **Mahalwari System:** It was introduced in 1822. Holt Mackenzie started this system in Punjab, Central Province, Agra, Awadh and Delhi. Under this system settlement were made estate (Mahal) by estate or village by village. The village community was the owner of the land and was called co - sharers.

List of some Important slogans/ statements	
Back to Vedas	Dayanand Saraswati
Dilli chalo	Subhash Chandra Bose
Jai Hind	Subhas Chandra Bose
Give me blood and I will give you freedom	Subhas Chandra Bose
Do or Die	Mahatma Gandhi (while launching Quit India movement in 1942)
My ultimate aim is to wipe every tear from every eye	Jawahar Lal Nehru
As dead as a doornail	Jawahar Lal Nehru
Rowlatt Act is a Preventive Murder	Edwin Samuel Montagu
Sawaraj is my birthright and I will have it	Bal Gangadhar Tilak
Every blow that is hurled on my back will be a nail in the coffin of the British Empire	Lala Lajpat Rai
Jai Jawan Jai Kisan	Lal Bahadur Shastri

Nicknames of Indian personalities

Name	Personality
Acharya	Vinoba Bhave
Desh Ratna, Ajatshatru	Dr. Rajendra Prasad
Badshah Khan / Frontier Gandhi	Abdul Ghaffar Khan
Bengal Kesari	Ashutosh Mukherji
Bismark of India	Vallabhai Patel
Biswa Kavi	Rabindranath Tagore
Desabandhu	C. R. Das
Grand Old Man of India	Dadabhai Naoroji
Gurudev	Rabindranath Tagore
Iron Man	Sardar Vallabhbhai Patel
Lokmanya	Bal Gangadhar Tilak
Loknayak	Jayaprakash Narayan
Mahamana	Madan Mohan Malaviya
Nightingale of India	Sarojini Naidu
Shaheed- I - Azam	Bhagat Singh
Rajaji	C. Rajagopalachari
Netaji Subhash Chandra Bose	
Morning Star of Indian Renaissance	Raja Ram Mohan Roy
Panjab Kesari	Lala Lajpat Rai

List of Books written by Freedom Fighters

- **M. K. Gandhi (Mahatma Gandhi):** Harijan, Navjivan, Hind Swaraj, My Experiments with Truth.
- **Bal Gangadhar Tilak:** Gita Rahasya, The Orion: Or Researches into the Antiquity of the Vedas, The Arctic Home in the Vedas.
- **Jawahar Lal Nehru:** Discovery of India,Glimpses of World History, Meri Kahani.
- **Maulana Abul Kalam Aazad:** Al Hilal, India Wins Freedom, Ghubar-e-Khatir
- **Lala Lajpat Rai:** Unhappy India
- **Dr. Rajendra Prasad:** India Divided, At the Feet of Mahatma Gandhi, Satyagraha in Champaran
- **Surendra Nath Banarje:** A Nation in Making
- **Veer Savarkar:** The Indian War of Independence
- **Bhagat Singh:** Why I am an Atheist
- **Ravindra Nath Tagore:** Geetanjali, The Home and The World, Gora, Hungry Stones, Chandalika, Visarjan, The Crescent Moon.
- **Madan Mohan Malviya:** Abhyuday, Hindustan, Leader.
- **Gopal Krishna Gokhale:** Nation
- **Keshav Chandra Sen:** Indian Mirror, Vaam Bodhini
- **Dinbandhu Mitra:** Neel Darpan
- **Muhammad Iqbal:** Tarana-e-Hind, Bang-e-Dara
- **Annie Besant:** The Commonwealth, New India
- **Subhash Chandra Bose:** Indian Struggle, An Indian Pilgrim
- **Muhammad Ali:** Comrade, Hamdard
- **Raja Ram Mohan Roy:** Tuhfat-ul-Muwahhiddin (a gift to deists), Samvad Kaumudi
- **Ishwarchadra Vidyasagar:** Som Prakash
- **Motilal Nehru:** Independent
- **Dada Bhai Naoroji:** Rust Goftar, Poverty and Un British Rule in India
- **Shishir Kumar Ghosh:** Amrit Bazar Patrika
- **Tarak Nath Das:** Free Hindustan
- **Sachindra Nath Sanyal:** The Revolutionary, Bandi Jeevan (A Life of Captivity)
- **Dayanand Saraswati:** Satyarth Prakash
- **Bankim Chandra Chattopadhyay:** Bang darshan, Anand Math, Devi Chaudharani, Durgesh Nandini
- **Bhartendu Harishchandra:** Bharat Durdasha
- **Sarojini Naidu:** The Golden Threshold, The Bird of Time, The Feather of the Dawn.
- **BR Ambedkar:** Annihilation of Caste, The Buddha and his Dhamma, Who were the Shudras?.
- **Sri Aurobindo (Aurobindo Ghose):** Love and Death, The Life Divine, Essays on the Gita, Savitri: A Legend and a Symbol.
- **Jayaprakash Narayan:** Why socialism
- **Bhagwati Charan Bohra:** Philosophy of the Bomb

List of Committees and Commissions in India before Independence

Name of Committees/ Commissions	Year	Governor-General/ Viceroy	Purpose
Wood Despatch	1854	Lord Dalhousie	Education
Hunter Commission	1882	Lord Ripon	Education
Campbell Commission	1866	Sir John Lawrence	Famine
Strachey Commission	1880	Lord Lytton	Famine
Lyall Commission	1886	Lord Dufferin	Famine
Raleigh Commission	1902	Lord Curzon	Education
Sadler Commission	1917	Lord Chelmsford	Education
Hartog Commission	1929	Lord Irwin	Education

Sargent Plan	1944	Lord Wavell	Education
MacDonnell Commission	1900	Lord Curzon	Famine
Mansfield Commission	1886	Lord Dufferin	Currency
Fowler Committee	1898	Lord Elgin-II	Currency
Fraser Commission	1902	Lord Curzon	Agriculture
Babington Smith Commission	1919	Lord Chelmsford	Currency
Hunter Committee Report	1919	Lord Chelmsford	Punjab Disturbances
Muddiman Committee	1924	Lord Reading	Examine the working of diarchy Montagu-Chelmsford reforms.
Butler Commission	1927	Lord Irwin	Indian States
Whitley Commission	1929	Lord Irwin	Labour
Simon Commission	1928	Lord Irwin	To investigate the progress of the governance scheme and suggest new steps for reform.
Sapru Commission	1935	Lord Linlithgow	Constitutional reforms, minorities
Hilton Young Commission	1926	Lord Reading	Currency
Chatfield Commission	1939	Lord Linlithgow	Army
Floud Commission	1940	Lord Linlithgow	Tenancy in Bengal

Nationalist Organisations

Organisation	Year	Founder	Place
Landholder's Society	1838	Dwarkanath Tagore	Calcutta
British India Society	1839	William Adam	London
Bengal British India Society	1843	George Thompson	Calcutta
British India Association	1851	Radhakant Deb	Calcutta
East India Association	1866	Dadabhai Naoroji	London
Poona Sarvajanik Sabha	1867	M. G. Ranade	Maharashtra
National Indian Association	1867	Mary Carpenter	London
Indian Society	1872	Anand Mohan Bose	London
Indian Association	1876	Anand Mohan Bose and Surendra Nath Banerjee	Calcutta
Indian National Conference	1883	Surendranath Banerjee	Calcutta
Madras Mahajan Sabha	1884	V. Raghvachari, S. Aiyyar and P. Anand Charlu	Madras
Bombay Presidency Association	1885	Pherozeshah Mehta, K. T. Telang, Badruddin Tyabji	Bombay
Indian National Congress	1885	A. O. Hume	Bombay
Servants of India Society	1905	Gopal Krishna Gokhale	Bombay
Home Rule League	1916	Anne Besant and B. G. Tilak	Pune
Uttar Pradesh Kisan Sabha	1918	Indra Narayan, Malviya and Gauri Shankar	Lucknow
Communist Party of India	1925	M. N. Roy	Kanpur
Awadh Kisan Sabha	1920	Ramchandra, Nehru, Gauri Shankar	Pratapgarh
Indian Trade Union Congress	1920	Founder: M. N. Joshi, President: Lala Lajpat Rai	Bombay
Swaraj Party	1923	Motilal Nehru and C. R. Das	Delhi

Rastriya Svayamsevak Sangh	1925	K. B. Hedgewar	Nagpur
Khudai Khidmatgars (Red Shirts)	1929	Khan Abdul Gaffar Khan (also known as Frontier Gandhi)	Peshawar
Congress Socialist Party	1934	Acharya Narendra Dev and Jai Prakash Narayan	
All India Kisan Sabha	1936	N. G. Ranga and Sahajanand	Lucknow
Forward Bloc	1939	Subash Chandra Bose	Calcutta
Radical Democratic Party	1940	M. N. Roy	Calcutta

Major Newspapers Published in India

Newspaper	Founder/Editor	Year	Place	Language
Bengal Gazette	James Augustus Hickey	1780	Calcutta	English
Samachar Darpan	John Clark Marshman	1818	Calcutta	Bengali
Digdarshan	John Clark Marshman	1818	Calcutta	Bengali
Samvad Kaumudi	Rajaram Mohan Roy	1821	Calcutta	Bengali
Mirat ul Akhbar	Rajaram Mohan Roy	1822	Calcutta	Persian
Bombay Samachar	Fardunjee Marzban	1822	Bombay	English, Gujarati
Rast Goftar	Dadabhai Naoroji	1851	Bombay	Gujarati
Satyaprakash	Karsandas Moolji	1852	Ahmedabad	Gujarati
Bombay Darpan	Balshastri Jambekar	1832	Bombay	Marathi
Indu Prakash	Ranade	1861	Bombay	Marathi
Indian Mirror	Devendranath Tagore	1862	Calcutta	English
Native Opinion	V. N. Manglik	1864	Bombay	English
Amrit Bazar Patrika	Sisir Kumar Ghosh & Motilal Ghosh	1868	Calcutta	Bengali, English
Som Prakash	Ishwar Chandra Vidyasagar	1859	Calcutta	Bengali
The Hindu	G. Subramania Iyer	1878	Madras	English
Kesari	Lokmanya Bal Gangadhar Tilak	1881	Bombay	Marathi
Maharatta	Lokmanya Bal Gangadhar Tilak	1881	Bombay	English
Bengalee	Surendranath Banerjee	1879	Calcutta	English
Kavi Vachan Sudha	Bhartendu Harishchandra	1867	UP	Hindi
Young India	Mahatma Gandhi	1919	Ahmedabad	English
Navjeevan	Mahatma Gandhi	1919	Ahmedabad	Hindi, Gujarati
Harijan	Mahatma Gandhi	1933	Poona	Hindi, Gujarati
Indian Opinion	Mahatma Gandhi	1903	South Africa	English
Hindu Patriot	Harishchandra Mukherjee	1855	Calcutta	English
The Punjabi	Lala Lajpat Rai	____	____	____
Banga Darshan	Bankim Chandra Chatterjee	1873	Calcutta	Bengali
The Tribune	Dayal Singh Majeethia	1877	Lahore	English
The Pioneer	George Allen	1865	Allahabad	English
Sudharak	Gopal Krishna Agarkar	1888	Bombay	Marathi
Statesman	Robert Knight	1878	Calcutta	English
Indian Sociologist	Shyamji Krishna Verma	1905	London	English
Bande Mataram	Hardayal, Shyamji Verma	1909	Paris	English

Yugantar	Barindra Kumar Ghosh, Bhupendranath Dutta	1906	Calcutta	Bengali
Ghadar	Lala Hardayal	1913	San Francisco	English
Bombay Chronicle	Pherozshah Mehta	1913	Bombay	English
Commenweal	Annie Besant	1914	Bombay	English
New India	Annie Besant	1914	Bombay	English
Hind Kesari	Ganga Prasad Gupta	1914	Kashi	Hindi
Servants of India	Srinivas Shastri	1918	Madras	English
Searchlight	Sacchidanand Sinha	1918	Bihar	English
National Herald	Jawaharlal Nehru	1938	Delhi	English
Sanjibani	K. K. Mitra	1883	Calcutta	Bengali
Hindustan Times	K. M. Panikar	1924	Delhi	English
Why I am Atheist	Bhagat Singh	1930	Lahore	English
My experiments with truth - An autobiography	Mahatma Gandhi	1925-29	Pune	Hindi, Gujarati
Life Divine	Aurobindo Ghosh	1939	Pondicherry	English
India: A Nation	Annie Besant	1916	Madras	English
Bandi Jeevan	Sachindra Nath Sanyal	1919-22	Port Blair	Bengali

History One Liners

- Swami Vivekananda attended the "Parliament of the World's Religions" in America in the year of 1893.
- J. B. Kripalani was the President of the Indian National Congress at the time of Mountbatten Plan was accepted.
- "Saare Jahan Se Accha" song written by Muhammad Iqbal.
- The Indian Trade Union Congress was founded on 31 October 1920 with Lala Lajpat Rai as its first president.
- Dadabhai Naoroji prepared the first estimates of National income of India.
- Mir Zafar betrayed Siraj-ud-Daulah in the battle of Plassey in 1757.
- The Bangladesh Liberation War ended on 16th December 1971.
- The Sepoy Mutiny started from Meerut on 10th may, 1857.
- The battle of Goa was occurred in 1510 between Portuguese Empire and Bijapur Sultanate.
- Lord William Bentick was the first Governor General of British India.
- Sardar Vallabh bhai Patel was the leader of Bardoli Satyagraha.
- The Poona pact was signed between Mahatma Gandhi and B. R. Ambedkar on 24th September 1932.
- The sati system was abolished by Lord William Bentinck in 1829.
- During their rule the British persuaded or forced cultivators to produce jute in Bengal, tea in Assam, sugarcane in Uttar Pradesh, wheat in Punjab, cotton in Maharashtra and Punjab, and rice in Madras.
- Simon Commission came to India in 1928 to review Government of India Act 1919.
- Gol Gumbaz is located in Karnataka.
- English education was introduced in India by Macaulay.
- Mahatma Gandhi gave the title of "Mahamana" to Madan Mohan Malviya.
- Lord Linlithgow was the Viceroy of the time of Quit India Movement.
- Madan Mohan Malaviya take loans for financing "The Hindustan Times" from Punjab national bank.
- Rowlatt Act 1919 was enacted during the period of Lord Chelmsford.
- In the year of 1991 Soviet Union disintegrate into 15 independent Republics.
- Pulakesin II was the greatest ruler of the Chalukya Dynasty.
- The Treaty of Seringapatam is associated with Third Anglo-Mysore War.
- Jawaharlal Nehru established the Indian Civil Liberties Union in 1936.
- The title 'Sardar' was given to Vallabhai Patel by the peasants and women of Bardoli village.
- Flag Satyagraha was held at Nagpur in 1923.
- Uraon tribes is associated with the "Tana Bhagat" movement.
- Shaheed Bhagat Singh founded the Naujawan Bharat Sabha.
- The Battle of Buxar was fought between British East India Company and Mir Qasim.
- Lord Lytton passed the Vernacular Press Act and the Arms Act of 1878.
- Lord Mayo was the only Viceroy of India to be murdered in office.
- In 1939 Subhash Chandra Bose was elected as President of the Congress Party defeating Pattabhi Sitharamayya.

- Raja Ram Mohan Roy was the founder of Brahmo Samaj.
- The famous book "Gulamgiri" was written by Jyotiba Phule.
- The first Muslim to be elected President of 'Indian National Congress' was Badruddin Tyabji.
- Sachindranath Sanyal was sent to the dreaded Cellular Jail in Port Blair for his involvement in Kakori train robbery.
- Ryotwari System was introduced by Thomas Munro in 1820.
- The National Archives of India (NAI) is located in New Delhi.
- The British officer who ended the menace of Thuggee was William Sleeman.
- Chittaranjan Das defended Aurobindo Ghosh in the Alipore conspiracy case.
- Dadabhai Naoroji in his Poverty and Un-British Rule in India explained how the English rulers were different from the earlier invaders.
- The Battle of Plassey was fought in 1757.
- Madam Cama is known as Mother of Indian Revolutionaries.
- The leader of revolt of 1857 in Lucknow was Begum Hazrat Mahal.
- Lord Cornwallis introduced Permanent Settlement in 1793.
- Lord Wavell convened the "Simla Conference" in 1945.
- 'Individual Satyagraha' began on 17 October 1940.
- The Two Nation Theory was propounded in Lahore Session, 1940 of the Muslim League.
- INA trials held at the Red Fort, New Delhi.
- The Cripps Mission visited India during the regime of Lord Linlithgow.
- Usha Mehta ran an underground radio station at Bombay during the Quit India Movement.
- Indian National Army (INA) was originally founded by Capt. Mohan Singh in Singapore in September 1942 with the help of Japan.
- Mahatma Gandhi gave the call "Do or Die" during the Quit India Movement.
- Satyendranath Tagore, the elder brother of poet Rabindranath Tagore, was the first Indian to pass the I.C.S. Examination in 1863.
- Ryotwari system was introduced by Thomas Munro and Captain Read in 1820. Major areas of introduction of Ryotwari system included Madras, Bombay, parts of Assam, and Coorg provinces of British India.
- Mahalwari system, a brain child of Holt Mackenzie was modified version of the Zamindari settlement introduced in the Ganga valley, the North-West Province, parts of the Central India and Punjab in 1822. Lord William Bentinck was to suggest radical changes in the Mahalwari system by the guidance of Robert Martins Bird in 1833.
- The first political murder of a European was committed in 1897, at Pune by the Chapekar brothers. Damodar and Balkishan. Their target was Mr. Rand, President of the Plague Commission, but Lt. Ayerst was accidentally shot.
- Mangal Pandey revolted in Barrackpore, near Calcutta.

❑❑❑

World History

Ancient World

Mesopotamian Civilization

- Mesopotamia, chiefly modern-day Iraq and Kuwait in particular, is generally cited as the cradle of civilization considering some of the most influential early city-states and empires first emerged there. The name comes from a Greek word meaning "between rivers", with reference to the land between the Tigris and Euphrates rivers.
- Mesopotamia was one of the first places to evolve the practice of agriculture, while it also offered as the crossroads for the Egyptian and the Indus Valley civilizations during that time period. This made civilization a hotspot of languages and cultures, all this piloted to the growth of writing, technology, language, trade, religion and practice of law.
- The crucial inventions which caused the world to change. Here it involved the concept of time, the wheel, math, maps, sailboats and writing. The Mesopotamians were well-approved for developing the first written scripts which took place 3500 to 3200 BCE in the wedge-shaped marks which are pressed into the clay tablets.
- **Sumerians** were one of the ancient civilizations that happened in the Mesopotamian age. They had built various ships which allowed the people to travel into the Persian Gulf and which backed them to trade with the other early civilizations, like the Harappans of the Indus Valley (present-day Pakistan and north-western India). The Sumerians have traded in the fields of textiles, leather goods and jewellery sectors besides in the Harappan society which traded the semi-precious stones, copper, pearls and ivories.
- **Akkadians**, which is termed after the city-state called Akkad. The Akkadian language is very much cordial to the modern Hebrew and Arabic languages. Their languages are termed the Semitic languages.
- The **Assyrian Empire** is named for its capital city, which is the ancient city of Ašur, this is also noted as the Ashur, the place is sited in northern Mesopotamia. After several hundred years of the breakdown of the great Akkadian Empire, Assyria then became a key empire in this area.
- Babylon was situated in the central part of Mesopotamia, this was a trivial city-state in 1894 BCE around that time it became important under the Amorites, and later rose to prominence under Hammurabi (c. 1792–1750 BCE).

Egyptian Civilization

- The Egyptian civilization advanced in Egypt was called "the gift of the Nile". This great river watered the land along its banks and in flood time it overflowed and dumped fertile soil on the fields. The farmers of ancient Egypt existed in one-story, mud-brick huts in villages along the river banks. The fields were parched and dry except in September when the river overflowed and flooded them with water carrying rich soil exceptional for growing crops.
- At first Egypt consisted simply of a number of autonomous, separate villages. In time, local rulers won control over nearby villages and then over larger areas. By 3100 BC two separate kingdoms had advanced. To the north lay Lower Egypt, which comprised the city of Memphis and the Nile delta, an area of land deposits at the mouth of the river.
- To the south lay Upper Egypt, which stretched along the river valley southward from Memphis to Aswan. About 3100 BC, the monarch of Upper Egypt, King Menes, united Upper and Lower Egypt and established a solitary capital city, Memphis. The reign of King Menes marked the first time in history that a robust government ruled so large an area.
- Artists carved fine statues and workmen wove soft linen cloth and made pottery with the practice of a potter's wheel. Since Egyptians of the Old Kingdom did not know how to make bronze, they continued to use stone tools. Still, they did make some implements from the copper that was mined in the Sinai Peninsula. As generations conceded, a ruling class of nobles and princes emerged.
- The Pyramids were constructed during the Old Kingdom as tombs for the pharaohs. The largest, made at Giza for Pharaoh Cheops, is about 455 feet high and each of its four sides measures 756 feet across at the base.

Harrapan Civilization / Indus Valley Civilization

- The Indus Valley Civilization flourished from approximately 3300 BCE to 1300 BCE. It thrived between 2600 BC and 1900 BC. The initial city to be excavated, Harappa (Punjab, Pakistan). Pre-Harappan civilization has been found in Mehrgarh, Pakistan which shows the first indication of cotton cultivation.
- In India: Kalibangan (Rajasthan), Lothal, Dholavira, Rangpur, Surkotda (Gujarat), Banawali (Haryana), Ropar (Punjab). In Pakistan: Harappa (on river Ravi), Mohenjodaro (on Indus River in Sindh), Chanhudaro (in Sindh).
- The civilization was first discovered through an excavation operation under Sir John Hubert Marshall in 1921–22 at Harappa following the unearthing of seals by J Fleet.
- Harappan ruins were discovered by Marshall, Rai Bahadur Daya Ram Sahni and Madho Sarup Vats.
- Mohenjodaro wrecks were excavated for the first time by R.D. Banerjee, E. J. H. MacKay and Marshall.
- The Indus Valley cities display a level of sophistication and advancement not seen in other contemporary civilizations.
- Most cities had comparable patterns. There were two parts: a citadel and the lower town.
- Mohenjodaro had a Great Bath.
- There were also granaries, 2-storied houses made of burnt bricks, closed drainage lines, outstanding storm water and wastewater supervision system, weights for measurements, toys, pots, etc.
- A great number of seals have been discovered.
- Agriculture was the most significant occupation. The first civilization to cultivate cotton.
- Animals were tamed like sheep, goats and pigs.
- Crops were wheat, barley, cotton, ragi, dates and peas.
- Trade was conducted with the Sumerians.

- Metal products were produced with copper, bronze, tin and lead. Gold and silver were also known. Iron was not identified to them.
- No constructions like temples or palaces have been found.
- The people worshipped male and female gods. A seal which was termed 'Pashupati Seal' has been excavated and it shows an image of a three-eyed figure. Marshall believed this to be an initial form of Lord Shiva.
- Exceptional pieces of red pottery designed in black have been excavated. Faience was used to make beads, bangles, earrings and vassals.
- Civilization also was progressive in making artworks. A statue termed 'Dancing Girl' has been found from Mohenjodaro and is supposed to be 4000 years old. A figure of a bearded Priest-King has also been found from Mohenjodaro.
- Lothal was a dockyard.
- Disposal of the dead was by burial in wooden coffins. Later on, in the H symmetry culture, bodies were burned in urns.
- The Indus Valley script has not yet been decrypted.

Chinese Civilization

- It thrived on the banks of river Hwang-Ho.
- The fertile plains of the river valley enabled agriculture, which became the base of this civilization.
- The Chinese were well-known for their silk production throughout the world. They were also skilled in weaving and making pottery.
- They used pictographic script which later advanced into ideographic script. The Chinese also formulated a calendar which consisted of 365 and a half days. Therefore, Chinese civilization was an advanced civilization of ancient time.

Greek and Roman Civilization

- From this world originated principles of law and government, fundamental concepts in science and mathematics, standards of art and architecture and the root words of several living languages.
- The Greeks established city-states on the rocky peninsula of Greece. Important findings were made in science, mathematics and medicine. Literature of enduring beauty and masterworks of sculpture and architecture were created. Brilliant philosophers, such as Socrates, Plato and Aristotle, inspired men to undertake the quest for truth and wisdom.
- Alexander attacked the huge Persian Empire and conquered it. Within a few years, he had extending from Greece through Asia Minor and Persia, into northwestern India (modern-day Pakistan).
- The Romans exhibited a genius for governing with justice the many different peoples in their empire. One of their utmost contributions to civilization was their comprehensive, flexible and enduring system of law.
- The Romans were also great constructors. They constructed splendid public buildings, massive engineering projects and durable roads. Even though they were not creative in the arts, philosophy, or science, they respected Greek cultural achievements and preserved them for future generations.

Seven Wonders of Ancient World

These Seven Wonders of the Ancient World were originally chosen by Hellenic travelers passing through Persian, Babylonian and Egyptian lands.

- **Great Pyramid of Giza:** The Great Pyramid of Giza is the only one of the Seven Wonders of the Ancient World that still survives. It remained the world's tallest human-made structure for nearly 4,000 years. Built around 2560 BCE on the west bank of the Nile River, it served as the tomb of the Fourth Dynasty Egyptian pharaoh Khufu (known to the Greeks as Cheops). It is the largest of the three pyramids at Giza Pyramid Complex.
- **Hanging Gardens of Babylon:** Despite being called one of the Seven Ancient Wonders, there is not much firsthand sign that the gardens actually existed. An amazing array of blooming flowers, luscious fruit, striking foliage and inspiring waterfalls were said to have filled them.
- **Statue of Zeus:** Housed in the Temple of Zeus at Olympia in western Greece, the statue displayed Zeus seated on a throne crusted in gold, precious gems, ivory and ebony. Zeus held a statue of Nike, the goddess of victory, in his right hand. A scepter topped by an eagle was held in his left hand.
- **Temple of Artemis:** The temple, originally built to celebrate Artemis, the Greek goddess of the hunt, became a revered place of worship.
- **Mausoleum of Halicarnassus:** The mausoleum was planned between 353 and 350 B.C.E. by the Greek architects Satyrus and Pythis. It was created for Maussollos, a governor in the Persian Empire and his wife and sister Artemisia II of Caria, who begun its construction upon her husband's death.
- **Colossus of Rhodes:** The statue was built c. 292–280 BCE to commemorate the successful defense against the siege of Demetrius I Poliorcetes (305–304 BCE).
- **Pharos (Lighthouse) of Alexandria:** This ancient lighthouse, considered a practical masterpiece that served as the model for all lighthouses that followed, was built on Pharos, an island in the harbor of Alexandria in Egypt, known as Kemet by its ancient citizens.

Medieval World

Medieval Europe

- Structure of the Feudal State in England - The king was the complete "owner" of land in the feudal system and all nobles, knights and other tenants, termed vassals, merely "held" land from the king, who was hence at the top of the feudal pyramid.
- Feudalism In France - In France, counties and duchies started to break down into smaller holdings as castellans and lesser seigneurs took control of local lands and (as comital families had done before them) lesser lords usurped/privatized a wide range of prerogatives and rights of the state—most importantly the highly lucrative rights of justice, but also travel dues, market dues, fees for using woodlands, obligations to use the lord's mill, etc. Power in this period became more personal and decentralized.
- The Crusades were a series of military campaigns planned by popes and Christian western powers to take Jerusalem and the Holy Land back from Muslim control and then secure those gains. There were seven to eight

major official crusades between 1095 and 1270, as well as several more unofficial ones.

- Relating emperors, kings and Europe's nobility, as well as thousands of knights and more humble warriors, the Crusades would have great consequences for all involved. The effects, besides the clear death, ruined lives, demolition and wasted resources, ranged from the collapse of the Byzantine Empire to a souring of relations and intolerance between religions and peoples in the East and West which still scars governments and societies today.

Arab Civilization

- In the seventh century, a new religion, Islam, formed in Arabia, leading to the foundation of a large empire.
- Muhammad, the Islamic Prophet, was born in Mecca in the year 570 AD.
- He experienced "visions of truth" and was converted into a prophet at the age of 40. His visions fully convinced Muhammad that Allah was the only god.
- He forbade the worship of idols and gained many detractors. He was eventually forced to flee Mecca and seek refuge in Medina. This event occurred in 622 AD and is known as the year of Hijri, or relocation, and Muslims use it to calculate their era (Hijri Samvat).
- The Quran, the holy book of Islam, is separated into a number of suras or chapters and contains the teachings of Muhammad. Besides the Quran, the life of a Muslim is directed by the Sunna, the practices of Muhammad and the Hadees, the sayings of Muhammad.
- Following his death (632 AD), his successors were known as Caliphs or Khalifas, and they wielded both religious and governmental power.
- Nearly all of Arabia had recognized the new religion and developed a unified state before the death of Prophet Muhammad in 632 AD.
- Islam expanded rapidly from Arabia to many other countries of the world. Muhammad assisted as both a political and religious leader.
- The Khalifas and their generals ruled over Iran, Syria, Egypt, Central Asia, North Africa and Spain within a century. The Arab empire was the prime that the world had seen so far.
- The first three Khalifas governed from the city of Medina Then the capital was shifted to Kufah.
- Damascus was the capital by 660 AD, as the Umayyad dynasty acquired control of the government.
- The Umayyads were defeated in 750 AD by the Abbasids, who established Baghdad as their capital. In several accounts, an Abbasid ruler named Harun Rashid was well-known in Baghdad.
- The Abbasids reigned for about 300 years, till the Seljuk Turks took over Baghdad and ended Arab rule. The Turks ruled the Islamic world for the next four centuries.
- The Ottoman Turks seized control of the majority of these lands in the 15th century. In 1453, the Ottoman Turks conquered Constantinople and ended the Eastern Roman Empire.

Medieval China

- "Medieval China" stands for that period in Chinese history between the descent of the Han dynasty (220 CE) and the fall of the Mongol (Yuan) dynasty (1368 CE).
- In northern China, these centuries were categorized by barbarian invasions and other upheavals, followed by the establishment of several kingdoms ruled by barbarian dynasties.
- The imperial bureaucracy, which had settled in ancient China along with the examination system with which it was inextricably linked, sustained to evolve. By the end of the period, Chinese officials were predominantly selected and promoted on merit and the civil service was dignified to take over the full running of the huge country.
- At times, particularly from later Han times and through the centuries of division, the ruling elite was molded by an aristocracy of influential landed families, whose hold on high office was unassailable. It was only with the fierce destruction of this class in the terrible years of the late Tang dynasty that the gentry class of minor landowners was able to come to the fore.
- The medieval era was a crucial time for Chinese culture. Under the Tang it saw poetry, painting and calligraphy; under the Song and Yuan Chinese fiction and drama made their arrival. The period also saw accumulating accomplishments in those literary branches established in ancient times, history and geography.

Medieval Japan

- The medieval period of Japan is measured by most historians to stretch from 1185 to 1603 CE.
- Stand out features of the period comprise the replacement of the aristocracy by the samurai class as the most influential social group, the formation of shogun military rulers and their regents, the failure in power of the emperors and Buddhist monasteries and a stratification of feudal society into lords and vassals as well as a lasting class distinction based on profession.
- The country saw long periods of civil wars as warlords and large estate owners (daimyo) fought for importance and the central government struggled to unify Japan.
- On the other hand, there were growths in agriculture, commerce and trade. The arts flourished, especially ink painting and performance arts.
- Finally, Japan's existence on the international stage became more involved with the Mongol Empire attacking Japan in the late 13th century CE and Japan attacking Korea in the late 16th century CE, both campaigns ending in failure.
- All in all, then, a busy period of development and one which saw the population of Japan upsurge from around 7 million at the beginning to around 25 million at the end of it.

Seven Wonders of Medieval World

- **Colosseum of Rome:** It is a glorious example of Roman engineering and the Roman Empire and it can be found in the heart of Rome, Italy. The well-known emperor Vespasian is thought to have built the amphitheater in the year 72 CE and was completed by Emperor Titus in 80 CE.. Gladiatorial competitions such as animal hunts, pretend sea battles, executions and recreations of well-known conflicts were held in the Colosseum.
- **Great Wall of China:** The Great Wall of China is the greatest visited place on earth. The Great Wall of China, which the Chinese Emperor Qin Shi Huang constructed between 220 and 206 BC, is well known across the whole world. In the time of the Emperor, the wall was restored.

- **Porcelain Tower of Nanjing:** The tower measures 97 metres in diameter and upsurges to a height of 260 feet with 9 storeys during the Ming Dynasty in the 15th century.
- **Stonehenge of England:** The Stonehenge monument was constructed between 3000 BC and 2000 BC, depending on the size of the individual stones. The Monument's design and features continue to be a mystery.
- **Mosque at St. Sophia (Constantinople):** This great mosque is in Istanbul, Turkey. Since 562, the famous mosque has served a variety of functions, counting as an Imperial Mosque, a Catholic Church, an Eastern Orthodox Cathedral and today, a museum.
- **Catacombs of Alexandria:** Southwest of the pillar are Alexandria's catacombs, frequently referred to as kom al-shoqafa.
- **Leaning Tower of Pisa:** One of the seven modern marvels, the leaning tower was also a marvel of the Middle Ages.

Modern World

Renaissance

- The Renaissance was an ardent period of European cultural, artistic, political and economic "rebirth" following the Middle Ages. Generally labelled as taking place from the 14th century to the 17th century, the Renaissance encouraged the rediscovery of classical philosophy, literature and art.
- During the 14th century, a cultural movement named humanism began to gain momentum in Italy. In 1450, the creation of the Gutenberg printing press allowed for better communication throughout Europe and for ideas to spread more rapidly.
- The Renaissance started in Florence, Italy, a place with a rich cultural history where rich citizens could afford to support budding artists.

Renaissance Geniuses

- **Leonardo da Vinci (1452–1519):** Italian painter, architect, inventor and "Renaissance man", accountable for painting "The Mona Lisa" and "The Last Supper".
- **Desiderius Erasmus (1466–1536):** Scholar from Holland who defined the humanist movement in Northern Europe. Interpreter of the New Testament into Greek.
- **Rene Descartes (1596–1650):** French philosopher and mathematician viewed as the father of modern philosophy. Famous for stating, "I think; therefore I am".
- **Galileo (1564-1642):** Italian astronomer, physicist and engineer whose ground breaking work with telescopes enabled him to describes the moons of Jupiter and rings of Saturn. Placed under house arrest for his views of a heliocentric universe.
- **Nicolaus Copernicus (1473–1543):** Mathematician and astronomer who made first modern scientific argument for the idea of a heliocentric solar system.
- **Thomas Hobbes (1588–1679):** English philosopher and author of "Leviathan".
- **Geoffrey Chaucer (1343–1400):** English poet and author of "The Canterbury Tales". He belonged to the Late Medieval period not the Renaissance. While he is historically recognized as a "morning star" or precursor to the English Renaissance.
- **Giotto (1267-1337):** Italian painter and architect whose more realistic portrayals of human emotions influenced generations of artists. Best recognized for his frescoes in the Scrovegni Chapel in Padua.
- **Dante (1265–1321):** Italian philosopher, poet, writer and political thinker who authored "The Divine Comedy".
- **Niccolo Machiavelli (1469–1527):** Italian diplomat and philosopher famous for writing "The Prince" and "The Discourses on Livy".
- **Titian (1488–1576):** Italian painter famous for his portraits of Pope Paul III and Charles I and his later religious and mythical paintings like "Venus and Adonis" and "Metamorphoses".
- **William Tyndale (1494–1536):** English biblical translator, humanist and scholar burned at the stake for interpreting the Bible into English.
- **William Byrd (1539/40–1623):** English composer known for his development of the English madrigal and his religious organ music.
- **John Milton (1608–1674):** English poet and historian who wrote the epic poem "Paradise Lost".
- **William Shakespeare (1564–1616):** England's "national poet" and the most well-known playwright of all time, famous for his sonnets and plays like "Romeo and Juliet", "Macbeth" and "Hamlet".
- **Donatello (1386–1466):** Italian sculptor famous for lifelike sculptures including the bronze statue of David, commissioned by the Medici family.
- **Sandro Botticelli (1445–1510):** Italian painter of "Birth of Venus".
- **Raphael (1483–1520):** Italian painter who learned from da Vinci and Michelangelo. Best recognized for his paintings of the Madonna and "The School of Athens".
- **Michelangelo (1475–1564):** Italian sculptor, painter and architect who carved "David" and painted The Sistine Chapel in Rome.
- Art, architecture and science were closely connected during the Renaissance. For instance, artists like da Vinci combined scientific principles, such as anatomy into their work, so they could reinvent the human body with extraordinary precision.
- Architects such as Filippo Brunelleschi studied mathematics to precisely engineer and design immense buildings with extensive domes.
- Scientific discoveries led to major changes in thinking: Galileo and Descartes presented a new view of astronomy and mathematics, while Copernicus proposed that the Sun, not the Earth, was the center of the solar system.
- While many artists and thinkers used their gifts to express new ideas, some Europeans took to the seas to learn more about the world around them. In a period known as the Age of Discovery, several important explorations were made.

Renaissance exploration

- Voyagers launched expeditions to travel the entire globe. They discovered new shipping routes to America, India and the Far East and explorers trekked across areas that weren't fully mapped.
- Well-known journeys were taken by Ferdinand Magellan, Christopher Columbus, Amerigo Vespucci (after whom America is named), Marco Polo, Ponce de Leon, Vasco Núñez de Balboa, Hernando De Soto and other explorers.

End of the Renaissance

- By the end of the 15th century, frequent wars had plagued the Italian peninsula. Spanish, French and German invaders battling for Italian territories caused disruption and instability in the region.
- Also, altering trade routes led to a period of economic decline and limited the amount of money that wealthy contributors could spend on the arts.
- Later, in a drive known as the Counter-Reformation, the Catholic church censored artists and writers in answer to the Protestant Reformation. Many Renaissance thinkers feared being too brave, which muffled creativity.
- Furthermore, in 1545, the Council of Trent established the Roman Inquisition, which made humanism and any views that tested the Catholic church as an act of heresy punishable by death.
- By the early 17th century, the Renaissance movement had expired out, giving way to the Age of Enlightenment.

Industrial Revolution

- The Industrial Revolution started in Great Britain and many of the technological innovations were of British origin.
- With the introduction of machineries like the flying shuttle, spinning jenny and power loom, weaving cloth and spinning yarn was made much easier and faster, while at the same time demanding less human labor.
- The effective and mechanized means of production could now meet the growing demand for cloth both at home and abroad. Britain's foreign colonies were also a captive market for the goods it produced now. Along with the textile industry, the iron industry accepted some innovations of its own as well.
- The first prototype of a modern steam engine was planned by Thomas Newcomen in the early 1700s. He named it as the "atmospheric steam engine" and was formerly created for pumping out water from mines.
- James Watt, an engineer from Scotland, worked on the steam engine created by Newcomen in the 1760s. By adding a water condenser to make it more effective, James Watt invented a steam engine that would be far more effective than any other models created so far.
- The demand for coal rose to planetary heights during this period as most of the machines were driven by these cheap sources of energy.
- The Industrial Revolution led to a development in Britain's road network, which was sub-standard before the advent of industrialization. The influx of new innovations, such as steam-powered locomotives, signaled a new era in transportation that saw an efficient movement of freights and people across Britain by 1815. These innovations also permitted to transport goods to overseas markets across the Atlantic Ocean and beyond.
- The later period of the Industrial Revolution saw many advances in long-distance communication. The first telegraphy system was patented by inventors William Cooke and Charles Wheatstone, while Samuel Morse operated on their version of the telegraph in the United States.
- The Industrial Revolution was a watershed moment in human history as every aspect of daily life felt its impact in one way or another. The average salary and the growth of the population, in general, saw unprecedented changes. Modern economists are of the belief that the standard of living of the general population began to change significantly for the first time in history even though it did not see an overall improvement until the beginning of the 20th century.

American Revolution

In the American Revolutionary War (1775–1783), usually known as the American Revolution, the Americans in the Thirteen Colonies defeated the British, gaining independence from the British Crown and creating the United States of America, the first modern constitutional liberal democracy.

American Revolution Causes

- **Political Causes**
  - The British Parliament did not comprise any representatives for the colonies.
  - Many claimed that the British government had no right to tax the colonies since they weren't characterized in the British parliament. The phrase "No Taxation without Representation" was used by them.
- **Economic Causes**
  - The economic growth of the colonies was stalled by English policies. Cotton, sugar and tobacco products were the only ones that could be shipped to England. Products from other colonies and outside of England are question to high import charges.
  - Stamp Act was passed by the British Parliament in 1765. Stamping was made compulsory for all official documents. Common protests followed, many of which turned violent.
- **Ideological Cause**
  - The general imagination was captured by enlightenment intellectuals like Locke, Harrington and Milton. They held that no authority should be permitted to violate the unalienable rights that all individuals possess.
- Philadelphia hosted the first continental convention (1774), which carried together members from 13 colonies. The king disregarded their request for fair treatment and considered their activities as mutiny. Colonial militias and British soldiers first involved in combat in the year 1775, which marked the beginning of the War.
- The Second Continental Congress (1776) saw the congress once more and on July 4, it declared independence. The statement held, among other things, that men have unalienable rights that needed to be safeguarded. The Bill of Rights later extended on this. The Bill of Rights of the United States was accepted by the Indian Constitution as fundamental rights.
- **Importance:** A republic based on the one of the earliest written constitution in history was recognized as a result of the revolution. In distinction to the other states where monarchies still held sway, this stood very clearly. People all across the world were driven by this to fight for democratic and republican forms of government. It formed a federal state where the central government and the states had identical authority. This presented a suitable model for power-sharing in many nations that needed intricate political systems.

French revolution

- The French Revolution was a time of social and political turmoil in France and its colonies that started in 1789 and ended in 1799. Inspired by liberal and radical ideas, its overthrow of the Monarchy influenced the decay of absolute Monarchies in other parts of Europe.

Causes Of French Revolution of 1789

- **Social:** The clergy and the nobility formed the first two Estates and were the utmost privileged classes in French society. They were exempted from payment of taxes to the State. On the other hand, the Third Estate that comprised of peasants and workers formed the mainstream of the population. They were burdened with extreme taxes with no political and social rights. As a result, they were tremendously discontent.
- **Economic:** As a result of frequent wars waged by Louis XVI the State coffers were empty. The condition was made even more complex by France's involvement in the American War of Independence and the faulty system of taxation. While the privileged classes were relieved from paying taxes, the Third Estate was more and more troubled with them.
- **Political:** The Bourbon king of France, Louis XVI was a very autocratic and weak-willed king who led a life of obscene luxury. This led to a lot of disenchantment amid the masses who then were leading life of massive poverty and widespread hunger.
- **Intellectual:** The 18th century was marked by a conscious rejection by French thinkers of the 'Divine Rights Theory'. Philosophers like Rousseau excluded the paradigm of absolute monarchy and promulgated the doctrine of equality of man and sovereignty of people.

French Revolution: A Brief Timeline

- **20 June 1789: Collapse of Estates-General**
  The Estates-General (France's equivalent to the British Parliament) collapses when members of the Third Estate – which signifies 'the people' – form their own National Assembly, to campaign for constitutional reform. This is a brave challenge to the King's authority. The French Revolution has commenced.
- **14 July 1789: Storming of Bastille**
  A wave of radical hysteria sweeps through Paris, leading to doubts of a military coup. In retaliation, rebels storm the prison fortress of the Bastille, a sign of royal authority. Paris falls from the King's control. Today this date is renowned as Bastille Day in France.
- **22 September 1792: French Republic established**
  After a long period of debate about how the new constitution will work, the French Revolution takes a sweeping turn when revolutionaries arrest the King. The following month, on 22 September 1792, the National Convention is established. This proclaimed the elimination of the monarchy and established the French Republic. The King is tried and, on 21 January 1793, he is executed as a traitor.
- **June 1793: Reign of Terror begins**
  Following the King's execution, France goes to war with several European powers. This signals the record violent phase of the French Revolution. Infighting inside the National Convention leads to the radical Montagnards taking power. This marks the start of the bloody Reign of Terror (la Terreur), a year-long period in which alleged enemies of the revolution are killed in their thousands.
- **1795: The Directory takes power**
  A new regime – the Directory – takes power in France in 1795. The internal political situation remains unstable, but is hushed by the army, now led by a young general Napoleon Bonaparte. There tracks a period of successes in war: what is now Belgium is seized, the Dutch Republic surrenders and peace is made with the Prussians and Spanish.
- **9 November 1799: Napoleonic Era begins**
  The Directory's four years in power are a failure, with them ceding much control to the military to keep order. On 9 November 1799, as frustration with their leadership spreads a fever pitch, Bonaparte stages a coup d'etat, eliminating the Directory and appointing himself France's 'first consul'. This letters the end of the French Revolution and the start of the Napoleonic era.

Unification of Italy

- The unification of Italy was the 19th-century socio-political movement that lead to in the consolidation of different states of the Italian Peninsula into the Kingdom of Italy.
- The Italian Peninsula had split into different city-states upon the death of the Western Roman Empire in 476 AD. Although briefly unified under the Ostrogothic Kingdom, it again fell to disunity resulting the invasion of the Eastern Roman Empire (Byzantine Empire) in the 500s.
- Towards the end of the French Revolution, Napoleon Bonaparte would begin a series of wars that would alter the political landscape of Europe for years to come. Napoleon ruled the Italian city-states and turned it into a single administrative unit. As part of the French Empire, the Italian people would imbibe many ideas of the revolution such as liberty, equality and fraternity.
- During the 1820s and 1830s, the movement for unification would grow finally concluding in revolutions break out in many Italian states in 1848. Giuseppe Garibaldi (1807-1882) was a radical who had taken part in 1848 insurrection but had to go into exile when it failed. Lending his support to King Victor Emmanuel II of Piedmont, he would return to Italy in 1860 carrying with him an army consisting of volunteers from Sicily and Naples. In 1858, Victor Emanuel, along with other northern Italian states, had allied with France to eternally end Austrian involvement in the region.
- The insurrection in 1860 would be a victory as Garibaldi and his army of Red shirts would master the island of Sicily and Naples. Meanwhile, the northern states had joined up with Piedmont-Sardinia and accepted Victor Emmanuel II as their King. Garibaldi offered Naples and Sicily to him in November 1860 and by 1861 Italy was professed as a kingdom. Only Venice and Rome would persist under foreign control and they became a share of Italy in 1866 and 1871 respectively. Thus, the Unification of Italy was accomplished.
- Although the reunification was a reality, it leads to total control of the Kingdom of Piedmont. Despite potentials that regional authorities would participate equally in the government, it was the ruling class of Piedmont that conquered the government during the initial years.
- The Italian people wanted a united Italy with a feeble central government and strong states. What they got

instead was a sturdy central government with little to no power exercised by the states.

- The new Kingdom of Italy was planned by renaming the old Kingdom of Sardinia and occupying all the new provinces into its structures. The first king was Victor Emmanuel II, who kept his old title.

Unification of Germany

- The Unification of Germany was declared on 18th January 1871. The country of Germany did not exist, but smaller kingdoms existed below their regional princes, united below the Holy Roman Empire. There was an absence of a homogenous sense of nationality.
- **Bismarck Takes Control:** In 1861, Wilhelm I succeeded Frederick William to the throne. The liberal parliament refused an increase in the military budget needed to pay for the already implemented reform of the army. Wilhelm saw the parliament's denial as a major challenge to his authority. He was braced in his view by the Junkers, powerfully conservative members of Prussia's wealthy landowning class. In 1862, Wilhelm chose a traditional Junker named Otto von Bismarck as his prime minister. Bismarck was a master of what came to be identified as realpolitik.
- In 1864, Bismarck took the first step in the direction of molding an empire. Prussia and Austria formed an association and went to war against Denmark to win two border provinces, Schleswig and Holstein. A quick victory improved national pride among Prussians. It also won new admiration from other Germans and borrowed support for Prussia as head of a unified Germany. After the victory, Prussia ruled Schleswig, while Austria controlled Holstein.
- **Seven Weeks War:** Bismarck deliberately stirred up border conflicts with Austria over Schleswig and Holstein. The strains provoked Austria into announcing war on Prussia in 1866. This conflict was identified as the Seven Weeks' War. The Prussians used their larger training and equipment to win a devastating victory. They mortified Austria. The Austrians lost the area of Venetia, which was assumed to Italy. They had to accept Prussian capture of more German territory.
- **The Franco-Prussian War:** By 1867, a few southern German states remained sovereign of Prussian control. The mainstream of southern Germans were Catholics. Many in the region battled domination by a Protestant Prussia. However, Bismarck felt he could triumph the support of southerners if they met a threat from outside. He reasoned that a conflict with France would rally the south.
- The Franco-Prussian War was the last stage in German unification. Now the patriotic fever also seized people in southern Germany. They finally acknowledged Prussian leadership. On January 18, 1871, at the took French palace of Versailles, King Wilhelm I of Prussia was crowned kaiser, or emperor. Germans called their empire the Second Reich.
- **A Shift in Power:** The 1815 Congress of Vienna had established five Great Powers in Europe— Britain, France, Austria, Prussia and Russia. In 1815, the Great Powers were nearly equal in strength. The wars of the mid-1800s greatly supported one of the Great Powers, as Prussia joined with other German states to form Germany.

First World War

The war was fought among Allied Powers and Central Powers.

Allied Powers- France, Russia, Japan and Britain. The United States joined after 1917. 'Italy' originally a part of the Triple Alliance later joined the Allied Powers in 1915.

Central Powers- Germany, Austria-Hungary, Ottoman Empire, Bulgaria.

Causes of First World War

- **Mutual Defence Alliance:** The Alliance of Austria-Hungary was argued by Serbia since Russia was in an alliance with Serbia it came to defend Serbia. Germany being in alliance with Austria – Hungary attacked Russia. France attacked Germany and both Austria – Hungary.
- Germany attacked Belgium and France which brought Britain into the war. Japan came to guard Britain. Lastly, Italy and the United States joined.
- **Imperialism:** The policy of extending one's own territorial boundary by means of power is known as imperialism. Africa and Asia were a point of conflict and involved many European Countries. The craving for power and increased competition was a major force in imitation of World War I.
- **Militarism:** By the start of the 20th century, countries were in a sort of arms race and there was a great show of military powers. Germany was winning the race trailed by Russia and France. The upsurge in military powers was also one of the causes that pushed the world into this catastrophic war.
- **Nationalism:** This can be considered one of the most significant causes of triggering war. The people of Bosnia and Herzegovina no longer desired to be part of Austria-Hungary but to be linked with Serbia. Each country in Europe subsidized to extending the war by proving their nationalism and trying to dominate others.
- **Immediate Cause:** Assassination of Archduke Franz Ferdinand - Franz Ferdinand was a associate of the royal Habsburg dynasty, which ruled the Austro-Hungarian Empire. After a first failed attempt to slay Ferdinand by a Serbian-nationalist terrorist group called the Black Hand, Ferdinand and his wife Sophie, Duchess of Hohenberg, were murdered in 1914 by a Serbian nationalist named Gavrilo Princip while they were in Sarajevo, Bosnia which was part of Austria-Hungary. This led to Austria-Hungary announcing war on Serbia while other countries were also mobilized to show their alliances.
- The course of World War I
- Start of War
- After the assassination, the following series of events took place:
  - July 28 – Austria open war on Serbia.
  - August 1 –Germany – Austria's ally announces war on Russia- an ally of Serbia.
  - August 3 – Germany announces war on France.
  - August 4 – Great Britain, an ally of France, announces war against Germany.
- President Wilson of The United States declared that they will continue neutral.
- Western and Eastern Fronts.
  - In West – Germany attacked Belgium and France.
  - In East – Russia attacked both Germany and both Austria-Hungary.

- The First Battle of the Marne (5–12 September 1914) took place in northeastern France and was part of the Western Front, not the Eastern Front. It stopped the German advance toward Paris.
- **Ottoman Empire:** During the 1915s allied powers rose contrary to the Ottomans in the Mediterranean as The Ottoman Entry into World War I occurred when the Ottoman Empire joined the Central Powers in late 1914. Russia declared war after Ottoman naval attacks on Russian Black Sea ports. A sequence of campaigns by the British was launched at Dardanelles, Gallipoli Peninsula and Mesopotamia. The British had some victory in their campaign excluding Dardanelles where they were defeated.
- **Trench Warfare:** Fight was fought in a succession of trenches dug from the North Sea through Belgium and France. Soldiers from dug-in positions gave them a slight benefit. The land between two enemy French lines was shielded with land mines and barbed fences and is termed as 'No Man's Land'.
- **United States Entrance and Russia's Exit:** In 1917 this war took a key turn when the United States, angered by an attack on its ship in the Atlantic Ocean opened War on Germany. Another was the drawing of Russia from the war due to the Bolshevik Revolution.
- **End of War and Armistice:** Such a long war spreading for a span of 4 years takes a toll both emotionally and physically on the troops fighting and is enough to demoralize them from stirring forward. Along with the soldiers being demoralized, there was a fatal spread of influenza which took the lives of soldiers on both sides and ultimately, both the parties Germany and Austria Hungary signed an armistice where Germany decided to surrender and give up their occupied territories.

Date	Events
28 June 1914	Austrian Archduke Franz Ferdinand and his wife Sophia are murdered by Black Hand Serbian nationalists.
28 July 1914	Austria announces war on Serbia along with Russia.
1 Aug 1914	Germany announces war on Russia.
3 Aug 1914	Germany announces war on France.
4 Aug 1914	Germany invades neutral Belgium so as to attack France. Britain announces war on Germany. The United States announces neutrality.
6 Aug 1914	Austria announces war on Russia.
12 Aug 1914	France and Britain announce war on Austria.
26-30 Aug 1914	Battle of Tannenberg between Russia and Germany. Russians are overpowered.
5-9 Sept 1914	First battle of Marne between German and allies of France and Britain. Germans were pushed back.
31 Oct 1914	First battle of Ypres among allies and Germany.
25 Dec 1914	Christmas Truce observed on Western front.
22 Apr-25 May 1915	Second Battle of Ypres. Poison gas was used by Germany.
7 May 1915	German U-Boat torpedoes the Lusitania.
21 Feb 1916	Battle of a Verdun where France effectively attacks of Germany.
10 May 1916	Germans suspends submarine warfare.
31 May 1916	Battle of Jutland Germans overpowered Britain.
24 June 1916	Battle of Somme between Britain and France in contrast to Germany begins.
15 Sept 1916	Britain positions tanks for the first time.
7 Nov 1916	The United States re-elect Woodrow Wilson as its president.
31 Jan 1917	Germany uses Submarine warfare unrestricted.
3 Feb 1917	Diplomatic relations between US and Germany is ended.
1 Mar 1917	The United States discovers Zimmerman Telegram plot.
2 Apr 1917	Wilson delivers war message in US congress.
6 Apr 1917	United States announces war on Germany.
15 Jun 1917	Congress enacts espionage act.
25 Jun 1917	First American troops lands in France.
31 July -10 Nov 1917	Third battle of Ypres by Britain counter to Germany.
25 Oct 1917	First American soldier murdered-James B Gresham.
2 Nov 1917	The Balfour Declaration accepted in London.
7 Nov 1917	Bolshevik seize power in Russia.
8 Jan 1918	President Wilson announces fourteen points.
3 Mar 1918	Treaty of Brest-Litovsk is signed between Russia and Germany.
28 May 1918	Battle of Cantigny, First American war in contrast to Germany.
6 Jun 1918	U.S. Marines launch attack at Belleau Wood.

18 Jun- Aug 5 1918	Allies launch Aisne-Marne offensive.
12-16 Sept 1918	Americans take offensive at St. Mihiel.
26 Sept 1918	First phase of the U.S. Meuse-Argonne offensive underway.
6 Oct 1918	Germany requests armistice – Allies refuse.
11 Nov 1918	Germany signs armistice.

End of the War

- In Germany, public were running short of food and fuel. The German navy mutinied and there was common unrest. On November 9, the German ruler, Kaiser William II, abdicated and on November 11. 1918 an armistice was signed amongst Germany and the allies, taking the fighting to an end. In January 1919, the Allies met at the Paris Peace Conference, which officially ended the war. It drew up the Treaty of Versailles, which levied a harsh peace upon Germany and laid the responsibility of starting the conflict squarely on Germany's shoulders.

Russian Revolution

- The Russian Revolution of 1917 is one of the most important events in modern history. Russia in the 1900s was the least industrialized. It was one of the most backward economies of Europe. The population comprised of landless agricultural laborer's and exploited industrial workers. Serfdom a form of feudalism was officially abolished in 1861 by Alexander II. However, peasants continued to face severe economic hardships afterward. Under serfdom, the landless agricultural peasants were required to work under the nobility. This practice ceased to occur in most parts of Europe by the end of the 16th century. Yet, it sustained to operate in Russia even in the 19th century.
- The system of serfdom was abolished in Russia in 1861. The emancipation of the serfs led to a sequence of events that came to be recognized as the Russian Revolution.
- The much-needed industrial revolution in Russia started throughout the nineteenth century. The changes in the industrial landscape carried with it many social and political changes. With the prosperous industrial revolution several changes came to fore. The population in the urban centers of Moscow and Saint Petersburg saws an exponential surge. It exerted too much stress on the infrastructure and formed problems of pollution and congestion.
- Hence, the new salaried middle class was becoming restless. The population boom also stressed the food supply chain. Providing a continuous food supply became one of the biggest challenges for the government. Fed up with non-action by the Tsar, a large group of Russian comprising of industrial workers began marching. They went on the way to the Winter Palace of Tsar Nicholas on 22nd January 1905.
- Seeing such a large crowd of people, the officers got frightened and panicked. The crowds refused to budge from the spot and the officer opened fire at the vulnerable group of people. Hundreds of protestors were killed and thousands were injured in the shootout carried out by Russian troops.
- This particular event is termed the Bloody Sunday Massacre. It demonstrated to be a turning point in Russia's modern history and the start of the downfall of the monarchy. Enraged by police brutality, people from all levels of society started a rebellion. The Russian Revolution of 1905 started. There were strikes in contrast to the Tsar throughout the country. These strikes exposed to derail the fragile Russian economy. Thus, Tsar Nicholas II agreed to install all the economic and political improvements. But as time passed people became doubtful of his intentions. This happened as he kept on postponing the reforms. He even dissolved the Parliament which would have introduced the reforms. In inference, the Bloody Sunday Massacre took place. The resulting revolution of the people had shaken the foundations of the Tsar.

The February Revolution

- The humiliating downfall at the hands of Germany in the First World War galvanized the people against the Tsar. They started a movement against the monarchy and it came to be recognized as February Revolution. It is said so as the movement occurred in February. Facing incredible pressure from the public, Tsar Nicholas II abdicated his throne. A provisional government comprising socialist and liberal factions was installed at the center. This government was run by Alexander Kerensky, the Chief of the Socialist Revolutionary Party.

The October Revolution

- In the October Revolution (November in the Gregorian calendar), the Bolsheviks, led by Vladimir Lenin and the workers' soviets defeated the Russian Provisional Government in Petrograd.
- The Bolsheviks appointed themselves as leaders of various government ministries and detained control of the countryside, establishing the Cheka to quash dissent.
- The October Revolution completed the phase of the revolution instigated in February, substituting Russia's short-lived provisional parliamentary government with government by soviets, local councils elected by bodies of workers and peasants.
- To end Russia's contribution in the First World War, the Bolshevik leaders signed the Treaty of Brest-Litovsk with Germany in March 1918.
- Soviet membership was primarily freely elected, but many members of the Socialist Revolutionary Party, anarchists and other leftists created hostility to the Bolsheviks through the soviets themselves.
- When it became clear that the Bolsheviks had little support outside of the commercial areas of Saint Petersburg and Moscow, they merely barred non-Bolsheviks from membership in the soviets.
- The new government soon passed the Decree on Peace and the Decree on Land, the latter of which reallocated land and wealth to peasants throughout Russia.
- A coalition of anti-Bolshevik groups attempted to unseat the new government in the Russian Civil War from 1918 to 1922.

Chinese Revolution

- Chinese revolution was the revolution that defeated Chinas last imperial dynasty Qing dynasty in 1912 and established the Republic of China.
- The revolution was called Xinhai because it occurred in 1911 the year of the Xinhai of the Chinese calendar.
- The government tried to reply to the new radical ideas by presenting reforms, promising democracy and setting up elected provincial assemblies. However, this only encouraged the provinces to detach themselves still further from the central government, which was now extremely unpopular.
- All through the 19th century the dynasty had been diminishing and upon the death of the empress dowager Cixi (1908) it lost its last able leader.
- In 1911 the emperor Puyi was a child and the regency was imperfect to guide the nation. The ineffective contests with foreign powers had shaken not only the dynasty but the complete machinery of the government.
- The revolution arose mainly in response to the deterioration of the Qing state which had proven unsuccessful in its efforts to modernize China and confront foreign aggression and was exacerbated by ethnic resentment against the ruling Manchu minority.
- The revolution involved of many revolts and uprisings and most provinces rapidly declared themselves independent of Beijing.
- A provisional republican government had been set up at Nanjing and the arch revolutionist Sun Yat-sen had returned from overseas and had been elected temporary president.
- The government reigning in behalf of the child emperor Puyi in desperation sought help from a retired general, Yuan Shikai who had been commander of the Chinese Northern Army and still had a lot of impact with the generals. He was made premier. However, the plan failed yuan who was still only in his early fifties turned out to have desires of his own, he did a deal with the revolutionaries – they agreed to him becoming the first president of the Chinese republic in re-occurrence for the abdication of Puyi and the end of Manchu dynasty.
- The provisional constitution was promulgated in March 1912 by the Nanjing parliament and in April the government was relocated to Beijing. This marked the commencement of Chinas early republican era. With the backing of the army, Yuan ruled as a military dictator from 1912 until 1915.
- The republic established with such startling rapidity and comparative ease, was intended in the succeeding decades to witness the progressive downfall of national unity an orderly government.

Turkish Revolution

- The Turkish War of Independence (19 May 1919 – 24 July 1923) was a sequence of military campaigns waged by the Turkish National Movement after parts of the Ottoman Empire were occupied and separated following its defeat in World War I. These campaigns were focused against Greece in the west, Armenia in the east, France in the south, loyalists and separatists in several provinces and British and Ottoman troops around Constantinople (Istanbul). They happened alongside with other resistance movements counter to the partitioning of the Ottoman Empire.
- This crisis reached a head when sultan Mehmed VI transmitted Mustafa Kemal Pasha (Ataturk), a well-respected and notable general, to Anatolia to restore order; however, Mustafa Kemal turn out to be an enabler and ultimately leader of Turkish nationalist resistance counter to the Ottoman government, Allied powers and Christian minorities.
- In an attempt to generate control over the power vacuum in Anatolia, the Allies convinced Greek Prime Minister Eleftherios Venizelos to launch a peacekeeping force into Anatolia and occupy Smyrna (İzmir), inflaming sectarian tensions and start the Turkish War of Independence.
- A nationalist counter government led by Mustafa Kemal was recognized in Ankara when it became clear the Ottoman government was appeasing the Allied powers.
- The Western Front of the independence war was identified as the Greco-Turkish War, in which Greek forces at first encountered unorganized resistance.
- However, Ismet Pasha (Inonu's) organization of militia into a regular military paid off when Ankara militaries fought the Greeks in the First and Second Battle of Inonu.
- The Allies evacuated Anatolia and Eastern Thrace, the Ottoman government was conquered and the monarchy eliminated and the Grand National Assembly of Turkey (which remains Turkey's primary legislative body today) stated the Republic of Turkey on 29 October 1923.
- With the war, a population exchange amongst Greece and Turkey, the partitioning of the Ottoman Empire and the elimination of the sultanate, the Ottoman era came to an end and with Ataturk's reforms, the Turks created the modern, secular nation-state of Turkey.
- On 3 March 1924, the Ottoman caliphate was also eliminated.

Economic depression of the world

- The Great Depression was a severe global economic depression that happened in 1929 and lasted until about 1939-1941. It started as a result of a sharp decay in American stock prices. The American stock market crash on October 29, 1929, known as Black Tuesday, prompted an economic slowdown throughout the world.

Causes of the Great Depression (1929–1939)

- The American economy was stunned by the stock market crash of 1929, which led to significant reductions in investment and spending.
- Early 1930s banking waves of panic led to the failure of numerous banks, which abridged the amount of money available for loans.
- In order to offset trade disparities with the United States, the gold standard forced foreign central banks to increase interest rates, which reduced consumption and investment in those nations.
- The Smoot-Hawley Tariff Act of 1930 placed high tariffs on various industrial and agricultural products, which prompted retaliatory actions that ultimately reduced output and led to a failure in international trade.
- In order to surge production after World War I, farmers acquired more machinery, which resulted in a debt

problem as, in the post-war economy, production was higher than demand.

- Due to overproduction brought on by the 1920s consumption flourishing, many companies were required to start selling goods at a loss.
- Losses and more layoffs effect in higher unemployment. For instance, the unemployment rate peaked in 1933 at 24.9 percent.
- Spending fell as a result of consumers' amplified debt load, which made the situation even worse by compelling more companies to close their doors or make budget cuts that gave rise to more job losses.
- Manufacturers and merchandisers detected an unintended increase in inventories as a result of a decrease in the general demand, which led to a decline in production.

Life During the Depression

- Many farmers lost their farms as an outcome of the Great Depression.
- The "Dust Bowl" in the Midwest was triggered by years of over-cultivation and drought at the same time, decimating agricultural production in a formerly fertile region.
- Thousands of these farmers, along with other unemployed workers, migrated to California in pursuit of employment.
- Many ended up existing as "hobos", or the homeless. Others relocated to slum communities known as "Hoovervilles", termed after the late President Herbert Hoover.
- Many shops permitted customers to pay with credit and kept track of the outstanding balance. People rarely paid back loans, but occasionally they did not. Some store owners eventually lost their businesses as a result.
- "Rich" grew into a family with a cow and a garden. These two benefits made all the difference between a family that had enough food and one that was on the edge of starvation.
- In order to endure, many started working as migrant farm laborers, traveling from harvest to harvest.
- Compared to wages, food costs were quite in height at that time, making living very tough for daily wage earners.

End of Great Depression

- From 1929 to 1939, the Great Depression continued for ten years. The GDP dropped by nearly 50 per cent over this ten-year period.
- Franklin D. Roosevelt was elected as president in 1932. In order to end the Great Depression, he pledged to launch federal government programs.
- He passed the New Deal into law within 100 days, launching 42 new agencies over its entire tenure.
- They were made to offer unemployment insurance, permit unionization and create jobs.
- These programs are still extensively used. They want to guard the economy and stop a new depression.
- These actions made it easier for the Federal Reserve to increase the money supply and move sluggishly in the direction of economic recovery.
- All of this helped the United States exit the depression by 1939 by slowing the descending spiral of price deflation.
- Many oppose that the New Deal did not end the Depression; rather, World War II did.
- Others uphold that the Depression would have ended if Franklin D. Roosevelt had invested as much in the New Deal as he did in the War.
- Franklin D. Roosevelt added $3 billion to the debt in the nine years between the start of the New Deal and the attack on Pearl Harbor. Defense expenditures in 1942 augmented the debt by $23 billion. It added an extra $64 billion in 1943.
- After the 1929 Great Depression ended, many people learned their lesson and understood how vital it was to secure their income, pay off debt, cut back on spending, keep cash on hand and diversify their sources of income.
- Following the end of the Great Depression, no nation has ever left the financial sector to its own devices and soon after that, the world saw an important development in terms of transportation, electronics and other mass-market goods.

Fascism in Italy

- Fascism emphasizes dangerous nationalism, militarism and the supremacy of both the nation and the single powerful leader over the individual citizen. It initiated in early 20th century Italy, with Benito Mussolini's Fascist Party and rapidly spread to other countries, counting Nazi Germany, Francoist Spain and Imperial Japan.
- The rise of fascism started during World War I when Mussolini shaped a political group supporting the war against Austria-Hungary and Germany. He founded the Fasci Italiani di Combattimento in 1919, which was reorganised into the National Fascist Party (PNF) in 1921 and won 35 seats. The political system and ideology of Benito Mussolini stimulated extreme nationalism and militarism shaping Italy along with hierarchical authoritarianism. The purpose was to fundamentally compete against liberalism and democracy in Italy. At the same time, it seemed to be a real danger of a left-wing revolution in an atmosphere of riots, affray and strikes. After World War I, many people looked-for for national unity and strong leadership in Europe.
- Italian fascism was built on Italian nationalism, national syndicalism and the zeal to develop Italian territories. The Italian fascists deemed it important for a nation to bring forward its strength and superiority and thereby escape from submitting to decay. For a large number of Italians, the fascists brought a loss of human rights and economic hardships to the country. The fascists are involved in political actions taking benefit of strikes to rouse violence across the country. However, they began to bring into line themselves with mainstream conservatives growing the membership exponentially around 1921.
- Fascism had a major influence on the people of Italy as it developed alarmingly as the days progressed. Between 1925 and 1929, fascism steadily outshined in

power in Italy and the opposition deputies were refused access to the parliament. However, censorship was merged and he became Prime Minister of Italy in 1922. The effects of fascism were so dangerous that the fascists proceeded to obtain several northern cities in Italy.

Nazism in Germany

- Nazism is a specific form of fascism that developed in Germany in the 1920s and 1930s under the control of the National Socialist German Workers' Party (NSDAP), commonly identified as the Nazi Party. Nazism was led by Adolf Hitler, who became the German Chancellor in 1933 and went on to become the dictator of Germany until his demise in 1945.
- At the termination of the war, Hitler settled in Munich. In early 1920, he joined a tiny right-wing political group. This group shared his belief that Germany had to downturn the Treaty of Versailles and combat communism. The group later termed itself the National Socialist German Workers' Party, termed Nazi for short. Its policies, braced by people in the middle and lower middle classes, formed the German brand of fascism identified as Nazism. The party assumed the swastika, or hooked cross, as its symbol. The Nazis also set up a private militia named the storm troopers or Brown shirts.
- Within a short time, Hitler's achievement as an organizer and speaker led him to be chosen der Führer, or the leader, of the Nazi party. These skills also assisted make the Nazis a increasing political force. Inspired by Mussolini's march on Rome, Hitler and the Nazis plotted to seize power in Munich in 1923. The effort failed and Hitler was arrested. He was tried for treason, but sympathetic judges punished him to only five years in prison. He served fewer than nine months.
- While in jail, Hitler penned Mein Kampf (My Struggle). This book set out his beliefs and his goals for Germany. It turned into the blueprint, or plan of action, for the Nazis. Hitler asserted that the Germans, particularly those who were blond and blue-eyed— whom he incorrectly called "Aryans"—were a "master race". He stated that non- Aryan "races"—such as Jews, Slavs and Gypsies—were lesser or subhuman. He called the Versailles Treaty an outrage and swore to recover the lands taken from Germany. Hitler also declared that Germany was overcrowded and desired more lebensraum, or living space. He assured to get that space by conquering eastern Europe and Russia.
- After leaving prison in 1924, Hitler rejuvenated the Nazi party. Most Germans ignored him and his angry message till the Depression ended the nation's brief postwar recovery. When American loans stopped, the German economy distorted. Factories ground to a halt and banks shut. Almost six million people, about 30 percent of Germany's workforce, were unemployed in 1932. Civil discontent broke out. Terrified and confused, Germans now turned to Hitler, wanting for security and firm leadership.
- The Nazis had become the major political party by 1932. Conservative leaders falsely believed they could control Hitler and use him for their purposes. In January 1933, they recommended President Paul von Hindenburg to name Hitler chancellor. Only Hitler, they said, could stand up to the robust Communist party in Germany. Thus, Hitler came to power officially, Soon after, General Erich Ludendorff, a former Hitler ally, wrote to Hindenburg.
- Once in office, Hitler acted swiftly to strengthen his position. He called for new elections, eager to win a parliamentary majority. Six days before the election, a fire ruined the Reichstag building the Parliament met. The Nazis blamed the Communists. By stirring up fear of the Communists, the Nazis and their allies won a thin majority.
- With majority control, Hitler commanded dictatorial, or absolute, power for four years. Only one deputy ventured to speak against the resulting Enabling Act. Hitler used his new authority to turn Germany into a totalitarian state. He barred all other political parties and had opponents arrested. In the meantime, an elite, black-uniformed unit called the SS (Schutzstaffel, or protection squad) was created. It was faithful only to Hitler. In 1934, the SS arrested and killed hundreds of Hitler's enemies. This brutal action and the terror functional by the Gestapo, the Nazi secret police, shocked most Germans into total compliance.
- The Nazis swiftly took command of the economy. New laws barred strikes, dissolved independent labor unions and offered the government authority over business and labor. Hitler put millions of Germans to work. They constructed factories, built highways, manufactured weapons and served in the military. As an effect, unemployment fell from about 6 to 1.5 million in 1936.
- The Fuhrer is Supreme: Hitler desired more than just economic and political power— he desired control over every aspect of German life. To shape public view and to win approval for his leadership, Hitler turned the press, radio, literature, painting and film into propaganda tools. Books that did not conform to Nazi beliefs were charred in huge bonfires. Churches were prohibited to criticize the Nazis or the government. Schoolchildren had to join the Hitler Youth (for boys) or the League of German Girls. Hitler was greatly inclined by Social Darwinism. He alleged that a continuous struggle brought victory to the strong. He twisted the philosophy of Friedrich Nietzsche to support his use of brute force to preserve power and his glorification of war.
- Hitler Makes War on the Jews: Hatred of Jews, or anti-Semitism, was a key part of Nazi ideology. Although Jews were fewer than one percent of the population, the Nazis used them as scapegoats for all Germany's plights since the war. This led to a upsurge of anti-Semitism across Germany. Beginning in 1933, the Nazis passed laws depriving Jews of maximum of their rights. Violence contrary to Jews mounted. On the night of November 9, 1938, Nazi mobs condemned Jews in their

homes and on the streets and demolished thousands of Jewish-owned buildings.

- This rampage, termed Kristallnacht (Night of the Broken Glass), signaled the real start of the process of removing the Jews from German life.

Militarism in Japan

- The decay of Feudalism led to the formation of a modern state with economic development and industry, as well as military domination at home. This led to speedy conquests and expansion, concluding in Japan's war with China. The growth of militarism in Japan was characterized by anti-democratic and authoritarian tendencies, with the army concentrating on war conquest and a focus on the empire's expansion. This led to the development of right-wing political parties and the army, which were dominated by ultra nationalism.
- Japanese militarism was anti-communist and pro-capitalist, with Russia as a natural rival and the upsurge of Bolsheviks further deteriorating relations. Japan was also troubled with colonial expansion based on capitalist lines, which was resented by Russia. This led to the signing of the Anti-Comintern Pact with Nazi Germany and Fascist Italy.
- The Minseito party won the 1936 elections, leading to a coup that ended in disappointment. The Hirota cabinet accepted the National Political Renovation program, which committed to increasing armament, stockpiling war materials and governing education. This led to the end of diplomatic isolation and amplified right-wing influence in Japan.
- The National Mobilization Act of 1938 concluded the parliamentary government, allowing the bureaucracy to take control from the legislature. The military controlled the industry and other government wings and by 1941, Japan saw single-party dominion. The Imperial Rule Assistance Association party, controlled by the army, directed Japan into the war.

Second World War

- World War II, also named Second World War, was a conflict that involved virtually every part of the world during the years 1939–45. The principal fighters were the Axis powers—Germany, Italy and Japan—and the Allies—France, Great Britain, the United States, the Soviet Union and, to a lesser extent, China. It was the major conflict in history that had lasted almost six years. Approximately some 100 million people had been militarized and 50 million had been killed.

Causes of War

- **Treaty of Versailles:** Germany had to accept guilt for the war and to pay compensations. Germany lost territory and was forbidden from having a large military.
- **Failure of the League of Nations:** The League of Nations was an international organization set up in 1919 to keep world peace. The League of Nations was a good idea, but ultimately a disappointment, as not all countries joined the league. Also, the League had no army to avoid military aggression such as Italy's invasion of Ethiopia in Africa or Japan's invasion of Manchuria in China.
- **Great Depression of 1929:** The wide-reaching economic depression of the 1930s took its toll in different ways in Europe and Asia.
- **Rise of Fascism:** Benito Mussolini recognized the first Fascist, European dictatorship throughout the interwar period in Italy in 1922.
- **Rise of Nazism:** Adolf Hitler, the Leader of the German National Socialist (Nazi) party, addressed a racist brand of fascism.
- **Policy of Appeasement:** Hitler openly condemned the Treaty of Versailles and began secretly building up Germany's army and weapons. Although Britain and France knew of Hitler's activities, they thought a stronger Germany would halt the spread of Communism from Russia.
- **The Start:** Three years of increasing international tension - encompassing the Spanish Civil War, the blending of Germany and Austria, Hitler's occupation of the Sudetenland and the attack of Czechoslovakia led to weakening of ties between Axis Power and Allied Powers. However, the German invasion of Poland on 1 September 1939 and subsequently two days later, Britain and France declared war on Germany. This marked the commencement of World War II.
- **Phoney War:** The western Europe was very quiet throughout the first few months of the war. This period of war is identified as 'phoney war'. Preparations for war sustained in earnest, but there were few signs of battle and civilians of the western European countries (allied powers) evacuated to safe places.
- **Ribbentrop Pact:** By the initial part of 1939 the German dictator Adolf Hitler had become strong minded to invade and occupy Poland. Poland, for its part, had assurances of French and British military backing when will it be attacked by Germany. Hitler planned to invade Poland anyway, but first he had to neutralize the likelihood that the Soviet Union would resist the attack of its western neighbour. Secret talks in August 1939, led to the signing of the German-Soviet Nonaggression Pact in Moscow. Additionally, Russia trailed Germany into Poland in September and Poland was carved up between the two invaders before the end of the year.
- **Winter War 1940:** The 'winter war' between Russia and Finland resolved in March and in the following month Germany attacked Denmark and Norway. Denmark submitted immediately, but the Norwegians fought on - with British and French assistance - surrendering in June 1940.
- **Fall of France 1940:** After war with Scandinavian countries ended, Germany invaded France, Belgium and Holland. During this time, the western Europe came across the Blitzkrieg - or 'lightning war'.
- **Blitzkrieg:** Germany's grouping of fast armored tanks on land and superiority in the air, made a unified attacking force that was both advanced and effective.

- In spite of greater numbers of air and army personnel in Allied powers, they showed no match for German Forces. In France an armistice was signed with Germany, with the puppet French Vichy government. Having occupied France, Hitler turned his attention to Britain and began arrangements for an invasion.
- **Battle of Britain 1940:** Lasting from July to October 1940, it was the first war to be fought exclusively in the air. German took choices to attack from airfields and factories to the major cities, but somehow the Royal Air Force succeeded to squeak a narrow victory. This ensured the - ultimately indefinite - deferment of the German invasion plans.
- **War Getting Global:** With continental Europe underneath Nazi control and Britain safe - for the time being - the war took on a more global dimension in 1941. Following the downfall of Mussolini's armies in Greece and Tobruk, German militaries arrived in North Africa and invaded Greece and Yugoslavia in April 1941.
- **Operation Barbarossa:** After facing loss in Britain, Hitler broke the Ribbentrop Pact and attacked Russia in 1941. The early advance was swift, with the fall of Sebastopol at the end of October and Moscow coming under attack at the end of the year. The bitter Russian winter, however, like the one that Napoleon had experienced a century and a half earlier, crippled the Germans. The Soviets counterattacked in December and the Eastern Front stagnated until the spring.
- **Pearl Harbour:** The Japanese, tired of American trade embargoes, mounted a surprise attack on the US Navy base of Pearl Harbor, in Hawaii, on 7 December 1941. This confirmed that global conflict commenced, with Germany announcing war on the US, a few days later. Also, within a week of Pearl Harbor, Japan had attacked the Philippines, Burma and Hong Kong.
- **American Entry into the War:** After the attack on Pearl Harbor (December 1941), the US entered World War II. The Battle of Midway in June 1942 marked a key turning point, in which US naval forces destroyed four Japanese aircraft carriers.
- **Reversal of German Fortunes:** By the second half of 1942, British forces seized the initiative in North Africa and Russian forces counterattacked at Stalingrad. In February 1943, Germany submitted at Stalingrad to Soviet Union. This was the first main defeat of Hitler's armies. Further, German and Italian forces in North Africa submitted to the Allies. As the Russian advance on the Eastern Front met pace, recapturing Kharkiv and Kiev from Germany. Moreover, Allied bombers started to attack German cities in enormous daylight air raids. The Russians reached Berlin (capital of Germany) on 21 April 1945. Hitler killed himself on the 30th, two days after Mussolini had been arrested and hanged by Italian partisans. Germany signed surrender documents on 7 May 1945, which took effect on 8 May 1945 (VE Day). The war in Europe ended.
- **Nuclear Bombing and The End:** Plans were being arranged for an Allied invasion of Japan, but fears of fierce battle and massive casualties impelled Harry Truman - the new American president to sanction the use of an atomic bomb against Japan. Such bombs had been in development since 1942 and on 6 August 1945 one of them was dropped on the Japanese city of Hiroshima. Three days later another was dropped on Nagasaki. No country could have endured such attacks and the Japanese surrendered on 15 August. With the submission of Japan, World War II was finally over.

Aftermath of World War II

- **New Superpowers:** World War II brought about variations in the status of countries and continents. Britain and France lost their positions of preeminence as superpowers and generated place to the USA and the USSR.
- **Start of Decolonization:** After the war, Britain and France were provoked with various domestic and external problems. Both of them could no longer hold onto their individual colonies Thus, the post-war world observed the end of colonialism in Africa and Asia.
- **Birth of UN:** One of the significant results of the war was the birth of the United Nations Organization. Although the League failed to deliver, mankind did not in total lose its hopes of making the world a safer and happier place to live in. The UN Charter enshrines the hopes and ideals of mankind on the basis of which countries can work collected to preserve lasting peace. However, the establishment of the UN was decided, much before the end of World War II under the Atlantic Charter.
- **Start of Cold War:** After the end of the war, a discussion was held in Potsdam, Germany, to set up peace treaties. The countries that fought with Hitler lost territory and had to pay compensations to the Allies. Germany and its capital Berlin were separated into four parts.
- The regions were to be controlled by Great Britain, the United States, France and the Soviet Union.
- The three western Allies and the Soviet Union disagreed on several things and as time went on Germany was divided into two discrete countries: East Germany, which had a Communist government and West Germany, which was a democratic state. This laid the basis of the Cold War.
- **New Economic World Order:** Bretton Woods Conference, officially United Nations Monetary and Financial Conference, meeting at Bretton Woods, New Hampshire (July 1–22, 1944), during World War II to make financial preparations for the postwar world after the anticipated defeat of Germany and Japan.
- It drew up a mission for the International Bank for Reconstruction and Development (IBRD-now known as World Bank) to make long-term capital accessible to states immediately needing such foreign aid and a project for the International Monetary Fund (IMF) to finance temporary differences in international payments in order to stabilize exchange rates.
- Also, the US dollar was recognized as a reserve currency for the world trade.

World History Timeline

- B.C.E
- **3000:** Construction of the Great Pyramids
- **776:** First Olympiad in Greece
- **753:** Establishment of Rome
- **490:** Battle of Marathon, Greeks defeated the Persians
- **360:** The period of Aristotle and Plato
- **332:** Egypt conquered by Alexander
- **323:** Death of Alexander at Babylon
- **214:** Construction of the Great Wall of China begins
- C.E.
- **375:** Huns' invasion of Europe
- **570:** Birth of Prophet Mohammed at Mecca
- **632:** Death of Prophet Mohammed
- **1267:** Roger Bacon recorded the first European formula for gunpowder (originally invented in China, c. 9th century CE).
- **1338:** Hundred Years' War
- **1348:** Black Death Plague
- **1453:** Turks captured Constantinople
- **1453:** Renaissance in Europe
- **1492:** Discovery of America by Columbus
- **1498:** Vasco-de-Gama discovered the sea route to India
- **1588:** Spanish Armada defeated
- **1600:** British East India Company established in India
- **1660:** Monarchy reinstated in England
- **1665:** The Great Plague of England
- **1688:** Glorious Revolution in England
- **1704:** Battle of Blenheim
- **1707:** Union of England and Scotland
- **1776:** Declaration of American Independence
- **1789:** French Revolution
- **1805:** Battle of Trafalgar
- **1815:** Battle of Waterloo
- **1832:** Reforms Bill passed in England
- **1837:** Queen Victoria's succession to the throne of England
- **1861:** American Civil War started
- **1863:** Slavery abolished in the USA
- **1865:** Assassination of Abraham Lincoln
- **1869:** Opening of the Suez Canal for traffic
- **1895:** X-rays were discovered by Roentgen
- **1896:** Marconi invented wireless
- **1904:** Russia-Japan war
- **1905:** Discovery of the Theory of Relativity by Einstein
- **1911:** Chinese Revolution
- **1912:** Republic of China established
- **1914:** Beginning of World War I
- **1917:** Russian Revolution
- **1918:** End of World War I
- **1919:** Treaty of Versailles signed
- **1920:** Formation of the League of Nations
- **1923:** Turkey declared Republic
- **1933:** Hitler became the Chancellor of Germany
- **1936:** Spanish Civil War broke out
- **1939:** World War II begins
- **1941:** Russia invaded by Hitler, Pearl Harbour invaded by Japan
- **1945:** Establishment of UNO, End of World War II, Death of President Roosevelt, First dropping of the Atom Bomb in Hiroshima and Nagasaki
- **1946:** Civil War in China
- **1948:** Ceylon and Burma get independence
- **1949:** The Communists capture power in China, Indonesia gets independence

❑❑❑

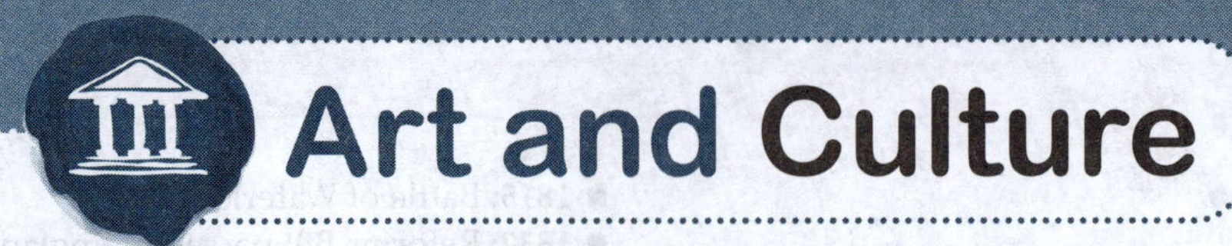

Art and Culture

Unit-1: Visual Arts

Indian Architecture, Sculpture and Pottery

Harappan Art and Architecture

- **Architecture:** Harappans were the first to introduce the concept of worker welfare by creating separate worker's quarters.
  Materials that were used for the construction of buildings:
  - Bricks,
  - baked bricks,
  - mud, stones, and
  - other mud-based materials.

Other remarkable features of Harrapan civilisations were:

- **Towns:** Towns were in rectangular patterns; roads ran in a north-south and east-west direction and cut each other at right angles.
- **Cities were divided into two parts:** The upper part (citadel) and lower part. Harappan sites did not have large monuments/palaces. Public baths were present in the sites: Great Bath was present in Mohenjo-Daro. It had advanced drainage system.
- **Sculpture:** Bearded Man was discovered in Mohenjo-Daro which was carved out of stone; numerous seals of different shapes and sizes, Bronze sculpture was made at most of the Harappan sites, Bronze casting was done using the Lost Wax Technique. Dancing Girl was a bronze sculpture found in Mohenjo-Daro. Terracotta Sculptures were mostly found in the sites of Gujarat and Kalibangan.
- **Pottery:** Two Types: Plain pottery and Painted pottery (Red and Black pottery).
- **Ornaments:** Both men and women wore ornaments, discovered in Chanhu-daro and Lothal; examples necklaces, fillets armlets and finger ring.

Mauryan Art and Architecture

Some of the notable features of Mauryan Art and Architecture are:

- **Architecture:** Wood was the main material used in the initial construction but later stone became prominent and several stupas were built in the Ashoka period.
- **Sculptures:** Mostly built for the decoration of Stupas, Yaksha and Yakshi are famous sculptures.
- **Palaces:** Palaces at Kumrahar; inspired by the Achaemenid palaces at Persepolis in Iran.
- **Caves:** Caves were used for viharas.
- **Pottery:** Northern Black Polished Ware (NBPW); highest level of pottery.

Post Mauryan Art

Some of the features of this period are:

- **Architecture:** Development of Chaitya and Vihara, Viharas were residential halls for Jain and Buddhist monks developed in the Mauryan period. Chaityas halls were developed in this period and were used as prayer halls. Stupas were bigger in this period and stone was mostly used for construction.
- **Sculpture:** Three different types of schools came up:
  - **Gandhara:** Influence of Greek, use of bluish grey schist but later mud and stucco were used, mostly Buddhist, patronized by Kushana rulers, developed in North West Frontier, Buddha shown in spiritual state with fewer ornaments.
  - **Mathura:** Indigenous, red sandstone was used, the influence of Hinduism; Jains and Buddhists; patronized by Kushana rulers; developed along Mathura, Buddha shown in a delighted mood with face and head shaven.
  - **Amravati:** Indigenous, white marble was used, mostly Buddhist, patronized by Satavahanas rulers, developed along Krishna-Godavari valley, and depicted life stories of Buddha and jataka tales.
- **Stupas:** Stone usage in place of wood and brick; torans was introduced by Shunga dynasty; Hellenistic influence; Bharhut stupa in Madhya Pradesh.

Gupta Art and Architecture

The Gupta period is often referred to as the Golden Age of India, during which art, literature, science, and architecture reached remarkable heights. Some unique features of this era are:

- **Cave Architecture:** Mural paintings on the cave walls; The caves of Ajanta and Ellora, Bagh Caves have some of the best examples of mural art.
- **Stupas:** Decline in stupas, Dhamek stupa at Sarnath.
- **Scupltures:** Metal and cream coloured sandstone usage.

Temple Architecture

- **Nagara:** North India, temples were built in the Panchayatan architecture, mandapas were meeting halls, no water tanks or reservoirs, temples constructed on raised platforms, did not have ornate boundary walls or gateways, curving Shikhara. Odisha school, Khajuraho school and Solanki school are three types of it.
- **Dravidian:** South India, temple surrounded by a high boundary wall, gopuram was entrance gateway, features a 'Vimana' that resembles a stepped pyramid, only one vimana on top of the main temple, presence of a water-tank. Chola rulers built in South India.
- **Vesara:** Influence of Nagara and Dravidian Styles, also known as Karnataka school of architecture. Chalukyas, Rashtrakutas and Hoysala Dynasty used such temple architecture.

Indo-Islamic Architecture

Some important features are:

- Introduction of arches and domes,
- Arcuate style replaced the Trabeate style,
- Minars were built,
- Mortar was used as a cementing agent,
- No human or animal figures,
- Importance to calligraphy, added spaciousness,
- Massiveness, and breadth to the architecture,
- Arabesque style in geometry was used, jaali art,
- Charbagh style of gardening
- Pietra-dura technique for the inlay

Modern Architecture

Important modern architecture are:

- **Portuguese:** Iberian architectural style; constructed trading terminals and warehouses along the coasts.
- **French:** Established the concept of anonymous architecture; the concept of urban city planning; constructed massive structures.
- **British:** Indo-Gothic Style (Victorian style, pointed arches, use of large windows, large buildings), Neo-Roman (Circular buildings, upturned dome, Edwin Lutyens and Herbert Baker famous architect).

Indian Paintings

Prehistoric Paintings

- **Upper Palaeolithic Period:** Caves were formed of quartzite, and red, white, yellow, and green colours were used. Red was used for hunters, white, dark red and green were used to depict large animals and green was used for dancers in human sculptures mostly.
- **Mesolithic Period:** Mostly hunters were depicted, size of paintings was smaller than Upper Palaeolithic Period. This period mainly saw the use of red colour.
- **Chalcolithic Period:** Green and yellow colours were mostly used, and most paintings depicted battle scenes, musical instruments were also depicted in the paintings.

Classification of Paintings

Paintings can be classified into:

- **Mural:** Painted on the walls of solid structures, Fresco technique is related to mural painting, paintings of Ajanta and Ellora caves are some examples.
- **Miniature paintings:** Executed on a very small scale on perishable material such as paper, not larger than 25 square inches.

Folk Painting

Some of the important paintings are:

- **Madhubani Paintings:** From Bihar; themes inspired by Hindu religion, traditionally painted on walls but later on paper also.
- **Pattachitra Paintings:** From Odisha; colours made from natural material; the brush is used to draw the outlines.
- **Kalamkari Paintings:** From Andhra Pradesh; bamboo is used to construct pen for colouring; colours are made with vegetable dyes; the base used for colouring is cotton fabric; images inspired by Hindu mythology.
- **Warli Painting:** From the Gujarat-Maharashtra border; resemblance prehistoric mural paintings at Bhimbetka; ritualistic paintings; traditionally done on walls using geometrical patterns.
- **Thangka Painting:** Practices in Sikkim, Himachal Pradesh, Ladakh region and Arunachal Pradesh, related to Buddhism's ideals.

Indian Handicrafts

Glassware: Mentioned in Mahabharata; evidence found in Painted Grey Ware Culture of the Ganges valley; no evidence in the early Harappan period; evidence of glass industry found in Maharashtra's Brahmapuri and Kolhapur; evidence found in Maski, a Chalcolithic site in the Deccan. Mughals preferred glassware in decorations; Panchkora or glass toys built in Saharanpur; Firozabad is also famous for glassworks. Tikuli is a glasswork from Bihar.

Cloth Handicrafts

- **Tie and Dye:** The process of tying and dying yarn or cloth; also known as bandh in Odisha; Ikat style is associated with it; creates beautiful patterns on fabrics; Bandhani or Bandhej is a tie and dye process and a famous art; Laharia is a type of tie and dye method of Jaipur and Jodhpur that creates ripples or wave-like patterns on the cloth; Kalamkari from Andhra Pradesh, uses the art of hand painting on fabrics with vegetable dyes of deep colours.
- **Embroidery Craft:** Embroidery is the skill of creating elevated patterns using threads or wooden blocks and is unique among textile crafts; Applique and Pipli embroidery technique is from Odisha; the Darning technique from Punjab and Haryana; Chikankari from Lucknow; Kashida embroidery from Kashmir.
- **Weaving:** It refers to the process of interlacing yarn to produce textiles and fabrics.

Ivory Carving

It has been practiced in India since the Vedic time when it was referred to as danta.

The inscription from Sanchi mentions the Vidisha guild of ivory workers and the carved sculptures in the Sanchi Stupa.

The ivory comb has been found in Taxila; Ivory was also used during the Mughal period. Other famous places for ivory are:

- **Kerala:** It is well-known for paintings on ivory.
- **Jodhpur:** It is famous for ivory bangles.
- **Jaipur:** It is well-known for its ivory jali work, which is used in homes and small art objects.

Silver Crafts

Filigree work is the famous work used in silver jewellery. Silver anklets known as painri and paijam are very popular in Odisha. Bidri art includes the work of silver from Karnataka.

Clay and Pottery Works

It is also known as the Lyric of handicrafts. Evidence has been found in Neolithic site of Mehrgarh. Painted Grey Ware pottery associated with the Vedic period is the most well-known ancient pottery; Roulette Pottery has been discovered in Southern India.

Bronze Crafts

Bronze metals were used more for spears and arrows in the ancient period. Dancing Girl from Mohenjodaro is a famous bronze art. Uttar Pradesh is the leading producer of bronze crafts. Tamil Nadu is another important centre.

Leather Products

Tigers and deer were among the first animals whose skins were tanned. However, camels also quickly became the most popular animal for skinning.

Rajasthan has the largest leather market where camel leather is used. Jaipur and Jodhpur are known for their Mojadis, a specialised type of leather footwear.

Kolhapuri chappals are popular in Maharashtra. Kanpur is also a famous leatherwork centre.

Wooden Work

Kashmiri latticework is an important woodwork, Gujarat is another famous centre for latticework.

Stoneware

The stonework was later shifted to marble work in the Mughal Period. Pietra Dura's Work is related to marble work used during the Mughal period.

Unit-2: Performing Arts

Indian Music

Introduction

The Vedic era, during which the reciting of chants was a crucial component of the Vedic ritual, can be regarded as the beginning of Indian music.

The following are some important aspects of Indian music:

- Epics like the Ramayana and Mahabharata contain references to the beginning and development of Indian classical music.
- Music instrument has been recovered from the site of the Indus Valley Civilization and from the Hela Civilization in Sri Lanka.
- All seven notes of the raga can be found in descending order in Samaveda. Sangama is a type of ritualistic music that evolved in the later Vedic Period.
- The first work that elaborated the subject of music was Bharata's Natyashastra. The 22 keys of octave are recognised as Shrutis in the Natyashastra.

Anatomy of Indian Music

There are three main pillars of Indian classical music: (i) Swara, (ii) Raga, and (iii) Tala.

- **Swara:** It defines the scale of degree in composition. Bharata in Natyashastra has divided Swara into a scale of 22 notes. At present, the national system of Hindustani music is defined by the seven swaras: sa, re, ga, ma, pa, dha, ni. These seven swaras are known as Saptak or Sargam.
- **Raga:** It forms the basis of melody while tala forms the basis of rhythm. Each raga represents a mood. There are 3 major types of ragas: Shuddha Raag, Chhayalag Raag and Sankeerna Raag.
  Raga is categorised on the basis of number of notes: Audava raga (raga containing five notes), Shadava raga (six notes), Sampurna raga (seven notes). Raga is divided into three speeds: Vilambit (slow), Madhya (medium), Drut (fast).
- **Tala:** Rhythmic groupings of beats are called tala.
- **Thaat:** It is the classification of ragas into different groups. Presently, in Hindustani music a 10-Thaat classification has been adopted.

Classification of Indian Music

Two different schools of India Music: Hindustani (Northern India) and Carnatic (Southern India).

Hindustani Music: It focuses more on the musical structure. There are different types of styles under it:

- **Dhrupad Style:** Oldest known forms of Hindustani music, finds mentions in Natyashastra, reached peak in the court of Akbar, essentially a poetic form of music, Tansen and Baiju Bawra are important musicians of this style.

Different types of gharana under this style are:

- **Dagari:** Dagars are Muslims who typically sing songs about Hindu Gods and Goddesses.
- **Darbhanga:** Emphasise on the raga alap, improvise by incorporating a variety of layakari.
- **Bettiah:** Perform the Nauhar and Khandar vani; some unique techniques.
- **Talwandi:** Based in Pakistan; sing the Khandar vani.
- **Khyal Style:** Amir Khusrau originated it, based on short songs, its composition is also referred to as Bandish, the theme is mostly romantic in nature, and Alap is given less importance compared to Dhrupad style.
  It is mainly of two types: Bada Khyal (sung in slow tempo) and Chhota Khyal (sung in fast tempo). Most of the performances are in Bada Khyal. Major gharanas under this style are:
  - **Gwalior:** One of the oldest; emphasis on melody and rhythm; prefers to perform simple ragas.
  - **Kirana:** Named after the town Kirana in Uttar Pradesh; precise tuning and expression of notes; slow tempo ragas.
  - **Agra:** Blend of Khyal and Dhrupad style; emphasis to Bandish.
  - **Patiala:** Greater rhythm; stress on emotions use alankaras; well known for Raga Darbari.
  - **Bhendi bazaar:** Sing long passages in a single breath; use some Carnatic ragas.
- **Tarana style:** Short melodies which are repeated many times; sung in fast tempo; invented by Amir Khusrau, also used by Guru Gobind Singh, Pandit Rattan Mohan Sharma is a famous singer.

Semi-Classical Hindustani Music

It is also based on swara, and uses lighter versions of tala and madhyam laya, the greatest emphasis on bhava and lyrics. Different styles of semi-classical music are:

- **Thumri:** Originated in Uttar Pradesh, based on mixed simple ragas, romantic or devotional in nature, inspired by the Bhakti movement, language of composition is Hindi or Braj Bhasha dialect, usually sung by females, linked to classical dance Kathak.
- **Tappa:** Rhythm plays an important role as compositions are based on fast notes; style is getting extinct.
- **Ghazal:** Consists of rhyming couplets; never exceeds the 12 ashaar. It reached its peak in the Mughal period, deals with just one subject. Amir Khusrau was a famous poet associated with it.

Carnatic Music

It is mainly associated with South India. Telugu, Kannada, Tamil or Sanskrit are the main languages. Carnatic music compositions are primarily based on the kriti form — a three-part musical composition consisting of pallavi, anupallavi, and charanam. It is also based on two elements like Hindustani music: raga and tala. It is usually played with mridangam.

The composition in Carnatic music has several parts to it:

- **Pallavi:** First or second line of the composition, it is often repeated.
- **Anu Pallavi:** It follows the Pallavi lines, not necessary to repeat it after every stanza.

- **Charana:** Final and the longest verse which concludes the song.
- **Varnam:** Sung at the beginning of a recital; two parts Purvanga first half and Uttaranga second half.
- **Ragamalika:** The concluding part.

Folk Music

This music form is a way in which rural people use oral tradition to perform, spread and preserve themselves. Some of the famous folk music are:

- **Baul:** Associated with West Bengal, Assam and Tripura, a type of Bengali religious sect, carry influences of Bhakti and the Sufi movements.
- **Wanawan:** Associated with Jammu and Kashmir and commonly sung in the weddings.
- **Pandavani:** Based on the epic Mahabharata with Bhima as the hero, associated with Chhattisgarh.
- **Alha:** Associated with Madhya Pradesh, uses heroic ballad song, can be sung in different languages (Awadhi, Bhojpuri), also related to epic Mahabharata.
- **Panihari:** Associated state Rajasthan, thematically related to water.
- **Ovi:** From Maharashtra and Goa, usually sung by women during their leisure time.
- **Pai:** From Madhya Pradesh, sung during festivals especially during rainy seasons for good monsoon and harvest.
- **Lavani:** From Maharashtra, combines dance and song.
- **Maand:** From Rajasthan, usually sung to the glory of Rajput rulers.
- **Dandiya:** From Gujarat, it is a featured dance of Navratri in western India along with Garba.
- **Powada:** From Maharashtra, sung for heroes like Shivaji.
- **Khongjom Parba:** From Manipur, it is a musical narration of the battle of Khongjom.
- **Bhavageete/Bhavgeet:** Sung in Karnataka and Maharashtra, they are close to Ghazals and sung on a lower pitch.
- **Mando:** Popular in Goa, a blend of Indian and Western musical traditions.
- **Kolattam:** From Andhra Pradesh, similar to Dandiya, an ancient dance form that involves rhythmic movements.

Fusion of Classical and Folk Music

- **Bhajan:** Originated with the Bhakti movement, usually sung in one or more raga, they are hymns in praise to God, Kabir and Surdas were expounders.
- **Shabad:** Songs dedicated to the Sikh gurus.
- **Qawwali:** Composed of single ragas, performed in Sufi shrines, sung both in solo and in groups. Amir Khusrau is the originator of Qawwali.

Musical Instruments

- **Avanaddha:** Membranophone instruments, contain an outer membrane which is beaten to produce a musical sound, also known as percussion instruments. Tabla and , Dhol come under this category.
- **Sushira Vadya:** Aerophones which include all the wind instruments such as flute, shehnai, etc.
- **Ghana Vadya:** Non-drum percussion instruments that do not require tuning.
- **Tata Vadya:** These are string instruments like the sitar.

Indian Dance Forms

Introduction

The first formal mention of dance is found in Bharatmuni's work Natya Shastra. The evidence of dance can be found in the Bhimbetka rock shelters and the bronze dancing girl of the Indus Valley civilization.

Important Terms

- **Lasya:** Denotes grace, bhava, rasa and abhinaya. Feminine features of the dance.
- **Tandava:** Male aspect of the dance form, more emphasis on rhythm and movement.
- **Nritta:** Basic dance steps, performed rhythmically but devoid of any expression or mood.
- **Natya:** Dramatic representation in the dance.
- **Nritya:** Sentiments and emotions evoked through dance.

Popular Indian Dance

Dance	State
Bihu	Assam
Bhangra	Punjab
Graba	Gujarat
Jhoomar	Punjab
Giddha	Punjab
Kummi	Tamil Nadu
Changu	Odisha
Therukoothu	Tamil Nadu
Chhau	Odisha, Jharkhand, and West Bengal
Yakshagana	Karnataka
Jatra	West Bengal
Bamboo dance/Cheraw	Mizoram
Ghommar	Rajasthan
Bhavai	Rajasthan
Kalbeliya	Rajasthan

There are eight classical dance forms. They are:

- **Bharatnatyam:** From Tamil Nadu, formerly known as Sadir or Dasiattam, equal emphasis is given to Tandava and Lasya aspects, knees are mostly bent.
- **Kuchipudi:** From Andhra Pradesh, involved difficult foot movements, usually performed in groups, based on stories of, Lasya and Tandava have equal importance, usually accompanied by Carnatic music.
- **Kathakali:** From Kerala, all-male group performance, elaborate facial make-up along with head gear, dance-drama performance, represents conflicts between good and evil, symbolizes elements of the sky.
- **Mohiniyattam:** From Kerala, solo dance, thumping of footsteps and gentle footwork, the feminine dance of Vishnu, Lasya aspect is dominant, symbolizes the element of air.
- **Odissi:** From Odisha; derives the name from Natya Shastra's Odra nritya, has tribhanga posture, dancers create geometrical shapes with the body, also known as mobile sculpture, accompanied by Hindustani music, symbolizes the element of water.
- **Manipuri:** From Manipur, usually performed by female dancers, with more emphasis on Lasya, Nagabandha mudra.
- **Kathak:** From Uttar Pradesh, accompanied by dhrupad music, elements of Kathak are: Aamad (introductory item), Todas and Tukdas (pieces of fast rhythm), Jugalbandi main attraction, Kramalaya (concluding performance). Different gharanas of Kathak: Lucknow, Jaipur, Raigarh, and Banaras.

- **Sattriya:** From Assam, usually performed by male monks, hand gestures and footwork play an important role, devotional in nature.

Indian Theatre

Important Ancient Sanskrit Plays

Swapnavasavadatta (written by Bhasa), Malavikagnimitram-Vikramorvasiyam-Abhigyana Shakuntalam (by Kalidasa), Mricchakatika (by Sudraka), Mudrarakshasa (by Vishakhadatta), Ratnavali-Nagananda-Priyadarsika (by Harshavardhana).

Important Folk Theatres

- **Assam:** Ankia Naat, Ojhapali, Bhaona
- **Uttar Pradesh:** Ramlila, Bhand
- **Gujarat:** Raslila, Garoda
- **Karnataka:** Bhuta Aradhana, Yakshagana, Bayalata.
- **Kerala:** Chavittu Natakam, Krishanattam.
- **Tamil Nadu:** Kuruvanji, Terukkuttu
- **Uttarakhand:** Ramman
- **Andhra Pradesh:** Burra Katha, Pagati Veshalu, Oggukatha
- **Maharashtra:** Tamasha, Powada, Dashavatar, Zadipatti
- **Gujarat:** Bhavai
- **Goa:** Ranmale, Tiatr

Indian Puppetry

- The evidence of puppetry have been found in the Indus Valley Civilization. There are four categories of puppets: **(i)** String Puppet, **(ii)** Shadow Puppet, **(iii)** Glove Puppet and **(iv)** Rod Puppet.
- **String Puppets:** Made out of wood, eight to nine inches long. Different types of string puppets are:
  - **Kathputli:** From Rajasthan, puppets do not have legs, strings are attached to the fingers of the puppeteer.
  - **Kundhei:** From Odisha, made up of wood and dressed in long skirts, has more joints making puppets flexible.
  - **Gombeyatta:** From Karnataka, more than one puppeteer to manipulate puppets.
  - **Bommalattam:** From Tamil Nadu, combines rod and string puppetry, the largest and heaviest marionettes found in India, puppets attached to the heads of the puppeteer.
- **Shadow puppets:** Flat figures, carved out of leather, painted on both sides, placed on a white screen with light from behind. Different types of puppets in this category are:
- **Tolpava Kuthu:** From Kerala, leather puppets, mainly performed in Bhadrakali temples of Kerala, Nair community associated with it.
- **Chamadyacha Bahulya:** From Maharashtra, leather puppet, Thakar tribal community associated with it.
- **Togalu Gombeyatta:** From Karnataka, puppets vary in size based on social status, the Killekyata community is mainly associated with it.
- **Ravanchhaya:** From Odisha, puppets made from deer-skin, do not have any joints, use of non-human puppets such as trees, etc.
- **Tholu Bommalata:** From Andhra Pradesh, themed around mythological and devotional tales.
- **Glove puppets:** Made up of cloth or wood, puppeteers wear puppets as a glove, accompanies by the beats of a drum. Important puppetry in this category is:
- **Pavakoothu:** From Kerala, decorated with colourful headgear, have the influence of Kathakali dance.
- **Rod Puppets:** Mainly popular in eastern India, larger than glove puppets, controlled by rods. Important puppets in this category are:
- **Yampuri:** From Bihar, made up of wood and do not have any joints, dressed in bright colour.
- **Putul Nachh:** From Bengal-Odisha-Assam, have joints.

Indian Circus

The great Indian Circus was the first modern circus in India. Founded by Vishnupant Chatre is called as the father of the Indian circus.

Major Circus companies in India

Three Ring Circus (the first and only six poles, three-ring circuses in Asia), Great Royal Circus, Great Bombay Circus (one of the largest circus companies in India), Gemini circus (the first Indian circus to attend the International Circus Festival of USSR), Jumbo Circus (The Pride of India, largest Indian circus of modern times).

Martial Arts in India

- **Kalarippayattu:** One of the oldest art from Kerala, not accompanied by drumming/song, footwork is very important.
- **Silambam:** It is from Tamil Nadu, a type of staff fencing, Pandyas, Cholas and Cheras promoted it, long staff is sued in fighting and self-defence.
- **Thang-ta and Sarit Sarak:** It is from Manipur. Thang-ta is armed martial while Sarit Sarak is unarmed, they both together is called Huyen Langlon.
- **Cheibi Gad-Ga:** Ancient martial art from Manipur, involves the use of a sword and shield.
- **Pari-khanda:** It is from Bihar, created by Rajputs, its steps and techniques are used in Chhau dance.
- **Thoda:** It is from Himachal Pradesh, a mixture of martial art, sports and culture, takes place during the Baisakhi festival. Depends on the player's skill in archery.
- **Gatka:** Performed by Sikhs of Punjab, involves use of stick, Kirpan, Talwar and Kataar.
- **Mardani Khel:** It is from Maharashtra, a unique feature, Patta (sword) and Vita (corded lance), performed by Shivaji.
- **Lathi:** Majorly practiced in Bengal.
- **Inbuan Wrestling:** It is from Mizoram.
- **Kuttu Varisai:** Mentioned in Sangam literature, practiced in Tamil Nadu, unarmed Dravidian martial art.
- **Musti Yuddha:** It is originated in Varanasi, resembles boxing.

UNESCO's List of Intangible Cultural Heritage

- **Koodiyattam:** Included in 2008, a dance drama from Kerala, performed by the Chakyars community, mainly performed inside the temples.
- **Ramlila:** Included in 2008, from Uttar Pradesh, enactment of Ramayan, mainly performed before Dussehra, usually performed by males.
- **The Tradition of Vedic Chanting:** Included in 2008.

- **Ramman:** Included in 2009, a religious festival and ritual theatre of Garhwal region, from Uttarakhand.
- **Mudiyettu:** Included in 2010, ritual theatre, from Kerala, folk dance and drama, performed in village temples, performers do heavy make ups.
- **Kalbelia:** Included in 2010, performed by the Kalbelia tribe in Rajasthan.
- **Chhau:** Included in 2010, a type of tribal martial art dance performed in Odisha, Jharkhand and West Bengal, mainly performed during the spring festival, performed by male dancers at night.
- **Buddhist Chanting of Ladakh:** Included in 2012, chanting related to Mahayana and Vajrayana.
- **Sankirtana:** Included in 2013, from Manipur, mainly practised in temples.
- **Traditional Brass and Copper Craft of Utensil Making:** It is included in 2014. The craft of the Thathelias of Jandiala Guru constitutes the traditional technique of manufacturing brass and copper utensils in Punjab.
- **Nowrouz:** Included in 2016, indicated the beginning of New Year for the Parsis, also celebrated as spring festival by the Kashmiri.
- **Yoga:** Included in 2016.
- **Kumbh Mela:** Included in 2017, performed at Prayagraj, Haridwar, Nashik and Ujjain, also known as Simhastha in Nashik and Ujjain, held after every 12 years.
- **Durga Puja:** Durga Puja in Kolkata was inscribed on the Representative List of Intangible Cultural Heritage of Humanity in 2021.
- **Garba:** Garba is a form of Gujarati dance which is included in the ICH in 2023.
- **Nowruz:** Persian New Year and spring festival, marking the vernal equinox (around 20–21 March). 2024
- **Deepavali (Diwali):** A Hindu festival. 2025

UNESCO's List of World Heritage Sites in India

Cultural Sites

- **1983:** Agra Fort, Ajanta Caves, Ellora Caves, Taj Mahal.
- **1984:** Monuments at Mahabalipuram, Sun Temple.
- **1986:** Fatehpur Sikri, Monuments at Hampi, Khajuraho Group of Temples, Churches and Convents of Goa.
- **1987:** Elephanta Caves, Great Living Chola Temples, Monuments at Pattadakal.
- **1989:** Buddhist Monuments of Sanchi.
- **1993:** Humayun's Tomb, QutbMinar and its Monuments.
- **1999:** Mountain Railways of India.
- **2002:** Mahabodhi Temple Complex, Bodh Gaya, Bihar.
- **2003:** Rock Shelters of Bhimbetka.
- **2004:** Chhatrapati Shivaji Terminus, Champaner-Pavagadh Archaeological Park.
- **2007:** Red Fort, Delhi.
- **2010:** Jantar Mantar, Rajasthan.
- **2013:** Hill Forts of Rajasthan.
- **2014:** Rani Ki Vav, Gujarat.
- **2016:** Nalanda University Archaeological Site, Archaeological Work of Le Corbusier, Chandigarh.
- **2017:** The Historic City of Ahmedabad.
- **2018:** Victorian Gothic and Art Deco Ensembles of Mumbai.
- **2019:** The Pink City, Jaipur.
- **2021:** Dholavira, Kakatiya Rudreshwara/Rampappa Temple.
- **2023:** Sacred Ensembles of the Hoysalas.
- **2023:** Santiniketan, The historic university town in West Bengal built by Rabindranath Tagore.
- **2024:** Moidams – The Mound-Burial System of the Ahom Dynasty.
- **2025:** Maratha Military Landscapes of India.

Unit-3: Culture of India

Languages in India

Language is a mode of communication using speech, a collection of sounds that have the same meaning for a set of people. A language family includes those languages which are related to a common ancestor and dialect is a form of language spoken in a local area. Language groups indigenous to the Indian sub-continent are:

Indo-Aryan Group of Languages

- **Old Indo-Aryan Group:** This group developed around 1500 B.C. Sanskrit was born out of this group, Sanskrit is the mother of many Indian Languages, even Upanishad Vedas, and Puranas are all written in Sanskrit.
- **Middle Indo-Aryan Group:** It developed around 600-1000 B.C. along with starting of the development of Prakrit. All Middle-Indo-Aryan group of all languages such as Ardha-Magadhi, Pali, etc. are clubbed into Prakrit. Prakrit was associated with common people. Prakrit and Ardha-Magadhi language is used in the Jain "Agamas".

■ Prakrit includes the following languages:

- **Pali:** Widely spoken in Magadha; closely related to Sanskrit; written in Brahmi script; Tripitaka of Buddhism were written in Pali.
- **Ardha-Magadhi or Magadhi:** Buddha delivered their preaching in this language. Court language of Mauryan dynasty; later evolved in languages of eastern India such as Assamese, Bengali, etc.
- **Shauraseni:** Used for writing dramas in medieval India; also referred to as dramatic Sanskrit; mostly used by Jain monks; Jain text 'Shatkhandgama' is written in this language.
- **Maharashtri Prakrit:** Spoken till 9th century; predecessor of Marathi and Konakani; official language of the Satavahanas dynasty; widely used in Western and Southern India.
- **Elu:** Ancient form of modern Sinhala language of Sri Lanka, and is similar to Pali.
- **Paishachi:** Referred to as Bhuta-bhasha or dead language; regarded as Prakrit.

- **Modern Indo-Aryan group:** Languages belonging to this group are Hindi, Bengali, Marathi, Assamese, Gujarati, Punjabi, Rajasthani, Sindhi, Odia, Urdu etc.; developed after 1000 AD.

Dravidian Group of Languages

It is usually spoken in the southern part of India. There are mainly three groups under it:

- **Northern Group:** Brahui, Malto, and Kurukh are three languages in this.
- **Central Group:** Consists eleven languages namely Gondi, Khond, Kui, Manda, Parji, Gadaba, Kolami, Pengo, Naiki, Kuvi, and Telugu.

- **Southern Group:** Kannada, Tamil, Malayalam, Tulu, Kodagu, Toda, and Kota belong to this group;
- **Malayalam:** Smallest and youngest Dravidian language.
- **Tamil:** Oldest Dravidian language
- **Telugu:** Most spoken Dravidian language

Sino-Tibetan Group of Languages

Languages in this group belong to Mongoloid family and are spoken all over the Himalayas, North Bengal, Assam, and North-East. These languages are considered to be older than the Indo-Aryan Languages.

This group is divided into following:

- Tibeto-Burmanese (Meitei or Manipuri is an important language).
- Siamese-Chinese (Ahom is an important language).

Austric Group of Languages

- Represents languages of Munda or Kol group and spoken in Central, Eastern, and North-Eastern India.
- They are called Nisadas in ancient Sanskrit literature.
- Important languages: Khasi and Santhali (Except these all other languages of this group are endangered).

Official Languages of India

- The Article 343 (1) of the Indian Constitution declares that the official language of the Union shall be Hindi in Devanagri script. For Sanskrit, there is a special status mentioned in article 351, whereby Sanskrit was given a position of the primary source language for many languages including Hindi.
- The Official Languages Act, 1963 declares that Hindi in Devanagari script will be the official language of the Union. English has been given the status of "subsidiary official language" of the Union.
- The Eighth Schedule of the Constitution includes 22 languages and India does not have a National language. States are free to adopt an official language. States can adopt languages other than listed in the Eighth schedule.
- English is not in the list of 22 languages. Arunachal Pradesh and Nagaland are the only states that have English as their only official language.

Criteria for Classical Languages in India

- The government of India currently follows the following criteria to determine the eligibility of language to be considered for classification as "classical language":
- High antiquity of its early texts/ recorded history over a period of 1500-2000 years;
- A body of ancient literature/ texts, which is considered a valuable heritage by generations of speakers;
- The literary tradition should be original and not borrowed from another speech community;
- The classical language and literature being distinct from modern, there may also be a discontinuity between the classical language and its later forms or its offshoots.
- Currently there are eleven classical languages:
- Tamil (since 2004)
- Sanskrit (since 2005)
- Telugu (since 2008)
- Kannada (since 2008)
- Malayalam (since 2013)
- Odia (since 2014)
- Marathi, Pali, Prakrit, Assamese, and Bengali (2024)

Ancient Scripts of India

The system of writing or orthography is called script. Two ancient scripts of India are Brahmi and Kharosthi script. Some important ancient scripts of India are:

- **Indus Script:** It is the collection of symbols produced by the people of the Indus Valley Civilization, and are extremely short scripts.
- **Brahmi Script:** It is the oldest writing system used in the Indian subcontinent and in Central Asia and is the mother of all scripts. It is present in rock-cut edicts of Ashoka, and is usually written from left to right in abugida.
- **Kharosthi Script (3rd Century BC- 3rd Century AD):** It is an ancient script used in the Gandhara region (Afghanistan and Pakistan), and is a sister script of Brahmi, written in abugida. It is mostly written from right to left.
- **Kadamba Script (4th - 6th Centuries):** It developed from Brahmi script. Kannada and Telugu script evolved from this script.
- **Vatteluttu Script:** It is abugida writing system which originated in South India, and developed from Tamil-Brahmi to write Granthi or Pallava alphabet and Tamil script.
- **Grantha Script (6th - 20th Centuries):** It was used by Tamil speakers to write Sanskrit and classical language 'Manipravalam', and Malayalam script evolved from this script (emerged around 1400s).
- **Sarada or Sharada script (8th Century):** It was used for writing Sanskrit and Kashmiri.
- **Gurumukhi script:** It developed from Sarada script and was standardised in the 16th Century. Guru Granth Sahib is written in this script.
- **Devanagari script:** It is abugida alphabet of Nepal and India which is written from left to right, abugida writing system around the 10th century CE. Hindi, Marathi, Nepali, Konkani, Pali, Bodo, Sindhi and Maithali is written in this script.
- **Modi scripts 16th to 17th century:** Till the 20th Century it was used to write the Marathi language, now Marathi is written based on Balbodh style of the Devanagari script.
- **Urdu script:** It is written from right to left, and is a modification of the Persian alphabet. In extended form, it is also known as Shahmukhi script.
- **Kaithi script:** It was widely used in parts of Northern and Eastern India for writing legal, administrative and private records during the Mughals.

Religion in India

Indian sub-continent 16th–mid 20th century has a variety of religions that are followed by the diverse population residing in this region. Some of them are:

Hinduism

It is derived from the word "Hindu" which depicts people living around the river Indus. The basic principles of Hinduism are derived from pre-Vedic and Vedic philosophies.There are four sects under Hinduism are:

- **Vaishnavism:** Followers of Vaishnavism consider Vishnu as Supreme Lord. Important sects under it are: Varkari Panthi, Ramanandi Sampradaya, Brahma Sampradaya, Pushtimarg Sampradaya, and Nimbarka Sampradaya.
- **Shaivism:** It considers Shiva as Supreme Lord, and originated before Vaishnavism. Important sects under it are: Nath Panthi, Lingayatism, Dashanami Sanyasis, Aghoris, Siddhas.
- **Shaktism:** Feminine power or Devi/goddess is considered as supreme.
- **Smartism:** It is based on the teachings of Puranas, and followers believe in worship of five deities: Shiva, Shakti, Ganesh, Vishnu and Surya.

Ajivikas

- Makkhali Gosala in 5th century BC founded this school. This school believes in Niyati (fate) doctrine, there is no free will and everything is pre-decided, hence it did not believe in karma.
- It is based on the theory of atoms, opposed Buddhism, Jainism, and were atheists, rejected the authority of Vedas, and believed in existence of the soul in the material form.
- Bindusara was its follower.
- Ajivikas are mentioned in Ashoka's 7th pillar edict.

Ajnanas

- This school believed in radical skepticism, it is impossible to attain knowledge about nature and ignorance is best.
- It was a rival of Jainism and Buddhism.

Islam

- Islam's origin can be traced back to the 7th century AD.
- It believes in monotheism, the day of Judgement, submission to God.
- Ramazan (month) and Eid are major festivals.

Christianity

- It is India's third largest religion that believes in only one God, and its sacred text is Bible.
- Bible consists of Old Testament and the New Testament.

Sikhism

- Guru Nanak was against the social order, and he believed that the ultimate purpose of human existence was salvation which can be achieved by right belief, right worship and right conduct. He said, there is no need to leave home to attain salvation.
- Khalsa was founded by Guru Gobind Singh, and Khalsa Sikh had to wear five k's i.e. kachcha, kesh, kangha, kirpan and kara. Baptized Sikh men are called Singh and women as Kaur.

Zoroastrianism

- This religion originated in Persia around 6-7th century BCE and is a monotheistic religion that believes in one God Ahura Mazda, Angra Mainyu the spirit of malice and bad behaviour.
- Followers known as Parsis and Iranis, Zenda Avesta (sacred texts) and Ahuna Vairyo (sacred chants); worship fire and consider fire and earth as sacred elements; only zorastrian open space in India is "Towers of Silence" in Mumbai where they performed 'Dakhma Nashini'.
- **Judaism:** Believes in one Yahwh (one true God); followers are called Jews; religious book is Torah; Talmud refers to brief history of Jews; synagogues is their place of worship; five major Communities:
  - Cochinis (Malayalam speaking)
  - Bene Israel (the children of Israel) is the largest Jews community in India (Marathi speaking)
  - Baghdadi Jews
  - Bneih Menashe (Children of Menasseh) also known as Manipuri Jews
  - Bene Ephraim (small group of Telugu speaking)

Buddhism and Jainism

Buddhism

- It was originated by Siddhartha who also came to be known as Buddha. It is the world's fourth-largest religion. In India, the majority of Buddhists live in Maharashtra.
- Buddha's teachings were compiled into three Pitakas. Vinaya, Sutta and Abhidhamma were combined into Tripitakas. All are written in Pali language.
- **Reason for rise:** Domination of Brahmanas, easy to understand.
- **Textual sources:** Canonical (directly linked to Gautama Buddha such as Tripitakas), Non-Canonical (comments and observation on canonical texts, not sayings of Buddha).
- **Philosophy:** Four major noble truths (truth of suffering, truth of the origin of suffering, truth of end of suffering truth of the path to end the suffering), rejected the authority of Vedas, rejects the concept of soul, believes in the Middle Path.
- **Eight Noble Path:** Right speech, right action, right livelihood, right effort, right mindfulness, right meditation, right thoughts, and right understanding.

Sects under Buddhism

- **Hinayana:** Lesser vehicle; orthodox school, followers of the original preaching of Buddha; do not believe in idol/ image worship; believe in individual salvation and attaining Nirvana; used Pali language.
- **Mahayana:** Greater vehicle; believes in Bodhisattva also called "Bodhisattvayana"; believe in idol/image worship; the concept of Bodhisattva led to the Mahayana Buddhism; believed in universal salvation, used Sanskrit language, Lotus Sutra and Mahavamsa are important texts, Kanishka was its followers.
  - **Bodhisattva** refers to the one who has a compassionate mind to attain Buddha hood, Important Bodhisattvas are: Avalokitesvara, Vajrapani, Manjusri, Samantabhadra, Ksitigrabha, Maitreya (future buddha) and Tara.
- **Theravada:** School of elder monks; used Pali language; the successor of Hinayana school; believes in seven stages of purification, the ultimate goal is the end of kleshas, concept of vibhajjavada i.e., "teaching of analysis".

- **Vajrayana:** Influenced by Hinduism, also known as tantric Buddhism, based on Mahayana Buddhist philosophy, main deity is Tara, a lady.

Jainism

- Mahavira was the 24th tirthankara but not the founder of Jainism. Jainism rejected the authority of Vedas. It believes in the existence of soul. Sallekhana and Pratikramana re the popular practices under Jainism.
- **Philosophy:** Believes in path of right belief, right knowledge and right conduct to achieve salvation. Five constraints required to follow are:

- non-violence,
- truthfulness,
- not stealing,
- non-acquisition,
- chaste living.

Sects under Jainism

- **Digambaras:** Monks do not wear clothes, Aryikas wear unstitched clothes, they follow all five constraints, believes that women cannot be tirthankaras, rules are more rigid. Sects under Digambaras are: Gumanapantha, Bispanthi, Terapanthi and Taranpanthi, Totapantha.
- **Svetambaras:** Believe in only four restraints to attain Kevalya; monks wear simple clothing; men and women both can be tirthankaras; rules are less rigid than Digambaras. Sects under Svetambaras are: Sthanakavasi, Deravasi and Terapanthi.

Indian Literature

Literature in Ancient India

- **Vedas:** Means knowledge, teaches people to live life, language is in symbols and myths, preach Vasudhaiva Kutumbakam.
- **Four Vedas are:** Rigveda, Yajurveda, Samaveda, and Atharvaveda. All of the Vedas emphasise yajna (sacrifice). Each Veda is accompanied by the Brahmanas, Upanishads and Aranyakas.
- **Types of Vedic Literature:** Shruti Literature (means to hear) and Smriti Literature (means to remember)

- **Rigveda:** Oldest of all Vedas, focuses on worldly prosperity and natural beauty; divided into ten books known as Mandalas; majority of the hymns are about life, death, creation, sacrifice, and seeking godly pleasure; Indra is the chief deity; several hymns dedicated to female goddesses as well e.g. Usha, Vak etc.
- **Atharvaveda:** Also known as Brahma Veda; concerned with the peace and prosperity of human society; includes all aspects of a man's daily life; focuses on the treatment of various ailments; concerned with healing and black and white magic; two different divisions: Paippalada and Saunakiya.
- **Yajurveda:** Focuses on the rites and mantras of various types of sacrifices; a ritual Veda; serving as a guide book for priests for conducting sacrificial rituals; two different divisions: Shukla (Vajasaneyi) and Krishna (Taittiriya)
- **Samaveda:** Derived from saman(melody); focus on melody or songs, known as the book of chants; helps trace the history of Indian music.

- **Brahmanas:** Part of Shruti literature; a mix of legends, facts, philosophy, and in-depth explanations of Vedic rituals; include instructions on how to properly perform rituals and explain the science of sacrifice.
- **Aranyakas:** Aranyaka means 'the forest'; related to the Vedas that describe the Vedic rituals and sacrifices from various perspectives; deal with ritualistic information on the birth and death cycles.
- **Upanishads:** Derived from Upani-sad that means 'to sit down near someone' also known as Vedanta; contains the truth about human life and point the way to salvation, or moksha; motto Satyameva jayate is taken from the Mundakopanishad.

Buddhist Literature

- Prakrit and Pali were the post-Vedic languages spoken by Indians; Buddhist literature were written in Pali.

Tripitakas

The canonical literature of Buddhists consists of Tripitaka written in Pali. Different Pitakas are:

- **Vinaya Pitaka:** Deals with rules and regulations to be followed by monks.
- **Sutta Pitaka:** Contains dialogues and speeches of Buddha that deals with morality and righteous dharma.
- **Abhidhamma Pitaka:** Focuses on philosophy and metaphysics.

- **Jatakas:** Jatakas are Buddhists non-canonical literature. Jataka contains stories of previous birth of Buddha, Bodhisattva or the future.

  The rise of Mahayana Buddhism included Sanskrit literature in Buddhism i.e., Buddhacharita by Aswaghosha.

Jain Literature

Written in Prakrit and Ardha Magadhi languages along with other languages. The teachings of the Tirthankaras before Mahavir are known as Purva. Jain Literature is called Jain Agamas. They are canonical texts of Jainism based on Mahavira's teachings. Between 9th-12th A.D. Jain monks extensively used Kannada.

Sikh Literature

There is no written record of Punjabi literature prior to Guru Nanak.

- **Adi Granth:** Completed by Guru Arjun Dev, written in the Gurumukhi script, predecessor to the Guru Granth Sahib.
- **Guru Granth Sahib:** Written in Gurumukhi script and in the Sant Bhasa language, includes the teachings of thirteen Bhakti saints known as Bhagats.
- **Dasam Granth:** Hymns written by Guru Gobind Singh.
- **Janamsakhis:** contains mythological stories of first guru i.e., Guru Nanak.

Dravidian Literature

It contains works in four major Dravidian languages: Tamil, Kannada, Telugu, and Malayalam.

Tamil (Sangam) Literature

- Gatherings/assemblies of poets and writers during the kingdoms of Pandya were known as Sangamas and the literature produced during these gatherings was known as Sangam literature.
- Two major schools of Sangam literature: Aham/agam (focuses on love, sexual relations, etc.) and Puram (deals with social life, ethics, etc.).
- Famous contributors to this literature: a Tamil saint Thiruvallurar, a female saint Avvaiyar.

Malayalam Literature

- It is commonly spoken in Kerala and its surrounding areas.
- Kokasandisan and Bhasa Kautilya are two major Malayalam works from the medieval period.
- Ramacharitam also a major literary work in Malayalam.
- Ezhuthachan is regarded as the father of Malayalam literature.

Telugu Literature

- Nannaya was the first Telugu poet. Vijayanagara period is known as the golden age of Telugu literature.
- Krishnadeva Raya produced exceptional poetry titled Amuktamalyada.

Kannada Literature

- Jain scholars wrote in Kannada Literature. Madhava's Dharmanathapurana is a biography of the fifteenth Tirthankara in Kannada Literature.
- **Ratnatraya consisted:** Pampa, Ponna and Ranna.
- Pampa is known as the "Father of Kannada", wrote Adipurana and Vikramarjuna Vijaya.
- Kannada literature grew due to the Vijayanagara empire's patronage.

Medieval Literature

It includes: Persian, Urdu and Hindi literatures.

- **Persian Literature:** It arrived in India with the arrival of Turks and Mongols. Amir Khusrau is a great Persian poet. It gained prominence in the Mughal era. Some examples are: Tuzuk-I-Babari (Babar), Tuzuk-I-Jahangiri (Jahangir), Humayun-nama (Gulbadan Begum), Ain-e Akbari and Akbarnama(Abul Fazl).
- **Urdu Literature:** Urdu arose from the interaction of Persian and Hindi. Amir Khusrau also wrote several texts in Urdu. Originally known as Dakkani because it was used by the Bahamani states of Ahmedabad, Golconda, Bijapur, and Bera. Mirza Ghalib, a greatest Urdu poet composed Diwan (collection of poetry). Another famous poet was Iqbal who wrote "Saare Jahan se Acha".
- **Hindi Literature:** Hindi evolved from the ancient apabhramsa language. Prithviraj Raso was the first Hindi book, documenting Prithviraj Chauhan's life and challenges. Bhakti movement gave boost to Hindi language.

Modern Literature

It is also known as Adhunik Kaal Sahitya. It includes:

- **Bengali Literature:** William Carey responsible for distribution of Bengal literature; Raja Ram Mohan Roy was one of the first to write in both Bengali and English; Rabindranath Tagore, the first Indian to receive the Nobel Prize, for his Bengali masterpiece Geetanjali.
- **Assamese Literature:** Dominated by Buranjis (court chronicles), Shankardev wrote devotional poetry in Assamese.
- **Odia Literature:** Sarala Das was the famous writer and wrote first major work Odia.
- **Gujarati Literature:** Narsingh Mehta is famous writer. K. M. Munshi's Prithvi Vallabha is a famous Gujarati work.
- **Rajasthani Literature:** Dingal and Pingal are two fictional writing form, Dhola Maru is a famous text. Stories of Rajasthani writers were oral in nature; spread through virkavya(victory poetic songs).
- **Sindhi Literature:** Influenced by the states of Rajasthan and Gujarat, Dewan Kauramal and Mirza Kalish Beg are two famous names in Sindhi literature.
- **Kashmiri Literature:** Kalhan's Rajatarangini from Kashmir is written in Sanskrit, influenced by Persian and Hindi dialects, Lal Ded was the first female poet. Dogri has reduced the importance of Kashmiri.
- **Punjabi Literature:** Composed in Persian and Gurmukhi. One of the greatest texts of Punjabi are Adi Granth in Gurmukhi. Famous literary works: Heer Ranjha (Waris Shah), Sassi Punnu, Sohni Mahiwal etc.
- **Marathi Literature:** Saint Jnaneshwar's work is the oldest known work in Marathi, Janabai is the oldest known female writer, Bal Gangadhar Tilak published his regional newspaper Kesari in Marathi.

Schools of Philosophy

Divided into two schools: Orthodox and heterodox.

Orthodox School

It is also known as Astika school. It believes in the authentication of Vedas. They had six sub-schools are: Samkhya, Yoga, Nyaya, Vaisheshika, Mimamsa, and Vedanta.

- **Samkhya School:**
  - Proposed by the philosopher Kapil Muni, developed into: Original Samkhya View and New Samkhya View,
  - Believes in dualism or dvaitavada (soul and matter are separate entities), Prakriti (Physiognomy of a woman) and Purusha (physiognomy of a man) are the absolute and independent basis of reality,
- **Yoga School:** Founded by Patanjali, believes in combination of meditation and the physical application of yogic practices; deals with asana(postures) and Pranayam(breathing excercises)
- **Nyaya School:** Believes in logical reasoning to obtain salvation, Gautama is the author of the Nyaya Sutra ; believes that God not only created but also sustains and destroys the Universe, emphasised on tools like inference, hearing and analogy.
- **Vaisheshika School:** Believes in the physicality of the Universe; founded by Kanada; believes that five

elements: fire, air, water, earth, and ether (sky) formed everything in the universe; developed atomic theory; believes in God, believes that the principles of karma govern the Universe; emphasis on metaphysics and naturalism.

- **Mimamsa School:** Focuses on analysis of Vedic writings such as the Samhita and Brahmana, believes that Vedas contain the eternal truth, believes that performing rituals can lead to salvation but it is also necessary to understanding the reasoning behind Vedic, believes in karma and attainment of salvation to be free from cycle of life and death.
- **Vedanta School:** Believes in the philosophies of Upanishads, believes that if a person achieves self-knowledge, he will understand Brahma and achieve salvation, believes that Brahma and Atma are indestructible and eternal, believed in the Theory of Karma and believed in the theory of rebirth.

Indian Cinema

It is one of the largest film industries in Asia.

- **History:** Lumiere Brothers, the inventors of the Cinematograph, introduced motion pictures to India. Harishchandra Bhatvadekar (Save Dada) was the first Indian to make a motion picture with the help of Edison Projecting Kinetoscope. Major Warwick opened the first film house in Madras.
- **Silent Films (1910-1920):** Not completely silent and were accompanied by music and dance, Raja Harishchandra was the first indigenous Indian silent film, produced by Dadasaheb Phalke, Fatima Begum was the first Indian woman to produce and direct her own film (Bulbul-e-Parastan).
- **Talking Films (Since 1931):** Alam Ara was the first talking film directed by Ardeshir Irani and produced by the Imperial Film Company and screened at Majestic Cinema in 1931, De de khuda ke naam par was the first recorded song written by W.M. Khan, first Indian color film but was processed and developed in Germany was Sairandhri made by Prabhat in 1933, Kisan Kanya was the first indigenously produced colour film produced by Ardeshir Irani.
- **Indian Cinematograph Act of 1952:** Enacted to regulate film certification, established the Central Board of Film Certification (CBFC), also known as the Censor Board of India, Censor Board certificate is required for all films including international films except films made specifically for Doordarshan, television shows and serials.
- First international Film Festival was held in Bombay in 1952. Do Bigha Zameen by Bimal Roy was the first film to win an award at Cannes. Mother India was nominated to the Oscars for Best Foreign Language film category. First President Gold Medal was received by Shorab Modi for Mirza Ghalib in 1954.

Calendars in India

The National Calendar of India is based on the Saka calendar, which is used as the country's official civil calendar.

The Calendar Reforms Committee set up by the Government of India adopted the Saka calendar as the National Calendar in 1957.

Types of Calendars

- **Vikram Samvat:** A luni-solar calendar; started 56 years before Christian era; has 354 days and divided in 12 months; each month divided into two halves (bright and dark).
- **Saka Samvat:** Both solar and lunar, Chaitra is the first month; by king Shalivahan in 78 AD; has a fixed number of days in each month; the number of days in year is 365/366.
- **Hijri Calendar:** In Arabic, lunar calendar; zero year for this calender is 622 A.D.; divided into 12 months and has 354 days (approximately); 4 months are considered as sacred
- **Gregorian Calendar:** Based on the birth of Jesus Christ, solar calendar, a year in this calendar is known as a civil year.

Fairs and Festivals of India

India is a secular nation, and a number of festivals associated with many religions and communities have been recognised holidays. Therefore festivals are divided into Religious and Secular Festivals.

- **Religious Festivals**
  - **Hindu festivals:** Diwali, Holi, Dussehra, Mahashivratri, etc.
  - **Muslim festivals:** Eid-ul-Fitr, Milad-Un-Nabi, Muharram, etc.
  - **Christian Festivals:** Christmas, Easter, Good Friday, etc.
  - **Sikh Festivals:** Gurpurab, Maghi, Hola Mohalla, Vaisakhi, etc.
  - **Jain Festivals:** Mahavir Jayanti, Paryushana, Mahamastakabhisheka, Gyana Panchami, Varshi Tapa, etc.
  - **Buddhist Festivals:** Buddha Purnima, Songkran, Ullambana, Losar Festival, etc.
  - **Sindhi Festivals:** Chaliho Sahib, Cheti Chand, etc.
  - **Zoroastrian Festivals:** Jamshedi Navroz, Zarthost No Deeso, Pateti, etc.
- **Secular Festivals:** Gangaur Festival, Khajuraho Dance Festival, New Year, Teej, Sair-e-Gulfaroshan, Raksha Bandhan, Onam, Pongal, etc.

Festivals of North-East India

- **Saga Dawa:** From Sikkim, performed by Buddhist group.
- **Losoong Festival:** Celebrated for New Year of Sikkim, performed by Bhutia tribe.
- **Bihu Festival:** From Assam, celebrated for Assamese New Year.

- **Hornbill Festival:** From Nagaland, named after bird.
- **Moatsu Festival:** Celebrated by Ao tribe of Nagaland.
- **Kharchi Puja:** From Tripura.
- **Cheiraoba Festival:** Celebrated in Manipur as a new year by Manipuri Tribes.
- **Wangala Festival:** From Meghalaya, celebrated by Garo Tribe.
- **Lui-Ngai-Ni Festival:** From Nagaland, celebrated by Naga tribes, gives the message of peace and harmony.
- **Dree Festival:** From Arunachal Pradesh, celebrated by Apatani tribe, biggest celebration in the Ziro valley.
- **Kang Chingba:** Celebrated in Manipur similar to Jagganath Puri Rath Yatra.
- **Ambubachi Mela:** Celebrated in Assam, the mahakumbh of the east.

Fairs of India

- **Kumbh Mela:** Held on rotational basis at Prayagraj, Haridwar, Nashik-Trimbak and Ujjain.
- **Sonepur Mela:** Held in Bihar, a cattle fair, takes place at the confluence of the Ganga and the Gandak rivers in Sonepur.
- **Chitra Vichitra Fair:** Gujarat's largest tribal fair, celebrated by Gharasia and Bhil tribes.
- **Pushkar Fair:** Annual fair in Rajasthan, one of the world's largest camel and cattle fairs.
- **Gangasagar Mela:** Takes place near the mouth of the Hooghly River in West Bengal on Makar Sankranti day.
- **Hemis Gompa Mela:** Related to Buddhist community.
- **Shamlaji Fair:** Celebrated by tribal community in Gujarat to honor God Shamlaji.
- **Goa Carnival:** Introduced by the Portuguese.

Awards and Honours

Both at the individual and collective levels, awards and honours are awarded as a sign of gratitude or acknowledgement for a remarkable effort.

Awards and Honours

- **Civilian Awards**
- **Bharat Ratna**
  - It is the highest civilian award of India. Instituted in 1954.
  - The first recipients of the Bharat Ratna were C. Rajagopalachari, Sarvepalli Radhakrishnan, and C. V. Raman.
  - The number of Bharat Ratna is restricted to a maximum of three nominees being awarded per year.
  - Pranab Mukharjee, Nanaji Deshmukh and Bhupen Hazarika was awarded Bharat Ratna in 2019.
  - Karpoori Thakur, Lal Krishna Advani, P. V. Narasimha Rao, Charan Singh, M. S. Swaminathan were awarded Bharat Ratna in 2024.

Padma Awards

- **Padma Vibhushan:** The Padma Vibhushan is the second-highest civilian award of India, second only to the Bharat Ratna. Instituted in 1954.
- **Padma Bhushan:** The Padma Bhushan is the third-highest civilian award of India, proceeded by the Bharat Ratna and the Padma Vibhushan and followed by the Padma Shri.
- **Padma Shri:** Padma Shri is the fourth highest civilian award in the Republic of India. Instituted in 1954.

National Sports Awards

- **Major Dhyan Chand Khel Ratna Award (Previously known as Rajiv Gandhi Khel Ratna)**
  - The Major Dhyan Chand Khel Ratna is the highest honour bestowed to a sportsperson for his/her achievements in India.
  - The first recipient of the Rajiv Gandhi Khel Ratna award is Viswanathan Anand.
- **Dhyan Chand Award:** The award that is given to the veteran sportspersons of India for their lifetime achievement in their respective field of sport is named as the Dhyan Chand Award for Life Time Achievement in Sports and Games.
- **Dronacharya Award**
  - This award is given to coaches and sports teachers for producing great skilled teams and individual players in various sports.
  - Dronacharya awards were initiated in 1985.
- **Arjuna Award:** The Arjuna Awards are given by the Ministry of Youth Affairs and Sports, Government of India to recognize outstanding achievement in sports. Instituted in 1961.
- **Literature Awards**
  - Jyanpith award
  - Saraswati Samman
  - Moortidevi Award
  - Bihari Puraskar
  - Sahitya Akademi Award
- **Gallantry awards**
  - Param vir chakra.
  - Mahavir chakra.
  - Vir chakra.
  - Ashoka chakra.
  - Kirti chakra.
  - Shaurya chakra.

Cultural Institutions in India

A cultural institution is an organisation that works for the preservation and promotion of culture.

- **The Archaeological Survey of India:** Comes under the Ministry of Culture; its responsibilities are the conservation; protection, and upkeep of Centrally protected monuments and sites.
- **All India Radio:** Run by the Indian Government's Ministry of Information and Broadcasting.
- **Sahitya Akademi:** Also known as the National Academy of Letters, undertakes literary activities in 24 languages (22 languages of the 8th schedule and English and Rajasthani).
- **Sangeet Natak Akademi:** Setup in 1952 and inaugurated in 1953 by Dr. Rajendra Prasad, the main goal was to establish an academy for Indian music, drama and dances.
- **Lalit Kala Akademi:** Also known as the National Academy of Art, whose objective is to promote fine arts in India, comes under the Ministry of Culture.

Coins in Ancient and Medieval India

Numismatics is the study of coins and medallions.

- **Punch Marked Coins:** Coins that have one to five markings or symbols punched onto one side are known as "punch-marked" coins. Two classifications:

- **Mahajanapada Coins:** Known as Puranas, Karshapanas and Pana, made of silver with diverse patterns, Punch-marked Magadhan coins became popular, mentioned in the Manusmriti and Buddhist Jataka Stories.
- **Coins during Mauryan Period:** Different coins were rupyarupa (silver), suvarnarupa (gold), tamrarupa (copper), and sisarupa (lead), mentioned in Arthashastra, Karshapanas were silver coins.
- **Indo-Greek Coins:** Silver, copper, nickel and lead were the most common metals for coins, Greek was written on one side and Pali on the other, one side had monarch and other side deity, Kanishka's coins were all written in Greek.
- **Coins By Satavahanas:** Lack of beauty and creativity; one side had figure of elephant, lion, horse or Chaittya and on another side. Ujjain symbol was present on the other side of the most coins; mostly used lead as a material.
- **Coins of the Gupta Age:** Mostly created gold coins but also issued silver and copper coins, one side had a monarch and the other side had goddess Lakshmi, inscriptions on the coins were written in Sanskrit.
- **Coins of the Vardhanas:** Silver coins had the head of the king on one side and the figure of a peacock on the other.
- **Coins of Chalukyas:** Legends and images of a temple or a lion appeared on one side of the coin. The backside was left blank.
- **Coins of Rajputs:** Usually made of gold, copper, or billion (a silver-copper alloy); on one side, the king's name was written in Sanskrit, while on the other, a deity was shown.
- **Coins of the Pandyas and Chola dynasty:** Fish and elephant were important symbols on their coins, inscriptions on the gold and silver coins were in Sanskrit, while the inscriptions on the copper coins were in Tamil.
- **Coins of the Vijayanagara Empire:** Gold, pure silver and copper coins.
- **Turkish and Delhi Sultanate Coins:** Based on Hijri calendar date, Gold, silver, copper, and billon coins were issued by the Sultans of Delhi, Iltutmish introduced Silver Tanka and Copper Jital, Muhammad ibn Tughlaq circulated bronze and copper coins, as well as paper currency.
- **Coins of The Mughals:** Mohur was the standard gold currency, had silver rupee, copper currency, round and square coins were minted by Akbar, Ilahi coins were gold coins made to promote Din-i-Illahi, the largest gold coin was the Shahanshah.

Foreign Travellers in India

- **Megasthenes (302-298 BC):** Greek Ambassdor, who visited the Mauryan capital Patliputra during the reign of Chandragupta Maurya, Indica is written by him.
- **Al-Masudi (10th century AD)**
  - He was An Arab traveller.
  - In his book Muruj-ul-Zehab, he has explained his journey.
- **Fa-Hien (399-414 AD):** From China, Record of Buddhistic Kingdoms in his book, visited during the reign of Chandragupta II.
- **Hiuen Tsang (630-645 AD):** From China, came to India through Silk Route, during the reign of Harshavardhana, Si-Yu-Ki is his book.
- **Nicolo Conti - 1420 A.D. – 1421 A.D.**
  - He was an Italian merchant.
  - He visited India during the reign of Deva Raya I of Vijayanagar.
- **Abdur Razzak 1443 A.D. – 1444 A.D.**
  - He was a Persian scholar.
  - He was also an ambassador of Persia.
  - He visited India during the rule of Deva Raya II of Vijayanagar.
- **Al Biruni (1024-1030 AD):** Fascinated by Indian culture and studied Sanskrit, Indian philosophy, Kitab-ul-Hind is written by him, tried to explain the caste system.
- **Marco Polo (1254-1324 AD):** Italian merchant, visited the Kakatiya kingdom; his book explained the economic history of India.
- **Ibn Battuta (1333-1347 AD):** Moroccan traveller, visited India during the reign of Muhammad bin Tughlaq, Rihla is the book written by him.

Unit-4: Miscellaneous

Bhakti and Sufi Movements

Bhakti Movement

It originated in the Southern part of India, especially in Tamil Nadu. Mentions in Katha, Upanishad and the Bhagavad Gita.

There were two groups within it in South India:

- Nayanars (Tamil saints devoted to Lord Shiva, believed in extreme asceticism),
- Alvars (propagated Vaishnavism and regarded Vishnu or Krishna as the supreme beings).

They both opposed Brahmanical domination, opposed Buddhism and Jainism and laid the foundation of the Bhakti movement.

- **Causes for origin:** In response to Brahmanical orthodoxy and rigidity in the caste system, emphasised the quality of mankind and attracted a marginalised section of the society.
- **Features of the Bhakti movement:** Love and devotion as a means of salvation, rejected rituals, believed in Universalism, against caste and gender discrimination, men and women both were followers, condemned the practice of Sati, believed in the idea of personal God, against priests who acted as a middleman.
- **Two schools of Bhakti were:**
  - **Nirguna** focus on acquiring knowledge; (believed God as formless with no attributes or qualities, condemned

every form of idol worship, Kabir, Guru Nanak and Dadu Dayal were from this school).

- **Saguna** stressed on love and devotion; (believed in the incarnation of God, believed in idols and image worship, accepted the authority of Vedas and need for human Guru. Ramanuja, Chaitanya Mahaprabhu belonged to it).
- **Impact of the Bhakti movement:** Able to uplift the position of women and lower strata of society, developed a philosophy of charity and service to humans.

Sufi Movement

Features: Ultimate goal was union with God, love of God meant love for humanity, believed in the spirit of tolerance, rejected elaborate rituals, secular in nature, believed in equality and universal brotherhood, believed in the purification of hearts.

There were three stages of Sufism: Khanqah, Tariqa and Tarifa.

- **Different types of Sufi Orders were:**
- **Ba-shara** (favoured Sharia law and law of Islam, silsilah orders founded by these) and
- **Be-shara** (against Sharia law, were wanderers and came to be known as babas, practiced harsh form asceticism).
- **Different Silsilah under Sufism are:**
- **Chishti** (founded by Khwaja Moinuddin Chishti, believes in 'panthetic monoism').
- **Suhrawardi Silsilah** (believed that three attributes of property, knowledge and hal should be owned by Sufis).
- **Qadiriyya Silsilah** (supported Wahadat al wajud).
- **Naqshbandi Silsilah** (Ahmad Sirhindi most popular saints, became popular during Akbar and Aurangzeb was its followers).
- **Sattari Silsilah** (Tansen was its followers, became popular in Malwa, Jaunpur and Bengal).
- **Kubrawiya Order** (also known as Firdausia silsilah).
- **Impact of Sufism:** Bridged the gap between Hindus and Muslims, brought peace and harmony in society and influenced people from urban and rural areas.

Important Personalities of India

- **Chanakya:** Royal advisor of the Mauryan dynasty, also known as Kautilya or Vishnugupta, Arthashastra and Chanakya Niti are his famous works.
- **Ashoka:** The greatest ruler of the Mauryan Empire, won the battle of Kalinga, made Buddhism as his state religion and built stupas and viharas for Buddhists.
- **Samudra Gupta:** Performed Ashvamedha, was a poet and musician, Harisena was his court poet, also known as Kaviraj.
- **Kalidasa:** The greatest Sanskrit poet of the world, belonged to the Gupta period, and have written many plays and poems.
- **Dharmapala:** Ruler of the Pala dynasty, follower of Buddhism, revived Nalanda University and founded the Vikramshila University.
- **Amir Khusrau:** Referred to as Parrot of India, father of Qawwali, invented sitar, originator of Khayal and Tarana style of music, Laila Majnu and Ashiqa was written by him, poet of Delhi Sultanate.
- **Marco Polo:** Italian traveller, who visited during the Pandyas.
- **Muhammad Bin Tughlaq:** Introduced token money in his kingdoms, and Ibn Battuta visited his court.
- **Akbar:** Followed Din-i-illahi, and had navratnas or nine jewels in his court. Akbarnama is the biography of Akbar written by Abul Fazl.
- **Ramakrishna Paramahamsa:** Swami Vivekananda was his disciple who founded Ramakrishna Mission.

Arts and Cultural Institutions in India

Institutions	Headquarters / Location
Anthropological Survey of India, 1945	Kolkata
Archaeological Survey of India, 1861	New Delhi
Asiatic Society, 1784	Kolkata
Indira Gandhi National Centre for Arts, 1985	New Delhi
Lalit Kala Academy, 1954	New Delhi
National Archives of India, 1981	New Delhi
National School of Drama, 1959	New Delhi
Sahitya Academy, 1954	New Delhi
Sangeet Natak Academy, 1953	New Delhi
Science City, 1997	Kolkata
Victoria Memorial Hall	Kolkata
Indian Council for Cultural Relations	New Delhi
Indian Institute of Islamic Studies	New Delhi
National Book Trust, 1957	New Delhi
National Gallery of Modern Art	New Delhi
National Handicrafts and Handlooms Museum	New Delhi
National Library of India	Kolkata
Central Institute of Buddhist Studies	Leh
Birla Industrial and Tech Museum	Kolkata
Centre for Cultural Resources and Training	New Delhi
Indian National Trust for Art and Cultural Heritage, 1984	New Delhi
National Museum of India	New Delhi
The Mehrangarh Museum Trust	Jodhpur
The Government Museum and Art Gallery	Chandigarh

One Liners

- The Sangai Festival is celebrated in Manipur.
- Elephant festival is celebrated annually in Jaipur.
- 'Me-Dam-Me-Phi' is a communal festival. It is observed by the Ahom or Tai-Ahom, ethnic community that is spread across the states of Assam and Arunachal Pradesh.
- Iron craft is the traditional work of the Agaria tribe.
- A Fire temple is a place of worship for Zoroastrians.
- The Barabar Hill Caves are the oldest surviving rock-cut caves in India.
- Matrimandir is located in Pondicherry.
- The Chapchar Kut is a festival of Mizoram. It is celebrated in March.
- The Bhimbetka rock shelters are an archaeological site of the Palaeolithic period. It is located in Madhya Pradesh.
- Kambala Sport is held in Karnataka.
- Castle Naggar heritage site is located in Himachal Pradesh.
- Gudi Padwa is celebrated on the first day of the month of Chaitra (March-April). The day is celebrated as New Year's Day for the people of Maharashtra.
- Christianity is currently the world's largest religion by number of followers.
- Chakan Gaan-Ngai, a post-harvest festival is celebrated in Manipur.
- Hornbill Festival is celebrated in Nagaland.
- Akshardham temple is situated in Delhi. It is dedicated to Hindu deity Swami Narayan.
- Rajgir Mahotsav is celebrated in Bihar.
- The birth place of Guru Nanak is Nankana Sahib.
- The famous painter Vincent van Gogh belonged to Netherlands.
- Pablo Picasso belonged to Spain.
- Nand Lal Bose, Manjit Bawa, Tyeb Mehta are Painters.
- Warli painting is a style of tribal art. This tribal art was originated in Maharashtra.
- Raja Harishchandra, an early Indian film was produced by Dada Saheb Phalke.
- Homi Vyarawalla is acclaimed as India's first Lady Photojournalist.
- Ikebana is Japanese art of flower arrangement.
- The technique of mural painting executed upon freshly laid lime plaster is known as Fresco.
- Ramkinker Baij was a well-known sculptor.
- Chamba is famous for embroidered handkerchief.
- Indian Council for Cultural Relations was founded by Maulana Abul Kalam Azad.
- Irula tribe well-known for snake-catching are native to Tamil Nadu.
- Kondapalli the place famous for toys is located in Andhra Pradesh.
- The city famous for its Chikankari work of embroidery is Lucknow.
- Film and Television Institute of India located in Pune.
- Japanese art of paper folding is known as Origami.
- Chatkora dance is the folk dance of Korku tribe of Madhya Pradesh.
- Devanagari script is used to write Haryanvi language.
- Lathmar Holi is celebrated in Barsana.
- Bihu is post-harvest folk dance in Assam.
- Aadiperukku commonly known as the Aadi Monson Festival is celebrated during months of July/ August in the Indian State of Tamil Nadu.
- Kajri is a song sung during rainy season.
- Maha Kumbh Mela is generally organized every 12 years.
- Piliya will be sung during occasion of birth.
- Jon Beel Mela is the only fair in India where barter system is still used. Jon Beel Mela is a three-day annual indigenous Tiwa Community fair held the weekend of Magh Bihu at a historic place known as Dayang Belguri at Joonbeel (Assam).

❑❑❑

World Geography

Unit-1: The Universe

Some Important Definitions

- **Cosmic:** This term is related to the universe or cosmos.
- **Cosmos:** Cosmos is another name of the Universe.
- **Cosmic Rays**
- Cosmic rays are very powerful atomic nuclei or other particles that move through space nearly at speed of light. Their speeds vary depending on their origin and interactions with magnetic fields. They originate from the Sun, from outside of the Solar System in our own galaxy,and from distant galaxies.
- It causes Cancer.
- **Cosmology:** The scientific study of the large scale properties of the universe as a whole.
- **Cosmological:** It is related to the origin and growth of the Universe.
- **Astronomy**
- Astronomy is the deep scientific study of celestial objects such as Star, planets, comets etc. and everything that originates outside the Earth's atmosphere like gravitational waves, solar winds etc.

Origin of Universe

There are three most famous theories related to the origination of Universe i.e.:

- Steady State Theory
- Pulsating or Oscillating Universe Theory
- Big Bang Theory
- **Steady State Theory:**
- It was given by Herman Bondi, Fred Hoyle and Thomas Gold.
- According to this theory, the universe has neither a beginning nor an end in which an old galaxy shifts apart and new galaxies are formed in the vacant region.
- **Pulsating or Oscillating Universe Theory**
- Pulsating universe theory is said that the universe expands and contracts alternately i.e it pulsates. The universe is expanding at present. It is explained by the phenomenon of the Red shift.The Collapse of matter is called the Big Crunch.
- **The Big Bang Theory**
- A big explosion occurred about 13.8 billion years ago. Due to this high intensity explosion the matter was broken into very small pieces which scattered in all directions with very high velocities and formed stars and galaxies. At present time they are still moving away from one another.
- The galaxies are receding away from each other; it is proven by the shift of the spectrum towards the red end.
- The majority of atoms produced by the Big Bang were hydrogen and helium along with trace amounts of lithium.

Galaxies

- The collection of the huge mass of stars, nebulae and interstellar material is known as Galaxy. About 1, 00, 000 stars are present in the smallest galaxies while the largest ones contain up to 3000 billion stars.

Types of Galaxies: 3 Types of Galaxies

- **Spiral Galaxies**
- Contain spiral arms of interstellar matter and are flattened discs.
- In the center of the spiral galaxy there is a great concentration of stars.
- Example: The Andromeda Galaxy and Milky Way Galaxy.
- **Elliptical Galaxies**
- These types of galaxies have a symmetrical elliptical or spheroidal shape with no clearly defined internal structures.
- It contains a big number of old red stars and has very little raw material for the formation of new stars.
- Approximately 15–20% of galaxies of our universe are elliptical.
- **Irregular Galaxies**
- These types of galaxies do not have a common axis so they don't spin regularly.
- Irregular galaxies are occupied with gases and layers of dust and they are comparatively lighter ones.

The Milky-way Galaxy

- It is a medium size spiral galaxy. It contains 100 billion stars and its diameter is 100,000 light years and thickness is 10,000 light years from the center.
- The Milky-way Galaxy has the shape of a flat disc with a central bulge. From the galactic center our solar system is 25,000 light years away.
- The sun completes one lap of the galaxy in about every 230 million years and is about 2/3rd out from the center.
- The Solar System is located in the Orion Arm, 25,000 light years from the centre (about two-third from the center) of the Milky Way galaxy.

Facts about Andromeda Galaxy

- The Andromeda Galaxy is the biggest among the local group of galaxies. Andromeda is also bigger than our galaxy (Milky-way).

  Note: "Andromeda was traditionally considered the largest galaxy in the Local Group, though recent studies suggest the Milky Way may be comparable in mass."
- This galaxy is 10 billion times more luminous than our Sun.
- Light from Andromeda takes 2.5 million years to reach the Earth.

Stars

- Stars are born in nebulae and they are bodies of hot glowing gas.
- Its surface temperature ranges from about 3,000°C to 50,000°C.
- Stars contain some gases they are:
- Hydrogen: 92.1%
- Helium: 7.8%
- Other Gases: 0.1%
- Proxima centauri is the nearest star to earth even when light comes from there takes 4.24 light years to reach us. There is a nuclear fusion of hydrogen into helium in the

star's core. Due to this reaction a huge amount of energy is released and stars become shining.

Star Life Cycle

- **Birth of a Star**
- The Cradle of stars are Nebulae because they have the same chemical composition as that of stars (mostly Hydrogen and Helium).
- The gravitational contraction from vast clouds of galactic gas and dust are the main reason behind star formation.
- **Protostars**
- A Protostar looks like a star, but its core is not yet hot enough for nuclear fusion to take place (nuclear fusion: the fusion of 2 hydrogen atoms into a helium atom with the liberation of a huge amount of energy. Nuclear fusion occurs only when the initial temperatures are very high – a few million degree Celsius. That is why it is hard to achieve and control).
- **Red Giant**
- Red giants have diameters between 100 to 1,000 times that of the Sun.
- They are very bright, although their surface temperature is lower than that of the Sun.
- A red giant is formed during the later stages of the evolution as it runs out of hydrogen fuel at its center.
- **White Dwarf**
- A white dwarf is a very small, hot star, the last stage in the life cycle of a star like the Sun. White dwarfs are the remains of normal stars, whose nuclear energy supplies have been used up. White dwarf consists of degenerate matter with a very high density due to gravitational effects, i.e. one spoonful has a mass of several tonnes.
- **Black Dwarf**
- The last stage of stellar evolution is a black dwarf.
- A black dwarf is a white dwarf that has sufficiently cooled that it no longer emits significant heat or light.
- **Massive Stars**
- These stars have an extremely high amount of energy and they have a mass at least three times that of a Sun. After passing through the main sequence stage a massive star becomes a red supergiant.
- It contracts to become a black hole when the core is greater than 3 solar masses.

Unit-2: The Solar System

- Our solar system consists of the sun, eight major planets, dwarf planets (Pluto, Ceres, Eris etc.), satellites and countless minor planets, asteroids, meteors, comets and debris.
- The mass of the solar system near about 99.85% is contained within the sun.

The Sun

- The Sun is at a distance of 25,000 light years from the center of our galaxy Milky-way and located in one of the spiral arms of it.
- In 230 million years the sun revolves around once to the centre of the galaxy. This time period is known as Cosmos Years.
- The distance between the sun and the earth is approximately 149.6 million kilometers (93 million miles) and the light coming from the sun takes 8 minutes and 20 seconds to reach the earth.
- The diameter of the sun is 13,91,016 km and its age is about 4.6 billion years.
- At its axis the sun completes a single rotation in about 27 days.

Chemical Composition of the Sun

- Hydrogen-92.1%
- Helium-7.8%
- Other Gases-0.1%
- Nuclear fusion is the main source of enormous energy of the Sun. Four hydrogen nuclei fuse to form a helium nucleus in this process of fusion.

Structure of the Sun

- **Core**
- Core is the centre region of the Sun and it forms 25% of the radius of the Sun.
- The temperature of the core is 15,000,000°C.
- **Photosphere**
- Photosphere is the visible surface of the Sun.
- The temperature of the photosphere surface is approximately 5500°C.
- **Chromosphere**
- The surface which is present above till 400-2100 kms the photosphere.
- Above 23,000 K, the Chromosphere consists of ionized hydrogen and helium atoms.
- **Corona**
- The corona is the outermost part of the Sun's atmosphere visible during the time of full solar eclipse.
- Corona is a region of highly rarefied and hot gasses which spreads millions of kilometers in space.
- It is a distinctive atmosphere of plasma that surrounds the Sun and other celestial bodies.
- **Sunspots**
- Sunspot is a dark patch on the surface of the Sun.
- Sunspots are relatively about 500-1500°C cooler than the surrounding chromosphere so it appears as a dark spot.
- The darker surface is known as Umbra and that region which is surrounded by a slightly less dark area is known as Penumbra.
- **Solar Wind**
- The Solar wind flows outward from the Sun at the speed of 900 km/s and at a temperature of 1 million degrees Celsius. It is made of ionized atoms called plasma.
- Effects of solar wind – Aurora

Bodies of the Solar System

- **Planets:** Mercury, Venus, Earth, Mars, Jupiter, Saturn, Uranus and Neptune.
- **Dwarf Planets:** Pluto, Ceres, Haumea, Eris, Makemake
- **Minor Bodies:** Satellites, meteors, comets, Asteroids, etc.

Planets

- All the planets are celestial bodies which revolve around the sun or star is known as a planet.
- According to their characteristics the planets of our solar system can be divisible in two groups:

- **Inner Planets**
- The planets which are made up of rocks and metals and they have relatively high density. As they lie between the sun and the belts of asteroids.
- The inner circle consists of four planets: i. Mercury, ii. Venus, iii. Earth, iv. Mars.
- **Outer Planets**
- Jupiter, Saturn, Uranus, Neptune and the dwarf planet Pluto are known as Outer Planets. They mainly consist of gas so the four outer planets are called the gas giants.
- The outer planets are composed mainly of hydrogen and helium which lack a solid surface but their moons are solid.
- Planets in increasing order according to their distance from the sun:

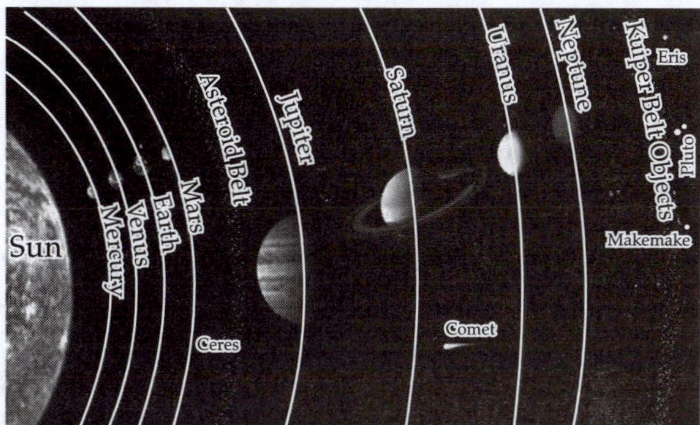

1. Mercury 2. Venus
3. Earth 4. Mars
5. Jupiter 6. Saturn
7. Uranus 8. Neptune

- Planets according to their Size (large to small):

1. Jupiter (Largest planet of our solar system)
2. Saturn 3. Uranus
4. Neptune 5. Earth
6. Venus 7. Mars
8. Mercury

- **Mercury**
- Mercury is also called God of Commerce and Skills.
- It is the nearest planet to the sun and also the smallest one.
- Mercury has no atmosphere to retain heat so its day temperature is about 430°C and the night temperature falls below 170°C.
- Mercury revolves around the sun in only 88 days and its rotational period is 59 days.
- On the surface of Mercury there are many craters. Caloris Basin Crater is the biggest among them with a diameter of 1300 km.
- **Venus**
- Venus is also known as the Veiled planet,Goddess Venus of beauty. It is similar to the Earth in size, mass and density so it is considered as Earth's twin.
- Venus is the third brightest object visible from earth after the sun and the moon.
- Just before the sunrise it is clearly visible so it is also known as the morning star.
- Venus is also visible immediately after sunset in the evening so it is also known as the evening star.
- Venus rotates very slowly and it takes 243 earth days to complete one rotation.
- It rotates in the opposite direction (clockwise or i.e from east to west) to most other planets.
- To complete a revolution around the Sun it takes 224.7 earth days.
- The highest place on Venus is Maxwell Montes which is nearly 800 km wide and 11 km high.
- The highest plateau of Venus is Lakshmi Planum.
- **Earth**
- Earth is also known as The Blue Planet.
- Earth is the fifth largest planet of the solar system and is the only planet where life exists.
- It is located in the life favored ecosphere of the Sun.
- The Earth's atmosphere is very dense and contains enough oxygen and water vapor.
- It is called Blue Planet because it has the largest and most continuous oceans in our solar system.
- In 23 hours 56 minutes and 4.1 seconds it completes one rotation and is inclined at an angle of 23.5 degrees.
- Stars appear as rotating along concentric circular paths when they are observed from one of the poles of the Earth. The celestial pole is the imaginary centre of such circular paths.
- **Satellite of the Earth**
- The Moon is the only satellite of the Earth.
- **Moon**
  - **Selenology** is the scientific study of the Moon.
  - Moon is about 3,84,400 km away from us.
  - Light takes only 1.3 second to reach us from the Moon.
  - It revolves around once to the Earth in 27 days, 7 hours, 43 minutes and also rotates on its own axis in the same period of time. Hence only one side of the moon is visible to us on the earth.
  - On 20 July 1969 Neil Armstrong was the first, and Buzz Aldrin was the second who stepped on the surface of the moon (Apollo 11 mission).
  - **Mons Huygens (18046 ft)** is the highest mountain on the moon.
  - Largest basins on the moon are The South Pole-Aitken (SPA) basin
- **Mars**
- Mars is also known as the Red Planet and God of War.
- The Mars surface glows with a reddish light due to the presence of iron rich red soil so it is called the Red Planet.
- Mars has only two satellites i.e.
  - Phobos
  - Deimos
- The atmosphere of Mars consists of:
  - 95.32% carbon dioxide,
  - 1.6% argon and
  - 2.7% nitrogen along with traces of oxygen and water.
- It rotates on its own axis once in 24 hours and 37 minutes while it is inclined at an angle of 25° to the plane of its orbit.
- Mars has seasons much like the Earth since this is much similar to Earth.
- **Jupiter**
- Jupiter is also known as the Giant Planets and Ruler of Gods.
- This is the biggest planet in our solar system.
- Jupiter contains mostly Hydrogen and Helium gases, it is a huge sphere of gas.It is composed mostly of gas and

liquid swirling in complex patterns with no solid surface.

- It takes about 11.9 terrestrial years while revolving around the Sun and it takes only 9.9 hours for a spin about its own axis.
- Due to its fast rotation, it causes a swirling storm of gasses that moves in a counter-clockwise direction which is known as the Great Red Spot.
- It is a source of radio waves.
- It has as many as 101 satellites. In 1610 Galileo discovered its four big satellites known as Galilean Satellites. Name of its four big satellites which was discovered by Galileo:
  - Lo
  - Europa
  - Ganymede
  - Callisto
- The largest satellite of Jupiter is Ganymede (5268 km in diameter)which is slightly bigger than Mercury.

- **Saturn**

- Saturn is also known as The Ringed Planet and God of Agriculture.
- It has the lowest density (0.687 g/cm^3) among the entire planets and also the second largest planet of the solar system.
- Its rings are probably made up of billions of particles of ice and ice-covered rocks.
- It is also a gaseous planet which contains mainly hydrogen and helium gases.
- Saturn rotates very fast and its spin period is 10 hours 32 minutes.
- Saturn's satellite Titan is the second-largest moon in the solar system and the only satellite with a substantial atmosphere. The total number of Saturn's satellites is 274.
- An Anne spot of red color, 6000 km long is seen on the surface of Saturn.

- **Uranus**

- Uranus is also known as The Green planet and God of Heaven.
- Uranus is the third largest planet in the solar system which was discovered by William Herschel in 1781.
- Venus and Uranus have a strange retrograde rotation (clockwise), i.e., opposite of the sun's rotation.
- To complete one revolution around the Sun Uranus takes 84 years and takes 17.25 hours for one rotation about its own axis.
- Uranus has 27 satellites and many rings around its equatorial plane which is formed by ice and large rocks, seen around the equator.
- Uranus atmosphere is very dense and its atmosphere contains:
  - Hydrogen- 83%
  - Helium- 15%
  - Methane- 2%
- Uranus's five most important satellites are:
  - Titania
  - Oberon
  - Ariel
  - Umbriel
  - Miranda

- **Neptune**

- Neptune is also known as a twin of Uranus and God of Sea.
- Neptune is surrounded by a thick atmosphere of hydrogen and helium and contains a higher proportion of "ices" such as water, ammonia, and methane ice giants" to emphasize this distinction.
- It was discovered by Johann Gottfried Galle, who used calculations by John Adams and Le verrier.
- In the order of distance from the sun Neptune is the eighth planet of the solar system.
- It has the strongest sustained winds (2,100 km/h) of any planet in the Solar System.
- Neptune has 16 satellites and 45 rings. Like Jupiter and Saturn, it also has an internal source of heat energy.
- Triton is the largest satellite of Neptune.

Dwarf Planets

- **IAU's definition of Dwarf planet:** Dwarf planet is an object that meets planetary criteria except that it has not cleared debris from its orbital neighborhood. Example, Pluto.

- **Pluto**

- When it discovered in 1930, it was considered to be the ninth planet; this changed in 2006 with the adoption of a formal definition of a planet.
- International Astronomical Union's definition of a Planet:
- A Planet is an object that:
  - orbits the sun;
  - has sufficient mass to assume hydrostatic equilibrium — a nearly round shape;
  - is not a satellite (moon) of another object, and
  - has removed debris and small objects from the area around its orbit.

- So, if Pluto is considered a planet, then many other objects like Eris will also have to be considered as planets.
- Hence, Pluto (diameter: 2,377 km) (Kuiper belt) was voted by IAU as a dwarf planet just like Ceres (asteroid belt) and Eris (diameter: 2,326 km) (Kuiper belt).
- Charon is the largest moon of Pluto.

- **Ceres**
- Ceres (2.77 AU) is the largest asteroid (946 km in diameter), a protoplanet, and a dwarf planet.
- Ceres has a mass large enough for its own gravity to pull it into a spherical shape.

Minor Bodies

- **Asteroids**

- They are heavenly bodies which formed between the orbits of Mars and Jupiter. Asteroids (planetoids — another term for an asteroid) are composed mainly of refractory rocky and metallic minerals, with some ice.
- **Amos:** Amos are those asteroids which meet the orbit of Mars.
- **Apollo:** Those asteroids which meet the orbit of Earth.
- **Athens:** Those asteroids which have orbits of radius less than that required to meet the orbit of Earth.
- The asteroid belt lies between 2.3 and 3.3 AU from the Sun.
- **Largest Asteroid:** Ceres (Diameter-946 km)

- **Comets**

- Comets are made of frozen gasses (water, ammonia, methane and carbon dioxide) which hold together small pieces of rocky and metallic minerals. They are celestial bodies which are chunks of ice, frozen gas and rock particles.
- When comets come near to the Sun, its frozen gas vaporizes due to the solar energy and produces a glowing head called the coma.
- Comets start burning with a tail that can stretch a million km. Its tail is always positioned away from the Sun.
- **Some Important Comets:**
  - Halley's Comet- It comes after every 76 years.
  - Shoemaker Levy-9
  - Hale-Bopp

- **Meteors**
  - Meteors are popularly known as shooting stars because when they are traveling at a great speed through space which becomes luminous during entering the atmosphere at about 200 km above the earth's surface due to heat produced by friction.
  - In some cases, the meteoroid does not burn up completely and makes its way to the Earth's surface. But a few larger ones reach the ground and are called meteorites.

Some Important Facts related to the Planets

Planets	Number of Satellites	Radius (km)	Rotation Days/ Hours	Revolution Days/Years	Distance from Sun Lakh km
Mercury	0	2,440	58.6 days	87.97 days	579
Venus	0	6,052	243 days	224.7 days	1082
Earth	1	6,371	23.9 hours	365.26 days	1496
Mars	2	3,390	24.6 hours	687 days	2279
Jupiter	**101**	69,911	9.9 hours	11.9 years	7786
Saturn	**274**	58,232	10 hours 32 minutes	29.5 years	14335
Uranus	**27**	25,362	17.2 hours	84 years	28725
Neptune	**16**	24,622	16.6 hours	164.8 years	44951

Asteroid Belt

- An area between Mars and Jupiter where many of these rocks orbit the Sun is known as the asteroid belt.

Kuiper Belt

- The Kuiper Belt is similar to the asteroid belt which is a circumstellar disc in the solar system beyond the planets.
- Kuiper Belt has three recognised dwarf planets:
  - Pluto
  - Haumea
  - Makemake
- It consists of remnants of the solar system's formation and small bodies.

Unit-3: Motion of the Earth, Imaginary Lines and Time-Zones

Rotational Motion

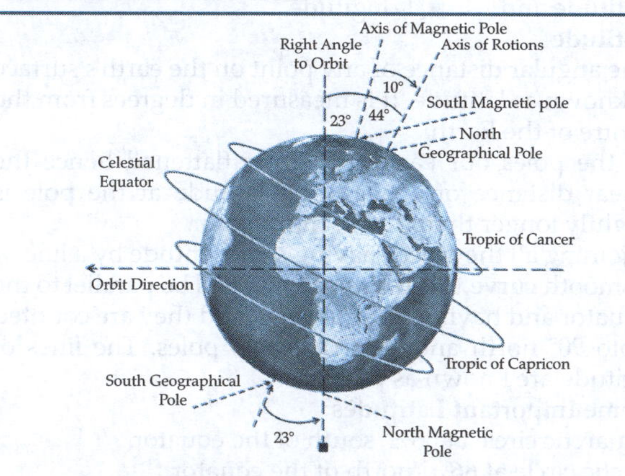

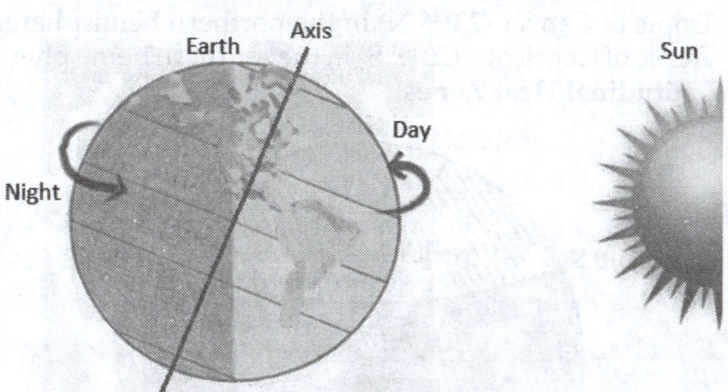

- In 23 hours, 56 minutes, and 4 seconds earth rotates on its own axis from west to east. This motion is known as rotation of the earth.
- It rotates on a tilted axis.
- The phenomenon of day and night occurring on the earth is due to its rotation on its axis.
- **Circle of illumination:** The circle that divides the day from night on the globe is called the circle of illumination.
- With the normal earth rotational axis,it makes an angle of 23.5° while with its orbit plane it makes an angle of 66.5°. The plan of Earth's orbit around the Sun is called the orbital plane.

Revolutional Motion of the Earth

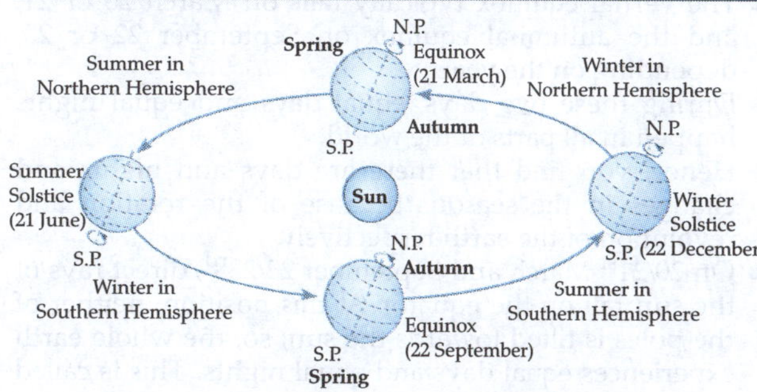

- In 365 days, 5 hours, 48 minutes and 46 seconds the earth revolves around the sun in an orbit. This motion of the Earth is known as revolutionary motion.
- Due to this motion the phenomenon of seasons change occurs on the earth.
- **Leap Year:** Every year during the revolution of the Sun,earth saves six hours which are added to make one day (24 hours) over a span of four years. This surplus day is added to the month of February. Due to this addition every fourth year, February is 29 days instead of 28 days. Such a year with 366 days is called a leap year.

Distance of the Earth from the Sun

- The distance between the Sun and the Earth changes due to the revolution motion of the Earth. We can divide this distance into two phases:

- **Perihelion:** Perihelion is the position of the earth where the distance between the sun and the earth is minimum and It is about 14.73 crore km. On January 3, every year the distance between them is minimum due to the elliptical orbit of the earth around the sun.
- **Aphelion:** Aphelion is the position of the earth in which the earth is farthest from the sun on July 4 every year. At this time the earth is said to be in Aphelion. During Aphelion the distance between them is 15.21 crore km.

Solstice

Solstice phenomenon can be divided into 2 types:

- Summer Solstice
- Winter Solstice
- **Summer Solstice**
- The North Pole of the Earth is tilted towards the sun on June 21 due to this recline,the sun is overhead at the Tropic of Cancer with an angle of 23.5°N. The rays of the sun fall directly on the Tropic of Cancer. As a result, these areas receive more heat.
- This day is known as Summer Solstice,during summer Solstice period, the northern hemisphere will have its longest day and shortest night.
- **Winter Solstice**
- The southern hemisphere of the Earth is tilted towards the sun on 22 December, while the sun is vertical at the Tropic of Capricorn with an angle of 23.5°S.
- A larger portion of the southern hemisphere of earth gets light. Hence, there is summer in the southern hemisphere with longer days and shorter nights while the reverse happens in the northern hemisphere. This position of the earth is called the winter solstice.

Equinox

- The vernal equinox typically falls on March 20 or 21, and the autumnal equinox on September 22 or 23, depending on the year.
- During these two days, equal days and equal nights happen in all parts of the world.
- Hence, you find that there are days and nights and changes in the seasons because of the rotation and revolution of the earth respectively.
- On 20/21st March and September 22/23rd, direct rays of the sun fall on the equator. At this position, neither of the poles is tilted towards the sun; so, the whole earth experiences equal days and equal nights. This is called an equinox.
- Equinox are basically of two types:
- Spring or Vernal Equinox
- Autumnal Equinox
- In the northern hemisphere there is spring season while autumn season in the Southern hemisphere on March 20 or 21.
- Hence the day is known as the Spring equinox.
- **Autumnal Equinox:**
- On 22 or 23rd September, there is autumn season in the northern hemisphere and spring season in the southern hemisphere.
- Thus the day is known as the Autumnal equinox.

Note

- **Earth's Rotation:** Causes Day and Night
- **Earth's Revolution:** Causes Season Change
- **Equinoxes:**
- All latitudes have equal day and night-12 hours.
- 20 or 21st March and 22 or 23rd September.

Duration of the Day

- At an angle of 66.5° the axis of the Earth is tilted to the plane of the ecliptic, due to this inclination it is gives different seasons and varying lengths of day and night.
- During the winter season (December)when one goes northwards in the northern hemisphere so the length of day gradually decreases.
- During the mid-winter of 22 December at the Arctic Circle (angle of 66.5°), there is darkness for the whole day and the sun never rises.
- Beyond the Arctic Circle the number of days with complete darkness increases until one reaches North Pole (90°N), when the half the year will have darkness.
- During the summer (June) there is a totally different phenomenon that occurs at the Arctic Circle, the conditions are totally reversed and daylight increases as one goes polewards. The sun never sets at mid-summer 21 June at the Arctic Circle and there is a whole 24-hour period of continuous daylight.
- The region north of the Arctic Circle is generally known as the Land of the Midnight Sun during summer seasons. Norway is known as the Land of the Midnight Sun.
- It is an interesting phenomenon that there will be six months of continuous daylight at the North Pole.
- Our Earth's shape is 'Geoid' so the location of a place on the earth can be mentioned with the help of latitudes and longitudes.
- Imaginary lines of the Earth can be divided into two types:
- Latitude and
- Longitude
- **Latitude**
- The angular distance of any point on the earth's surface is known as latitude. It is measured in degrees from the centre of the Earth.
- At the poles our earth is slightly flattened hence the linear distance of a degree of latitude at the pole is slightly longer than that at the equator.
- If joining all the places having same latitude by a line or a smooth curve,this produced line will be parallel to the equator and having an angle of 0° and they are counted upto 90° north and south,the two poles. The lines of latitude are known as parallels.
- **Some Important Latitudes:**
- Antarctic circle at 66½° south of the equator.
- Arctic circle at 66½° north of the equator.
- Tropic of Cancer (23½° N) in the northern hemisphere.
- Tropic of Capricorn (23½° S) in the southern hemisphere.
- **Latitudinal Heat Zones:**

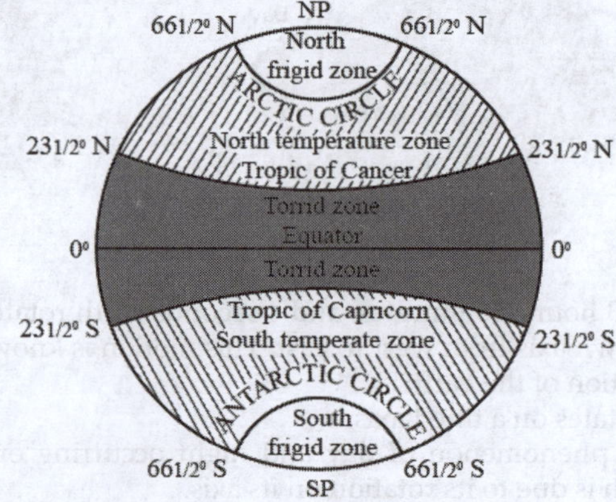

Heat zones.

- **Torrid Zone:** In all latitudes which are present in between the region of the Tropic of Cancer and the Tropic of Capricorn, here the mid-day sun is exactly overhead at least once a year. Hence this region receives the maximum heat and this is called the torrid zone.
- **Temperate Zone:** On any latitude beyond the Tropic of Cancer and the Tropic of Capricorn here the mid-day sun never shines overhead. Towards the poles the angel of the sun's rays goes on decreasing. Due to this reason, the area bounded by the Tropic of Capricorn and the Antarctic Circle in the southern hemisphere and the Tropic of Cancer and the Arctic Circle in the northern hemisphere have moderate temperatures. These are called temperate zones.
- **Frigid Zone:** These zones are very cold, lying between the Arctic Circle and the North Pole in the northern hemisphere and the area of the Antarctic Circle and the South Pole in the southern hemisphere because at the horizon the Sun does not rise much above so its rays are always slanting. These are called frigid zones.
- **Longitude**

- It is an angular distance of a pole, measured in degrees along the equator earth east or west of the Prime Meridian.
- When observing the globe the longitudinal lines are shown as a series of semi circles which pass through pole to pole and cut through the equator. Such lines are known as longitudinal lines.
- Prime Meridian: It is 0° longitude that runs through Greenwich near London where the British Royal Observatory is situated.
- The British Royal Observatory has a very important function that determines local time in relation to G.M.T. or Greenwich Mean Time, which is sometimes referred to as World Time.
- Meridians are separated by 1°of longitude at the equator which is about 111.32 km apart between two meridians.
- Meridians are those lines, joining all places that are situated at the same longitude.

Longitudes and Time

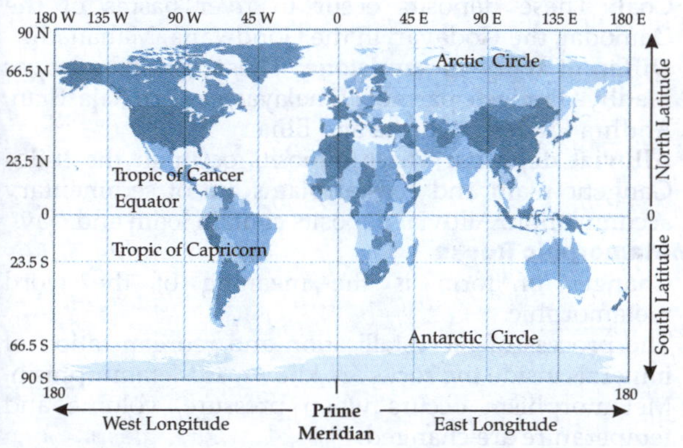

- **Local Time:**

- In one day or 24 hours the earth makes its one complete revolution of 360° and crosses through 15° in one hour or 1° in 4 minutes.
- As we know that the earth rotates from west to east on its own axis, so when we go every 15° eastwards, local time advances by one hour. on the contrary, when we go westwards, local time is retarded by one hour.
- For example: At Prime Meridian if there is 1.00 noon, it will be 2.00 p.m., in all places on the 15°E longitude while 12.00 p.m., in all places on the 15°W longitude.

- **Standard Time**

- There would be much difference in local time between one town and the other if each town were to keep the time of its own meridian.
- A system of standard time is observed by all countries to avoid all these problems.
- Standard Time is the uniform time which is fixed by each country with the relation to the mean time of a central meridian or the meridian which is chosen in such a way that on which the most important city is located.
- It would be inconvenient to have a single time zone in larger countries such as Canada, U.S.A., China, and U.S.S.R., So these countries have multiple time zones.
- This central meridian is divisible by 7.5° hence the standard time differs from GMT in multiples of 30 minutes.

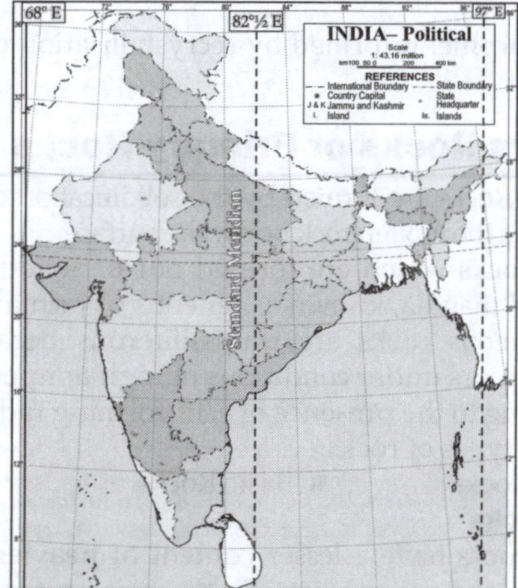

- **Indian Standard Time (IST)**

- The meridian of 82.5°East has been accepted by the Indian Government as the standard time of India which is ahead of Greenwich Mean Time by 5 hours 30 minutes.
- This meridian passes through Naini (Praygraj).

- **The International Date Line**

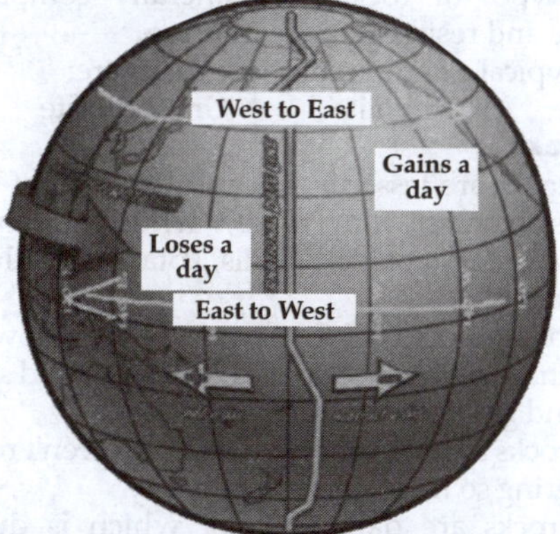

- To avoid the confusion of the difference of one day while traveling across the world by people, the concept of the International Date Line has been produced.
- It correlates with the 180°E or W meridian of longitude; it falls on the opposite side of the Greenwich meridian,

as this line is crossed so the date changes by 1 day or 24 hours.

- The date to the east of it is one day ahead than to its west when it has been counted from the Prime Meridian.
- If we travel westwards of Prime Meridian up to 180°W, we have to put our watch back by 12 hours and while traveling eastwards up to 180°E have to put our watch 12 hours forward.
- The International Date Line in the mid-Pacific curves from the normal 180° meridian at the Bering Strait, Fiji, Tonga and other islands to prevent confusion of day and date in some of the island groups that are cut through by the meridian.

Unit-4: Rocks

- The aggregate of one or more minerals that are held together by chemical bonds are called Rocks.
- The most common minerals found in rocks are
  - Quartz
  - Feldspar
- Petrology is the scientific study of rocks.
- There are three major groups of rocks are defined based on the mode of their formation, they are:
  - **Igneous or primary rocks:** It formed by the solidification of magma and lava.
  - **Sedimentary:** It formed by deposition of fragments of rocks.
  - **Metamorphic:** It formed by recrystallisation of existing rocks.

Igneous Rocks or Primary Rocks

- Igneous Rocks are formed by the solidification of magma. Magma is the molten rock below the surface.
- Those rocks which are formed out of solidification of lava and magma, known as Igneous or primary rocks.
- The igneous rocks are unfossiliferous because their origin occurs under conditions of high temperatures.
- According to the presence of acid-forming radical, there are two types of rocks:
  - Acidic Rocks
  - Basic Rocks

Acidic Rocks

- Acidic rocks have a lesser content of heavier minerals like iron and magnesium. So these rocks are lighter in color than basic rocks and are less dense.
- These rocks are distinguished by high content of silica up to 80%.
- Acidic magma cools fast due to the excess presence of silicon. It does not spread far away and also does not flow.
- The SiAl portion of the crust is made of acidic rocks.
- These types of rocks are generally compact, hard, massive and resistant to weathering.
- Some typical examples of these rocks are:
  - Granite
  - Rhyolite
  - Granodiorite

Basic Rocks

- Basic Rocks are lesser in silica. It has 40% of silica and magnesia content is up to 40% while the remaining is spread over Iron oxide, Alkalis, Potassium, Aluminium, Lime etc.
- The cooling process of these rocks is very slow which is due to the low presence of silica, so it flows and spreads far away and gives rise to plateaus.
- These rocks are not very hard and also aren't resistant to weathering so it weathers very easily.
- These rocks are dark in color which is due to the presence of heavy elements.
- Some typical examples of these rocks are
  - Basalt
  - Gabbro
  - Dolerite

Economic Significance of Igneous Rocks

- Many great economic value minerals are found in igneous rocks, because magma is the main source of metal ores.
- These valuable minerals are
  - Magnetic iron
  - Nickel
  - Copper
  - Lead Zinc
  - Chromite
  - Manganese
  - Gold
  - Diamond and
  - Platinum
- Amygdales (almond-shaped bubbles) are formed in basalt which are filled with minerals. These bubbles are formed in basalt due to escape of gasses.
- The old rocks of the great Indian peninsula are rich in these crystallized minerals or metals.
- Many igneous rocks like granite are used as building materials as they come in beautiful shades.

Sedimentary Rocks or Detrital Rocks

- These rocks are formed by compaction of sediments and lithification consolidation. So they are found in layers or stratified of varying thickness.
- Some examples of it
  - Sandstone
  - Shale
- Sediments are due to the denudation of all types of rocks. Weathering and erosion is known as denudation.
- 75% of Earth's crust is covered by these rocks. They are available only in the upper part of the crust hence it has volumetrically occupied only 5 percent of the crust.

Characteristics of Sedimentary Rocks

- These rocks consist of many layers or strata called stratified.
- These Rocks have the most important geological records due to the presence of marks left behind by many geophysical and biological activities like fossils.
- Sedimentary Rocks allow water to percolate through them and also are porous.
- These rocks have fossils of animals and plants so are known as fossiliferous.

Sedimentary Rocks in India

- **Coal:** These deposits occur in river basins of the Damodar, the Godavari in the Gondwana, Mahanadi.
- **Different types of sandstone:** These are spread over Madhya Pradesh, parts of Himalayas, eastern Rajasthan, Andhra Pradesh, Odisha and Bihar.
- **Alluvial deposits:** These deposits occur in the Indo-Gangetic plain and coastal plains are of sedimentary accumulation. Alluvial deposits contain loam and clay.

Metamorphic Rocks

- Changes of form is the meaning of the word metamorphic.
- The process of recrystallisation and reorganization of minerals inside the rocks are known as Metamorphism.
- Metamorphism occurs when pressure, volume and temperature are changed.

Metamorphosis occurs when

- Rocks are forced down to lower levels by tectonic processes.
- The magma rising through the crust comes in contact with the crustal rocks.
- Some important examples of metamorphic rocks are
  - Gneissoid
  - Slate
  - Schist
  - Marble
  - Quartzsite

Rock Cycle

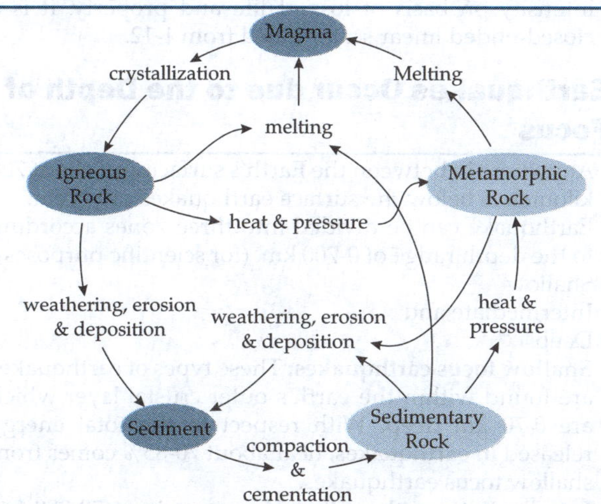

- It is an uninterrupted process where old rocks are transformed into new ones.
- Other rocks are formed from igneous rocks. Igneous rocks are primary rocks.
- Igneous rocks can be changed into sedimentary or metamorphic rocks.
- Sedimentary and igneous rocks can be changed into metamorphic rocks.
- Sedimentary Rocks are also formed by the fragments derived out of igneous and metamorphic rocks.

Minerals that Formed Rocks

- **Quartz:** Quartz is an hexagonal crystalline structure and has two elements silicon and oxygen. Mostly these rocks are uncleaved, white or colorless. It is present in sand, granite and cracks like glass. Quartz crystals are used in manufacturing radio oscillators and radar equipment due to their piezoelectric properties
- **Bauxite:** It is a hydrous oxide of aluminium and also the ore of aluminium. These rocks occur in small pellets and are non-crystalline.
- **Feldspar:** Feldspar main constituents are silicon, oxygen, sodium, potassium, calcium and aluminium. Feldspar rocks are used for ceramics and gloss making. These rocks are lighter in color and half the crust is composed of it.
- **Gypsum:** Gypsum is used in cement, fertilizer and chemical industries. These rocks are hydrous calcium sulphate.
- **Cinnabar or Mercury sulphide:** Cinnabar color is brown and mercury is derived from it.
- **Haematite:** Red ore of iron.
- **Magnetite:** Black ore of iron.
- **Mica:** Earth's 4% crust is formed from it. It is largely used in electrical instruments and it is generally found in igneous and metamorphic rocks. It consists of potassium, aluminium, magnesium, iron, silica etc.
- **Dolomite:** Dolomite is used in cement, iron and steel industries. Color of the dolomite is white. It is a double carbonate of calcium and magnesium.
- **Pyroxene:** The color of Pyroxenes are green or black. It consists of Aluminium, Magnesium, Silica and Iron.
- **Amphibole:** It consists of Aluminium, Calcium, Silica, Iron and Magnesium. 7% of Earth's crust forms of it. Certain fibrous varieties of amphibole minerals are used in the asbestos industry.
- **Olivine:** It is generally a greenish crystal and it consists of Magnesium, Iron and Silica.
- **Other minerals present in rocks are:** Chlorite, Magnetite, Bauxite, Calcite, Hematite, Barite etc.

Unit-5: Earthquake

- **Seismograph:** It is an instrument to detect and record earthquakes.
- **Focus:** Focus is the point of earthquakes from which energy is released. It is also known as the hypocentre of an earthquake.
- **Epicenter:** Epicenter is the point on the earth's surface which is present directly above the focus. It is the surface point which experiences the earthquake waves first.
- **Isoseismal line:** All points are connected on the surface through a line where the intensity of earthquakes are the same is known as isoseismic line.

Aftershocks and Foreshocks

- **Aftershocks:** Many lesser-size earthquakes occur after a major or even moderate earthquake. These lesser-size earthquakes are called Aftershocks.
- **Foreshocks:** When a mild earthquake occurs just before the violent shaking movement of an earthquake. This mild earthquake is known as Foreshock.

Earthquake Swarms

- Sometimes a considerable number of small earthquakes occur in a region without any major earthquakes. These series of earthquakes are called earthquake swarms.
- Such earthquakes that are associated with volcanic activity, these types of earthquakes often occur in swarms.
- It may also serves as markers for the location of the flowing magma throughout the volcanoes.

Causes of Earthquakes

There are mainly four important causes of Earthquakes. They are

- Fault Zones
- Volcanic activity
- Plate tectonics
- Human raised Earthquakes

- **Fault Zones**
  - The sudden release of stress along a fault rupture in the earth's crust is the immediate cause of most shallow earthquakes.
  - The constant change in volume and density of rocks due to intense temperature and pressure in the earth's interior as a result sudden slipped of rock formations along fault rupture in the earth's crust.
  - The resulting magnitude of earthquakes are as higher as the longer the length and the wider the width of the faulted area.
  - Along with the thrust fault, the longest earthquake ruptures are approximately 1000 km.
  - When the longest earthquake ruptures on the strike, slip faults are half to one third as long as the lengths along the thrust fault.

- **Volcanic Activity**
  - Earthquakes can also occur due to volcanic activity but these types of earthquakes are generally less severe and more limited in extent than those occurred by fracturing of the earth's crust.
  - The consequent release of elastic strain energy both by tectonic faults and the movement of magma in volcanoes are the major cause of earthquakes in volcanic regions.
  - These types of earthquakes give an early warning of volcanic eruptions; it was seen in the 1980 eruption of Mount St. Helens.
  - Particularly in the Circum-Pacific Belt and along oceanic ridges there is clear correspondence between the geographic distribution of volcanoes and major earthquakes.
- **Plate Tectonics**
  - Transform boundaries convergent boundaries and divergence along with the faultline and Slipping of land are the main reasons behind earthquakes.
  - The most powerful earthquakes and megathrust earthquakes of magnitude 8 or more are associated with reverse faults or convergent boundaries.
  - Earthquakes associated with normal faults are generally less than magnitude 7.
  - Subduction zones are those zones where the Mega thrust earthquakes occur in which one tectonic plate is forced underneath another. For example: Indian Ocean earthquake 2004.
  - Major earthquakes up to about magnitude 8 can occur due to the strike-slip faults, particularly continental transforms.
  - The Pacific plate and North American plate move horizontally relative to each other at the San Andreas Fault, as a result earthquakes occur along the fault lines.
- **Human Induced Earthquakes**
  - Human activity such as nuclear tests, mining large scale petroleum extraction, artificial lakes or reservoirs, etc. cause typically minor earthquakes and tremors.

Reservoirs-Induced Seismicity

- In a large and deep artificial lake the pressure applied by a column of water alters stresses along an existing fault or fracture. Also the soil structure is weakened by the percolation of water, it also lubricates the faults.
- There is a significant change in stress while loading and unloading of water, it leads to a sudden movement along the fault or fracture.As a result an earthquake occurs.
- In 1967, Koynanagar earthquake occurred near the Koyna Dam reservoir in Maharashtra with the magnitude 6.5. There have been many earthquakes of smaller magnitude since then. In this earthquake more than 150 lives were lost.

Measurement of Earthquake

- Richter Scale is used to measure the magnitude of an earthquake or to measure the strength of the earthquake or the amount of energy released during the earthquake. It is determined by the base 10 logarithm of the amplitude of waves recorded.
- This corresponds to the 31.6 times energy released for each unit level increase in magnitude.
- For example, if the magnitude of an earthquake registered at 7 on the Richter scale means its magnitude is 10 times the earthquake on the Richter scale 6, corresponding to the 31.6 times energy released by the lesser earthquake.
- The Mercalli scale is a 12-step measure of earthquake intensity on basis of loss of life and property. It is a closed-ended linear scale, scaled from 1-12.

Earthquakes Occur due to the Depth of Focus

- Anywhere in between the Earth's surface and about 700 kilometers below the surface earthquakes can occur.
- Earthquake can be divided into three zones according to the depth range of 0-700 km. (for scientific purposes):
  - Shallow
  - Intermediate and
  - Deep
- **Shallow focus earthquakes:** These types of earthquakes are found within the earth's outer crustal layer which are 0-70 km deep. With respect to the total energy released in earthquakes, near about 70-85% comes from shallow focus earthquakes.
- **Intermediate earthquakes:** It occurs about 70-300 km deep. About 12-15% energy comes from intermediate earthquakes with respect to the total energy released in earthquakes.
- **Deep Earthquakes:** These types of earthquakes often occur 300-700 km deep. It occurs within the deeper subduction zones of the earth.
- Energy release from the earthquake depends not only on the energy released, it also depends on location, distance from the epicenter and depth.

Conclusion of both earthquake

- The Italy earthquake had originated within 10 kilometers underground and it was a very shallow focus earthquake. Hence it is considered as a destructive earthquake.
- While the earthquake in Myanmar was 84 kilometers deep. So it wasn't very destructive.

Earthquakes Along The Convergent Boundary: Wadati-Benioff Zone

- Wadati Benioff zone is the most sensitive zone in which the most powerful earthquakes can occur along the convergent boundary. It is a zone of subduction along which earthquakes are common.
- These types of zones can occur by slipping along the subduction thrust fault or slip on faults within the downgoing plate.
- A numerous earthquakes can occur by the differential motion along the zone and its foci may be as deep as about 700 kilometers.

Major Earthquake Zones

- Where the belts coincide with the margins of tectonic plates in which mainly earth's major earthquakes occur.
- **The Circum-Pacific Belt:** The Circum-Pacific Belt is the most important earthquake belt. Its effects occur around the Pacific Ocean populated coastal regions such as:
  - New Zealand
  - New Guinea
  - Japan
  - The Aleutian islands
  - Alaska and
  - The western coasts of North and South America
- **The Alpine Belt:** It is the second most important earthquake belt in which the energy released in

earthquakes from this belt is about 15% of the world total. It is also known as the mid-world mountain belt.

- It extends parallel to the equator from Mexico across following:
  - The Atlantic Ocean
  - The Mediterranean Sea from Alpine-Caucasus ranges to the Caspian
  - Himalayas mountain and adjoining lands.
- Some Striking connected belts of seismic activity along oceanic ridges are as follows:
  - The Western Indian Ocean
  - Along The rift valleys of East Africa
  - The Arctic Ocean and
  - The Atlantic Ocean

Earthquake in India

- The latest seismic zone map prepared by the National Disaster Management Authority reveals that nearly 59% of India's land area is prone to moderate or severe earthquakes.
- India has been divided into four seismic zones (II, III, IV, and V) based on scientific inputs relating to seismicity, earthquakes occurred in the past and tectonic setup of the region. V being most vulnerable area and II being lease vulnerable area.

Volcanism

Volcanism is the phenomenon of eruption of molten rock, pyroclastics and volcanic gases to the surface through a vent.

Causes

- Huge temperature difference between the inner layers and the outer layers of the earth resulting in convective activity.
- Weak zones on earth's crust(convergent/divergent boundaries).
- Earthquake and Faulting.

Type of Lava

Acidic Lava	Basic Lava
Highly Viscous, High melting point.	Hottest lava with high viscosity, very fluid.
Light colour, low density, high silica.	Dark coloured basalt, rich in iron and magnesium but poor in silica.
Forms stratovolcano, steep sloping volcano.	Thin sheets at great distance, gentle sloping volcano.
Violent eruptions.	Silent eruptions.

Types of Volcano

- On basis of activity
  - Active volcanoes erupt frequently and are mostly located around the Ring of Fire.
  - Dormant volcano is one that has not erupted in a long time but there is a possibility it can erupt in the future.
  - Dead volcano is an extinct volcano.
- On basis of occurrence
  - Extrusive (above surface of earth)
    - **Central Type:** Strombolian (Composite cone), Hawaiian (Shield type) (Hawaiian can occur as central type and fissure type as well).
    - **Fissure Type:** Lava Plateaus, basalt tablelands.
  - Intrusive (Below the surface of the earth).

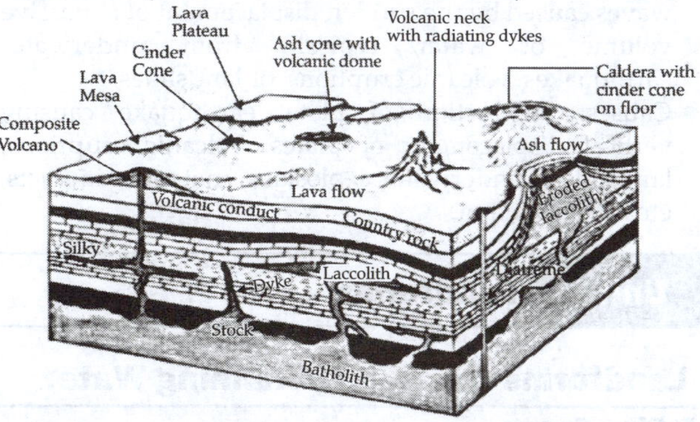

Figure: Extrusive and Intrusive Volcanic features

Effects of Volcanism

- Acid Rain, Ozone Destruction.
- Air Pollution- gases released sulphur dioxide, carbon dioxide, and hydrogen fluoride.
- Creation of fertile land like deccan trap, and volcanic soil.
- Creation of Hot Springs and Geysers.
- Potential for geothermal energy.

Some Additional Features

- Crater -vent through which the magma flows out.
- Caldera- enlarged crater.
- Lava domes-viscous magma piles up around the vent.
- Cinder cone - a steep circular or oval-shaped hill of loose pyroclastic fragments built around a volcanic vent.

Additional Information

- Mantle plume is the convection of abnormally hot rock (magma) within the Earth's mantle. They are Volcanic Hotspots.
- Pseudo volcanic features are certain topographic features that resemble volcanic forms but are of non-volcanic origin. They include meteorite crater, salt plugs, and mud-volcanoes.
- The Himalayan region and the Indian peninsula are both devoid of volcanoes.
- Barren Island in Andaman islands is the only active volcano in India. Barren Island has erupted multiple times after 2004, including significant eruptions in 2017, 2018, and 2019 and most recently in 2024 and 2025.

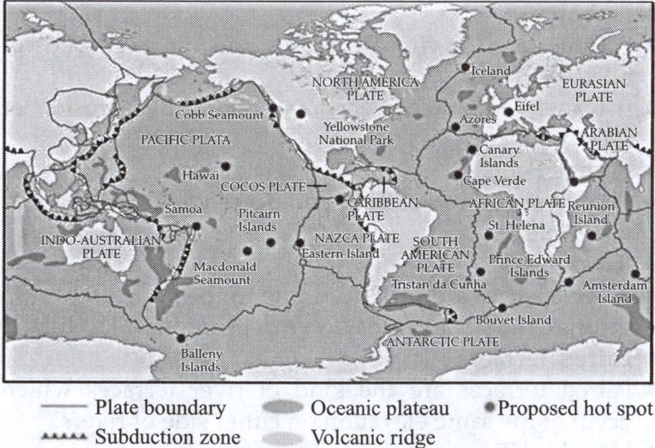

Figure: Distribution of hotspots
(Credits: K. Cantner, Earth Magazine)

Tsunami

- A tsunami is a series of extremely long-wavelength waves caused by the sudden displacement of a massive volume of water, typically from underwater earthquakes, volcanic eruptions, or landslides.
- Causes: Subduction of plate, earthquake causing vertical displacement of plates, Volcanic eruptions, landslides, underwater explosions, meteorite impacts, etc cause tsunami.
- The sea level decreased before the tsunami. In open ocean the speed of the wave is more and wave height is less but as the wave arrives never shallow water the speed reduces and the wave height increases, i.e. it becomes killer waves in shallow water.
- NOAA has developed the 'Deep Ocean Assessment and Reporting of Tsunamis' (DART) gauge.
- Indian National Centre for Ocean Information Services (INCOIS), Hyderabad, the tsunami warning system.

Unit-6: Landforms

Landforms Created by Running Water

A. River Course

- **Upper Course or The Young Stage**
  - During this stage gorges and canyons are formed, it is a deep cleft between escarpments or cliffs resulting from weathering and the erosive activity of a river.
  - A natural diversion of the headwaters of one stream into the channel of another is known as the river capture. This is typically resulting from rapid headward erosion by the latter stream.
  - **Waterfall:** It is a vertical drop in a streambed. Waterfalls are the sites of vigorous erosion.
  - **Rapids:** Stream sections with extremely strong currents and numerous obstacles that step in their streambeds are known as rapids. They also are the sites of vigorous erosion.
- **Valley or Middle Course**
  - A winding curve or bend of a river is known as meanders.
  - River Cliffs and slip-off slopes.
- **Plain or Lower Course**
  - **Flood Plains:** It is a low-lying ground area which is adjacent to a river, formed mainly of river sediments and subject to flooding.
  - **Ox-bow Lakes:** These types of lakes form when a wide meander from the main stem of a river is cut off and creates a free-standing body of water. It is usually a U-shaped lake.
  - **Delta:** At the mouth of a river a triangular tract of sediment deposited occurs and diverges into several outlets. The triangular tract of sediment deposits is known as delta.

B. Erosional Landforms of Running Water

- **Potholes**
  - Potholes are the circular depressions on rocky beds of hills.
  - It forms when steam erosion is aided by abrasion of rock fragments.
- **Plunge Pools**
  - Plunge pools are the large and deep holes at the base of waterfalls.
- **River Terraces**
  - River terraces are produced due to the vertical erosion through the stream into its own depositional Floodplain.
- **Paired Terraces**
  - Paired terraces are the kind of river terraces which occur at the same elevation on either side of rivers.
- **Unpaired Terraces**
  - Such river terraces which occur at different elevations.

C. Depositional Landforms of Running Water

- **Alluvial Fans**
  - When streams flow from higher levels and break into foot slope plains of low gradient, then the load gets dumped as a broad low to high cone shaped deposit as a result alluvial fans are formed.
- **Natural Levees**
  - Natural levees are the ridges of coarse deposits along the banks of rivers.
  - They are parallel, low and linear ridges coarse deposits.
- **Point Bars**
  - Bar points are generally found on the convex side of meanders of large rivers.
  - They formed when the sediments deposited in a linear fashion through flowing waters along the bank of rivers.
- **Braided Channels**
  - Braided channels formed when the thread-like streams of water rejoined and subdivided repeatedly, as a result braided pattern formed.
  - A bunch of braided patterns are called braided channels.

Glaciers

- A large perennial accumulation of crystalline ice, snow, rock, sediment and liquid water are called glaciers.
- They originate on land and move down slopes under the influence of their own weight and gravity.
- At present there are only two major ice caps are present
  - Antarctica
  - Greenland
- **Piedmont glacier:** Several glaciers may converge to form an extensive ice-mass at the foot of the mountain glacier, these glaciers are known as the Piedmont glacier.

A. Landforms of Glaciations

- **Corrie or Cirque**
  - Corrie is a depression or lower land where snow accumulates.
- **Aretes and Pyramidal Peaks**
  - Knife-edged ridges peaks are formed when two corries cut back on each other;these knife-edged ridges peaks are called aretes.
- **Bergschrund**
  - When snow starts to leave the corrie and a deep vertical crack occurs at the head of a glacier. These deep vertical cracks are called bergschrunds.
- **U-shaped Glacial Trough**
  - These types of valleys are a geological formation characterized by high and steep sides and a rounded or flat valley bottom.
  - These types of glacial trough are located all over the world specially in high area mountains because these areas are geographically ideal for glacier formation.

■ Some examples of U-shaped valleys are as follows
➢ Zezere Valley in Portugal;
➢ Leh Valley in India ; and
➢ Nant Ffrancon Valley in Wales.

● **Hanging Valley**
■ Hanging valleys also are the U-shaped valleys above their respective main valleys.
■ At the point where the two valleys meet, there is a steep wall.
■ Basically these valleys are found in regions of high altitude in mountainous regions.
■ Hanging valleys are natural crevices through which rivers flow.
■ Where the two valleys meet the rivers dramatically drop to form waterfalls at the cliff meeting point.

● **Moraines**
■ They are formed by the debris that was previously carried along by a glacier.
■ Lateral moraines and terminal moraines are marking the maximum advance of the glacier.
■ At the side of the ice flow where lateral moraines are formed while at the foot, terminal moraines are formed.

B. Landforms of Glaciated Lowlands

● **Roche Mountains**
■ They are glaciated bedrock surfaces.
■ They are generally in the form of rounded knobs.

● **Craig and Tail**
■ They are isolated from other high ground and are generally a rocky hill or mountain.

● **Boulder Clay or Glacial till**
■ Many large stones and boulders are contained by the boulder clay.
■ They formed by deposition from melting glaciers and ice sheets.

● **Erratic**
■ A piece of rock that eroded and transported by a glacier to a different area is known as erratic.

● **Drumlins**
■ Elongated, teardrop-shaped hills of rock, sand and gravel that formed under moving glacier ice are known as drumlins.

● **Eskers**
■ It is formed through a long, winding ridge of stratified sand and gravel.

● **Outwash Plains**
■ At the terminus of a glacier a plain formed of glacial sediments deposited by meltwater outwash. Such types of plains are called outwash plains.

Desert or Arid Landforms

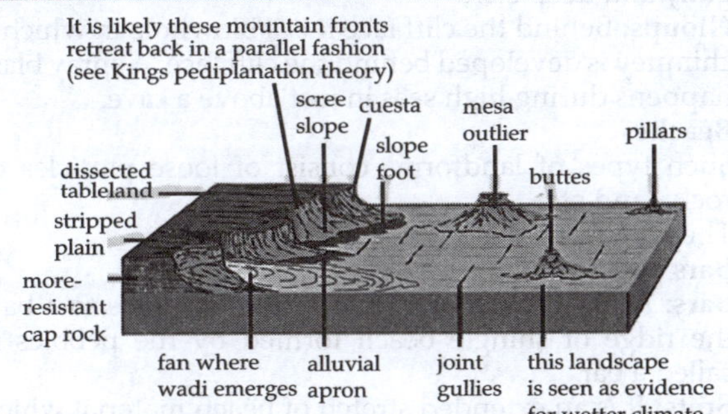

● In between 15 to 30 degrees north and south of the equator, on the western margins almost all deserts are located.
● Deserts mainly lie in the trade wind belt on the western part of the continents in which trade winds are off-shore. Here the cold currents bathed it and these currents are devoid of any moisture.

A. Types of Desert

● **Hamada or Rocky Desert**
■ Hamada desert is a type of desert landscape where most of the sand is removed by deflation.
■ It consists of high, largely barren and hard rocky plateaus.

● **Reg or Stony Desert**
■ Interlocking angular or rounded rock fragments of pebble and cobble size cover the surface of these types of deserts.

● **Sandy or Erg Desert**
■ These types of deserts are mainly covered with wind-swept sand with little or no vegetative cover.
■ A sandy desert is a broad and flat area.

● **Badlands**
■ In badlands soft sedimentary rocks and clay-rich soils are eroded through wind and water.
■ They are a type of dry terrain where rocks have been eroded slowly by wind and water.

● **Mountain Desert**
■ These types of deserts are usually found on plateaus and mountain ranges.
■ Steep slopes, irregular and sharp peaks are the major characteristics of mountain desert.

B. Landforms of Wind Erosion in Deserts

● Rock Pedestals or Mushroom Rocks or Gour
■ They are naturally occurring rocks and also called a mushroom rock whose shape resembles a mushroom by weathering and erosion.

● Zeugen
■ A Zeugen forms in those desert areas where the alternating horizontal layers of hard and soft rocks occur.

● Yardangs
■ It is an irregular and sharp ridge of sand that is formed by the wind erosion of adjacent material which is less resistant.
■ It forms in the direction of the prevailing wind that is exposed in desert areas.

● Mesas and Buttes
■ Mesas: Mesa is comparatively smaller in area than a plateau. It is an isolated, flat-topped hill or mountain with steep sides.
■ Buttes: It is also a flat-topped hill with steep sides but smaller in area as compared to mesa.

● Insel Berg
■ It is a small mountain similar to the knob and ridge mountain that rises abruptly from a virtually level surrounding plain or gentle sloping.

● Venti Facts
■ Ventifacts are formed by the erosive action of wind-blown sand.

● Deflation Hollows
■ Deflation hollows are the place where a layer of sand particles are too heavy for the wind to move it, the sand prevents the surface from being lowered further because these sand particles are removed by wind to a level where a layer of particles becomes too heavy for the wind to move to stabilize it.

C. Landforms of Wind Deposition in Deserts

- **Beaches**
  - They are Crescent shaped dunes.
- Seif
  - It is a long narrow sand dune formed by the wind.
  - Seif is formed in a parallel to the wind that is responsible for its construction.
- Parabolic Dunes
  - Reversed barchans with wind direction being the same.
- Longitudinal Dunes
  - These types of dunes are generally low in height but appear as long ridges of considerable length.
- Transverse Dunes
  - Transverse dunes are aligned perpendicular to the wind direction.
- Loess
  - Those surfaces which are covered by the deposits of wind transported silt which are settled out from dust storms over many thousands of years.
  - Such types of depositions are known as the loess.

D. Limestone and Chalk Landform

- Both are organic sedimentary rocks. They origin from the accumulation of corals and shells in the sea.
- Calcite or calcium carbonate is the pure form of limestone but it is termed dolomite when magnesium is also present in it.
- Chalk is pure white in color as well as it is a very pure form of limestone which is soft in nature.
- Limestone is soluble in rain-water so when it comes in direct contact with carbon dioxide from the air then it forms a weak acid.

Karst Region

- It is a very distinct type of topography in the region of a large stretch of limestone.
- These regions have a bleak landscape generally with absence of surface drainage as a result most of the surface water goes underground.
- Karst regions cut their way along the joints and fissures of the rock for the greater part of their course. As a result, the underground channel system comes to an end.

Characteristics of Karst Region

- **Limestone Pavements**
  - They are formed by a combination of chemical weathering and erosion which is a flat expense of exposed limestone.
- **Grikes and Clints**
  - Both are the separate but integral parts of pavement.
  - **Grikes:** They are the fissures that isolate the individual clints.
  - **Clints:** The blocks of limestone are known as clints that constitute the paving.
- **Swallow Holes**
  - Swallow holes are small carved on limestone which is formed by solution.
  - At the weak zone of limestone where rain water enters inside the small hole. It is also known as sinkholes.
- **Limestone Gorges**
  - When the roof of a large underground cavern collapses, as a result it forms a steep-sided gorge with a river running in the bottom. In this region limestone gorges are formed.
- **Resurgence**
  - They are formed when water passes down through a swallow hole and it flows underground along bedding planes and down joints.
- **Uvala**
  - Uvala is a closed karst depression which is generally a terrain form of elongated or compound structure.
  - It is larger in size than that of sinkholes.
- **Polje**
  - Polje is an elongated basin which consists of a flat floor and steep walls.
- **Stalactites**
  - An icicle-shaped mineral deposit that hangs downward from the ceiling of a cave is called a stalactite.
- **Stalagmites**
  - Cone-shaped formations that rise upward from the floor of a cave, formed by mineral deposits from dripping water falling from the ceiling.

Landforms in Coastal Regions

- Any relief features present along the coast are known as coastal landforms.
- There are some examples of coastal landforms as follows:
- **Capes and Bays**
  - **Cape:** It is an adjacent point of land that extends beyond the adjacent coast into a sea or lake.
  - **Bay:** It is a body of water and its more or three-quarters are surrounded by land.
- **Cliffs and Wave-cut platforms**
  - **Cliffs:** Cliffs are generally formed by rock that is resistant to weathering and erosion. So they are formed as erosion landforms by the processes of weathering and erosion.
  - **Wave-cut platforms:** These platforms are formed when destructive waves hit against the cliff face and it causes an undercut between the high and low water marks as a result of corrosion, abrasion and hydraulic action making a wave-cut notch.
- **Cave, Arch, Stack and Stump**
  - **Cave:** When in the cliff face, waves force their way into cracks as a result of sand and other materials associated with water that grind away at the rock until the cracks become a cave.
  - **Arch:** When the formation region of the cave is a headland then it eventually breaks through to the other side, as a result an arch will form.
  - **Stack:** When the arch slowly becomes bigger until it no longer supports the top of the arch, after some time the arch collapses and leaves a headland on one side forming a stack.
  - **Stump:** Stump will form when the stack will be attacked at the base in the same way that a wave-cut notch is formed, as a result this weakens the structure and it will eventually collapse and form a stump.
- **Geos and Gloups**
  - **Geous:** In the face of a cliff it is an inlet, a narrow or a gully and deep cleft.
  - **Gloups:** Behind the cliff face it is a blowhole in which a chimney is developed behind the cliff face. A spray blast happens during high seas in just above a cave.
- **Beaches**
  - Such types of landforms consist of loose particles of rock, sand etc.
  - They are formed alongside a body of water.
- **Bars and Spits**
  - **Bars:** At the mouth of a river or the entrance to a bay, the ridge of shingle beach formed by the pebbles is called a bar.
  - **Spits:** It is an extended stretch of beach material which projects out to sea and it is joined to the mainland at one end.

- **Marine Dunes and Dunes Belt**
- A large amount of coastal sand is driven landwards due to the force of on-shore winds and forming extensive marine dunes that stretch into dune belts.

Types of Coasts

- **Coastlines of Submergence**
- These types of submergence coasts have been flooded by ocean waters because of a relative rise in the elevation of sea level at that location.
- **Coastlines of Emergence**
- These types of coasts occur due to the local tectonic uplift of the land surface or a fall in the elevation of sea level. It is because of a reduction in the water volume of ocean basins.
- Also emergent coasts associated with rocky coastlines, cliffs and nearly flat platforms that extend inland in which tectonically raised older coastal plains have been elevated above the modern land and water interface.

Coastlines of Submergence

- **Ria Coasts**
- These types of coasts are generally found along an un-glaciated land. They are a coastal formation which was once as a river valley.
- **Fiord Coasts**
- It is a submerged U-shaped glacial trough which makes the path of glaciers that plunged down from the highlands.
- **Dalmatian Coasts**
- It forms when a continental fold region is submerged but the terrain basically preserves its correspondence to the tectonic structures.
- **Estuarine Coasts**
- It is a partially enclosed coastal body of brackish water. One or more rivers or streams flowing into it with a free connection to the open sea.

Islands and Coral Reefs

- Those lands which are surrounded by water on all sides and may occur individually or in a group.

Coral Reefs

- Shell forming creatures, lime secreting tiny animals and Coral Polyps – calcareous algae live in large colonies. Skeletons of polyp are cemented into coralline limestone.
- Precious coral of the Pacific Ocean and the Red coral of the Mediterranean sea are non reef building species.

Types of Coral Reefs

- **Fringing Reefs**
- It lies near the coast and increases outwards from the mainland separated by shallow lagoons.
- It becomes wide when fringing protruding headland but absent while facing the mouth of the stream.
- **Patch Reefs**
- Isolated Outcroppings of coral are known as Patch Reefs which are in close proximity to each other but they are physically separated by sand rings.
- **Barrier Reefs**
- They are physically separated by wider and deeper Reefs channels but they are partially submerged and there are narrow gaps at several places which allow water to enter inside it.
- Example: Great Barrier Reef off the coast of Queensland.
- **Atolls**
- Atolls are circular and enclose shallow lagoons without any land in the centre.

Condition For Coral Formation

- There are several factors behind coral reef formation. Some Important factors are as follows:
- Temperature of the water must not be below 20°C.
- Less than 100 feet of shallow water is ideal.
- Depth of water should not exceed 30 fathoms or 180 feet as beyond it sunlight is too faint.
- Coral Reefs survive best in warmer tropical seas.
- Water must be free from sediments.
- Water should be saltish.

Unit-7: Interior of the Earth

Scientists have some sources of information about the interior of the earth they are as follows:

Direct Sources

- Volcanic eruptions
- Rocks from mining area

Indirect Sources

- **By analyzing the rate of change of pressure and temperature**
- Scientists have a fair idea about the interior of the earth by absorbing the rate of change of pressure and temperature from the surface towards the interior of the earth.
- **Gravity Anomaly**
- Gravity anomaly gives us fair information about the materials in the earth's interior in which scientists measure the changes in gravity value according to the mass of material.
- **By analyzing the Meteors**
- Scientists also analyze the material of meteors because they belong to the same type of materials earth is made of.
- **Gravitational Force**
- Earth's gravitational forces are greater near poles and less at the equator. By the help of variation of the gravitational forces scientists have been able to determine a fair idea about the interior of the earth.

Magnetic sources

- **Seismic Waves:**
- With the help of seismic waves or Primary and secondary waves scientists research about the state of materials in the interior of the earth.

Structure of the earth's interior

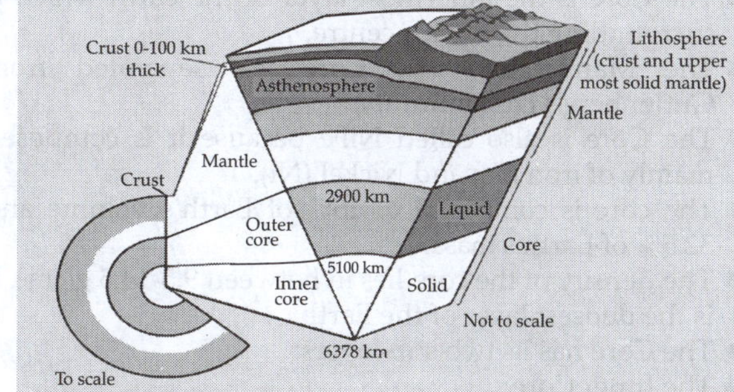

- According to the some scientific researches, structure of the earth's interior is fundamentally divided into three layers:
- Crust
- Mantle
- Core

- **Crust**
- This layer is almost 8 to 40 km thick and is the outermost solid part of the earth.
- Under the oceanic and continental areas the thickness of the crust is different.
- The continental crust (about 30 km) is thicker as compared to the oceanic crust (about 5 km).
- The nature of the crust is brittle.
- Silica and Aluminium are the major constituent elements of the crust so, it is also termed as SiAl.
- SiAl is the region comprising the crust and uppermost solid mantle and is a part of the lithosphere.
- Almost 0.5% of Earth's mass and 1% of the earth's volume are made of the crust.
- 2.7 g/cm^3 is the mean density of the materials in the crust.
- The Conrad Discontinuity is the discontinuity between the upper crust and the lower crust.
- **Mantle**
- Mantle is the portion of the interior beyond the crust.
- Mohorovich Discontinuity is a discontinuity between the crust and mantle. It is also known as Moho discontinuity.
- The thickness of the earth's mantle is near about 2900 km.
- The mantle of the earth occupied 84% of the earth's volume and 67% of the earth's mass.
- Silicon and Magnesium and the major constituent elements of the mantle so, it is also called SiMa.
- The density of the mantle varies from 3.3 – 5.7 g/cm^3 and its density is higher than the crust.
- The lithosphere consists of the uppermost solid part of the mantle and the entire crust.
- Repetti Discontinuity is the discontinuity that is found in between the upper mantle and the lower mantle.
- The asthenosphere is a deforming region of the upper mantle. The thickness of the asthenosphere is in between 80 to 200 kms and it is mechanically weak, highly viscous and ductile which is found just below the lithosphere.
- Magma is erupted from the asthenosphere and also it is the main source of magma.
- The asthenosphere is the layer over which the continental plates or lithospheric plates (Plate tectonics) move.
- The Mesosphere is the region just above the core and it lies just below the lithosphere and asthenosphere, called the Mesosphere. It is also a portion of the mantle.
- **Core**
- The Core is the innermost layer of the earth which is surrounding the earth's centre.
- The Mantle and the Core are separated from Guttenberg's Discontinuity.
- The Core is also called NiFe because it is composed mainly of iron (Fe) and Nickel (Ni).
- The core is composed of 15% of Earth's volume and 32.5% of Earth's mass.
- The density of the core lies in between 9.5-14.5 g/cm^3. It is the densest layer of the Earth.
- The Core has its two sub-layers:
- The Inner Core
- The Outer Core

The Inner Core

- It is in a solid state which extends from the centre of the earth until 5100 kms below the earth's surface.
- It believes that the inner core is composed of iron (80%) and some Nickel.
- S-waves cannot travel through the liquid outer core, but P-waves slow down significantly.
- The inner core can transmit shear waves or transverse seismic waves.
- As compared to the rotation of the surface the inner core rotates slightly fast.
- Barysphere is generally used to indicate the core of the earth or sometimes the whole interior.
- The solid inner core doesn't have a magnetic field because it is too hot to hold a permanent magnetic field.
- Inner Core Density: The density of the Earth's inner core lies in between 12.6 g/cm^3 to 13 g/cm^3.
- Lehmann Discontinuity is the discontinuity which is found in between the inner core and the outer core.
- The inner iron core is as hot as the Sun, having a temperature of 6000°C but the crushing pressure produced by earth's gravity prevents it from becoming liquid.
- **Note:** The melting point of a solid will increase when there will increase in ambient pressure, and vice-versa. But ice is one exception. Increasing the ambient pressure will lower its melting point in the case of ice.

The Outer Core

- It is the core which is surrounding the inner core.
- The outer core lies between 2900 km to 5100 km below the earth's surface.
- It consists of iron mixed with nickel and along with trace amounts of lighter elements.
- The outer core has a composition similar to the inner core but it is liquid in nature because it does not have enough pressure to be solid.
- Dynamic Theory: According to the Dynamic Theory when the convection in the outer core is combined with the Coriolis effect then it gives rise to Earth's magnetic field.
- Till 9.9 g/cm^3 to 12.2 g/cm^3 is the range of the density of the outer core.
- The temperature of the earth's outer core lies from 4400°C (in the outer regions) to 6000°C near the inner core.

Seismic Discontinuities

- **Seismic discontinuities** are that region of the earth where due to a marked change in physical or chemical properties, the seismic waves behave a lot different as compared to the surrounding regions.

Mohorovicic Discontinuity (Moho)

- Moho discontinuity separates the crust from the mantle and it works as the boundary between the Earth's crust and the mantle.
- Mohorovicic Discontinuity was discovered by Andreaja Mohorovicic who was a Croatian Scientist.
- It shows a change in seismic waves velocity from the crust to the uppermost mantle.

Temperature, Pressure and Density of the Earth's Interior

Temperature

- It is observed in deep wells and mines that there is a rise in temperature when increasing in the depth of them.
- We have evidence for the temperature that increases when we will go towards the centre of the earth. It is

well proved by the molten lava erupted from the earth's interior.

- According to the different observations, scientists come to a conclusion that the rate of increase of temperature is not uniform from the surface towards the centre of the earth because it is slower at some places while faster at other places.
- The rate of increase of temperature will increase at an average rate of 1°C for every 32 m increase in depth.
- While the temperature will increase at the rate of 120°C per km in the upper 100 kms and also it will increase at the rate of 200°C per km in the next 300 kms.
- After the depth of 300 km, if going further deep, this rate of increase of temperature will have decreased at the rate of 100° C per km.
- Internal temperature at the centre of the earth 6000°C. The temperature of the centre is much higher due to the chemical reactions under high-pressure conditions.
- The materials at the centre are in solid state even in such a high temperature, due to the heavy pressure of the overlying materials.

Pressure

- The pressure increases when going from the surface towards the centre of the earth, due to the enormous weight of the overlying materials (rocks, sea water, soil etc).
- The materials beneath the surface are melted towards the centre of the earth at very high temperature but these molten materials come to have the properties of a solid and they are probably in a plastic state.
- According to some scientific study it is probably possible that in the deeper portions of the earth, the pressure is enormously very high and it is nearly about 3 to 4 million times more than that of the pressure of the atmosphere at sea level.

Density

- The density of the earth's layers also increases towards the centre, it is due to the increase in pressure and the presence of heavier materials like Iron and Nickel towards the centre.
- At the very centre, the average density of the layers is nearly 14.5 g/cm^3.
- It is also proved that the average density of the layers increases from crust towards the core.

Unit-8: Geomorphology

Origin of Continents and Oceans

- The seven main divisions of Earth's land are continents.
- We can classified to all continents by their size, from largest to smallest Number the continents insted of bullet

1. Asia 2. Africa 3. North America
4. South America 5. Antarctica 6. Europe and
7. Australia

- About 148 million square kilometers of land add up by the continents.

Building the Continents

- The Formation of earth occurred 4.6 billion years ago from a cloud of dust and gas.
- The inside of Earth heated up due to the continuous smashing of space debris and the pull of gravity.
- During this period as the heat of space debris continuously increased, it melted some of Earth's rocky materials and rose to the surface and cooled to form the crust.
- Heavier materials sank toward Earth's center during the formation of Earth's three main layers. These layers are:

■ The Core ■ The Mantle and ■ The Crust

- **Tectonic Plates**

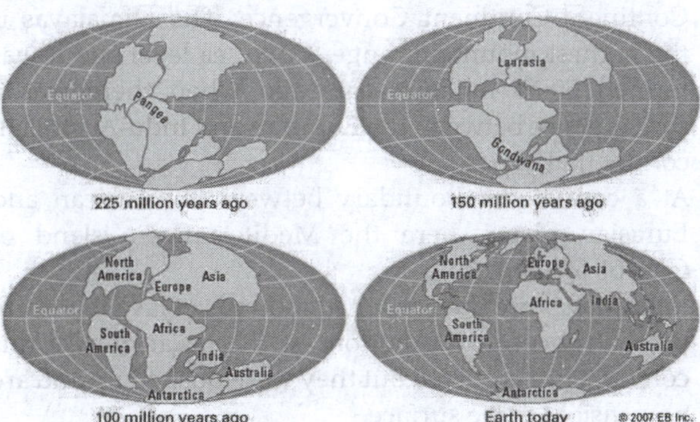

225 million years ago 150 million years ago
100 million years ago Earth today © 2007 EB Inc.

■ A rigid shell around the earth is formed by the crust and the top portion of the mantle, these rigid shells are broken up into huge sections which are called tectonic plates.

■ Due to the massive heat produced inside the earth, the movement of plates to slide around on the molten mantle.

■ The plates are sliding around on the molten mantle when the massive heat production occurs from inside the earth.

■ At present still tectonic plates are sliding very slowly and continuously just around the surface. This phenomenon has been happening continuously for hundreds of millions of years.

■ According to some geologists, the creation of continents happened by the interaction of the plates, which is known as plate tectonics.

- 71% of Earth's surface is covered by the Ocean in which about 1.35 billion cubic kilometers of water is retained on the surface of all oceans. It is about 97% of all the water on Earth.
- The ocean makes the earth appear blue when viewed from space and also it makes possible all life on Earth.
- In our solar system, earth is the only planet that contains has consistent, stable bodies of liquid water.
- The oceans are one continuous body of water and they have been divided into four principal areas by the oceanographers

■ The Pacific Ocean
■ The Atlantic Ocean
■ The Indian Ocean and
■ The Arctic Ocean

- **Note:** The Pacific, Atlantic and Indian Oceans have been joined together into icy waters around Antarctica. The region of their consolidation is defined as a fifth ocean by some oceanographers. This region is most commonly known as the Southern Ocean.

Ocean Formation

- About 4.6 Billion years ago while the earth began to form, during this period it gradually separated into layers of heavier and lighter rocks.
- The heavier rock sank inside the earth and formed the Earth's core and mantle while the light rock rose and formed the Earth's crust.
- As the molten rocks cooled, they released water vapor and gases. The oceanic water came from rocks inside the newly forming Earth.
- In this water forming process, the water vapor that comes out from the molten rocks is condensed to form ocean water that covers the crust with a primitive ocean.
- Still at present time, warm gases continuously come out from the earth's interior that produce new water at the bottom of the ocean.

Continental Drift Theory

- Alfred Wegener in 1912, propounded the continental Drift Theory (CDT) stating existance of Pangea (Superland) surrounded by Panthalasa (superocean), which further disintegrated into Gondwanaland (S. America, Africa, Arabia, India, Oceania, Antartica) and Laurasia (N. America, Eurasia) divided by Tethys sea.
- Drift started around 200 million years ago (Mesozoic Era, Triassic Period, Late Triassic Epoch), and the continents began to break up and drift away from one another.

Prominent Evidence in Support of Continental Drift Theory

- **Jig saw fit:** S Shape of atlantic ocean and clear fit of South America and Africa. This was supported by superimposed faunal succession, mesosauras fossil remains found in Brazil and Guenia.Similar gold rich stratas and placer gold found in Brazil. Fit of block mountains along both coastlines.
- **Paleoclimatic evidance:** Pole like conditions wandering and shift of poles, evidance of simultaneous glacial and intraglacial period, presence of coal feild in temperate (Europe/Canada/USA/China) regions even if coal formation being more prominant to tropical latitudes.
- **Argument against the concept:** No description of mechanism of drift, entire theory is Sial floating over Sima(it is lithosphere over asthenosphere), west ward drift due to tides and equator ward pull due to gravity were practically invalid. Ocean crust was considered as passive. Could not explain formation of 2nd order relief features.
- The theory was discarded due to impractical approach and explaination. Though due to Geomagneic evidences explaining magnetic propert of eath and west ward drift of continents due to spinning of iron rich interior and paleomagnetism explaining the wandering of the magnetic north pole and south pole in different time period helped in revival of CDT.
- Sea floor spreading of Herry Hess explained the activity of oceanic crust by studying the challenger ridge in Atlantic ocean and let to complete revival of CDT.

Plate Tectonics

- It states that the Earth's lithosphere is broken into distinct plates which are floating on a ductile layer called asthenosphere the upper portion of the mantle. Plates move horizontally over the asthenosphere as rigid units. Convection currents in the mantle are the driving force of plate movement.The plate boundries are divided as convergent, divergent and transform boundries. These are various interactions between Ocean- Ocean, Continent - Continent, Continent - Ocean boundries.
- **Divergent Boundries:** Two plates moving away from each other. Also known as constructive plate boundries.
- Formation of New sea floor, mid oceanic ridges, and rift valleys, faults and block mountain.
- Also gives rise to Shallow focus earthquakes and volcanism.
- Plates separate from a narrow rift valley at the divergent boundaries. Here some materials like magma, molten rock and spurt superheated water are released from the mantle and all these materials are solidified into basalt and as a result formed a new crust. Hence at divergent boundaries new oceanic crust is formed.
- **The Earth's longest mountain range:** The mid-ocean ridge is the longest mountain range on Earth, stretching 65,000 kilometers (40,390 miles) long and 1,500 kilometers (932 miles) wide.
- **Convergent boundaries:** Plates are collided one another at the Convergent boundary.
- After the collision of plates occurs it blocks the edge of one or both plates and forms a mountain range or subducting one of the plates under the other and creates a deep seafloor trench.
- Continental crust and oceanic crust converges, oceanic crust is pulled below the continental crust casusing distruction of oceanic crust. This activity also causes formation of trench and gives rise to active earthquake and volcanism.
- This boundary gives rise to reverse fault and block mountains.
- Subducts, and becomes magma. Ocean-Ocean Convergence forms volcanic island arcs, for example, Japanese Island Arc, Indonesian Archipelago, Philippine Island Arc and Caribbean Islands.
- Chains of volcanoes and major earthquakes also occur due to the movement of convergent plates. Continent-Ocean Convergence forms mountains (Rockys and Andes) and Continental Arcs.
- Continent-Continent Convergence: The Himalayas is the highest mountain range above sea level and it was formed 50-55 million years ago when there was a convergence between the Eurasian and Indo-Australian continental plates.
- At a convergent boundary between the African and Eurasian plates, here the Mediterranean island of Cyprus formed.
- Pillow lavas are the hardened mounds of lava that were present once on the bottom of the ocean where this convergence occurred but they were pushed up and are now visible at the surface.

Rates of Plate Movement

- **Fastest Rates of Plate Movement:** East Pacific Rise in the South Pacific Ocean has the fastest rate of plate movement. It is more than 15 cm/year.
- **Slowest Rate of Plate Movement:** The Arctic Ridge has the slowest rate of plate movement. It is less than 2.5 cm/year.

Force For Plate Movement

Convection Currents: It is generated due to the thermal gradients on the surface of the mantle.

Minor Tectonic Plates

- Minor tectonic plates are formed due to stress created by converging major plates. For example, due to the compressive force exerted by Eurasian and African plates, as result the Mediterranean Sea is divided into numerous minor plates.
- At present there are many minor tectonic plates. Some Important examples of them are as follows
- **Philippine plate:** Between the Asiatic and Pacific plate.
- **Fuji plate:** North-east of Australia.
- **Cocos plate:** Between Central America and Pacific plate.
- **Caroline plate:** Between the Philippine and Indian plate (North of New Guinea).
- **Iranian plate:** covering the modern-day countries of Iran and Afghanistan, and parts of Iraq and Pakistan.
- **Caribbean plate:** Underlying Central America and the Caribbean Sea off the northern coast of South America.
- **Nazca plate:** Between South America and Pacific plate.
- **Aegean plate:** Mediterranean region.
- Turkish plate.
- **Arabian plate:** Mostly the Saudi Arabian landmass.
- **Juan de Fuca plate:** Between Pacific and North American plates.

Major Tectonic Plates

- Pacific Plate
- India-Australia-New Zealand Plate
- South American Plate
- North American Plate
- Antarctica and the surrounding oceanic plate
- Eurasian and the adjacent oceanic plate
- Africa with the adjacent oceanic plate

Isostasy

- Beneath the Earth's surface lies a hidden equalizer known as the compensation depth, where pressure becomes uniform despite changes in topography. This magical point acts like a balancing scale, ensuring equal downward force regardless of mountains towering above or valleys plunging below. When the weight on the crust fluctuates, like through erosion or glacial shifts, the crust responds with an isostatic adjustment, rising or sinking to restore this perfect equilibrium. This dynamic process, known as isostatic rebound, constantly sculpts the Earth's surface, ensuring a never-ending balance between weight, pressure, and the ever-shifting landscape.
- While the depth of lithosphere varies and also the boundary (Mohorovicic Discontinuity) between the mantle and crust don't have an uniform depth.
- Isostatic elaborate us on the physical, chemical and mechanical differences between the mantle and crust.
- Isostatic describes that how the earth's crust are floating on the more malleable mantle and also tell us that not all regions of Earth are balanced in isostatic equilibrium.
- This equilibrium depends on the thickness and density of the earth's crust, as well as on the dynamic forces that work in the mantle.

Unit-9: Oceanography

- 71% of Earth's surface is covered by water so it is often referred to as the water planet.
- Only 29% of Earth's surface is land.
- The Northern Hemisphere is referred to as the land hemisphere because it contains 61% land and 39% water.
- While the Southern Hemisphere is referred to as the water hemisphere because it contains 81% water and 19% land.
- 3800 m is the average depth of oceans while the average height of the lithosphere is 840 m.

Major Oceans

- Pacific ocean is the largest ocean followed by Atlantic, Indian, Arctic.
- According to depth pacific ocean is deepest followed by Indian, Atlantic and Arctic.

The Relief of the Ocean

- Hypsographic or Hypsometric Curves are those curves that represent the different height and depth zones of the lithosphere and the hydrosphere.
- The floor of the oceans may be divided into 4 parts according to the hypsographic curve:
- Continental shelf
- Continental slope
- Deep sea plains
- Oceanic deeps

Continental Shelf

- Continental shelf is the seaward extension of the continent from the shoreline to the continental edge.
- Average width of continental shelves is 65 kilometers (40 miles).
- Average depth of continental shelves is 150 to 200 m and slope is 1°.
- The relief of the coastal land decides the width of continental shelves, they are:
- **Wider Shelves:** They present where coast lands are wide plains.
- **Narrow Shelves:** The shelves are narrow where the high mountains are very close and parallel to the coast. Example, due to the presence of the Andes mountain, the Pacific continental shelf along western coast of South America is 16 km narrow.
- These shelves have the richest fishing grounds in the world. For example, Dogger Bank in the North sea, Grand Banks off Newfoundland.
- 7.6% of the ocean floor is occupied by the continental shelves.

Continental Slope

- Continental slope is the region of steep slope that extends from the continental shelf to the deep sea plains.
- Submarine canyons are the major significant relief features of continental slope.
- 8.5% of the total area of the ocean basins is occupied by this slope.
- Variation of its gradient from 2° to 5°.
- Over continental slopes the depth of water varies from 200 m to 3000 m.

Deep Sea Plains

- 75.9% of the total area of the ocean basins is occupied by this plain. Hence, It is the most extensive relief zone of the ocean.
- The depth of water varies from 3000 m to 6000 m.
- Some significant relief features are Ridges, guyots, seamounts, trenches etc.

Oceanic Deeps

- Oceanic Deeps are indicated to the depressions and trenches on the ocean floor.
- Oceanic Deeps are the deepest zones of the ocean basins and cover about 7% of the ocean basins.
- Oceanic Deeps can be divided into two categories according to their sizes:
- **Deeps:** They are very deep but less extensive depressions.
- **Trenches:** They are long but narrow linear depressions.

Major Ocean Trenches

Trenches	Depth (m)	Location
Mariana	11034	North Pacific Ocean
Tonga (Aldrich)	10882	Central South Pacific Ocean
Ramapo (Japan)	10554	North Pacific Ocean
Kurile	10542	Off Sakhalin, Kamchatka, Pacific Ocean
Mindanao	10540	Pacific Ocean
Swire (Philippines)	10475	North West Pacific Ocean
Kermadec	10047	Pacific Ocean
Puerto Rico (Nares)	8,376	Atlantic Ocean
Diamantina	5,800	Indian Ocean
Aleutian	8,109	Pacific Ocean
Cayman	7,686	Atlantic Ocean
Atacama	8,065	South Pacific Ocean
Romanche (Tizard)	7,758	South Atlantic Ocean
Java (Sunda)	7,290	East Indian Ocean

Distribution of Water on Earth

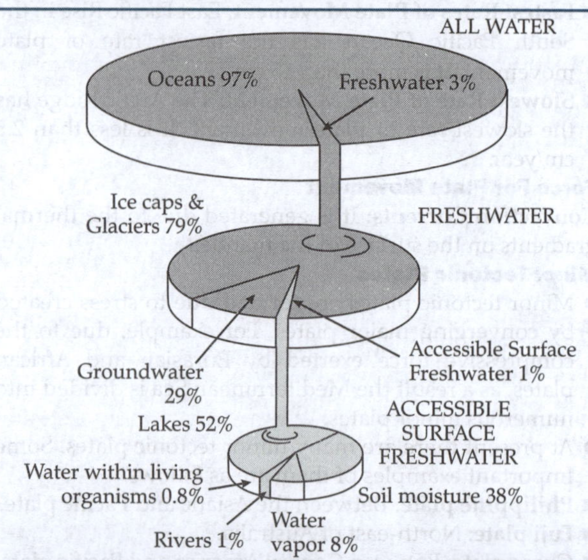

Basin	Volume (Ten Lakh Cubic km)	% of Total
Oceans	1370	97.25
Glaciers and ice caps	29	2.05
Groundwater	9.5	0.68
Lakes	0.125	0.01
Soil moisture	0.065	0.005
Atmosphere	0.013	0.001
Rivers	0.0017	0.0001
Biosphere	0.0006	0.00004

Some Important Features of Relief

- **Submarine Canyons:** Submarine canyons are basically the steep-sided erosional gorges which cut into the continental slope, sediments and rocks of the shelf. Some Important examples are: Congo Canyon, Nazare Canyon, Hudson Canyon, Bering Canyon, Monterey Canyon etc.
- **Oceanic Ridges:** These are most extensive in the Atlantic and the Indian Ocean. Oceanic Ridges are a long elevation of deep-sea floor having less regular topography than a rise and steeper sides. Above the ocean surface they form islands at many places such as Azores islands.

Oceans

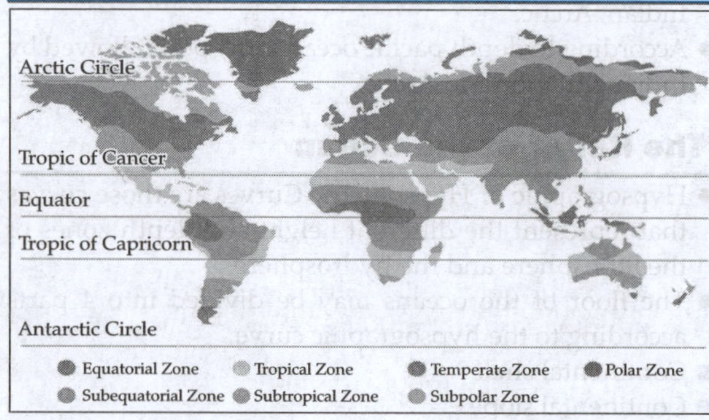

Pacific Ocean

- It is the largest ocean of all the oceans.
- Earth's 1/3rd area is occupied by it.
- Overall shape of the Pacific Ocean is triangular.
- In the east coasts of Asia and in the west to west coasts of Americas in the east it extends 16000 km from east to west.
- It extends 14880 km from north to south between the Bering Strait in the north to Cape Adre (Antarctica) in the south.
- Marginal seas are found on the western margin of the Pacific Ocean. on the eastern side of this ocean, the Gulf of California is the only marginal sea. e.g. Coral Sea, Sea of Okhotsk, Bering Sea, Sea of Japan, Yellow Sea, China Sea, Bass Strait, Arafura Sea etc.
- **East Pacific Rise:** Central or mid-oceanic ridges are not found in the Pacific Ocean like the Indian and Atlantic Oceans however few scattered ridges are found here. Albatross Plateau or the east Pacific Ridge of it. Albatross Plateau extends from north of New Zealand to California coast.
- **Pacific Ridges and Rises name:**

1. Bonin
2. East Pacific
3. Macquarie
4. Fanning
5. Hawaii
6. Fiji

Important Trenches and Basins of the Pacific Ocean:

	Deep Sea Trenches		Deep Sea Basins
1.	Japan	1.	Tasman
2.	Mariana	2.	Central Pacific
3.	Aleutian	3.	Coral
4.	Chile	4.	Celebes
5.	Peru (Atacama)	5.	Banda
6.	Philippine	6.	Fiji
7.	Kurile	7.	Philippines
8.	Tonga	8.	Caroline
9.	Kermadec	9.	South Pacific
10.	Riukiu	10.	Peru

Atlantic Ocean

- About 1/6th of the total area of the earth is covered by the Atlantic Ocean.
- This ocean has an area of 106,460,000 km² which is about 50% of the Pacific Ocean.
- The shape of the Atlantic Ocean is 'S' and it narrows towards the equator while it widens to the south of the equator with the maximum width of 5920 km at 35° latitude.
- But in between the Liberian coast and the Cape Sao Roque it is only 2560 km wide.
- **Marginal seas are:**

- Hudson Bay
- Baltic Sea
- Baffin Bay
- North Sea
- Mediterranean Sea
- Davis Strait.

- **Islands on the Atlantic Ocean:** Atlantic Ocean contain a few islands such as:

- Georgia
- British Isles
- South orkneys
- Saint Helena Islands
- Sandwich
- Falklands
- Shetlands
- New-Foundland etc.

Atlantic Ocean's Deep Sea Basins, Ridges and Rises

Deep Sea Basins	Ridges and Rises
Brazil	Rio Grande
Agulhas	Sierra Leone
North America	North and South Atlantic
Cape Verde	Walvis
Sierra Leone	Guinea
South Antilles	

Atlantic Ocean Deep Sea Trenches and Troughs

Deep Sea Trenches	Deep Sea Troughs
Romanche Trench	Caymon Trough
Vema Deep	Valdivia Deep
Buchanan Deep	Puerto Rico Deep
Columbia Deep	Hatteras Deep
Moseley Deep	Nares Deep

Mid Atlantic Ridge

- Mid Atlantic Ridge is extended for 14,400 km from Iceland in the north to Bouvet Island in the south and has an S shaped structure.
- In the bottom relief of the Atlantic ocean, the presence of a longitudinal mid-Atlantic Ridge is the most characteristic feature. It has many branches like:

- **Challenger Rise:** It is present to the south of the equator.
- **Dolphin Rise:** It is present to the North of the equator.
- **Wyville-Thomson Ridge:** It is present in between Iceland and Scotland.
- **Telegraphic Plateau:** This Plateau is situated to the south of Greenland.
- **Newfoundland Rise:** It is a branch of the central ridge lies near 50°N latitude.
- **Azores Rise:** It extends upto Azores Islands and bifurcates from the mid-Atlantic Ridge to the south of 40°N latitude.
- **Walvis Ridge:** It spreads from Tristan da cunha to the west coast of Africa at 40° S latitude.
- **Rio Grande Rise:** This ridge extends upto South American coast.

- The higher parts of the mid-Atlantic Ridge rising above the water surface are as follows

- The Azores in the north and
- Ascension and Tristan da cunha Islands in the south.

- **Pico Islands of Azores:** It is the highest island peak of the Azores which raises 213.36 m above sea level and 8229.6 m above the sea floor.

Indian Ocean

- It is smaller than the Atlantic and Pacific Oceans.
- About 20% of the total area of all the oceans of the world is covered by it.
- On all of its sides is bounded by Asia in the north, Africa in the west, Asia in the east, Australia in the south-east and Antarctica in the south.
- Andaman Sea is the basin enclosed between the Andaman-Nicobar arc and the Kra Isthmus.
- **Central Ridge:** It is also known as Mid-Indian Oceanic Ridge and it extends from the southern tip of the Indian peninsula in the north to Antarctica in the south.

Branches of Central Ridge

- Seychelles-Mauritius Ridge
- **Socotra Chagos Ridge:** It is also known as Carlsberg Ridge.
- Southwest Indian Ridge
- **Madagascar Ridge:** Prime Edward-Crozet Ridge is the southward extension of it which lies between 40°S to 48°S latitudes.
- **Ninety East Ridge:** It merges with Amsterdam-St. Paul Plateau and extends upto the continental shelf off the Irrawaddy river mouth. The length of the ridge is almost 4000 km long. In the south it joins with West Australian Ridge or The Broken Ridge. Kerguelen is the western branch of it. The Central Ridge bifurcates to the south of 50° S latitude. Eastern branch of the central ridge and Gaussberg ridge is also known as Indian-Antarctic ridge.
- **Islands:** As compared to the Pacific and Atlantic ocean, it has far less number of islands. Some of them are as follows:
  - Madagascar
  - Sri Lanka
  - Socotra
  - Maldives
  - Chagos
  - New Amsterdam
  - St. Paul
  - Kerguelen
  - Mauritius (also known as volcanic island)
  - Reunion or Volcanic island
  - Laccadives etc.
- **Indian Ocean's Deep Sea Basins, Ridges and Deep Sea Trenches**

Deep Sea Basins	Ridges	Deep Sea Trenches
Arabian	South West Indian Ridge	Amirante
India-Australian	Crozet	Nicobar
Somali	Carlsberg	Sunda
Madagascar	Mascarene	Ob
	Diego Garcia	
	Ninety East	
	Kerguelen- Gaussberg	
	Macquarie	

Arctic Ocean

- The shape of the Arctic Ocean is almost circular that surrounds the North Pole of the Earth.
- Total area of the Arctic Ocean is about 14 million km².
- By land masses it is surrounded on all sides hence there are a few places where it is connected with the Pacific and Atlantic Oceans.
- It is connected with the Pacific Ocean through the Bering Strait at 170° W.
- By a central ridge and Ellesmere Land it is divided into two basins. Central Ridge extends from the front Novosibirsk Islands through the North Pole to Greenland. It is also named as Lomonosov Ridge and has a length of 1800 km.

Arctic Ocean's Marginal seas and Islands

Marginal Seas	Islands
Eastern Siberian Sea	New Siberian Islands
Beaufort Sea off Alaska	Bear Island
Barents Sea (Between Norway and Spitsbergen)	Canadian Archipelago
Laptev Sea (along Siberian coast)	Novaya Zemlya
Kara Sea (Between mouth of river Ob and island of Novaya Zemlya)	Jan Mayen
	Spitsbergen

- **Ridges And Basin:** The geographic North Pole is located in the Fram Basin which is 2345 fathoms deep. It is surrounded by Nansen and Lomonosov Ridges.

Salinity of Ocean

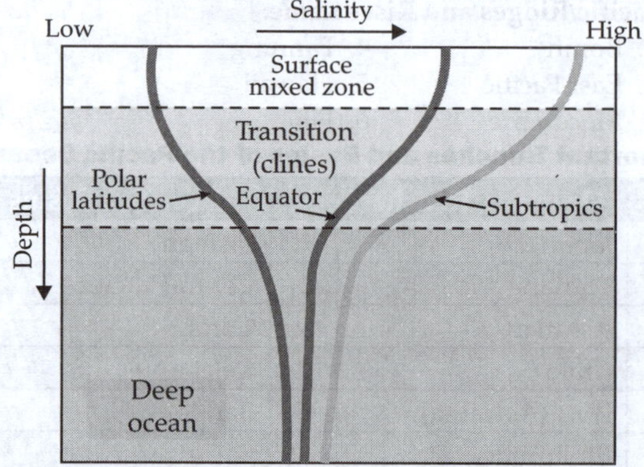

- Salinity is the degree of saltiness in water.
- Due to free movement, salts remain remarkably constant in all oceans and even at great depths but degree of concentration varies.
- NaCl or common salt form 77% of dissolved mineral matter and other salts include magnesium, calcium and potassium.
- Average salinity is 35.2 parts per thousand.
- **Salinity of some famous Seas**
  - **Red Sea:** Its much surface evaporation and fewer rivers draining into it: salinity is 39 parts per thousand.
  - **Dead Sea:** Its salinity varies between 300–400 ppt.
  - **Baltic Sea:** It is dilution of fresh water and has salinity of 6 to 20 parts per thousand.
  - **Caspian Sea:** Enclosed sea with salinity at 180.
  - **Lake Van:** Lake Van at 330 parts per thousand highest salinity.
  - Due to the high density in Lake Van and Dead Sea it is impossible to sink so beginner swimmers find it easier to float.
- Salinity is Affected by following factors:
  - **Fresh water is added by precipitation, streams and icebergs:** Salinity is low in the equatorial region due to heavy rainfall and high relative humidity. Baltic, Arctic and Antarctic waters have low salinity due to colder climate and little evaporation-as water is added by melting of icebergs and rivers.

- **Rate of evaporation:** Water fringing the high-pressure belts of trade wind deserts have high salinity caused by high temperature and low humidity. Temperate oceans have low salinity due to lower evaporation & temperature.
- **Degree of water mixing by currents:** Water does not mix freely with ocean waters in enclosed seas and salinity is high.

Factors Increasing or Decreasing Salinity

Increasing Salinity	Decreasing Salinity
Ice Formation	Ice Melting
Evaporation	Precipitation
Solution of salt deposits	Inflow of fresh water from land
Mixing with more saline deep water	Mixing with less saline deep water
Surface Circulation (Advection of more saline water)	Surface Circulation (Advection of less Saline water)

Significant Salts of the Oceans

Salts	Amount (% per 1000g of water)	Percentage
Sodium Chloride	27.213	77.8
Magnesium Chloride	3.807	10.9
Magnesium Sulphide	1.658	4.7
Calcium Sulphate	1.260	3.6
Potassium Sulphate	0.863	2.5
Calcium Carbonate	0.123	0.3
Magnesium Bromide	0.076	0.2
Total	**35.00**	**100.00**

Temperature of the Oceanic Water

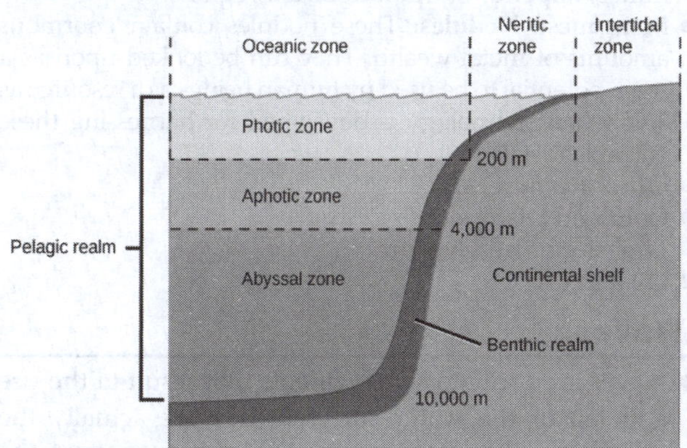

- The temperature of the oceanic water is important for marine organisms including phytoplanktons and zooplanktons (animals).
- The temperature of ocean water also affects the climate of the coastal areas.
- The daily range of temperature of surface water of oceans is insignificant, as it is only 1° C.
- Maximum temperature is recorded at 2 p.m., and minimum temperature recorded at 5 a.m., in the morning. In the northern hemisphere the maximum and minimum annual temperatures of ocean water is recorded in August and February respectively.
- Annual range of temperature is much smaller-less than –12° C for open seas but there are regional variations.
- Cold current as Labrador current reduces surface water temperature and warm current like North Atlantic Drift raises the temperature making Norwegian coast ice free year round.
- Highest water temperatures are seen in tropics: Red Sea with 30° C to 38° C.
- Temperature varies vertically with increasing depth 80% ocean water has temperature 35°F to 40°F.

Based on Temperature there are Two Types of Currents

- **Cold Currents**
- Bring cold water into warm water areas.
- These currents are usually found on the west coast of the continents in the low and middle latitudes (in both hemispheres) and on the east coast in the higher latitudes in the northern hemisphere.
- **Warm Currents**
- Bring warm water into cold water areas.
- Usually observed on the east coast of continents in the low and middle latitudes (in both hemispheres).
- In the northern hemisphere they are found on west coasts of continents in high latitudes.
- Based on depth there are two types of currents
- **Surface Currents:** Upper 400 m of the ocean constitute about 10% of water in the ocean.
- **Deep Water Currents:** Constitute 90% of ocean waters.

Major Oceans Currents of the World

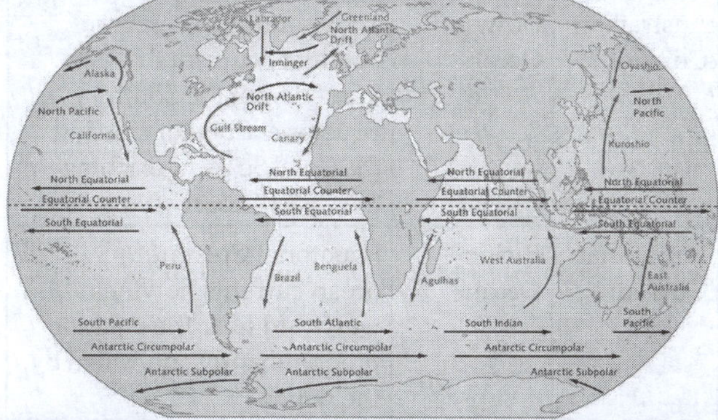

Cold Currents

Name	Ocean	Description
California Current	North Pacific Ocean	Southward flowing current off the west coast of the United States in the Pacific Ocean.
Canaries Current	North Atlantic Ocean	The Canary Current is a wind-driven surface Current that is part of the North Atlantic Gyre.
Humboldt Current	South Pacific Ocean	The Humboldt Current, also known as the Peru Current, flows northward along the western coast of South America.
Labrador Current	North Atlantic Ocean	Flowing from the Arctic Ocean south along the east coast of Canada.

Oyashio (Kamchatka) Current	North Pacific Ocean	Oyashio or the Kurile current, is a cold subarctic ocean current that flows south in the western North Pacific Ocean.
West Australian Current	Indian Ocean	It is a cool surface current of the Southern Ocean and Southern Indian Ocean.
West Wind Drift	South Pacific Ocean	Surface oceanic current encircling Antarctica and flowing from west to east.

Warm Currents

Name	Oceans	Description
Agulhas Current	Indian Ocean	The Agulhas Current is the western boundary current of the southwest Indian Ocean. It flows down the east coast of Africa.
Alaska Current	North Pacific Ocean	Southwest warm water current off the coast of Alaska and west coast of Canada.
Brazil Current	South Atlantic Ocean	Flows south along the Brazil South coast to the mouth of the Rio de la plata.
East Austrailian Current	South Pacific Ocean	The East Australian Current is the southward western boundary current that is formed from the South Equatorial Current crossing the Coral Sea and reaching the eastern coast of Australia.
Equatorial Current	Pacific Ocean	Equatorial Current, ocean currents flowing westward near the equator, predominantly controlled by the winds.
Gulf Stream	North Atlantic Ocean	Warm ocean currents originating in the Gulf of Mexico along the east coast of the United States.
Kuroshio Current	North Pacific Ocean	North-Flowing warm current off the coast of Japan in the Pacific.
North Atlantic Current (NAC)	North Atlantic Ocean	The North Atlantic current warms the western boundary within the Atlantic Ocean that extends the Gulf Stream north-eastward.
North Pacific Drift	North Pacific Ocean	The North Pacific Current is a slow warm water

Movements of Ocean Currents

- Circulate in a regular pattern.
- Warm current flows from the equatorial region to poles.
- Cold currents flow from Polar Regions to the equator and have low surface.

- **Underlying Factors**
- **Temperature:** Warm water is lighter and rises while cold water is denser and sinks.
- **Salinity:** Water of high salinity is denser than water of low salinity. Low salinity water flows on the surface of waters and high salinity water flows at the bottom.
- **Planetary Winds:** Trade winds which move equatorial waters pole ward and westwards and warm eastern coast of continents. Example: South Equatorial Current warms eastern coast of Brazil as warm Brazilian current. Westerlies in temperate are less reliable than trade Winds-result in north-easterly flow of water in the northern hemisphere, so the Gulf Stream is driven to Western Europe.
- **Land:** Landmass obstructs and diverts a current. Example: Tip of south Chile diverts west wind Drift northward as Peruvian current.
- **Earth's Rotation and Influence of Coriolis Force:** It deflects freely moving objects including ocean currents to the right. In the north hemisphere it is clockwise (Gulf Stream and Canaries Current)while in the south hemisphere it is anti-clockwise (Brazilian current and West Wind Drift).

Ocean Resources

- **Potassium:** Potassium is also one of the most abundant minerals like salt. Although potassium cannot be directly extracted as salt.
- **Sand:** The sea beaches can be understood as the residual deposits of sand.
- **Salt:** Salt is chemically known as sodium chloride. It is one of the most abundant minerals found in the ocean water. Salt can be either directly extracted or could be mines, depending upon different regions.
- **Manganese Nodules:** These nodules contain enormous amounts of metal wealth. They can be looked upon as a huge potential to be used by human beings as a resource as and when technology is developed for harnessing these valuable metals.
- **Other Resources:**
- Gold and Diamonds
- Limestone and Gypsum
- Oil and Gas

Waves

- Waves are oscillatory movements that result in the rise and fall of the water surface. They are actually the energy, not the water as such, which moves across the ocean surface.
- Note: waves and ocean currents are horizontal movement of ocean water, tides are vertical movement of ocean water.

Wave speed

- Rate at which wave moves->measured in knots.

Wave frequency

- Number of waves passing a given point during 1 second time.

Wave amplitude

- One half of the wave height.

Tides

- Tides are the periodical rise and fall of sea levels caused by the combined effects of the gravitational forces exerted by the Moon and the Sun, and the rotation of the Earth and associated centrifugal forces.
- Note: Spring tides occur twice monthly, during full moon and new moon. Neap tides occur during the first and third quarter moon phases.
- Tides help in navigation, desilting, fishing, and generation of electrical power.

Spring Tides	When sun, moon and earth are in straight line occurs on full moon day and new moon day. Highest high tide.
Neap Tide	A period of moderate tides when the sun and moon are at right angles to each other.
Surges	The movement of water caused by meteorological effects.
Ebb	The time between the high tide and low tide when the water level is falling.
Flow or Flood	The time between low tide and the high tide when the tide is rising.

Unit-10: Climatology

- **Climate:** Average weather conditions of a specified area for a considerable time.
- **Weather:** Pertains to the condition of the atmosphere in any place or any time.

Elements of Weather and Climate

- **Humidity:** Dampness of the atmosphere. Measured using a hygrometer.
- **Rainfall:** Form of precipitation (snow, sleet and hail) measured by rain gauge.
- **Absolute humidity:** Amount of water vapor present in air.
- **Relative humidity:** the ratio between actual amount of water vapor and maximum amount the air can hold at that temperature.
- When relative humidity is 100% then air is said to be saturated and air temperature is at dew point.
- **Wind:** Air in motion with direction and speed. Wind direction is measured by wind vane or weather. Winds are named from the direction where they blow as east wind blows from east to west.
- Anemometer is used to measure speed of wind.
- **Clouds:** After dew point cooling leads to condensation of water vapor in atmosphere tiny drops will suspend as clouds-form, shape, height and movement tell us about the sky conditions.
- Cloud cover is expressed in eights or oktas.

Other Elements Pertaining to Visibility

- **Mist:** Visibility greater than 1 km less than 2 km. Condensation of water vapor in air, forms drops of water to float above clouds at ground level.
- **Haze:** Visibility is 2 km to 5 km, due to smoke and dust in industrial areas which causes unequal refraction of light.
- **Fog:** Visibility less than 1 km. Water condensing on dust and other particles forming dense clouds near the ground surface. Fogs are more common over sea than land and most prevalent over coastal areas. Dense fogs are more in high and mid latitude rather than tropics.
- **Frost:** Forms on cold surfaces when condensation takes place below freezing point (0°C).
- **Smog:** Fog and smoke together is called smog.

Classification of Clouds

High Clouds 6000-12000 m	Middle Clouds 2100-6000 m	Low Clouds Below 2100 m	Clouds with great Vertical Extent 1500-9000 m
Cirrus: Composed of small ice crystals, white, wispy and fibrous in appearance.	**Altocumulus:** Composed of water droplets in layers and patches.	**Stratocumulus:** Large globular masses, bumpy, looking soft and gray in appearance, regular and sometimes wavy pattern.	**Cumulus:** Round topped and flat based forming a whitish gray globular mass, it consists of individual cloud units.
Cirro Cumulus: Composed of ice crystals, but globular or rippled in appearance.	**Alto-Stratus:** Composed of water droplets, forming sheets of gray or watery looking clouds.	**Nimbostratus:** They are known as 'Rain Clouds' and they are dark, thick and accompanied by light to moderately falling precipitation.	**Cumulonimbus:** They have great vertical extent, white or black globular masses, whose rounded tops often spread out in the form of anvil. It is characterized by conventional rain, lighting and thunder.
Cirrus Stratus: Looking like a thin white, almost transparent sheet, which causes the sun and moon to have holes		**Stratus:** These are low, gray and layered, with a fog-like appearance, bringing dull weather and often accompanied by drizzle.	

Atmosphere

- Atmosphere is composed of gases, water vapour and dust particles.

Water Vapour

- Decreases with altitude. In warm and wet tropics it accounts for 4%, in dry and cold areas less than 1%.
- It decreases from equator to poles. It acts as a blanket for earth by absorbing some incoming radiation and preserves earth radiated heat.
- It contributes to stability and instability of air.

Gases

Constituent	Formula	Percentage by Volume
Nitrogen	N_2	78.084
Oxygen	O_2	20.946
Argon	Ar	0.934
Carbon dioxide	CO_2	0.042%
Neon	Ne	0.002
Helium	He	0.0005
Krypto	Kr	0.001
Xenon	Xe	0.00009
Hydrogen	H_2	0.00005

- Carbon dioxide is transparent to incoming solar radiation and opaque to outgoing terrestrial radiation. It absorbs part of terrestrial radiation and reflects back the rest.
- Nitrogen is present highest by volume.

Dust Particles

- It includes sea salts, fine soil, ash, pollen, smoke soot etc.
- Higher concentrations of dust particles are found in subtropical and temperate regions.
- These act as hygroscopic nuclei around which water vapour condenses to form clouds.

Structure of the Atmosphere

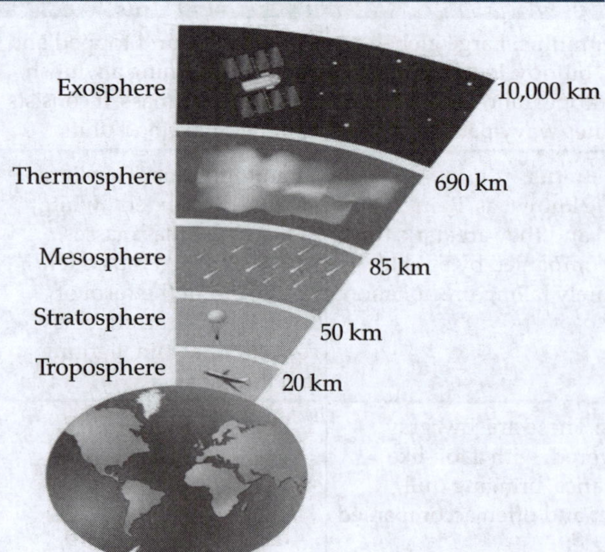

Troposphere

- Lowermost layer of the atmosphere, with average height of 13 km.
- Its thickness is greater at the equator (18 km), because the heated air rises to greater heights by strong convection currents. Whereas at the poles it is at 8 km.
- It is associated with climatic and weather phenomena.
- The troposphere ends with the Tropopause.

Stratosphere

- Found above the troposphere, it is cloudless, thin air, without dust and vapour.
- The temperature in this layer remains constant for some distance but then rises, due to the presence of ozone (harmful ultraviolet radiation is absorbed by ozone).
- This layer is almost free from clouds and associated weather phenomenon, making conditions most ideal for flying aeroplanes.
- So airplanes fly in the lower stratosphere, sometimes in the upper troposphere where the weather is calm.

Mesosphere

- This is an intermediate layer beyond the ozone layer and continues up to an altitude of 80 km from the earth's surface.
- The temperature gradually falls to -100°C at 80 km altitude.
- Upper layer of the mesosphere is Mesopause.

Thermosphere

- In the thermosphere temperature rises very rapidly with increasing height.
- **Ionosphere:** It contains electrically charged particles called ions, which make short wave radio transmission possible over long distances.
- It extends between 80-400 km.
- Meteors burn in this region.

Exosphere

- This is the uppermost layer of the atmosphere extending beyond the ionosphere above a height of about 400 km.
- The air is extremely rarefied and the temperature gradually increases through the layer.
- Light gases like helium and hydrogen float into space from here. This layer coincides with space.

Insolation

- Insolation is the incoming solar radiation (short wavelength: visible and UV radiations).
- The earth absorbs short wave radiation during daytime and reflects back the heat received into space as long-wave radiation (mostly infrared radiation) during night.
- The maximum insolation is received over subtropical deserts, where the cloudiness is least.
- Equator receives comparatively less insolation than the tropics.
- **Aphelion:** On 4th July earth is farthest from the sun.
- **Perihelion:** On 3rd January, the earth is the nearest to the sun.

Variability of Insolation at the Surface of the Earth

The factors that cause these variations in insolation are

- Angle of inclination of the sun's rays:
  - The higher the latitude, the less is the angle they make with the surface of the earth resulting in slant sun rays.
  - The area covered by the vertical rays is always less than the slant rays.

- **Rotation of earth on its axis**
- Earth makes an angle of 66.5 degree with the plane of its orbit around the sun.
- **Transparency of the atmosphere**
- The transparency of the atmosphere depends upon the cloud cover and its thickness, dust particles, water vapour etc.
- They reflect, absorb or transmit insolation. Thick clouds hinder the solar radiation to reach the earth's surface.
- Similarly, water vapour absorbs solar radiation resulting in less amount of insolation reaching the surface.
- When the solar radiation passes through the atmosphere, water vapour, ozone and other gasses absorb much of the near infrared radiation (mainly in the troposphere).
- Very small suspended particles in the troposphere scatter visible spectrum both to space and towards the earth's surface.
- This process adds colour to the sky. The red colour of the rising and the setting sun and the blue colour of the sky are the results of scattering of the light within the atmosphere.
- **Configuration of land in terms of its aspects**
- Sun facing slopes receive more vertical rays of sun, the other side receives less insolation.
- **Note:** Sun's rays, like a spotlight, shine brightest on the subtropical deserts, where skies are clear and cloudless. Surprisingly, the equator, despite its proximity to the sun, receives less direct sunlight than the tropics due to its vertical angle and frequent cloud cover. Additionally, at the same latitude, landmasses tend to bask in more sunshine than oceans, as water reflects more radiation back into space. Winter, however, casts a dimmer light on the mid- and higher latitudes, with their tilted angles receiving significantly less solar energy compared to summer's bounty.
- **Duration of the day**
- The longer the duration of the day, the greater is the amount of insolation received.
- Conversely shorter the duration of the day leads to receipt of less insolation.

Heating and Cooling of the Atmosphere

Four Different Ways

- **Convection**
- Vertical heating of the atmosphere. Air in contact with the earth rises vertically on heating, in the form of currents and further transmits heat to the atmosphere.
- **Terrestrial radiation**
- Earth heats up with incoming short wave solar radiation, and becomes a radiating body. It radiates energy to the atmosphere in the long wave form.
- **Conduction**
- When two bodies of unequal temperature are in contact with one another, there is flow of energy from warm body to cooler body.
- Earth after being heated by insolation transmits heat to the lower layers of the atmosphere in long wave form.
- **Advection**
- Transfer of heat through horizontal movement of the air.

Elements of Climate and Factors Affecting Temperature of The Earth

The temperature of air at any place is influenced by:

- **Altitude**
- The atmosphere is indirectly heated by terrestrial radiation from below through conduction. The temperature generally decreases with increasing height.
- **Latitude**
- The temperature of a place depends on the insolation received. Wherever there are vertical rays of sun, intense heating happens. Slant rays cause less heating and temperature also less.
- **Ocean Currents and Air Mass**
- Like the land and sea breezes, the passage of air masses also affects the temperature.
- The places, which come under the influence of warm air-masses experience higher temperature and the places that come under the influence of cold air masses experience low temperature.
- Similarly, the places located on the coast where the warm ocean currents flow record higher temperature than the places located on the coast where the cold currents flow.
- **Continentality**
- Land is heated more quickly than water, because of higher specific heat of water.
- Thereby causing warm summers, cool winters and great temperature range for continental interiors.
- **Distance from the Sea**
- Compared to land, the sea gets heated slowly and loses heat slowly. Land heats up and cools down quickly.
- Therefore, the variation in temperature over the sea is less compared to land. The places situated near the sea come under the moderating influence of the sea and land breezes which moderate the temperature.
- **Slope, Shelter and Aspect**
- Steep slope experiences a rapid change in temperature. Mountain ranges having East west alignment have higher temperatures on the south facing sunny slope (good for vine cultivation) than the north facing sheltered slope.
- Hot day followed by calm night, air cools more rapidly over higher grounds and may induce cold heavy air to flow down the slope and accumulate in valley bottom pushing warm air upwards (temperature would be lower in valley than above this reversal of lapse rate is called as Temperature Inversion).
- **Natural Vegetation and Soil**
- Thick foliage of Amazon cuts incoming insolation and sunlight does not reach ground.
- In the day trees lose water by evapo-transpiration so the air above is cooled. Light soil reflects more heat than darker soil which is better absorbers.
- Dry soil like sand is more sensitive to temperature changes while wet soil retains moisture and warms up and cools down more slowly.

Albedo

- Reflected amount of radiation from the earth surface.
- The value of albedo will be different for different surfaces.
- Because of the effect of albedo, highly developed areas such as urban cities can experience higher average temperatures than the surrounding suburban or rural

areas, a phenomenon known as the "Urban Heat Island Effect".

- **Highest albedo:** snow > clouds> sand > grass > crops > forest.

Inversion of Temperature

- Normally, temperature decreases with increase in elevation. It is called normal lapse rate. It is 6.5°C per 1,000 m.
- At times, the situation is reversed and the normal lapse rate is inverted. It is called inversion of temperature.
- A long winter night with clear skies and still air is an ideal situation for inversion.
- The heat of the day is radiated off during the night, and by early morning hours, the earth is cooler than the air above. Over polar areas, temperature inversion is normal throughout the year.
- Smoke and dust particles get collected beneath the inversion layer and spread horizontally to fill the lower strata of the atmosphere.
- The inversion takes place in hills and mountains due to air drainage. Cold air at the hills and mountains, produced during night, flows under the influence of gravity.

Precipitation

- The process of continuous condensation in free air helps the condensed particles to grow in size.
- When the resistance of the air fails to hold them against the force of gravity, they fall onto the earth's surface.
- So after the condensation of water vapour, the release of moisture is known as precipitation.
- In simple terms we can summarize precipitation as the following

Virga	Raindrops evaporate before reaching the earth.
Rainfall	Drop size more than 0.5 mm.
Mist	Evaporation occurs before reaching the ground leading to foggy weather.
Hail	Precipitation in the form of hard rounded pellets is known as hail; 5 mm and 50 mm.
Drizzle	Light rainfall, drop size less than 0.5 mm.
Sleet	Frozen raindrops and refrozen melted snow mixture of snow and rain or merely partially melted snow.
Snowfall	Fine flakes of snow fall when the temperature is less than 0°C.

Types of Rainfall

On the basis of origin, rainfall may be classified into three main types:

- **Nimbo-Stratus:** Dark gray and rainy looking, dense and shapeless, often gives continuous rains.
- **Orographic rainfall or relief rain**
  - When the saturated air mass comes across a mountain, it is forced to ascend and as it rises, it expands; the temperature falls and the moisture is condensed.
  - After giving rain on the windward side, when these winds reach the other slope, they descend, and their temperature rises, leeward slopes remain rainless and dry.Leeward side also called as rain shadow region.
- **Convectional rainfall**
  - The air on being heated, becomes light and rises up in convection currents. As it rises, it expands and loses heat and consequently, condensation takes place and cumulus clouds are formed. With thunder and lightning, heavy rainfall takes place.
  - Common in summer/hot days/equatorial regions/earth's interiors.
- **Cyclonic or Frontal Rain:**
  - Purely associated with cyclonic activity.
  - Tropical regions with cyclones and temperate regions with depressions.
  - When two air masses with different temperatures meet, turbulent conditions are produced.
  - Along the front convection occurs and causes precipitation. This is called frontal rainfall.

Tornadoes and Thunderstorms

- Thunderstorms and tornadoes are severe local storms. They are of short duration, occurring over a small area but are violent.
- **Tornadoes**
  - From severe thunderstorms sometimes spiraling wind descends like a trunk of an elephant with great force, with very low pressure at the centre, causing massive destruction on its way. Such a phenomenon is called a tornado.
  - Tornadoes generally occur in middle latitudes. The tornado over the sea is called water sprouts.
- **Thunderstorms**
  - Thunderstorms mostly occur on ground where the temperature is high with thunder and lightning.
  - Thunderstorms are less frequent on water bodies due to low temperature.

Polar Vortex

- The Earth's atmosphere has two polar vortices which are overlying the North and South Poles.
- Each polar vortex is a persistent, large-scale, low-pressure zone that rotates counter-clockwise at the North Pole (called a cyclone) and clockwise at the South Pole; both polar vortices rotate eastward around the poles.
- These cold blasts of arctic air are bottled up by the strong jet stream or polar jet stream which is circulated at the high latitudes.
- Even though research claims that there is no direct relation between the Polar Vortex and Indian weather, the Arctic winds influence atmospheric circulations, weather systems, including the western disturbance.

Factors affecting Wind Velocity and Direction

- Air in motion is called wind. As wind blows from high pressure to low pressure it experiences a combined effect of three forces, in addition to gravitational forces.
- **Frictional forces**
  - Wind at the surface experiences friction. It affects the speed of the wind.
- **Coriolis force**
  - Rotation of earth about its axis affects wind direction. It deflects the wind to the right in the northern hemisphere and to the left in the southern hemisphere.
  - Coriolis force is directly proportional to the angle of latitude. It is maximum at the poles and absent at the equator.
  - Since Coriolis force is zero, winds blow perpendicular to the isobars. Low pressure gets filled instead of getting

intensified because of which tropical cyclones do not originate near the equator.

- Note: over low pressure areas air will converge and rise and at the high pressure area air will subside from above and diverge at the surface.

- **Pressure gradient force (PGF)**
- Rate of change of pressure with respect to distance is PGF.
- Higher the PGF, more is the velocity of the wind and larger is deflection in direction of the wind.

Atmospheric circulation and weather systems

- Air expands when heated and gets compressed when cooled.
- The pressure decreases with height.

Pressure Belts

- There are distinctly identifiable zones of homogeneous horizontal pressure regimes or 'pressure belts' on the earth's surface, the following are the various pressure belts.
- The subtropical highs.
- Equatorial low.
- Polar High-Pressure.
- The Sub-Polar Low-Pressure.

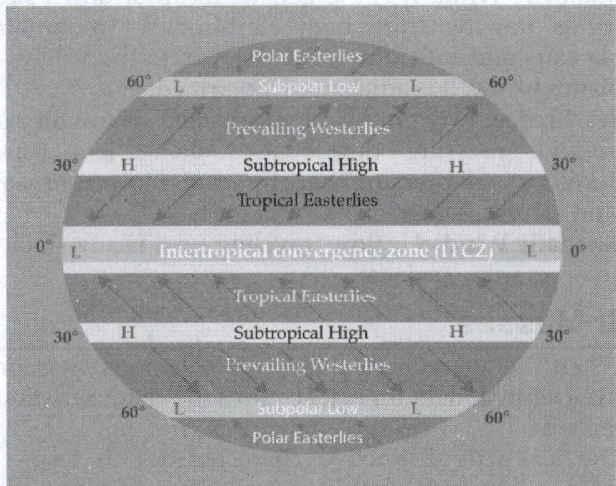

- **Sub-Tropical High-Pressure Belt or Horse Latitudes**
- The subtropical high-pressure belts, located around 30°N and 30°S, are also known as 'horse latitudes,' a term historically associated with becalmed sailing ships in these regions.
- After saturation (complete loss of moisture) at the Inter Tropical Convergence Zone (ITCZ), the air moving away from equatorial low-pressure belts in the upper troposphere becomes dry and cold.
- This dry and cold wind subsides at 30°N and S.
- So the high pressure along this belt is due to subsidence of air coming from the equatorial region which descends after becoming heavy.
- The high pressure is also due to the blocking effect of air at upper levels because of the Coriolis force.
- The subsiding air is warm and dry; therefore, most of the deserts are present along this belt, in both hemispheres.
- This belt is frequently invaded by tropical and extratropical disturbances.

- **Equatorial Low Pressure Belt or 'Doldrums'**
- Lies between 10°N and 10°S latitudes.
- Width may vary between 5N and 5°S and 20°N and 20°S.
- This belt happens to be the zone of convergence of trade winds from two hemispheres from subtropical high pressure belts.
- This belt is also called the Doldrums, because of the extremely calm air movements.
- The position of the belt varies with the apparent movement of the Sun.
- **Formation:** As this region lies along the equator, it receives the highest amount of insolation.
- Due to intense heating, air gets warmed up and rises over the equatorial region (convection).
- Whenever there is vertically upward movement of air, the region at the surface will be at low pressure.
- Thus the belt along the equator is called equatorial low pressure belt.
- **Climate:** This belt is characterized by extremely low pressure with calm conditions.
- Vertical winds (convection) carrying moisture form cumulonimbus clouds and lead to thunderstorms (convectional rainfall).

- **Polar High-Pressure Belt**
- The polar highs are small in area and extend around the poles. They lie around poles between 80-90° N and S latitudes.
- The air from sub-polar low-pressure belts after saturation becomes dry. This dry air becomes cold while moving towards poles through the upper troposphere.
- The lowest temperatures are found over the poles.

- **Sub-Polar Low-Pressure Belt:** Located between 45°N and S latitudes and the Arctic and the Antarctic circles (66.5° N and S latitudes). These are dynamically produced due to:
- Coriolis Force produced by rotation of the earth on its axis,
- Ascent of air as a result of convergence of Westerlies and polar easterlies.

- Due to a great contrast between the temperatures of the winds from subtropical and polar source regions, extra tropical cyclonic storms or lows (temperate cyclones or frontal cyclones) are produced in this region.

General Circulation of the Atmosphere

- The air at the Inter Tropical Convergence Zone (ITCZ) rises because of convection caused by high insolation and a low pressure.
- The winds from the tropics converge at this low pressure zone.
- The converged air rises along with the convective cell. It reaches the top of the troposphere and moves towards the poles. This causes accumulation of air at about 30° N and S.
- Part of the accumulated air sinks to the ground and forms a subtropical high.
- Another reason for sinking is the cooling of air when it reaches 30° N and S latitudes.
- Down below near the land surface the air flows towards the equator as the easterlies.

- The easterlies from either side of the equator converge in the Inter Tropical Convergence Zone (ITCZ).
- Such circulations from the surface upwards and vice-versa are called cells. Such a cell in the tropics is called Hadley Cell.
- In the middle latitudes the circulation is that of sinking cold air that comes from the poles and the rising warm air that blows from the subtropical high. At the surface these winds are called westerlies and the cell is known as the Ferrel cell.
- At polar latitudes the cold dense air subsides near the poles and blows towards middle latitudes as the polar easterlies. This cell is called the polar cell.
- These three cells set the pattern for the general circulation of the atmosphere. The transfer of heat energy from lower latitudes to higher latitudes maintains the general circulation.

Planetary Winds

Generalized Sketch of
Global Atmospheric Circulation

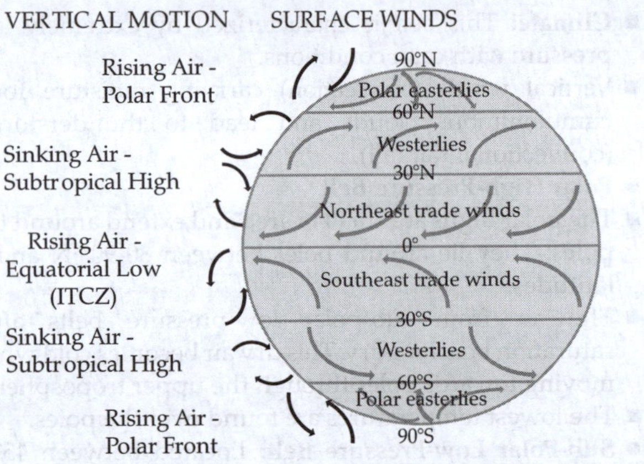

VERTICAL MOTION SURFACE WINDS

Rising Air - Polar Front
Sinking Air - Subtropical High
Rising Air - Equatorial Low (ITCZ)
Sinking Air - Subtropical High
Rising Air - Polar Front

90°N
Polar easterlies
60°N
Westerlies
30°N
Northeast trade winds
0°
Southeast trade winds
30°S
Westerlies
60°S
Polar easterlies
90°S

- The winds blowing throughout the year from high pressure belts to low pressure belts in the same direction are called "planetary or prevailing winds".
- Due to the effect of the rotation of the earth, the direction of the winds tends to deflect, instead of blowing directly from one pressure belt to another.
- These winds blow throughout the year and are controlled by the latitudinal pressure belts. They blow over vast areas of continents and oceans.

The Main Planetary Winds Are

- **Westerlies**
  - Westerlies blow from sub-tropical high-pressure belts towards sub-polar low-pressure belts.
  - The Westerlies of the Southern Hemisphere blow with greater strength and constant direction than the Northern Hemisphere.
  - Under the Coriolis force effect, the Westerlies become the South-Westerlies in the northern hemisphere and the North-Westerlies in the southern hemisphere.
  - Westerlies winds are named as roaring forties, furious fifties, screaming sixties based on the speed of the wind.
- **Polar Easterlies**
  - The Polar easterlies are dry, cold prevailing winds that blow from the Polar high-pressure belts to the Temperature low pressure belts.
  - There are extremely cold winds as they blow from the Tundra and Icecap regions. The Polar Easterlies are more regular in the southern hemisphere than in the northern hemisphere.
  - Unlike the Westerlies, the polar easterlies are often weak and irregular.
- **Trade Winds**
  - Trade winds blow in a belt lying between 5°N-30°N in the northern hemisphere and 5°S-30°S in the southern hemisphere.
  - There is low pressure on the equator, while high pressure at the sub tropics. So, air moves from the tropics toward the equator.
  - The trade winds in the Northern-Hemisphere blow from the north-east direction due to the deflection of the wind caused by the rotation of the Earth and so are called North-East Trades.
  - Similarly, the trade winds in the Southern-Hemisphere blow from the South-East direction and are thus called south-East Trades.
  - They are also known as Tropical easterlies.

Local Winds

- Local winds occur on a small spatial scale.
- The main types of local winds are: Sea breezes and land breezes, Anabatic and katabatic winds and other local winds. Due to differential heating of land surface.
  - **Land Breeze:** Night-land cools faster than sea, high pressure over land, low pressure over ocean-winds blow from land towards sea.
  - **Katabatic Wind:** It is the generic term for down slope winds flowing from high elevations of mountains, plateaus and hills down their slopes to the valleys or planes below. It is adiabatically warmed.
  - **Sea Breeze:** Day time-land gets heated -warm air rises up-Low pressure develops-sea being less warm, develops high pressure there by winds blow from sea to land causing sea breeze.
  - **Anabatic Wind:** Air flow traveling up a facing slope of an orographic surface.

Air Masses

- When the air remains over a homogenous area for a sufficiently longer time, it acquires the characteristics of the area.
- The air with distinctive characteristics in terms of temperature and humidity is called an air mass. It is a large body of air having little horizontal variation in temperature and moisture.
- The main source regions are the high-pressure belts in the subtropics (giving rise to tropical air masses) and around the poles (the source for polar air masses).
- Areas with high pressure but little pressure difference or pressure gradient are ideal source regions for development of air masses. Tropical air masses are warm and polar air masses are cold.

Air Masses and Source Region

- There are five major source regions. These are:
  - The subtropical hot deserts.
  - The relatively cold high latitude oceans.
  - Warm tropical and subtropical oceans.
  - Permanently ice-covered continents in the Arctic and Antarctica.
  - The very cold snow-covered continents in high latitudes.

4 Types of Fronts

- **Warm front:** The contact zone where the warm air mass moves towards the cold air mass.
- **Cold front:** The contact zone when the cold air moves towards the warm air mass.

- **Occluded front:** If an air mass is fully lifted above the land surface.
- **Stationary front:** When the front remains stationary.

Influence of Air Mass and World Weather

- The air masses carry atmospheric moisture from oceans to continents and cause precipitation over landmasses.
- They transport latent heat, thus removing the latitudinal heat balance.
- Most of the migratory atmospheric disturbances such as temperate cyclones and storms originate at the contact zone between different air masses and the weather associated with these disturbances is determined by characteristics of the air masses involved.
- **Fronts:** When two different air masses meet the boundary zone between them is called front.
- **Frontogenesis:** The process of formation of fronts.

Jet Stream

- Jet streams are relatively narrow bands of strong wind in the upper levels of the atmosphere.
- The winds blow from west to east in jet streams but the flow often shifts to the north and south. Jet streams follow the boundaries between hot and cold air.
- Since these hot and cold air boundaries are most pronounced in winter, jet streams are the strongest for both the northern and southern hemisphere winters.
- The strongest jet streams are the polar jets, weaker is subtropical jets.

Jet Streams and its Influence on Indian Monsoons

- **SubTropical Jet Streams:** Lowest latitudinal jet stream,present throughout the year, gives rossby waves characteristics,flows at lowest isobaric levels, dry weather conditions in the entire influence zone,and transports western disturbance of Mediterranean sea. Shifts northward during high sun season. However, the continentality of India causes exceptional bends and displaces this jetstream in central asia and replaces it with tropical Easterly Jet stream.
- Polar front jet stream is thermal indirect jet stream and is extention of polar night jet stream. This Jet stream has well defined life cycle. It occurs in between 40 to 60 degree latitudes.
- Polar night jet stream- heighest latitudinal, thermal direct, whith very high velocity and are in the convergence zone above the sub-polar low pressure belt.
- **Somali Jet**
  - The progress of the southwest monsoon towards India is greatly aided by the onset of the Somali jet that transits Kenya, Somalia and Sahel region.
  - It strengthens permanent high near Madagascar and also helps to drive S-W monsoons towards India at a greater pace and intensity.
  - The peculiar feature of Somali Current is reversal in direction with the onset of the summer monsoon.
- **Tropical easterly jet stream**
  - There are major high velocity winds in the lower troposphere called low-level jets (LLJs).
  - In the tropics, the most prominent of these are the Somali Jet and the African Easterly Jet [Tropical Easterly Jet].
  - The formation of TEJ results in the reversal of upper air circulation patterns [High pressure switches to low pressure] and leads to the quick onset of monsoons.
  - The easterly jet come into existence during high sun season in northern hemisphere and affects the occurrence of rainfall in India ensuring 3 months of continuous monsoon ladned wind.

Tropical Cyclone: Features of a Cyclone

- It is a large system of winds that circulates about a centre of low atmospheric pressure in a counter-clockwise direction north of the Equator and in a clockwise direction to the south.
- Cyclonic winds move across nearly all regions of the Earth except the equatorial belt.
- Anticyclones, wind systems that rotate about a high-pressure centre. Anticyclones have a flow opposite to that of cyclones-i.e., an outward-spiralling motion, with the winds rotating clockwise in the Northern Hemisphere and counter-clockwise in the Southern.

Conditions Ideal for the Formation of Cyclones

- Sufficiently warm sea surface temperatures higher than 27°C.
- Atmospheric instability.
- High humidity in the lower to middle levels of the troposphere.
- Enough Coriolis force to develop a low-pressure centre.
- A pre-existing low-level focus or disturbance.
- Low vertical wind shear.
- Upper divergence above the sea level system.

Energy source of Cyclones

- The temperature difference between the warm rising air and the cooler environment causes the rising air to become buoyant, further enhancing its upward movement.
- The fuel for a tropical cyclone is provided by a transfer of water vapour and heat from the warm ocean to the overlying air, primarily by evaporation from the sea surface.

Anticyclones

- An anticyclone, as a high-pressure area is a large atmospheric circulation system with the wind flowing clockwise around it in the Northern Hemisphere, and counter-clockwise in the Southern Hemisphere.
- Anticyclones form from air masses cooler than their surroundings, leading to contraction of air making it denser, thereby increasing surface air pressure.
- Calm settled weather is usually synonymous with anticyclones in temperate latitudes.
- Anticyclones are typically relatively slow-moving features.

Formation-Polar Front Theory

- The warm-humid air masses from the tropics meet the dry-cold air masses from the poles and thus a polar front is formed.
- The cold air mass is denser and heavier and due to this reason, warm air mass is pushed up.
- This interaction of cold and warm air masses creates instability and a low pressure is created at the junction particularly in the center of interactions.
- Thus, a void is created because of lessening of pressure. The surrounding air rushed in to occupy this void and coupled with the earth's rotation a cyclone is formed.

Temperate Cyclone

- Temperate cyclone and polar front theory come under the head of temperate cyclone, here they are given under the subhead of tropical cyclones.
- They are also known as Extra-tropical cyclones where the term "Extra-tropical" signifies that this type of cyclone generally occurs outside the tropics with a latitude range between 30° and 60°.
- They occur more strongly during winter season.
- Jet streams influence path of temperate cyclone.
- They are caused due to front formation.
- **Stationary front:** When both warm and cold arimass are in front of each other, causes frontal precipitation.
- Frontogenesis - convergence of warm and cold airm colums.
- **Stage of division of front:** This generated divison in temperate cyclone cold front - part of cold airmass penetrating in warmer latitude, causes thunder storm; Warm front- part of warm airmass penetrating in colder latitude, has increased temperature, and slight precipitation and has Cirrostratus clouds; Cold sector-remaining part of cold airmass, warm sector- remaining part of warm airmass
- Quick shift of cold front
- Closing down of warm sector.
- Stage of occlusion - merging of warm and cold fronts.It has a mixture of cold front type and warm front type weather.
- Frontolisis - death of temperate cyclone where warm air has completely rised and cold air ahd completely subsided.
- **Difference between Tropical and Temperate cyclones**

Tropical Cyclones	Temperate Cyclones
Tropical cyclones developed in the Inter Tropical Convergence (ITCZ) due to the differential heating of land and sea. As the ITCZ migrates to tropical and subtropical latitudes and even beyond during the respective hemisphere's summer season, increasing Coriolis force makes the formation tropical cyclones within this zone more possible. Tropical cyclones form between 5° and 30° latitude.	Temperate cyclones are formed in mid-latitude between 35°C and 65°N and S.
The Wind decreases with height.	The wind increase with height.
The eye of the Cyclone is Characterized by light wind and clear skies. The eyewall is where winds are strongest and rainfall is heaviest.	These cyclones have rising air at the center which result in clouds and rain.
Tropical cyclones have strongest winds in the lower troposphere near the top of the boundary layer.	Temperate cyclones have strongest winds at the top of the troposphere in the core of the jet stream.
These cyclones have much more intense rainfall than Temperate cyclones. Isobars are in complete circles and the pressure gradient is steep. Center of cyclone is hotter than the surrounding area.	These cyclones tend to have much more moderate rainfall still destructive enough to cause flooding. Isobars are usually 'V' shaped and the pressure gradient is low.

El Nino Southern-Oscillation (ENSO)

Indian Monsoon Mechanism

- Monsoon are seasonal monsoon ladened winds peculiar to Indian Subcontinent, South East Asia, parts of Central Western Africa.

Mechanism

- Differential heating of land and water, Intense heating of Tibetian plateau causing bend in ITCZ.
- This shifts the whole pressure belt system, making the equator shift 5° north to actual geographical equator, also called as monsoonal trough.
- The south east winds from the subtropical high pressure belt travell to reach ITCZ and change their direction to south west after crossing the equator(due to corriolis force).
- These winds are attracted to Indian subcontinent owing to the low pressure generated over Tibetian plateau causing burst of Indian Monsoon.
- Sub tropical westerly jet is replaces by subtropical eastery jet stream.
- The winds pick up moisture while travelling over the sea and drop it over the Indian Subcontinent.
- The Indian Monsoon is divided into Arabian sea and Bay of Bengal Branch.
- Due to shift of monsoonal trough there occurs break in Indian Monsoon for a short period of time.

Retreating Monssons

- Are also called as north ease monsoon. They are caused by Formation and strengthening of high pressure cells over Tibetan plateau and Siberian Plateau in winter; Westward migration and subsequent weakening of high pressure cell in the Southern Indian Ocean; Migration of ITCZ to the south of India.
- Majorly south india especially Tamil Nadu recieves december rains due to retreating monsoon.
- India recieves rainfall through 3 ways -
- South west monsson- regular monsoon
- North east monsson - retreating monsoon
- Western disturbances- temperate cyclonic precipitation.
- El Nino and La Nina are opposite phases of what is known as the El Nino-Southern Oscillation (ENSO) cycle.
- The ENSO cycle is a scientific term that describes the fluctuations in temperature between the ocean in the east-central Equatorial Pacific.
- **El Nino**
- It refers to a periodic warming in sea surface temperatures across the east-central Equatorial Pacific, with increase in temperature of more than 0.5°C.

- The warm ocean conditions in the equatorial Pacific induce large-scale anomalies in the atmosphere. Rainfall increases many fold in Ecuador and northern Peru, california causing coastal flooding and erosion and Severe droughts occur in Australia, Indonesia, India and southern Africa.
- El Nino events occur irregularly at two-to seven-year intervals.
- Strong El Nino events are associated with droughts in Indonesia, Australia, and north-eastern South America and with altered patterns of tropical storms in the tropical belt. El Nino is negative for Indian monsoons.

- **La Nina**

- It is a cyclic counterpart to El Nino, consisting of a cooling of surface waters of the Pacific Ocean along the western coast of South America.
- La Nina has less effect in Europe but it does tend to lead to milder winters in Northern Europe and colder winters in southern/western Europe, leading to snow in the Mediterranean region.
- Elsewhere in the world, areas that are affected by La Nina experience the opposite of the effects they experience with El Nino.
- It does not occur as often as El Nino. It causes abnormally heavy monsoons in India and Southeast Asia and winter draught in southern USA.

Madden-Julian Oscillation

- The Madden-Julian oscillation (MJO) is the largest element of the intra-seasonal (30 to 90-day) variability in the tropical atmosphere.
- **Unlike a standing pattern like the El Nino:** Southern Oscillation (ENSO), the Madden-Julian oscillation is a travelling pattern that propagates eastward, through the atmosphere above the warm parts of the Indian and Pacific oceans.
- This overall circulation pattern manifests itself most clearly as anomalous rainfall.
- Heavy tropical rainfall associated with the MJO shifts eastward from the eastern Indian Ocean to the western tropical Pacific.

Indian Ocean Dipole (IOD)

- The Indian Ocean Dipole (IOD), also known as the Indian Nino, is an irregular oscillation of sea-surface temperatures in which the western Indian Ocean becomes alternately warmer and then colder than the eastern part of the ocean.
- The IOD involves an aperiodic oscillation of sea-surface temperatures (SST), between "positive", "neutral" and "negative" phases.
- A positive phase sees greater-than-average sea-surface temperatures and greater precipitation in the western Indian Ocean region, with a corresponding cooling of waters in the eastern Indian Ocean, which tends to cause droughts in adjacent land areas of Indonesia and Australia.
- The negative phase of the IOD brings about the opposite conditions, with warmer water and greater precipitation in the eastern Indian Ocean, and cooler and drier conditions in the west.
- The IOD also affects the strength of monsoons over the Indian subcontinent.
- The IOD is one aspect of the general cycle of global climate, interacting with similar phenomena like the El Nino-Southern Oscillation (ENSO) in the Pacific Ocean.
- El Niño Modoki- strong warming in the central tropical Pacific and cooling in the eastern and western tropical Pacific. It results into two-cell Walker Circulation.
- La Nina Modoki - cooling of central tropical ocean and warming of eastern and western tropical Pacific.
- Walker Cell Circulation is caused due to generation of a high pressure system over the eastern Pacific ocean, and a low pressure system over Indonesia.Walker cell is associated with southern oscillation.

Unit-11: World Climate

Tropical Monsoon & Tropical Marine Climate

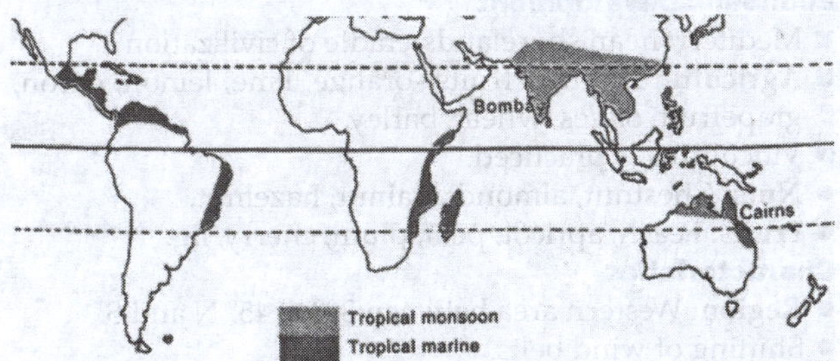

- **Climate-Tropical Monsoon:** Landmass is heated in summer in Northern Hemisphere, Low pressure develops in Central Asia & High Pressure in seas,which warm up much slower, remain comparatively at high pressure, and high pressure in southern hemisphere in Australia. Leading to seasonal reversal of winds. Temperatures range from 30-45° C in summer and 15-30° C in winter. Annual mean rainfall ranges from 200-250 cm.
- **Seasons: 1.** Tropical Monsoon: Cool Dry (Oct to Feb), Hot Dry Climate (March to June), Rainy (June to Sept). **2.** Retreating Monsoon: After mid Sept (North East monsoon).
- **Climate-Tropical Marine:** on the east coast of tropical lands, it receives evenly distrbuted rain from trade winds all time. It has maximum of summer without any distinct dry period. Favorable for habitation. Occurs severe tropical cyclones hurricanes or typhoons.
- **Vegetation:** Tropical Monsoon Forests-Drought-deciduous forest; dry forest; dry-deciduous forest; tropical deciduous forest, Broad-leaved. With a decrease in rainfall in summer, the forests thin out into thorny scrubland or savanna with scattered trees and tall grass.

- Tropical marine - The vegetation includes deciduous trees and durable hardwoods like teak, Sal, acacia, varieties of eucalyptus, and bamboo.
- **Location:**
- Monsoon: India, Burma, Vietnam, Thailand, Laos, Cambodia, South China, North Australia.
- Maritime: Central America, West Indies, North Eastern Australia, Philippines, Eastern Africa, Madagascar, Guinea & East Brazil.

Hot, Wet Equatorial Climate between 5-10 degree North and South of Equatorial regions

Climate and Rainfall	Vegetation	Life & Development	Factors Affecting Development
Uniform temperature throughout the year with average of 27° C, no winter, heavy precipitation,and small diurnal range of temperature. **Convectional Rainfall:** Mostly in Afternoon. Annual average is always above 150 cm with maximum rainfall in April and October, [shortly after the equinox] and least rain fall in June and December [solstice].	**Variety:** Evergreen hardwoods like mahogany, ebony; small palm trees; climbing lianas epiphytic or parasitic; ferns, orchids and Lalangs. **Distinct Layer:** thick canopy, struggle for sunlight **Multiple Species:** No pure strand; commercial exploitation is difficult; hardwood don't float on water and haulage expensive making tropical nations net timber importers.	**Amazon:** Indian Tribes gather wild rubber. **Congo**: Pygmies gather nuts. **Malaysia:** Orang Asli (Orang Asli are the indigenous people and the oldest inhabitants of Peninsular Malaysia) -cane products.	**Climate:** High heat & humidity; sun-stroke; perspire and lose energy; malaria) yellow fever. **Bacteria and insect pests:** Injurious to crops, diseases; plage **Jungle hinders development**: Lalang (tall grass) & thick undergrowth choke crops. Deterioration of tropical soil Difficult lumbering & livestock farming.

Savanna or Sudan Climate

- **Vegetation:**
- Tall grass-6 to 12 ft.-elephant grass-long roots, Short trees broad trunks, deciduous in nature, grasslands are also called as bushveld.
- African Savanna, South American Savanna (Llanos in Venezuela and Campos in Brazil).
- **Climate:** Warm year-round (avg. >18°C) with hottest months being April in Northern Hemisphere and October in Southern Hemisphere. Rain (80-160 cm) decreases with increasing distance from equator. With a wet season in northern hemisphere from May-Sept and Oct-Mar in the southern hemisphere.
- **Human Life:**
- Tribes-Masai - Eastern Africa Hausa of northern Nigeria
- Agriculture is barely practiced, potential for plantation agriculture of cotton, cane sugar, coffee, oil palm, groundnuts and even tropical fruits.
- Cattle rearing practiced.
- **Characteristics:**
- Transitional type of climate found between Equatorial forest and Hot deserts.
- Distinct Dry and wet season transition, onshore winds bring summer rains and off-shore winds in winter keep the climate dry. Extreme diurnal temperature. Experiencing local hot wind-Harmattan.
- Trade winds bring rain to coastal areas-strong in summer and dry in continental interior Trade winds are easterlies – flow from east to west. So rainfall decreases from east to west here.

Warm Temperate

Natural Vegetation

- Climate is not extreme(18°C- 10°C), precipitation range from 35 – 90 cm,winter rain climate.
- Trees with small broad leaves, no shade. Growth restricted to autumn and spring-good moisture and high temperature.
- **Mediterranean evergreen:** Open woodlands-evergreen oaks.
- **Evergreen coniferous trees:** Pines, firs, cedar and cypress.
- **Mediterranean bushes:** low bush in scattered clump-laurel, lavender, rosemary and scrubs.

Economic Development

- Mediterranean shorelands-cradle of civilization
- **Agriculture:** Citrus fruits -orange, lime, lemon, citron, grapefruit, olives, wheat, barley.
- Viticulture is practiced.
- **Nuts:** Chestnut, almond, walnut, hazelnut.
- **Fruits:** Peach, apricot, pear, plum, cherry, fig.

Characteristics

- **Region:** Western area between 30° to 45° N and S.
- Shifting of wind belts.
- Winter rain with on shore westerlies (cyclonic, orographic rainfall), Dry Warm Summer with offshore trades (no rain, dry air, intense heat, low relative humidity).
- Climate is transition between Trade wind hot desert (S) and Cool temperate maritime (N).

Hot Desert & Mid-latitude Desert

Vegetation Climate

- Hot Desert Climate-due to the effects of off-shore Trade Winds. The major hot deserts of the world are located on the western coasts of continents between latitudes 15° and 30°N. and S. They include- Sahara Desert , Great Australian Desert, Arabian Desert, Iranian Desert, Thar Desert, Kalahari and Namib Deserts, Atacama, Mexican.
- Mid-Latitude Desert Climate - are temperate deserts mainly due to continentiality (Gobi desert) or rain-shadow effect (Patagonian desert).
- Overll Climate - annual precipitation of less than 25 cm, average summer temperature is 30°C, extreme diurnal range of temperature
- Scrub and herbs, Dormant vegetation, Xerophytic or drought-resistant scrub cactus, thorns, trees are rare and date palms.
- Leaves are waxy and leathery, needle shaped-reduce transpiration.
- **Salinity of soil:** Salt accumulates-hard pans.
- Deficient in humus.

Life of Human

- Major tribes practising nomadic herdsmen include Bedouin of Arab. Tuaregs of sahara, Gobi Mongols.
- Nomadic Hunters
- Gatherers tribe include Bushmen of Kalahari and Bindibu of Australia.
- Bindibu of Australia
- The settled cultivators cultivate date,maize, barley, wheat, cotton, cane sugar, fruits and vegetables. Mining settlers are observed.

Characteristics

- Cause of aridity-Offshore trade winds (trade wind desert) and located in interior region a clear, cloudless sky, intense insolation, dry air and a rapid rate of evaporation.

Warm Temperate Continental (Steppe) Climate

Climate

- Continental interiors, temperature extremes - Summers are warm, winters are cold. The average rainfall is from 25 cm to 75 cm, due to Convection and westerlies depression occasionally brings about an 2.5 cm of precipitation in form of snow.
- **Mildura:** Fringe of Mallee scrub of Great Australian Desert.
- Local Winds: Chinook (Snow eaters) (USA and Canada) hot wind, melt snow covered areas around rockies.
- Fohn (Switzerland).

Economical Development

- **Prairies:** Granaries of world (wheat and maize). In the Prairies, the Argentinian Pampas, the Ukrainian Steppes and the Downs of Australia, agriculture is completely mechanized and has extensive ranching.
- Ranching region of world where tuft grass is replaceb by more nutritious Lucerne or alfalfa grass for cattle and sheep rearing.
- Pastoral Farming
- Dairy products
- Leading world in export of beef, meat processing factories in coastal ports.
- **Australia and New Zealand:** World's leading wool exporter (one third of total production).

Characteristics

- Border desert and lie in interior of continents: Temperate Grasslands Lie on Westerly belt.
- Away from maritime influence and are treeless.
- **South Hemisphere:** Moderate climate.
- **North hemisphere:** Extensive and continental.

Natural Vegetation

- Scanty vegetation. Grass is tall, fresh and nutritious. Greatest difference from the tropical savanna is that steppes are practically treeless and the grasses are much shorter.

Locations

- **Steppes (Eurasia):** Black Sea to Altai
- **Prairies (North America):** Rockies and Great Lakes
- **Pampas:** Argentina and Uruguay
- **South Africa:** Between Drakensberg and Kalahari (Bushveld in north and Highveld in south)
- **Downs:** Australia (Murray Darling Basin)
- **Canterbury:** New Zealand
- **Pustaz:** Hungary

Warm Temperate Western Margin (British) Climate

Climate

- Moderately warm summers and fairly mild winters. Mean annual temperature 5° C and 15° C.
- Warming effect of warm North Atlantic Drift and South Westerlies. Weather conditions can vary so much from day to day, as well as from season to season that is it sometimes said that the British Isles have no climate only weather.
- **Precipitation:** Rainfall throughout the year. Western margins have highest rainfall (as rain bearing winds come from west), thereby western slopes of Southern Alps have more rainfall compared to Canterbury plains (rain shadow area). There is a tendency towards an autumn or winter maximum of rainfall.

Economical Development

- **North-west Europe:** Little surplus for export and a net importer of food crop mainly wheat.
- **Fishing:** Britain, Norway & British Columbia.
- **Netherlands:** Horticultural and Dairy Industry (Britain, Denmark).
- **Australia:** High speed boats ply across Bass Strait and Tasmania named as garden state.
- **Mixed Farming:**
- Commercial lumbering.
- Paper and pulp industry.
- Manufacturing industry automobile, textile.
- Very less agriculture.
- Market gardening.
- Sheep and cattle raring
- Beet sugar cultivation.
- Both arable farming (potato, wheat, barley, beet sugar, cash crop and fodder crop etc.) and pastoral farming (pigs, poultry, sheep rearing). Climate is very favorable for maximum human output.

Natural Vegetation

- **Deciduous forest:** Shed leaves in winters-to protect against snow and frost.
- **Valuable temperate hardwood:** Oak, elm, birch, beech, poplar, Willows, Alder, Aspen.
- Other species-elsewhere-chestnut, maple, lime, eucalyptus, conifers.

Characteristics

- Under permanent influence of Westerlies, frontal Cyclonic activity, Oceanic influence.
- Also called North-West European Maritime Climate.
- North America, Southern hemisphere-New Zealand, Tasmania and Chile.

Warm Temperate Eastern Margin (China) Climate

Climate

- Warm moist summer and cool dry winters, with strong maritime influence. with mean monthly temperature varies between 4°C and 25°C.
- Uniform rainfall throughout the year (except Central China with distinct dry season) due to convection, orographic and occasional depressions.
- Rain by conventional source or orographic rain in summer & by depressions in prolonged showers in winter. Rainfall is from 60 cm to 150 cm and fairly uniform distribution of rainfall throughout the year.
- In summer, the regions are under the influence of moist, maritime airflow from the subtropical anticyclonic cells.
- Local storms- typhoons (tropical cyclones), and hurricanes

Natural Vegetation

- Eastern margins have more rainfall.
- Timber species, with broad leaved and deciduous forest at lowlands and conifers at highlands.
- Palm trees, chestnut, ironwood, blackwood and wattle trees, Eucalyptus, walnut, oak, pines, used most productive and intensively tilled parts of earth.

Characteristics

- Modified monsoonal climate-Temperate monsoon or China type Also known as Gulf climate in China and Japan.
- Natal Type Climate-in south-eastern U.S.A., bordering the Gulf of Mexico where continental heating in summer induces an inflow of air from the cooler Atlantic Ocean.
- Natal type Climate in New South Wales (Australia), Natal (South Africa), Parana-Paraguay-Uruguay basin (South America).
- Natal type is different from temperate monsoon or China type as it receives rainfall from on-shore Trade Winds all the year round.

Three Types of Region

- **China Type**
  - Central and North China including South Japan, Continental in nature.
  - Intense heat in interiors of Asia - Tibet and desert region creates low pressure in summer and brings South East monsoon, causing moderate rain.
  - Winter-pressure gradient between cold Mongolia, Siberia and warm Pacific, there is outflow of air as North West monsoon (cold and dry).
  - Occurrence of Typhoons-intense tropical cyclone in Pacific Ocean and move westward bordering South China Sea during July to September.
- **Gulf Type**
  - South Eastern USA-similar to China type-with less monsoonal characteristics.
  - No complete seasonal reversal of wind as pressure gradient between America and Atlantic is less marked.
  - Narrow range of temperature.
  - Thunderstorms in summer and hurricanes in September and October.
- **Natal Type**
  - Includes Natal, Eastern Australia, Brazil-Paraguay-Uruguay and Northern Argentina, all warm temperate eastern climate in southern hemisphere.
  - No monsoonal characteristics-narrowness of continent and dominance of maritime influence.
  - South East Trade winds bring even distribution of rainfall.
  - Depression along southern edges lead to autumn or winter maximum (wettest month from March to July).
  - Small annual temperature range.
  - Violent local storms-Southerly Buster (Cold wind along coast of New South Wales), Pampero (cold wind along Argentina and Uruguay), Berg (hot, dry wind in eastern Africa): comparable to Fohn or Chinook-bring unpleasant high temperature and oppressive weather.

Economical Development

- Most productive and intensively tilled parts of earth.
- World's greatest rice growing areas, warm wet and lowland favors rice cultivation.
- **Agriculture in the Gulf (USA):** Export crops (rice in Mississippi delta), Corn (half of world's corn production, used to fatten animals) or Maize, cotton, sugarcane, market gardening.
- Gulf-tobacco is native crop.
- Cropping/pastoral in Southern Hemisphere: cane sugar, cotton, tobacco, maize, produce from cattle and sheep. Famous for dairy products.

Cool Temperate Eastern Margin (Laurentian)

Climate

- Cold dry winters-temperature below freezing point, winds are dry westerlies from continental interior.
- Warm wet summers (has cooling effect of offshore cold currents).
- Rainfall-year-round rainging from from 75 to 150 cm.

Economical Development

- Lumbering-timber, paper and pulp industries less Agriculture.
- Annapolis valley in Nova Scotia-world's most renowned region of apples.
- **Fishing:** major activity in this region-as warm and cold current mixes. World's largest fishing ground on Grand Banks of Newfoundland.
- Seaweed weed cultivation, oyster cultivation etc. is most common specifically in Japan (with rich plankton growth on continental shelves, upwelling of waters).

Characteristics

- Intermediate between British and Siberian climate. Both maritime and continental.
- Only in 2 regions: **1.** North Eastern USA, Eastern Canada or America Region and **2.** Eastern Asia, Eastern Siberia, North China, Manchuria, Korea & North Japan-Asiatic Region. Absent in Southern Hemisphere-small section of continents, oceanic influence and climate is equable.
- Only exception could be Eastern Patagonia-Westerlies don't reach causing aridity (rain shadow desert).

Natural Vegetation

- Cool temperate forest. Coniferous trees north of latitude.
- Fir, spruce and larch, oak, beech, maple, birch are the trees found.
- Trees occur in pure stands-easy commercial exploitation Canada-greater reserve of coniferous.

Cool Temperate Continental (Siberian) Climate

- Due to extreme climatic condition-cold pole of earth.

Climate

- Cold long winters and cool brief summers. Snow falls are heaviest in the northern tundra and Siberian taiga.
- No maritime influence, frontal precipitation.
- Winds-Blizzards of Canada and Buran of Europe.
- Low temperature, low evaporation and high relative humidity.
- Permanent snowfields are absent (as in Alps and Himalayas) due to melting in spring and summer.
- Frozen rivers are thawed causing rise in water level and floods.

Natural Vegetation

- Greatest softwood production-Russia, USA, Canada, Finland, Norway, Sweden.
- Taiga (Siberia) -richest source of temperate softwood Occur in pure strands-good for commercial exploitation. 4 main species-Pine, Fir, Spruce & Larch.
- **Evergreen Coniferous Forest**
- Uniform, straight, tall.
- No annual replacement of new leaves. Food stored in trunks and bark is thick to protect trunk from cold.
- Conical in shape to prevent snow accumulation.
- Leaves are small, thick, leathery and needle-shaped.

Economical Development

- Many areas are untouched in Canada, Eastern Europe and Asiatic Russia. Lumbering-transported to sawmills.
- Fur farms, paper making, matches and newsprint firms are well established little agriculture.

Characteristics

- Broad Eastern-Western spread-Merge with Arctic tundra in north and Steppes in south, also called subarctic.
- Evergreen coniferous-continuous belt in north Called Taiga-Siberia.
- Absent in South Hemisphere-narrowness of southern continents in high latitude and strong oceanic influence.
- Coniferous trees are found (South Hemisphere) only in mountain uplands.

Arctic or Polar Climate

Climate

- Very low temperature. Winters -long and severe (weeks of continuous darkness).
- Summers-cool and brief.
- Convectional rainfall is generally absent due to less rate of evapouration and lack of moisture.
- Frost and blizzards are commonly seen.
- Coastal Areas-Warm water meets cold land then thick fog develops.
- Precipitation as snow in winters and varies from ice crystals to snowflakes.
- Anticyclones over ice caps.
- Coastal areas-cyclones.

Human Activities

- **Confined to coasts:** Plateaus and mountains are inhabitable and snow covered.
- **Semi-nomadic life:** Eskimos-Canada, Alaska, Greenland.
- **Nomads of Eurasia:** Lapps-Norway, Sweden, Finland and Russia.
- Yakuts in Northern Siberia. Koryak and Chukchi in Russia.
- **Discovery of minerals** has given rise to new settlements.
- Trying to grow hardy cereals for local needs in Arctic lowlands with warm currents and higher temperatures.

Natural Vegetation

- Tundra type-few plants can survive-deficiency in heat, frozen soil.
- No trees, Mosses, lichens and sedges are present.
- Drainage is poor-subsoil is permanently frozen Birch, willow and alder, reindeer moss, arctic flowers as arctic prairies are commonly found.

Characteristics

- **North of Arctic Circle:** Ice-Caps-Greenland and highland of high latitude regions-permanent snow cover.
- **Tundra Climate:** Lowlands with few ice free months-coastal Greenland, North Canada, Alaska and Arctic seaboard of Eurasia.

Local Winds

- **Hot Winds**
  - Siroco: Hot, dry dusty wind-from Sahara-most frequent in spring-accompanied by depression.
  - Chinook (Snow eaters)-USA
  - Ghibli-Libya
  - Harmattan (Guinea Doctor) West Africa
  - Khamsin-Egypt & Malta
  - Gharbi-Adriatic & Aegean Sea-cause fog & rain -blood rain (red dust)
- **Cold Winds**
  - Mistral-Cold wind from north-down to Rhone valley (40-80 miles/hr) - funneling effect (b/w Alps & Central Massif).
  - Bora-cold north-easterly wind along Adriatic coast-difference in pressure b/w continental Europe and Mediterranean-occur in winter
  - **Blizzard**-Tundra region
  - **Purga**-Russia

Unit-12: Miscellaneous

Locations

List of Deserts in the World Ranked on the basis of Area

Rank	Desert	Location
1.	Antarctica	Antarctica
2.	Arctic	Alaska, Canada, Greenland, Iceland, Norway, Sweden, Finland, Russia
3.	Sahara	Algeria, Chad, Egypt, Eritrea, Libya, Mali, Mauritania, Morocco, Niger, Sudan, Tunisia
4.	Arabian Desert	Iraq, Jordan, Kuwait, Oman, Qatar, Saudi Arabia, United Arab Emirates and Yemen
5.	Gobi Desert	Mongolia and China
6.	Kalahari Desert	Angola, Botswana, Namibia and South Africa
7.	Great Victoria Desert	Australia
8.	Patagonian Desert	Argentina and Chile

9.	Syrian Desert	Iraq, Jordan, and Syria
10.	Great Basin Desert	United States
11.	Chihuahuan Desert	Mexico and United States
12.	Great Sandy Desert	Australia
13.	Karakum Desert	Turkmenistan
14.	Colorado Plateau	United States
15.	Sonoran Desert	Mexico and United States
16.	Kyzylkum Desert	Kazakhstan, Turkmenistan and Uzbekistan
17.	Taklamakan Desert	China
18.	Thar Desert	India, Pakistan
19.	Gibson Desert	Australia
20.	Dasht-e Margo	Afghanistan
21.	Registan Desert	Afghanistan
22.	Simpson Desert	Australia
23.	Atacama Desert	Chile and Peru
24.	Mojave Desert	United States
25.	Namib Desert	Angola and Namibia

Major Lakes of the World

Lake	Location
Great Slave	Canada
Baikal	Russia
Caspian Sea	Azerbaijan, Iran, Kazakhstan, Russia and Turkmenistan
Aral Sea	Kazakhstan and Uzbekistan
Victoria	Kenya, Uganda, Tanzania
Great Bear	Canada
Superior	Canada and USA
Tanganyika	Burundi, Democratic Republic of the Congo (DRC), Tanzania and Zambia
Huron	Canada and USA

Deepest Point on the Ocean

Ocean	Deepest Point
Pacific Ocean	Mariana Trench (11034 meters)
Atlantic	Puerto Rio Trench (8400 meters)
Indian	Java Trench (7,450 meters)
Arctic	Molloy Deep (5,550 meters)

Canals and Straits

Strait / Canal	Country	Water Bodies Joined
Suez Canal	Egypt	Mediterranean and Red Sea
Kiel Canal	Runs through Germany	North Sea and Baltic Sea
Bering Strait	Alaska and Siberia	Pacific and Arctic
Palk Strait	India and Sri Lanka	Bay of Bengal and Gulf of Mannar

Continent's Highest Point (m) and Lowest Point (m)

Continent	Highest point (m)	Lowest point (m)
Asia	Mt Everest	Dead Sea
Africa	Mt Kilimanjaro	Lake Assal
North America	Mt Mckinley	Death Valley
South America	Mt Aconcagua	Valdes Peninsula
Antarctica	Vinson Massif	Denman Glacier
Europe	Mt El's Brus	Caspian Sea
Australian	Kosciuszko	Lake Eyre

Some Important Facts

Related Fact	Name of the Lake
Deepest lake in the world	Baikal (fresh water) in Russia.
Largest fresh water lake	Lake Superior, between Canada and the USA.
Largest lake in the world	Caspian Sea, bounded by Iran, Russia, Kazhakistan, Azerbaijan and Turkmenistan.
Saltiest lake in the world	Dead Sea bounded by Israel, Jordan and west bank.
Lowest lake in the world	Dead Sea between Israel and Jordan.
Largest lake in India	The largest lake of India (Area wise) is Vembanad Lake in Kerala. Sambhar Salt Lake is India's largest inland saline lake. Manasbal lake is the deepest lake in India.
Largest fresh-water lake in India	Wular Lake in Jammu and Kashmir.
Largest coastal lagoon / Brackish Lake in India	Chilka lake in Odisha.
Sriharikota island is located in	Pulicat lake in Andhra Pradesh.

Some Important Features

Feature	Name
Largest Continent	Asia
Largest Ocean	Pacific Ocean
Largest Bay	Bay of Bengal
Largest Gulf	Gulf of Mexico
Largest Peninsula	Arabian Peninsula
Largest Island	Greenland
Largest Coral Reef	Great Barrier Reef (Australia)
Largest and Highest Plateau	Tibetan Plateau

Distinctive names of countries & towns (world)

Distinctive Names	Countries / Towns
Britain of the South	New Zealand
The Battlefield of Europe	Belgium
City of the Golden Gate	San Francisco
City of Magnificent Distances	Washington D.C.
City of Popes	Rome
City of Seven Hills	Rome
City of Skyscrapers	New York
Cockpit of Europe	Belgium
Dark Continent	Africa
Dairy of Northern Europe	Denmark
Emerald Island	Ireland
Empire City	New York
Eternal City	Rome, Italy
Forbidden City	Lhasa (Tibet)
Garden of England	Kent (England)
Gate of Tears	Babel-Mandab, Jerusalem
Granite City	Aberdeen (Scotland)
Gift of Nile	Egypt
Gibraltar of the Indian Ocean	Aden
Herring Pond	Atlantic Ocean
Hermit Kingdom	Korea
Land of Cakes	Scotland
Land of the Golden Pagoda	Myanmar (Burma)
Land of Kangaroos	Australia
Land of Lilies	Canada
Land of the Midnight Sun	Norway
Land of the Rising Sun	Japan
Land of a Thousand Lakes	Finland
Land of Thunderbolt	Bhutan
Land of White Elephants	Thailand
Lady of Snow	Canada
Playground of Europe	Switzerland
Pearl of the Pacific	Guayaquil Port (Ecuador)
Quaker City	Philadelphia
Queen of the Arabian Sea	Kochi (India)
Roof of the World	Pamir (Tibet)
The Sea of Mountains	British Columbia
Sorrow of China	River Hwang Ho
Sugar Bowl of the World	Cuba
Venice of the North	Stockholm
Yellow River	Hwang Ho (China)
The Imperial City	Rome
City of Arabian Nights	Baghdad
The Modern Babylon	London

Tribes and races of the world

Tribe	Area Inhabited
Abhors	Mongolians living in the Assam region
Afridis	Inhabitants of the north-west frontier in Pakistan (tribal area of Waziristan)
Afrikaner	Dutch-born South African race
Anglo-Saxon	People who invaded Britain after the withdrawal of the Romans AD 410. Now living in England, Canada, USA and Australia
Bantus	Negroes of central and south Africa (Black race)
Bedouins	Wandering tribe of Arabia and North Africa
Bhils	Ancient Dravidians of central India
Cossacks	Inhabitants of southern and eastern frontiers of Russia
Croats	Inhabitants of Croatia
Dravidians	Ancient people of South India (non-Aryans)
Eskimos	Inhabitants of the Arctic Circle and Greenland
Filipinos	Natives of Philippines
Flemish	Inhabitants of Belgium
Garos	Hill tribe of Assam
Gorkhas	Martial race of Nepal
Hottentots	Pastoral nomads of south-west Africa
Kaffris	Martial race of South Africa
Kardars	Descendants of Austric race, now living in the forests of central and northern India
Khasis	Tribes of Assam
Khirgiz	Tribe living in Central Asia
Kiwis	People of New Zealand
Magyars	Inhabitants of Hungary
Masuds	Tribe living in Waziristan (Pakistan)
Maoris	Natives of New Zealand
Moor	A mixed tribe of Arab and Berber people of Morocco
Negroes	Dark-skinned race of Africa
Nipponese	People living in Japan
Red Indians	Original inhabitants of North America. They were named so by Columbus who thought that he had discovered India
Sherpas	Tribe on the border of Tibet and Nepal
Slovenes	People of Slavic origin living in former Yugoslavia
Swahili	People living in parts of Kenya and Tanzania
Todas	Natives of Nilgiris Hills
Zulus	People living in South Africa, belonging to the Bantu family

Geography One Liners

- Loktak Lake situated in Manipur.
- 10° Channel separates the Andaman from the Nicobar.
- Standard Meridian of India (82°30'E) passing through Mirzapur (in Uttar Pradesh) is taken as the standard time for the whole country.
- Mawsynram in Meghalaya receives the highest rainfall in the world.
- Loo is the local name of the wind blowing in the northern plains during summers.
- Reason of rainfall during winters in north-western part of India is Western disturbances.
- 68° 7' E is the westernmost longitude of India.
- The Southernmost Himalayas are known as Shiwaliks.
- Western Ghats is another name of Sahyadris.
- Palk Strait lies between India and Sri Lanka.
- Aravali Mountains is the oldest mountain range in India.
- The Azoic era is the era of the origin of the continental shelf.
- Antarctica is the India's permanent research station Dakshin Gangotri.
- The Duncan Pass is located between South Andaman and Little Andaman.
- Secunderabad is popularly known as twin city of Hyderabad.
- Uttar Pradesh is called the sugar bowl of India.
- Tehri dam is the highest dam in India.
- Western Ghats of Kerala is famous for the lion-tailed macaque.
- Silent valley located in Kerala.
- Chilka Lake is the largest Brackish lake in India.
- Digboi is the India's oldest oil Refinery in India.
- Jog Falls is created by the Sharavathi River.
- Godavari is the largest river basin of Indian peninsular region.
- The Damodar River is called the Sorrow of Bengal.
- The Asia's largest fresh water lake "Wular lake" is located in Jammu and Kashmir.
- River Narmada originated from Amarkantak.
- Sambhar Lake is a salt water lake.
- Krishna Raja Sagara Dam, located in Karnataka is built on river Cauvery.
- Ganga river is the home for fresh water dolphins.
- Godavari river is known as Dakshina Ganga.
- Indira Sagar Dam located in Madhya Pradesh is built on Narmada.
- Bhakra Nangal dam is situated on River Satluj.
- River Koshi is known as – Sorrow of Bihar.
- The Radcliffe Line is the international border between India and Pakistan.
- The average salinity of sea water is 3.50%.
- Tropical Moist Deciduous Forest covers the maximum area in India.
  Suez Canal joins Red & Mediterranean Sea.
- Aravallis mountain range stretches from Gujarat in west to Delhi in the north.
- Black Soil is also known as Regur.
- Congo river crosses the equator twice.
- Brazil is the only country that passes through both the equator and a tropic of Capricorn.
- Strait of Gibraltar separates Africa from Europe.
- The fertile land between two rivers is called Doab.
- Limpopo river crosses tropic of Capricorn twice.
- Madagascar is the largest island in the Indian Ocean.
- Tropical Rain forests is found in silent valley of Kerala.
- Gulf of Khambat separates the Daman & Diu.
- Port Blair – the capital of Andaman and Nicobar Islands, is located in South Andaman.
- Damodar river basin is called 'Ruhr of India'.
- Valley of flowers is located in Uttrakhand.
- Atlantic Ocean is called Herring Pond.
- Jaisalmer district of Rajasthan gets the least rainfall in India.
- Guru Shikhar Peak located in Rajasthan.
- Lake Superior is the largest fresh water lake in the world.
- The Sivasamudram Falls is located on River Cauvery.
- Bering strait separates the Asia from North America.
- Australia is the largest producer of Bauxite.
- The cool temperate grasslands of South America are known as Pampas.
- Tides are caused by the gravitational pull of the Sun and Moon on the Earth.
- World's largest Mangrove forest is located in Sundarbans.
- Highest railway bridge in the world constructed in Jammu and Kashmir on Chenab River.
- Koyali oil refinery located in Gujarat.
- The longest dam in India is Hirakund Dam.
- Savannah is the tropical grassland.
- The great Victoria Desert is located in Australia.
- Earth is known as the 'Blue planet' due to Presence of huge amount of water on it.
- Mount Etna, one of the world's most active volcanoes, is located in Italy.
- Bab El-Mandeb strait connects Red Sea and Indian Ocean.
- Lesotho is a country completely surrounded by South Africa.
- The most densely populated island of the World is Java.
- The Prime Meridian passes through Greenwich.
- The atmospheric air is held to the Earth by Gravity.
- Pachmarhi hill station is called as the Queen of the Satpuras.
- The famous species of tree 'Sundari' is found in Sunderbans delta formed by the rivers Ganga and Brahmaputra in West Bengal.
- The Nanda Devi Peak is located in Uttarakhand.
- Majuli, the largest river island in the world is located in Assam.
- Baglihar Dam is built on Chenab River in the Doda district of Jammu and Kashmir.
- Bum La Pass connects Tawang with Lhasa.
- Alluvial soil is best suited for rice cultivation.
- Diphu pass is located at the tri junction of India, Myanmar and china and it is located on the Mcmohan border line.
- The Friendship Highway is a road that connects China to Nepal.
- Gujarat has the longest mainland coastline in India.
- China has the world's largest number of International Borders.

- The river ganga emerges from Gangotri Glacier and drains into Bay of Bengal.
- Ganga is 2525 kilometres long and is the longest river of India.
- The (Western Ghats) Sahyadri mountains starts near the Songadh town of Gujarat and covers the states of Maharashtra, Goa, Karnataka, Kerala and Tamil Nadu.
- Kiblithu is the easternmost point of India. It is located in Arunanchal Pradesh.
- Rajasthan is the largest in terms of the total area covered.
- India has longest international border with Bangladesh.
- Red data book contains data of all plant endangered species.
- The final boundary between the Earth and the outer space is called magnetosphere created due to solar wind.
- Himalayan mountain range falls under Fold Mountain.
- A difference between 2 longitudes at the equator is nearly equivalent to 111 km.
- Alps is the highest mountain range that lies entirely in Europe and stretching across eight Alpine countries (from west to east): France, Switzerland, Italy, Monaco, Liechtenstein, Austria, Germany and Slovenia.
- Mount Blanc is the highest mountain peak of Alps.
- Saddle Peak which has a height of 737 metres is the highest peak in Andaman and Nicobar Islands. It is located in North Andaman Island and is covered by saddle national park which has a wide variety of flora and fauna.
- The Patkai hills belong to Purvanchal mountain ranges.
- Kosi river originates in Nepal and flows into the Ganges.
- Dachigam National Park is located in Jammu and Kashmir.
- The Keoladeo National Park formerly known as the Bharatpur Bird Sanctuary in Rajasthan.
- The Sankosh river forms boundary between Assam and Arunachal Pradesh.
- The northernmost point of India is Indira Col.
- Karnataka is largest producer of Coffee in India.
- Paradip Port is located on the delta of Mahanadi.
- The salal project is on the river Chenab River.
- The state having a largest area of forest cover in India is Madhya Pradesh.
- Sugarcane crops needs maximum water per hectare.
- Deccan plateau is the most ideal region for the cultivation of cotton in India.
- Canada has longest coastline in world.
- The Great Victoria Desert is located in Australia.
- Khasi hills located in Meghalaya.
- Adam's bridge locate between India and Sri Lanka.

❑❑❑

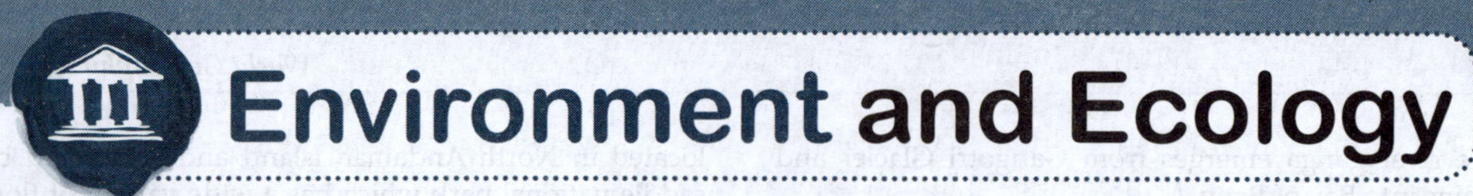

Environment and Ecology

Unit-1: Ecosystem

Ecology: Components and Functions

- **Ecology:** The term was coined by the German biologist Ernst Haeckel in 1866.
- It may be defined as the scientific study of the relationship among the living organisms and with their environment.
- **Environment:** The conditions or surroundings in which an organism operates or lives.
- It includes both biotic (living) and abiotic (non-living) components.
- **Ecological Hierarchy:** The formation of grouping of organisms due to the synergy of organisms with their environment.
- **Individual:** The Individual organism is the first level of ecological hierarchy.
- **Population:** A group of individuals that live in a definite area, interact with each other and belong to the same species.
- **Community:** A group of organisms that live in an area, that interacts with each other and containing several different species.
- **Ecosystem:** A collection or group of organisms and their environment, interacting with each as one of the ecological unit. The term 'Ecosystem' was coined by A.G. Tansley in 1935.
- **Biosphere:** A relatively thin life supporting stratum of the surface of the Earth that extends from the deep sea vents in the ocean to a few kilometres into the atmosphere.
- **Biome:** Group of similar ecosystems with the same general type of environment anywhere in the world.
- **Habitat:** It is the physical space in which the animal resides and which includes its environment.
- **Niche:** The role played by an organism in a community. The niche of an species describes how it fits within its environment.
- **Species:** It is a group of organism capable of inter-breeding and producing fertile offsprings.
- Every species has a specific set of genetic characteristics that distinguishes it from other species.
- **Species Diversity:** The different kinds of organisms present in a community represents the diversity of species.
- **Amensalism:** One species harms or limits the existence of the other species without being harmed or adversely affected.
- It is a negative relationship between the two species.
- **Predation:** Predator catches, kills and consumes a prey animal of a different species. Prey suffers but the predator profits from this kind of relationship.
- **Parasitism:** One species suffers while the other profits. It includes a parasite which lives on other living species known as the host.
- **Competition:** Both the species gets adversely affected when both need a vital resource which is in short supply.
- It can be intra-specific or inter-specific.
- **Commensalism:** One species (the host) is neither harmed nor inhibited while the other species (commensal) benefits.
- **Mutualism:** That kind of biotic interaction in which both species gets benefited.
- **Neutralism:** A kind of relationship between the two organisms in which they appears to be no influence on each other.
- **Gross Primary Productivity (GPP):** The rate of production of an organic matter during photosynthesis.
- **Net Primary Productivity (NPP):** It is the biomass which is available for the consumption by the heterotrophs (decomposers and the herbivores).
- Gross Primary Productivity (GPP) minus the respiration losses (R) is equal to the NPP.
- **Ecological Efficiency (Lindeman's Efficiency):** The ratio between the amount of energy acquired from lower trophic level and that transferred from the higher trophic level.
- It follows a 10% rule.
- **10 Percent Rule:** If 100 cal is produced by the autotrophs, the herbivores will store only 10 cal and the carnivores will store only 1 cal.
- **Trophic Level:** A particular position of an organism in a food chain based on the source of their nutrition or food.
- **Food Chain:** A food chain is a series of organisms where all the organisms are dependent on next organism as a source of food. Food chain Start with producers.
- **Food Web:** In an ecosystem, the trophic levels do not always follow a linear relationship.
- They are linked together and form a food web.
- It is a matrix of the inter-connected food chains.
- **Ecological Pyramids:** These are the graphic illustrations of the trophic levels. The base of pyramids are made up of producers.
- **Bio-accumulation** is the mechanism of increase in the concentration of a chemical in a biological organism over time, compared to the chemical's concentration in the environment. Compounds are taken ups and stored by the organisms.
- **Biomagnification:** There is an increase in the concentration of a pollutant from one trophic level to the another trophic level.
- **Nutrient/Biogeochemical Cycles:** The movement of the nutrient elements through the various ecosystem components. In a perfect nutrient cycle, the replacement of the nutrients is at the same rate as they are used.
- Examples of these cycles include Water Cycle, Carbon Cycle, Nitrogen Cycle, Phosphorus Cycle, etc.
- **Ecological Succession:** It is the mechanism through which animal and plant species, in a given region, are replaced or transformed into another over time.
- **Pioneer Community:** The community which initially inhabits the bare area. After some time, this community gets replaced by another community and the process continues.

- **Climax Community:** The community which forms the final or terminal stage of succession.
- **Sere:** The complete sequence of communities in each area succeeding each other during the succession.
- **Homeostasis:** It refers to the ecosystems ability to self-regulate. The ability to control the function and structure of their own organisms.

Types of Ecosystems

Ecosystem can be classified into two types:

- Terrestrial Ecosystem
- Aquatic Ecosystem

Terrestrial Ecosystem:

- **Forest Terrestrial Ecosystem:** A forest ecosystem is made up of several plants, especially trees, animals and microorganisms that coexist with the environment's abiotic factors. Forests help in keeping up with the temperature of the earth and are the significant carbon sink.
- **Tundra Ecosystem:** The tundra is a type of ecosystem that lacks trees and is typically located in cold climates or areas with low rainfall, resulting in most of the year being covered in snow. It can be found in the Arctic or on mountain tops.
- **Grassland Ecosystem:** In a grassland ecosystem, the vegetation is dominated by grasses and herbs. Temperate grasslands and tropical or savanna grasslands are examples of grassland ecosystems.
- **Desert Ecosystem:** Deserts are found throughout the world. These are regions with little rainfall and scarce vegetation. The days are hot and the nights are cold.
- **Natural Ecosystem:** It is a collection of living and non living entities that naturally exists and inside which each of the components interact as a single unit through physical, chemical and biological processes.
- **Artificial Ecosystem:** These are also termed as the man-engineered or man-made ecosystems. Examples include the croplands.
- **Aquaculture:** Practice of raising aquatic plants or animals in a managed environment.

Aquatic Ecosystem

- **Freshwater Ecosystem:** The freshwater ecosystem is an aquatic ecosystem that includes lakes, ponds, rivers, streams and wetlands. These have no salt content in contrast with the marine ecosystem.
- **Marine Ecosystem:** The marine ecosystem includes seas and oceans. These have a more substantial salt content and greater biodiversity in comparison to the freshwater ecosystem.

Components of Ecosystem

There are two components of ecosystem are Abiotic and biotic:

- Biotic components (living organisms)
- Abiotic components (non - living components)

Abiotic components (non - living components)

- The abiotic component can be grouped into following categories:
  - Inorganic substances
  - Organic substances
  - Physical factors
  - Lithosphere
  - Hydrosphere
  - Atmosphere
- **Inorganic Substances:** Examples: Carbon dioxide, nitrogen, oxygen, phosphorus, sulphur, water, rock, soil and other minerals.
- **Organic Substances:** Examples: Carbohydrates, proteins, lipids and Humic substances.
- **Physical Factors:** Examples: Sun light, temperature, rainfall, humidity and pressure. They are influence the growth and development of organisms of biological communities.
- **Lithosphere:** The lithosphere is the outer most part of the Earth. It is made up of rocks and minerals. It is covered by a thin layer of soil.
- **Hydrosphere:** Hydrosphere is made up of all the water and watery layers of the Earth. All of the oceans, lakes, seas and clouds are an example of the hydrosphere. The hydrosphere covers 71 percent of the Earth's surface.
- **Atmosphere:** Atmosphere is a mixture of gases, water vapour and dust particles in different proportions. It is held near the surface of the planet by Earth's gravitational attraction. Nitrogen (78%) and Oxygen (21%) are permanent gases of the atmosphere. They constitute 99% of the total composition and their percentages always remain the same without any change. The remaining one percentage is occupied by Argon (0.93%), Carbon-di-oxide, (0.042%), Neon (0.0018%), Helium (0.0005%), Ozone (0.00006%) and Hydrogen (0.00005%).
- **Biotic components (Living organisms)**

  The biotic component can be grouped into following categories:
  - Producers
  - Consumers
  - Decomposers
- **Producers:** Producers (Green plants) are organisms that make their own food through the photosynthesis. They are also known as autotrophs. Green plants are called autotrophs, as they absorb water and nutrients from the soil, carbon dioxide from the air, and capture solar energy for this process. Examples: Green plants, Trees
- **Consumers:** Consumers are called heterotrophs and they consume food synthesized by the autotrophs. It can be divided into three categories:
  - Herbivores or Primary Consumer
  - Carnivores or Secondary consumers
  - Omnivores
- **Herbivores or Primary Consumer:** A herbivore is gets its energy from eating plants. Examples: Cow, Goat, Horses, Deer, Rhinoceros, Sheep, Rabbit.
- **Carnivores or Secondary consumers:** Secondary consumers are organisms that eat primary consumers (Herbivores) for energy. Examples: Spider, Eagles, Owls, Cat, Snake, lizard, Dog.
- **Omnivores:** Omnivores defined as the animals that eat on plants and other animals for nutrition. Examples: Chickens, Crows, Humans, Bear, Pigs.
- **Decomposers:** Decomposers are the organisms that break down dead plants and animals. Examples: Bacteria, Fungi.

Unit-2: Biodiversity

Biodiversity Levels

- **Biodiversity or Biological Diversity:** It is described as the huge variety of life on Earth. It applies to all of the organisms in a single ecosystem.
  Scientists have estimated that there are around 8.7 million species of animals and plants on Earth.
- **Biodiversity Levels:** The levels in which the biodiversity is mainly found to exist.
- **Genetic Diversity:** The variety of genes present within species of animals, plants and micro-organisms.
  Genetic diversity permits the species which are present, to adapt to different environments.
- **Species Diversity:** Different variety of species within a geographical area.
  There is difference in between the species, mainly in the genetic makeup and they do not inter-breed in nature.
- **Species Richness:** The count of various species in a given area. Further, it can be classified into alpha, beta and gamma diversity.
- **Alpha Diversity:** It is usually denoted by the count of species (species richness) in a specific area or a particular ecosystem.
- **Beta Diversity:** It usually compares the diversity between different ecosystems, which is generally measured by the variation in the species count between the ecosystems.
- **Gamma Diversity:** Within a region, it measures the overall diversity of the different ecosystems on a very large scale.
- **Exotic Species:** The term "exotic species" refers to alien species, commonly referred to as "invasive species", "non-indigenous species", or "bioinvaders". These species thrive in non-native environments.
- **Species Abundance:** It implies the relative numbers among different species. For an instance, the number of animal species, plant and other micro-organisms might be more in an area than that in the other area.
- **Taxonomic Diversity:** It implies the genetic relationships between various species.
  When the taxonomically unrelated species are present in an area, the area exhibits higher species diversity as compared to an area represented by the related species.
- **Ecosystem Diversity:** It refers to the presence of the different types of ecosystems.
  For example, compared to the desert ecosystem, which has quite less number of animal and plant species, the tropical southern India has rich species diversity with different structure.
- **The Evil Quartet:** Four major causes for loss of biodiversity are Habitat loss and fragmentation, Over exploitation, Co-extinctions and Alien species invasions.
- **Ways in which Biodiversity Loss can be caused:**
  - **Direct Ways:** Hunting, deforestation and commercial exploitation.
  - **Indirect Ways:** Introduction of the exotic species, loss of the natural habitats, pollution, etc.
  - **Natural Causes:** Natural disaster, climate change, etc.
- **Sixth Mass Extinction:** It is considered different from the previous five mass extinction episodes as in the present mass extinction the species extinction rates are estimated to be about 100-1000 times faster than the pre human times.
- **Ecosystem Services:** They are the services provided directly or indirectly benefitting human well being. They being provisioning, regulating, cultural and supporting services. Protection of natural resources like water, recycle and storage of nutrients, pollution breakdown, climate stability, recovery from unpredictable events, etc.
- **Biological Services:** Food production, medicinal resources and pharmaceutical drugs, wood products, ornamental plants, breeding, etc.
- **Social Services:** Research, education and monitoring, recreation activities and tourism.
- **Facts about Biodiversity:**
  - The species density, in general, is greater in the Southern Hemisphere.
  - UNEP identified 17 mega diverse coundries accounting to almost 84% of biodiversity. Australia, Brazil, China, Colombia, Ecuador, United States, Philippines, India, Indonesia, Madagascar, Malaysia, Mexico, Papua New Guinea, Peru, Democratic Republic of Congo.
  - There are 25,000 plant species in the Hindu Kush-Himalayan region as a whole, which accounts for 10% of the world's flora.
  - According to National Center for Biotechnology Information (NCBI), Two-thirds of the estimated 250,000 plant species are found in tropical regions.
  - In a 52-hectare plot in Lambir Hills National Park, Sarawak (Malaysian Borneo), 1,200 species of trees have been documented as the highest tree diversity to date.
  - About 50 to 90 percent of all species are thought to be contained in tropical rainforests.
  - About 2,600 bird species, or 30% of all bird species, depend on tropical forests.

Biodiversity Hotspots

- Biodiversity hotspots refer to regions that exhibit an exceptional concentration of endemic species and are currently experiencing a significant loss of habitat. These regions are characterized by high species richness and a high degree of endemism.
- The concept of biodiversity hotspots was introduced by Norman Myers in 1988 when he observed a decline in plant species and habitat in tropical forests.
- The Red Data Book, which is prepared by the IUCN, is an important resource for tracking threatened species. Biodiversity hotspots are crucial to human survival because biodiversity is fundamental to all life on Earth, providing air, food and water, among other essentials. Hotspots, which contain the highest levels of biodiversity and are under the greatest threat, are particularly important.

Biodiversity Hotspots in India

As of the most recent CEPF (Critical Ecosystem Partnership Fund) update, there are 36 global biodiversity hotspots (updated from 34). The four hotspots intersecting India remain as listed:

- **Himalaya:** Includes the entire Indian Himalayan region (and that falling in Pakistan, Tibet, Nepal, Bhutan, China and Myanmar).
- **Indo-Burma:** Includes entire North-eastern India, except Assam and Andaman group of Islands (Myanmar, Thailand, Vietnam, Laos, Cambodia and Southern China).
- **Western Ghats and Sri Lanka:** Includes entire Western Ghats (and Sri Lanka).
- **Sundalands:** Includes Nicobar group of Islands (and Indonesia, Malaysia, Singapore, Brunei, Philippines).

Unit-3: Protected Area Network

- **Biodiversity Conservation:** The proper management of natural resources to retain the balance in nature and diversity.
  It includes the rational use of natural resources.
- **In-situ Conservation:** Protection of animals and plants within their natural or protected areas.
- **Ex-situ Conservation:** Conservation of animals and plants outside their natural habitats.
  Examples include zoos, botanical gardens, gene banks, seed banks, cryopreservation and tissue culture.
- **National Parks:** IUCN in 1975 defined National Park as a relatively large area where several or one ecosystem is not altered by human occupation or exploitation.
  State governments and central government declares the National Parks under the Wildlife (Protection) Act of 1972.
- **Wildlife Sanctuaries:** Conservation inside these sanctuaries is species-oriented, and its boundary is not limited by state legislation.
  Under the Wildlife (Protection) Act of 1972 the State Government declares an area as the Wildlife Sanctuaries.
- **Biosphere Reserves:** Natural areas which are undisturbed and are dedicated to conservation of biological diversity and genetic integrity of animals, micro-organisms and plants in their totality.
- Traditionally, the biosphere reserves are grouped into three inter-related zones:
  Core Area: Natural area of the biosphere reserve that is fully protected and least disturbed by human activities.
- Entry inside it is allowed only with special permission.
- Scientific investigations carrying out the destructive sampling is strictly prohibited.
- Buffer Zone: It surrounds the core zone and is managed to provide some room for a greater variety of resource-use strategies, educational activities and researches.
- Transition Zone: The outer-most part of the biosphere reserve which is an area of active engagement between the locals and the reserve management.
- Other activities like cropping, settlements, recreation, forestry, etc. are carried out in harmony with the conservation goals.
- **The main functions of Biosphere Reserves are:**
- Conservation: Conservation of the biodiversity and ecosystems around the world.
- Development: Associating the environment with the development.
- Education, Monitoring and Scientific Research: International network of research and monitoring.
- **Conservation Reserves:** Area under the State Government besides the National Parks and Sanctuaries for protecting the seascape, landscape and the habitats of animals and the plants.
  Conservation Reserve Management Committee manages these reserves.
- **Community Reserve:** A community land or a private land may be notified by the State Government as a community reserve with an aim of protecting the flora and fauna of the reserve and also to improve the socio-economic conditions of the people living in that particular areas.
- **Sacred Forests:** Protected by the local communities because of their beliefs and rituals that runs through several generations. These areas are free from all disturbances.
- **Sacred lakes:** Several water bodies have been declared sacred by the local people leading to protection of aquatic flora and fauna.
- **Critical Tiger Habitat (CTH):** These are also referred to as the core areas of the tiger reserves.
- These are identified under the Wildlife Protection Act of 1972.
- State government in consultation with the expert committee notifies an area as the CTH.
- **Marine Protected Areas (MPAs):** As defined by the IUCN, is a region of the ocean that is set aside for long-term conservation goals. MPAs help with climate change adaptation and mitigation, and provide other ecosystem services. Primarily, the MPAs in India are classified into following four categories:
- Category-I: It covers Sanctuaries and the National Parks that have areas in sub-tidal/inter-tidal or mangroves, creeks, coral reefs, algal beds, seagrass beds, lagoons and estuaries.
- Category-II: This category includes that islands, the major portion of which comes under marine ecosystems and some parts in terrestrial ecosystems.
- Category-IIIA: It includes the sandy beaches beyond the inter-tidal line but occasionally interacting with the seawater.
- Category-IIIB: This category has evergreen or semi-evergreen forests of islands.
- **Botanical Garden:** The scientifically planned collection of living shrubs, trees, climbers, herbs and other plants from various parts of the world.
- **Gene Banks:** Preservation and ex-situ collection of the genetic resources is carried out in these banks.
- **Cryopreservation:** Storage of the materials at the ultra-low temperatures of liquid nitrogen and it essentially involves suspension of all metabolic activities.
- **Biodiversity Hotspots:** This concept was introduced in 1988 by Norman Myers.
  It refers to that bio-geographic region which contains in it the significant levels of biodiversity which is threatened by the human habitation.
- **Biodiversity Hotspots in India:**
- The Eastern Himalayas
- Indo-Burma

- Western Ghats and Srilanka
- Sundalands
- **Man and Biosphere Programme (MAB):** It is an inter-governmental scientific programme, launched in 1971 by UNESCO, that aims to establish a scientific basis for improving the relationship between people and their environments.
- It combines the natural and social sciences with a view to improving human livelihoods and safeguarding natural and managed ecosystems, thus promoting innovative approaches to economic development that are socially and culturally appropriate and environmentally sustainable.
- Currently, the World Network of Biosphere Reserves has 784 sites located in 142 countries around the globe.
- **IUCN's Red List of Threatened Species:** It was formed in 1964 to become the world's most comprehensive information source about the global conservation status of fungi, animal and plant species. It has few categories:
- **Extinct (EX):** A taxon is considered as extinct when there is no doubt that the last individual has passed.
- **Extinct in the Wild (EW):** When the exhaustive and extensive surveys in the known or expected habitats have failed to record even a single individual.
- **Critically Endangered (CR):** When a taxon has been facing high risk of extinction in the wild in the immediate future or will decrease by 80% within three generations.
- **Endangered (EN):** When the taxon in question is not critically endangered but it is facing a very high risk of extinction in the wild in near future due to low in numbers, or threatened by changing environmental or predation parameters.
- **Vulnerable (VU):** When the taxon is not critically endangered or endangered but it is facing a high risk of extinction in the wild in medium term future unless the circumstances threatening its survival and reproduction improve.
- **Lower Risk:** When the taxon has been evaluated and does not seems to be falling in the categories such as CR, EN or VU, then it is considered to be at lower risk of extinction.
- **Data Deficient:** When there is inadequate availability of information about a taxon to make any direct or indirect assessment of its risk of extinction.
- **Not Evaluated:** The taxon is not put to any evaluation when it has not been assessed as per the above mentioned criterias.
- **Colour Codes in the List according to the risk of extinction:**
- **Black:** Extinct (EX) - No living individuals remaining anywhere in the world.
- **Green Pages:** Lowest risk; widespread, abundant, and not currently facing significant threats.
- **Purple (Dark):** Extinct in the Wild (EW) - Species only survive in captivity or as naturalized populations outside their historical range.
- **Red:** Critically Endangered (CR) - Extremely high risk of extinction in the wild.
- **Orange:** Endangered (EN) - High risk of extinction in the wild.
- **Yellow:** Vulnerable (VU) - High risk of endangerment in the wild.
- **Red List Index:** It measures the trends in the overall extinction risk of the set of species as an indicator of trends in the biodiversity status.
  It helps the governments in tracking the progress in achieving targets that reduce the biodiversity loss.
- **This index is available for five taxonomic groups:**
- Birds
- Mammals
- Amphibians
- Cycads
- Warm-water reef-forming Corals
- **Red List Index = 1:** All species qualifying as Least Concern (LC).
- **Red List Index = 0:** All species have gone Extinct.
- **National Conservation Efforts:** Initially, there was no provision in the Indian Constitution to protect or to promote the environment. In 1976, the 42nd Amendment added forest and Protection of Wild Animals and Birdsas concurrent subject, and added DPSP 48A for maintaining a well-protected and safe environment.
- **Constitutional Provisions:** After the UN Conference on Human Environment held in Stockholm in 1972, which is also known as Stockholm Conference, the Indian Constitution was amended to include protection of the environment as a Constitutional mandate.
- **Article 51A (g):** It made it a fundamental duty of every Indian to protect and improve the natural environment. "It shall be the duty of every citizen in India to protect and improve the natural environment including forests, lakes, rivers, and wildlife and have compassion for living creatures".
- **Article 48A (DPSP):** "The States shall endeavour to protect and improve the environment and to safeguard the forests and the wildlife of the country".
- **Project Tiger:** It is a Centrally Sponsored Scheme launched by the Ministry of Environment, Forests and Climate Change (MoEFCC). India is having 58 reserves which are all run under the Project Tiger.
- **Launched:** 1973
- **Aim:** To protect the Bengal tigers from extinction and maintaining a stable population in their habitats.
- **Number of Tigers:** Madhya Pradesh>Karnataka >Uttarakhand >Maharashtra
- **Tiger Census:** The NTCA conducts this census across India every four years.
- Conservation Status of Tigers:
- **IUCN Red List:** Endangered
- **CITES:** Appendix I
- **Wildlife (Protection) Act, 1972:** Schedule I
- **Project Elephant**: It is a Centrally-Sponsored Scheme which offers a financial and technical help to States.
- **Launched:** 1992
- **Implemented In:** 16 States
- **Corridors Set-up:** 150
- **Programmes:** MIKE (Monitoring of Illegal Killing of Elephants), 'Haathi Mere Saathi' by MoEFCC and Wildlife Trust of India.
- Conservation Status of Elephants:
- **IUCN Red List:** Endangered
- **CITES:** Appendix I
- **Wildlife (Protection) Act, 1972:** Schedule I
- **Indian Rhino Vision 2020**: It was launched with a view to increase rhino population from 2000 to 3000 by 2020 in seven protected areas of Assam:
- Kaziranga National Park
- Pobitora National Park

- Orang National Park
- Manas National Park
- Burachapori Wildlife Sanctuary
- Laokhowa Wildlife Sanctuary
- Dibru-Saikhowa Wildlife Sanctuary
- **Project Snow Leopard:**
- **Launched:** 2009
- **Aim:** To strengthen wildlife conservation in High altitudes regions.
- **Found:** In Central Asian and Himalayan mountains
- **In Western and Trans Himalayans:** At an altitude around 3000 metres
- **In Eastern Himalayas:** Above 4000 metres
- Conservation Status:
- **IUCN Red List:** Vulnerable (VU)
- **CITES:** Appendix I
- **Wildlife Protection Act, 1972:** Schedule I
- **Sea-Turtle Project:** Olive Ridley Turtle visits Indian coasts for hatching during winters.
- **Launched:** 1999
- **Started By:** Environment Ministry in collaboration with UNDP
- **Implementing agency:** Wildlife Institute of India (WII), Dehradun
- **IUCN Status:** Vulnerable (VU)

Unit-4: Environmental Issues

Climate Change and Forests

- Climate change refers to long-term shifts in the Earth's climate system, including changes in temperature, precipitation and weather patterns, that are primarily caused by human activities, such as burning fossil fuels and deforestation. These activities release large amounts of greenhouse gases, such as carbon dioxide, into the atmosphere, trapping heat and causing the Earth's average temperature to rise. Climate change also includes the impacts of these changes, such as rising sea levels, increased frequency and severity of natural disasters, and changes in ecosystems and biodiversity.
- **Deforestation:** It includes the issues like tree felling, lopping, grazing, browsing, trampling of seedlings and clearing of the forest debris.
  Removal or damage of vegetation in a forest to the extent that the forest's natural flora and fauna is no longer supported.
- **Causes of Deforestation:** Agriculture, Overgrazing, Urbanisation and developmental projects, fuel (firewood) requirements, raw material requirements, etc.
- **Consequences of Deforestation:**
- Soil Erosion and Flash Floods
- Climatic Change and Forests Destruction
- Loss of Biodiversity
- **Shifting Cultivation:** It is also known as Jhoom Farming or the Slash and Burn farming. In this method, the wild and forested land is cleared and any remaining vegetation burned.
- This type of farming is often intended to meet the on-site demands or needs.

India State of Forest Report

- **India State of Forest Report (ISFR):** It is a biennial publication by the Forest Survey of India, which is a part of the Ministry of Environment, Forests and Climate Change (MoEF&CC).
  It assesses the country's land and tree inventory, including wall to wall forest cover mapping.
- **Forest Area:** As per the Government records, the legal status of the land as forest.
- **Forest Cover:** The forest cover is defined as 'all land, more than one hectare in area, with a tree canopy density of more than 10 percent irrespective of ownership and legal status.
- **Key Findings of the ISFR 2023:**
  Increase in the Forest and the Tree Area: Countrywide, there is an increasing forest and tree cover. Over the last two years, there has been a rise in cover of 1,445 square kilometres.
- India's forest cover has increased to 7,15,343 sq km (21.76% of geographical area).
- The term "tree cover" refers to all tree patches less than one hectare in size that occur outside the recorded forest area. This applies to all tree formations, including scattered trees.
- Increase or Decrease in Forests:
- The highest increase in forest cover have been shown by Chhattisgarh (683.62 km^2), followed by Uttar Pradesh (559.19 km^2) and Odisha (558.57 km^2).
- Loss of Forest cover have been shown by Madhya Pradesh (612.41 km^2) and Karnataka (459.36 km^2).
- States with Highest Forest Area/Cover:
- Area wise top three states having largest forest cover are Madhya Pradesh (77,073 sq km) followed by Arunachal Pradesh (65,882 sq km) and Chhattisgarh (55,812 sq km).
- In terms of percentage of forest cover with respect to total geographical area, Lakshadweep (91.33 percent) has the highest forest cover followed by Mizoram (85.34 percent) and Andaman & Nicobar Island (81.62 percent).
- **Mangroves:** With an increase of 16.68 sq. km, India's total mangrove cover touched 4,991.68 sq. km.
- **Total Carbon Stock:** The amount of carbon that has been removed from the atmosphere and stored in the forest ecosystem is known as the forest carbon stock.
- India's carbon stock has reached 30.43 billion tonnes of CO_2 equivalent.
- **Bamboo Forests:** The extent of bamboo bearing area for the country has been estimated as 1,54,670 sq km. As compared to the last assessment done in 2021 there is an increase of 5,227 sq km in bamboo area.
- **Desertification:** The destruction or reduction of the biological capacity of a land, which can eventually lead to desert-like conditions. It is resulted by excessive felling of trees.
- Human-induced desertification has affected about 76.15% of the total Indian desert.
- **Control Measures against Desertification:** India is one of the signatory to the United Nations Convention to Combat Desertification (UNCCD).
- In order to take appropriate action in resolving desertification issues, the National Action Plan for Combating Desertification commenced in 2001.

- National Afforestation Programme
- Integrated Watershed Management Programme
- National Mission for Green India
- The Mahatma Gandhi National Rural Employment Guarantee Scheme
- Soil Conservation in the Catchment of River Valley Project and Flood Prone River
- National Watershed Development Project for Rainfed Areas
- Desert Development Programme
- Fodder and Feed Development Scheme
- **Natural Desertification:** In the Asia-Pacific region, an area of approximately 4.361 lakhs hectare has resulted from the natural desertification. These are type of deserts, the topic is about desertification, not relevant, already covered in geography.

Coral Bleaching

- **Coral Bleaching:** When the corals are subjected to stressful conditions by changes in temperature, light, or nutrients, they throw out the symbiotic algae living in their tissues, causing the corals to turn white completely.
- The Zooxanthellae and the Coral live in a mutualistic symbiotic relationship which helps each other in their survival.
- **Causes of Coral Bleaching:**
- Increased temperature in the ocean which is the result of Climate Change is the most common trigger for Coral bleaching.
- Storm Run-off and Pollution are damaging for the corals.
- High Solar-irradiance caused by the over-exposure to sunlight bleaches the shallow water corals.
- Increased Sedimentation
- Ocean Acidification
- Infectious Diseases
- Chemical Pollution
- Sub-aerial Exposure
- **Protection Measures for Corals:**
- The Ministry of Environment, Forests and Climate Change (MoEF&CC) provides the financial support to UTs/Coastal States for Coral Reef and Mangrove protection and management.
- The Coral reef has been granted the highest level of protection under the Schedule I of the Wildlife (Protection) Act, 1972.
- Protected Areas have been developed across the country to preserve the Marine life, including Coral Reefs, under the provisions of the Wildlife (Protection) Act, 1972.
- The Wildlife Crime Control Bureau was formed to improve the law enforcement in the fight against illegal wildlife trade and poaching activities.
- **Ocean Acidification:** The acidity of the ocean water increases due to the absorption of more carbon dioxide which eventually inhibits the ability of the corals to produce the calcareous skeletons, which is essential for their survival.
- **Eutrophication:** It is that condition of a water body which gets enriched with nutrients.
- This excessive enrichment with nutrients facilitates the growth of water hyacinth, algae, phytoplankton and other aquatic plants.
- **Oligotrophication:** The process of nutrient reduction or depletion in rates of cycling of nutrients in the aquatic ecosystems.
- It is considered as the partial reduction of the eutrophication process.
- **Red Tide:** It is a phenomenon where a particular phytoplankton species containing pigments and which bloom and the human eye perceives the water to get discoloured.
- **Biological Oxygen Demand (BOD):** The term "biochemical oxygen demand" (BOD) refers to how much oxygen is used by bacteria and other microorganisms during the aerobic (oxygen-containing) decomposition of organic matter at a specific temperature.
- Decrease in the dissolved oxygen (DO) causes a large number of aquatic species to die abruptly which releases an unpleasant odour eventually rendering the water unfit for human consumption.
- Algal Blooms or water blooms are effected by the explosive growth of algae and phytoplankton, which gives water a green colour.
- It covers the surface layer and prevents the sunlight from entering and gas from the atmosphere to diffuse.
- **Harmful Algal Blooms (HABs):** Phytoplankton blooms that are harmful or toxic. When colonies of algae grow out of control and have toxic or harmful effects on people, fish, shellfish, marine mammals, and birds, this is known as a hazardous algal bloom, or HAB.
- Scientists prefer the term "harmful algal bloom" even though many people refer to these blooms as "red tides".
- A dinoflagellate species called Karenia brevis is the agent for this type of bloom.
- The most common causes of blooms in freshwater lakes and reservoirs is blue-green algae (also known as cyanobacteria).
- Run-off from agriculture and urban areas is directly related to blue-green algae blooms.
- Cyanobacterial development is promoted by nutrient pollution.

Unit-5: Environmental Pollution

Classification of Pollutants

- **Acid Rain:** A precipitation that is unusually acidic containing high levels of hydrogen ions. It usually has a pH levels between 4-5.
- Sulphur dioxide and Nitrogen oxide emissions when react with water molecules in the atmosphere to form the acids which results in the acid rain.
- **Air Pollution:** A composition of any gaseous, liquid or solid substances in the atmosphere in concentrations that are considered harmful to humans, other living organisms, plants, property, that usually interferes with normal environmental processes.
- **Photochemical Smog:** Air pollution that occurs when volatile organic compounds (VOCs) react to sunlight creating a brown haze above cities.

- **Primary Pollutant:** Air pollutant that is emitted directly from the source. Example includes nitrogen oxides, VOCs, etc.
- **Secondary Pollutant:** Pollutant which is formed when the other primary pollutants reacts in the atmosphere.
- Example includes Ozone, Peroxyacetyl nitrate (PAN), etc.
- **Volatile Organic Compounds (VOCs):** These are formed by the evaporation of naturally occurring compounds like terpenes and the incompletely burned fossil fuels.
- **Non-Attainment Cities:** Those cities which are marked by Central Pollution Control Board (CPCB) for falling short of the National Ambient Air Quality Standards (NAAQS) for NO_2 and PM10 over 5 years.

Types of Pollution

- **Air pollution**
- Air pollution is a mixture of solid particles and gases in the air.
- Car emissions, chemicals from factories, dust and pollen and mold spores may be suspended as particles.
- Common gaseous pollutants include carbon monoxide, sulfur dioxide, chlorofluorocarbons (CFCs) and nitrogen oxides produced by industry and motor vehicles.
- **Water pollution**
- Water pollution occurs when toxic substances enter water bodies such as lakes, rivers, oceans and so on, getting dissolved in them, lying suspended in the water or depositing on the bed.
- Common pollutants include discharges of untreated sewage and chemical contaminants, release of waste and contaminants into surface runoff flowing to surface waters, groundwater pollution from waste disposal and leaching into the ground.
- **Soil pollution**
- It is the presence of toxic chemicals (pollutants or contaminants) in soil, in high enough concentrations to pose a risk to human health and/or the ecosystem.
- The contaminants include metals, inorganic ions and salts (e.g. phosphates, carbonates, sulfates, nitrates) and many organic compounds (such as lipids, proteins, DNA, fatty acids, hydrocarbons, PAHs, alcohols, etc.).
- **Thermal pollution**
- Thermal pollution, sometimes called "thermal enrichment", is the degradation of water quality by any process that changes ambient water temperature.
- A common cause of thermal pollution is the use of water as a coolant by power plants and industrial manufacturers.
- Deforestation eliminates shade, which exposes the water to sunlight.
- Water on hot paved surfaces gets hot and then runs off into nearby bodies of water, raising the water temperature.
- Retention ponds can also be a source of thermal shock because the relatively small and shallow bodies of water can absorb quite a bit of heat energy from the sun.
- **Noise pollution**
- Noise pollution happens when the sound coming from planes, industry or other sources reaches harmful levels.
- WHO Noise Environmental Burden on Disease working group found that noise pollution may contribute to hundreds of thousands of deaths per year by increasing the rates of coronary heart disease.
- Underwater noise pollution coming from ships has been shown to upset whale's navigation systems and kill other species that depend on the natural underwater world.
- **Light pollution**
- Light pollution is the excess amount of light in the night sky.
- Light pollution, also called photo-pollution, is almost always found in urban areas.
- Light pollution can disrupt ecosystems by confusing the distinction between night and day.
- **Land Pollution**
- This involves the decline in the quality of the earth's land surfaces in terms of use, landscape and ability to support life forms.
- Land pollution takes place when waste and garbage is not disposed of in the right manner thus, introducing toxins and chemicals on the land.
- Also, Mineral exploitation equally leads to a decline in the quality of the earth's land surfaces.
- **Point-Source Pollution:** It is said to occur when pollutants gets discharged from a particular location such as a drain pipe containing the effluents from industries and discharge directly into the water body.
- **Non-Point Source Pollution:** When waste discharges from the diffused sources or from a broader area such as from a farm field, pasture land, building site, abandoned mines and dumps and streets and roads.

Pollution Control Measures

- **For Air Pollution:** Afforestation or planting more trees should be encouraged to maintain a balance in the ecosystem and manage the effect caused by the rising greenhouse gases. The government also took initiatives to control air pollution, including the National ambient air quality standards (NAAQS) and the National air quality monitoring program (NAMP).
- **For Water Pollution:** Water consumption must be minimized or reduced by revising the strategies involved in controlling the environmental pollution of water. Wastewater should be treated well to be reused.
- Various programmes like National River Conservation Programme (NRCP), National Lake Conservation Programme (NLCP), Atal Mission for Rejuvenation and Urban Transformation (AMRUT), Smart Cities Mission, Mahatma Gandhi National Rural Employment Guarantee Scheme (MGNREGS), Repair, Renovation and Restoration (RRR) schemes.
- **For Soil Pollution:** To control the environmental pollution of soil, we must stop plastic usage. The use of plastic should be reduced to prevent soil pollution, and sewage should be appropriately treated before its utilization as fertilizer on cultivated grounds.
- Soil Conservation Act 1951, Soil Health Card (SHC) scheme (2015), Rashtriya Krishi Vigyan Yojana (RKVY) (2007), National Afforestation Program, Green India Mission, and Watershed Development Component of Pradhan Mantri Krishi Sinchayee Yojana (PMKSY).

- **For Thermal Pollution:** Thermal environmental pollution can be prevented using a few scientific approaches, like cooling ponds or buildings and constructing artificial lakes. These lakes are man-made water sources that provide a possible alternative for cooling power plants.
- **For Noise Pollution:** Noise pollution can be decreased by properly maintaining roadside vehicles and using soundproof equipment in noisy places. Horns should be used minimally on roads. Automobiles and industrial equipment must be fitted with silencers to avoid excessive noise.
- **For Light Pollution:** Lights should be turned off whenever unused, especially at night. The over utilization of indoor lights should be minimized.
- Lights should be pointed towards the ground whenever you are going outside your home.
- **For Land Pollution:** Organic fertilizers, an incorporated pest management technique and crop rotation can all be used by farmers.
- The 3 R's should be embraced by all households – reduce, reuse and recycle, to generate less waste.
- People should use products as much as possible to generate less waste individually.
- We should pick materials that can be easily recycled, for instance, paper, glass, plastics and electronic items and transform them into new products.

Ozone Depletion

- **Ozone Depletion:** The thinning of the atmosphere's protective ozone layer is referred to as ozone layer depletion.

  This occurs when certain chemicals interact with ozone and destroy it.
- **Ozone Hole:** It primarily occurs over Antarctica (and to a lesser extent the Arctic) during spring months (September -November in the Southern Hemisphere).
- **Polar Stratospheric Clouds:** Clouds present at an altitude of 12-22 kms containing water, nitric acid and sulphuric acid. They are formed generally during winter.

Waste Management

- **Bioremediation:** The usage of natural or genetically engineered micro-organisms (bacteria or fungi) to downgrade environmental pollutants into relatively less harmful types.
- **Bioventing:** Air and nutrients are supplied to contaminated soil via wells to stimulate the development of local bacteria.

  It can be applied if contamination is found deeply below the surface and is employed for simple hydrocarbons.
- **Biosparging:** An in-situ remediation technique called biosparging employs indigenous micro-organisms to break down organic constituents in the saturated zone. In order to boost the biological activity of the indigenous microorganisms, air (or oxygen) and nutrients (if needed) are injected into the saturated zone during biosparging.
- **Bioaugmentation:** Adding cultured microorganisms to the subsurface with the purpose of biodegrading certain contaminants in the soil and groundwater is known as bioaugmentation.
- **Oil Zapper:** Oil zapping is the new term for the technique of cleaning up an oil spill using bacteria.

  Oil zapping is a bio-remediation technique that employs microorganisms that "zap" oil.
- **Landfarming:** It is an ex-situ waste treatment method that is carried out in biotreatment cells or the upper soil zone.

  Transported to the land farming site, contaminated soils, sediments, or sludge are mixed into the soil surface and periodically turned over to aerate the mixture.
- **Bioreactors:** A bioreactor is a vessel in which raw materials are transformed into products under controlled conditions by living cells (microorganisms, mammalian, plant cells, algae and stem cells) or by cellular components like enzymes.
- **Composting:** The natural process of recycling organic matter, such as leaves and food scraps, into a valuable fertiliser that can enrich soil and plants is known as composting.
- **Phytoaccumulation:** When the contaminants accumulates in the above ground shoots or leaves and roots of plants.
- **Phytoremediation:** When the plants are employed to extract toxins from the soil and water, the process is termed as phytoremediation.
- **Coagulation:** When alum is introduced in the untreated water, the dirt particles in the water stick together or coagulates.
- **Flocculation:** Following the coagulation, the clusters of dirt particles clump together and forms the larger particles called the flocs, which proves to be easier to extract by filtration or by settling.
- **Electronic Waste or E-Waste:** These are generally the discarded electrical or electronic equipments.
- **Extended Producer Responsibility (EPR):** Under the EPR principle, the manufacturers are bound to collect a certain percentage of e-waste produced by their products till the time they reach their end of life.
- **Solid waste:** Those materials that have been discarded or are called the waste-like.
- **Vermiculture:** In this process, the earthworms are added to the compost, which break down the waste and the excrement of these worms enriches the compost with nutrients.
- **Sanitary Land Filling:** Garbage is spread out in thin layers, compacted and covered with clay or plastic foam in a sanitary landfill. The bottom of modern landfills is lined with an impermeable liner, which is usually made up of several layers of clay, thick plastic and sand. The liner prevents leachate from percolating into the groundwater, contaminating it.
- The bottom leachate is pumped and sent for treatment. To prevent water seepage, the landfill is covered with clay, sand, gravel and top soil once it is full. Several wells near the landfill site are being drilled to see if any leakage is contaminating ground water. Anaerobic decomposition produces methane, which is collected and burned to generate electricity or heat.

- **Incineration:** The term incinerates refers to the act of burning something until it is reduced to ashes. An incinerator is a device or facility that burns trash and other waste until it turns to ash. An incinerator is made of heavy, well-insulated materials to avoid releasing excessive amounts of heat into the environment.
- **Pyrolysis:** Pyrolysis is a type of incineration in which organic materials are chemically decomposed by heat in the absence of oxygen. Pyrolysis occurs most commonly under pressure and at temperatures above 430°C (806°F).

Unit-6: Climate Change

Global Warming & Greenhouse Effect

- **Climate:** The long-term average of the weather events of a place is termed as climate. Due to natural forces like ice age glaciations, sunspots, etc. the world has shifted several times over billions of years.
- **Climate Change:** Change of climate directly or indirectly due to human activities that changes the composition of the atmosphere and which is in addition to the natural climate variability observed over comparable period of time.
- ■ A change in long term weather trends is known as climate change.
- **Global Warming:** Increase in the temperature of the atmosphere near the surface of the Earth and in the troposphere which affects the climate patterns around the world.
- ■ It can be caused by both natural and man-made factors.
- ■ Generally, it is caused due to increased emissions of greenhouse gases from anthropogenic activities.
- **Greenhouse Effect:** The naturally-occurring phenomena that blankets the earth's lower atmosphere and warms it, holding it at a temperature suitable for life.
- **Greenhouse Gases:** Water Vapour, Carbon Dioxide, Methane, Nitrous Oxide, Fluorinated gases, Black carbon, Brown Carbon, etc.
- **Global warming Potential (GWP):** The heat that any greenhouse gas in the atmosphere absorbs, expressed as a multiple of the heat that the same mass of carbon dioxide would absorb, is known as its global warming potential.
- **Polar Vortex:** It is an area of low pressure arctic air which is normally centred around the North pole.
- ■ It is held in its place by a jet stream passing around 60° N, 25000 to 30000 feet above ground and divides the cold air and warm air.
- ■ The Jet stream is pushed in a wavy manner by a high pressure and a low pressure system, which leads the polar vortex much southwards than normal.
- ■ Arctic Invasion: When a portion of the vortex is brought into North America and causes the temperatures in the mid-west and the eastern United States to dive below zero.

Impacts of Climate Change

- Agriculture and Food security
- Sea Levels, Oceans and Coastal Areas
- Water Stress and Water Insecurity
- Biological Diversity Affected
- Health Issues Encountered
- **Social Cost of Carbon:** Under this calculation, it is generally tried to add-up all the quantifiable costs and benefits of emitting one additional tonne of CO_2 in monetary terms.
- ■ This value can then be used to weigh the advantages of reduced warming against the costs of cutting emissions.
- ■ It is generally estimated as the net present value of the impacts of the climate change over the next 100 years of one additional tonne of carbon emitted to the atmosphere today.
- ■ It is marginal damage cost of carbon emissions.
- ■ Objective: To assist the policy-makers in assessing whether a policy designed to curb climate change is justified or not.

Climate Change Mitigation Strategies

- Lowering the amount of Green House Gas (GHG) emissions that contribute to global warming.
- Retrofitting buildings to make them more energy-efficient.
- Embracing the various renewable energy sources such as solar, wind and small hydro.
- Assisting communities in creating more sustainable transportation solutions, such as electric cars, bus rapid transit and bio-fuels.
- Promoting more sustainable use of forests and land.
- **Carbon Sequestration:** The process of capturing CO_2 gas in the atmosphere. It is also termed so when the CO_2 is captured from the existing and new power plants and the factories before they are released into the atmosphere.
- ■ Once the Carbon dioxide gas has been contained it is placed in to long term storage.
- ■ Carbon Sequestration is aimed at eliminating harmful human-introduced carbon from our atmosphere by disrupting the carbon cycle.
- **Types of Carbon Sequestration:**
- ■ Terrestrial Sequestration: The plants and trees store CO2 in their roots and in their bodies.
- ■ Geologic Sequestration: Carbon dioxide gas is buried thousand feet underground.
- **Carbon Sink:** Anything that absorbs more carbon than it releases in the form of carbon dioxide.
- ■ These sinks are essential for controlling atmospheric carbon dioxide levels.
- ■ Common carbon sinks include undisturbed soils and forests, the ocean, untapped fossil fuel sources, and terrestrial plant photosynthesis.
- **Carbon Credit:** Permits that allow the owner to emit a specific amount of carbon dioxide or other greenhouse gases are known as carbon credits, commonly referred to as carbon offsets.
- ■ One carbon dioxide credit, or its equivalent in other greenhouse gases, allows for the emission of one tonne of carbon dioxide.
- ■ The carbon credit is half of a so-called cap-and-trade programme.

- Companies that pollute are given credits that allow them to do so up to a limit that is periodically reduced.
- In the meantime, the company may sell any credits it doesn't require to another company that needs them.
- In order to reduce greenhouse gas emissions, carbon credits were devised.
- Companies are given a set number of credits, which decrease with time. Any extra credits can be sold to another company.
- Companies have a monetary incentive to cut their carbon emissions attributable to carbon credits. Those that find it difficult to cut emissions can still operate, although at a higher cost.
- The cap-and-trade model, which was employed in the 1990s to reduce sulphur pollution, is the basis for carbon credits.
- The creation of a global carbon credit offset trading market was decided upon by negotiators in the Glasgow COP26 climate change summit in November 2021.

• **Carbon Offsetting:** Through carbon offset programmes, individuals and companies can make investments in environmental projects all over the world to offset their own carbon footprints.

- Carbon offset programmes assist in the fight against global warming while also supporting local communities.
- These projects frequently provide underdeveloped communities with much-needed jobs, health improvements, biodiversity, reforestation and broad social benefits.

• **Carbon Tax**: A tax on burning fuels containing carbon is known as a carbon tax (coal, oil, gas).

- It is thought to be the main policy for reducing and ultimately eliminating the use of fossil fuels, the burning of which is degrading and destabilising our climate.
- Emission trading, which entails setting a maximum quantity of permissible effluents from industries and permitting those with low emissions to sell their extra space, is another method of pricing carbon.
- Economic activities such as the usage of coal can be subject to a carbon tax, as is the case in Canada and Sweden.

• **Geo-Engineering:** It is the large scale intervention in the Earth system to counteract the human-led climate change. There are two basic techniques to intervene:

• **Carbon Dioxide Removal:** Under this, the carbon dioxide is removed from the atmosphere and stored for a long time. Techniques included are:

- Ocean Fertilization
- Afforestation
- Air Capture

• **Solar Radiation Management:** By reflecting some sunlight back to space the global warming is counteracted. Techniques included are:

- Marine Cloud Brightening
- Stratospheric Aerosol
- Space Reflector

Global Response to Climate Change

• **United Nation Framework Convention on Climate Change (UNFCCC):**

- In Force: 1994
- Secretariat: Bonn, Germany
- Ratified by: 198 Parties (197 countries)
- Convention: Legally non-binding
- Aim: To stabilize GHG concentrations in the atmosphere.
- Annex-I Countries: Industrialized Nations and economies in transition.
- Annex-II Countries: Developed countries which pay for costs of the developing countries.
- Non-Annex Countries: Developing countries.

• **Kyoto Protocol:**

- Adopted: 1997
- In Force: 2005
- Parties: 192
- Task: It sets the binding goals for the Annex-I countries.
- Aim: To combat global warming it aims to reduce the greenhouse gas emissions.
- Concept for Protocol: Common but Differentiated Responsibilities.
- GHGs included in Protocol:
  - Methane
  - Carbon Dioxide
  - Sulphur Hexafluoride
  - Nitrous Oxide Hydrofluorocarbons Perfluorocarbons

• **UN-REDD:** REDD stands for Reducing Emissions from Deforestation in Developing Countries.

- Formed: 2008
- HQ: Geneva
- Membership: 65 Countries
- Type: Multi-lateral collaborative programme of the FAO, UNDP and UNEP.
- Objective: Partners with the developing countries to support them in creating the technical capacities needed to implement REDD+ and meet UNFCCC requirements for REDD+ results based payments.

• **Global Environment Facility (GEF):** The Global Environment Facility (GEF) was created to offer fresh grants and additional concessional funding to meet the additional costs associated with transforming a project with national benefits into one with global environmental benefits.

- The GEF unites 186 member nations in collaboration with global organisations, non-governmental organizations and the private sector.

• **Green Climate Fund (GCF):** The GCF was established in 2010 as part of the UNFCCC's financial mechanism to provide funding from developed countries to developing countries so they can both combat climate change and adapt to its effects.

- The Green Climate Fund will use thematic funding windows to support projects, programmes, policies, and other activities in developing country Parties.

• **Intergovernmental Panel on Climate Change (IPCC):**

- Formed: 1988
- By: WMO and UNEP
- Objective: To provide policymakers with regular assessments of the scientific basis of climate change, its future risks and impacts and options for adaptation and mitigation.
- The United Nations Framework Convention on Climate Change (UNFCCC) negotiations are based on IPCC assessments, which give governments of all levels a scientific basis for developing climate-related policies.

- **Paris Agreement:** An international agreement address climate change is known as the Paris Agreement.
- The governments of 195 countries met in Paris, France, at the UN Climate Change Conference (COP21), to examine the possibility of a new global climate change agreement that would reduce greenhouse gas emissions worldwide and reduce the threat of dangerous climate change.
- Aim(s):
  - Limit the increase in the global temperature this century to no more than 2 degrees Celsius over the pre-industrial level.
  - Attempt to limit the temperature rise to 1.5 degrees Celsius or less.
  - Bolster ability of the countries to deal with the effects of climate change.

Indian Initiatives

- **National Action Plan on Climate Change (NAPCC):** The Prime Minister's Council on Climate Change launched the National Action Plan on Climate Change (NAPCC) in 2008.
- It aims to create awareness of the threat posed by climate change and the steps to counter it among representatives of the public, different government agencies, scientists, industry and communities.
- The NAPCC is comprised of eight national missions, which together offer multi-pronged, long-term, integrated strategies for attaining key climate change goals. These are:
- National Solar Mission
- National Mission for Enhanced Energy Efficiency (NMEEE)
- National Mission on Sustainable Habitat
- National Water Mission
- National Mission for Sustaining the Himalayan Ecosystem
- National Mission for a Green India
- National Mission for Sustainable Agriculture
- National Mission on Strategic Knowledge for Climate Change.
- **Intended Nationally Determined Contribution (INDC):** Intended Nationally Determined Contributions, or INDCs, are declarations made by individual countries indicating the climate actions they expect to undertake as part of a new international agreement.
- With the aim of reducing greenhouse gas emissions enough to keep global temperature rise under 2 degrees Celsius, the INDCs combine the top-down system of a United Nations climate agreement with bottom-up system-in elements, allowing countries to present their agreements in light of their own national circumstances, capabilities and priorities.
- India's Proposed Targets:
  - Reduce the GDP's emissions intensity by 45% by 2030 compared to 2005 levels.
  - With the help of technology transfer and low-cost international finance, achieve an installed capacity of non-fossil fuel-based energy resources equal to about 50% of the total by 2030.
  - By 2030, create additional 2.5 to 3 billion tonnes of CO_2 equivalent of forest and tree cover to serve as a carbon sink.
- **Green Building:** A "green" building is one that reduces or eliminates negative effects on our climate and natural environment during design, construction, or operation. It can also have positive impacts.
- Green buildings preserve precious natural resources and raise our quality of life.
- Green building is the process of creating and constructing structures while employing processes that are resource-efficient and environmentally responsible at every stage of a building's life cycle, from siting to design to construction to operation to maintenance to renovation to deconstruction.
- **Green Rating for Integrated Habitat Assessment (GRIHA):** It is India's official national rating system for finished buildings.
- In India's Intended Nationally Determined Contributions (INDC) presented to the United Nations Framework Convention on Climate Change, GRIHA is recognized as the country's own green building rating system.
- The Energy and Resources Institute (TERI) came up with the concept and the Ministry of New and Renewable Energy worked jointly with TERI to create it.
- **BSE-GREENEX:** The first environmentally friendly equity index, "BSE-Greenex", was launched by the country's premier stock exchange, BSE Ltd.
- It would allow investors make better informed decisions in India's green theme.
- The BSE has created BSE-Greenex in association with gTrade (supported by GIZ promoted by Germany, Observer Research Foundation, and IIM Ahmedabad), with the goal of promoting green investing while placing an emphasis on financial performance and long-term viability of companies.
- To assess carbon performance, it is based purely on quantitative and objective performance signals.

Unit-7: Sustainable Development

Definition

- **Sustainable Development:** Development that meets present needs without compromising the ability of future generation to meet their own needs.
- The Brundtland Commission provided this most widely accepted definition of sustainable development in its report 'Our Common Future' (1987).
- In order to create an inclusive, sustainable, and resilient future for people and the planet, sustainable development (SD) calls for coordinated efforts.
- **Core Elements of Sustainable Development:**
- Economic growth, social inclusion and environment protection are the three pillars of sustainable development. It is essential to bring them together.
- Sustainable development emphasises living in harmony with nature, achieving sustainable livelihoods, and using the appropriate technologies.

UN-SDGs

- **United Nations-Sustainable Development Goals (UN-SDGs):** The Sustainable Development Goals (SDGs), also known as the 'Global Goals', were adopted by the United Nations in 2015 as a universal call to action to end poverty, protect the planet and ensure that by 2030 all people enjoy peace and prosperity.
- The 17 SDGs are integrated, they recognise that action in one area will affect outcomes in others and that development must balance social, economic and environmental sustainability.
- Countries have committed to prioritize progress for those who're furthest behind. The SDGs are designed to end poverty, hunger, AIDS and discrimination against women and girls.
- The 17 UN-SDGs are listed below:
- **SDG 1:** No Poverty
- **SDG 2:** Zero Hunger
- **SDG 3:** Good Health and Well Being
- **SDG 4:** Quality Education
- **SDG 5:** Gender Equality
- **SDG 6:** Clean Water and Sanitation
- **SDG 7:** Affordable and Clean Energy
- **SDG 8:** Decent Work and Economic Growth
- **SDG 9:** Industry, Innovation and Infrastructure
- **SDG 10:** Reduced Inequalities
- **SDG 11:** Sustainable Cities and Communities
- **SDG 12:** Responsible Consumption and Production
- **SDG 13:** Climate Action
- **SDG 14:** Life below Water
- **SDG 15:** Life on Land
- **SDG 16:** Peace, Justice and Strong Institutions
- **SDG 17:** Partnerships for the Goals
- **Efforts at the Individual Level:**
- Conserve Fossil Fuels
- Conserve Water
- Save Trees
- Keep the Air Clean
- Reduce Garbage
- Spread Awareness

NITI Aayog's SDG Index

- **NITI Aayog's Sustainable Development Goal India Index (SDG India Index):** SDG India Index look to provide a holistic view on the Social, Economic and Environmental status of the country and its States. The SDG India Index provides a State's or UT's present situation on each of the indicators taken into account, and later versions will reflect incremental change. This Index spans across 13 out of 17 SDGs not taking into its fold the goals 12, 13, 14 and 17.
- **Developed By:** Ministry of Statistics & Programme Implementation, NITI Aayog, United Nations-India and Global Green Growth Institute.
- **Classification Criteria:**
- Aspirant: 0-49
- Performer: 50-64
- Front-Runner: 65-99
- Achiever: 100
- **SDG India Index 2.0:** NITI Aayog has released SDG India Index versions beyond 2.0. The SDG India Index 3.0 (2020 -21) and subsequent editions cover all 17 SDGs.

Unit-8: Environmental Organisations

United Nations Environment Programme (UNEP)

- **United Nations Environment Programme (UNEP):**
- Established: 1972 (as an outcome of the Stockholm Conference)
- HQ: Kenya (Nairobi)
- Achievements:
  - One of the several implementing agencies for the Global Environmental facility (GEF).
  - International Cyanide Management Code was developed under its auspices.
  - Contributed to the creation of treaties and recommendations on topics such as Contamination of International Waterways, International Trade in potentially hazardous substance, etc.

World Meteorological Organisation (WMO)

- **World Meteorological Organization (WMO):**
- Formed: 1950
- HQ: Geneva, Switzerland
- Type: Inter-governmental organisation
- Membership: 193 states and territories
- Importance: Provides an international forum for co-operation in meteorology.

World Wide Fund for Nature

- **World Wide Fund for Nature (WWF):**
- Formed: 1961
- HQ: Gland, Switzerland
- Mission: To halt and reverse the destruction of our environment.
- Type: International Non-Governmental Organisation
- Tasked with: Wilderness preservation and reducing the human's footprint on the environment.
- It is a type of charity with around 60% of its funding coming from the voluntary donations by private individuals.
- **International Union for Conservation of Nature (IUCN):**
- Formed: 1948
- HQ: Gland, Switzerland
- Type: Membership union comprising both Governments and Civil Society Organisations.
- IUCN Red List of Threatened Species: It is the most comprehensive inventory of the global conservation status of animal and plant species.
  - It assesses the likelihood of species extinction using a set of quantitative criteria. All species and geographical regions around the world find these criteria as relevant.
  - The extinction risk of a species is defined by the IUCN Red List Categories. The range of nine categories comprises NE (Not Evaluated) to EX (Extinct).

➢ Species that are deemed to be at risk of extinction include those that are Critically Endangered (CR), Endangered (EN), and Vulnerable (VU).

- **Global Tiger Forum:** The GTF is the only inter-governmental international body created with members from willing nations to launch a global campaign to preserve the tiger.
  - Formed: 1994
  - HQ: New Delhi
- **International Whaling Commission (IWC):** It is an international organisation created in accordance with the International Convention for the Regulation of Whaling (ICRW).
  - HQ: Cambridge, England
  - Functions: The ICRW governs the 89 member nations' commercial, scientific, and subsistence whaling practices.
  - It enacted a moratorium on commercial whaling in 1986. This ban is still in effect.
- **International Solar Alliance (ISA):** It is an action oriented, member-driven, collaborative platform to increase deployment of solar energy based technologies. It was conceived as a joint effort by France and India to mobilize efforts against climate change through employment of solar energy solutions.
  - **Aim:** To facilitate energy access, ensure energy security and drive energy transition in its member countries.
  - **Vision:** 'Let us together make the sun brighter'.
  - **Mission:** 'Every home, no matter how far away, will have a light at home'.
  - **Headquarters:** India (Gurugram)
  - **Member Nations:** 120 countries (Out of 120 nations, 100 have signed and ratified the ISA Framework Agreement)
  - **Eligibility:** All member states of the United Nations are eligible to join the ISA.

Unit-9: Miscellaneous

Important Acts related to Environment

- **Wildlife (Protection) Act, 1972:** The Act was passed in order to save various plant and animal species. Except for the State of Jammu and Kashmir, it covers the entirety of India. India only had five recognised national parks prior to the passage of this legislation.
  - Authorities Appointed Under the Act:
    - ➢ **By Central Government:** The Director of Wildlife Preservation
    - ➢ **By State Governments:** The Chief Wildlife Warden (CWLW)
  - **Schedules Under the Act:** The WPA of 1972 has divided the protection status of various animals and plants under the below-mentioned six categories:
    - ➢ Schedule-I ➢ Schedule-II ➢ Schedule-III
    - ➢ Schedule-IV ➢ Schedule-V ➢ Schedule-VI
- **Environmental Protection Act 1986:** It was enacted by the Government of India after the Bhopal Gas Tragedy.
  - It establishes the framework for studying, planning and putting into practise long-term environmental safety requirements as well as prescribing a system of timely and appropriate reaction to environmental hazards.
  - The EPA Act was passed in accordance with Article 253 of the Indian Constitution, which provides for the enactment of legislation to implement international agreements.
  - The EPA grants the Central Government the power to establish authorities tasked with preventing environmental pollution in all of its forms and addressing particular environmental problems that are peculiar to various regions of the country.

Coastal Regulation Zone (CRZ)

- **Coastal Regulation Zone (CRZ):** The land between the low tide line (LTL) and the high tide line, as well as the coastal areas including seas, bays, creeks, rivers, and backwaters that are exposed to tides up to 500 metres from the high tide line (HTL), have been designated as coastal regulation zone (CRZ) from 1991.
  - The Ministry of Environment, Forest, and Climate Change has established the coastal regulation zones in accordance with the Environment Protection Act of 1986.
  - The state government's Coastal Zone Management Authorities are responsible for ensuring that the CRZ Rules are implemented, even though the Union Environment Ministry creates them.
  - Classification of Coastal Zones under CRZ Notification 2011:
    - ➢ **CRZ-I:** Ecologically Sensitive Areas.
    - ➢ **CRZ-II:** Shore Line Areas.
    - ➢ **CRZ-III:** Undisturbed Areas.
    - ➢ **CRZ-IV:** Aquatic area from low tide line up to territorial limits.

Organizations

Animal Welfare Board of India (AWBI)

- **Established in 1962 + HQ:** Ballabhgarh in Haryana (earlier based at Chennai).
- **Key person:** Rukmini Devi Arundale (also the 1st Chairperson of AWBI).
- AWBI is a statutory advisory body under The Prevention of Cruelty to Animals Act, 1960 under the Ministry of Fisheries, Animal Husbandry and Dairying.
- **Functions:** Its advices governments on the matters related to Animal welfare + Provides grants to Animal Welfare Organizations.

Central Zoo Authority (CZA)

- Established in 1992 (HQ: New Delhi).
- CZA is a statuary body + under 1991 Amendment to Wildlife (Protection) Act 1972 + under MoEF&CC.
- Objectives: To complement the national effort in conservation of wild life + To maintain Indian Zoos on

par with International standards + Exchange of animals between Indian and foreign zoos. Regulates the establishment and management of zoos in India, Ensures animal welfare and conservation of zoos, Promotes scientific research on zoo animals.

- The Authority consists: Chairman: Minister of Environment + 10 members & a member Secretary.

Forest Survey of India (FSI)

- Established in 1981 + HQ: Dehradun in Uttarakhand + under MoEF&CC.
- It started as 'Pre-Investment Survey of Forest Resources (PISFR)' in 1965 before re-organized as FSI in 1981.
- **Objective:** To conduct survey and assessment of forest resources.
- **Forest Survey Report:** Released by FSI since 1987, biennially (once in two years).

Botanical Survey of India (BSI)

- Established in 1890 (under the direction of Sir George King) + HQ: Kolkata + under MoEF&CC.
- BSI is the apex taxonomic research organization of the country.
- **Mandate:** Biosystematics research, floristic studies, documentation of flora, digitization of herbarium specimens, & advisory services etc.,
- BSI publishes 'Red Data Book of Indian Plants'.

Zoological Survey of India (ZSI)

- Established in 1916 + HQ: Kolkata + under MoEF&CC
- **Objective:** To promote the survey, exploration and research of the fauna.
- The history of ZSI goes back to Asiatic Society of Bengal founded by Sir William Jones in 1784.

National Biodiversity Authority (NBA)

- Established in 2003 + HQ: Chennai + under MoEF&CC
- NBA is a statutory body under Biological Diversity Act, 2002.
- The act was enacted to give effect-to the Convention on Biological Diversity (CBD) (India signed it in 1992). Regulates access to biological resources and their conservation, Promotes sustainable use of biodiversity, Creates databases of biodiversity
- **Mandate:** To perform regulatory & advisory functions for the GoI on issues of conservation, sustainable use of biological resources.
- NBA supports creation of State Biodiversity Boards (SBBs).
- **Biodiversity Heritage Sites:** Notified by State Governments in consultation with local bodies.

Wildlife Crime Control Bureau (WCCB)

- Established in 2006 + HQ: New Delhi + under MoEF&CC
- WCCB is a statutory body constituted under the Wildlife (Protection) Act 1972 (WPA 2006, Amendment).
- Have five regional offices at Delhi, Kolkata, Mumbai, Chennai & Jabalpur.
- **Objective:** to combat organized wildlife crime.
- Additional Director General (Wild Life) is the ex-officio director of the WCCB.
- WCCB is the nodal point for SAWEN (South Asia Wildlife Enforcement Network) in India.
- WCCB has conducted Operation Save Kurma, Thunder Bird, Wild-Net, Lesknow, Birbil, Clean Art.
- It also assists & advises the Customs authorities in inspection of the consignments of flora & fauna as per the provisions of WPA, CITES & EXIM Policy.
- UNEP has awarded WCCB with 'Asia Environment Enforcement Awards' in 2018.

National Plan for Conservation of Aquatic Eco-Systems (NPCA)

- NPCA was launched in 2013 by merging National Lake Conservation Plan (NLCP) and National Wetlands Conservation Programme (NWCP)
- **Objective:** Holistic conservation & restoration of lakes, wetlands to enhance water quality besides improving biodiversity and the ecosystem.
- NPCA is presently operational on cost sharing between Central and respective state governments.

National Ganga River Basin Authority

- Established in 2009 + HQ: New Delhi + under Ministry of Jal Shakti
- Mandate: Abatement of pollution & conservation of the river Ganga.
- The NGRBA is chaired by the Prime Minister.
- Members include: Union Ministers concerned, the Chief Ministers of the States through which Ganga flows.
- **Work/Objectives:** Regulates and manages the Ganga River Basin, Implements measures for pollution control and rejuvenation of the Ganga River, Facilitates community participation in conservation.

National Board for Wildlife (NBWL)

- Established in 2003 + HQ: New Delhi + under MoEF&CC
- It replaced the 'Indian Board for Wildlife', which was formed in 1952 as an advisory board.
- NBWL is a statutory body constituted under the WPA, 1972.
- NBWL Composition: Chair Person: the Prime Minister | Vice-Chair: Minister of Environment | 45 other members including 19 ex-officio members, 3 MPs (2 from LS & 1 from RS), 5 NGOs.
- **Objective:** To promote the conservation and development of wildlife and forests.
- It has power to review all wildlife-related matters and approve projects in and around national parks and sanctuaries.
- No alternation of boundaries in National Parks and Wildlife Sanctuaries can be done without approval of the NBWL.

National Tiger Conservation Authority (NTCA)

- Established in 2005 + HQ: New Delhi + under MoEF&CC
- NTCA is a statutory body constituted under the WPA, 1972 (Amendment Act, 2006).

- **Chairperson:** Minister of Environment
- It provides statutory authority to Project Tiger.

Environmental Impact Assessment (EIA)

- **Environmental Impact Assessment (EIA):** According to the UNEP (United Nations Environment Programme) EIA is a tool used to identify the environmental, social and economic impacts of a project prior to decision-making.
- **Aim:** To predict environmental impacts at an early stage in project planning and design, find ways and means to reduce adverse impacts, shape projects to suit the local environment and present the predictions and options to decision-makers.
- Process:
  - 1st **Stage-Screening:** It tells us whether the proposed project requires an EIA and if it does then the level of assessment required.
  - 2nd **Stage-Scoping:** This stage identifies the key impacts and issues that should be further investigated further. It also explains the boundary and time-limit of the study.
  - 3rd **Stage-Impact analysis:** Identifies and predicts the likely social and environmental impact of the proposed project and evaluates the importance.
  - 4th **Stage-Mitigation:** Recommends the steps to reduce and avoid the potential adverse consequences on the environment of the development activities.
  - 5th **Stage-Reporting:** Presents the result of EIA through a report to the decision-making body and other parties.
  - 6th **Stage-Public hearing:** On completion of the EIA report, environmental and public groups living close to project site may be informed and then consulted.
  - 7th **Stage-Review of EIA:** It examines the effectiveness and adequacy of the EIA report and provides the necessary information for the decision-making process.
  - 8th **Stage-Decision-making:** It decides whether the concerned project is approved, rejected or needs any further changes.
  - 9th **Stage-Post monitoring:** This stage comes into picture when the project is commissioned. It checks to confirm that the impacts of the project does not exceed the legal standards and implementation of the mitigation measures are in the way described in the report.

Agriculture

- Agriculture is the science, art and practice of cultivating plants and livestock. Agriculture was the key development in the rise of sedentary human civilization, whereby farming of domesticated species created food surpluses that enabled people to live in cities.

Salient Features of Indian Agriculture

- Subsistence type of agriculture.
- Dependent on unreliable and erratic monsoon (about 60 percent).
- India's vast relief, varying climate and soil conditions produce a variety of crops.
- All tropical, subtropical and temperate crops are grown across geographical areas.
- Predominance of food crop → about $2/3^{rd}$ of total cropped area.
- Backbone of rural economy.
- Plays critical role in ensuring food security.
- Poor electricity, storage, water, credit & marketing infrastructure.
- Supports allied sectors and activities – cattle, poultry etc.
- Major involvement of women in Indian agriculture sector.
- Characterized by poor mechanization, inadequate Agricultural research and extension services.
- Fragmented nature of agricultural holding.

Productivity of Agriculture

- Productivity of Agriculture is defined as the number of crops produced per unit land.
- Productivity levels in Indian agriculture are very low as compared to the productivity levels of other countries – China, USA etc.
- Like in 2018, average productivity in India was approximately 2600 kg/ha while world average was approximately 3500-4000 kg/ha.
- Fertiliser use, irrigation and rainfall cause significant variation in productivity.
- Productivity in the regions of Green revolution are certainly higher than other areas. Other high productivity regions are Tamil Nadu, Kerala, West Bengal and Maharashtra.
- The productivity in Gangetic plain is reducing because of Land bifurcation leading to reduced size of land holdings.
- Key issues affecting agricultural productivity include the decreasing sizes of agricultural land holdings, continued dependence on the monsoon, inadequate access to irrigation, imbalanced use of soil nutrients resulting in loss of fertility of soil, uneven access to modern technology in different parts of the country, lack of access to formal agricultural credit, limited procurement of food grains by government agencies, and failure to provide remunerative prices to farmers.

Cropping Intensity

- The ratio of the gross cropped area to the net sown area.
- As the land is cropped multiple times, the cropping intensity increases.
- It depends on factors like climate, demand of crops, availability of irrigation and other inputs etc.

Renewable Energy Sources

- **Solar Energy:** Solar energy is the most plentiful energy source available and may be used in cloudy conditions. The Earth absorbs solar energy at a pace that is around 10,000 times greater than the rate at which people use.
- The quantity of solar energy that reaches the surface of the globe in a single hour exceeds the planet's whole annual energy.

- **Wind Energy:** Wind energy is the process of harnessing the kinetic energy of moving air by means of massive wind turbines that are installed on land (onshore), in salt water, or in freshwater (offshore). Despite the fact that wind energy has been used for thousands of years, onshore and offshore wind energy technology has lately progressed to maximize the quantity of electricity produced, with higher turbines and larger rotor diameters.
- **Hydro-Power Energy:** The largest renewable energy source in the electricity sector at the moment is hydro-power. It is dependent on typically consistent rainfall patterns. The energy of water flowing from higher elevations to lower elevations is captured by hydro-power.
- **Ocean Energy/ Tidal Energy:** Tidal energy is now at the research and development (R&D) stage in India, according to the Ministry of New and Renewable Energy. Low to moderate tidal wave power is predicted for the Gulf of Khambat, Gulf of Kutch, southern Gujarat, Palk Bay and Mannar Channel in Tamil Nadu, Hooghly River, South Haldia and the Sunderbans in West Bengal.
- **Geothermal Energy:** Geothermal energy uses the thermal energy that exists within the Earth's interior. Warming geothermal reservoirs can be accomplished using wells and other methods.
- **Biomass Energy:** Bioenergy is made from various organic resources, known as biomass, including wood, charcoal, dung and other manures for the production of heat and power, as well as agricultural crops for the creation of liquid biofuels. The majority of biomass is used for cooking, lighting and space heating by the poorest people in developing countries rural areas.

Organization/ Program	History	Aims/Objectives
National Wildlife Action Plan	• First NWAP was launched in 1983, and the latest version was launched in 2017. • The plan is prepared by the Ministry of Environment, Forest and Climate Change, and is based on inputs from various stakeholders.	• Aims to conserve wildlife and their habitats. • Identifies and prioritizes areas for conservation. • Promotes community participation in conservation.
CAMPA	• Established in 2004 under the Forest (Conservation) Act headquarters is located in New Delhi, India. • Governed by a Governing Council, is chaired by the Union Minister for Environment, Forest and Climate Change.	• Funds afforestation and forest conservation activities. • Compensates states for loss of revenue due to forest conservation measures.
National Afforestation and Eco-Development Board	• Established in 1992 by the Government of India as a statutory body under the Ministry of Environment and Forests. • Has implemented several successful afforestation and eco-development projects in collaboration with state governments, NGOs, and other stakeholders. • Some of its notable initiatives include the Green India Mission, National Mission for a Green India, and the National Agroforestry Policy.	• Promotes afforestation and eco-development activities. • Facilitates community Participation in afforestation and eco-development projects.
National Bamboo Mission	• Launched in 2006 as a sub-scheme of the National Mission on Bamboo.	• Promotes bamboo cultivation and utilization, Develops bamboo-based industries. • Generates employment opportunities through bamboo.
Mangroves for the Future	• Established in 2006 as a partnership program between IUCN and UNDP.	• Promotes the conservation and sustainable use of mangrove forests. • Builds capacity for mangrove management. • Facilitates knowledge sharing.
Joint Forest Management	• Introduced in 1990.	• Involves local communities in the management of forests. • Promotes sustainable forest management, Generates income for local communities.

Social Forestry	• First introduced in 1976 during 5th Five Year Plan.	• Involves communities in afforestation and forest conservation activities. • Generates income for local communities.
National Mission for Electric Mobility	• Launched in 2013 as a mission under the Ministry of Heavy Industries and Public Enterprises.	• Promotes the adoption of electric vehicles. • Develops charging infrastructure for electric vehicles. • Develops a domestic manufacturing base for electric vehicles.
Eco Mark	• Launched in 1991 as a certification scheme for environmentally friendly products.	• Certifies environmentally friendly products. • Promotes the adoption of eco-friendly products. • Encourages sustainable production practices.
National Lake Conservation Plan	• Launched in 2001 under the Ministry of Environment and Forests.	• Aims to conserve lakes in India, • Identifies and prioritizes lakes for conservation. • Implements conservation measures for lakes.

Tiger Reserve in India

- Andhra Pradesh
  - Nagarjuna Sagar Srisailam
- Arunachal Pradesh
  - Namdapha
  - Kamlang Tiger Reserve
  - Pakke
  - Pakhui
- Assam
  - Manas
  - Nameri
  - Orang Tiger Reserve
  - Kaziranga
- Bihar
  - Valmiki
- Chhattisgarh
  - Udanti- Sitanadi
  - Achanakmar
  - Indravati
  - Guru Ghasidas
- Jharkhand
  - Palamau
- Karnataka
  - Bandipur
  - Bhadra
  - Dandeli – Anshi
  - Nagarhole
  - Kudremukha
  - Biligiriranga Hills
- Kerala
  - Periyar
  - Parambikulam
- Madhya Pradesh
  - Kanha
  - Pench
  - Bandhavgarh
  - Panna
  - Bori- Satpura
  - Sanjay- dubri
  - Ratapani
- Maharashtra
  - Melghat
  - Tadoba- Andhari
  - Sahyadri
  - Bor
  - Nawegaon- Nazgira
- Mizoram
  - Dampa
- Odisha
  - Similipal
  - Satkosia
  - Sunabeda
- Rajasthan
  - Ranthambore
  - Sariska
  - Mukandra Hills
  - Darrah
  - Ramgarh Vishdhari
- Tamil Nadu
  - Kalakad- Mundanthurai
  - Anamalai
  - Mudumalai
  - Sathyamangalam
  - Meghamalai
- Uttar Pradesh
  - Dudhwa
  - Philibhit
  - Amangarh (Buffer of Corbett Tiger Reserve)
  - Katerniaghat
- Uttarakhand
  - Corbett
  - Rajaji
- West Bengal
  - Sunderbans
  - Buxa

National Parks in India

- Andaman and Nicobar Islands
  - Galathea National Park
  - Mahatma Gandhi Marine (Wandoor) National Park
  - Campbell Bay National Park
  - Mount Harriet National Park
  - Rani Jhansi Marine National Park
  - Saddle peak National Park
  - Middle Button Island National Park

- North Button Island National Park
- South Button Island National Park
- Andhra Pradesh
- Papikonda National Park
- Sri Venkateswara National Park
- Rajiv Gandhi (Rameswaram) National Park
- Arunachal Pradesh
- Mouling National Park
- Namdapha National Park
- Assam
- Nameri National Park
- Manas National Park
- Dibru- Saikhowa National Park
- Kaziranga National Park
- Orang National Park
- Dihing Patkai National Park
- Raimona National Park
- Bihar
- Valmiki National Park
- Chhattisgarh
- Indravati National Park
- Kanger Valley National Park
- Guru Ghasi Das (Sanjay) National Park
- Goa
- Bhagwan Mahavir (Mollem) National Park
- Gujarat Gir National Park
- Blackbuck National Park
- Gulf of Kutch National Park
- Gujrat
- Gujarat Gir National Park
- Blackbuck National Park
- Gulf of Kutch National Park
- Haryana
- Sultanpur National Park
- Kalesar National Park
- Himachal Pradesh
- Pin Valley National Pak
- Simbalbara National Park
- Inderkilla National Park
- Khirganga National Park
- Great Himalayan National Park
- Jammu and Kashmir
- Dachigam National Park
- Salim Ali National Park
- Kishtwar National Park
- Ladakh
- Hemis National Park
- Jharkhand
- Betla National Park
- Hazaribagh National Park
- Karnataka
- Bandipur National Park
- Anshi National Park
- Bannerghata National Park
- Kudremukh National Park
- Nagarhole(Rajiv Gandhi) National Park
- Kerala
- Eravikulam National Park
- Mathikettan Shola National Park
- Periyar National Park
- Silent Valley National Park
- Anamudi Shola National Park
- Pambadum Shola National Park
- Madhya Pradesh
- Pench (Priyaradharshini) National Park
- Bandhavgarh National Park
- Kanha National Park
- Panna National Park
- Sanjay National Park
- Satpura National Park
- Madhav National Park
- Van Vihar National Park
- Maharashtra
- Navegaon national Park
- Sanjay Gandhi (Borivilli) National Park
- Chandoli National Park
- Gugamal National Park
- Tadoba National Park
- Manipur
- Sirohi National Park
- KeibulLamjao National Park
- Meghalaya
- Nokrek National Park
- Balphakram National Park
- Mizoram
- Murlen National Park
- Nagaland
- Ntangki National Park
- Odisha
- Simlipal National Park
- Bhitarkanika National Park
- Nandankanan National Park
- Punjab
- Abohar National Park
- Rajasthan
- Sariska Tiger Reserve
- Ranthambore National Park
- MukundraHils (Darrah) National Park
- Keoladeo Ghana National Park
- Sikkim
- Khangchendzonga National Park
- Tamil Nadu
- Mudumalai National Park
- Mukurthi National Park
- Indira Gandhi (Anamalai) National Park
- Guindy National Park
- Gulf of Mannar Marine National Park
- Palani Hills National Park
- Uttar Pradesh
- Dudhwa National Park
- Uttarakhand
- Jim Corbett National Park
- Gangotri National Park
- Govind Pashu Vihar
- Rajaji National Park
- Valley of Flowers National Park
- Nanda Devi National Park
- West Bengal
- Buxa National Park
- Neora Valley National Park
- Gorumara National Park

- Singalila National Park
- Jaldapara National Park
- Sunderbans National Park

Important One Liner

- World Environment Day is celebrated on June 5.
- World Wetland Day is celebrated on February 2.
- International Day for biodiversity is observed on May 22.
- Two components of ecosystem are Abiotic and biotic.
- The term Ecology was coined by Haeckel.
- The earth is surrounded by huge blanket of air is called atmosphere.
- Part of earth having water resources like ocean, river, pond and lakes are called Hydrosphere.
- The part of the earth where all life is found is called the biosphere.
- Lichens used as air pollution indicator.
- Pollution of river water is measured by dissolved amount of Oxygen.
- E-wastes are generated from Discarded electronic equipment.
- Ecosystem consists of producers, consumers, Decomposers and Abiotic factors.
- Energy flows in an Ecosystem is always unidirectional.
- Largest share in global mangrove areas is found in Indonesia.
- The Montreal Protocol is a global agreement to protect the stratospheric ozone layer.
- The 'thickness' of Ozone layer is measured in Dobson unit.
- The ozone layer is a region of Earth's stratosphere that absorbs the Sun's ultraviolet radiation.
- Ozone Layer is made up of three oxygen atoms.
- Food chain Start with producers.
- In food chain humans are Primary and secondary consumer.
- Bacteria and fungi are called Decomposers.
- Food web is Interlinked arrangement of food chain.
- The major pollutant from automobile exhaust is carbon monoxide.
- Acid rain is formed due to the contribution from oxides of Sulphur and nitrogen.
- Source of geothermal Energy is Earth.
- Problem of solid waste disposal can be reduced through Recycling.
- Sewage treatment is the process of treatment of waste water.
- Gas that traps heat in the atmosphere is called Greenhouse gases. These greenhouse gases include water vapor, CO_2, methane, nitrous oxide (N_2O), Chlorofluorocarbons.
- Greenhouse gas chlorofluorocarbon is produced from Refrigerator.
- Ozone layer depletion causes increased UV radiation levels at the Earth's surface. which is damaging to human health. which includes skin cancers, eye cataracts and immunodeficiency disorders.
- Deforestation causes Soil erosion, Loss of biodiversity and Disturbance in hydrological cycle.
- Consumers that eat animal flesh as well as plants and plant products are called omnivores.
- All Carnivorous animals are Predators.
- Thunderstorm and lightning convert atmospheric nitrogen into nitrates.
- Volcano is natural source of pollution.
- Noise pollution is created if noise is in excess to 80-99 db.
- Fish aquarium is an example of artificial ecosystem.
- Natural gas, coal and petroleum are the example of fossil fuels.
- Constant flow of energy is from producer to consumer.
- Representation of biomass energy present in different levels of food chain is classified as biological pyramid.
- More than 70 % of worlds freshwater are contained in polar ice and glaciers and about 30% is found in ground water.
- BOD stands for Biochemical oxygen demand.
- A river with high BOD value is highly polluted.
- Lichen is the best indicator of SO_2 pollution.
- Oceans are considered to be the most stable ecosystem in nature.
- The conservation of selected plants and animals in selected areas outside their natural habitat is known as ex- situ conservation. It includes botanical gardens, zoological gardens and germplasm bank.
- The conservation with in natural habitat is known as In-situ conservation. It includes national parks, wildlife sanctuaries, biospheres reserve etc.
- The earthworm is referred as a farmer's friend.
- A primary pollutant is an air pollutant emitted directly from a source. Examples: Hydrocarbons, Carbon monoxide, Sulphur oxides, Nitrogen oxides, lead.
- A secondary pollutant is not directly emitted as such, it forms when other pollutants (primary pollutants) react in the atmosphere Examples: ozone, nitrogen dioxide, sulphur trioxide.
- Trophic levels are formed by different organisms linked in a food chain.
- The Pyramid of energy is always upright.
- Salim Ali Was an Indian ornithologist and naturalist.
- Earth Day is an annual event celebrated around the world on April 22 to demonstrate support for environmental protection.
- The lowest layer of the atmosphere is known as troposphere.
- Photosynthesis is a process used by the plants make food with the help of the Sun.
- The Green Gold revolution is related to the Promotion and trade of Bamboo.

- Savanna grasslands are found between tropical rainforest and desert. They are mostly located near the equator. The largest savanna is located in Africa.
- Eutrophication means enrichment of plants nutrients in water bodies. The most common nutrients causing eutrophication are nitrogen and phosphorus.
- Biotic components are the living things that shape an ecosystem. Examples of biotic components include animals, plants, fungi, and bacteria etc.
- Abiotic components are non-living components that influence an ecosystem. Examples of abiotic factors are temperature, air currents, and minerals.
- Percentage of Nitrogen in earth atmosphere is 78%.
- Largest reservoir of Nitrogen in Atmosphere.
- Roots Of plant contains nitrogen fixing bacteria.
- Percentage of Oxygen in earth atmosphere is 21%.
- Percentage of carbon dioxide present in atmosphere is 0.042%.
- Earth's body temperature is approximately equal to 16.4°C.
- Bhopal gas tragedy occurred due to the leakage of Methyl Isocyanate. Bhopal Gas Tragedy happened on 2 December 1984.
- Estuary means the tidal mouth of a large river.
- As per BIS recommendation, the pH for drinking water should be of the range 6.5 to 8.5.
- Compressed Natural Gas (CNG) is the best environmentally clean alternative fuel.
- Hydrogen is considered as energy source of future.
- Hydrogen is found on earth in combination with Oxygen. Most of the hydrogen on Earth is in the form of water.
- Methane is the main component in natural gas. Percentage of methane content of biogas is 50–75 %.
- Biodegradable pollutants are pollutants that are broken down naturally by micro-organisms and are not harmful to the environment. Examples are sewage, paper products, vegetables, juice, seeds and leaves.
- The non-biodegradable pollutants are the one that cannot be broken down into smaller, harmless and simpler substances.
- The loudness of a sound that a person can withstand without discomfort is about 80 db.
- 3R of Energy conservation is reduce, reuse and recycle.

❑❑❑

Polity

Historical Background

1608	The British came to India as traders in the form of East India Company.
1765	East India Company obtained 'diwani rights'. • Rights over revenue and civil justice of Bengal, Bihar and Orissa. • Mughal emperor Shah Alam II granted these rights after losing the Battle of Buxar against East India Company.
1773 - 1858	Company Rule
1858	After the "sepoy mutiny" the British crown assumed direct responsibility for the governance of India.
1858 - 1947	Crown Rule

The Company Rule (1773 – 1858)

Regulating Act 1773
Amending Act of 1781
Pitt's India Act 1784
Act of 1786
Charter Act of 1793
Charter Act 1813
Charter Act 1833
Charter Act 1853

The Crown Rule (1858 – 1947)

Government of India Act 1858
Indian Council Acts (1861, 1892, 1909)
Government of India Act 1919
Government of India Act 1935
Indian Independence Act 1947

The Company Rule (1773 – 1858)

Regulating Act of 1773

- **Key points**
- The beginning of parliamentary control over the Government of the Company.
- The British government laid the foundations of central administration in India.
- First time, the British government recognised the political and administrative functions of the EIC.
- **Features of the Act**
- Governor of Bengal was made 'Governor- General of Bengal' and governors of Bombay and Madras presidencies were made his subordinates.
- During this period, the Supreme Court (1774) was established in Calcutta (with Original and Appellate jurisdiction) and it had a chief justice (Elijah Impey) and three other judges.
- It also introduced the four-member council.
- The Court of Directors should report all affairs (revenue, civil, and military) to the British government.

Amending Act, 1781

- To address the shortcomings of the Regulating Act of 1773, the British Parliament enacted the Amending Act of 1781, also known as the Act of Settlement or Declaratory Act.
- This legislation granted immunity to the Governor-General and the Council, shielding them from the jurisdiction of the Supreme Court for their official actions. Additionally, it exempted the company's servants from Supreme Court jurisdiction regarding their official actions.
- The Act specifically excluded revenue matters and issues related to revenue collection from the Supreme Court's jurisdiction.
- Hindus to be tried under Hindu law and Muslims under Mohammedan law.
- It vested the Governor-General-in-Council with the power to formulate regulations for the Provincial Courts and Councils.

Pitt's India Act 1784

Features of the Act

- The Company's activities were divided into commercial and political activities.
- Reiterated the supremacy of the British Parliament over the administration of the company.
- Reduced the strength of the council from four to three.
- Company's territories in India were for the first time called the 'British possessions in India'.
- Allowed the Court of Directors (CoD) to manage the commercial affairs and created a new body called Board of Control (BoC) (6 members) to manage the political affairs- to supervise and direct all operations of the civil and military government or revenues of the British possessions in India. Thus, it established a system of dual government.

Act of 1786

- In 1786, Lord Cornwallis assumed the role of Governor-General of Bengal, accompanied by two demands for accepting the position.
- Firstly, he sought the authority to override his council's decisions in special cases.
- Secondly, he desired to hold the position of Commander-in-Chief.
- To accommodate these requests, the Act of 1786 was enacted, incorporating both provisions.

Charter Act of 1793

- It expanded the overriding authority initially granted to Lord Cornwallis over his council, applying it to all future Governor-Generals and Governors of Presidencies. This move aimed to enhance the powers and control of the Governor-General over subordinate Presidencies like Bombay and Madras.
- The Act prolonged the East India Company's trade monopoly in India for an additional 20 years.
- It stipulated that the Commander-in-Chief would not automatically be a member of the Governor-General's council unless specifically appointed.
- The Act mandated that the members of the Board of Control and their staff would be compensated from Indian revenues moving forward.

Charter Act of 1813

Features of the Act

- It put an end to the East India Company's monopoly in India, with the exception of "trade with China" and "trade in tea with India".
- The Act affirmed the British Crown's sovereignty over the Company's territories in India, marking the explicit

definition of the constitutional position of British territories in India for the first time.

- The Act facilitated the spread of Western education among the residents of British territories in India, allocating 1 lakh rupees for education in native India.
- It granted authority to Local Governments in India to levy taxes on individuals and empowered them to enforce penalties on those who failed to pay their taxes.
- Indian trade was thrown open to all the British subjects.
- Missionaries allowed to preach in India.
- The Company rule extended for another 20 years.

Charter Act of 1833

Features of the Act

- Governor-General of Bengal designated as Governor-General of India (GGI), with Lord William Bentinck being the first.
- Final step towards Centralization.
- Legislative powers of the Governors of Bombay and Madras were revoked.
- It transformed the East India Company from a commercial entity to a purely administrative one.
- A Law Member, represented by Macaulay, was introduced into the Governor General's Council.
- The provision for open competition was nullified by this act due to opposition from the Court of Directors.
- Restrictions on the immigration of Europeans and property acquisition were lifted.
- Indian laws were codified and consolidated.
- No Indian was denied employment under the company based on religion or color.
- Slavery was abolished.
- The first faint beginnings of a Central Legislature for India.
- The First Law Commission was pioneered in 1834 under the chairmanship of Lord Macaulay.

Charter Act of 1853

Features of the Act

- It delineated the legislative and executive functions of the Governor General's council, establishing a clear separation.
- The act allowed for the addition of six new members, termed legislative councilors, to the council, which became known as the Indian (Central) Legislative Council.
- It marked the initiation of local representation in the Indian (Central) Legislative Council.
- The Act introduced open competition for civil services, opening up the coveted civil service positions to Indians.
- The Governor General was granted the authority to veto bills.

The Crown Rule (1858 – 1947)

Government of India Act 1858

Features of the Act

- Also known as the Act for the Good Government of India.
- Rule of company was replaced by the Rule of crown.
- Changed the designation of the Governor-General of India to that of Viceroy of India. Viceroy became the agent of the crown (Lord Canning being the first Viceroy).
- This Act abolished the East India Company, and transferred the powers of government, territories and revenues to the British Crown.
- This act abolished the dual government of the Pitt's India Act.
- This act also ended the doctrine of lapse.
- The Secretary of State was a member of the British cabinet and was ultimately responsible to the British Parliament. Established a 15-member Council of India to assist the Secretary of State for India.
- Secretary of state can be sued in India and in England.

Indian Council (1861, 1892, 1909)

Features of Indian Councils Act of 1861

- This Act made a beginning of representative institutions – it associated Indians with the lawmaking process. Viceroy nominated some Indians as non-official members of his expanded council. Three Indians nominated were —the Raja of Banaras, the Maharaja of Patiala, and Sir Dinkar Rao.
- The trend of decentralisation was initiated by this act, which restored the legislative powers of the Bombay and Madras presidencies.
- It thus reversed the centralising tendency that started from the Regulating Act of 1773.
- It recognized the Portfolio System introduced by Lord Canning in 1859.
- Empowered the Viceroy to frame the Rules of Business (the same power is given to the President of India under Art 77).
- New legislative councils for Bengal, NWFP, Punjab.
- The Act empowered the VOI to make ordinance during an emergency. However, the life of such an ordinance was six months.

Features of Indian Councils Act of 1892

- Enlarge the size and functions of central and provincial councils.
- The council to have the right to discuss the budget under certain conditions.
- Members of the council granted the right to ask questions.
- The members had the power to form new laws and alter or repeal old laws with Governor-General's permission.

Features of Indian Councils Act of 1909: (Morley-Minto Reforms)

- First attempt at introducing a representative and popular element.
- Councils, for the first time, were referred to as "legislative councils".
- Members were allowed to ask supplementary questions, move resolutions on the budget, and so on.
- ICA 1909 introduced a system of communal representation for Muslims -- concept of 'separate electorate'.
- The Beginning of non-official resolutions in the Council. It provided for the first time, association of Indians with the Executive Councils of the Viceroy and Governors. (Satyendra Prasad Sinha became the first Indian to join the Viceroy's Executive Council. He was appointed as the law member).

Government of India Act -1919

Features of Government of India Act of 1919 (Montagu-Chelmsford Reforms)

- Demarcation of separate central and provincial subjects: Central and provincial legislatures can make laws on their respective list of subjects Responsible Government.

- Office of the High Commissioner of India was created in London.
- Dyarchy was applied on a state-by-state basis. Dyarchy refers to the presence of two governments in which one is responsible and the other is not. Transferred subjects- (Governor with ministers Responsible) Reserved subjects- Governor with Executives.
- Extended communal representation or separate electorate to Sikhs, Indian Christians, Anglo-Indians and Europeans.
- Upper House and Lower House: First time, bicameralism and direct elections in the country were introduced (only at Centre).
- It separated, for the first time, provincial budgets from the Central budget and authorised the provincial legislatures to enact their budgets.
- It provided for the establishment of a public service commission.
- It provided for the appointment of a statutory commission to inquire into and report on its working after ten years of its coming into force. Granted franchise to a limited number of people on the basis of property, tax or education.

Simon Commission

- The Simon Commission, commissioned by the British government in 1927 and led by Chairman John Simon, was tasked with reviewing the functioning of the Government of India Act 1919 and proposing future measures.
- Comprising seven British Members of Parliament, including the Chairman, the commission extended the timeline for provincial governance.
- Among its recommendations were the establishment of a federation encompassing British India and the princely states, with the communal electorate persisting. Subsequently, the British government announced the organization of Three Round Table Conferences to assess the proposals put forth by the Simon Commission. This process culminated in the publication of a White Paper outlining the agreed-upon constitutional reforms.
- These initiatives collectively laid the groundwork for the subsequent Government of India Act in 1935.

Communal Award

- The Communal Award was created by the British prime minister Ramsay MacDonald on 16 August 1932. Also known as the MacDonald Award.
- It extended the separate electorates to depressed classes (Scheduled Castes) as well (with Muslims, Sikhs, Indian Christians, Anglo-Indians and Europeans).

Government of India Act -1935

Features of Government of India Act of 1935

- The Act intended to bring completely responsible government in India. Abolished dyarchy in the provinces and introduced 'provincial autonomy' in its place (started dyarchy at the centre).
- It provided for the establishment of an All India federation consisting of provinces and princely states as units. (Note: Princely States did not join and so Federation didn't come into existence).
- Bicameralism was introduced in six provinces- Bengal, Bombay, Madras, Bihar, Assam and the United Provinces.
- It divided the powers between the centre and units in terms of three lists- Federal list, Provincial List and the Concurrent List.
- Extended separate electorates for depressed classes (scheduled castes), women and labour (workers).
- Establishment of a Reserve Bank of India to control the currency and credit of the country.
- Establishment of a Federal Court (in 1937).
- Federal PSC + Provincial PSC (on lines of UPSC + SPSC).

Indian Independence Act of 1947

Features of Indian Independence Act of 1947

- It ended the British rule in India and declared India as an independent and sovereign state from August 15, 1947.
- It provided for partition of India and creation of two new dominions- India and Pakistan.
- It proclaimed the lapse of British paramountcy over the Indian princely states and treaty relations with tribal areas from August 15,1947.
- It granted freedom to the Indian princely states either to join the Dominion of India or Dominion of Pakistan or to remain independent.
- It abolished the office of viceroy and provided for each dominion, a Governor-General, who was to be appointed by the British King on the advice of the dominion cabinet.
- It empowered the constituent assemblies of the two dominions to frame and adopt any constitution for their respective nations and to repeal any act of the British parliament, including the independence act itself.
- Governance of each dominion was to be conducted based on the provisions of the GoI Act, 1935.
- The British monarch could no longer ask for bills or veto them. However, this was reserved for the Governor-General.
- It designated the Governor-General of India and the provincial Governors as constitutional (nominal) heads of the states. They were made to act on the advice of the respective council of ministers in all matters.

Interim Government (1946)

Members	Portfolios Held
Jawaharlal Nehru	Vice-President of the Council, External Affairs & Commonwealth Relations
Sardar Vallabhbhai Patel	Home, Information & Broadcasting
Dr. Rajendra Prasad	Food & Agriculture
Dr. John Mathai	Industries & Supplies
Jagjivan Ram	Labour
Sardar Baldev Singh	Defence
C. H. Bhabha	Works, Mines & Power
Liaquat Ali Khan	Finance
Abdur Rab Nishtar	Posts & Air
Asaf Ali	Railways & Transport

C. Rajagopalachari	Education & Arts
I. I. Chundrigar	Commerce
Ghaznafar Ali Khan	Health
Joginder Nath Mandal	Law

The members of the interim Government were members of the Viceroy's Executive Council. The Viceroy continued to be the head of the Council.

First Cabinet of Free India (1947)

Members	Portfolios Held
Jawaharlal Nehru	Prime Minister, External Affairs & Commonwealth Relations, Scientific Research
Sardar Vallabhbhai Patel	Home, Information & Broadcasting States
Dr. Rajendra Prasad	Food and Agriculture
Maulana Abul Kalam Azad	Education
Dr. John Mathai	Railways & Transport
R. K. Shanmugham Chetty	Finance
Dr. B.R. Ambedkar	Law
Jagjivan Ram	Labour
Sardar Baldev Singh	Defence
Raj Kumari Amrit Kaur	Health
C. H. Bhabha	Commerce
Rafi Ahmed Kidwai	Communication
V. N. Gadgil	Works, Mines & Power
Dr. Shayama Prasad Mukherji	Industries & Supplies

Indian Constitution

- The Constitution of India is the supreme law of India. This document lays down the framework which demarcates fundamental political code, structure, procedures, powers and duties of government institutions.
- The Indian Constitution is unique in both spirit and content.
- The Indian Constitution replaced the Government of India Act 1935 as the country's fundamental governing document and the Dominion of India became the Republic of India.
- The Constitution of India contains 395 articles in 22 parts.
- Additional articles and parts are inserted later through various amendments.
- There are also 12 schedules in the Indian Constitution.
- Adoption Date of the Constitution of India: November 26, 1949.

Making of the Constitution

1934	The idea of a Constituent Assembly for India was put forward for the first time by M. N. Roy.
1935	The Indian National Congress (INC), for the first time, officially demanded a Constituent Assembly to frame the Constitution of India.
1938	Jawaharlal Nehru on behalf of INC declared that the Constitution of free India must be framed, without outside interference, by a Constituent Assembly elected on the basis of adult franchise'.
1940	August Offer. The demand was finally accepted by the British Government.
1942	Sir Stafford Cripps, a Member of the Cabinet, came to India with a draft proposal of the British Government on the framing of an independent Constitution to be adopted after World War II.
1946	The Constituent Assembly was constituted in November 1946 under the scheme formulated by the Cabinet Mission.

Composition of the Constituent Assembly Features

- The total strength of the Constituent Assembly was to be 389.
- Out of these 296 seats were to be allotted to British India and 93 seats to the Princely states and out of the 296 seats allotted to British India, 292 members were to be drawn from 11 governors' provinces namely Madras, Bombay, UP, Central Provinces, Bihar, Orissa, Punjab, North West Frontier Province, Sindh, Bengal and Assam) and 4 from the four chief commissioner's provinces, (one from each Delhi, Ajmer-Merwar, Coorg and British Baluchistan).
- After the partition of India in 1947, the effective membership was reduced to 299.
- Each province and princely state (or group of states in case of small states) were to be allotted seats in proportion to their respective population.
- Seats allocated to each British province were to be divided among the three principal communities– Muslims, Sikhs and General (all except Muslims and Sikhs), in proportion to their population.
- The Constituent Assembly was to be a partly elected and partly nominated body.
- Although the Constituent Assembly was not directly elected by the people of India on the basis of adult franchise.
- The voting was to be done by the method of proportional representation by means of single transferable vote.
- The representatives of princely states were to be nominated by heads of the princely states.
- Thus, the Constituent Assembly was a partly elected and partly nominated body.
- The representatives of the princely states were to be nominated by the heads of the princely states.
- Indian Independence Act of 1947- Constituent Assembly was made a fully sovereign body, Assembly also became a legislative body, the Assembly became the first Parliament of free India (Dominion Legislature).

- Whenever the Assembly met as the Constituent body it was chaired by Dr. Rajendra Prasad and when it met as the legislative body, it was chaired by G.V. Mavalankar. These two functions continued till November 26, 1949.

Election to Constituent Assembly

- The election to the Constituent Assembly was held in July-August 1946, for 296 seats allotted to the British Indian Provinces.
- In this election Indian National Congress won 208 seats whereas Muslim League won 73 seats.
- It is important to note that Constituent Assembly included almost all important personalities of India at that time except Mahatma Gandhi and M. A. Jinnah.

Working of the Constituent Assembly

9 December 1946	First meeting of the Constituent Assembly.
13 December 1946	Jawaharlal Nehru moved the historic 'Objectives Resolution' in the Assembly.
22 January 1947	This Resolution was unanimously adopted by the Assembly.

Objectives Resolution

- Jawaharlal Nehru moved this historic resolution on December 13, 1946 in the assembly.
- It contained the fundamentals and philosophy of Constitutional structure. This resolution was adopted on January 22, 1947 by assembly.
- Our Preamble is the modified version of Objective Resolution.

Salient Features

- The Salient Features of the Constitution the Indian Constitution is unique in its contents and spirit.
- The salient features of the Constitution, as it stands today, are as follows:
- Lengthiest Written Constitution
  - Constitutions are classified into written, like the American Constitution, or unwritten, like the British Constitution.
  - The Constitution of India is the lengthiest of all the written Constitutions of the world.
  - Four factors have contributed to the elephantine size of our Constitution. They are:
    - Geographical factors
    - Historical factors
    - Single Constitution for both the Centre and the states
    - Dominance of legal luminaries in the Constituent Assembly.
- **Committees of the Constituent Assembly:** To cope up with the wide range of specialized tasks, the Constituent Assembly set up major committees to outline the proposed constitution.
- **Major Committees**
  - Union Powers Committee - Jawaharlal Nehru
  - Union Constitution Committee - Jawaharlal Nehru
  - States Committee - Jawaharlal Nehru
  - Rules of Procedure Committee - Rajendra Prasad
  - Steering Committee - Rajendra Prasad
  - Provincial Constitution Committee - Sardar Patel
  - Drafting Committee - Dr. B. R. Ambedkar
  - Advisory Committee on FRs, Minorities & Tribal & Excluded Areas - Sardar Patel
- The Drafting Committee was the most important. It was set up on 29, August 1947.
- **It consisted of 7 members:**
  - Dr. B. R. Ambedkar (Chairman)
  - N. Gopalaswamy Ayyangar
  - Alladi Krishnaswamy Ayyar
  - Dr. K. M. Munshi
  - Syed Mohammad Saadullah
  - N. Madhava Rau (He replaced B. L. Mitra)
  - T. T. Krishnamachari (He replaced D. P. Khaitan)
- Some important facts about Constituent Assembly:
  - Elephant was adopted as the symbol for Constituent Assembly.
  - Sir B. N. Rau was appointed as the Constitutional Adviser to Constituent Assembly.
  - H. V. R. Iyengar was the Secretary to Constituent Assembly.
  - S. N. Mukherjee was chief draftsman of constitution in Constituent Assembly.
  - Prem Behari Raizada was the calligrapher of the Constitution. The Hindi version calligraphy was done by Vasant Krishan Vaidya and illuminated by Nand Lal Bose.
  - Nand Lal Bose and B. R. Sinha decorated and beautified the Constitution.

Constituents of the Objectives Resolution

- India is an independent, sovereign, republic.
- It declared the aim of the Constituent Assembly to write a constitution which fosters unity of the nation and ensures its economic and political security.
- All powers and authority of sovereign and independent India and its constitution shall flow from the people.
- India has a Federal form of government with Division of Powers between the Centre and the States.
- All people of India shall be guaranteed and secured social, economic and political justice, equality of status and opportunities and equality before the law, and fundamental freedoms – of speech, expression, belief, faith, worship, vocation, association and action – subject to law and public morality.
- The minorities, backward and tribal areas, depressed and other backward classes shall be provided adequate safeguards.
- To maintain the integrity of the territory of the Republic and the sovereign rights on land, sea and air according to the law of civilized nations.
- To attain a rightful and honoured place in the world and make a willing contribution to the promotion of world peace and the welfare of mankind.

Other Functions Performed

May 1949	It ratified the India's membership of the Commonwealth
22 July 1947	It adopted the national flag
24 January 1950	It adopted the national anthem
24 January 1950	It adopted the national song
24 January 1950	It elected Dr. Rajendra Prasad as the first President of India
24 January 1950	The Constituent Assembly held its final session.

- The Constitution as adopted on November 26, 1949, contained a Preamble, 22 Parts, 395 Articles and 8 Schedules. The Preamble was enacted after the entire Constitution was already enacted.
- Some provisions of the Constitution pertaining to citizenship, elections, provisional parliament, temporary and transitional provisions and short title contained in Articles 5, 6, 7, 8, 9, 60, 324, 366, 367, 379, 380, 388, 391, 392 and 393 came into force on November 26, 1949, itself.
- In all, the Constituent Assembly had 11 sessions over 2 years, 11 months and 18 days.
- The total expenditure incurred on making the Constitution amounted to ₹ 64 lakh.
- The oldest member Dr. Sachchidanand Sinha was elected as the interim President of the Constituent Assembly. Later , on December 11, 1946 Dr. Rajendra Prasad was elected as the President, H. C. Mukherjee as the Vice-President of the Constituent Assembly.
- The Constitution contains not only the fundamental principles of governance, but also detailed administrative provisions.

Salient Features of The Indian Constitution

- **Drawn From Various Sources**
  - The Constitution borrowed from almost every Constitution of the world.

Sources	Features Borrowed
Government of India Act, 1935	Federal Scheme, Office of Governor, Judiciary, Public Service Commissions, Emergency provisions and administrative details.
British Constitution	Parliamentary government, Rule of Law, Legislative procedure, Single citizenship, Cabinet System, Prerogative writs, Parliamentary privileges and Bicameralism.
US Constitution	Fundamental rights, Independence of judiciary, Judicial review, Impeachment of the President, Removal of Supreme Court and High Court judges and Post of Vice president.
Irish Constitution	Directive Principles of State Policy, Nomination of members to Rajya Sabha and Method of election of President.
Canadian Constitution	Federation with a strong Centre, Vesting of residuary powers in the Centre, Appointment of state Governors by the Centre, and Advisory jurisdiction of the Supreme Court.
Australian Constitution	Concurrent List, Freedom of trade, Commerce and Inter-course, and Joint sitting of the two Houses of Parliament.
Weimar Constitution of Germany	Suspension of Fundamental Rights during Emergency.
Soviet Constitution (USSR, now Russia)	Fundamental duties and the ideal of justice (social, economic and political) in the Preamble.
French Constitution	Republic and the ideals of liberty, equality and fraternity in the Preamble.
South African Constitution	Procedure for amendment of the Constitution and Election of members of Rajya Sabha.
Japanese Constitution	Procedure established by Law.

- **Blend of Rigidity and Flexibility**
  - Constitutions are also classified into rigid and flexible.
    - A rigid Constitution is one that requires a special procedure for its amendment, as for example, the American Constitution.
    - A flexible constitution, on the other hand, is one that can be amended in the same manner as the ordinary laws are made, as for example, the British Constitution.
  - The Constitution of India is neither rigid nor flexible, but a synthesis of both'.
  - Article 368 provides for two types of amendments:
    - Some provisions can be amended by a special majority of the Parliament, i.e., a two-third majority of the members of each House present and voting, and a majority of the total membership of each House.
    - Some other provisions can be amended by a special majority of the Parliament and with the ratification by half of the total states.
  - Some provisions of the Constitution can be amended by a simple majority of the Parliament in the manner of ordinary legislative process.
- **Federal System with Unitary Bias**
  - The Constitution of India establishes a federal system of Government.

Federal Feature

- Two Government,
- Division of powers,
- Written Constitution,
- Supremacy of Constitution,
- Rigidity of Constitution,
- Independent judiciary,
- Bicameralism.

Unitary Features

- A Strong Centre,
- Single Constitution,
- Single Citizenship,
- Flexibility of Constitution
- Integrated Judiciary
- Appointment of State Governor by the Centre
- All-India Services,
- Emergency Provisions.

- The Indian Constitution has been variously described as 'federal in form but, unitary in spirit', therefore known as 'Quasi-federal'.
- **Parliamentary Form of Government**
  - The Constitution of India has opted for the British Parliamentary System of Government.

- The features of parliamentary government in India are:
  - Presence of nominal and real executives
  - Majority party rule
  - Collective responsibility of the executive to the legislature
  - Membership of the ministers in the legislature
  - Leadership of the Prime Minister or the Chief Minister
  - Dissolution of the lower House (Lok Sabha or Assembly).

- **Integrated and Independent Judiciary**

- The Indian Constitution establishes a judicial system that is integrated as well as independent.
- The Supreme Court stands at the top of the integrated judicial system in the country.

- **Single Citizenship**

- It provides for only a single citizenship, that is, Indian citizenship.

- **Independent Bodies**

- The Indian Constitution not only provides for the legislative, executive and judicial organs of the Government (Central and state) but also establishes certain independent bodies.
- Independent bodies like:
  - Election Commission
  - Comptroller and Auditor-General of India
  - Union Public Service Commission
  - State Public Service Commission

- **Co-operative Societies**

- The 97th Constitutional Amendment Act of 2011 gave constitutional status and protection to co-operative societies.
- It made the following three changes in the Constitution:

Article 19 (1) (c)	Right to form co-operative societies a fundamental right
Article 43-B	Directive Principle of State Policy on promotion of co-operative societies
Articles 243-ZH to 243-ZT Part IX-B	It empowers the Parliament in respect of multi-state cooperative societies and the state legislatures in respect of other co-operative societies to make the appropriate law.

- **Three-tier Government**

- The 73rd and 74th Constitutional Amendment Acts (1992) have added a third-tier of Government (i.e., local government) which is not found in any other Constitution of the world.
- The 73rd Amendment Act of 1992 gave constitutional recognition to the panchayats (rural local governments) by adding a new Part IX and a new Schedule 11 to the Constitution.
- The 74th Amendment Act of 1992 gave constitutional recognition to the municipalities (urban local governments) by adding a new Part IX-A and a new Schedule 12 to the Constitution.

Parts of Indian Constitution:

Part	Subject	Articles
Part I	The Union and its territory	Art. 1 to 4
Part II	Citizenship	Art. 5 to 11
Part III	Fundamental Rights	Art. 12 to 35
Part IV	Directive Principles	Art. 36 to 51
Part IVA	Fundamental Duties	Art. 51A
Part V	The Union Chapter I - The Executive (Art. 52 to 78) Chapter II - Parliament (Art. 79 to 122) Chapter III - Legislative Powers of President (Art. 123) Chapter IV - The Union Judiciary (Art. 124 to 147) Chapter V - Comptroller and Auditor-General of India (Art. 148 to 151)	Art. 52 to 151
Part VI	The States Chapter I - General (Art. 152) Chapter II - The Executive (Art. 153 to 167) Chapter III - The State Legislature (Art. 168 to 212) Chapter IV - Legislative Powers of Governor (Art. 213) Chapter V - The High Courts (Art. 214 to 232) Chapter VI - Subordinate Courts (Art. 233 to 237)	Art. 152 to 237
Part VII	States in the B part of the First schedule [Repealed by Const. (7th Amendment) Act, 1956]	Art. 238 (deleted)
Part VIII	The Union Territories	Art. 239 to 242
Part IX	The Panchayats	Art. 243 to 243O
Part IXA	The Municipalities	Art. 243P to 243ZG
Part IXB	Co-operative Societies	Art. 243ZH to 243ZT
Part X	The Scheduled and Tribal Areas	Art. 244 to 244A
Part XI	Relations between the Union and the States Chapter I - Legislative Relations (Art. 245 to 255) Chapter II - Administrative Relations (Art. 256 to 263)	Art. 245 to 263

Part XII	Finance, Property, Contracts and Suits Chapter I - Finance (Art. 264 to 291) Chapter II - Borrowing (Art. 292 to 293) Chapter III - Property, Contracts, Rights, Liabilities, Obligations and Suits (Art. 294 to 300) Chapter IV - Right to Property (Art.300-A)	Art. 264 to 300A
Part XIII	Trade, Commerce and Intercourse within the Territory of India	Art. 301 to 307
Part XIV	Services under the Union and the States	Art. 308 to 323
Part XIVA	Tribunals	Art. 323A to 323B
Part XV	Elections	Art. 324 to 329A
Part XVI	Special provisions relation to certain classes	Art. 330 to 342
Part XVII	Official Language Chapter I - Language of the Union (Art. 343 to 344) Chapter II - Regional Languages (Art. 345 to 347) Chapter III-Language of the Supreme Court, High Courts, and so on (Art. 348 to 349) Chapter IV-Special Directives (Art. 350 to 351)	Art. 343 to 351
Part XVIII	Emergency Provisions	Art. 352 to 360
Part XIX	Miscellaneous	Art. 361 to 367
Part XX	Amendment of the Constitution	Art. 368
Part XXI	Temporary, Transitional and Special Provisions	Art. 369 to 392
Part XXII	Short title, commencement, authoritative text in Hindi and repeals	Art. 393 to 395

- When India became newly independent, there were many princely states and independent territories, making it difficult to define the territorial boundaries of India. When the constitution was drafted, the states were classified into four types- A, B, C and D.
- Part VII deals with the states mentioned under Para B of the classification of states. Part B Indian territory consisted of princely states like Jammu and Kashmir, Hyderabad, Travancore-Cochin, Central India, Saurashtra, Mysore, Rajasthan, East Punjab Union, and Patiala.
- The 7th Part of the Indian Constitution is called "The States in Part B of the First Schedule" and contains only one article i.e. Article 238. It is one of the 22 basic parts added by our Constitution Committee. Since then, this part is the only one that has been repealed and It was repealed by the 7th Constitutional Amendment Act in 1956.

Trick to remember Parts of Indian constitution

- U Can Fly Directly From US to UP to Meet Child of Shyam and Ram, (from part I to part XI)
- Fruits Taste Sweet To Eat So Only Eat Maggi As Tasty Snack (from part XII to part XXII)

- U - Union & Its Territory
- Can - Citizenship
- Fly - Fundamental Rights
- Directly - Directive Principles of State Policies
- From - Fundamental Duties
- U - Union, S - States
- U - Union Territories, P - Panchayats
- Meet - Municipalities
- Child - Co-operative Societies
- Shyam - Scheduled and Tribal Areas
- Ram - Relation between Union & States
- Fruits - Finance, Property, Contracts and Suits
- Taste - Trade, Commerce, and Intercourse within the territory of India
- Sweet - Services under the Union and States
- To - Tribunals
- Eat - Elections
- So - Special Provisions relating to certain classes
- Only - Official Languages
- Eat - Emergency Provisions
- Maggi - Miscellaneous
- As - Amendment of the Constitution
- Tasty - Temporary, Transitional, and Special Provisions
- Snack - Short title, Commencement, Authoritative Text in Hindi and Repeals

Schedules

First Schedule: Names and territory of – a) States b) Union Territories.

Second Schedule: Salaries and allowances of certain dignitaries.

- President, Governors, Speaker and Deputy Speaker (Lok Sabha), Chairman and Deputy chairman (Rajya Sabha), Speaker and Deputy Speaker (Legislative Assembly), Chairman and Deputy Chairman (Legislative council), Supreme court judges, High court judges, CAG.
- **Third Schedule:** Forms of oath and affirmation.
- Union ministers, State ministers, MPs, MLAs, Judges of Supreme Court and High Court, Candidates for Election to Parliament and State Legislature.

Fourth Schedule: Allocation of seats in Rajya Sabha to the state and union territories.

Fifth Schedule: Provisions as to Administration of scheduled areas and Scheduled Tribes.

Sixth Schedule: Provisions as to the Administration of Tribal areas in the state of Assam, Meghalaya, Tripura and Mizoram.

Seventh Schedule [Article 246]: Distribution of power between the Union and states in terms of Union list, State list and Concurrent List.

Eighth Schedule: 22 languages in the schedule:

- 21st Constitutional Amendment Act, 1967 - Sindhi.
- 71st Constitutional Amendment Act,1992 - Manipuri, Nepali, Konkani.
- 92nd Constitutional Amendment Act 2003 – Dogri, Bodo, Maithli, Santhali.
- 96th Constitutional Amendment Act, 2011 - 'Odia'.

Ninth Schedule: Contains a list of central and state laws which cannot be challenged in courts (added by the 1st Constitutional Amendment Act, 1951).

- R Coelho case, 2007 [Laws placed subsequent to 24th April 1973 can be challenged on grounds of violation of Basic structure]. Laws placed before 24th April 1973 would continue to enjoy Blanket immunity.

Tenth Schedule: Lays down the process by which legislators may be disqualified on grounds of defection by the Presiding Officer of a legislature.

- The Tenth Schedule was inserted in the Constitution in 1985 by the 52nd Amendment Act.

Eleventh Schedule [Article 243G] – Contains the provisions that specify the powers, authority and responsibilities of Panchayats.

- It has 29 matters.
- Added by the 73rd Constitutional Amendment Act of 1992.

Twelfth Schedule [Article 243W]: Deals with the provisions that specify the powers, authority and responsibilities of Municipalities.

- It has 18 matters.
- Added by the 74th Constitutional Amendment Act of 1992.

Preamble

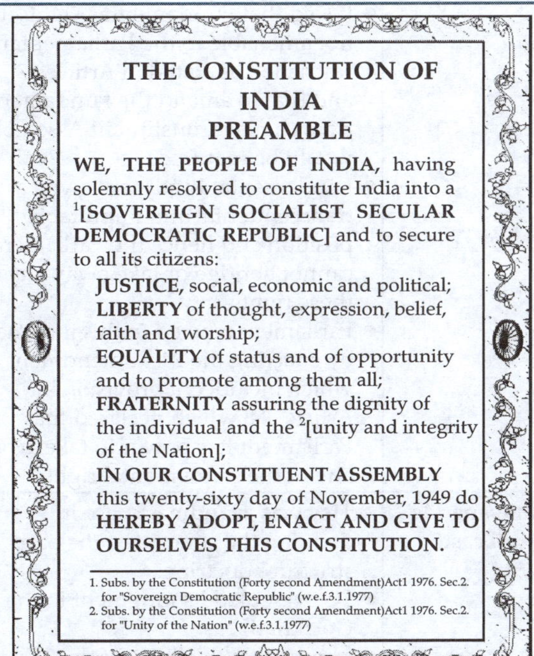

THE CONSTITUTION OF INDIA
PREAMBLE

WE, THE PEOPLE OF INDIA, having solemnly resolved to constitute India into a [1]**[SOVEREIGN SOCIALIST SECULAR DEMOCRATIC REPUBLIC]** and to secure to all its citizens:

JUSTICE, social, economic and political;
LIBERTY of thought, expression, belief, faith and worship;
EQUALITY of status and of opportunity and to promote among them all;
FRATERNITY assuring the dignity of the individual and the [2][unity and integrity of the Nation];
IN OUR CONSTITUENT ASSEMBLY this twenty-sixty day of November, 1949 do **HEREBY ADOPT, ENACT AND GIVE TO OURSELVES THIS CONSTITUTION.**

1. Subs. by the Constitution (Forty second Amendment)Act1 1976. Sec.2. for "Sovereign Democratic Republic" (w.e.f.3.1.1977)
2. Subs. by the Constitution (Forty second Amendment)Act1 1976. Sec.2. for "Unity of the Nation" (w.e.f.3.1.1977)

Key Points

- A preamble is an introductory statement that explains the document's philosophy and objectives of Constitution.
- It contains the summary of the essence of the Constitution.

Two important information should be noted

- The Preamble is neither a source of power to legislature nor a prohibition upon the powers of legislature.
- It is non-justiciable, that is, its provisions are not enforceable in courts of law.

The Preamble, in brief, explains the objectives of the Constitution in two ways:

- The Constitution is the supreme law and it helps to maintain integrity in the society and to promote unity among the citizens to build a great nation.
- The other, about the structure of the governance.

Important key words in the Preamble

Sovereignty	• Independent authority (not a dominion of any other external power). • Government which is not controlled by any other power. • A country cannot have its own constitution without being sovereign.
Socialist	• This word was added in the Preamble by 42nd Amendment, 1976. • The word 'Socialism' had been used in the context of economic planning. • It holds faith in a mixed economy where both private and public sectors co-exist side by side.
Secularism	• In India there will be no 'State' religion. • All the religions in India get equal respect, protection and support from the state. • State will not discriminate against any individual or group on the basis of religion. • It was incorporated in the Preamble by 42nd Constitutional Amendment, 1976.
Democratic Republic	• "Republic" - indicates a government by the people and for the people. • Government is elected by the people, it is responsible and accountable to the people. • Preamble declares India as a Republic - It means that the head of the State is the President who is indirectly elected and he is not a hereditary ruler as in case of the British Monarch.
Justice	• Justice in the Preamble means social, political and economic justice. ▪ **Social Justice:** Social justice means that the Constitution wants to create a society without discrimination on any grounds like caste, creed, gender, religion, etc. ▪ **Economic Justice:** Every person must be paid equally for an equal position and all people must get opportunities to earn for their living. ▪ **Political Justice:** Political Justice means all the people have an equal, free and fair right without any discrimination to participate in political opportunities.

Liberty	• 5 liberties - Thought, Expression, Belief, Faith and Worship • The ideals of liberty, equality and fraternity in our Preamble have been taken from the French Revolution (1789–1799). • The term 'Liberty' means freedom for the people to choose their way of life, have political views and behavior in society. • Liberty is the essential requirement of democratic and free society.
Equality	• Everyone is equal before the law. • 'Equality' means no section of society has any special privileges and all the people have been given equal cpportunities for everything without any discrimination. • The Preamble secures to all citizens of India equality of status and opportunity.
Fraternity	• The term 'Fraternity' means a feeling of brotherhood and an emotional attachment with the country and all the people. • Fraternity helps to promote dignity and unity in the nation. • The term 'Fraternity' draws inspiration from the French Revolutionary ideals and resonates with Article 1 of the Universal Declaration of Human Rights, 1948.

Preamble as Part of the Constitution

- The Preamble is as to whether it is a part of the Constitution or not.

Berubari Union case (1960)	The Supreme Court specifically opined that Preamble is not a part of the Constitution. The Supreme Court said that the Preamble shows the general purposes behind the several provisions in the Constitution, and is thus a key to the minds of the makers of the Constitution.
Kesavananda Bharati case (1973)	The Supreme Court rejected the earlier opinion and held that Preamble is a part of the Constitution.
LIC of India case (1995)	The Supreme Court again held that the Preamble is an integral part of the Constitution.

- The Preamble is neither a source of power to legislature nor a prohibition upon the powers of legislature.
- It is non-justiciable, that is, its provisions are not enforceable in courts of law.

Amenability of The Preamble

- Preamble can be amended, subject to the condition that no amendment is done to the 'basic features'- the fundamental features of the Constitution as contained in the Preamble cannot be altered by an amendment under Article 368 .
- Preamble has been amended only once so far, in 1976, by the 42nd Constitutional Amendment Act, which has added three new words–Socialist, Secular and Integrity–to the Preamble.

Basic Structure

Doctrine of Basic Structure

- The parliament's unlimited power to amend the constitution is subject to only one restriction i.e. it should not dilute or violate the basic structure of the constitution.
- Or the effects of the amendment should not be abrogating or disturbing in nature towards the basic structure.

Emergence of the Basic Structure

Shankari Prasad case (1951)	• In this case, the SC contended that the Parliament's power of amending the Constitution under Article 368 included the power to amend the Fundamental Rights guaranteed in Part III as well. • It based its judgment on the logic that the word 'law' mentioned in Article 13 includes only ordinary laws and not constitutional amendment acts.
Golaknath case (1967)	• In this case, the court reversed its earlier stance that the Fundamental Rights can be amended. • It said that Fundamental Rights are not amenable to the Parliamentary restriction as stated in Article 13 and that to amend the Fundamental rights a new Constituent Assembly would be required. • Fundamental Rights are given a transcendental and immutable position and hence the Parliament cannot abridge or take away any of these rights. • Parliament reacted to this judgment by enacting the 24th amendment act which included a provision in Article 368 which declared that Parliament has power to take away any of the fundamental rights.
Keshavananda Bharati case (1973)	• This was a landmark case in defining the concept of the basic structure doctrine. • SC overruled its judgment in the Golaknath case. • It upheld the validity of the 24th amendment act and opined that parliament is empowered to take away or abridge any of the fundamental right. However, such changes should not alter the 'basic structure' of the constitution.

	• The constituent power of Parliament under Article 368 does not enable it to alter the "basic structure" of the Constitution.
42nd CAA 1976	• Amended Article 368 – no limitation on the constituent power of Parliament. • Any amendment cannot be questioned in any court on any ground.
Minerva mills case (1980)	• Parliament reacted to the above case by enacting 42nd amendment act which declared under article 368 that there is no limitation on the constituent power of Parliament and it barred the courts from questioning such amendments. • This provision was invalidated by the SC stating that Parliament cannot take away the 'judicial review' power of the constitution since it is part of the 'basic structure of the doctrine'. • The judges ruled that a limited amending power itself is a basic feature of the Constitution.
Waman Rao case 1981	• SC clarified that doctrine would be applicable to constitutional amendments enacted after April 24, 1973 (Kesavananda Bharati case) (Including 9th schedule).
Indra Sawhney case 1992	• SC examined the scope and extent of Article 16(4), which provides for the reservation of jobs in favour of backward classes. It upheld the constitutional validity of 27% reservation for the OBCs with certain conditions (like creamy layer exclusion, no reservation in promotion, total reserved quota should not exceed 50%, etc.) • Here, 'Rule of Law' was added to the list of basic features of the constitution.

Elements of Basic Structure

From the various judgments, the following have emerged as "Basic features" of the Constitution or elements of the "Basic structure" of the constitution:

- Supremacy of the constitution.
- Rule of law.
- Sovereignty, liberty and republic nature of Indian polity.
- Judicial review.
- Harmony and Balance between fundamental rights and directive principles.
- Separation of power.
- Federal character.
- Parliamentary system.
- Rule of equality.
- Unity and integrity of the nation.
- Free and fair elections.
- Powers of SC under Article 32, 136, 141, 142.
- Power of High Court under Article 226 and 227.
- Limited power of parliament to amend the constitution.
- Welfare state.
- Freedom and dignity of an individual.

Significance of Basic Structure

- The basic doctrine saved the Indian democracy.
- It strengthens our democracy by delineating a true separation of power where Judiciary is independent of other two organs.
- By restraining the amending powers of the legislative organ of State, it provided basic Rights to Citizens which no organ of State can overrule.
- Being dynamic in nature, it is more progressive and open to changes in time unlike the rigid nature of earlier judgements.

Amendment of the Constitution

- The Constitution of India also provides for its amendment in order to adjust itself to the changing conditions and needs.
- It was borrowed from the South African constitution

Procedure for Amending the Indian Constitution

Procedure for Amending the Indian Constitution

Article 368 in Part XX of the Constitution deals with the power of parliament to amend the constitution and its procedures:

- It states that the Parliament may amend the Constitution by way of addition, variation or repeal of any provision in accordance with the procedure laid down for the purpose.
- The Supreme Court in the Kesavananda Bharati case (1973), the Parliament cannot amend those provisions which form the 'Basic structure' of the Constitution.

Types of Amendments

The Constitution can be amended in three ways:

- Amendment by simple majority of the Parliament,
- Amendment by special majority of the Parliament.
- Amendment by special majority of the Parliament and the ratification of half of the state legislatures.

Simple Majority A number of provisions in the Constitution can be amended by a simple majority of the two Houses of Parliament outside the scope of Article 368.	• Formation of new states and alteration of areas, boundaries or names of existing states, • Abolition or creation of legislative councils in states, • Use of official language, • Citizenship – acquisition, and termination, • Elections to Parliament and state legislatures, • Fifth Schedule – administration of scheduled areas and scheduled tribes, • Sixth Schedule – administration of tribal areas.

Special Majority Under Article 368(2), Parliament can amend the Constitution by passing a Bill with a special majority.	• Fundamental Rights, • Directive Principles of State Policy.
Special Majority with Consent of Half of States Amended by a special majority of the Parliament and also with the consent of half of the state legislatures by a simple majority. There is no time limit within which states should give their consent to the bill.	• Election of the President and its manner. • Extent of the executive power of the Union and the states. • Extent of the powers of Supreme Court and high courts. • Distribution of legislative powers between the Union and the states. • Goods and Services Tax Council. • Any of the lists in the Seventh Schedule. • Representation of states in Parliament. • Power of Parliament to amend the Constitution and its procedure (Article 368 itself).

- **Recent Important Constitutional Amendments**

The Constitution (100th Amendment) Act, 2015	Land Boundary Agreement (LBA) between India and Bangladesh.
The Constitution (101th Amendment) Act, 2017	Introduced the Goods and Services Tax.
The Constitution (102th Amendment) Act, 2018	Constitutional status to National Commission for Backward Classes.
The Constitution (103th Amendment) Act, 2019	10% Reservation for Economically Weaker Sections (EWSs).
The Constitution (104th Amendment) Act, 2020	It extended the reservation of seats for SCs and STs in the Lok Sabha and states assemblies.

- **105th Constitutional Amendment (2021):** Restored the power of State governments to identify and notify Other Backward Classes (OBCs) within their respective states.
- **106th Constitutional Amendment (2023):** To reserve one-third of the seats in the Lok Sabha (330A), state legislative assemblies (332A) and Delhi Legislative Assembly (239AA) for women for a period of 15 years after coming to effect (334A).

Union of States

- Article 1 describes India, that is, Bharat as a 'Union of States' rather than a 'Federation of States'.
- First schedule of Constitution lists the names of states and their territories phrase 'Union of States' has been preferred to 'Federation of States' for two reasons: one, the Indian Federation is not the result of an agreement among the states like the American Federation, and two, the states have no right to secede from the federation.

Union and Its Territory

Articles 1 to 4 under Part I of the Constitution explains the Union and its Territory.

Article 1(1)	India, that is Bharat, shall be a Union of States.
Article 1(2)	The States and the territories will be specified in the First Schedule.
Article 1(3)	The territory of India will comprise the following: • The territories of the States, • The Union territories mentioned in the First Schedule, and • Such other territories may be acquired.

- **Article 2:** It deals with admission or establishment of new States. Parliament may by law admit into the Union, or establish, new States based on terms and conditions.
- Article 3 authorises the Parliament to:
  - Form a new state by separation of territory from any state or by uniting two or more states or parts of states or by uniting any territory to a part of any state,
  - Increase the area of any state,
  - Diminish the area of any state,
  - Alter the boundaries of any state, and
  - Alter the name of any state.
- Article 3 lays down two conditions in this regard:
  - One, a bill contemplating the above changes can be introduced in the Parliament only with the prior recommendation of the President.
  - Two, before recommending the bill, the President has to refer the same to the state legislature concerned for expressing its views within a specified period.
  - The President (or Parliament) is not bound by the views of the state legislature and may either accept or reject them, even if the views are received in time.

> **100th Constitutional Amendment Act (2015)** was enacted to give effect to the acquiring of certain territories by India and transfer of certain other territories to Bangladesh in pursuance of the agreement and its protocol entered into between the Governments of India and Bangladesh.

Article 4: Itself declares that laws made for admission or establishment of new states **(under Article 2)** and formation of new states and alteration of areas, boundaries or names of existing states **(under Article 3)** are not to be considered as amendments of the Constitution under Article 368. This means that such laws can be passed by a simple majority and by the ordinary legislative process.

Dhar Commission and JVP Committee (1948)

- The integration of princely states with the rest of India has purely an ad hoc arrangement.
- Government of India appointed the Linguistic Provinces Commission under the Chairmanship of Justice S.K.

Dhar in 1948 to examine the feasibility and evolution of an objective criteria.

- Committee recommended the reorganization of states on the basis of administrative convenience rather than linguistic factors.

Fazl Ali Commission (1953)

- It identified four major factors that can be taken into account:
- Preservation and strengthening of the unity and security of the country.
- Linguistic and cultural homogeneity.
- Financial, economic and administrative considerations.
- Planning and promotion of the welfare of the people in each state as well as of the nation as a whole.
- **States Reorganization Act (1956):** It was a major reform of the boundaries of India's states and territories, organising them along linguistic lines. The Act came into effect at the same time as the Constitution (Seventh Amendment) Act, 1956.

Andhra State Act, 1953 – Formed the first linguistic state, known as the State of Andhra, by taking out the Telugu speaking areas from the State of Madras. Kurnool was the capital of Andhra State and the state high court was established at Guntur.

Citizenship

- India has two kinds of people–citizens and aliens.
- Citizens are full members of the Indian State and owe allegiance to it. They enjoy all civil and political rights.
- Aliens, on the other hand, are the citizens of some other state and hence, do not enjoy all the civil and political rights.
- Citizenship is listed in the Constitution's Union List and hence falls within Parliament's sole control.
- The term "citizen" is not defined in the Constitution, however, Part 2 describes the numerous types of people who are eligible for citizenship (Articles 5 to 11).
- Unlike other parts of the Constitution, which took effect on January 26, 1950, these articles were put into effect on November 26, 1949, the day the Constitution was signed.

Article 5	• Citizenship was granted to all persons who were born and raised in India. • Even people who were domiciled in India but not born there, yet had one of their parents born there, were considered citizens. • Anyone who had lived in India for more than five years was also eligible to seek citizenship.
Article 6	• It granted citizenship rights to certain Pakistani migrants to India. • Because of Partition and migration prior to Independence, Article 6 stated that anyone who migrated to India prior to July 19, 1949, automatically became an Indian citizen if one of his parents or ancestors was born in India. • Those who arrived in India after this date, on the other hand, had to register.
Article 7	• It Provided certain migrants to Pakistan with the right to citizenship. • Those who migrated to Pakistan after March 1, 1947 and later returned on resettlement permits were included in the citizenship net. • The law was more sympathetic to those who migrated from Pakistan and were referred to as refugees than to those who were stranded in Pakistan or went there but decided to return soon.
Article 8	• Provided certain persons of Indian origin residing outside India with the right to citizenship. • Any Person of Indian Origin residing outside India who was born in India, or either of his or her parents or grandparents, could register as an Indian citizen with the Indian Diplomatic Mission.
Article 9	• Article 9 states that if a person voluntarily obtains the citizenship of a foreign state, he or she will no longer be a citizen of India.
Article 10	• Article 10 states that any person who is or is deemed to be a citizen of India under any of the preceding provisions of this Part shall continue to be such a citizen, subject to the provisions of any law made by Parliament.
Article 11	• It gives Parliament the authority to make any provision regarding the acquisition and termination of citizenship, as well as all matters pertaining to it.

- The Citizenship Act, 1955 provides for the acquisition and determination of Indian citizenship.

Acquisition and Determination of Indian Citizenship

There are four ways in which Indian citizenship can be acquired: birth, descent, registration and naturalisation. The provisions are listed under the Citizenship Act, 1955.

By Birth

- Every person born in India on or after 26.01.1950 but before 01.07.1987 is an Indian citizen irrespective of the nationality of his/her parents.
- Every person born in India between 01.07.1987 and 02.12.2004 is a citizen of India given that either of his/her parents is a citizen of the country at the time of his/her birth.
- Every person born in India on or after 3.12.2004 is a citizen of the country given both his/her parents are Indians or at least one parent is a citizen and the other is not an illegal migrant at the time of birth.

By Registration

Citizenship can also be acquired by registration. Some of the mandatory rules are:

- A person of Indian origin who has been a resident of India for 7 years before applying for registration.
- A person of Indian origin who is a resident of any country outside undivided India.
- A person who is married to an Indian citizen and is ordinarily resident for 7 years before applying for registration. Minor children of persons who are citizens of India.

By Descent

- A person born outside India on or after January 26, 1950 is a citizen of India by descent if his/her father was a citizen of India by birth.
- A person born outside India on or after December 10, 1992, but before December 3, 2004 if either of his/her parents was a citizen of India by birth.
- If a person born outside India or after December 3, 2004 has to acquire citizenship, his/her parents have to declare that the minor does not hold a passport of another country and his/her birth is registered at an Indian consulate within one year of birth.

By Naturalisation

- A person can acquire citizenship by naturalisation if he/she is ordinarily resident of India for 12 years (throughout 12 months preceding the date of application and 11 years in the aggregate) and fulfils all qualifications in the third schedule of the Citizenship Act.
- The Act does not provide for dual citizenship or dual nationality. It only allows citizenship for a person listed under the provisions above i.e., by birth, descent, registration or naturalisation.

  Note: The act has been amended four times — in 1986, 2003, 2005, and 2015.

  Citizenship (Amendment) Act 2019: The amendment proposes to permit members of six communities — Hindus, Sikhs, Buddhists, Jains, Parsis and Christians from Pakistan, Bangladesh and Afghanistan — to continue to live in India if they entered India before December 31, 2014. It also reduces the requirement for citizenship from 11 years to just 6 years. Two notifications also exempted these migrants from the Passport Act and Foreigners Act. A large number of organisations in Assam protested against this Bill as it may grant citizenship to Bangladeshi Hindu illegal migrants. The justification given for the bill is that Hindus and Buddhists are minorities in Bangladesh, and fled to India to avoid religious persecution, but Muslims are a majority in Bangladesh and so the same cannot be said about them.

The Citizenship Act, 1955: Termination

By Renunciation

- Any citizen of India of full age and capacity can make a declaration renouncing his Indian citizenship.
- Upon the registration of that declaration, that person ceases to be a citizen of India.
- However, if such a declaration is made during a war in which India is engaged, its registration shall be withheld by the Central Government.
- Further, when a person renounces his Indian citizenship, every minor child of that person also loses Indian citizenship.
- However, when such a child attains the age of eighteen, he may resume Indian citizenship.

  By Termination: An Indian citizen's citizenship can be revoked if he or she knowingly or voluntarily adopts the citizenship of another country.

The Constitution of India, like Canada, has introduced the system of single citizenship and provided uniform rights (barring some exceptions) for the people of India to promote the feeling of fraternity and unity among them and to build an integrated Indian nation.

- This provision, however, does not apply during a war in which India is engaged.

By Deprivation

It is a compulsory termination of Indian citizenship by the Central government, if:

- The citizen has obtained the citizenship by fraud,
- The citizen has shown disloyalty to the Constitution of India,
- The citizen has unlawfully traded or communicated with the enemy during a war,
- The citizen has, within five years after registration or naturalisation, been imprisoned in any country for two years,
- The citizen has been ordinarily resident out of India for seven years continuously.

National Register of Citizens (NRC)

- The National Register of Citizens, 1951 is a register prepared after the conduct of the Census of 1951 in respect of each village, showing the houses or holdings in a serial order and indicating against each house or holding the number and names of persons staying therein.
- The national NRC was published only once in 1951 but a state-level NRC for Assam was updated and published in 2019.
- The NRC of 1951 and the Electoral Roll of 1971 (up to midnight of 24 March 1971) are together called Legacy Data.
- Persons and their descendants whose names appeared in these documents are certified as Indian citizens.

PIO Card (Persons of Indian Origin)

- If a person meets the following criteria, he or she is qualified for the PIO card:
- Is of Indian descent and a citizen of any nation other than Pakistan, Sri Lanka, Nepal, Bangladesh, Bhutan, China, or Afghanistan, or has previously held an Indian passport, or is the spouse of an Indian citizen or a person of Indian heritage.
- PIO cardholders can enter India many times for a period of fifteen years. They do not need to obtain a second visa.

Overseas Citizen of India (OCI) Card

- The OCI Card is for overseas people who were eligible for Indian citizenship on or after January 26, 1950, or who were already citizens of India.
- The OCI Card is not available to citizens of Pakistan or Bangladesh. The holder of an OCI card does not have voting privileges.
- OCI isn't the same as dual citizenship. OCI cardholders are not citizens of India.
- The OCI Card is a multipurpose, multiple entry visa that allows you to enter India for the rest of your life.
- In terms of financial, educational, and economic considerations, people having OCI Cards enjoy the same privileges as NRIs. However, they are unable to obtain agricultural land in India.

Conceptual Elements of Constitution

Fundamental Rights are enshrined in Part III (described as the Magna Carta of India) of the Constitution from Articles 12 to 35.

Fundamental Rights

- The concept of fundamental rights first came into being in Magna Carta in England in 1215.
- Fundamental Rights in Indian Constitution is inspired by the 'Bill of Rights' (Fundamental Rights) included in the Constitution of the USA.
- Fundamental Rights is defined as the basic human rights of all citizens. These rights, defined in Part III of the Constitution are guaranteed by the Constitution to all persons without any discrimination.
- Originally there are 7 Fundamental Rights, but presently there are 6 Fundamental Rights. Right to property as a fundamental rights was deleted by 44th Constitutional Amendment Act 1978 . Presently Right to property was, Legal right under Article 300A.

Features of Fundamental Rights

- Some of them are available only to the citizens while others are available to all persons whether citizens, foreigners or legal persons like corporations or companies .
- They are not absolute but qualified. The state can impose reasonable restrictions on them.
- All of them are available against the arbitrary action of the state. Some of them are also against the actions of private individuals.
- Some of them are negative in character, that is, place limitations on the authority of the State.
- They are justiciable in nature.
- They are not sacrosanct or permanent. The Parliament can curtail or repeal them but only by a constitutional amendment act and not by an ordinary act.
- They can be suspended during the operation of a National Emergency except the rights guaranteed by Articles 20 and 21. Further, the six rights guaranteed by Article 19 can be suspended only when emergency is declared on the grounds of war or external aggression .
- Their application can be restricted while martial law is in force in any area.
- Right given to citizens only:
- Few are available only to citizens not to foreigners (Article 15, 16, 19, 29 and 30).
- Citizens and foreigners (Not for enemies): Available to citizens and foreigners too but not enemy aliens (Article 14, 20, 21, 21A, 22, 23, 24, 25, 26, 27, 28).
- Fundamental rights Against citizens: Fundamental rights available against private citizens too – Article 15, 17, 23, 24, 32 (Only Habeas Corpus).

Article 12	• **Definition of State** ■ Executive and legislative organs of the union. ■ Executive and legislative organs of the state. ■ All local bodies. ■ All statutory and non-statutory authorities. ■ Private body or agency working as an instrument of state can fall within the meaning of the state.
Article 13	• Declares that all laws that are inconsistent with or in derogation of any of the fundamental rights shall be void. The term 'Law' in Article 13 has been given a wide connotation so as to include the following: • Permanent laws enacted by Parliament or state legislatures. • Temporary laws like ordinances issued by President or the Governors. • Statutory instruments in the nature of delegated legislation. • Non-legislative sources of law. **Note:** Even constitutional amendment act can be challenged (Keshavananda Bharati case). **Laws Include** • Laws of parliament and state legislature, Ordinances, Non legislative sources of law i.e (Convention). • Delegated legislation. • The word law do not apply for personal laws.
Article 14	**Right to equality: Equality before law and equal protection of laws** • Includes legal persons as well. • Equality before law: British version. • Equal protection of laws: American constitution. • It permits reasonable classification of persons, objects and transactions by the law but it should not be arbitrary. **Exceptions to equality** • President and Governor are not answerable to court for their official acts. • No criminal proceedings shall be instituted or continued against the President or the Governor in any court during his term of office. • No process for the arrest or imprisonment of the President or Governor. • Civil proceeding on personal acts can be initiated only after two months notice. • No liability of true reporting in newspapers. • No member of Parliament shall be liable for anything said or vote in Parliament. • Article 31C. • Foreign sovereigns enjoy immunity, this includes even UNO.
Article 15	**No citizen of India shall be discriminated on the basis of religion, race, caste, sex or place of birth** • Usage of two keywords- 'Discrimination' and 'Only'. • Ground mentioned in the article: religion, race, caste, sex or place of birth.

	• The second provision in this article is applicable to even private individuals and legal persons. **Exceptions** • Special provisions for women and children. • Advancement of socially and educationally backward classes of citizens or for the SC and ST. • Provision for education of the above could be made for education in aided and unaided.
Article 16	**Equality of opportunity in public employment** • Addition of two more grounds: Descent or residence. **Exceptions:** • Parliament can prescribe residence as condition for certain employment. • State can provide reservation for any backward classes if they are inadequately represented. • Religious denomination exception.
Article 16(2)	It guarantees equal treatment under law in matters of public employment, and prohibits the state from discriminating on grounds of place of birth or residence.
Article 16(3)	It provides an exception by saying that Parliament may make a law "prescribing" a requirement of residence for jobs in a particular state.
Article 16(4)	"Nothing in this article shall prevent the State from making any provision for the reservation of appointments or posts in favor of any backward class of citizens which, in the opinion of the State, is not adequately represented in the services under the State".
Article 17	**Abolition of untouchability** • Protection of civil rights act, 1955. • Term untouchability has not been defined anywhere in the constitution. • It is available against even private individuals.
Article 18	**Abolition of titles** • State cannot confer titles until it is military or academic. • Prohibits a citizen of India from accepting titles from foreign countries. • Foreigner who holds office of profit should take consent of the President. • No gift also for a foreigner without President's approval.
Article 19	**Right to freedom** • It has six rights within it. • Right to hold property was deleted by the 44th amendment act of 1978. • These rights are not applicable to aliens, legal corporation. • These are not available against private individuals. • Reasonable restrictions can be imposed on enjoyment of these rights. • Restrictions should be based on the grounds mentioned in article 19 and not on any other grounds. **Freedom of speech and expression** Constitution imposes reasonable restriction on Right of speech and expression when it comes to: • Includes freedom of commercial advertisements. • Right against bandh (Strike) called by a political party. • Freedom of silence. • It does not include right to strike. **Reasonable restrictions** **Constitution imposes reasonable restriction on Right of speech and expression when it comes to:** • Sovereignty and integrity of India. • Security of the state. • Friendly relations with foreign states. • Public order. • Decency or morality. • Contempt of court. • Defamation and. • Incitement to an offence. **Freedom of assembly** • Can be exercised only on public land. • Assembly must be peaceful and unarmed. • Reasonable restriction: sovereignty and integrity of India and public order. **Freedom of association** • Right to obtain recognition of the association is not a fundamental right. • Right to strike is not a constitutional right can be regulated by appropriate law. **Reasonable restriction** • Interest of general public and protection of interests of any scheduled tribes. • Article 19 does not deal with movement outside the country. • Freedom of residence is complementary to the above right. • Freedom of profession.
Article 20	**Protection in respect of conviction for offences** • Grants protection against arbitrary and excessive punishment to an accused person. • Applicable to almost everyone. ■ No ex-post facto law (not on civil or tax laws or even on criminal trials, preventive detention cases). ■ No double jeopardy (not available in proceedings before departmental or administrative authorities). ■ No self-incrimination (not applicable to civil proceedings).

Article 21	**Protection of life and personal liberty** ● "Procedure established by law". ● Gopalan case (1950): not available against arbitrary legislative action. ● Maneka Gandhi case (1978): wider interpretation of article 21 (just, fair and reasonable). ● Various rights included under this are: ■ Right to live with human dignity. ■ Right to a decent environment including pollution-free water and air and protection against hazardous industries. ■ Right to livelihood. ■ Right to shelter. ■ Right to health. ■ Right to free education up to 14 years of age. ■ Right to free legal aid. ■ Right against solitary confinement. ■ Right to a speedy trial. ■ Right to travel abroad. ■ Right against bonded labor. ■ Right against custodial harassment. ■ Right to a fair trial. ■ Right of prisoners to have necessities of life. ■ Right of women to be treated with decency and dignity. ■ Right against public hanging. ■ Right to information. ■ Right to reputation. ■ Right to Privacy.
Article 21A	**Right to education** ● Free and compulsory education to all children in the age group of 6-14 years. ● Added by 86th Constitutional amendment act, 2002.
Article 22	**Protection against arrest and detention** ● Two types of detention: punitive and preventive. **First part of article 22** ● Right to be informed of the grounds of arrest. ● Right to consult and be defended by a legal practitioner. ● Right to be produced before a magistrate within 24 hours. ● Right to be released after 24 hours unless the magistrate authorizes further detention. These are applicable to those acts which are of a criminal or quasi-criminal nature. These safeguards are not available to a person detained under preventive detention law and also to an alien. Preventive detention provisions are applicable to both citizens as well as aliens. ● Detention of a person cannot exceed three months unless an advisory board recommends the same (the board is to consist of judges of a high court). ● Ground of detention should be communicated to Detenu. However, facts considered important may not be communicated. ● Opportunity for representation should be provided. Constitution has divided the legislative power with regard to preventive detention between Parliament (exclusively for defence, foreign affairs and security of India) and the state legislatures.
Article 23	**Prohibition of traffic in Human beings and Forced Labour** ● Protection against private actions as well. ● Compulsion arising from economic reasons are also included. ● Exception: compulsory military service.
Article 24	**Prohibition of employment of children in factories etc.** ● Does not prohibit employment in harmless activities. ● Commission for Protection of Child rights act, 2005 was enacted to provide for a national commission and state commission for child rights.
Right to freedom of religion Article 25 to Article 28	**Article 25: Freedom of Conscience and Free profession, Practice and Propagation of Religion** ● No forcible conversions allowed. ● Available to both citizens and non-citizens. ● Covers both rituals and practices. ● It guarantees rights of individuals. ● State can regulate these religious institutions. ● State can provide for social welfare and reform. **Article 26: Freedom to manage religious affairs** ● To establish institutions. ● To manage its religious affairs. ● To own property. ● To administer such property. ● It guarantees rights of religious denominations. ● These are not subject to other provisions relating to FRs. **Religious denomination** ● Group of people with common belief. ● Common organization. ● Distinctive name. **Article 27: Freedom of taxation for promotion of a religion** ● It prohibits levy of a tax and not fee. **Article 28: Freedom from attending religious instruction** ● Institution wholly setup by use of state funds: prohibited. ● Institution administered by state but established by a trust: allowed. ● Institutions recognized by a state: voluntary basis. ● Institution receiving aid from state: voluntary basis.

Cultural and educational rights Article 29-30	**Article 29: Right to conserve distinct language, script or culture of its own** ● No discrimination can be made on the basis of language in educational institutions. ● This is applicable to not just to minorities. ● It provides protection to both religious and linguistic minorities. **Article 30: To administer educational institutions** ● Applicable to both religious and linguistic minorities. ● Here, protection is confined only to minorities.
Article 32	**Right to constitutional remedies** ● Most important part of the Fundamental Rights. ● Parliament can empower any other court to issue directions, orders and writs of all kinds. ● President can suspend the enforcement of Fundamental rights during a national emergency (Article 359). ● Article 32 can be invoked in only those cases where there is violation of FRs. **Writs** ● Before 1950, only the high courts of Bombay, Madras and Calcutta could issue writs. ● Idea borrowed from Britishers. ● Writ jurisdiction of Supreme Court is narrower than High court. ● Territorial jurisdiction of Supreme Court is much greater than High Court. ● SC is the defender and guarantor of fundamental rights. **Habeas Corpus** ● Tool of individual liberty against arbitrary detention. ● Can be issued against both public and private individuals. ● The writ cannot be issued in the following cases: ■ Detention is lawful. ■ Proceedings is for contempt of legislature or court. ■ Detention is by a competent of court. ■ Detention is outside court jurisdiction. **Mandamus** ● Demanding a public official to perform a duty which he has failed to perform. ● Can be issued against an inferior court also. ● Mandamus cannot be issued against: a private individual or body; to enforce a departmental instruction that does not possess statutory force; when the duty is discretionary; to enforce a contractual obligation; against the President or Governor; or against the Chief Justice of India or a judge of a High Court acting in a judicial capacity. **Prohibition** ● It means 'to forbid'. ● Issued by a higher court to a lower court. ● To prevent exceeding jurisdiction. ● Only against judicial and quasi-judicial bodies. ● Not available against administrative authorities, legislative bodies and private individuals or bodies. **Certiorari** ● Much like above but it is curative as well. ● Available against administrative authorities as well. **Quo-Warranto** ● To adjudicate the legality of a claim of a person to public office. ● It can be issued against public office of substantive character. ● Cannot be issued against ministerial or private office. ● Any interested person can seek the application of this.
Armed Forces & FR	● Article 33 gives Parliament the authority to limit or abolish the basic rights of members of the armed forces, paramilitary forces, police forces, intelligence agencies, and similar entities. ● Objective behind this article is to ensure proper discharge of their duties and maintenance of discipline among them. ● Power to make laws under this is conferred only to Parliament.
Martial Law & FR	● Article 34 imposes limits on FRs while martial rule is in effect in any portion of India's jurisdiction. ● Parliament has the authority to reimburse any government official for restoring peace and order while martial rule is in effect, even if such acts violated FRs. ● The concept of Martial law has been borrowed from Britishers. ● Despite its mention, the term 'martial law' has not been defined in the Constitution. ● There are no justifications given for the establishment of martial law. ● During the period of martial law, military officials have extraordinary authority to conduct any required actions. However, the SC held Habeas Corpus is not suspended when martial law is in force.
Article 35	**Effecting certain fundamental rights** In the following sections, the parliament shall have the rights and the state legislature shall not have the power to pass legislation. ● Prescribing residence as a condition for certain employments or appointments in a union territory or local authority or other authority.

	• Allows courts other than the Supreme Court and high courts to issue various directives, orders, and writs. • Restriction or abolition of the applicability of basic rights to members of the armed services, police forces, and so forth. • Indemnifying any government or any other person for any act done during the operation of martial law in any area. • Punishment for acts involving untouchability. • Traffic in human beings and forced labour.

Exceptions of FR

Article 31A, 31B and 31C

Article 31A: Saving of laws providing for acquisition of estates etc.

- It protects five types of legislation from being challenged and annulled on the basis of violations of articles 14 and 19.
- The state acquires states and associated rights.
- Taking over the management of properties by the state.
- Amalgamation of corporations.
- Extinguishment or modification of corporate directors' or shareholders' rights. Extinguishment or modification of mining leases.

Article 31B: Validation of certain acts and regulations

- It protects the acts and regulations in the 9th schedule from being challenged and annulled for violating any of the fundamental rights.
- The Supreme Court concluded in one of its decisions that there could be no blanket immunity. Laws adopted after the Keshavananda Bharati decision can be challenged in court if they infringe the fundamental rights provided by Articles 14, 15, 19, and 21.

Article 31C: Saving of laws giving effect to certain directive principles

- It contains following two provisions:
- No legislation shall be declared unlawful if it strives to give effect to Articles 39 (b) or 39 (c), even if it breaches Articles 14 or 19.
- Courts are barred from challenging such legislation, so that such a policy is not implemented. (This clause was deemed illegal by the court in the Keshavananda Bharati judgement).

Directive Principles of State Policy (DPSP)

The Directive Principles of State Policy are enumerated in Part IV of the Constitution from Articles 36 to 51.

- Borrowed from the Ireland's constitution.
- Part IV of the Indian Constitution (Articles 36-51).
- Socioeconomic democracy is enshrined.
- They are a 'instrument of instructions' as defined by the Government of India Act of 1935.
- Their breach is not legally enforced by the courts.
- The DPSP's objective is to establish a "Welfare State".
- **Sapru committee Report (1945):** Which gave us both Fundamental Rights (justiciable) and DPSP(s) (non-justiciable).
- Article 37 of the Indian Constitution states unequivocally that "DPSPs are fundamental in the governance of the country, and it shall be the duty of the state to apply these principles in making laws".
- Directive Principles are not classified in the Constitution as per their underlying philosophies. However, they can be classified into:

■ Socialistic. ■ Gandhian. ■ Liberal-intellectual.

Socialistic principles	**Article 38:** Promoting welfare of the society by securing a social order permeated by justice. **Article 39:** To secure. • Right of adequate means of livelihood. ■ Equitable distribution of material resources of the community for the common good. ■ Prevention of concentration of wealth and means of production. ■ Equal pay for equal work for men and women. ■ Preservation of health and strength of workers and children against forcible abuse. ■ Opportunities for healthy development of the child. **Article 39A:** To promote equal justice and to provide free legal aid to the poor. **Article 41:** To secure the right to work, to education and to public assistance in cases of unemployment, old age, sickness and disablement. **Article 42:** Make provisions for just and humane conditions for work and maternity relief. **Article 43:** To secure a living wage, a decent standard of life and social and cultural opportunities for all workers. **Article 43A:** Steps to secure participation of workers in the management of industries. **Article 47:** Raise the level of nutrition and the standard of living of people and to improve public health.
Gandhian principles	**Article 40:** To organize village panchayats and endow them with necessary powers **Article 43:** To promote cottage industries on an individual and cooperative basis **Article 43B:** To promote functioning of cooperative societies **Article 46:** To promote educational and economic interests of SCs, STs and other weaker sections **Article 47:** To prohibit the consumption of intoxicating drinks and drugs **Article 48:** To prohibit the slaughter of cows, calves and other milch and draught cattle and to improve their breeds

Liberal-Intellectual principles	**Article 44**: To secure a uniform civil code for all. **Article 45**: To provide early childhood care until 6 years of age. **Article 48:** To organize agriculture and animal husbandry on modern scientific lines. **Article 48A**: To protect and improve the environment and to safeguard forests and wildlife. **Article 49**: To protect monuments, places and objects of artistic or historic interest. **Article 50**: To separate judiciary from the executive. **Article 51**: To promote international peace and security.

DPSP and Amendment

42nd Constitutional Amendment, 1976	**Added four new DPSP** Article 39: To secure opportunities for healthy development of children. Article 39A: To provide free legal aid to the poor. Article 43A: Participation of workers in management of Industries. Article 48A: To protect and improve the environment.
44th Constitutional Amendment, 1978	Article 38: To minimize inequalities in income, status, facilities and opportunities.
86th Amendment Act of 2002	Changed the subject-matter and made elementary education a fundamental right under Article 21A. The amendment directed state to provide early childhood care until the completion of six years.
97th Amendment Act of 2011	Article 43B: cooperative societies

Fundamental Duties

- The Fundamental Duties are an important part of the Indian Constitution.
- No Duties of the Citizen were incorporated in the original constitution of India at the time of its commencement in 1950.
- The Fundamental Duties of citizens were added to the Constitution by the 42nd Amendment in 1976, upon the recommendations of the **Swaran Singh Committee** that was constituted by the government earlier that year.
- The idea of this section was borrowed from USSR constitution.
- Enumerated in Part IV(A) and consists of single Article 51 A.
- Fundamental duties like DPSP are non-justiciable
- Japanese constitution is one of the other democratic nations which have a provision dealing with the duties of its citizens.
- Fundamental duties apply only to citizens and Do Not Extend To Foreigners.

1. To abide by the Constitution and respect its ideals and institutions, the National Flag and the National Anthem.
2. To cherish and follow the noble ideals which inspired our national struggle for freedom.
3. To uphold and protect the sovereignty, unity and integrity of India.
4. To defend the country and render national service when called upon to do so.
5. To promote harmony and the spirit of common brotherhood amongst all people of India transcending religious, linguistic and regional or sectional diversities and to renounce practices derogatory to the dignity of women.
6. To value and preserve the rich heritage of our composite culture.
7. To protect and improve the natural environment including forests, lakes, rivers and wildlife and to have compassion for living creatures.
8. To develop the scientific temper, humanism and the spirit of inquiry and reform.
9. To safeguard public property and to abjure violence.
10. To strive towards excellence in all spheres of individual and collective activity, so that the nation constantly rises to higher levels of endeavor and achievement.
11. Subsequently, another duty was added by the 86th Constitutional Amendment Act of 2002: For a parent or guardian to provide opportunities for education of the child or ward between the age of six to fourteen (It was added when under Article 21A Right to education was made a FR).

- Both moral and civic duties have been laid down under the fundamental duties.
- The fundamental duties are not enforceable in nature. No legal sanction can be enforced by the government in case of their violation.

System of Government

Parliamentary and Federal System

Parliamentary System

- The Constitution of India provides for a parliamentary form of government, both at the Centre and in the states.
- Articles 74 and 75 deal with the parliamentary system at the Centre and Articles 163 and 164 in the states.

Features of Parliamentary Government

Nominal and Real Executives	• The President is the nominal executive officer. • The Prime minister is the actual executive officer (de facto executive officer). • Article 74 provides for the Council of Ministers headed by the Prime Minister to assist the President in performing his duties and to advise him.
	• The proposal made in this way is binding on the President.

Majority Party Rule	• The political party which secures majority seats in the Lok Sabha forms the government. • The leader of that party is appointed as the Prime Minister by the President, other ministers are appointed by the President on the advice of the prime minister. • If no single party gets the majority, a coalition of parties may be invited by the President to form the government.
Collective Responsibility	• The ministers are collectively accountable to the entire legislature, particularly the People's Chamber (Article 75). • They sink and swim together as a group.
Political Homogeneity	• Members of the Council of Ministers often belong to the same political party and so have the same political world view. • In the case of a coalition government, the ministers are bound by consensus.
Double Membership	• Ministers are members of both the legislative and executive branches of government. • This means that if a person is not a member of Parliament, he cannot be a minister. • The constitution stipulates that ministers will no longer serve as ministers if they do not serve as members of Parliament for six consecutive months.
The Prime Minister's Leadership	• The leader of this form of government is the Prime Minister.
Dissolution of the Lok Sabha	• The lower house of the Parliament (Lok Sabha) can be dissolved by the President on recommendation of the Prime Minister.
Secrecy	• Ministers are bound by the concept of procedural secrecy and are not permitted to provide information regarding their procedures, policies, or decisions. • Before entering their office, they swore an oath of secrecy. The president administers the oath of secrecy to the ministers.

Federal System

- A federal government is one in which powers are divided between the national government and the regional governments by the Constitution itself and both operate in their respective jurisdictions.

Features of Federal System

Dual Polity	• The Constitution establishes a dual polity consisting the Union at the Centre and the states at the periphery.
Written Constitution	• Indian Constitution is not only a written document but also the lengthiest Constitution of the world. • It specifies the structure, organisation, powers and functions of both the Central and state governments and prescribes the limits within which they must operate.
Division of Powers	• The Constitution divided the powers between the Centre and the states in terms of the Union List, State List and Concurrent List in the Seventh Schedule.
Supremacy of the Constitution	• The Constitution is the supreme (or the highest) law of the land. The laws enacted by the Centre and the states must conform to its provisions.
Independent Judiciary	• The Constitution establishes an independent judiciary headed by the Supreme Court to settle the disputes between the Centre and the states or between the states.

However, the India federal system of government has a power tilt towards the centre:

Strong Centre	**The division of powers is in favor of the Centre as:** • The Union List contains more subjects than the State List. • The more important subjects have been included in the Union List. • The Centre has overriding authority over the Concurrent List. • Finally, the residuary powers have also been left with the Centre.
States Not Indestructible	• The states in India have no right to territorial integrity. The Parliament can by unilateral action change the area, boundaries or name of any state.
Flexibility of the Constitution	• The Constitution can be amended by the unilateral action of the Parliament, either by simple majority or by special majority. • Further, the power to initiate an amendment to the Constitution lies only with the Centre.
No Equality of State Representation	• The states are given representation in the Rajya Sabha on the basis of population.

Emergency Provisions	• During an emergency, the Central government becomes all powerful and the states go into the total control of the Centre. It converts the federal structure into a unitary one without a formal amendment of the Constitution.
Parliament's Authority Over State List	• The Parliament is empowered to legislate on any subject of the State List if Rajya Sabha passes a resolution to that effect in the national Interest. • This means that the legislative competence of the Parliament can be extended without amending the Constitution.
Veto Over State Bills	• The Governor is empowered to reserve certain types of bills passed by the state legislature for the consideration of the President. • The President can withhold his assent to such bills not only in the first instance but also in the second instance.
	• Further, Article 250 states the Parliament shall have power to make laws for the whole or any part of the territory of India with respect to any of the matters enumerated in the State List during the Emergency.

Centre-State Relations and Inter-State Relations

- The constitution of India divides all powers- legislative, executive and financial between the centre and the states.
- Articles 245 to 263 of Part XI and Articles 268 to 293 of Part XII describe the types of Centre-State relations.
- Centre-state relations can be better understood under the following three heads:
  - Legislative relations
  - Administrative relations
  - Financial relations

Legislative relations (Articles 245 to 255)	• Article 245 (1) states that Subject to the provisions of this Constitution, Parliament may make laws for the whole or any part of the territory of India, and the Legislature of a State may make laws for the whole or any part of the State. • Article 245 (2) No law made by Parliament shall be deemed to be invalid on the ground that it would have extra territorial operation. • Article 246 states that the Parliament has exclusive power to make laws with respect to any of the matters enumerated in List I (Union List) and List III (Concurrent List) of the Seventh Schedule. • Article 248 states that the Parliament has exclusive power to make any law with respect to any matter not enumerated in the Concurrent List or State List.
Administrative relations (Articles 255 to 263)	• Article 256 states that the executive power of every State shall be so exercised as to ensure compliance with the laws made by Parliament and any existing laws which apply in that State, and the executive power of the Union shall extend to the giving of such directions to a State as may appear to the Government of India to be necessary for that purpose. • Article 257(1) states that the executive power of every State shall be so exercised as not to impede or prejudice the exercise of the executive power of the Union, and the executive power of the Union shall extend to the giving of such directions to a State as may appear to the Government of India to be necessary for that purpose. • Article 258(2) states that a law made by Parliament which applies in any State may, notwithstanding that it relates to a matter with respect to which the Legislature of the State has no power to make laws, confer powers and impose duties, or authorise the conferring of powers and the imposition of duties, upon the State or officers and authorities thereof. • Article 261(3) states that final judgments or orders delivered or passed by civil courts in any part of the territory of India shall be capable of execution anywhere within that territory according to law Disputes relating to Waters. • Article 262(1) states that Parliament may by law provide for the adjudication of any dispute or complaint with respect to the use, distribution or control of the waters of, or in, any inter-State river or river valley. • Article 262(2) states that Notwithstanding anything in this Constitution, Parliament may by law provide that neither the Supreme Court nor any other court shall exercise jurisdiction in respect of any such dispute or complaint as is referred to in clause (1) Coordination between States.

Financial relations	• **Article 268** describes the Duties levied by the Union but collected and appropriated by the States. • **Article 269** describes the Taxes levied and collected by the Union but assigned to the States. • **Article 269-A** describes Levy and Collection of Goods and Services Tax in Course of Inter-State Trade or Commerce. • **Article 270** describes the Taxes levied and distributed between the Union and the States. • 80th Amendment Act of 2000 and the 101st Amendment Act of 2016.

Inter-state Relations

For ensuring harmonious relations and close cooperation between the Centre and the states the Constitution makes the following provisions with regard to inter-state relations:

- Adjudication of inter-state water disputes.
- Coordination through inter-state councils.
- Mutual recognition of public acts, records and judicial proceedings.
- Freedom of inter-state trade, commerce and intercourse.

Inter-state water dispute

Article 262 provides for the adjudication of inter-state water disputes. It has two following provisions:

- Parliament may by law provide for the adjudication of any dispute or complaint with respect to the use, distribution and control of waters of any inter-state river and river valley.
- Parliament may also provide that neither the Supreme Court nor any other court is to exercise jurisdiction in respect of any such dispute or complaint.

River Boards Act (1956)	• Provides for the establishment of river boards for the regulation and development of inter-state river and river valleys. • A river board is established by the Central government on the request of the state governments concerned to advise them.
Inter-State Water Disputes Act (1956)	• Empowers the Central government to set up an ad hoc tribunal for the adjudication of a dispute between two or more states in relation to the waters of an inter-state river or river valley. The decision of the tribunal would be final and binding. • Moreover, neither the Supreme Court nor any other court is to have jurisdiction in respect of any water dispute which may be referred to such a tribunal under this Act.

Inter-State Water Dispute Tribunals Set-up So Far

Name	Set-up in	States Involved
Krishna Water Disputes Tribunal-I	1969	Maharashtra, Karnataka and Andhra Pradesh
Godavari Water Disputes Tribunal	1969	Maharashtra, Karnataka, Andhra Pradesh, Madhya Pradesh and Odisha
Narmada Water Disputes Tribunal	1969	Rajasthan, Gujarat, Madhya Pradesh and Maharashtra
Ravi and Beas Water Disputes Tribunal	1986	Punjab, Haryana and Rajasthan
Cauvery Water Disputes Tribunal	1990	Karnataka, Kerala, Tamil Nadu and Puducherry
Krishna Water Disputes Tribunal-II	2004	Maharashtra, Karnataka and Andhra Pradesh
Vansadhara Water Disputes Tribunal	2010	Odisha and Andhra Pradesh
Mahadayi Water Disputes Tribunal	2010	Goa, Karnataka and Maharashtra
Mahanadi Water Disputes Tribunal	2018	Odisha and Chhattisgarh

Inter-state Council

- Article 263 contemplates the establishment of an inter-state council (ISC) to effect coordination between the states and between Centre and States.
- The President can establish such a council at any time it appears to him that public interest would be served by its establishment.
- The ISC is the only multilateral centre-state forum that operates directly within the framework of the Constitution (Article 263 (b) and (c)) where topics like the GST and contemporary issues like disaster management, terrorism and internal security can be taken up.

Duties for the council	• Inquiring into and advising upon disputes which may arise between the states. • Investigation and discussing subjects in which the states or the centre and the states have a common interest. • Making recommendation on any subject for the better co-ordination of policy and action.
Composition of the council	• PM as Chairman. • CM of all the states. • CM of UTS having legislative assemblies. • Administrators of UTs not having legislative assemblies.

	• Governors of states under President's rule. • Six Central cabinet ministers, including the home minister, to be nominated by the PM. • Five ministers of the cabinet rank are permanent invitees of the council. The council meeting is supposed to be held thrice a year and its decisions on all questions are decided by consensus. Standing committee of ISC: Home Minister+5 cabinet ministers+9 Cm of states ISC Secretariat: headed by secretary of Government, also works as secretary to Zonal council

Inter-state Trade and Commerce

- Article 301 to 307 in Part XIII of the Constitution deal with the trade, commerce and intercourse within the territory of India.
- Article 301 declares that trade, commerce and intercourse throughout the territory of India shall be free. The freedom afforded by this applies to between the states and also within the state.
- However, Article 302-305 imposes some restrictions on the above. These restrictions are:
  - Restriction can be imposed by the Parliament to safeguard public interest. However, no discrimination can be made between states while imposing restrictions.
  - Legislature of a state can impose reasonable restrictions on the freedom afforded by Article 301 to safeguard public interest. But, a bill for this purpose can only be introduced in the legislature with the prior recommendation of the President of India.
  - Legislature of a state can impose tax on import of goods and services from other states in those cases where similar taxes are imposed by the state on their goods and services.
- Article 307 empowers Parliament to appoint by law such authority as it deems necessary to carry out the purposes of Articles 301, 302, 303, and 304, as well as to confer on that authority such powers and duties as it deems necessary. So far, this provision has not been invoked.

Zonal Councils

- They are statutory bodies established by an act of parliament (State reorganization Act of 1956).
- The home minister of central government is the common chairman of all the zonal councils.
- Other members include: The Chief Ministers of the States included in each zone act as Vice-Chairman of the Zonal Council for that zone by rotation, each holding office for a period of one year at a time, Chief Minister and two other Ministers as nominated by the Governor from each of the States and two members from Union Territories included in the zone.
- At present there are five zonal councils: Northern, Central, Eastern, Western and Southern.
- In addition to above Zonal councils, a north-Eastern council was created by a separate Act of 1971 (NEC became functional in 1972). Its functions are similar to those of the zonal councils, but with a few additions.

Various Commission Reports On Center-State Relations

Administrative Reform Commission 1966	• Under chairmanship of Morarji Desai (followed by K Hanumanthayya) • Recommendation: ▪ Establish Inter State Council ▪ Appointment of Governors(non Partisan) ▪ Maximum powers to state, more financial resources to states
Rajamannar Committee 1969	1969, TN govt. appointed committee identified centralisation trend in center-state relation , hence recommended: • Finance commission to permanent body • Omit President's Rule • Abolish All India Services • Residuary powers to state
Sarkaria Commission 1983	• Permanent Inter State Council • Extreme/rare use of president's rule • Strengthen All India services • Armed forces to deploy without consent of states • 3 language formula • Center to consult state before laws on concurrent list • Other residuary powers vested in concurrent list • Appointment of Governors: he should be outside of state, not be eligible for any office of profit, can appoint for second term
Punchhi Commission 2007	Took help of sarkaria commission. Report and 2nd ARC Co-operative Federalism is key for unity. • Selection of Governors on the basis of Sarkaria Commission. Recommendation • Governor impeachment procedure same as president • Governor not to be chancellor of university • Create new All India Services • Setting up Interstate Trade and commerce commission

Emergency Provisions

Introduction

- Emergency provisions are borrowed from the Govt. of India Act 1935.
- Constitutional provisions: Part XVIII- Articles 352 to 360.
- "Suspension of Fundamental Rights during proclamation of emergency" provision borrowed from Weimer constitution (Now Germany).
- During emergency, Central government becomes all powerful and states are in the complete control of the union.
- The federal structure becomes unitary without a formal amendment to the Constitution.

National Emergency (Article 352)	President's Rule (Article 356)	Financial Emergency (Article 360)
Grounds of Declaration ● Article 352: Changed "internal disturbance" to External Aggression or Armed Rebellion (44th Amendment) ● 42nd Amendment 1976: President can limit operation of National emergency to particular area. ● National Emergency 1975: due to Internal Disturbance. ● The President can proclaim only after receiving a written recommendation from Cabinet (44th Amendment). ● Proclamation of National emergency brought under Judicial Review (44th Amendment)	**Grounds of Declaration** ● It is also known as state Emergency. ● Article 355: Duty on center to ensure state Govt. is Working in accordance to constitution. ● Article 356: Duty of center to take over state govt. in case of Constitution failure in state. ● 2 grounds to proclaim president's rule: ■ Article 356: President to proclaim, if SATISFIED action with/without Governor's Report. ■ Article 365: State fails to comply with directions of center.	**Grounds of Declaration** ● President to proclaim financial emergency, if he 'SATISFIED' that situation arised.
Approval ● Must be approved by both houses within 1 Month from date of issue (44th Amendment). ● If approved continues for 6 months, can be extended to infinite with the approval for every 6 months (periodic parliamentary approval (44th Amendment). ● Approval for Continuous by either of the houses by Special Majority (44th Amendment).	**Approval** ● Must be approved by both houses within 2 months from date of issue. ● If approved, it will continue for 6 months, can be extended for maximum 3 Years with approval of Parliament. ● Continuation: either house, by Simple Majority. ● Condition For Continuance: ■ National emergency in whole country. ■ Election commission to certify that no general elections due to difficulties.	**Approval** ● Must approved by Both Houses of Parliament within 2 Months. ● Resolution of approval can be passed by simple majority. ● Continues indefinitely till it revoked. ● No Maximum period specified. ● No Parliamentary approval needed for continuation.
Revocation ● President must revoke if LOKSABHA (1/10th Of total members of Lok Sabha give written notice to Speaker)- 44th Amendment. ● Revocation by simple majority.	**Revocation** ● Revoked by President ANY TIME (NO PARLIAMENTARY APPROVAL NEEDED).	**Revocation** ● Financial emergencies can be revoked by the president ANY TIME without parliamentary Approval.
Effects on Center-State relations Executive- Center extends its executive power to states, give directions to states on ANY matter, (STATE GOVT. IS NOT SUSPENDED BUT COMPLETE CONTROL BY CENTER). Legislative: Parliament make laws on state list however legislative power of state is not suspended, laws of parliament inoperative 6 months after emergency ceased, President can issue ordinance on state subjects. Financial: President can modify (reduce/cancel) distribution of revenues of states- such order, president has to laid before parliament.	**Effects on State Assembly** ● President dismisses state council of ministers. ● Governor on behalf of center carry Administration with help of chief secretary (authority of parliament) and advisor appointed by President. ● President either suspend /Dissolve State assembly ● Removal of Council of ministers of SLA State Legislative Assembly not dissolves automatically. ● 44th Constitutional Amendment 1978: 'Satisfaction of President' this provision is brought under JUDICIAL REVIEW.	**Effects** Center extends executive authority: Directing states to observe financial propriety. **Direction to President** Reduction of salaries & allowances reservation of all money/ other financial bills for consideration of presidents. Reduction of salaries & allowances for union & state and Judges of SC & HC.

Effect on Loksabha and State Assembly: Loksabha may extend for 1 year at a time, Extension can not continue beyond 6 months after emergency ceased to operate Parliament may extend tenure of state assembly. **Effects on Fundamental Rights:** Article 358 & Article 359 effects on FR during national emergency. ● Article 358: automatically suspends 6 rights of FR under Article 19 only when national emergency on External aggression, Article 19 suspends for entire duration of emergency and extended to entire country. ● Article 359: Suspension of other FR except Article 20 & 21, Suspends FR at both cases(armed rebellion or external), President may specify duration and the suspension of FR may applied to entire country or any part of country. ● 44th Amendment : Automatic suspension of Article 19 only on External aggression and Article 359: President suspend Right to seek Remedy Except for Article 20 & 21.		PROCLAMATION OF FINANCIAL EMERGENCY –ARTICLE 360.

Central Executive

President

- The President of India is the head of state of the Republic of India.
- The President is the formal head of the executive, legislature and judiciary of India and is also the commander-in-chief of the Indian Armed Forces.

Article 52	● There shall be a President of India.
Article 53 : Executive Power of the Union	● The executive power of the Union shall be vested in the President and shall be exercised by him either directly or through officers subordinate to him in accordance with this Constitution. ● Without prejudice to the generality of the foregoing provision, the supreme command of the Defence Forces of the Union Shall be vested in the President and the exercise thereof shall be regulated by law. ● Nothing in this Article shall: ■ Be deemed to transfer to the President any functions conferred by any existing law on the Government of any State or other authority, or ■ Prevent Parliament from conferring by law functions on authorities other than the President.

Article 54 : Election of President	● The President shall be elected by the members of an electoral college consisting of: ■ The elected members of both Houses of Parliament, and ■ The elected members of the Legislative Assemblies of the States. **Explanation:** In this Article and in Article 55, "State" includes the National Capital Territory of Delhi and the Union territory of Pondicherry.
Article 55 : Manner of Election Of President	● As per Article 55(3) of the Constitution of India, the election of the President shall be held in accordance with the system of proportional representation by means of single transferable vote and the voting at such election shall be by secret ballot.
Article 56 : Term of Office of President	● The President shall hold office for a term of five years from the date on which he enters upon his office: Provided that: ■ The President may, by writing under his hand addressed to the Vice-President, resign his office,

	■ The President may, for violation of the Constitution, be removed from office by impeachment in the manner provided in Article 61. ■ The President shall, notwithstanding the expiration of his term, continue to hold office until his successor enters upon his office. ● Any resignation addressed to the Vice-President under clause (a) of the provision to clause (1) shall forthwith be communicated by him to the Speaker of the House of the People.
Article 57 : Eligibility for Re-Election	● A person who holds, or who has held, office as President shall, subject to the other provisions of this Constitution be eligible for re-election to that office.
Article 58 : Qualifications for Election as President	● No person shall be eligible for election as President unless he: ■ Is a citizen of India, ■ Has completed the age of thirty-five years, and. ■ Is qualified for election as a member of the House of the People. ● A person shall not be eligible for election as President if he holds any office of profit under the Government of India or the Government of any State or under any local or other authority subject to the control of any of the said Governments. **Explanation:** For the purposes of this Article, a person shall not be deemed to hold any office of profit by reason only that he is the President or Vice-President of the Union or the Governor of any State or is a Minister either for the Union or for any State.
Article 59 : Conditions of President's Office	● He should not be a member of either House of Parliament or a House of the state legislature. If any such person is elected as President, he is deemed to have vacated his seat therein house on the date on which he enters upon his office as President. ● He should not hold any other office of profit. ● He is entitled, without payment of rent, to the use of his official residence (the Rastrapati Bhavan). ● He is entitled to such emoluments, allowances and privileges as may be determined by Parliament. ● His emoluments and allowances cannot be diminished during his term of office.

Article 60 : Oath or Affirmation by the President	● The oath to the President is administered by the Chief Justice of India and in his absence, by the senior most judge of the SUPREME COURT. In his oath, the President swears: ● To faithfully execute the office, ● To preserve, protect and defend the Constitution and the law, ● To devote himself to the service and well-being of the people of India.
Article 61 : Procedure For Impeachment of the President	● The President can be removed from his office before the expiry of his term only on the grounds of violation of the constitution. ● However, the Constitution does not define the meaning of the phrase 'violation of the constitution'. ● The impeachment process can be started from any house of the parliament by levelling charges against him. ● The notice bearing the charges against the President must be signed by at least a quarter of the members of the house. ● Before that house passes the resolution a 14 days' notice must be given to the President. ● The resolution to impeach the President must be passed by a special majority (two-thirds) in the originating house. ● Next, it is sent to the other house for consideration. which should investigate the charges. A select committee is formed to investigate the charges labelled against the President. ● If the other house passes the resolution by a two-thirds majority after the investigation by the select committee, the President of India is impeached.
Article 62: Vacancy in The President's Office	● In case of completion of President's term for five years in the office. ● In case of resignation to the Vice-president of India. ● If Lok Sabha/Rajya Sabha initiates an impeachment charge and they stand valid, he is removed. ● In case of he dies during his tenure. ● Invalidation of election by Supreme Court. In case of vacancy by resignation, removal, death or otherwise, the Vice-President acts as the President until a new President is elected.

	• Vacancy by the expiration of the term of the sitting President – election to fill the vacancy must be held before the expiration of the term. • Vacancy by resignation, removal, death or otherwise – election to fill the vacancy should be held within six months from the date of the occurrence of such a vacancy.

Powers and Functions of President

- President is executive head (Article 53).
- Act on Aid and advice of Council of Ministers (Article 74).
- All executive action taken in his name, make rules for convenient transaction of business of Government of India (Article 77).
- Power of appointment and removal of various dignitaries. Example, Comptroller and Auditor General of India, Chief Election Commissioner and Election Commissioners, Attorney General, Members of Union Public Service Commission, Joint Public Service Commission, Judges of Supreme Court and High Courts etc.
- Administers Union Territories directly (Article 239).
- Enjoys special powers with regard to administration of scheduled areas.

Legislative Power

- Integral Part of Parliament, Bill will become Act only after his Assent.
- Sessions of parliament, prorogation and Dissolution (Article 85).
- Right of the President to Address and Send messages to the House (Article 86).
- Special address by President (Article 87).
- Power of Nomination of members of the house.
- Lok Sabha: 2 members from Anglo Indian Community (Article 331). This provision is no longer in effect. It was abolished with the passage of the 104th Constitutional Amendment Act, 2019.
- Rajya Sabha: 12 members (Art, Science, literature and Social Service) (Article 80).
- Prior Sanction for Introduction of Certain Legislature. Example:
- Bill for creation of new states (Article 3).
- Introduction of certain Financial Bills (Article 117).
- Power of president to Assent Legislations (Article 111).
- Give Assent.
- Withhold the Assent.
- Return for reconsideration.
- **Type of veto:** Absolute, Qualified, Suspensive, Pocket.
- Indian President: Absolute, Suspensive and Pocket.
- President Veto power with regards to Bills Passed by State Legislature. (Article 201).
- Governor's power to Assent (Article 200).
- Give Assent.
- Withhold the Assent.
- Send for Reconsideration.
- Reserve Bill for Consideration of the President.
- Reserving bill for Consideration of President (Article 201 – Options with the President).
- Give Assent.
- Withhold the Assent.
- Send for Reconsideration (State Legislature to pass it again within 6 months).
- If sent again for reconsideration, it is not mandatory for the President to give his assent.
- President Shall Convene Joint Sitting (Article 108).
- Ordinance Making power of President and Governor (Article 123 and 213).
- Legislative Power in the hands of Executive (Conditions).
- Recess of the parliament.
- Any one House is not in Session.
- Temporary in nature, (6 months and 6 weeks – Maximum).
- Not parallel powers of legislation, Coextensive with legislative Power of Parliament, no Constitutional Amendment.
- Borrowed from GoI Act 1935, Aid and Advice of 'Council of Ministers'.
- Subject to judicial Review on malafide Grounds. (R. C. Cooper Case 1970).
- 38th Constitutional amendment act 1975, President satisfaction final and beyond judicial Review.
- 44th Constitutional amendment act, 1978 Repealed the above Permission.
- Present position: Subject to the judicial review on malafide grounds. [D. C. Wadhwa case (1987)].
- Re-promulgation of ordinance is a fraud and Violation of the Constitution.
- Exceptional powers to be sparingly used (No Substitute for Legislative Power).
- The Supreme Court reiterated the same in Krishna Kumar case, 2017.
- Governor enjoys similar powers under Article 213 except – on certain legislations where prior approval of the president is required, prior instruction may be taken from the President before passing the ordinance.

Pardoning power of the President Article 72.

- President under Article 72 (pardon, Commute, Remit, Reprieve and Respite).

• **Pardon:** With the grant of pardon convicts both conviction and sentence completely absolved. • **Commutation:** With this nature of the punishment of the convict can be changed. • **Remission:** Reduces the term of the imprisonment. • **Respite:** Awards lesser punishment than original punishment by looking at the special condition of a convict. • **Reprieve:** Stays the execution of the awarded sentence for a temporary period.

- In cases of:
- Court martial.
- Prosecuting agency is the Central Govt. (Executive power of union extends).
- All cases where punishment is the sentence of death.
- President power under Article 72 is Subject to limited power of Judicial review (Maru Ram case 1980).
- Exercised based on Aid and Advice of Council of ministers (Devinder Pal Singh Case, 2013).
- Powers to be exercised within a reasonable time frame (V. Sriharan case 2014).
- Remission power are also available under article 432 and 433 of CrPC irrespective of Article 72 and Article 161 (V. Sriharan Case, 2015).

- No right to oral hearing (Kehar Singh case 1989).
- Governor has powers of (Pardon, Commute, Remit, Reprieve and respite) in all Case where the prosecuting agency is the state authorities.
- No power with regard to court martial.
- No power to pardon capital punishment (where the presenting agency is central government).

Vice-President

- Article 63: There shall be a Vice President.
- Ex officio chairman of Rajya Sabha.
- Acts as President during death, resignation removal (or) otherwise of the incumbent President (Article 65).
- Vice President may also discharge the duties of the President during his absence, illness or any other cause (Article 65).
- Election of Vice President (Article 66):
- Electoral college, proportional representation single Transferable vote, secret ballot.
- Electoral College – Member of both houses of the parliament (elected and nominated).
- Eligibility Criteria – similar to that of President.
- Exception: He should be qualified for the election of member of Rajya Sabha.
- Oath to be administered by the President (or) any person appointed on that behalf by the President.
- **Term of Office of Vice President (Article 67)**
- 5 Year.
- Resignation to President.
- Removed by resolution introduced only in Rajya Sabha, 14 days prior notice, effective majority (majority of all existing members of the Rajya Sabha).
- Continue to hold office until his successor assume office (on expiration).
- **Vacancy to Office of Vice President (Article 68)**
- Expiry of term – Vacancy to be filled before such expiration.
- Death.
- Resignation.
- Removal.
- Otherwise.

Note – Election in case of vacancy other than the end of term shall be held as soon as possible (and not within 6 months). Newly elected Vice-President occupies Office for a full 5 -year term.

Prime Minister

The Prime minister is both the head of government and the real executive of the Indian system.

- Article 74 states that "There shall be a Council of Ministers with the Prime Minister as the head to aid and advise the President"

Appointment	• **Indirect election:** The Prime Minister is appointed by the President. • According to the Constitution, the Prime Minister may serve in either of the two Houses of Parliament. • Three Prime Ministers, for example, were Rajya Sabha members: Indira Gandhi (1966), Deve Gowda (1996), and Manmohan Singh (2004).
Qualifications	• He must be a citizen of India. • He must be a member of either Rajya Sabha or Lok Sabha at the time of taking oath or should be a member of any house within six months. • He should have completed his 30 years if he is a member of the Rajya Sabha or can be 25 years of age if he is a member of the Lok Sabha.
Oath	• Before entering upon his office, the Prime minister has to make and subscribe to an oath or affirmation. • The President of India administered the oath of office to the Prime Minister.
Terms of Office	• The term of office of the PM is not fixed. • The Prime Minister holds office during the pleasure of the President. • President can't dismiss the PM, he can hold the position till he enjoys the majority in the Lok Sabha, • He must resign if he loses the confidence in Lok Sabha.
Salary and allowance	• The Prime Minister's salary and allowances are set by Parliament on a regular basis. • He is paid the same salary and allowances as a member of Parliament. • He also receives a stipend, free housing, a travel allowance, medical care, and other benefits.

Power and Functions of the Prime Minister

With Respect to the Council of Minister	• The PM recommends a person to the President for appointment as ministers. • The PM can ask for the resignation of any minister. • He guides, directs, controls and coordinates the activities of all the ministers. • If the PM resigned from his office the Council of Ministers also collapsed.
In relation with the President	• **Chief Advisor:** The PM acts as a principal channel of communication between the President and Council of Ministers.

	• The PM has to communicate the decision of the Council of Ministers relating to administration of affairs of the Union and proposal for legislation to the President.
With Respect to the Parliament	• The Prime Minister is the leader of the lower house. • The PM can recommend the President about the prorogued and summoning the sessions of the Parliament. • The PM can recommend the dissolution of the Lok Sabha at any time to the President. • The PM announces the government policies on the floor of the houses.

Some other functions and powers of the PM

- The PM is the chairman of Niti Aayog, National Development Council, National Integration Council, National Water Resource Council and Inter-state council.
- The PM also acts as chief spokesman of the Union government.

Council of Ministers – Cabinet

Article 74 deals with the status of the council of ministers while Article 75 deals with the appointment, tenure, responsibility, qualification, oath and salaries and allowances of the ministers.

Article 74 (council of ministers to aid and advise President)	• The President may require the council of ministers to reconsider such advice and the President shall act in accordance with the advice tendered after such reconsideration.
Article 75 (Other Provisions as to Ministers)	The PM shall be appointed by the President and the other Ministers shall be appointed by the President on the advice of the PM. • The total number of ministers, including the Prime Minister, in the council of ministers shall not exceed 15% of the total strength of the Lok Sabha. ■ This provision was added by the 91st Amendment Act of 2003.
Article 77 (Conduct of Business of the Government of India)	The President shall make rules for the more convenient transaction of the business of the Government of India, and for the allocation among Ministers of the said business.
Article 78 (Duties of Prime Minister)	To communicate to the President all decisions of the council of ministers relating to the administration of the affairs of the Union and proposals for legislation.
Article 88 (Rights of Ministers as Respects the Houses)	Every minister shall have the right to speak and take part in the proceedings of either House, any joint sitting of the Houses and any Committee of Parliament of which he may be named a member. But he shall not be entitled to vote.

Note:- A minister who is not a member of the Parliament (either house) for any period of six consecutive months shall cease to be a minister.

Oath and Salary of Ministers

- Parliament decides the salary and allowances of the council of ministers.
- The President administers to them the oaths of office and secrecy.

Responsibility of Ministers

- **Collective Responsibility:** Article 75 clearly states that the council of ministers is collectively responsible to the Lok Sabha.
- **Individual Responsibility:** Article 75 also contains the principle of individual responsibility. It states that the ministers hold office during the pleasure of the President, which means that the President can remove a minister even at a time when the council of ministers enjoys the confidence of the Lok Sabha.
  - ■ However, the President removes a minister only on the advice of the Prime Minister.

Kitchen Cabinet

- Every Indian Prime Minister has had an 'Inner Cabinet'–a circle within a circle. The 'Inner Cabinet', also known as the 'Kitchen Cabinet', was particularly powerful during Indira Gandhi's tenure.
- It is made up of cabinet ministers as well as outsiders such as the prime minister's friends and family members.
- The Kitchen Cabinet does not have constitutional status.

Cabinet Committees

- A Cabinet committee is a group of ministers which can take collective decisions that are binding across various ministries/departments.
- They are an organizational device to reduce the enormous workload of the Cabinet which also facilitates in-depth examination of policy issues and effective coordination.

List of Cabinet Committees

Cabinet Committee on Political Affairs	• It examines economic and political issues that require a wider perspective but have no internal or external security implications.
Cabinet Committee on Economic Affairs	• It is supposed to review economic trends, problems and prospects for evolving a consistent and integrated economic policy, coordinate all activities requiring policy decisions at the highest level, deal with fixation of prices of agricultural produce and prices of essential commodities.

	• It considers proposals for investment of more than ` 1,000 crore, deals with industrial licensing policies and reviews rural development and the Public Distribution System.
Appointments Committee of the Cabinet	• It makes appointments to posts of the three service chiefs, Director General of Military Operations, chiefs of all Air and Army Commands, Director General of Defence Intelligence Agency, etc. • It decides on all important empanelments and shifts of officers serving on Central deputation.
Cabinet Committee on Security	• It deals with issues relating to law and order, internal security and policy matters concerning foreign affairs with internal or external security implications and also goes into economic and political issues related to national security.
Cabinet Committee on Parliamentary Affairs	• It draws the schedule for Parliament sessions and monitors the progress of government business in Parliament. • It scrutinizes non-government business and decides which official Bills and resolutions are to be presented.
Cabinet Committee on Accommodation	• It determines the guidelines or rules with regard to the allotment of government accommodation.
Cabinet Committee on Investment and Growth	• It will identify key projects required to be implemented on a time-bound basis, involving investments of ` 1,000 crore or more, or any other critical projects, as may be specified by it, with regard to infrastructure and manufacturing.
Cabinet Committee on Employment and Skill Development	• It is supposed to provide direction to all policies, programs, schemes and initiatives for skill development aimed at increasing the employability of the workforce for effectively meeting the emerging requirements of the rapidly growing economy and mapping the benefits of demographic dividend. • Currently, the Cabinet Committee on Accommodation is headed by the Home Minister and the Cabinet Committee on Parliamentary Affairs is the Defence Minister.

Groups of Ministers (GoMs)

- These are ad hoc bodies formed to give recommendations to the cabinet on certain emerging issues and critical problem areas.
- Ministers heading the concerned ministries are inducted into the relevant GoMs and when the advice is crystallised they are disbanded.
- In the past two decades, the institution of GoMs has become a viable and effective instrument of coordination among the ministries.
- Some of these GoMs have been empowered to take decisions on behalf of the Cabinet whereas the others make recommendations to the Cabinet.

Attorney General of India

- The Attorney General (AG) of India is a part of the Union Executive. AG is the highest law officer in the country.
- Article 76 of the Constitution provides for the office of AG of India.

Appointment	• The Attorney General (AG) of India appointed by the President on the advice of the Government.
Eligibility	• Qualified to be appointed as Supreme Court judge. • Citizen of India. • Judge of High Court for 5 years/ advocate High Court for 10 years/ eminent jurist in President's opinion.
Functions	• Advise Government on legal matters. • Perform legal duties assigned by the President. • Appear on behalf of Government in all cases in Supreme Court or High Court. • Represent Government under Article 143 (Power of President to consult SC). • Discharge functions conferred by Constitution or law.
Rights	• Right to Speak & take part in proceedings of both Houses of Parliament/joint sitting/any committee of Parliament of which he/she may be named a member. • Enjoys privileges & immunities of a member of Parliament. • Not a Government servant & not debarred from private legal practice.
Limitations	• No Right to Vote in House proceedings/committees. • Should not advise against or hold a brief against the Government. • Should not defend accused persons in criminal prosecutions without the permission of the Government of India. • Should not accept appointment as a director in any company or corporation without the permission of the Government of India.

Removal	• Holds office during President's pleasure & can be removed by President at any time. • No grounds for removal or procedure mentioned in the Constitution.

State Executive

Governor

- The Governor is the constitutional head of the State Government.
- He plays a two-fold function as the constitutional head of the State Government and as a link between the Centre and the State government.
- The Governor of a State is appointed by the President by warrant under his hand and seal.

Articles 153	• Articles 153 says that there should be a Governor for each state. • But under the 7th Amendment Act, 1956, the same person can be appointed as Governor of one or more States.
Article 156 – Term of Office	■ Normally holds office for five years but can be removed at any time before that by the President. ■ Thus, Governors remain in office during the pleasure of the President. ■ The Governor may resign at any time by writing to the President.
Article 157 Appointment	**Qualifications:** In order to be appointed as Governor, a person: • Must be a citizen of India, • Must have completed the age of 35 years. • In addition, there are two conventions that have come to develop with regard to appointment of the Governor:- ■ Must not belong to the state where he is appointed and, ■ Consult the Chief Minister of the concerned state where he is going to be appointed.

Conditions of Office

- Should not be a member of the Houses of Parliament or state legislatures. If any such person is appointed as Governor, he or she is presumed to have relinquished his or her position in that House on the date he or she takes office as Governor.
- Should not hold any other office of profit.
- Entitled without payment of rent to the use of official residence (the Raj Bhavan).
- Entitled to such emoluments, allowances and privileges as may be determined by Parliament.
- When the same individual is appointed as Governor of two or more states, the states share the emoluments and allowances payable to him in the proportion established by the President.
- Emoluments and allowances cannot be diminished during his term of office.
- During his or her tenure of office, he or she is exempt from criminal prosecution, including for personal activities, and cannot be detained or imprisoned.

■ However, after giving two months' notice, civil proceedings can be instituted him against during the term of office in respect of his personal acts.

Functions and Powers

Executive Powers	• All executive activities of the State Government are taken formally in his or her name. • Can make rules for more convenient transactions of the business of a State government. • Appoints the Chief Minister and other ministers, as well as the Attorney General, to serve at his or her leisure. • The State Election Commissioner (SEC) is appointed by the governor. However, the SEC may only be dismissed in the same way and on the same grounds as a high court judge. • Appoints the Chairman and members of the State Public Service Commission, who can be removed only by the President and not by a Governor. • Can recommend to the President declaring a state of constitutional emergency. As an agent of the President, the Governor has significant executive powers in a state during the President's reign. • Acts as the Chancellor of universities in the State and appoints the Vice-Chancellors (VCs).
Legislative Powers	• **Article 174:** Power to prorogue the state legislature and dissolve the state legislative assemblies. • **Article 176:** He addresses the state legislature at the first session of every year. • He can send messages to the house or houses of the state legislatures, with respect to a bill pending in the legislature or otherwise. • If the speaker of the legislative assembly is absent and the same is Deputy Speaker, then the Governor appoints a person to preside over the session. • Governor appoints 1/6th of the total members of the legislative council from the fields of – Literature, Science, Art, Cooperative Movement and Social Service.

	• Governor nominates 1 member in the state legislative assembly from the Anglo-Indian Community. • He can consult Election Commission for the disqualification of members. • **Article 200:** With respect to the bill introduced in the state legislature, he can: ▪ Give his assent. ▪ Withhold his assent. ▪ Return the bill. • **Article 201:** Reserve the bill for the President's consideration (In instances where the bill introduced in the state legislature endangers the position of state High Court). Governor can reserve the bill for the President's consideration in the following cases When provisions mentioned in the bill: • Violates the constitution (Ultra-Vires). • Oppose Directive Principles of State Policy. • Hinders the larger interests of the country. • Of grave the national importance. • Mention the acquisition of property that is dealt with Article 31A in the Constitution. • **Article 213:** An ordinance can be promulgated by him when either the Legislative Assembly or Council (Unicameral/Bicameral) are not in session. • The following reports are laid by him before the state legislatures: ▪ State Finance Commission. ▪ State Public Service Commission. ▪ Comptroller and Auditor General (Concerning the state finance).
Financial Powers	• He looks over the state budget being laid in the state legislature. • Money bills can be introduced in the State Legislature only with his/her prior recommendation. • No demand for a grant can be made except on his/her recommendation. • Can make advances out of the Contingency Fund of the State to meet any unforeseen expenditure. • Constitutes a Finance Commission after every five years to review the financial position of the panchayats and the municipalities.
Judicial Powers	• President consults the Governor while appointing judges of High Court. • In Consultation with state High Court, Governor makes appointments, postings and promotions of the district judges. • In consultation with the state high court and state public service commission, he also appoints persons to the judicial services.
Pardoning Power (Article 161)	• Power to grant pardons, reprieves, respites or remissions of punishment or to suspend, remit or commute the sentence of any person convicted in any offence against a state law.

Difference between Pardoning Powers of President and Governor

- The scope of the pardoning power of the President under Article 72 is wider than the pardoning power of the Governor under Article 161. The power differs in the following two ways:
- The power of the President to grant pardon extends in cases where the punishment or sentence is by a Court Martial but Article 161 does not provide any such power to the Governor.
- The President can grant pardon in all cases where the sentence given is sentence of death but pardoning power of the Governor does not extend to death sentence cases.

Chief Minister

The Chief Minister's position in the state is comparable to that of the Prime Minister at the centre.

Appointment	• Article 164 of the Constitution envisages that the Chief Minister shall be appointed by the Governor. • A leader of the party that has got the majority share of votes in the assembly elections, is appointed as the Chief Minister of the state.
Term of the CM	• The Chief Minister is not fixed and he holds office during the pleasure of the Governor. • The State Legislative Assembly can also remove him by passing a vote of no-confidence against him.
Powers and Functions	**With Respect to Council of Ministers** • The Governor appoints only those persons as ministers who are recommended by the Chief Minister. • He allocates and reshuffles the portfolios among ministers. • He can bring about the collapse of the council of ministers by resigning from office, since the Chief Minister is the head of the council of ministers.

	With Respect to Governor • Under Article 167 of the Constitution, the Chief Minister acts as a link between the Governor and state council of ministers. • CM advises the Governor regarding the appointment of important officials like Advocate General, Chairman and members of the State Public Service Commission, State Election Commission, etc. **With Respect to State Legislature** • All the policies are announced by him on the floor of the house. • He recommends dissolution of legislative assembly to the Governor. **Other Functions** • He is the Chairman of the State Planning Board. • He acts as a Vice-chairman of the concerned zonal council by rotation, holding office for a period of one year at a time. • He is a member of the Inter-State Council and the Governing Council of NITI Aayog, both headed by the Prime minister.

State Council of Ministers

Article 163 – Council of Ministers to Aid and Advise Governor	• There shall be a Council of Ministers with the Chief Minister as the head to aid and advise the Governor in the exercise of his functions, except in so far as he is required to exercise his functions in his discretion.
Article 164 – Other Provisions as to Ministers	• The Chief Minister shall be appointed by the Governor and the other Ministers shall be appointed by the Governor on the advice of the Chief Minister. • The ministers shall hold office during the pleasure of the Governor. • The council of ministers shall be collectively responsible to the State Legislative Assembly. • A minister who is not a member of the state legislature for any period of six consecutive months shall cease to be a minister.
Article 166– Conduct of Business of the Government of a State	• All executive action of the Government of a State shall be expressed to be taken in the name of the Governor. • Orders and other instruments made and executed in the name of the Governor shall be authenticated in such manner as may be specified in rules to be made by the Governor. • Moreover, the validity of an order or instrument which is so authenticated shall not be called in question on the ground that it is not an order or instrument made or executed by the Governor. • The Governor shall make rules for the more convenient transaction of the business of the government of the state, and for the allocation among ministers of the said business.
Article 167–Duties of Chief Minister	It shall be the duty of the Chief Minister of each state: • To communicate to the Governor of the state all decisions of the council of ministers relating to the administration of the affairs of the state and proposals for legislation. • To furnish such information relating to the administration of the affairs of the state and proposals for legislation as the Governor may call for. • If the Governor so requires, to submit for the consideration of the council of ministers any matter on which a decision has been taken by a minister but which has not been considered by the council.
Article 177– Rights of Ministers as Respects the Houses	• Every minister shall have the right to speak and take part in the proceedings of the Assembly (and also the Council where it exists) and any Committee of the State Legislature of which he may be named a member. But he shall not be entitled to vote.

91st Constitutional Amendment ACT 2003

- The total number of ministers, including the Chief Minister, in the council of ministers in a state shall not exceed 15 percent of the total strength of the legislative assembly of that state.
- However, the number of ministers, including the Chief Minister, in a state shall not be less than 12.
- A member of either House of state legislature belonging to any political party who is disqualified on the ground of defection shall also be disqualified to be appointed as a minister.

Oath and Salary of Ministers

- The oath to every new minister is administered by the Governor of State.
- "Oath of Secrecy" of ministers should be replace by "Oath of Transparency" – Second ARC.
- **Salary:** The salaries and allowances of ministers shall be determined by the state legislature.

Dismissal of a Minister

- A Minister holds office during the pleasure of the Governor. Actually this pleasure is the consent of the Chief Minister.
- It is the Chief Minister who selects the members of his team. This power is given to the Chief Minister to uphold the Collective Responsibility in the legislature.
- No person shall be retained as a member of council, if the Chief Minister wants to dismiss a sitting member.

- If he loses elections.
- Cannot get elected or nominated (in case of Legislative Council) within 6 months.

Advocate General

- Article 165 has provided for the office of the Advocate General.
- Highest law officer in the state.

Appointment	• The advocate general is appointed by the Governor.
Qualification	• He must be a person who is qualified to be appointed a judge of a high court. • He must be a citizen of India. • He must have held a judicial office for ten years or been an advocate of a high court for ten years.
Term of office	• The term of office of the Advocate General is not fixed by the Constitution. • He holds office during the pleasure of the Governor. • He may also quit his office by submitting his resignation to the Governor.
Remuneration	• The remuneration of the advocate general is not fixed by the Constitution. • He receives such remuneration as the Governor may determine.

Duties and Functions

The duties of the advocate general include the following:

- To give advice to the government of the state upon such legal matters which are referred to him by the Governor.
- To perform such other duties of a legal character that are assigned to him by the Governor.
- To discharge the functions conferred on him by the Constitution or any other law.
- The Advocate General is entitled to appear before any court of law within the state.
- He has the right to speak and to take part in the proceedings of both the Houses of the state legislature but without a right to vote.
- He enjoys all the privileges and immunities that are available to a member of the state legislature.

Parliament

The Parliament is the legislative organ of a Union government and the Parliament of India is its supreme legislative body.

- It occupies a pre-eminent and central position in the Indian democratic political system due to the adoption of the Parliamentary form of Government ('Westminster' model of government).
- Articles 79 to 122 in Part V of the Constitution deal with the organisation, composition, duration, officers, procedures, privileges, powers and so on of the Parliament.

Organs of Parliament

- President (discussed) • Rajya Sabha • Lok Sabha

Rajya Sabha

It is the Upper House (Second Chamber or House of Elders) and it represents the states and union territories of the Indian Union.

- The Rajya Sabha is called the permanent House of the Parliament as it is never fully dissolved.
- The IV Schedule of the Indian Constitution deals with the allocation of seats in the Rajya Sabha to the states and UTs.

Composition	• The maximum strength of Rajya Sabha is 250 (Out of which 238 members are representatives of the states & UTs (elected indirectly) and 12 are nominated by the President). ■ The members nominated by the President are those who have special knowledge or practical experience in art, literature, science and social service.
Election of Representatives	• The representatives of states are elected by the members of state legislative assemblies. • Only three UTs (Delhi, Puducherry and Jammu and Kashmir) have representation in Rajya Sabha (others don't have enough population).
Functions	• Rajya Sabha has an important role of reviewing and altering the laws initiated by the Lok Sabha.
Powers	• State Related Matters: The Rajya Sabha provides representation to the States. Therefore, any matter that affects the States must be referred to it for its consent and approval. ■ If the Union Parliament wishes to remove/transfer a matter from the State list, the approval of the Rajya Sabha is necessary. • Additional All-India Services are being developed on the request of Rajya Sabha (Article 312).
Qualifications	• She/He should be a citizen of India and at least 30 years of age. ■ She/He should make an oath or affirmation stating that she/he will bear true faith and allegiance to the Constitution of India. ■ According to the Representation of People Act, 1951, she/he should be registered as a voter in the State from which she/he is seeking election to the Rajya Sabha. ➢ However, in 2003, a provision was made declaring, any Indian citizen can contest the Rajya Sabha elections irrespective of the State in which she/he resides.

Tenure	● Every member of Rajya Sabha enjoys a safe tenure of six years. ■ One-third of its members retire after every two years. They are entitled to contest again for the membership.
Officials	● The Vice-President of India is the ex-officio Chairman of the Rajya Sabha. She/He presides over the meetings of Rajya Sabha. ● In his absence the Deputy Chairman (elected by its members from amongst themselves) presides over the meeting of the House.

Lok Sabha (The House of the People)

It is the Lower House (First Chamber or Popular House) and it represents the people of India as a whole.

Composition	● The maximum strength of the Lok Sabha is fixed at 550 out of which 530 members are to be the representatives of the states and 20 of the UTs (current strength of Lok Sabha is 543). ● Earlier, the President also nominated two members from the Anglo-Indian community, but by the 95th Amendment Act, 2009, this provision was valid till 2020 only (ceased through 104th Constitutional Amendment Act, 2020).
Election of Representatives	● The representatives of states are directly elected by the people from the territorial constituencies in the states.
Functions	● Lok Sabha is to select the executive, a group of persons who work together to implement the laws made by the Parliament.
Powers	● **Power in Money Matters:** Lok Sabha exercises more powers in money matters (Money Bill). Once the Lok Sabha passes the budget of the government or any other money related law, the Rajya Sabha cannot reject it. ■ The Rajya Sabha can only delay it by 14 days or suggest changes in it, however, the former may or may not accept these changes. ● **Power over Council of Ministers:** The Lok Sabha controls the Council of Ministers. ■ If the majority of the Lok Sabha members say they have 'no confidence' in the Council of Ministers, all ministers including the Prime Minister, have to quit. ■ The Rajya Sabha does not have this power.
Qualifications	She/He should be not less than 25 years of age. ● She/He should declare through an oath or affirmation that she/he has true faith and allegiance in the Constitution and that she/he will uphold the sovereignty and integrity of India. ● She/He must possess such other qualifications as may be laid down by the Parliament by law and must be registered as a voter in any constituency in India. ● Person contesting from the reserved seat should belong to the Scheduled Caste or Scheduled Tribe.
Tenure	● The normal term of Lok Sabha is five years. But the President, on the advice of the Council of Ministers, may dissolve it before the expiry of five years. ■ In the case of national emergency, its term can be extended for one year at a time. But it will not exceed six months after the emergency is over.
Officials	The presiding officer of Lok Sabha is known as Speaker. ● She/He remains the Speaker even after Lok Sabha is dissolved till the next House elects a new Speaker in her/his place. ● In the speaker's absence, a Deputy Speaker (elected by the House) presides over the meetings.

Powers/Functions of Parliament

Legislative Functions: Only Parliament can make laws on the subjects of the Union List. Along with the State Legislatures, the Parliament is empowered to make laws on the Concurrent List.

Financial Functions: It is the custodian of the public money. The Government can neither impose any tax on the public nor spend the money without the approval of the Parliament.

- The budget is approved by the Parliament every year.

  Electoral Functions: It participates in the election of the President and Vice-President of India.
- The Lok Sabha elects its Speaker and Deputy Speaker and the Rajya Sabha elects its Deputy Chairman.

  Power of Removal: It can remove the President, Judges of the Supreme Court and High Courts through impeachment for violation of the Constitution.

  Amendment of the Constitution: Parliament can amend the Constitution provisions but cannot change the basic structure of the Constitution.

  Power over Executive: Parliament exercises control over the Executive through Question-hour, Zero hour, Calling attention notice, Adjournment motion etc.

Sessions of Parliament

- **Summoning**
- Summoning is the process of calling all members of the Parliament to meet.
- The summoning of Parliament is specified in Article 85 of the Constitution.
- The President summons each House of the Parliament from time to time.
- However, the maximum gap between two sessions of Parliament cannot be more than six months.
- **Sessions**
- **Budget Session:** Longest session, starts towards the end of January, and concludes by the end of April.
- **Monsoon Session:** Second session, usually begins in July and finishes in August.
- **Winter Session:** Third session, held from November to December.
- **Adjournment**
- An adjournment suspends the work in a sitting for a specified time, which may be hours, days or weeks.
- When the meeting is terminated without any definite time/date fixed for the next meeting, it is called Adjournment sine die.
- The power of adjournment as well as adjournment sine die lies with the presiding officer (Speaker or Chairman) of the House.
- **Prorogation**
- Unlike adjournment, Prorogation terminates a sitting as well as the session of the House.
- It is done by the President of India.
- Prorogation is different from the dissolution (of Lok Sabha).
- **Quorum**
- Quorum refers to the minimum number of the members required to be present for conducting a meeting of the house.
- The Constitution has fixed one-tenth strength as quorum for both Lok Sabha and Rajya Sabha.

Joint Session of Parliament

- The Constitution of India, under Article 108, provides for the joint sitting of the Lok Sabha and the Rajya Sabha, in order to break any deadlock between the two house.
- The joint sitting is called by the President and is presided over by the Lok Sabha Speaker.
- In the speaker's absence, the Deputy Speaker of the Lok Sabha presides over the meeting.
- In the absence of both, it is presided over by the Deputy Chairman of the Rajya Sabha.

Lame Duck Session: It refers to the last session of the existing Lok Sabha, after a new Lok Sabha has been elected.

- Those members of the existing Lok Sabha who could not get re-elected to the new Lok Sabha are called lame-ducks.

Devices of Parliamentary Proceedings

Type of bills

Public Bill

- It is introduced in the Parliament by a minister.
- It reflects the policies of the government (ruling party).
- It has a greater chance to be approved by the Parliament.
- Its rejection by the House amounts to the expression of want of parliamentary confidence in the government and may lead to its resignation.
- Its introduction in the House requires seven days' notice.
- It is drafted by the concerned department in consultation with the law department.

Private Bill:

- It is introduced by any member of Parliament other than a minister.
- It reflects the stand of the opposition party on public matters.
- It has lesser chance to be approved by the Parliament.
- Its rejection by the House has no implication on the parliamentary confidence in the government or its resignation.
- Its introduction in the House requires one month's notice.
- Its drafting is the responsibility of the member concerned.

Question Hour

- The first hour of every parliamentary sitting is termed as Question hour. It is mentioned in the Rules of Procedure of the House.

Starred questions	These are distinguished by an asterisk and require oral answers. Hence supplementary questions can follow.
Unstarred questions	It requires a written answer and hence, supplementary questions cannot follow.
Short notice questions	These are asked by giving a notice of less than ten days and are answered orally.

Zero Hour

- The zero hour starts immediately after the question hour.
- Under this, the Members of Parliament (MPs) can raise matters without any prior notice.

Half-an-Hour Discussion

- Discussing a matter of sufficient public importance.
- The Speaker can allot three days in a week for such discussions. There is no formal motion or voting before the House.

Short Duration Discussion

- It is also known as two-hour discussion as the time allotted for such a discussion should not exceed two hours.
- The Speaker can allot two days in a week for such discussions. There is neither a formal motion before the house nor voting.
- This device has been in existence since 1953.

Legislative Procedure in Parliament

- The legislative procedure is identical in both the Houses of Parliament. Every bill has to pass through the same stages in each House.
- **Motions:** To express opinions on various issues by ministers/private members 3 principal categories of motions

- **Substantive Motion:** Matter like Impeachment of president, removal of chief election commissioner.
- **Substitute Motion:** Moved in substitute to original motion and passes alternative to it.
- **Subsidiary Motion:** Reference to original motion.
- **Closure Motion:** To cut short debate on provisions of bills Kangaroo closure- only important clause taken for debate and voting, other clauses skipped Guillotine closure- Undiscussed clauses of bill put to vote along discussed clauses due to matter of time.
- **Privilege Motion:** Concerned with breach of parliamentary privileges by Minister- by withholding facts or giving wrong facts, used against Minister.
- **Calling Attention Motion:** To call attention of minister on matter of urgent public importance, it is Indian innovation to parliamentary procedure, it is mentioned in Rules of procedure.
- **Adjourned Motion:** To draw attention of house to definite matter of urgent public importance, It is an Extraordinary device as interrupts normal business of house, It is used only In Lok Sabha- RS is not permitted to use this motion.
- **No Confidence Motion:** This motion is not mentioned in Constitution, In Lok Sabha, removal of minister by passing this motion, Motion needs support of 50 members to be admitted, there is no need to state reasons for adoption of this motion, this motion can be moved against entire council, if passed in LS then council of minister Must resign.
- **Censure Motion:** There is need to state the reason for adoption of this motion, Can be moved against individual or group of ministers, it means censuring council for specific policies, if passed in LS then entire Council of Ministers need not to Resign from office.
- **Motion of Thanks:** President addresses motion of thanks in the first session after every general election and first session of every fiscal year, It is discussed in both houses, Motion outlines Government Policies, Motion Must be passed otherwise it amounts defeat of Government.
- **Point of Order:** Members can raise point of order when proceedings of house do not follow normal rule of procedure, Usually Leader of Opposition raise this device, It is an extraordinary device.
- **Special Mention:** A matter which is cannot be raised during any other rules of business, can be raised in special Mention in Rajyasabha, it is equivalent to notice device of Loksabha.
- **Resolutions:** Private member Resolution discussed on alternative Fridays, Government Resolution moved by ministers from Monday to Thursday, All Resolution came in category of substantive motion, All motions need not to be voted upon but all Resolutions required to Voted upon.
- **Bill:** A bill is a proposal for legislation that becomes an act or law when duly enacted.

■ **Types of Bills:** Bills introduced in the Parliament are of two kinds, public bills (government bills) and private bills.

■ **Classification:** The bills introduced in the Parliament can be classified into four categories:

➢ **Ordinary bills:** Concerned with any matter other than financial subjects.

➢ **Money bills:** Concerned with financial matters like taxation, public expenditure, etc.

➢ **Financial bills:** Concerned with financial matters (but are different from Money bills).

➢ **Constitution Amendment Bills:** Concerned with the amendment of the provisions of the Constitution.

Difference between Money bills and Financial Bills

Characteristics	Money Bills	Financial Bills	
		Financial Bill-I	Financial Bill-II
Constitutional Provisions	Article 110 deals with money bills.	Article 117(1) deals with Finance Bill.	Article 117(3) deals with Finance Bills-II.
	Deals 'only' with the provisions of Article 110.	Also deals with matters of general legislation (along with provisions of Article 110).	Contains provisions involving expenditure from Consolidated Fund of India but are not included in Article 110.
Certification of Speaker	He decides whether a bill is a money bill or not.	No Certification required.	No Certification required.
Introduced in	Only in Lok Sabha.	Only in Lok Sabha.	In both houses.
President's Recommendation	Required	Required.	Not required.
Bills in Rajya Sabha	Cannot be amended or rejected.	Can be amended or rejected.	Can be amended or rejected.
President's Power	Can either accept or reject a money bill but cannot return it for reconsideration.	Can return it for reconsideration.	Can return it for reconsideration.
Joint Sitting of the Houses	No provision to resolve the deadlock.	The President can summon.	The President can summon.

Constitutional Amendment Bills

- **About:** As per the Constitution of India, Constitution Amendment Bills can be of three types requiring:
  - A Simple majority for their passage in each House.
  - A Special majority for their passage in each House.
  - A Special majority for their passage and ratification by Legislatures of not less than one-half of the States by resolutions to that effect passed by those Legislatures.
- **House of Introduction:** Under Article 368, it can be introduced in either House of Parliament and has to be passed by each House by special majority.
  - There is no provision of joint sittings on a Constitution Amending Bill (or in a Money Bill).

Joint Sitting of Two Houses

- Joint sitting is extraordinary machinery provided by the Constitution to resolve a deadlock between the two Houses over the passage of a bill.
- The provision of joint sitting is applicable to ordinary bills or financial bills only and not to money bills or Constitutional amendment bills.
- The Speaker of Lok Sabha presides over a joint sitting of the two Houses and the Deputy Speaker, in his absence.

Parliament Committees

Parliamentary committee means a committee that:

- Is appointed or elected by the House or nominated by the Speaker/Chairman.
- Works under the direction of the Speaker / Chairman
- Presents its report to the House or to the Speaker / Chairman.
- Has a secretariat provided by the Lok Sabha / Rajya Sabha.

The consultative committees, which also consist of members of Parliament, are not parliamentary committees as they do not fulfill above four conditions.

Financial Committee	**PUBLIC ACCOUNTS COMMITTEE** ● 22 members (15 (Lok Sabha) + 7 (Rajya Sabha)). ● Term (1 year), No membership of minister, Chairman appointed by Speaker, Chairman from opposition (Convention). ● Functions. ■ Scrutinize CAG report on Appropriation and Revenue. **ESTIMATES COMMITTEE** ● 30 Members (Lok Sabha). ● Members elected by Proportional representation, Term (1 year), No Membership of minister, Chairman appointed by Speaker. ● Function. ■ Scrutinizes the Estimates Presented in the Budget. **COMMITTEE ON PUBLIC UNDERTAKING** ● 22 members (15 Lok Sabha + 7 Rajya Sabha). ● Functions. ■ Scrutinize CAG report on public undertakings.
Departmentally Related Standing Committees (DRSC's)	● 24 Committees – 16 Lok Sabha + 8 Rajya Sabha (21 Lok Sabha + 10 Rajya Sabha – members). ● DRSC in LS – Agriculture, Chemical and Fertilizers, Coal and Steel, Defense, Energy, External Affairs, Finance, Food, Consumer Affairs and Public Distribution, Information Technology, Labor, Petroleum and Natural Gas, Railways, Rural Development, Social Justice and empowerment, Urban Development, Water Resources. ● DRSC in RS – Commerce, Health and family welfare, Home affair, Human resource development, Industry, Personnel, Public grievance, Law and justice, Science and technology, Environment, Forest and climate change, Transport, Tourism and culture. **Functions** ● Examine the bills referred to them. ● Examine the implementation of various policies. ● Examine budgeting outlays for department.
Ad Hoc Committees	● Temporary in nature. ● Dissolved after their purpose is served. **Example:** Joint Parliamentary Committee, select committee etc.
Administrative Committees/ Standing Committee (Others)	● **Business advisory committee:** Help the presiding officer in the planning of the business of the house. ● **Committee on government assurance:** Make govt. accountable on any assurance given in the house of the parliament. ● **Committee on subordinate legislations:** Ensure executive accountability on various subordinate legislations. ● **Privilege committee:** Any question/ motion of privilege are generally referred to the committee. ● **Rules committee:** Frames the rules of the house, procedure and conduct of the house. ● **Ethics committee:** Oversees moral and ethical conduct of members, prepares code of conduct for members, looks into cases of alleged breach of code of conduct.

	• **General purpose committee:** To look into and advice on those matters referred to by the presiding officer from time to time.

Parliamentary Forums

The purpose of the Parliamentary Forums is to provide members information and knowledge on specific problems of national interest, as well as to assist them in taking a result-oriented approach to relevant issues.

Composition of the Parliamentary Forums

- Except for the Parliamentary Forum on Population and Public Health, where the Chairman of Rajya Sabha is the ex-officio President and the Speaker is the ex-officio Co-President, all Forums have an ex-officio President.
- The ex-officio Vice-Presidents of the respective forums are the Deputy Chairman of Rajya Sabha, the Deputy Speaker of Lok Sabha, the concerned Ministers, and the Chairman of department-related Standing Committees..
- Each forum has a maximum of 31 participants (excluding the President, Co-President, and Vice-President).
- Members of the forum serve for the same amount of time as their membership in the respective Houses.
- By writing to the Speaker and Chairman, a member may also resign from the forum.

Parliamentary Forum on Water Conservation and Management (2005)	• To identify water-related issues and propose recommendations for consideration and appropriate action by the relevant governments and organizations.
Parliamentary Forum on Youth (2006)	• To have focused deliberations on strategies to leverage human capital in the youth for accelerating development initiatives.
Parliamentary Forum on Children (2006)	• To provide an organized forum for Parliamentarians to exchange ideas, perspectives, experiences, and expert practices in regard to children through workshops, seminars, and orientation programs, among other things.
Parliamentary Forum on Population and Public Health (2006)	• To raise public understanding on propulsion control and public health in all segments of society, particularly at the grass-roots level.
Parliamentary Forum on Global Warming and Climate Change (2008)	• To identify issues related to global warming and climate change, and to give suggestions/ recommendations for consideration and appropriate action by the government/ organizations responsible in order to decrease the extent of global warming.
Parliamentary Forum on Disaster Management (2011)	• To hold seminars/workshops to raise awareness among Members of Parliament on the causes and effects of disasters.
Parliamentary Forum on Artisans and Crafts-people (2013)	• To raise Parliamentarians' awareness of and attention to crucial issues facing artisans and crafts people so that traditional art and crafts can be preserved and promoted through various channels.
Parliamentary Forum on Millennium Development Goals (2013)	• To provide Parliamentarians, a platform to engage with civil society on issues related to the Millennium Development Goals, such as poverty eradication, hunger alleviation, universal education, women's empowerment, HIV/AIDS, Malaria, and other diseases, and the development of a long-term development partnership.

Parliamentary Groups

Indian Parliamentary Group (IPG) was established as an autonomous entity in 1949, following a decision passed by the Constituent Assembly (Legislative) on August 16, 1948.

Composition	• The Speaker of the Lok Sabha is the ex-officio President of the group. • The deputy Speaker of Lok Sabha and the deputy chairman of Rajya Sabha are the ex-officio vice president of the group. • The secretary general of Lok Sabha acts as the ex- officio secretary general of the group.
Objectives of the group	• To promote personal contacts between members of the Parliament of India. • To study questions of public importance that are likely to come up before the Parliament, arrange seminars, discussions and orientation courses, and bring out publications for the dissemination of information to the members of the group. • To arrange lectures on political, defence, economics, social and educational problems by the members of Parliament and distinguished persons. • To arrange visas to foreign countries with a view to develop contacts with members of other Parliaments.

Functions	• The group acts as a link between the Parliament of Indian and the various parliaments of the world. • Seminars and symposium on parliamentary subjects are organized periodically at national as well as international levels. • Members of the Group, when visiting abroad are given letters of introduction to the Secretaries of the National Groups of the IPU and Secretaries of the CPA branches. • Only Members of the Parliamentary Group for at least six months standing at the time of the composition of the delegation, may be included in the Indian Parliamentary Delegations.

Inter Parliamentary Union (IPU)

The Inter Parliamentary Union is an international organisation of parliaments of sovereign states. At Present, the IPU consists of 183 Member Parliaments and 15 Associate Members.

State Legislature

Articles 168 to 212 in Part VI of the Constitution deal with the organisation, composition, duration, officers, procedures, privileges, powers and so on of the state legislature.

Article 168: Constitution of Legislatures in States.	• Governor. • Legislature Assembly. • Legislative council (Only in certain States).
Article 169: Abolition or Creation of Legislative Council.	• Parliament may by law provide for the abolition of the Legislative Council of a State having such a Council or for the creation of such a Council in a State having no such Council, if the Legislative Assembly of the State passes a resolution with special majority. • Not to be considered a Constitutional Amendment Act under Article 368.
Article 170: Composition of Legislative Assembly.	• Not more than 500, or less than 60 Members, Direct Election from territorial Constituencies. • 1971 census – Number of seats in Legislative Assembly. • 2001 census – Adjustment of territorial constituencies. • The delimitation of constituencies has been frozen until the first census after 2026 (under the 84th Amendment Act, 2001, as subsequently extended).
Article 171: Composition of Legislative Council.	• Not more than 1/3rd of Members of the Legislative Assembly and not less than 40. • Composition (Under Parliament otherwise Provides). • **Electoral College** ■ 1/3rd Electorates Comprising member of municipalities, District boards and other Local Authorities (Parliament may by law specify). ■ 1/3rd Elected by members of Legislative Assembly. ■ 1/12th by Electorates consisting of graduates (3 years in possession of degree). ■ 1/12th of electorates consisting of teachers not less than Secondary level. ■ 1/6th nominated by Governor.
Article 172: Duration of State Legislatures.	Legislative Assembly of every State: 5 years. • During the Emergency a period can be extended one year at one time but not exceed six months after the Proclamation has ceased to operate. The Legislative Council of a State shall not be subject to dissolution.
Article 173: Qualification for membership of the State Legislature.	• Citizen of India. • For the Legislative Assembly, not less than twenty-five years of age and, in the case of a seat in the Legislative Council, not less than thirty years of age. • Possesses such other qualifications as may be prescribed in that behalf by or under any law made by Parliament.

Judiciary

India is a federal State with a single and unified judicial system with three-tier structure- SUPREME COURT (at top), HIGH COURT (at state/s level) and SUBORDINATE COURTS (at district level).

Supreme Court

- **Regulating Act of 1773:** Established the Supreme Court of Judicature at Calcutta as a Court of Record, with full power & authority.
- **GoI Act 1935:** Federal Court of India with jurisdiction to solve disputes between provinces and federal states and hear appeals against Judgements from High Courts.
- Integrated judicial system adopted from the GoI Act of 1935.
- Supreme Court of India- came into existence on 26 January 1950 (first sitting was held on 28 January 1950).

Constitutional Provisions	• Part V (The Union) and Chapter 6 (The Union Judiciary). • Part V spanning from Article 124 to Article 147. • 124 (1)– There shall be a Supreme Court of India constituting of a Chief Justice of India and, until PARLIAMENT by law prescribes a larger number, of not more than seven other Judges. (1+7). • Supreme Court (Number of Judges) Act of 2019 has added four judges to increase the judicial strength from 31 to 34 including the Chief Justice of India.

	• The Supreme Court (Number of Judges) Amendment Ordinance, 2026 was promulgated by President Droupadi Murmu, increasing the sanctioned strength of the Supreme Court of India from 34 to 38 judges. • Supreme Court is guarantor of the Fundamental Right of the citizens and guardian of the Constitution. • Parliament is authorised to regulate organisation, independence, jurisdiction, powers, procedures of Supreme Court.
Seat of Supreme Court	• Delhi is the seat of the **Supreme Court** as per the constitution. • However, the Constitution empowers the Chief Justice of India to declare other cities as seats of the Supreme Court with the prior permission of the President of India.
Appointment of Judges	• The judges of the Supreme Court are appointed by the President. • The Chief justice is appointed by the President after consultation with such judges of the Supreme Court and High Court as he deems necessary. • The other judges of the Supreme Court are appointed by the President after consultation with the Chief justice and such other judges of the Supreme Court. • The consultation with the Chief justice is obligatory in the case of appointment of a judge other than Chief Justice.
Collegium System of Supreme Court	• The Collegium system was evolved through three landmark cases (1982, 1993, 1998) and has been in practice in its current form since 1993, with the collegium composition finalized in 1998. • It is used for appointments and transfers of judges in High Court and Supreme Court . • No mention of the Collegium either in the original Constitution of India or in successive amendments. • Supreme Court collegium – Headed by the Chief Justice of India and comprises four other senior most judges of the Supreme court (1+4).
Evolution of Collegium System	• **First judges case (1982):** The court held that consultation does not mean concurrence and it only implies exchange of views. • **Second judges case (1993):** The court reversed its earlier ruling and changed the meaning of the word consultation to concurrence. Hence, it ruled that the advice tendered by the Chief Justice of India is binding on the President in matters of appointment of Supreme Court judges. But any such advice would be tendered after Chief Justice of India consults with two of his most senior-judges. It was also decided in the case that the President should appoint the senior-most judge in the Supreme Court as the Chief Justice of India. • **Third judges case (1998):** The consultation process to be employed should be based on plurality of judges. He should consult a collegium of four senior-most judges before making a recommendation to the President and even if two judges give an adverse opinion, he should not send the recommendation to the President.
Qualification of judges	• He should be a citizen of India. • He should have been judge of a High Court for five years, or He should have been an advocate of a High Court for ten years. • He should be distinguished jurist in the opinion of the President. • Oath: It is administered by the President of India or some person appointed by him for this purpose.
Tenure of judges	• He holds office until he attains the age of 65 years. Any questions pertaining to his age will be determined by such authority as decided by Parliament. • He can resign his office by writing to the President. • He can be removed from his office by the President on the recommendation of the Parliament.
Salaries and allowances of the judges	• They are determined by the Parliament. • The salaries and emoluments of the judges cannot be varied to their disadvantage after their appointment except during the financial emergency.
Article 127: Ad hoc judge	• When there is a lack of quorum, the Chief Justice of India can appoint a judge of High Court to the Supreme Court bench. • Such a step can be taken only with the prior permission of the President and consultation with the Chief Justice of the concerned High Court. • While performing this duty, the newly appointed judge receives the salary, powers and privileges of a judge of the Supreme Court.

Retired judges	• The Chief Justice of India can request a retired judge of the Supreme Court or retired judge of the Hight Court to act as a judge of the Supreme Court for a temporary period. • He can take this step after getting consent from the President of India and also of the person to be so appointed. • The appointed person in this case will receive such salary and allowances as determined by the President of India.
Removal of Judges	• By an order of President, • A removal motion needs to be passed in both the Houses of the Parliament by a special majority in the same session, • On grounds of proved misbehavior or incapacity. • Parliament may provide by law to regulate the procedure for the presentation and address and investigation of such charges. • The Judges Enquiry Act (1968) regulates the procedure relating to the removal of a judge of the Supreme Court by the process of impeachment: • No judge of the Supreme Court has been impeached so far.
Independence of the Supreme Court	• **Security of Tenure:** Once appointed, the judges cannot be removed from the office except by an order of the President on the ground of proven misbehavior and incapacity (Articles 124 and 217). • The salaries and allowances of the judges are fixed and are not subject to a vote of the legislature. • **Powers and Jurisdiction of Supreme Court:** Parliament can only add to the powers and jurisdiction of the Supreme Court but cannot curtail them. • No discussion in the Parliament and legislature of the state with respect to the conduct of any judge of the Supreme Court or of a High Court in the discharge of his duties. • Both the Supreme Court and the High Court have the power to punish any person for their contempt.

Jurisdiction and Powers of Supreme Court

Article 131: Original jurisdiction of the Supreme Court	The Supreme Court shall, to the exclusion of any other court, have original jurisdiction in any dispute: • between the Government of India and one or more States, or. • between the Government of India and any State on one side and one or more other States on the other, or. • between two or more States. **However, this jurisdiction does not extend in the following situations:** • A dispute arising out of any pre-Constitution treaty, agreement, covenant, engagement, sanad or other similar instrument. • A dispute arising out of any treaty, agreement, etc., which specifically provides that the said jurisdiction does not extend to such a dispute. • Inter-state water disputes. • Matters referred to the Finance Commission. • Adjustment of certain expenses and pensions between the Centre and the states. • Ordinary dispute of Commercial nature between the Centre and the states. • Recovery of damages by a state against the Centre.
Article 132: Appellate jurisdiction of Supreme Court in appeals from High Court in certain cases	• Appeals in civil cases. Disputes relating to property, marriage, money, contract and service etc. are called civil cases. • Appeals in criminal cases. ▪ If a High Court sets aside an appeal or an order of acquittal passed by a lower court and awards a death sentence to the accused, he may bring an appeal to the Supreme Court by right. ▪ Appeal can also be made to the Supreme Court if the High Court withdraws a case from a lower court to itself, declares the accused guilty and awards death sentence. In this situation appeals can be made as a matter of right and without certificate from the High Court. • Appeals in constitutional cases. It is a case arising out of different interpretations of the Constitution, mainly regarding the fundamental rights. In such Constitutional Cases an appeal can be taken to the Supreme Court only if a High Court certifies that the matter in dispute involves a substantial question of law.

	• Appeal by special leave (Article 136). Supreme Court is authorized to grant in its discretion special leave to appeal from any judgment in any matter passed by any court or tribunal in the country (except in the case of military tribunal). Some of the aspects related to this power are: • It is a discretionary power and hence cannot be claimed as a matter of right. • It can be granted in any judgment-final or interlocutory. • It can be related to any matter. • It can be granted against any court (except the military tribunal).
Writ Jurisdiction	• If there is a violation of fundamental rights a person under Article 32 can ask the Supreme Court to issue writs. • But this applies only if the fundamental rights of a person are infringed.
Advisory jurisdiction	The Constitution under Article 143 authorizes the President to seek the opinion of the Supreme Court in the two categories of matters: • On any question of law or fact of public importance which has arisen or which is likely to arise. • On any dispute arising out of any pre-constitution treaty, agreement, covenant, engagement, sanad or other similar instruments. The court may refuse to give its advice on the first matter, while it is bound to give advice in the second matter. In case, the advice or the opinion of the Court is sent to the President, he may or may not accept it. The advice of the Court is not binding on the President. So far, whenever the Court has given its advice, the President has always accepted it.
Court of Record	• All the proceedings of the Supreme Court are recorded and assume the form of case law. Such decisions are binding on all courts in India.
Contempt of Court	**Contempt of court can be of two kinds** • Civil, which is the willful disobedience of a court order or judgment or willful breach of an undertaking given to a court. • Criminal, that is written or spoken words or any act that scandalizes the court or lowers its authority or prejudices or interferes with the due course of a judicial proceeding or interferes/obstructs the administration of justice'.
	• Article 129 and 215 of the Constitution of India empowers the Supreme Court and High Court respectively to punish people for their respective contempt.

High Courts

- The institution of the High Court originated in India in 1862 when the High Courts were set up at Bombay, Calcutta and Madras.
- The constitution of India provides a high court for each state, however, the Parliament is authorized to declare a common High Court for two or more states.
- The Parliament has been empowered to extend or curtail the jurisdiction of a High Court over a Union Territory.

Organization of a High Court	• The number of judges in a high court unlike Supreme Court is decided by the President of India rather than the parliament.
Appointment of HC Judges	• Article 217 of the Constitution: It states that the Judge of a High Court shall be appointed by the President in consultation with the Chief Justice of India (CJI) and the Governor of the State. • In case of appointment of other judges to High Court, it was opined that CJI should consult a collegium of two senior-most judges of the Supreme Court before recommending a name to the President of India in the third judges case.
Collegium System of HC	• A High Court collegium is led by its Chief Justice and four other senior most judges of that court. • Names recommended for appointment by a HC collegium reaches the government only after approval by the Chief Justice of India and the Supreme Court collegium.
Qualification of judges	• He should be a citizen of India. • He should have held a judicial office in the territory of India for ten years or. • He should have been an advocate of a High Court for ten years.
Tenure of judges	• The Constitution has not fixed the tenure of a judge of a High Court. • He holds office until he attains the age of 62 years (65 years in case of Supreme Court). Any questions regarding his age are to be decided by the President after consultation with the Chief Justice of India and the decision of the President is final (Determine by parliament in case of Supreme Court). • Resignation – By writing to the President.

	• He can be removed from his office by the President on the recommendation of the Parliament.
Removal of judges	• The process of impeachment of a High Court judge is similar to that of a judge of Supreme Court.
Salaries and allowances	• Salaries and allowances are determined by the parliament and cannot be varied to the detriment of the judges once they are appointed. However, this does not apply during the times of financial emergency. **Note:** Though the salary of a judge is charged on the consolidated fund of the state, the pension is charged on the consolidated fund of India.
Transfer of judges	• **Constitutional provisions:** Transfer of Judges from one High Court to another High Court is made by the President after consultations with the Chief Justice of India under Article 222 (1) of the Constitution.
Additional and acting judges	The President can appoint duly qualified persons as additional judges of a High Court for a temporary period (not exceeding two years) when: • There is a temporary increase in the business of the High Court. • There are arrears of work in the High Court. The President can also appoint a duly qualified person as an acting judge of a High Court when a judge of that High Court is: • Unable to perform the duties of his office due to absence or any other reasons, or • Appointed to act temporarily as Chief Justice of that High Court. In both the cases, the additional or acting judge cannot hold office beyond 62 years of age.
Independence of High Court	• Mode of appointment. • **Security of tenure:** They can be removed in the same manner as Supreme Court judges. • Fixed service conditions. • Expenses charged on Consolidated Fund. • Conduct of judges cannot be discussed in state legislature. • Ban on practice after retirement: The retired permanent judges of a high court are prohibited from pleading or acting in any court or before any authority in India except the Supreme Court and the other High Courts. • Power to punish for its contempt. • Freedom to appoint its staff. • Its jurisdiction cannot be curtailed: ■ The jurisdiction and powers provided by the Constitution to High Court cannot be curtailed by either the Parliament or the state legislature. ■ However, the jurisdiction and powers of a high court can be changed both by the Parliament and the state legislature.

Jurisdiction of High Court

Original jurisdiction of High Court	• Original jurisdiction entails power of High Court to hear disputes in the first instances (applicant can directly go to the High Court not by the way of appeal). • It is mostly applicable for cases related to the election disputes of State Legislative Assembly and parliament, marriages, enforcement of Fundamental Right (Article 226), revenue matters, contempt of court and transfer cases from other courts.
Writ jurisdiction	• Constitution under Article 226 of the empowers a High Court to issue writs including Habeas Corpus, Mandamus, Certiorari, Prohibition and Quo warranto for the enforcement of the Fundamental Right and "for any other purpose" (enforcement of an ordinary legal right). • **Chandra Kumar case (1997):** The Supreme Court ruled that writ jurisdiction of both the High Court and Supreme Court constitute a part of the basic structure of the Constitution.
Appellate Jurisdiction	The appellate jurisdiction of the High Court extends to both civil and criminal cases. • In civil cases, its jurisdiction extends to cases decided by Courts of Munsifs and District judges. • In the criminal cases it extends to cases decided by Sessions and Additional Sessions Judges.
Supervisory Jurisdiction	• High Court has the power of superintendence over all courts and tribunals functioning in its territorial jurisdiction (except military courts or tribunals). • The supervisory power of a High Court is very broad. It extends to all courts and tribunals whether they are subject to the appellate jurisdiction of the High Court or not. • It covers administrative

	• superintendence as well as judicial superintendence. • It is a revisional jurisdiction. • It can be suo-motu (on its own) and not necessarily on the application of a party.
Court Of Record (Article 215)	• It involves recording the judgments, proceedings and acts of High Court for perpetual memory. • These records are admitted to be of evidentiary value and cannot be questioned when produced before any subordinate court. They are recognised as legal precedents and legal references.

Erosion of High Court's Jurisdiction in recent times Due to Tribunalization

- Tribunals have replaced High Courts for disputes under the Companies Act, Competition Act, SEBI Act, Electricity Act and Consumer Protection Act among others.
- Any person aggrieved by an order of an appellate tribunal can directly appeal to the Supreme Court, side-stepping the High Court.

Subordinate Courts

- Appointment of District Judges (Article 233).
- Appointment to district judge is made by the Governor in consultation with the High Court of the concerned state.
- Criteria – At Least 7 years an advocate (recommended by High Court).
- Recruitment of persons other than District Judges to the Judicial Service (Article 234).
- Appointment of persons other than District judges, shall be made by the Governor (Sub judicial service) in accordance with rules made by him in consultation with the State Public Service Commission and concerned High Court.

Local Government

- Local Self Government is the management of local affairs by such local bodies who have been elected by the local people.
- The local self-Government includes both rural and urban government.
- It is the third level of the government.
- There are 2 types of local government in operation – panchayats in rural areas and Municipalities in urban areas.

Panchayati Raj

- Panchayati Raj Institution (PRI) is a system of rural local self-government in India.
- PRI was constitutionalized through the 73rd Constitutional Amendment Act, 1992 to build democracy at the grass roots level and was entrusted with the task of rural development in the country.
- This act has added a new Part-IX to the Constitution of India. This part is entitled as 'The Panchayats' and consists of provisions from Articles 243 to 243 O.
- In addition, the act has also added a new Eleventh Schedule to the Constitution. This schedule contains 29 functional items of the panchayats. It deals with Article 243-G.

Municipalities

- Urban Local Governments were established with the purpose of democratic decentralisation.
- There are eight types of urban local governments in India – Municipal Corporation, Municipality, Notified Area Committee, Town Area Committee, Cantonment Board, Township, Port trust, Special purpose agency.
- The 74th Amendment Act pertaining to urban local government was passed during the regime of P. V. Narsimha Rao's government in 1992. It came into force on 1st June, 1993.
- Added Part IX -A and consists of provisions from articles 243-P to 243-ZG.
- Added 12th Schedule to the Constitution. It contains 18 functional items of Municipalities and deals with Article 243 W.

Committees formed to materialize PRIs

- **Balwant Rai Mehta Committee (1957).**
  - Recommended a three-tier Panchayat Raj institutional structure consisting of Gram Panchayat, Panchayat Samiti and Zila Parishad.
- **Ashok Mehta Committee (1977)**
  - Recommended a two-tier Panchayat Raj institutional structure consisting of Zilla Parishad and Mandal Panchayat.
- **G. V. K. Rao Committee (1985)**
  - Recommended making the "District" as the basic unit of planning and also holding regular elections.
- **L. M. Singhvi Committee (1986)**
  - Recommended providing more financial resources and constitutional status to the panchayats to strengthen them.

Constitutional/Non-Constitutional Bodies

Constitutional Bodies

Election Commission of India

The Constitution provides the Election Commission of India with the power of direction, superintendence and control of elections to Parliament, State Legislatures, the office of President of India and the office of Vice-president of India.

- Permanent, independent body established under Article 324.
- The body consists of one Chief Election Commissioner (CEC) and such members as the President may fix. Appointments of CEC and Election commissioners are is also done by the President. Currently there are 2 Election Commissioners (EC) in addition to the CEC.
- The CEC and ECs have the same powers and emoluments including salaries, which are the same as a Supreme Court judge.
- The constitution doesn't mention any qualification for either of the commissioners, nor does it restrict retiring commissioners from taking further appointments under the government.
- They hold the office for a period of 6 years or till 65, whichever is earlier.

- The Chief Election Commissioner and Other Election Commissioners (Appointment, Conditions of Service and Term of Office) Act, 2023 changed the appointment process significantly. Under this Act, the selection committee now comprises: (1) Prime Minister, (2) a Union Cabinet Minister nominated by PM, and (3) Leader of Opposition in Lok Sabha — replacing the earlier convention where the Supreme Court Chief Justice was part of the process (as recommended by the Supreme Court in Anoop Baranwal case, 2023).
- The Chief Election Commissioner cannot be removed except in the same manner as judge of the Supreme Court.
- The other commissioners can be removed only after advice of the Chief Election Commissioner.
- It must be noted here that the election commission is not concerned with the elections to panchayats and municipalities in the states. For this, the Constitution of India provides for a separate State Election Commission. It conducts elections to Panchayats Bodies and Urban Local Bodies in accordance with 73rd and 74th Constitutional Amendments.

Powers and Functions	• To decide the territorial areas of the electoral constituencies throughout the country on the basis of the Delimitation Commission Act of Parliament. • Preparing and periodically revising electoral rolls and registering all eligible voters. • To act as a court for settling disputes related to granting of recognition to political parties and allotment of election symbol to them. • It issues the Model Code of Conduct in every election for political parties and candidates so that the decorum of democracy is maintained. • To advise the President and the Governors relating to disqualification of MPs or MLAs. • Advising the President on whether elections can be held in a state that is under the President's rule, in order to extend the period of emergency after 1 year.

Comptroller and Auditor General of India (CAG)

- Article 148 of the Constitution provides for an independent Comptroller and Auditor General of India.
- Appointed by the President for a period of 6 years or up to the age of 65 years, whichever is earlier.
- He can be removed from his office in the same manner as a judge of the Supreme Court (on the grounds of proved misbehavior).
- His salary and terms of service cannot be altered to his disadvantage after his appointment.
- Not eligible for further office under Government of India or under the Government of state.
- Office expenses, salaries and allowances of members of the office, charged on the Consolidated Fund of India.
- Article 149 deals with Duties and Powers of the Comptroller and Auditor-General of India.
- Article 150 says that the accounts of the Union and of the States shall be kept in such form as the President may on the advice of the CAG prescribe.
- Article 151 says that the reports of the Comptroller and Auditor-General of India relating to the accounts of the Union shall be submitted to the President, who shall cause them to be laid before each House of Parliament.
- **Article 279:** Calculation of "net proceeds" is ascertained and certified by the Comptroller and Auditor-General of India, whose certificate is final.
- His administrative powers and the conditions of service of persons serving in the Indian Audit and Accounts Department are prescribed by the President only after consulting him.

Functions and Power of CAG	• **CAG derives its audit mandate from different sources like** ▪ Constitution (Articles 148 to 151). ▪ The CAG (Duties, Powers and Conditions of Service) Act, 1971. ▪ Important Judgments. ▪ Instructions of Government of India. ▪ Regulations on Audit and Accounts-2007. • CAG audits the accounts related to all expenditure from: ▪ Consolidated Fund of India,. ▪ Consolidated Fund of each state and UT's having a legislative assembly. • He audits all expenditure from the Contingency Fund of India and the Public Account of India as well as the Contingency Fund and Public Account of each state. • He audits departments of the Central Government and the state governments and all bodies and authorities substantially financed from the Central or State revenues, government companies, other corporations and bodies, when so required by related laws. • He audits the accounts of any other authority when requested by the President or Governor example, Local bodies. • He submits his audit reports relating to the accounts of the Centre to the President, who shall, in turn, place them before both the houses of Parliament (To Governor in states). • CAG also acts as a guide, friend and philosopher of the Public Accounts Committee of the Parliament.

Union Public Service Commission (UPSC)

- Mandated to be the prime recruiting agency of the government of India.
- Consist of Chairman and other members as appointed by the President of India.
- The constitution doesn't specify the strength.
- Only mandating that half of the members should be people who've held office under the government of India or state for at least 10 years in the past.

- The chairman and member hold office until the age of 65 years or 6 years from the date of appointment, whichever is earlier.
- Removal by the President for:
  - Getting adjudged insolvent,
  - Engaging in Paid employment outside the office or,
  - Is of infirm mind in the opinion of the President, and
  - Misbehavior, however in this case, a formal Supreme Court enquiry is needed.
- The salary and term of office cannot be varied to the members' disadvantage.
- The chairman of UPSC is not eligible for any future appointment under the union or the state, the member can be however appointed as the chairman.

Functions	• The UPSC conducts examinations for All-India Services Central Services and Public Services for different Indian states and Union territories. • The UPSC serves the interests of the State on the demand of the Governor and with the consent of the President of India. • The UPSC shall be consulted in the matters of: ■ Demands for compensation of legal express obtained by a civil servant in defending proceedings instituted against him. ■ Matters relating to the interim appointments for period exceeding one year. ■ Matters of personnel management etc.

State Public Service Commission

- An independent constitutional body mandated to be the prime recruiting agency of the government of states.
- The SPSC's consist of chairman and other members as appointed by the Governor of the state.
- The chairman and member hold office until the age of 62 years or 6 years from the date of appointment, whichever is earlier.
- The Constitution specifically mandates the appointment to be done by the governor and the removal by the president of members and chairman alike.
- The chairman of SPSC is eligible for appointment under as member or chairperson of the UPSC, the members can be however appointed as the chairman of SPSC or member or chairperson of UPSC.

Joint State Public Service Commission

- The Constitution provides for the establishment of JPSC for two or more states.
- JPSC is created by an act of parliament on the request of the state legislature concerned, thus JPSC are statutory body and not a constitutional body.
- The chairman and the members are appointed by the President. They hold office for a period of 6 years or 62 years whichever is earlier.
- They can be suspended or removed by the President. The number of members and condition of service are determined by the President.

Finance Commission

- Article 280 provides for establishing a finance commission every 5 years by the President.
- Finance Commission is required to make recommendations to the President of India on issues:
  - Distribution of the net proceeds of taxes between the Centre and states.
  - The principles of grants-in-aid to states by the Centre.
  - It also provides advice on any other matter referred by the President.
- The commission consists of a Chairman and Four other members appointed by the President.
- The constitution authorizes the parliament to fix the qualification and as per the provisions contained in the Finance Commission [Miscellaneous Provisions] Act, 1951:
  - The chairman should be a person experienced in public affairs.
  - 4 Members:

• A judge of the High Court or one qualified to be appointed. • One who has specialised knowledge of finance and accounts of the govt. • One who has wide experience in financial matters and administration. • One who has special knowledge of economics.

- The tenure of the office of the Member of the Finance Commission is specified by the President of India and in some cases, the members are also re-appointed.
- The role of Finance Commission is purely advisory in nature.

National Commission for Scheduled Castes (NCSC)

- National Commission for Scheduled Castes is a constitutional body directly established under Article 338.
- The 89th Constitutional Amendment Act, 2003 bifurcated the combined national commission for Schedule Castes and Schedule Tribes into two separate bodies.
- Apart from the Chairman, there is a Vice-chairman and three other members.

Functions	• Investigating and monitoring all matters relating to the constitutional and legal safeguards for the Scheduled Castes. • It also seeks to participate and advise on the planning process of socio-economic development of the Schedule Castes. • It annually presents a report to the President on working of safeguards mentioned for the scheduled castes in the Constitution. • The commission is also expected to discharge the similar functions with respect to the Anglo-Indian community. The power for Other Backward Castes was transferred to NCBC after it was accorded constitutional status.

National Commission for Scheduled Tribes (NCST)

- National commission for scheduled tribes is a constitutional body directly established by Article 338-A.
- The functions include investigating and monitoring all matters relating to the constitutional and legal safeguards for the scheduled tribes.
- It also seeks to participate and advise on the planning process of socio-economic development of the Schedule Tribes.
- It annually presents a report to the President on working of safeguards mentioned for the scheduled tribes in the constitution.
- The central and state governments are required to consult NCST on matters pertaining to Scheduled Tribes.

NON-CONSTITUTIONAL BODIES

A non-constitutional body is an organisation or institution which is not mentioned in the Constitution of India.

NITI AAYOG

- Planning Commission was replaced by a new institution – NITI AAYOG on January 1, 2015 with emphasis on 'Bottom –Up' approach to envisage the vision of Maximum Governance, Minimum Government, echoing the spirit of 'Cooperative Federalism'.
- The composition of NITI Aayog is as follows:
  - **Chairperson:** Prime Minister.
  - **Vice-Chairperson:** To be appointed by Prime-Minister.
  - **Governing Council:** Chief Ministers of all states and Lt. Governors of Union Territories.
  - **Regional Council:** To address specific regional issues, Comprising Chief Ministers and Lt. Governors Chaired by the Prime Minister or his nominee.
  - **Ad hoc Membership:** Two members in ex-officio capacity from leading Research institutions on rotational basis.
  - **Ex-Officio membership:** Maximum four from the Union council of ministers to be nominated by the Prime minister.
  - **Chief Executive Officer:** Appointed by Prime Minister for a fixed tenure, in rank of Secretary to Government of India.
  - **Special Invitees:** Experts, Specialists with domain knowledge nominated by the Prime-minister.

National Human Rights Commission (NHRC)

- NHRC of India is an independent statutory body established on 12 October, 1993 as per provisions of Protection of Human Rights Act, 1993, later amended in 2006.

Structure of the Commission

- The NHRC comprises a Chairperson, five full-time Members, and seven deemed Members. The statute lays down qualifications for the appointment of the Chairperson and Members of the Commission.
- The President appoints the Chairman and members of NHRC on recommendation of a high-powered committee. Headed by Prime Minister. Other members of committee are:
- Speaker of Lok Sabha.
- Deputy Chairman of Rajya Sabha.
- Leader of Opposition in both the houses of Parliament and.
- Union Home Minister.
- **Ex Officio Members:** Chairpersons of the below national commissions:
  - National Commission for Minorities.
  - National Commission for Scheduled Castes.
  - National Commission for Scheduled Tribes.
  - National Commission for Women.
  - National Commission for Backward Classes.
  - Chairperson of the National Commission for Protection of Child Rights.
  - Chief Commissioner for Persons with Disabilities.
- **Tenure of the Chairperson and the members:** 3 years or till the age of 70 years, whichever is earlier. They remain eligible for re-appointment.
- The Chairperson should be a Retired Judge or Retired Chief Justice of India, and members should be serving or retired judges of the Supreme Court, a serving or retired chief justice of the high court and two persons having knowledge or practical experience with respect to human rights.
- They can be removed only on the charges of proved misbehavior or incapacity,
  - If proved by an inquiry conducted by a Supreme Court Judge.
- Commission also has five Specialized Divisions i.e. Law Division, Investigation Division, Policy Research & Programmes Division, Training Division and Administration Division.

> The chairman and the members of State Human Rights Commission are appointed by the Governor in consultation with the Chief Minister, Home Minister, Speaker of Legislative Assembly and Leader of the Opposition in the State Legislative Assembly.
> - The chairperson should be a retired judge or retired Chief Justice of a High Court.
> - The other members should be:
>   - A serving or retired judge of a High Court or a District Judge in the state with a minimum of seven years' experience as District judge.
>   - A person having practical experience or knowledge related to human rights.

Central Information Commission (CIC)

- The Central Information Commission was established by the Central Government in 2005. It was constituted through an Official Gazette Notification under the provisions of the Right to Information Act (2005).
- The CIC is headed by the Chief Information Commissioner.
- He is assisted by Ten Information Commissioners.
- The Chief Information Commissioner (and an Information Commissioners) holds the office for five years or until they attain the age of 65 years.
- They are not eligible for reappointment.
- The commissioners are appointed by the President of India on the recommendation of a committee comprising of:
  - Prime Minister (Chairperson),
  - Leader of the Opposition in the Lok Sabha,
  - and a Union Cabinet Minister nominated by the Prime Minister.
- They should be Persons of Eminence in public life with wide knowledge and experience in law, science and technology, social service, management, journalism, mass media or administration and governance.

- They can be removed on the charges of proved misbehavior or incapacity, if proved by an inquiry conducted by a Supreme Court Judge.
- The CIC also submits an annual report to the GOI on the implementations of the provisions of the Act. This report is then placed before both the Houses of Parliament.

Powers and Functions

- Power to examine any record under the control of the public authority. All such records have to be given to the Commission during examination and nothing shall be withheld.
- The CIC has the powers of a civil court, such as the powers to:
  Summon and enforce the attendance of persons, and compel them to give oral or written evidence on oath and produce documents or things.

Central Vigilance Commission CVC

- Central Vigilance Commission is the apex vigilance institution, free of control from any executive authority, monitoring all vigilance activity under the Central Government.
- The CVC was set up by the Government in February, 1964 on the recommendations of the Committee on Prevention of Corruption, headed by Shri K. Santhanam.
- In 2003, the Parliament enacted CVC Act conferring statutory status to the CVC.
- The Central Vigilance Commissioner and the Vigilance Commissioners (not more than two) are appointed by the President on the recommendations of a committee consisting of:
  - Prime Minister (Chairperson),
  - Minister of Home Affairs (Member) and,
  - Leader of the Opposition in the House of the People (Member).
- The term of office of the Central Vigilance Commissioner and the Vigilance Commissioners is four years from the date on which they enter their office or till they attain the age of 65 years, whichever is earlier.
- They can be removed on the charges of proven misbehavior or incapacity, if proved by an inquiry conducted by a Supreme Court Judge.

The following are the works of CVC members:

- They inquire or investigate whenever a public servant (Central Government employee) commits an offence under the Prevention of Corruption Act, 1988.
- They superintend, direct and review the functioning of Delhi Special Police Establishment (CBI) in cases related to Prevention of Corruption Act, 1988.
- They review the progress of those applications that are pending with competent authorities for sanction under Prevention of Corruption Act, 1988.
- Central Government and its authorities are advised on matters as they refer to CVC members.
- They also superintend vigilance departments of government ministries.
- CVC members are part of the selection committee which is responsible to recommend appointment of Director of Enforcement (ED).
- The Commission acts as an authority to receive information that is related to suspicious transactions under the Prevention of Money Laundering Act, 2002.

Central Bureau of Investigation (CBI)

- The CBI was established as the Special Police Establishment in 1941, to investigate cases of corruption in the procurement during the Second World War.
- Later, the Santhanam Committee on Prevention of Corruption recommended the establishment of the CBI.
- The Central Bureau of Investigation (CBI) was set up in 1963 by a resolution of the Ministry of Home Affairs. CBI founded on 1 April 1963.
- A high powered committee chaired by the prime minister will recommend the selection of the director of CBI.
- It functions under the superintendence of the Dept. of Personnel Training (DoPT), Ministry of Personnel, Pension & Public Grievances, Government of India – which falls under the prime minister's office.
- However, for investigations of offences under the Prevention of Corruption Act 1988, its superintendence vests with the Central Vigilance Commission.
- It is also the nodal police agency in India which coordinates investigations on behalf of Interpol Member countries.

Director of CBI

- Director, CBI as Inspector General of Police, Delhi Special Police Establishment, is responsible for the administration of the organisation.
- Till 2014, the CBI Director was appointed on the basis of the DSPE Act, 1946.
- In 2003, DSPE Act was revised on the Supreme Court's recommendation in the Vineet Narain case.
- A committee that had members from Central Vigilance Commission, Secretaries from Home Ministry, Ministry of Personnel and Public Grievances would send recommendations to the Central Government for the appointment of CBI Director.
- In 2014, the Lokpal Act provided a committee for appointment of CBI Director:
  - Headed by Prime Minister.
  - Other members – Leader of Opposition/ Leader of the single largest opposition party, Chief Justice of India/ a Supreme Court Judge.
- The Home Ministry sends a list of eligible candidates to DoPT. Then, the DoPT prepares the final list on the basis of seniority, integrity, and experience in the investigation of anti-corruption cases, and sends it to the committee.
- Director of CBI has been provided security of two- year tenure, by the CVC Act, 2003.

Cases Handled by the CBI

- **Anti-Corruption Crimes:** Cases under the Prevention of Corruption Act, 1988.
- **Economic Crimes:** Major financial scams and serious economic frauds, Bank Frauds and Cyber Crime, Import Export & Foreign Exchange violations, etc.
- **Special Crimes:** Serious and organized crime under the Indian Penal Code and other laws on the requests of State Governments or on the orders of the Supreme Court and High Courts.
- **Suo Moto Cases:** CBI can Suo moto take up investigation of offences only in the Union Territories.
- The Central Government can authorize CBI to investigate a crime in a State but only with the consent of the concerned State Government.
- The Supreme Court and High Courts, however, can order CBI to investigate a crime anywhere in the country without the consent of the State.

Lokpal and Lokayuktas

- The Lokpal and Lokayukta Act, 2013 provided for the establishment of Lokpal for the Union and Lokayukta for States.
- These institutions are statutory bodies without any constitutional status.
- They perform the function of an "Ombudsman" and inquire into allegations of corruption against certain public functionaries and for related matters.

Structure of Lokpal

- Lokpal is a multi-member body that consists of one Chairperson and a maximum of 8 members.
- **Chairperson:** Either a former Chief Justice of India or the former Judge of Supreme Court or an eminent person.
- Out of the maximum eight members, half will be judicial members and minimum 50% of the Members will be from SC/ ST/ OBC/ Minorities and women.
- The judicial member of the Lokpal is either a former Judge of the Supreme Court or a former Chief Justice of a High Court. The non-judicial member should be an eminent person.
- The term of office for Lokpal Chairman and Members is 5 years or till the age of 70 years.
- The members are appointed by the President on the recommendation of a Selection Committee:
  - Prime Minister who is the Chairperson,
  - Speaker of Lok Sabha,
  - Leader of Opposition in Lok Sabha,
  - Chief Justice of India or a Judge nominated by him/her and,
  - One eminent jurist.
- For selecting the Chairperson and the members, the selection committee constitutes a search panel of at least eight persons.
- The Act states that not less than 50% of the members of the Lokpal should be from among persons belonging to the SCs, the STs, OBCs, minorities and women.
- A search committee will prepare a panel of candidates, a selection committee will recommend names from among this panel and the President will appoint these as members.

Jurisdiction and Powers

- Jurisdiction of Lokpal includes Prime Minister, Ministers, members of Parliament, Groups A, B, C and D officers and officials of Central Government.
- Jurisdiction of the Lokpal included the Prime Minister except on allegations of corruption relating to international relations, security, the public order, atomic energy and space.
- The Lokpal does not have jurisdiction over Ministers and MPs in the matter of anything said in Parliament or a vote given there.
- The Lokpal Act mandates that all public officials should furnish the assets and liabilities of themselves as well as their respective dependents.
- It has the powers to superintendence over, and to give direction to CBI.
- If Lokpal has referred a case to CBI, the investigating officer in such case cannot be transferred without the approval of Lokpal.
- The Inquiry Wing of the Lokpal has been vested with the powers of a civil court.
- Lokpal has powers of confiscation of assets, proceeds, receipts and benefits arisen or procured by means of corruption in special circumstances.
- Lokpal has the power to recommend transfer or suspension of public servant connected with allegation of corruption.
- Lokpal has the power to give directions to prevent the destruction of records during the preliminary inquiry.

Lokayuktas

- These are the state equivalents of the central Lokpal.
- Every State shall establish a body to be known as the Lokayukta for the State.
- The establishment of the institution of the Lokayukta including any appointment therein falls within the domain of the states.

Political Dynamics

Political Parties

- The Election Commission of India (ECI) registers political parties for the purpose of elections and grants them recognition as national or state parties on the basis of their poll performance.
- The other parties are simply declared as registered-unrecognised parties.
- As per the Representation of People Act 1951, Registered political parties, in course of time, can get recognition as 'State Party' or' National Party'.

Registration of political parties	• Section 29A of the Representation of the People Act, 1951 governs the registration of political parties. • The Election Commission of India in exercise of the powers conferred by Article 324 and Section 29A of the Representation of the People Act, 1951.
To be eligible for a National Political Party of India	• It receives at least 6% of the valid votes cast in any four or more states in a general election to the House of People or the State Legislative Assembly. • Furthermore, it obtains at least four representatives in the House of People from any state or states. • It wins at least two percent seats in the House of the People (i.e., 11 seats in the existing House having 543 members), and these members are elected from at least three different States.
To be eligible for a State Political Party	• It obtains at least 6% of the legitimate votes cast in the State in a general election, either to the House of the People or to the Legislative Assembly of the State in question. • Furthermore, it gained at least two seats in the State's Legislative Assembly. • It obtains at least three percent (3%) of the total number of seats in the State Legislative Assembly, or at least three seats in the Assembly, whichever is greater. • If it receives 6% of the legitimate votes cast in the state in a general election to the Lok Sabha from the state in question, as well as 1 seat in the Lok Sabha from the state in question.

	• If it wins one Lok Sabha seat for every 25 seats or portion thereof assigned to the state in a general election to the Lok Sabha from the state in question. • If it secures 8% of the total valid votes polled in the state at a General Election to the Lok Sabha from the state or to the legislative assembly of the state.

Elections

Electoral System

- Articles 324 to 329 in Part XV of the Constitution.
- The following provisions with regard to the electoral system in our country:
  - The Constitution (Article 324) provides for an independent Election Commission in order to ensure free and fair elections in the country.
  - The power of superintendence, direction and conduct of elections to the Parliament, the state legislatures, the office of the President and the office of the Vice-President is vested in the Commission.
  - There is to be only one general electoral roll for every territorial constituency for election to the Parliament and the state legislatures.
  - No person is to be ineligible for inclusion in the electoral roll on grounds only of religion, race, caste, sex or any of them (Article 325).
  - The elections to the Lok Sabha and the state assemblies are to be on the basis of adult franchise (Article 326).
  - Parliament may make provision with respect to all matters relating to elections to the Parliament and the state legislatures including the preparation of electoral rolls, the delimitation of constituencies and all other matters necessary for securing their due Constitution.
  - The state legislatures can also make provision with respect to all matters relating to elections to the state legislatures including the preparation of electoral rolls and all other matters necessary for securing their due Constitution.
  - The Constitution declares that the validity of any law relating to the delimitation of constituencies or the allotment of seats to such constituencies cannot be challenged in any court (Article 329).
  - The Constitution states that no election to the Parliament or the state legislature may be challenged except by an election petition presented to such authority and in such manner as the appropriate legislature provides.
- **Article 323B** empowers the appropriate legislature (Parliament or state legislature) to establish a tribunal for the adjudication of election disputes.

Election Commission of India	• The Election Commission of India is an autonomous constitutional institution in India that is in charge of managing Union and State election procedures. • The organisation is in charge of elections to India's Lok Sabha, Rajya Sabha, and State Legislative Assemblies, as well as the positions of President and Vice President. • The Election Commission was established in accordance with the Constitution on 25th January 1950. • Article 324 to 329 of the constitution deals with powers, function, tenure, eligibility, etc. of the commission and the members.
Composition	• The commission originally had only one Election Commissioner, but with the Election Commissioner Amendment Act 1989, it became a multimember body. • One Chief Election Commissioner and two Election Commissioners make up the commission.
Appointment and Tenure	• The President appoints Chief Election Commissioner and Election Commissioners. • They have a set term of six years, or until they reach the age of 65, whichever comes first. • They have the same status, as well as the same salaries and benefits as Supreme Court of India judges.
Removal	• The Chief Election Commissioner can only be removed from office through a procedure identical to that used to remove a Supreme Court judge by Parliament. • Removal requires a special majority of 2/3rd members present and voting supported by more than 50% of the total strength of the house.

Election Laws in India

To regulate elections in India certain laws in India have been passed.

- Representation of the People Act, 1950.
- Representation of the People Act, 1951.
- Delimitation Act, 2002.

Representation of the People Act, 1950

- Articles 81 and 170 of the Constitution of India lay down the maximum number of seats in Parliament and in Legislative Assemblies of States.
- Article 171 of the Constitution of India lays down the maximum and minimum number of seats in the Legislative council of States.
- Sought to confer on the President the powers to delimit, after consultation with the Election Commission.
- Provided for the registration of electors for Parliamentary Constituencies and for the Assembly and Council Constituencies and the qualifications and disqualifications for such registration.
- Barring the jurisdiction of civil courts.
- Manner of filling seats in the Council of States to be filled by representatives of Union territories.

Representation of the People Act, 1951

- Qualifications and disqualifications for membership of Parliament and State Legislatures.
- Notification of general elections.
- Administrative machinery for the conduct of elections.
- Registration of Political Parties.
- Conduct of elections.
- Free supply of certain material to candidates of recognised political parties.
- Disputes regarding elections.
- Corrupt practices and electoral offences.
- Powers of Election Commission in connection with inquiries as to disqualifications of members.
- By-elections and time limit for filling to elections.
- Barring the jurisdiction of civil courts.

Delimitation Act, 2002

- Article 82 and 170 of the Constitution of India provide for readjustment and the division of each State into territorial constituencies (Parliamentary constituencies and Assembly Constituencies) on the basis of the 2001 census.

- Articles 330 and 332 of the Constitution of India provide for re-fixing the number of seats reserved for the Scheduled Castes and the Scheduled Tribes.

Election Laws (Amendment) Bill, 2021.

- **Linking Aadhaar to the Voter ID:** The Election Laws (Amendment) Bill also seeks to allow the electoral registration officers to ask for Aadhaar number from persons already included in the electoral roll for the purposes of authentication of entries in the electoral roll.
  - And also, to identify registration of names of the same person in the electoral roll of more than one constituency or more than once in the same constituency.
- **Voluntarily link Aadhaar data to electoral rolls:** Amendment bill makes it clear that no application for inclusion of name in the electoral roll shall be denied and no entries in the electoral roll shall be deleted for inability of an individual to furnish or intimate Aadhaar number due to such sufficient cause as may be prescribed.
  - Such people will be allowed to furnish other documents as may be prescribed.
- **Representation of the People Act, 1950 and 1951:** Various sections of the Representation of the People Act, 1950 and 1951 will be amended.
  - Section 23 of the Representation of the People Act, 1950 will be amended to allow linking of electoral roll data with the Aadhaar ecosystem "to curb the menace of multiple enrolment of the same person in different places.
  - Section 14 of the Representation of the People Act, 1950 will allow having four "qualifying" dates for eligible people to register as voters.

Electoral Reforms

Electoral reforms in India refer to the evolution and positive change in election processes in order to promote greater democracy, clean politics, ideal members of legislative chambers, and equal representation, among other things. Elections and electoral reforms are covered in Articles 324-329.

Electoral Reforms After 2010

The ceiling on election expenditure	For the Lok Sabha elections, it is ₹ 70-95 lakhs (depending on the state they are contesting the Lok Sabha seat from), and ₹ 28-40 lakh for an assembly election.
Restriction on exit polls	The Election Commission issued a statement before the 2019 Lok Sabha elections saying that exit poll results could be broadcast only after the final phase of the elections were over.
Voting through postal ballot	In 2013, The Election Commission decided to expand the ambit of postal ballot voting in the country.
Awareness Creation	The government decided to observe January 25th as 'National Voters Day' to mark The Election Commission's founding day.
Introduction of NOTA	It was introduced in India following the 2013 Supreme Court directive in the People's Union for Civil Liberties Vs. Union of India judgment.
Introduction of VVPAT (Voter Verified Paper Audit Trail)	Voter verifiable paper audit trail (VVPAT) is a method of providing feedback to voters using EVMs.
Transparency in election funding	Electoral bonds Government introduced an Electoral Bond Scheme in January 2018, purportedly with a view to cleansing the prevailing culture of political sponsorship. **Note:** The Electoral Bond Scheme, introduced in 2018, was struck down as unconstitutional by the Supreme Court of India on February 15, 2024.

Various Committees on Electoral Reforms

Dinesh Goswami Committee
Jeevan Reddy Committee
Tarkunde Committee

Voting Behaviour

Voting behaviour is also known as electoral behaviour. It is a form of political behaviour. It implies the behaviour of voters in the context of elections in a democratic political system.

Determinants of Voting Behaviour

Voting behaviour in India is determined or influenced by multiple factors.

Miscellaneous

Anti-Defection Law

Origin	• "Aaya Ram Gaya Ram" was a phrase that became popular in Indian politics after a Haryana MLA Gaya Lal changed his party thrice within the same day in 1967. • The Anti-defection law sought to prevent such political defections which may be due to reward of office or other similar considerations.
10th Schedule	**Constitutional basis** • The 52nd Amendment Act of 1985 added the Tenth Schedule to the Constitution. **Lays down the Procedure** • It establishes the procedure for disqualifying parliamentarians on the basis of defection by the Presiding Officer of a legislature upon the petition of any other member of the House.
Condition of Defection	• A legislator is deemed to have defected if he either voluntarily gives up the membership of his party or disobeys the directives of the party leadership on a vote. • This implies that a legislator defying (abstaining or voting against) the party whip on any issue can lose his membership of the House.
Applicable	The legislation applies to both Parliament and state legislatures.

Exceptions in Law	• In specific conditions, legislators may shift parties without fear of disqualification. • The legislation enables a party to combine with or into another party if at least two-thirds of its lawmakers support the merger. • In such a scenario, neither the members who decide to merge, nor the ones who stay with the original party will face disqualification.

Important Constitutional Amendments

- **First Amendment Act 1951**
  - Added Ninth Schedule to protect the land reform and other laws included in it from the judicial review.
  - Empowered the state to make special provisions for the advancement of socially and economically backward classes.
- **Fourth Amendment Act,1955:** Authorized the state to nationalize any trade.
- **Seventh Amendment Act,1956**
  - It was necessitated on account of reorganization of states on a linguistic basis and changed first and fourth schedules.
  - Provided for the establishment of a common high court for two or more states.
  - Extended the jurisdiction of high courts to union territories.
- **Eighth Amendment Act, 1960:** Extended reservation of SC, ST & Anglo Indians in Lok Sabha and the state legislative assemblies for a period of 10 years.
- **Ninth Amendment Act, 1960:** Transferred certain territories to Pakistan following September 1958 Indo-Pak Agreement.
- **Tenth Amendment Act, 1961:** Incorporated Dadra and Nagar Haveli in the Indian Union.
- **Twelfth Amendment Act, 1962:** Incorporated Goa, Daman and Diu in the Indian Union.
- **Thirteenth Amendment Act, 1962:** Gave the status of a state to Nagaland and made special provisions for it
- **Fourteenth Amendment Act, 1962:** Incorporated Puducherry in the Indian Union.
- **Fifteenth Amendment Act, 1963**
  - Enabled the high courts to issue writs to any person or authority even outside its territorial jurisdiction if the cause of action arises within its territorial limits.
  - The retirement age of high court judges from 60 to 62 years.
- **Seventeenth Amendment Act, 1964:** Amended right to property and added more provisions in 9th schedule.
- **Nineteenth Amendment Act, 1966:** Abolished the system of Election Tribunals and vested the power to hear election petitions in the High Courts
- **Twenty-First Amendment Act, 1967:** Included Sindhi as the 15th language in the Eight Schedule.
- **Twenty-Second Amendment Act, 1969:** Created a sub state of Meghalaya within Assam.
- **Twenty-Fifth Amendment Act, 1971:** Curtailed the fundamental right to property.
- **Twenty-Sixth Amendment Act, 1971:** Abolished titles and special privileges of former rulers of princely states.
- **Twenty-Seventh Amendment, 1971:** Made certain special provisions for new Union Territories of Arunachal Pradesh and Mizoram.
- **Thirty-First Amendment Act, 1972:** Increased the number of Lok Sabha seats from 525 to 545.
- **Thirty-Fifth Amendment Act, 1974:** Terminated the protectorate status of Sikkim and conferred on it the status of an associate state of the Indian Union.
- **Thirty-Sixth Amendment Act, 1975:** Made Sikkim a full-fledged State of the Indian Union.
- **Forty-First Amendment Act, 1976:** Increase in retirement age of members of State Public Service Commission and Joint Public Service Commission from 60 to 62.
- **Forty-Second Amendment Act, 1976:** Added three new words (socialist, secular and integrity) in the Preamble.
  - **Added Fundamental Duties by the citizens (new Part IV A).**
  - Froze the seats in the Lok Sabha and state legislative assemblies on the basis of 1971 census till 2001.
  - Provided that the laws made for the implementation of Directive Principles cannot be declared invalid by the courts on the ground of violation of some Fundamental Rights.
- **Forty-Fourth Amendment Act, 1978**
  - Provided that the fundamental rights guaranteed by Articles 20 and 21 cannot be suspended during a national emergency.
  - Deleted the right to property from the list of Fundamental Rights and made it only a legal right.
- **Fifty-Second Amendment Act, 1985:** Provided for disqualification of members of Parliament and state legislatures on the ground of defection and added a new Tenth Schedule containing the details in this regard.
- **Fifty-Sixth Amendment Act, 1987**
  - Goa was made full-fledged State.
  - Fixed the strength of the Goa Legislative Assembly at a minimum of 30 members.
- **Sixty-First Amendment Act, 1989:** Reduced the voting age from 21 years to 18 years for the Lok Sabha and state legislative assembly elections.
- **Sixty-Fifth Amendment Act, 1990:** Establishment of National Commission for SCs & STs.
- **Sixty-Ninth Amendment Act, 1991:** Special status to the Union Territory of Delhi by designing it as the National Capital Territory.
- **Seventy-First Amendment Act, 1992:** Included Konkani, Manipuri and Nepali languages in the Eight Schedule.
- **Seventy-Third Amendment Act, 1992**
  - Granted constitutional status and protection to the panchayat raj institutions.
  - The Amendment has added a new Part-IX entitled as 'the panchayats 'and added new 11th Schedule.
- **Seventy-Fourth Amendment Act, 1992**
  - Granted constitutional status and protection to the urban local bodies.
  - The Amendment has added a new Part IX-A entitled as 'the municipalities 'and a new 12th Schedule.
- **Eighty-Sixth Amendment Act, 2002**
  - Made elementary education a fundamental right. The newly-added Article 21-A declares that –the State shall provide free and compulsory education to all children of the age of six to fourteen years in such manner as the State may determine.
  - Added a new fundamental duty under Article 51-A which reads— It shall be the duty of every citizen of India who is a parent or guardian to provide opportunities for education to his child or ward between the age of six and fourteen years.
- **Eighty-Ninth Amendment Act, 2003:** Bifurcated the erstwhile combined National Commission for Scheduled Castes and Scheduled Tribes into two separate bodies.

- **Ninety-First Amendment Act, 2003**
  - The total number of ministers, including the Prime Minister, in the Central Council of Ministers shall not exceed 15% of the total strength of the Lok Sabha.
  - The total number of ministers, including the Chief Minister, in the Council of Ministers in a state shall not exceed 15% of the total strength of the legislative Assembly of that state.
- **Ninety-Second Amendment Act, 2003:** Included four more languages in the Eighth Schedule. They are Bodo, Dogri (Dongri), Mathilli (Maithili) and Santhali.
- **One Hundredth Amendment Act, 2015**
  - Land boundary agreement between India and Bangladesh and Amended 1st schedule of constitution 36.
  - **101st Constitution Amendment Act, 2016**
  - Goods and Services Tax (GST) has commenced with the enactment of the 101st Constitution Amendment Act, 2016.
  - Articles 246A, 269A and 279A were added in the constitution.
- **102th constitutional amendment Act 2018:** Grant constitutional status to National Commission on Backward classes.
- **103th constitutional amendment Act 2019:** 10% Reservation for Economically Weaker Section.
- (104 to 106 are covered earlier in the book)

Indian Polity One Liner

- An amendment of the constitution may be initiated by the introduction of a bill in either House of Parliament.
- The salary and allowances of the Governor are charged from the Consolidated Fund of the State.
- G. V. K. Rao committee on Panchayat raj is constituted on 1985.
- A member of the council of ministers can hold office without being a member of the state legislature for a maximum period of six months.
- Six fundamental Rights are mentioned in Indian constitution.
- Article 72 deals with the pardoning power of the President.
- The independence of Judiciary in Indian constitution is taken from USA.
- Preamble of the constitution describes India as a secular state.
- The first Parliamentary Forum on Youth constituted on 2006.
- Arvind Panagariya was the first Vice Chairman of NITI Aayog.
- The Panchayat Raj system exists in all the states except Nagaland, Meghalaya and Mizoram and in all the Union territories except Delhi.
- The Panchayat Raj system was first adopted by the state of Rajasthan.
- High Courts issue writs under Article 226.
- Governor of the state appoints the Lokayukta and Upalokayukta.
- Article 44 of the Constitution is directed to establish Uniform Civil Code.
- Articles 36 to 51 of the Indian Constitution contains Directive principles of State policy.
- Directive principles of State Policy is mentioned in Part IV of the Indian constitution.
- Indian constitution taken the concept of single citizenship from UK.
- Article 5 to 11 part II of Indian constitution deals with Citizenship.
- Right to property according to the constitution is Legal right (Article 300-A).
- The total number of Schedules in the constitution are 12.
- The Central Bureau of Investigation (CBI) comes under the administrative control of Department of Personnel and Training (DoPT) of the Ministry of Personnel.
- Anti-Defection law passed in the year of 1985.
- Article 83 lays down the qualifications for membership of the two Houses of Parliament.
- National Commission for Other Backward Class came into effect from 1993.
- Procedure for the amendment of the Constitution is taken from South Africa.
- Farming is mainly served by the Co-operative Societies in India.
- State reorganisation committee was appointed on 1953.
- Central Vigilance Commission established on 1964.
- Central Information Commission is established by the central government under the Right to Information Act 2005.
- The Attorney General of India is the highest law officer of the country.
- Jawahar Lal Nehru prepared the preamble of the Indian Constitution.
- Government of India act 1935 is called the mini constitution of India.
- The Council of Ministers is responsible to the Lok Sabha.
- The Ninth Schedule to the Indian Constitution was added by First Amendment.
- The representative from states in Rajya Sabha is elected by the Elected members of the state legislative Assembly.
- Article 249 of Indian constitution says that Parliament has the power to make laws on any matter in the state list if a proclamation of emergency is in operation.
- Article 275 has the provision that the union government will provide grants-in-aid to state government.
- Joint session of the parliament is arranged under the Article 108.
- The Chairman of the National Human Rights Commission (NHRC) must be Retired Judge or Retired Chief Justice of Supreme Court.
- National Human Rights Commission was established in the year of 1993.
- Andhra Pradesh was the first linguistic state.
- Sarojini Naidu was the first woman governor in independent India.
- The Estimates Committee is the largest Committee of the Parliament.
- The salaries of the Judges of the Supreme Court drawn from Consolidated Fund.
- The first session of the Constituent Assembly held at New Delhi.
- The year of the Shimla pact between India and Pakistan is 1972.
- The Union Public Service Commission presents its report to President.
- The maximum number of elected members in a State Assembly is 500.
- First woman to become a Chief Minister of any State in India is Sucheta Kripalani (Uttar Pradesh).
- Dr. Rajendra Prasad was the first President of the Indian Union.
- Dr. Saravapalli Radhakrishnan was the first Vice-President of the Indian Union.

❑❑❑

Economy

Unit-1: Basic Concepts and Planning

Basic Economic Concept

Introduction

Economics and Economy

- Economics monitors the activities and performance of many economic sectors. Its primary goal is to examine economic aspects. Economics is divided into two categories: macroeconomics and microeconomics.
- The economy is defined as a region in which various activities such as production, consumption, distribution, and trading of products take place. These activities are carried out by several economic sectors. It is seen as a social domain responsible for emphasising practises linked with the production and administration of various resources.

Classification of Sectors of Economy

- **On the basis of Nature of Job**

■ **Primary Sector**

- It deals with the extraction of raw materials.
- The agriculture contribute major role in this sector, that's why Primary sector is also called the Agriculture and allied sector.
- Agriculture, mining, fishing, forestry, dairy etc., are some examples of the primary sector.
- The jobs produced in this sector called "Red Collar Job". The employment in this sector is outdoor in nature.

■ **Secondary Sector**

- It includes the industries where finished products are made from raw material produced in the primary sector.
- Secondary sector is also known as industrial sector.
- Industrial production, textile, sugar, bread, automobiles, oil refinery etc., comes under this sector.
- The jobs produced in sector sector called "Blue Collar Job". The employment in this sector is mostly indoor in nature.

■ **Tertiary Sector (or Service Sector)**

- This sector's activities help in the development of the primary and secondary sectors.
- These activities, by themselves, do not produce good but they are an aid or a support for the production process.

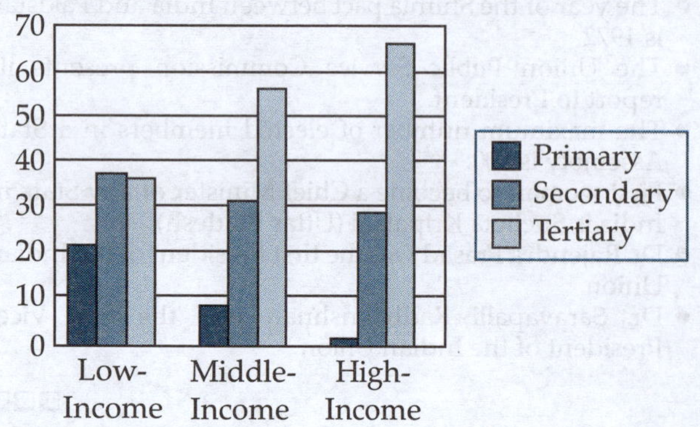

In nations with elevated levels of socio-economic development, there is typically a lower proportion of their economies dedicated to the primary and secondary sectors, with a greater emphasis on the tertiary sector. Conversely, less developed countries often display the opposite trend, allocating a higher percentage of their economic activity to the primary and secondary sectors.

- Transport, storage, communication, banking, insurance and trade are some examples of tertiary activities.

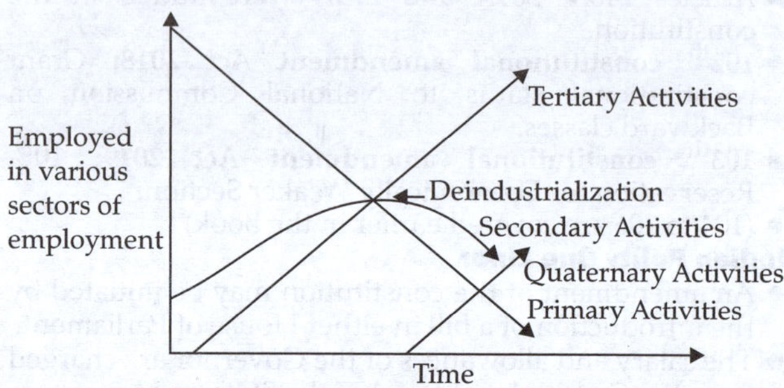

- These activities generate services rather than goods, therefore, the tertiary sector is also called the service sector.
- The jobs produced in sector sector called "White Collar Job". The employment in this sector is both indoor and outdoor in nature.

- **On the basis of working condition**

■ **Organised Sector**

- Employment arrangements in this industry are set and consistent, and employees have guaranteed work and social security.
- It is a government-registered industry, and specific laws apply to the businesses.
- This industry gives job stability.
- It is also known as formal sector.

■ **Unorganised Sector**

- This sector includes home-based workers, self-employed workers, and wage workers in the unorganised economy.
- It also covers an organized-sector worker who is not protected by any benefit plan.
- Low wages, insecure and irregular work, and a lack of protection from legislation or trade unions characterise this industry.
- It is sometimes referred to as the informal sector.

- **On the basis of ownership**

■ **Public Sector**

- In this case, the government controls the majority of the assets and provides all services.
- Railways and post offices are examples of public sector enterprises.
- The goal of the public sector is not only to make money. Governments collect funds through taxes and other means to cover the costs of the services they provide.

■ **Private Sector**

➢ Private persons or corporations hold the assets and provide the services in this case.

➢ Privately held firms include Tata Iron and Steel Company Limited (TISCO) and Reliance Industries Limited (RIL).

➢ Profit is the driving force behind private-sector activities.

Economic Systems

- Economic System refers to the manner in which individuals and institutions are connected together to carry out economic activities in a particular area. It is the methodology of doing economic activities to meet the needs of the society.
- There are three major types of economic systems. They are:

■ Capitalistic Economy

■ Socialistic Economy

■ Mixed Economy

Capitalistic Economy

- Adam Smith is the 'Father of Capitalism'.
- Capitalistic economy is also termed as a free economy or market economy where the role of the government is minimum and market determines the economic activities.
- The means of production in a capitalistic economy are privately owned. Manufacturers produce goods and services with profit motive. The private individual has the freedom to undertake any occupation and develop any skill.

Socialistic Economy

- The Father of Socialism is Karl Marx.
- Socialism is defined as a way of organizing a society in which major industries are owned and controlled by the government, A Socialistic economy is also known as 'Planned Economy'.
- In a socialistic economy, all the resources are owned and operated by the government. Public welfare is the main motive behind all economic activities.
- It aims at equality in the distribution of income and wealth and equal opportunity for all.

Mixed Economy

- In a mixed economy system both private and public sectors co-exist and work together towards economic development.
- In these economies, resources are owned by individuals and the government.

Economic Indicators

Economic indicators detail a country's economic performance and are issued on a regular basis by governmental or commercial organisations.

- **Gross Domestic Product (GDP):** It is the total market value of all final goods and services produced within a country's borders in a year.
- **Industrial Production**

■ The reports released by government bodies alter based on the production of factories, mines, and utilities in the country, and this data is an indicator of price hikes or supply shortages in the near future, Slack/Tightening of the Economy, and so on.

- **Employment Data:** Rapid increases in employment indicate prosperous economic growth and potential contractions may be imminent if significant decreases occur.
- **Consumer Price Index (CPI)**

■ This is the baseline for assessing inflation since it monitors the level of retail price fluctuations and consumer expenses.

■ This index is an important economic indicator and its release can increase volatility in equity, fixed income and forex markets.

Branches of Economics

- **Microeconomics**

■ Microeconomics is the study of how individual customers and organisations allocate resources.

■ Economists may examine how individuals, households, and businesses respond to price changes and why they want what they do at specific price levels.

- **Macroeconomics**

■ Macroeconomics is the discipline of economics that investigates the overall behaviour and performance of an economy.

■ Its major focus is the cyclical nature of the economy. Economic expansion and development on a large scale.

■ John Maynard Keynes is regarded as the founder of macroeconomics.

■ *Note:* The terms 'micro economics' and 'macro economics' were first used in economics by Norwegian economist RagnAr Frisch in 1933.

Economic Growth

- Economic growth is defined as a rise in the production of economic products and services from one period of time to the next.
- It can be quantified in nominal or real (inflation-adjusted) terms.

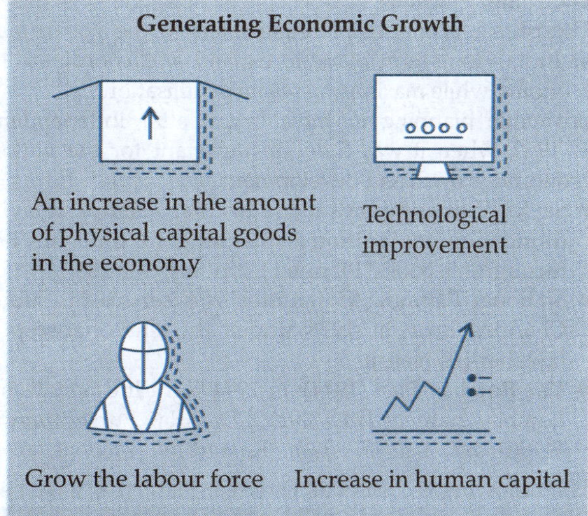

Economic Development

- Economic development is described as a consistent improvement in society's material well-being.
- In summary, economic development is a long chain of interconnected changes in fundamental supply variables and demand structure that contribute to an increase in a country's net national product in the long term.

Law of Supply and Demand

- The law of supply and demand is a theory that describes the relationship between sellers and purchasers of a resource.
- The theory defines the relationship between the price of a given good or product and the willingness of people to

either buy or sell it. Generally, as price increases, people are willing to supply more and more.

Law of Supply and Demand

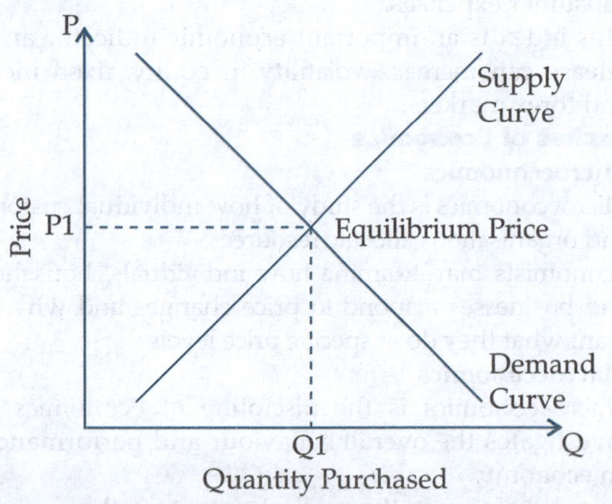

Importance of concept of Supply and Demand

- The Law of Supply and Demand is important because it assists investors, entrepreneurs, and economists in understanding and forecasting market situations.
- For example, a corporation releasing a new product may purposefully attempt to raise the price of their product by building consumer demand through advertising.
- At the same time, they may try to raise their prices even higher by purposely limiting the quantity of units sold in order to reduce supply.

Planning and National Income

Economic Planning

The phrase economic planning refers to the government of India's long-term plans to expand and coordinate the economy while maximising resource utilisation.

Economic planning in India began after independence in 1950, when it was thought important for the nation's economic growth and development.

- Sir M. Vishveshwarya made his first attempt in laying foundation for economic planning in India in 1934 through his book, "Planned Economy of India".
- National Planning Committee was set up by Subhas Chandra Bose in 1938 under the chairmanship of Jawahar Lal Nehru.
- **The Bombay Plan (1944):** In 1944 Eight Industrialists of Bombay namely JRD Tata, GD Birla, Purshottamdas Thakurdas, Lala Shriram, Kasturbhai Lalbhai, A. D. Shroff, Ardeshir Dalal and John Mathai working together prepared a plan known as "Bombay Plan".
- **Gandhian Plan (1944):** S. N. Agarwal, principal of Wardha Commercial College, created this idea. Its primary focus is on decentralisation, with a priority on rural development through the growth of cottage enterprises.
- **People's Plan (1945):** M. N. Roy was the author. It placed equal emphasis on agriculture and industry. This was a ten-year plan.
- **Sarvodaya Plan (1950):** Jaiprakash Narayan composed it. This proposal was influenced by Gandhi's plan and Vinoba Bhave's Sarvodaya idea. This strategy focuses on agriculture as well as small and cottage enterprises.

Economic Planning in India – Five-Year Plans

- Post-independence, India began a Five-Year Plan program to make the most use of the country's resources and achieve rapid economic development.
- In India, development plans were designed and implemented within the mixed economy framework.
- Economic planning was implemented in India in the form of Five-Year Plans and was viewed as a development tool for a variety of reasons.
- Since the year 2012, when the 12th Five Year Plan (2012-2017) was adopted by the NDC (National Development Council) on December 27, 2012, 12th Five-Year Plans have been formulated.

The following are the long-term goals of India's Five-Year Plans:

- To raise the living standards of India's citizens, a high growth rate is required.
- For prosperity, there must be economic stability.
- An economy that is self-sufficient.
- Reducing inequality and promoting social justice
- The economy is being modernized.

> The concept of five-year economic planning was taken from the Soviet Union by first Prime Minister Pt. Jawahar Lal Nehru, who was a socialist.

The first eight Indian five-year plans concentrated on increasing the public sector through huge investments in heavy and fundamental sectors, but the focus has shifted from the commencement of the Ninth five-year plan in 1997 to making the government a growth facilitator.

The following is a list of all Five-Year Plans that have been executed in India:

Five-Year Plans	Years	Assessment	Objective
First Five-Year Plan	1951-1956	Targets and objectives were mostly met. With the state playing an active role in all economic areas. As significant technological institutes, IIT Kharagpur was established in 1951.	Rehabilitating refugees, achieving food self-sufficiency in the quickest period feasible, and controlling inflation are all priorities.
Second Five-Year Plan	1956-1961	This plan faced implementation challenges due to foreign exchange shortages. Targets have to be reduced. Nonetheless, hydroelectric power plants and five steel mills were developed at Bhilai, Durgapur, and Rourkela.	The Nehru-Mahalanobis model was implemented. Rapid industrialization, with a focus on the growth of fundamental and heavy industries. The Industrial Policy of 1956 identified as the objective of economic policy the construction of a socialistic form of society.

Third Five-Year Plan	1961-1966	Failures include wars and droughts. Nonetheless, Panchayat elections have begun. State electricity and secondary education boards were established.	'Establishment of a self-reliant and self-generating economy'.
Plan Holidays – Annual Plans	1966-1969	A new agriculture plan was put in place. It entailed the dissemination of high-yielding seed types, intensive fertiliser usage, irrigation potential utilisation, and soil conservation measures.	Crisis in agriculture and serious food shortage required attention.
Fourth Five-Year Plan	1969-1974	Growth of 3.3 percent was achieved, although it was hampered by inflation. Indira Gandhi's administration nationalised 14 major Indian banks, and the Green Revolution boosted agriculture in India.	'Growth with stability' and progressive achievement of self-reliance. Garibi HataoTarget: 5.6 percent.
Fifth Five-Year Plan	1974-1979	High inflation. Was terminated by the Janta govt. Yet, the Indian national highway system was introduced for the first time.	'Removal of poverty and attainment of self-reliance'.
Sixth Five-Year Plan	1980-1985	Most targets achieved. Growth: 5.7 percent. Family planning was also expanded in order to prevent overpopulation.	'A direct attack on the problem of poverty by fostering economic growth'.
Seventh Five-Year Plan	1985-1990	This plan was effective despite severe drought circumstances for the first three years in a row, with a growth rate of 6.01%. This strategy included programmes such as the Jawahar Rozgar Yojana (1989).	Emphasis on policies and programs that would accelerate the growth in foodgrains production, increase employment opportunities and raise productivity.
Annual Plans	1989-1991	It was the beginning of privatization and liberalization in India.	No plan due to political uncertainties.
Eighth Five-Year Plan	1992-1997	Partly success. An average annual growth rate of 6.78% against the target 5.6% was achieved.	Rapid economic growth, high growth in agricultural and related sectors, high growth in the manufacturing sector, growth in exports and imports, improvement in trade and current account deficit to achieve 5.6% annual average growth. Indicative planning was applied for the first time.
Ninth Five-Year Plan	1997-2002	It obtained a lower-than-expected GDP growth rate of 5.4%. Nonetheless, industrial growth was 4.5%, which was more than the 3% forecast. The service industry grew at a 7.8% annual pace. An yearly growth rate of 6.7% was achieved on average.	Quality of life, generation of productive employment, regional balance and self-reliance. Growth with social justice and equality growth target 6.5%.
Tenth Five-Year Plan	2002-2007	It was successful in reducing the poverty ratio by 5%, increasing forest cover to 25%, increasing literacy rates to 75 % and the economic growth of the country over 7.7%.	To achieve 8% GDP growth rate, Reduce poverty by 5 points and increase the literacy rate in the country.
Eleventh Five-Year Plan	2007-2012	India has recorded an average annual economic growth rate of 7.9%, farm sector grew at an average rate of 3.3% as against 4% targeted. The industry grew with an annual average growth of 7.2% against 10% targeted.	Rapid and inclusive expansion. Education and skill development provide empowerment. Reduced gender inequality. The long-term viability of the environment. To boost agricultural, industrial, and service growth rates to 4%, 10%, and 9%, respectively. By 2009, all people will have access to safe drinking water.
Twelfth Five-Year Plan	2012-2017	Its growth rate target was 8%.	"Faster, sustainable and more inclusive growth". Increasing agricultural production by 4% and industrial output by 10%. The goal was to add more than 88,000 MW of electricity producing capacity.

Comparison of Planning Commission and NITI Aayog

Planning Commission	NITI Aayog
Prepared the Five-Year Plans of India	NITI Aayog Composition: Prime Minister of India as the Chairperson. Vice-chairperson is to be appointed by the PM. Governing Council comprising the Chief Ministers of all the States and Lt. Governors of Union Territories. Experts, specialists and practitioners with relevant domain knowledge as special invitees nominated by the Prime Minister. Regional Councils will be formed to address specific issues and contingencies impacting more than one state or a region. NITI Aayog has delegated responsibilities for the following draft: ● Three Year Action Agenda (2017-20). ● Seven Year Strategy Document. ● Fifteen Year Vision Document (2017-32). ● 2018: Drafted Strategy for New India @ 75 covering the period 2017 to 2022-23. ● 2023: Drafted Strategy for Viksit Bharat @2047 initiative.
How much funding should the union provide to each state for the execution of centrally sponsored schemes (CSS)? How much money should the union allocate to state governments' five-year plans? PC would respond to these queries using the Gadgil Mukherjee formula (created in the 8th FYP) depending on a state's population, per capita income, particular difficulties, and so on.	The NITI Aayog does not decide how much money should be distributed to each state. That component is decided by the Finance Commission (tax devolution and grants) and Finance Ministry (Allocations for schemes). NITI Aayog primarily functions as a think tank, assisting in policy formulation. Its dashboard aids in monitoring plan execution. e.g. 'School Education Quality Index', 'SDG India Index', 'Digital Transformation Index' etc.

National Income

It is the sum of the money received by its citizens from factor services supplied to production units both within and outside the country's geographical limits.

National Income provides a comprehensive measure of the economic activities of a nation. It represents the purchasing power of the country. The pace at which an economy's real national income rises over time is used to quantify economic growth.

- **National:** It refers to the residents whose economic interests lie within the country in which they live.
- **Factor Income:** It is the income generated from factors of production such as land, labour, capital, and entrepreneurship.

Measure of National Income

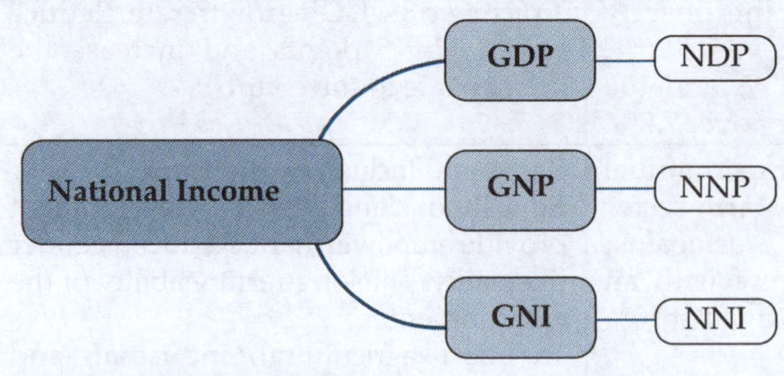

Gross Value Added (GVA)

- It is a measure of the economy's overall output and revenue.
- It gives a rupee value to the quantity of products and services generated in an economy after deducting the cost of inputs and raw materials used in their production.
- It gives a sector-specific picture of growth in an area such as industry, agriculture, manufacturing etc.

- **Classification of Good or Service as Intermediate Consumption**
  - It is purchased or acquired from another production unit.
  - It is obtained for resale, which equates to being completely consumed in the process of manufacturing within the accounting period.

GVA = Value of Gross Output – Value of Intermediate Consumption

- The National Statistical Office (NSO) revised National Accounts Statistics and determined that for estimating GDP, sector-specific estimates of Gross Value Added (GVA) will now be presented at basic prices rather than factor cost.
- GVA at basic prices will include production taxes and exclude production subsidies available on the commodity.

GVA (at Basic Price) = GVA (at Factor Cost) + Production Taxes – Production Subsidies

- GVA at factor cost includes no taxes and excludes no subsidies.
- While calculating GDP at market prices, it includes both production and product taxes and excludes both production and product subsidies.

Gross Domestic Product (GDP)

- It is the market value of all final products and services produced inside the country's borders within a fiscal year.
- It can, however, be calculated quarterly or semi-annually.
- It is estimated by the National Statistical Office (NSO).
- The Ministry of Finance uses the GDP numbers (at current prices) to peg the financial targets [as per the Fiscal Responsibility and Budget Management Act (FRBM), 2003].

Methods of Calculating GDP

- **Production or Output Method:** This method sums the value of all goods and services produced within a country's borders. It accounts for the market value of all final goods and services produced in various sectors of the economy. Calculating GDP by this method involves adding up the value-added at each stage of production across industries.
- **Income Method:** GDP can also be calculated by summing up all incomes earned within an economy. This includes employee compensation (wages, salaries, benefits), corporate profits, rental income, and taxes (less subsidies) on production and imports. The income approach aims to measure the total income earned by individuals and entities contributing to the production of goods and services.
- **Expenditure Method:** This method calculates GDP by summing up all expenditures in an economy. It accounts for the total spending on consumption (household spending), investments (business spending on capital goods), government spending on goods and services, and net exports (exports minus imports). This approach is represented by the equation: GDP = C + I + G + (X - M), where C is consumption, I is investment, G is government spending, X is exports, and M is imports.

Net Domestic Product (NDP)

- NDP is the value of net output of the economy during the year. Some of the country's capital equipment wears out or becomes obsolete each year during the production process. The value of this capital consumption is some percentage of gross investment which is deducted from GDP. Thus

Net Domestic Product = GDP at Factor Cost – Depreciation

Nominal GDP

- Nominal gross domestic product is GDP that is evaluated at the present market prices. GDP is the financial equivalent of all the complete products and services generated within a nation in a definite time.
- The nominal varies from the real and incorporates changes in cost prices due to an increase in the complete cost price. Generally, economists utilize a gross domestic factor to change the nominal GDP to the real GDP, which is also known as current dollar GDP or chained dollar GDP.

Real GDP

- Real GDP is an inflation-adjusted calculation that analyses the rate of all commodities and services manufactured in a country for a fixed year. It is expressed in foundation year prices and referred to as a fixed cost price.
- It is also known as inflation-corrected GDP or constant price GDP. The real GDP is regarded as a reliable indicator of a nation's economic growth as it solely considers production and is free from currency fluctuations.

GDP Deflator

- The GDP deflator, also called implicit price deflator, is a measure of inflation. It is the ratio of the value of goods and services an economy produces in a particular year at current prices to that of prices that prevailed during the base year.
- The GDP deflator is an index of price changes of goods and services included in GDP. It is a price index which is calculated by dividing the nominal GDP in a given year by the real GDP for the same year and multiplying it by 100.

GDP deflator = Nominal GDP/ Real GDP × 100

Gross National Product (GNP)

- The total value of all goods and services generated by citizens and enterprises in a country, regardless of where they are produced, is referred to as the gross national product (GNP).
- The Gross National Product (GNP) accounts for investments made by enterprises and citizens of the country, both inside and outside the country. It also takes into account the value of products generated by domestically based industries.
- GNP does not include revenue made by foreign nationals in the country or any products manufactured by a foreign business in the country's manufacturing units.
- Only the final commodities and services are taken into account when calculating GNP. Double counting is prevented by avoiding intermediate products.

GNP = Consumption Expenditure + Investment + Government Expenditure + Net Exports + Net Income

Net National Product

NNP is the total value of completed products and services generated by a country's inhabitants both abroad and at home during a certain time period, excluding depreciation. NNP is obtained by subtracting depreciation from GNP.

Net National Product (Market Price) = Gross National Product – Depreciation

Personal Income

- Personal Income is the part of National Income which is received by the households.

Personal income (PI) = National Income – Undistributed profits (profits utilised by manufacturers for further production) – Net interest payments made by households – Corporate tax + Transfer payments to the households from the government and firms (old-age pensions, unemployment compensation, relief payment etc.).

Personal Disposable Income

- Personal Disposable Income is the amount of money available to households to spend as they see fit.
- Individuals do not have access to all of their Personal Income. They must pay taxes (e.g., income tax) as well as non-tax payments such as penalties.
- The formula for Personal Disposable Income is

Personal Disposable Income (PDI) = PI – Personal tax payments – Non-tax payments (such as fines etc.).

- Thus, Personal Disposable Income is the portion of total income that belongs to families. They may opt to eat some of it and store the remainder.

National Disposable Income

- National Disposable Income is the total of all resident and institutional disposable incomes.
- National Disposable Income indicates the greatest quantity of goods and services available to the domestic economy.

National Disposable Income = Net National Product at market prices + Other current transfers from the rest of the world

- Current transfers from the rest of the world includes items such as gifts, aids etc.

Private Income

- Private income is the sum of all factor and transfer earnings obtained by the private sector (private company and families) both inside and outside the country.

Private Income = Factor income from net domestic product accruing to the private sector + National debt interest + Net factor income from abroad + Current transfers from government + Other net transfers from the rest of the world

Private income is a bigger term than personal income since it includes personal income + profit tax + undistributed profit.

- National income accounting equation is an equation that shows the relationship between income and expense of an economy and other categories. It is represented by the following equation:

$$Y = C + I + G + (X - M)$$

Where

Y = National Income

C = Personal Consumption Expenditure

I = Private Investment

G = Government Spending

X = Net Exports

M = Imports

GDP, GNP, NNP, disposable income, and personal income are the most essential indicators defined by national income accounting. In the following lines, please explain these topics in more detail.

Unit-2: Money Circulation in Economy

Fiscal Policy

Introduction

- Fiscal policy is the use of government revenue collection (mainly taxes but also non-tax revenues such as disinvestment, loans) and expenditure (spending) to influence the economy.
- Through fiscal policy, the government of a country controls the flow of tax revenues and public expenditure to navigate the economy.

The major fiscal measures are:

Public Expenditure	The government spends money on a wide range of activities, including the military and police, as well as services like as education and health care, as well as transfer payments such as social benefits.
Taxation	The government levies new taxes and raises the rates of existing taxes. The government's expenditures are paid by the levy of taxes.
Public Borrowing	Government also raises money from the population or from abroad through Bonds, NSC, Kisan Vikas Patra, etc.
Other Measures	**Other measures adopted by the government are:** • Rationing and price control • Regulation of wages • Increase the production of good and services.

Types of Fiscal Policy

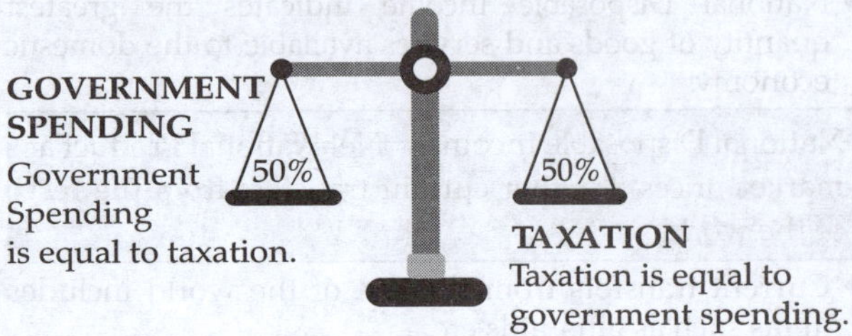

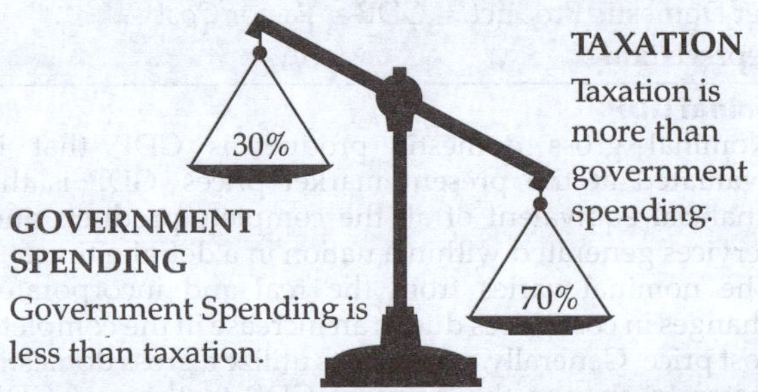

Objectives of Fiscal policy	**To promote economic growth:** • The government fosters economic growth by establishing fundamental and heavy industries such as steel, chemicals, fertilisers, machine tools, and so on. • It also constructs infrastructure such as roads, canals, trains, airports, education and health facilities, water and energy supply, telecommunications, and so on, all of which promote economic growth. • To reduce income and wealth inequalities **To provide employment opportunities:** • The government expands employment prospects in a variety of ways, and jobs are produced when it establishes public-sector firms. • It also fosters the establishment of small-scale, cottage, and village enterprises by job-seekers.

	To ensure stability in prices: The government maintains price stability for important commodities and services by controlling their supply. **To correct balance of payments deficit:** ● A country's balance of payments account documents its receipts and payments to other governments. ● The balance of payments account is considered to be in deficit when payments to foreigners exceed revenues from foreigners. To provide for effective administration: Government incurs expenditures on police, defence, legislatures, judiciary, etc. to provide effective administration.

Components of Fiscal Policy

The components of the Fiscal Policy can be categorized as:

- Government Receipts
- Government Expenditures
- Public Accounts of India

Government Receipts

- The income of the government in the form of taxes, interest and earnings on investments, cess, and other receipts for services given is referred to as government receipts.
- This is the total amount of money that the government receives from all sources.
- Government receipts are divided into two groups—**Revenue Receipts and Capital Receipts.**

Revenue Receipts	● Receipts that neither generate nor diminish liabilities. ● Revenue receipts are classified as either tax or non-tax. ● There are two sorts of tax revenues: direct and indirect taxes. ● Non Tax revenue sources are interest and dividend on government investment, cess and other receipts for services rendered by the government, income through licenses, permits, fines, penalties, etc.
Capital Receipts	● Capital receipts are sometimes referred to as incoming cash flows. ● Borrowings, loans, and so on are all considered debt receipts since the government is required to repay this money, along with interest in some situations.

Government Expenditure

Government expenditure is classified in two ways: Capital Expenditure and Revenue Expenditure.

Revenue Expenditure	● When the government incurs expenditure that neither creates any asset nor reduces any liability, such expenditure is known as revenue expenditure. ● **Example:** Salaries and employee wages, utilities, rents, property taxes on government-owned properties, etc. ● These do not create any public asset.
Capital Expenditure	● Investments made by the government in capital to maintain or to expand its business and generate additional revenue. ● Purchase of long-term assets, buying fixed assets, which are physical assets such as equipment. As a result, capital expenditures are typically for larger amounts than revenue expenditures. ● **Example:** purchase of factory equipment, purchases for business, other government purchases like furniture, spending on infrastructure, etc.

Public Accounts of India (Public Debt)

- This fund was established in accordance with Article 266(2) of the Constitution. It considers flows for transactions in which the government just acts as a banker.
- Examples include minor savings, provident funds, etc.
- This money doesn't belong to the government; instead, they must be returned to their original owners at some point.
- Consequently, the Parliament is not required to authorize spending from the public account.

Deficit

Revenue Deficit: It refers to the excess of total revenue expenditure of the government over its total revenue receipts.

Revenue Deficit = Total Revenue Expenditure – Total Revenue Receipts. OR Revenue Deficit = Total Revenue Expenditure – (Tax Revenue + Non-Tax Revenue)

Fiscal Deficit: Fiscal deficit is defined as excess of total expenditure over total receipts excluding borrowings during a fiscal year.

● Fiscal deficit = Total budget expenditure – Total budget receipts excluding borrowings OR Fiscal Deficit = (Revenue expenditure + Capital expenditure) – (Revenue Receipts + Capital receipts excluding borrowings). ● The fiscal deficit represents the government's borrowing needs for the fiscal year. ● The fiscal deficit shows the government's borrowing needs for funding expenditures, including interest payments. ● Fiscal deficit = Revenue expenditure + capital expenditure – Revenue receipts – capital Receipts excluding borrowings OR Fiscal deficit = Revenue expenditure + capital expenditure – Tax Revenue – Non-Tax Revenue – recovery of loans – disinvestment OR ● Fiscal deficit = Total borrowing requirement of the government

- The fiscal deficit denotes the additional financial resources required to fulfil government expenditure.
- It is an indication of the government's future responsibilities for interest payments and loan repayment.
- The government must repay the borrowed funds with interest in the future.
- As a result, the government must either borrow more from the people or tax them more in the future to pay the interest and loan amount.

Primary Deficit

- The primary deficit is calculated by subtracting the fiscal deficit from the interest paid on earlier borrowings.
- The primary deficit reflects the government's borrowing needs to fulfil expenditures, excluding interest payments.
- Gross Primary deficit = Fiscal deficit – Interest payments.

Net Primary deficit = Fiscal deficit + Interest received – Interest payments It shows the total amount that the central government needs to borrow.

Three Ways to Finance Deficit

- Borrowing from Public and Foreign Governments.
- Withdrawing Cash Balances held with the Reserve Bank of India (R.B.I.).
- Borrowing from the Reserve Bank of India (R.B.I.).

Fiscal Responsibility and Budget Management Act, 2003 (FRBMA)

- The Fiscal Responsibility and Budget Management Act, 2003 (FRBMA) is an Act of the Indian Parliament enacted to institutionalise financial discipline, lower India's fiscal deficit, enhance macroeconomic management, and improve overall management of public finances by moving towards a balanced budget.

Major Provisions of the FRBM Act, 2003	• The FRBM regulation established a fiscal deficit reduction objective of 3% of GDP by 2008-09. But the current fiscal deficit target under the revised FRBM framework is 4.5% of GDP by 2025-26. • Revenue deficit has to be reduced by 0.5% of the GDP per year with complete elimination by 2008-09. But the specific statutory targets for the revenue deficit were largely removed, making the fiscal deficit and overall debt-to-GDP ratios the primary anchors by N.K. Singh Committee. • Reduction of Public Debt. • The government must take necessary steps to minimise the fiscal deficit and revenue deficit in order to erase the revenue deficit by 2008-09 and generate a large revenue surplus thereafter. • It required the establishment of yearly objectives for the reduction of the fiscal and revenue deficits, contingent liabilities, and total liabilities. • The government shall end its borrowing from the RBI except for temporary advances. • After 2006, the RBI was not supposed to subscribe to principal offerings of central government securities. • The revenue deficit and budget deficit may exceed the laws' goals only in cases of national security, catastrophe, or other extraordinary circumstances designated by the Central government.
Objectives of FRBM Act	• In the country, establish transparent fiscal management methods. • Give the country's debts a more equal and manageable distribution over time. • Ensure India's long-term budgetary stability. • Furthermore, the act was supposed to provide the Reserve Bank of India with the required flexibility in managing inflation in India.

- **Amendments to FRBM Act:** The Fiscal Responsibility and Budget Management Act of 2003 was amended in 2012 to require the Central Government to present to the Houses of Parliament the Macro-Economic Framework Statement, Medium Term Fiscal Policy Statement, and Fiscal Policy Strategy Statement, in addition to the Annual Financial Statement and Grant Demands.
- **N. K. Singh Committee**, which was set up in 2016 to review the FRBM Act, recommended that the government must target a fiscal deficit of 3% of the GDP in the years up to March 31, 2020, subsequently cut it to 2.8% in 2020-21 and to 2.5% by 2023. But these targets were not met due to COVID-19 and economic disruptions.

Monetary Policy and Banking

Concept of Money

Money is anything that is generally accepted as payment for goods and services and repayment of debts and that serves as a medium of exchange.

Major Functions of Money

- It is used as a medium of exchange.
- It gives a common measure of value.
- It is used as a standard of deferred payments.
- It can also be used as a store of value.

Commodity Money

- The value of commodity money is derived from the product from which it is created.
- Gold, silver, copper, salt, precious stones, and other commodities that have been used as a means of trade include gold, silver, copper, salt, precious stones, and so on.

Representative Money

- Token coins or other tangible tokens, such as certificates, that can be securely exchanged for a defined amount/ quantity of a commodity, such as gold and silver, are included.
- It is used against the backing of equivalent values of gold and silver.

Fiat Money

- Paper Money is sometimes referred to as fiat money since its worth is not derived from any inherent value or promise that it may be changed into a valued commodity such as gold. It obtains its worth, which is solely determined by government decree.
- Fiat money is money that has been proclaimed legal tender. This covers any type of circulating cash, such as paper money or coins.
- Legal tender means something which cannot be refused as an option for payment, for example Indian Rupee, US Dollar etc.

Cryptocurrency

- Crypto-currencies, such as bitcoin, are peer-to-peer money.
- This form of money is based on electronic accounting records and may be used as a medium of trade.
- It is based on block chain technology, which is a decentralised database with an ever-growing list of entries.
- In India Crypto-currencies are not legal tenders.

Measures of Money Supply

- The total stock of all sorts of money, such as currency and demand deposits held by the public and banks, is referred to as the money supply.
- The stock of money held by the government and the RBI, for example, is not included in the money supply since it is not in active circulation in the economy.

The Government

- It produces coins of all denominations and the One Rupee notes.
- The government of India has sole authority over currency minting.
- However, in lieu of the RBI Act, they are only available for distribution through the Reserve Bank.

RBI

- The Reserve Bank of India was established on April 1, 1935, in accordance with the provisions of the Reserve Bank of India Act, 1934.
- The Central Office of the Reserve Bank was initially established in Kolkata but Headquarter moved from Calcutta to Mumbai in 1937.
- Osborne Smith was the first Governor of Reserve Bank of India.
- CD Deshmukh was the first Indian Governor of RBI.
- Sanjay Malhotra is the current Governor of RBI.
- RBI was nationalised on 1 January 1949.
- Except for one rupee notes, which are issued by the Ministry of Finance, it is the sole authority with the ability to issue currency notes.
- However, the RBI uses a minimum reserve method while issuing notes. It is only required to have ₹200 crores in gold and foreign exchange reserves, with gold reserves of ₹115 crores.
- Functions of Reserve Bank of India
- Monetary Authority
- The issuer of currency
- The issuer of Banking License
- Bank of the banks
- Banker to the Government
- Lender of last resort
- Act as clearing house
- Custodian of foreign exchange reserves
- Regulator of Economy
- Publisher of monetary data and other data
- **Commercial Banks:** These create the credit as per the demand deposits.

Monetary Aggregates	
M0	• It is referred to as the monetary basis or reserve money. • It is also known as high-powered money or main money. • It includes all physical money like coins and currency along with demand deposits and other liquid assets held by the central bank.
M1	• It is also known as narrow money. • Narrow money comprises just the most liquid financial assets that are easily accessible on demand. • It comprises all currency notes in circulation on any given day, demand deposits with commercial banks (including savings and current account deposits), and other bank deposits held with the RBI. • Narrow money is the most liquid part of the money supply because the demand deposits can be withdrawn anytime during the banking hours.
M2 and M3	• When Post office Savings Deposits are also added to M1, it becomes M2. ▪ M2 = M1 + Savings Deposits of Post Office Savings account. • When time deposits in narrow money (M1) are added together, we get wide money, which is indicated by M3. ▪ M3 = M1 + Time deposits of public with the banks. • Interbank deposits are not included in broad money. At the same time, public time deposits with banks, including cooperative banks, are included in Broad money. • M1, M2 and M3 are also called fortnight money as these three aggregates are computed or compiled fortnightly.
M4	• When we add total savings deposits with post offices with M3 we get M4 Money. ▪ M4 = M3 + Total Saving deposits with Post offices • M3 Money, often known as Broad money, is the most commonly used measure of money supply. • M1 and M3 are currently widely utilised for policy objectives and are important indices of money supply in India.

Banks' key sector targets and sub-targets are as follows:

- Scheduled commercial banks' goals.
- The following are the priority sector lending objectives and sub-targets for all scheduled commercial banks in India:

Table: Targets and Sub targets under Priority Sector

Categories	Domestic scheduled commercial banks and foreign banks with 20 branches and above	Foreign banks with less than 20 branches	Regional Rural Banks	Small Finance Banks
Total Priority Sector	40% of Adjusted Net Bank Credit or the Credit Equivalent Amount of Off-Balance-Sheet Exposure, whichever is greater.	40% of Adjusted Net Bank Credit or Credit Equivalent Amount of Off-Balance-Sheet Exposure, whichever is greater; up to 32% of which can be in the form of loans to Exports and no less than 8% to any other priority sector.	75 per cent of ANBC as computed in para 6 below or CEOBE whichever is higher; However, lending to Medium Enterprises, Social Infrastructure, and Renewable Energy shall be counted for priority sector accomplishment only up to 15% of ANBC.	75 per cent of ANBC as computed in para 6 below or CEOBE whichever is higher.
Agriculture	18% of ANBC or the Credit Equivalent Amount of Off-Balance-Sheet Exposure, whichever is greater. For Small and Marginal Farmers, a target of 8% of ANBC or Credit Equivalent Amount of Off-Balance-Sheet Exposure, whichever is greater, is mandated within the 18% objective for agriculture.	Not applicable	18 per cent of ANBC or Credit Equivalent Amount of Off-Balance Sheet Exposure, whichever is higher.	18 per cent of ANBC or Credit Equivalent Amount of Off-Balance Sheet Exposure, whichever is higher.
Micro Enterprises	7.5 per cent of ANBC or Credit Equivalent Amount of Off-Balance Sheet Exposure, whichever is higher.	Not applicable	7.5 per cent of ANBC or Credit Equivalent Amount of Off-Balance Sheet Exposure, whichever is higher.	7.5 percent of ANBC or the Credit Equivalent Amount of Off-Balance-Sheet Exposure, whichever is greater.
Advances to Weaker Sections	12 percent of ANBC or Credit Equivalent Amount of Off-Balance Sheet Exposure, whichever is higher.	Not applicable	15 percent of ANBC or Credit Equivalent Amount of Off-Balance Sheet Exposure, whichever is higher.	12 percent of ANBC or the Credit Equivalent Amount of Off-Balance-Sheet Exposure, whichever is greater.

BANKING

Commercial banks can be broadly divided into public sector, private sector, foreign banks and RRBs.

Historical evolution of Banking System in India

Phase 1: Pre – Independence Phase	• The first bank, known as the Bank of Hindustan, was formed in Calcutta in 1770. • It was closed in 1832. • India's first commercial bank was the Oudh Commercial Bank (1881).
Phase 2: Post-Independence Phase	• The Government of India recognised that many groups were financially excluded in 1975. Between 1982 and 1990, it established banking entities with specialised roles in response to the expansion of India's financial services. ▪ NABARD ▪ EXIM Bank etc.

Phase 3: The LPG Era (1991 till date)	• The Indian economy saw a seismic shift beginning in 1991. • The Indian government has urged private investors to invest in the country. The RBI has approved ten private banks. • A few notable names that have survived this liberalisation include HDFC, Axis Bank, ICICI, DCB, and IndusInd Bank. • In the early to mid-2000s, two other banks, Kotak Mahindra Bank (2001) and Yes Bank (2004) received their licenses. IDFC and Bandhan banks were also given licenses in 2013-14. Other notable changes are: • Foreign banks such as Citibank, HSBC, and Bank of America established branches in India. • The nationalisation of banks has come to a halt. Banks began to digitalize transactions and various other related banking operation.

- **Basel Norms:** Basel Committee on Banking Supervision is an international committee formed in 1974 to develop standards for banking regulation.
  - It consists of central bankers from 45 member institutions across 28 jurisdictions.
  - It is headquartered in the office of Bank for International Settlements (BIS) in Basel, Switzerland.
  - It developed a series of policy recommendations with respect to Capital risk, market risk and operational risk known as Basel Accords.
- **Tier 1 capital:** It can absorb losses without a bank being required to cease trading.
- **Tier 2 capital:** It can absorb losses in the event of winding up, which provide lesser degree of protection to depositors.
- **Tier 3 capital:** They are used to meet market risk, commodity risk and foreign currency risk.

Classification of Banks in India

Scheduled Banks

- Scheduled banks are those mentioned in the Reserve Bank of India Act, 1934's second schedule.
- To qualify as a scheduled bank, the bank's paid-up capital and raised funds must be at least '5 lakh.
- Scheduled banks are eligible for low-interest Reserve Bank of India loans and membership in clearinghouses.
- Bank must, however, meet certain requirements, such as maintaining an average daily CRR (Cash Reserve Ratio) balance with the central bank at the rates set by it. RBI allows Scheduled Banks to raise debts and loans at bank rates.
- All commercial banks, including nationalized, international, cooperative and regional rural banks, fall under scheduled banks.

Non-scheduled Banks

- Non-scheduled banks, by definition, are those that do not adhere to the RBI's regulations.
- They are not mentioned in the Second Schedule of the RBI Act, 1934 and are therefore deemed incapable of serving and protecting depositors' interests.
- Non-scheduled banks must also meet the cash reserve requirement, but not with reserve banks, but with themselves.
- They are generally smaller in size and have a range of influence that is somewhat narrow.
- They are risky to do business with due to their financial limitations. The reserve capital of these banks is less than 5 lakh rupees.

Functions of Banks in an Economy

Collection of the Savings of the Community	• People nowadays do not save their savings at home. They put them in banks. As a result, the chance of loss (from theft, etc.) is reduced. • Furthermore, some interest is earned. • There are several types of deposits. • Some are short-term deposits.
Loans and Investment	• Banks make loans to merchants, business owners, and others. • Lending is done in a variety of ways. Sometimes an account is formed in the borrower's name and he is authorised to write checks on it. • Banks put money into company stock and debentures, as well as government promissory notes. They lend money to industrial firms in exchange for Government Promissory Notes, shares, debentures, gold, finished items, and so on. Private persons can also get loans against G. P. Notes, shares, debentures, life insurance policies, and gold.
Creation of Money	• Formerly banks could print and issue notes payable by them on demand. • The notes were used as a medium of exchange. Nowadays only the central bank of the country can issue notes.
Other Functions	Banks retain assets in safe custody, such as lockers, shares, debentures, G.P. Notes, and so on, and use them to pay insurance premiums, bills, and so on. They also serve as executors and trustees of wills and exchange currency from foreign nations.

Nationalization of Banks

The transfer of public sector assets to be operated or held by the state or central government is referred to as nationalisation. In India, the act of nationalisation moved banks formerly operating in the private sector to the public sector, resulting in the establishment of nationalised banks.

Reasons for the Nationalization of Banks:

- For Social Welfare
- For Developing Banking Habits
- For Expansion of Banking Sector
- For Controlling Private Monopolies
- To Reduce Regional Imbalance
- For Prioritizing Sector Lending

On July 19, 1969, the government nationalised the 14 main commercial banks under the Banking Companies (Acquisition and Transfer of Undertakings) Ordinance. These lenders controlled more than 80% of the country's bank deposits. The Banking Companies (Acquisition and Transfer of Undertaking) Bill was quickly enacted by parliament and got presidential sanction on August 9, 1969.

Allahabad Bank, Bank of Baroda, Bank of India, Bank of Maharashtra, Central Bank of India, Canara Bank, Dena Bank, Indian Bank, Indian Overseas Bank, Punjab National Bank, Syndicate Bank, UCO Bank, Union Bank, and United Bank of India were among the banks nationalised.

Following that, on April 15, 1980, six other banks were nationalised: Punjab and Sind Bank, Vijaya Bank, Oriental Bank of India, Corporation Bank, Andhra Bank, and New Bank of India.

Regional Rural Banks

- The Regional Rural Banks (RRBs) were first set up on 2 October, 1975 (only 5 in numbers).
- RRBs were established based on the recommendations of Narsimha Committee working group.
- RRBs were set up as regional based rural lending institutions under the Regional Rural Banks Act, 1976.
- The Government of India, the concerned state government and the sponsoring nationalised bank contribute the share capital of the RRBs in the proportion of 50 per cent, 15 per cent and 35 per cent, respectively. The area of operation of the RRB is limited to notified few districts in a state.
- First RRB: Prathama Grameen Bank.

Small finance & Payment Banks

- In 2014, the RBI issued the draft guidelines for setting up small banks and payment banks. The guidelines said that both are 'niche' or 'differentiated' banks with the common objective of furthering financial inclusion.
- **Small finance banks:** Small finance banks are a type of niche banks in India. Banks with a small finance bank license can provide basic banking service of acceptance of deposits and lending. The aim behind these to provide financial inclusion to sections of the economy not being served by other banks, such as small business units, small and marginal farmers, micro and small industries and unorganized sector entities
- **Payments Banks:**
  - The objective of payments banks is to increase financial inclusion by providing small savings accounts, payment/remittance services to migrant labour, low-income households, small businesses, other unorganized sector entities and other users by enabling high volume-low value transactions in deposits and payments/remittance services in a secured technology-driven environment.
  - Payments Banks can accept demand deposits (only current account and savings accounts). They would initially be restricted to holding a maximum balance of 1 lakhs per customer. Based on performance, the RBI could enhance this limit.
  - The Payments Banks would be required to use the word 'Payments' in its name to differentiate it from other banks.
  - No credit lending is allowed for Payments Banks.
  - Payments Banks Formation - Nachiket Mor Committee.

MUDRA (Micro Units Development and Refinance Agency)

- Pradhan Mantri MUDRA Yojana (PMMY) is a scheme launched by the Honorable Prime Minister on April 8, 2015 for providing loans non-corporate, non-farm small/micro-enterprises.
- These loans are classified as MUDRA loans under PMMY. These loans are given by Commercial Banks, RRBs, Small Finance Banks, MFIs and NBFCs.
- The products designed under it are categorized into three buckets of finance named Shishu (loan up to ₹50,000), Kishor (₹50,000 to ₹5 lakh) and Tarun (₹5 lakh to ₹10 lakh).
- The newest category of PMMY- Tarun Plus category, started in 2024, extends loans above ₹10 lakh and up to ₹20 lakh to borrowers who have successfully repaid previous loans under the Tarun category.
- The scheme's objective is to refinance collateral-free loans given by the lenders to small borrowers.
- Though the scheme covers the traders of fruits and vegetables, in general, it does not refinance the agriculture sector.

NBFCs (Non-Banking Financial Companies)

- A non-bank financial company (NBFC) is a financial institution that does not have a full banking license or is not supervised by the central bank.
- It is company under companies Act,1956.

NABARD (National Bank for Agriculture and Rural Development)

- NABARD was established on the recommendation of B. Sivaraman Committee on 12 July 1982.
- NABARD set up in July 1982 by an Act of parliament to take over the functions of ARDC and the refinancing functions of RBI in relation to co-operative banks and RRBs.
- NABARD is linked organically with the RBI by the latter contributing half of its share capital the other half being contributed by the Government of India.
- Deputy Governor of RBI is appointed as Chairman of NABARD.

The committees that proposed the banking sector reforms are as mentioned below:

- The First Narasimham Committee- 1991
- The Verma Committee – 1996
- The Khan Committee – 1997
- The Second Narasimham Committee – 1998

Banking Reforms introduced in India in recent times

Some of the steps taken by the government to bring reforms in the banking sector are:

- The Ministry of Finance in its **Economic Survey 2015-16** suggested four R's – Recognition, Recapitalization, Resolution and Reform to address the problem of NPAs.
- In October 2015, the Government announced Mission Indradhanush under which 7 key strategies were proposed to reform public sector banks (PSBs).
- In May 2015, the RBI advised all PSBs to appoint an internal Ombudsman to further boost the quality of customer service and to ensure that there is undivided attention to the resolution of customer complaints in banks.

- The Government announced its intention to introduce a comprehensive Insolvency and Bankruptcy Bill in the Parliament based on the recommendations of the Dr. T. K. Viswanathan-headed Bankruptcy Law Reforms Committee (BLRC).
- In order to rein in corruption, the Supreme Court on 23 February 2016 ruled that the top officials and employees of private banks will be considered as public servants for the purposes of the Prevention of Corruption Act, 1988.

Monetary Policy

- Monetary policy is a process implemented by the central bank to manage the money supply in order to achieve specific goals such as limiting inflation, maintaining an appropriate exchange rate, creating jobs and promoting economic growth.
- Monetary policy entails changing interest rates, either directly or indirectly, through open market operations, reserve requirements or foreign exchange trading.

Objective of Monetary Policy

- Monetary policy is concerned with making money available to the market at reasonable rates and in sufficient quantities at the appropriate time in order to achieve:
  - Price stability
  - Accelerating growth of economy
  - Exchange rate stabilization
  - Balancing savings and investment
  - Generating employment
  - Financial stability
- The primary goal of monetary policy is to maintain price stability while keeping growth in mind. Price stability is a prerequisite for long-term growth.
- In order to maintain price stability, inflation must be kept under control.
- Every five years, the Indian government sets an inflation target.
- The Reserve Bank of India (RBI) plays an important role in the consultation process for inflation targeting. The current inflation-targeting framework in India is flexible.

Reserve Bank of India

- The Reserve Bank of India was founded on April 1, 1935, under the terms of the Reserve Bank of India Act, 1934.
- The Reserve Bank's Central Office was first located in Calcutta but was permanently relocated to Mumbai in 1937. The Governor sits in the Central Office, where policies are developed.
- Though originally privately held, the Reserve Bank has been wholly owned by the Government of India since its nationalisation in 1949.

Amendments introduced in RBI act over the years.

- In May 2016, an amendment to the RBI Act of 1934 was adopted, providing the statutory foundation for the adoption of the flexible inflation-targeting framework.
- **Banking Regulation (Amendment) Bill, 2020:** The bill was approved by the Lok Sabha. The Bill supersedes an ordinance to that effect that was passed on June 26. The Bill proposes changes to the Banking Regulation Act of 1949. The federal government intends to put cooperative banks under the jurisdiction of the Reserve Bank of India (RBI) with this new Bill.

Main Functions of the RBI

Monetary Authority	• It executes and monitors monetary policy and guarantees price stability while keeping growth in mind. • In May 2016, an amendment to the RBI Act of 1934 was adopted, providing the statutory foundation for the adoption of the flexible inflation targeting framework. • Section 45ZB of the amended RBI Act, 1934, also provides for an empowered six-member Monetary Policy Committee (MPC) to be constituted by the Central Government by notification in the Official Gazette.
Regulator and Supervisor of the Financial System	• Prescribes general parameters of banking operations within which the country's banking and financial system works, such as licence issuance, branch growth, asset liquidity, bank merger, and so on. • Maintain public trust in the system, safeguard depositors' interests, and provide cost-effective banking services to the public such as commercial banking and cooperative banking.
Manager of Foreign Exchange	• Manages India's Foreign Exchange Reserves. • It fosters the orderly growth and upkeep of India's foreign exchange market and enables overseas commerce and payment. • It also keeps the rupee's external value stable.
Issue of Currency	• Issues and exchanges or destroys currency and coins not fit for circulation. • Objective: To give the public adequate quantities of supplies of currency notes and coins and in good quality.
Related Functions	• Government banker: provides merchant banking activities for the federal and state governments. • It is in charge of the central government's money, remittances, exchange, and public debt management. • Banker to banks: Maintains all scheduled banks' banking accounts. It also serves as a lender of last resort, supplying cash to banks.

RBI Constitute

- **Official Directors (Central Board of Directors)**
- Full-time: Governor and not more than four Deputy Governors.
- **Non-Official Directors**
- **Nominated by Government:** Ten Directors from various fields and two government Official.
- Two Finance Ministry Representatives
- **Others: Four Directors** – One each from four local boards (regional).

How does the RBI get its mandate to implement Monetary Policy?

- The Reserve Bank of India (RBI) is charged with implementing monetary policy. The Reserve Bank of India Act of 1934 expressly mandates this responsibility.
- There have recently been many changes in the way India's monetary policy is formed, with the introduction of the Monetary Policy Framework (MPF), Monetary Policy Committee (MPC) and Monetary Policy Process (MPP).

Monetary Policy Committee (MPC)

- The Monetary Policy Committee now determines the policy interest rate required to achieve the inflation target in India.
- The MPC is a six-person committee appointed by the Central Government (Section 45ZB of the amended RBI Act, 1934).
- The MPC must meet at least four times per year. The MPC meeting requires a quorum of four members. Each MPC member has one vote and in the event of a tie, the Governor has a second or casting vote.
- Following the conclusion of each MPC meeting, the resolution adopted by the MPC is published.
- The Reserve Bank is required to publish a document called the Monetary Policy Report once every six months to explain:
- the sources of inflation; and
- the forecast of inflation for the next 6-18 months.

Monetary Policy Instruments

Monetary policy is implemented using a variety of direct and indirect instruments.

Repo Rate

- The (fixed) interest rate at which the Reserve Bank provides short-term liquidity to banks in exchange for the government and other approved securities as collateral under the liquidity adjustment facility (LAF).

Reverse Repo Rate

- The (fixed) interest rate at which the Reserve Bank absorbs liquidity from banks on an overnight basis in exchange for eligible government securities under the LAF.

Liquidity Adjustment Facility (LAF)

- The LAF is made up of both overnight and term repo auctions.
- The Reserve Bank has gradually increased the proportion of liquidity injected through fine-tuning variable rate repo auctions of various tenors.
- The goal of the term repo is to help develop the inter-bank term money market, which in turn can set market-based benchmarks for loan and deposit pricing and thus improve monetary policy transmission.
- The Reserve Bank also conducts variable interest rate reverse repo auctions as market conditions dictate.

Marginal Standing Facility (MSF)

- A facility through which scheduled commercial banks can borrow an additional amount of overnight money from the Reserve Bank by dipping into their Statutory Liquidity Ratio (SLR) portfolio up to a certain limit at a penal rate of interest.
- This acts as a safety valve for the banking system in the event of unexpected liquidity shocks.

Corridor

- The corridor for the daily movement in the weighted average call money rate is determined by the MSF rate and the reverse repo rate.

Bank Rate

- It is the rate at which the Reserve Bank is willing to purchase or rediscount bills of exchange or other commercial papers.
- This rate has been aligned with the MSF rate and, as a result, changes automatically when the MSF rate and the policy repo rate change.

Cash Reserve Ratio (CRR)

- Cash reserve Ratio (CRR) is the amount of Cash that the banks have to keep with RBI.
- The commercial banks as per the statute has to maintain reserves based on their demand deposit and fixed deposit with central bank is called as Cash Reserve Ratio.
- If the CRR is high, the commercial bank's capacity to create credit will be less and if the CRR is low, the commercial bank's capacity to create credit will be high.

Statutory Liquidity Ratio (SLR)

- Statutory Liquidity Ratio (SLR) is the amount which a bank has to maintain in the form of cash, gold or approved securities. The quantum is specified as some percentage of the total demand and time liabilities of a bank.
- SLR is used to control the bank's leverage for credit expansion.

Open Market Operations (OMOs)

- These include the outright purchase and sale of government securities for the purpose of injecting and absorbing long-term liquidity, respectively.

Market Stabilisation Scheme (MSS)

- This monetary management tool was introduced in 2004.
- Short-term government securities and treasury bills are sold to absorb longer-term surplus liquidity resulting from large capital inflows.
- The money raised in this manner is kept in a separate government account of the Reserve Bank.

What is a Digital Currency?

Digital currency is any currency that's available exclusively in electronic form.

- Crypto-currency is a type of digital currency.
- The majority of currencies in this world are digital. As per an estimate, around 92% of the world's currency is already in digital form. Only 8% is in cash.

What is a Central Bank Digital Currency (CBDC)?

Following the success of decentralized digital currencies like Bitcoin, Ethereum, etc. countries over the world are thinking to introduce their own digital currencies known as Central Bank Digital Currency (CBDC) or national digital currency in India.

- CBDC is simply the digital form of a country's fiat currency. Instead of printing paper currency or minting coins, the central bank issues electronic tokens.
- This token value is backed by the full faith and credit of the government.

Note: Please keep in mind that Crypto-currency (like Bitcoin, Dogecoin etc.) is a type of digital currency. They are not the same.

Cryptocurrency vs Digital Currency

Here are some key differences:

- **Decentralization:** Digital Currencies are centralized meaning they are regulated and issued by a single entity like a central bank.
- **Openness:** In Crypto-currencies, one can see all the transactions as the directory (ledger) is kept open. This functionality is an integral feature of blockchain where every block contains information about the previous transaction. In Digital Currencies, one would not be able to visualize the entire chain of transactions.
- **Legal framework:** Most Crypto-currencies have no legal frameworks while a digital currency is backed by an appropriate legal framework.

Public Finance

- The administration of a country's revenue, expenditures, and debt through different government and quasi-government organisations, policies, and instruments is known as public finance.
- Components of public finance: public expenditure + public revenue + financial scrutiny + fiscal policy + financial administration + public borrowing.

Annual Financial Statement (Budget): Article 112

- The phrase budget appears nowhere in the Constitution.
- Article 112 of the constitution refers to the budget as the Annual Financial Statement.
- In 1924, the Acworth Committee recommended that the Rail Budget be seperated from the General Budget.
- However, it was merged again in 2017.
- The Budget is a statement of the Government estimated receipts and expenditure in a financial year starting from April 1 and ending on 31 March.
- The revenue account (also known as the revenue budget) includes just receipts and expenditures for the current fiscal year.
- Those relating to the government's assets and obligations in the capital account (also known as the capital budget).

Budget

Receipt
- Revenue Receipt
- Tax Revenue
- Non-Tax Revenue
- Non-Revenue Receipt

Expenditure
- Capital Expenditure
- Revenue Expenditure (both discussed in Fiscal Policy)

Tax Revenue

- A tax is a legal obligation that individuals and corporations must pay to a country's government without obtaining any immediate benefit in return. It is imposed on the people by the government.
- A government collects taxes such as income tax, sales tax, service tax, excise duty, and customs duty.
  - Historically, taxation has been the primary source of government finance.
  - Those who earn income such as wages, salaries, rent, interest and profit are subject to income tax.
  - The tax on the sale of goods is known as sales tax. When we buy something, a portion of our money goes to the government as sales tax.
  - Service tax is the fee we pay when we use a service, such as a telephone.
  - Excise duty is a tax paid by the maker of a product.
  - Customs tax is paid when a product is imported or exported.
- **All taxes are of two kinds:**
  - Direct taxes
  - Indirect taxes
- **This distinction between taxes depends on:**
  - the liability of payment of tax to the government and
  - the actual burden of the tax.

Direct Taxes

Direct taxes are charged on a person's or a company's property and revenue. Direct taxes are collected on businesses and people and are paid to the government directly. People's purchasing power and income levels are affected by direct taxes. It also aids in the adjustment of the economy's aggregate demand. Direct taxation can be proportional, progressive or regressive. The Central Board of Direct Taxes (CBDT), which is part of the Ministry of Finance in the Government of India, makes recommendations on Direct Tax programmes and policies. Income tax, corporate tax, property tax, and gift tax are all examples.

Indirect Taxes

Indirect taxes are those that influence an individual's income or the income and property of a firm through their consumer expenditure. Products and services are subject to indirect taxes, sometimes known as forced payments. An example of an indirect tax is the service tax. Direct taxation aids in the management of inflation.

Sources of Tax Revenue

- Corporation tax, income tax, customs, union excise charges, service tax, and a variety of other taxes all generate significant revenue.
- Real estate taxes, wealth taxes on various types of wealth, and gift taxes are all examples of wealth taxes. Import duties, basic tariffs, and fees on specific commodities all contribute to customs income. Export levies and a cess on exports are additional factors.
- Goods and Services Tax (GST) on a wide range of products and services also contributes to tax revenue.

Non-Tax Revenue

Non-Tax Revenue is the government's recurring revenue from sources other than taxes. They are revenue collections that are not received from regular population taxation. The following are some of the most important non-tax revenue sources:

- Interest on loans granted to state governments, UTs, private firms, and the general public is a substantial source of nontax revenue for the government.
- Fees received by the central power authority of any country are included in this category. This comprises fees received by the Central Electricity Authority in India.
- **Fees:** These are fees charged by the government to cover the expense of ongoing services. It is an obligatory tax-like contribution.
- **License Fee:** A license fee is a type of tax levied by the government and its affiliated entities for engaging in a certain activity, such as starting a restaurant or operating a heavy vehicle.
- **Penalties and fines:** Fines are most typically used in criminal law, when a court of law imposes a fine on a person guilty of a crime.
- In contrast, the penalty is used in both civil and criminal law. It includes both financial and physical sanctions.
- **Escheats:** When a person dies without leaving a legally binding will or legal heirs, escheats are the transfer of estate assets or property to the government.

- International organisations and foreign countries provide funding to the government. Such grants are rarely a steady source of funding and are often awarded in reaction to a national catastrophe such as war, flood, or natural disaster.

- **Forfeitures:** A forfeiture is the uncompensated loss of property as a result of failing to satisfy contractual commitments or as a punishment for illegal behaviour. A defaulting party's responsibility to cede ownership of an asset or cash flows from an asset in compensation for the other party's losses is referred to as forfeiture under contract provisions.
- **Interests:** This category includes interest on loans and insurance supplied to the government for non-planned and planned schemes, as well as interest on loans, advanced to PSEs and other statutory entities.
- **Communication Services Fees:** The majority of this is made up of licence fees from telecom operators for spectrum use prices that licenced Telecom Service Providers pay to the government ministry in charge of telecommunications.

Non Revenue Receipts

Amounts received that either incur an obligation that must be met at some future date or change the form of an asset from property to cash and therefore decrease the amount and value of property.

Objectives of Budget

- Resource Allocation For Public Goods
- Redistribution Of Income
- Stabilisation In The Economy

Golden Rule of Budget

The Golden Rule is a guideline for the operation of fiscal policy, especially in countries who uses high borrowing to run the budget. It states that over the economic cycle, the Government should borrow only to invest and not to fund current spending (current expenditure means day to day running expenses). In layman's terms, this means that the government should borrow to finance investment that benefits future generations.

Balanced Budget	The government may spend an amount equal to the revenue it collects.
Surplus Budget	If the expected government revenues exceed the estimated government expenditure in a particular financial year.
Deficit Budget	If the estimated government expenditure exceeds the expected government revenue in a particular financial year.
Outcome Budget	It is a budget that converts outlays into outcomes by planning the expenditure, fixing appropriate targets, quantifying deliverables in each scheme and bringing to the knowledge of all the outcomes for each scheme/programme under various ministries.
Gender Budgeting	It is not an accounting exercise but an ongoing process of keeping a gender perspective in policy/programme formulation, its implementation and review.
Zero Based Budgeting	All expenses are evaluated each time a budget is made and expenses must be justified for each new period.
Sunset Budgeting	Schemes are announced with a deadline, designed to self-destruct within a prescribed time.

Inflation

- Inflation refers to the rise in the prices of most goods and services of daily or common use, such as food, clothing, housing, recreation, transport, consumer staples, etc.
- Inflation measures the average price change in a basket of commodities and services over time.
- The opposite and rare fall in the price index of this basket of items is called 'deflation'. Inflation is indicative of the decrease in the purchasing power of a unit of a country's currency.

- This example clearly explains the fall in the purchasing power of money. For ₹ 100 you could get 5 kg rice before, but now only 4 kg. So the purchasing power of money got reduced. This is inflation.

- This is measured in percentage.

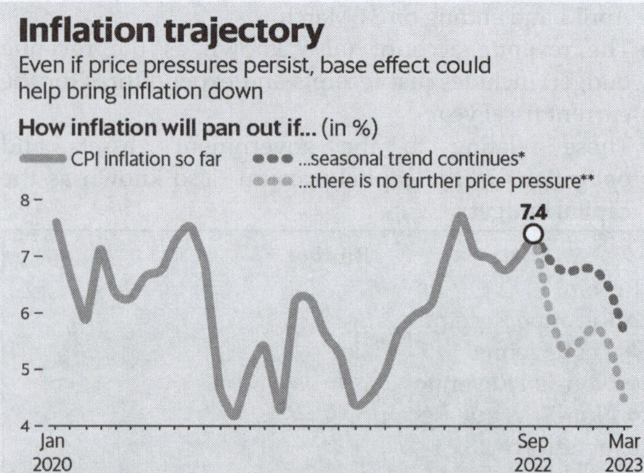

Types of inflation	**Based on demand and supply** ● **Demand Pull Inflation:** Demand pull inflation occurs when aggregate demand in the economy exceeds aggregate supply. ● **Cost Push Inflation:** When there is a drop in the aggregate supply of goods and services, the cost of production rises. **Based on Speed or Intensity, the types of inflation are as follows:** ● **Creeping or Mild Inflation** ■ Creeping inflation occurs when the rate of price increases is gradual yet significant. ■ It is beneficial to economic progress. ■ Prices rise at a very small rate (<3%). ● **Walking or Trotting Inflation** ■ When prices rise moderately and the annual inflation rate rises by a single digit. ■ It is the time when the government should focus on the issue. ■ Price rises at a moderate rate (3% to 10%). ● **Running Inflation** ■ Running inflation occurs when prices grow at a pace of 10% - 20% per year, similar to the speed of a horse. ● **Galloping and Hyperinflation** ■ When creeping and walking inflation are uncontrolled, the rate rises beyond 10%, which is referred to as galloping inflation. ■ As a result, the economy becomes unstable. ■ Hyperinflation is when the prices of goods and services rise more than 50% per month. ■ It is the last stage of inflation. ■ Examples: Germany in the 1920s, Zimbabwe in the 2000s, the American Civil War, and Venezuela in 2018 are all examples. ■ Prices climb at an alarming rate (20% to 100%). On the basis of inducement ● **Credit inflation** ■ When banks are liberal in lending credit, the money supply increases and thereby rising prices. ● **Currency inflation** ■ The excess supply of money in circulation causes rise in price level. This type of inflation is caused by the printing of currency notes. ● **Deficit induced inflation** ■ The deficit budget is generally financed through printing of currency by the Central Banks. As a result, prices rise ● Tax induced inflation. Increase in indirect taxes like excise duty, custom duty, GST and sales tax may lead to rise in price (Ex. petrol and diesel). This is called tax induced inflation. ● **Scarcity induced inflation** ■ The scarcity of goods happen either due to a fall in production (Ex. farm goods) or due to hoarding and black marketing. This also pushes up the price. ● **Profit induced inflation** ■ When the firms aim at higher profit, they fix the price with a higher margin. So prices go up.
Causes of Inflation	**Demand-Pull Inflation** Various variables might cause an increase in aggregate demand. Some of them are: ● Fiscal Stimulus ● Population Pressure ● Increase in Net Exports ● Monetary Stimulus ● Policy Decisions **Cost-Push Inflation** The fundamental cause of cost-push inflation is rising production costs. The following reasons can cause production costs to rise. ● Employees' salaries being raised ● Raw material prices increasing ● Firms profit margins ● Import prices ● Increase in indirect taxes **Built-In Inflation** ● As the price of goods and services increases, labor expects and demands more wages to maintain their cost of living, increasing prices and the wage-price spiral continues. **Monetary Inflation** ● Reserve Bank of India printing more money (deficit financing) can trigger inflation. It is a sustained increase in the money supply of a country or currency area.
How inflation is measured?	● **In India, inflation is primarily measured by two main indices —** WPI (Wholesale Price Index) and CPI (Consumer Price Index), are able to monitor wholesale and retail pricing fluctuations, respectively. ● The CPI measures the difference in the prices of items and services purchased by Indian consumers for usage, such as food, medical care, education, and gadgets. ● The WPI, on the other hand, captures the items or services sold by firms to smaller businesses for resale. ● WPI is still published but CPI is now the official inflation benchmark since 2014.

	• **Producer Price Index:** It measures the average price changes in the selling prices over time received by the domestic producer. India does not officially publish a Producer Price Index (PPI), it uses WPI as a producer-level price index.
Effect of Inflation in Indian Economy	• The buying power of a currency unit declines as commodities and services become more expensive. • This has an effect on the cost of living in a country. When inflation is strong, the cost of living rises along with it, resulting in a slowing of economic growth. • A certain degree of inflation is essential in the economy to guarantee that spending is encouraged and savings are discouraged. • **Repo Rate** ▪ It is expected to push up interest rates in the banking system. Equated Monthly Installments (EMIs) on home, vehicle and other personal and corporate loans are likely to go up. ▪ Deposit rates, mainly fixed term rates, are also set to rise. • **CRR (Cash Reserve Ratio)** ▪ The cost of funds will go up and banks' net interest margins could get adversely impacted.
Advantages and Disadvantages of Inflation	• Inflation targeting is a monetary strategy in which a central bank sets an explicit medium-term inflation objective and discloses it to the public. • The primary aim of monetary policy will be price stability. **Advantages:** • It will result in more openness and accountability. • Policy will be tied to medium/long term aims, but with significant flexibility in the short term. • People tend to have low inflation expectations when inflation targeting is in effect. People may have higher inflation expectations if there is no inflation objective, prompting workers to demand higher pay and businesses to raise prices. • It also helps in avoiding boom and bust cycles. • Inflation may create a variety of economic consequences, including uncertainty, which leads to fewer investment, a loss of international competitiveness, and a decrease in the value of savings. This is also avoidable with targeting. • Inflation objectives can offer a variety of advantages, particularly under 'normal' economic conditions. However, the extended recession after the 2008 financial crunch has put inflation objectives to the test.

	Disadvantages: • It puts too much weight on inflation relative to other goals. Central Banks start to ignore more pressing problems like unemployment. • Inflation targets reduce "flexibility". It has the potential to constrain policy in some circumstances in which it would not be desirable to do so. • Cost-push inflation may cause a temporary blip in inflation. • It cannot help remove supply bottlenecks and shortages. • It cannot help external shocks, exchange rate might suffer in the short run. • Growth and employment might take hits in the short run.
Various methods of combating inflation	• **Monetary Policy:** Monetary policy is one of the most commonly used measures taken by the government to control inflation. It uses tools like – Bank rate, Repo Rate, Open Market Operations, etc. • **Fiscal Policy:** The two main components of fiscal policy are government revenue and government expenditure. In fiscal policy, the government controls inflation either by reducing private spending or by decreasing government expenditure or by using both. It reduces private spending by increasing taxes on private businesses. When private spending is more, the government reduces its expenditure to control inflation. However, in the present scenario, reducing government expenditure is not possible because there may be certain on-going projects for social welfare that cannot be postponed. • **Price Control :** In this method, inflation is suppressed by price control, but cannot be controlled for the long term. The historical evidence has shown that price control alone cannot control inflation, but only reduces the extent of inflation.
Terms Related to Inflation	Some terms related to Inflation are as follows: • **Disinflation:** Decrease in the rate. • **Deflation:** Negative inflation or persistent price level decrease. • **Reflation:** This happens when the Price level increases because the economy recovers from recession. • **Stagflation:** When stagnation and inflation coexist in the economy. Stagnation- low national income growth and high unemployment. Inflation + Recession (Unemployment)

	• **Misery Index:** Rate of inflation + Rate of unemployment • **Inflationary Gap:** Aggregate demand > Aggregate supply • **Deflationary Gap:** Aggregate supply > Aggregate demand

	• **Suppressed/Repressed Inflation:** Aggregate demand > Aggregate supply. The government will not allow the rising of prices in this. • **Open Inflation:** Situation where price level rises without any price control measures by the government.

Unit-3: Market

Financial Markets

- The financial market is the market in an economy where funds are exchanged between fund-surplus and fund-scarce individuals and groups.

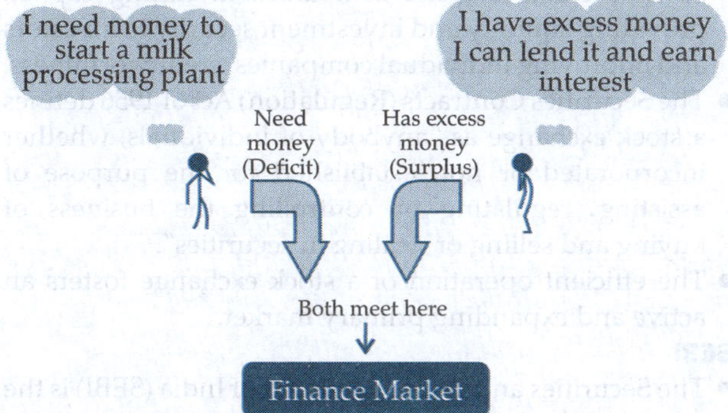

Types of financial markets

A financial market is of two types:
- Money Market
- Capital Market

There can be one more type of classification of financial market:
- Organized financial market – Regulated and controlled by any regulatory body like RBI. This organized market can be further divided into the following two categories:
  - Money Market
  - Capital Market
- Unorganised financial market – Unregulated and not governed by any laws. Private moneylenders etc. come under this category.

Money Market

In a money market, short term financial assets that are close substitutes of money are sold & bought (upto 365 days or less).
- Close substitutes mean those financial assets that can be quickly converted to cash with minimum transaction cost.
- Short-term financial assets mean maturity period is less than a year. Examples include treasury bills, certificates of deposit, etc.
- This market is characterised by buying and selling of products with high liquidity (easily convertible to cash) and short-maturity (less than a year).

In simplest terms, the money market fulfills borrowing and lending needs of less than a year.

Types of Maturity

Borrowing and lending can be done for various time periods within 365 days. On the basis of these we define few terms:
- Call money or overnight call money – Here lending and borrowing is done on an overnight basis i.e., 1 day
- Notice money – Time period here is between 1 – 14 days (i.e., 2 to 13 days)
- Term money – Time period here is between 14 – 365 days (i.e., 15 to 364 days)

Types of Money Market Instruments

- Treasury Bills
- Commercial Bills
- Certificate of Deposit (CD)
- Commercial Paper (CP)
- Banker's Acceptances
- Bills of Exchange
- Money Market Mutual Funds
- Repurchase Agreements (Repos)

Capital Market

It is a market in which lending or borrowing is done for a period of more than 365 days.
- The capital market is characterized by long term financial assets like bonds, debentures, etc.
- This market is critical for our economy because it provides the financial resources required for the long-term sustainable development of the economy.
- The capital market consists of development banks, commercial banks and stock exchanges.
- Indian Capital Markets are regulated and monitored by the Ministry of Finance, The Securities and Exchange Board of India (SEBI) and RBI.

Types of Capital Market

Capital market is generally of two types:
- Primary market
- Secondary market

Primary Market

In this market, securities are issued for the first time.
- The investors in this market are banks, financial institutions, insurance companies, mutual funds and individuals.

Secondary Market

It deals with the buying and selling of existing or previously issued securities.
- This market is also known as the stock market or stock exchange.

Capital Market Instruments

Capital market instruments are of three types:
- **Pure instruments:** These include shares, bonds and debentures. They do not share features of one another. They are pure.
- **Hybrid instruments:** They have a combination of features like a combination of bond & equity.
- **Derivatives:** These instruments have no value of their own but derive their value from one or more financial assets. Some examples of derivatives include futures and options.

Major Terminologies – Financial Market

- **Treasury Bills:** They are short-term promissory notes issued by the RBI on behalf of the government and sold to banks and the general public. The maturation period spans from 14 and 364 days. They are negotiable instruments, which means they may be freely transferred. Such banknotes bear no interest, but they are issued at a reduction from their face value.
- **Commercial Bills:** They are sometimes referred to as Trade Bills or Bills of Exchange. Commercial bills are issued by one company to another in place of credit transactions. It is a written acknowledgement of debt by the creator ordering the payment of a certain quantity of money to a specific individual. They are short-term instruments generally issued for 90 days. These are freely marketable. Banks provide working capital finance to firms by purchasing the commercial bills at a discount; this is called 'discounting of bills'.
- **Commercial Paper (CP):** The Vaghul Committee recommended the introduction of the CP in 1990. A commercial paper is an unsecured promissory note issued by a corporation having a net value of at least ₹ 100 crore for short-term financing. These are provided at a discount from face value for a term ranging from 7 days to 12 months. These are granted in 1 lakh increments with a minimum of 25 lakh.
- **Certificate of Deposit (CD):** The Vaghul Committee recommended the introduction of the CD in 1989.
- These are issued by banks in exchange for deposits held by individuals and institutions for periods ranging from 15 days to three years. These are similar to Fixed Deposits, except they may be negotiated and traded. These are granted in multiples of1 lakh, subject to a minimum of ₹ 25 lakh.
- **Discount and Finance House of India Ltd.:** On the advice of the Vaghul Committee, DFHI was established as a subsidiary of the RBI in 1988. Its goal is to boost money market activity by supplying liquidity to the money market instrument. It purchases bills and short-term securities from banks and financial institutions, creating a secondary market for them.

Gilt-Edged Market

The Gilt-edged market refers to the market for government and semi-government securities, backed by the RBI. The term gilt-edged means 'of the best quality'. It is known so because the government securities do not suffer from the risk of default and are highly liquid. The RBI is the sole provider of these securities. Commercial banks, insurance firms, provident funds, and mutual funds all require them. The gilt-edged market may be separated into two parts: Treasury bills and government bonds.

Treasury bills are issued to cover the government's short-term funding needs, whilst government bonds are issued to support long-term development investment.

Stock Exchanges

- A stock exchange is an organisation that provides a marketplace for the purchase and sale of existing securities.
- The stock exchange facilitates the conversion of a security (share, debenture, etc.) into money and vice-versa.
- Stock exchanges assist companies in raising capital, providing liquidity and investment security to investors and improving individual companies' creditworthiness.
- The Securities Contracts (Regulation) Act of 1956 defines a stock exchange as "anybody of individuals, whether incorporated or not, established for the purpose of assisting, regulating or controlling the business of buying and selling or dealing in securities".
- The efficient operation of a stock exchange fosters an active and expanding primary market.

SEBI

- The Securities and Exchange Board of India (SEBI) is the regulatory body for securities and commodity market in India under the ownership of Ministry of Finance within the Government of India. It was established on 12 April 1988 as an executive body and was given statutory powers on 30 January 1992 through the SEBI Act, 1992. SEBI has its headquarters in Mumbai.
- For the discharge of its functions efficiently, SEBI has been vested with the following powers:
  - To approve by–laws of Securities exchanges.
  - To require the Securities exchange to amend their by–laws.
  - Inspect the books of accounts and call for periodical returns from recognised Securities exchanges.
  - Inspect the books of accounts of financial intermediaries.
  - Compel certain companies to list their shares in one or more Securities exchanges.
  - Registration of Brokers and subrokers.

Unit-4: Different Aspects of the Indian Economy

Poverty and Unemployment

Poverty

- Poverty is defined as a lack of a normal or socially acceptable quantity of money or material belongings.
- Poverty is defined as a lack of resources to meet one's fundamental necessities.

On the basis of social, economic and political aspects, poverty can be classified as follows:

Absolute Poverty	• Extreme poverty, often known as abject poverty, is defined by a lack of essential food, clean water, health, housing, education, and knowledge. • Those who live in abject poverty struggle to survive, and many children die from avoidable ailments. • Absolute poverty is unusual in wealthy countries.
Relative Poverty	• It is defined from a social standpoint, that is, living standards in comparison to the economic standards of the surrounding population. As a result, it is a measure of income disparity.

	• Typically, relative poverty is defined as the percentage of the population earning less than a certain percentage of median income. • It is a frequently used metric for determining poverty rates in affluent industrialised countries.
Situational Poverty	• It is a sort of temporary poverty caused by an unpleasant event such as an environmental disaster, job loss, or significant health difficulties. • People can help themselves even with a small assistance, as the poverty comes because of unfortunate event.
Generational Poverty	• It is passed on from generation to generation to people and families. • This is more complex since there is no way out because the individuals are caught in the cause and lack access to the tools needed to escape.
Rural Poverty	• This occurs in rural areas, where there are less job opportunities, less access to services, less support for disabilities and quality education opportunities.
Urban Poverty	• The key obstacles that urban residents confront as a result of poverty include: ▪ Limited access to health and education. ▪ Housing and services are inadequate. ▪ Overcrowding creates a violent and toxic atmosphere, with little or no social protective mechanisms.

Various committees on the Poverty

Working Group (1962)	• This Group defined the poverty line in India for the first time in 1962, in terms of a basic necessity (food and non-food) of persons for healthy living. • The Group established distinct poverty levels for rural and urban regions ('20 and '25 per capita per month in 1960-61 prices) with no geographical variance. • The poverty line excluded expenditure on health and education, both of which were to be provided by the State.
Lakdawala Expert Group (1993)	• It did not redefine the poverty standard and kept the Alagh Committee's recommendation of separate rural and urban poverty lines at the national level based on minimal nutritional requirements. • However, it disaggregated them into state-specific poverty lines in order to reflect the inter-state price differentials. • Over the years, this method lost credibility. The price data were flawed and successive poverty lines failed to preserve the original calorie norms.
Tendulkar Expert Group (2009)	• It advocated for a change away from basing poverty lines on calorie standards, which had been used in all poverty estimates since 1979, and towards focusing on nutritional outcomes instead. • Instead of two different poverty line baskets (PLBs) for rural and urban poverty lines, it proposed a single all-India urban PLB that would apply to both rural and urban India. • It recommended using Mixed Reference Period (MRP) based estimates, as opposed to Uniform Reference Period (URP) based estimates used in earlier methods for estimating poverty. • It suggested that when assessing poverty, private investment on health and education be included. • It verified the poverty lines by comparing real private consumer spending per capita at the poverty line on food, education, and health to normative expenditures consistent with nutritional, educational, and health results. • Instead of monthly household consumption, consumption expenditure was broken up into per person per day consumption, resulting in the figure of ₹ 32 and ₹ 26 a day for urban and rural areas. • As a result, the national poverty line for 2011-12 was estimated at ₹ 816 per capita per month for rural areas and ₹ 1,000 per capita per month for urban areas.
Rangarajan Committee (2014)	• Because of considerable criticism of the Tendulkar Committee's methodology, as well as changing circumstances and people's expectations in India. In 2012, the Rangarajan Committee was formed. • It went back to using distinct all-India rural and urban poverty line baskets and producing state-level rural and urban estimates from them. • It recommended separate consumption baskets for rural and urban areas which include food items that ensure recommended calorie, protein & fat intake and non-food items like clothing, education, health, housing and transport.

	• This committee increased daily per capita expenditure to ₹47 for urban and ₹32 for rural from ₹32 and ₹26 in 2011-12 prices. • At the national level, a monthly per capita consumption expenditure of ₹972 in rural regions and ₹1407 in urban areas is indicated as the poverty line. • However, the government did not act on the Rangarajan Committee's report.

Various Programme and Schemes for Poverty Alleviation Since Independence

- Since the early 1950s, the Indian government has established, supported, and developed several planning projects to assist the poor in achieving self-sufficiency in food acquisition and overcoming hunger and poverty.
- All the Five year plans introduced in India, had elements in them to reduce Poverty; of which the following Five-Year Plans (FYP) had explicit provisions in them aimed at Poverty alleviation:

Fifth Plan (1974–1978)

- It emphasised job creation, poverty reduction (Garibi Hatao), and justice.
- It also guaranteed a monthly minimum income of '40 per person at 1972-73 prices.

Seventh Plan (1985–1990)

- The Seventh Five-Year Plan's main thrust areas were social justice, oppression of the weak, use of modern technology, agricultural development, anti-poverty programmes, full supply of food, clothing, and shelter, increasing productivity of small- and large-scale farmers, and making India an independent economy.
- From the perspective of poverty, it aimed at improving the living standards of the poor with a significant reduction in the incidence of poverty.

Eighth Plan (1992–1997)

- The primary goals included population control, poverty alleviation, job creation, and so on.

Ninth Plan (1997–2002)

- It offered strong support to the social spheres of the country in an effort to achieve the complete elimination of poverty.

Tenth Plan (2002–2007)

- One of the main objectives of the plan, was reduction of poverty rate by 5% by 2007.

Eleventh Plan (2007–2012)

- Its goal was to achieve rapid and inclusive growth (poverty reduction).

Twelfth Plan (2012–2017)

- The government intended to reduce poverty by 10% during the tenure of the plan.

Scheme/Programme	Year	Objective/Provisions
Public Distribution System	Pre-Independence	• This project began in 1945, during World War II, and was introduced in its current form after 1947. • After the Green Revolution increased agricultural productivity, the PDS outreach was expanded to tribal blocks and areas of high poverty incidence in the 1970s and 1980s.
Integrated Rural Development Programme (IRDP)	1978	• It was one of the most ambitious programmes in the world for alleviating rural poverty by distributing income-generating assets to the poorest of the poor. • The scheme's main goal was to keep families from falling into poverty by generating long-term chances for self-employment in the rural sector.
Rural Landless Employment Guarantee Programme	1983	• This was launched to generate additional employment opportunities for the landless people in the villages.
Indira Awaas Yojana	1985	• It originally started as a sub-scheme of the Rural Landless Employment Guarantee Programme (RLEGP) to provide houses for Scheduled Castes (SCs), Scheduled Tribes (STs), and freed bonded labourers. In 2016, the scheme was restructured and renamed as the Pradhan Mantri Awaas Yojana-Gramin (PMAY-G).
Jawahar Rozgar Yojna	1989	• This was launched with the objective of providing 90-100 Days Employment per person particularly in backward districts. • People Below Poverty Line were main targets.
Revamped Public Distribution System	1992	• The Revamped PDS was begun in 1992 with the goal of strengthening and streamlining the PDS as well as improving its reach in rural, mountainous, and inaccessible areas where a significant portion of the poor dwell.

Targeted Public Distribution System(TPDS)	1997	• In 1997, RPDS was renamed TPDS (Targeted PDS), and Fair Price Shops were established to provide food grains at subsidised rates. • The major purpose was to provide critical food commodities such as rice, wheat and paraffin at heavily subsidised costs to persons living in poverty. This poverty-relief programme has aided in tackling the issue of food insecurity in rural India.
National Maternity Benefit Scheme	1999-2000	• It is for families below the poverty line. • This scheme provides a sum of ₹ 6000 to a pregnant mother in three installments. • The scheme was updated in 2005-06 into Janani Suraksha Yojana.
Jawahar Gram Samridhi Yojana (JGSY)	1999	• The main aim of this program was the development of infrastructure rural areas like roads, schools and hospitals. • Its secondary objective was to give out sustained wage employment.
Annapurna Scheme	1999-2000	• This initiative was established to offer meals to older adults who are unable to care for themselves, are not covered by the National Old Age Pension initiative (NOAPS), and have no one to care for them in their community. • The scheme mostly targeted groups of 'poorest of the poor and 'indigent senior citizens'.
Antyodaya Anna Yojana (AAY)	2000	• This scheme provides food grains at a highly subsidized rate of ₹ 2.00 per kg for wheat and ₹ 3.00 per kg for rice to the poor families under the Targeted Public Distribution System (TPDS).
Sampoorna Gramin Rozgar Yojana (SGRY)	2001	• The Government of India created this plan with the goal of creating productive work for the rural poor. • It was created by combining provisions from the Employment Assurance Scheme (EAS) and the Jawahar Gramme Samridhi Yojana (JGSY). • The plan is self-targeting in design, with the goal of providing jobs and food to persons living below the poverty line in rural regions.
Mahatma Gandhi National Rural Employment Guarantee Act (MGNREGA)	2005	• It seeks to improve rural livelihood stability by offering at least 100 days of pay employment each fiscal year to every household whose adult members volunteer to conduct unskilled manual labour. • Another goal of MGNREGA is to build long-lasting assets (such as roads, canals, ponds, and wells). • Through the process of providing employment on works that address causes of chronic poverty such as drought, deforestation and soil erosion, the Act seeks to strengthen the natural resource base of rural livelihood and create durable assets in rural areas. Effectively implemented, MGNREGA has the potential to transform the geography of poverty. • It is replaced by Viksit Bharat – Guarantee for Rozgar and Aajeevika Mission (Gramin) (VB-G RAM G).
National Rural Livelihood Mission	2011	• It was founded with the goal, "To reduce poverty by enabling the poor households to access gainful self- employment and skilled wage employment opportunities resulting in appreciable improvement in their livelihoods on a sustainable basis, through building strong and sustainable grassroots institutions of the poor" .
National Urban Livelihood Mission	2013	• It focuses on organizing urban poor into Self Help Groups, creating opportunities for skill development leading to market-based employment and helping them to set up self-employment ventures by ensuring easy access to credit.
Pradhan Mantri Ujjwala Yojana (PMUY)	2016	• It was launched to distribute 50 million LPG connections to women of Below Poverty Line (BPL) families.

Unemployment

- Unemployment happens when a person actively looking for job is unable to find work.
- Unemployment is frequently used to gauge the state of the economy.
- NSO defines employment and unemployment on the following activity statuses of an individual:
  - Working (involved in an economic activity), often known as 'Employed'.
  - 'Unemployed' means looking for or available for employment.
  - Neither looking for nor available for job.
- ➢ The first two constitute the labour force and unemployment rate is the percent of the labour force that is without work.

➢ Unemployment rate = (Unemployed Workers / Total labour force) × 100.

Different Types of Unemployment

Disguised Unemployment	• It is a phenomena in which more individuals are hired than are really required. • It is largely found in India's rural and unorganised industries.
Seasonal Unemployment	• It is an unemployment that occurs during certain seasons of the year. • Agricultural labourers in India rarely have work throughout the year.
Structural Unemployment	• It is a type of unemployment caused by a mismatch between the jobs offered in the market and the abilities of the available workers. • Many individuals in India are unemployed because they lack the necessary skills, and training them is difficult owing to a lack of knowledge.
Cyclical Unemployment	• It is the outcome of the business cycle, in which unemployment rises during recessions and falls during expansions. • In India, cyclical unemployment is low. It is a phenomena that is prevalent in capitalist economies.
Technological Unemployment	• It is the loss of jobs due to changes in technology. • In 2016, World Bank data predicted that the proportion of jobs threatened by automation in India is 69% year-on-year.
Frictional Unemployment	• Frictional unemployment, also known as Search Unemployment, refers to the time gap between jobs while an individual is looking for a new work or moving jobs. • In other words, when an employee needs time to look for a new job or transition from one position to another, the unavoidable time lag generates frictional unemployment.
Vulnerable Employment	• This means, people working informally, without proper job contracts and thus sans any legal protection. • These people are classified as "unemployed" since no records of their job are kept. • It is one of the most prevalent kinds of unemployment in India.

Major Causes of Unemployment in India

- Rapid Growth of Population
- Dominance of Agriculture
- Fall of Cottage and Small Industries
- Immobility of Labour
- Defects in Education System

Government's Initiatives to Curb Unemployment

- Support for Marginalized Individuals for Livelihood and Enterprise (SMILE)
- Pradhan Mantri Dakshta Aur Kushalta Sampann Hitgrahi (PM-DAKSH)
- Viksit Bharat – Guarantee for Rozgar and Aajeevika Mission (Gramin) (VB-G RAM G).
- Pradhan Mantri Kaushal Vikas Yojana (PMKVY)
- Start Up India Scheme
- Rozgar Mela

Agriculture

- Agriculture plays a vital role in the Indian economy.
- As per Economic Survey 2022-23 and NSO data: Agriculture's share in GDP was approximately 18.3% in 2022-23 (GVA at basic prices). Employment figures from Periodic Labour Force Survey (PLFS) 2021-22 show approximately 45.5% of workforce in agriculture.
- The foodgrains production has increased from 51 million tonnes (MT) in 1950-51 to 357.73 MT in 2024-25 highest ever since independence.
- The share of agriculture in GDP increased to 18 per cent in 2024-25 from 17.8 per cent in 2019-20. The last time the contribution of the agriculture sector in GDP was at 20 per cent was in 2003-04.
- Over 70 per cent of the rural households depend on agriculture.

Characteristics and features of Indian Agriculture

Source of livelihood	Agriculture is the most common employment. It employs around 61% of the entire population. It accounts for 25% of national income.
Dependence on monsoon	Agriculture in India mainly depends on monsoon because irrigation facilities are quite inadequate.
Labour intensive cultivation	Due to the increase in population the pressure on land holding increased. Land holdings get fragmented and subdivided and become uneconomical. Machinery and equipment can not be used on such farms.
Under employment	Farmers find work just a few months of the year because of insufficient irrigation facilities and unpredictable rains. Their labour potential cannot be fully used. Underemployment and disguised unemployment exist in agriculture.
Small size of holdings	Due to large scale sub-division and fragmentation of holdings, land holding size is quite small.
Traditional methods of production	Agriculture producing methods and equipment are traditional in India. It is related to people's poverty and ignorance. The major cause of poor productivity is traditional technology.

Low Agricultural production	In India, agricultural production is low. Per acre, India produces 27 quarts of wheat. An agricultural laborer's average yearly production in India is 162 dollars, 973 dollars in Norway, and 2408 dollars in the United States.
Dominance of food crops	75% of the cultivated area is under food crops like Wheat, Rice and Bajra while 25% of cultivated area is under commercial crops. This pattern is the cause of backward agriculture.

Types of Farming in India

Some of the major types of farming are:

Subsistence Farming

- Landholdings are tiny and fragmented in this style of farming, and agricultural practises are rudimentary and unsophisticated.
- There is a complete lack of modern farm equipment, such as tractors, as well as farm inputs such as chemical fertilisers, insecticides, and pesticides. Farmers mostly farmed grains, as well as oilseeds, legumes, vegetables, and sugarcane, in this farming.
- Subsistence farming is further classified into:

Intensive

- Intensive subsistence agriculture is done on small lands with simple tools and more labour.
- The produce is enough for local consumption and to be sold outside.

Primitive

- Primitive subsistence agriculture is done on small plots of land using primitive technologies such as rudimentary digging tools and communal or family work.
- This style of farming is dependent on the monsoon, as well as soil fertility and other environmental factors.

Intensive and Extensive Farming

- The primary distinction between these two methods of farming is the quantity of output per unit of land.
- Extensive farming is when a huge area of land is used for cultivation. Because of the bigger area, total output may be high, but per unit production is low.
- Intensive farming produces a lot of food per acre of land. An example of intense agriculture may be seen in Kerala, where agricultural land is scarce.

Commercial Farming

- In this system, farmers use inputs like irrigation, chemical fertilizers, insecticides, pesticides, High Yielding Varieties of seeds, etc.
- Cotton, jute, sugarcane, groundnut, and other significant commercial crops are cultivated in various locations of India.
- Rice planting in Haryana is mostly for commercial purposes because the inhabitants of this region eat wheat.

Plantation Farming

- In this type, a single cash crop is grown for sale in national and international markets.
- This type of agriculture involves the growing and processing of a single cash crop purely meant for sale.
- Tea, coffee, rubber, banana and spices are all examples of plantation crops. Most of these crops were introduced in India by the britishers in the 19th century.

Mixed Farming

- Mixed farming refers to the practise of cultivating crops and animals at the same time. Farmers that practise mixed farming benefit financially as well.
- For example, Banana is a plantation type of farming but can also be classified as commercial farming.

Contribution of Agriculture to Indian Economy

The Economic Survey of India 2024-25 report stated that:

- The agriculture and allied sectors grew at an average annual rate of around 4.4% at constant prices over the last five years.
- Survey states that India's net agricultural exports exceeded USD 50 billion, reaching USD 51.1 billion in the fiscal year.
- India recorded unprecedented foodgrain output of 357.73 million metric tonnes, an increase of 25.43 million metric tonnes from the preceding year. Similarly, combined foodgrain and oilseed output reached a record high of over 400 million metric tonnes, driven by favourable monsoons, improved input management, and sustained productivity gains.
- Survey of India confirmed that institutional agricultural credit has consistently increased, reaching a ground-level disbursement of ₹28.67 lakh crore in FY24-25, reflecting a structural expansion of formal finance to the farm sector.

Challenges of Indian Agriculture

Instability	• Agriculture in India is heavily reliant on the monsoon. • As a result, food grain output varies from year to year. • A year of high crop output is frequently followed by a year of severe shortfall.
Cropping Pattern	• The crops that are grown in India are divided into two broad categories: food crops and non-food crops. While the former comprise food-grains, sugarcane and other beverages, the latter includes different kinds of fibers and oilseeds.
Land Ownership	• Inequality in land distribution is also caused by frequent changes in land ownership in India. • It is claimed that significant tracts of land in India are held by a very small group of wealthy farmers, landlords, and moneylenders, whereas the great majority of farmers possess very little or no land at all.

Conditions of Agricultural Labourers	• The majority of farm labourers in India have deplorable working conditions. There is also the issue of excess labour, commonly known as disguised unemployment. • As a result, wage rates fall below subsistence levels.
Manures, Fertilizers and Biocides	• Indian soils have been used for growing crops over thousands of years without caring much for replenishing. • This has resulted in soil depletion and fatigue, leading in low output. • Almost all crop average yields are among the lowest in the world. This is a major issue that may be addressed by utilising additional manures and fertilisers.
Irrigation	• India is the second largest irrigated country of the world after China, only one-third of the cropped area is under irrigation.
Lack of Mechanisation	• Little or no use of machines is made in ploughing, sowing, irrigating, thinning and pruning, weeding, harvesting threshing and transporting the crops.
Agricultural Marketing	• Agricultural marketing in rural India is still in poor shape. • In the lack of good marketing infrastructure, farmers must rely on local traders and intermediaries to dispose of their farm produce, which is sold at a loss.
Inadequate Transport	• One of the major challenges for Indian agriculture is the absence of affordable and effective transportation. • Even now, there are thousands of villages that are not adequately connected to big routes or market hubs.

Government Initiatives, Policies and Measures

The Government of India is giving more priority for the welfare of farmers. In this regard it is implementing several farmers welfare schemes to re-vitalize agriculture sector and to improve their economic conditions. Therefore, the government has rolled out new initiatives, schemes, programmes and plans to benefit all the farmers.

National Agriculture Market (eNAM)	National Agriculture Market (eNAM) is a pan-India electronic trading system that connects the current APMC mandis to form a unified national agricultural market. Small Farmers Agribusiness Consortium (SFAC) is the lead agency for implementing eNAM under the aegis of Ministry of Agriculture and Farmers' Welfare, Government of India. **Vision:** • Increasing standardisation in agricultural marketing by simplifying operations across integrated marketplaces. • Eliminating information imbalance between buyers and sellers, allowing for real-time price discovery based on actual demand and supply.
National Mission for Sustainable Agriculture (NMSA)	The National Mission for Sustainable Agriculture (NMSA) was created to increase agricultural output, particularly in rainfed areas, by focusing on integrated farming, water usage efficiency, soil health management, and resource synergy. **Schemes under NMSA:** • **Rainfed Area Development (RAD):** RAD is being implemented by RFS Division. • **Soil Health Management (SHM):** SHM is being implemented by INM Division. • **Sub Mission on Agro-Forestry (SMAF):** SMAF is being implemented by NRM Division. • **Paramparagat Krishi Vikas Yojana (PKVY):** PKVY is being implemented by INM Division. • **Soil and Land Use Survey of India (SLUSI):** Being implemented by RFS Division. • **National Rainfed Area Authority (NRAA):** Being implemented by RFS Division. • **Mission Organic Value Chain Development in North Eastern Region (MOVCDNER):** Being implemented by INM Division. • **National Centre of Organic Farming (NCOF):** Being implemented by INM Division. • **Central Fertilizer Quality Control and Training Institute (CFQC&TI):** Implemented by INM Division.
Pradhan Mantri Krishi Sinchai Yojana (PMKSY)	The Pradhan Mantri Krishi Sinchayi Yojana (PMKSY) was created with the goal of expanding irrigation coverage of 'Har Khet Ko Pani' and increasing water usage efficiency. 'More crop per drop' with an end-to-end solution on source generation, distribution, management, field application, and extension activities. **Objectives:** • Achieve convergence of investments in irrigation at the field level (preparation of district level and, if required, sub district level water use plans).

	• Improve physical availability to water on the farm and extend cultivable land under guaranteed irrigation (Har Khet Ko Pani). • Water supply, distribution, and efficient usage are all integrated to make the best use of water through appropriate technology and practises. • Improve the efficiency of on-farm water use to decrease waste and enhance availability in both duration and extent. • Enhance the adoption of precision – irrigation and other water saving technologies (More crop per drop). • Enhance recharge of aquifers and introduce sustainable water conservation practices.
Paramparagat Krishi Vikas Yojana (PKVY)	The NDA administration introduced the Paramparagat Krishi Vikas Yojana (PKVY) in 2015, an attempt to encourage organic farming in the country. Farmers would be encouraged to create groups or clusters and use organic agricultural practises throughout huge regions of the country, according to the programme. **Objectives:** • Promotion of commercial organic production through certified organic farming. • The produce will be pesticide residue free and will contribute to improve the health of consumers. • It will raise farmer's income and create a potential market for traders. • It will motivate the farmers for natural resource mobilization for input production.
Pradhan Mantri Fasal Bima Yojana (PMFBY)	The Pradhan Mantri Fasal Bima Yojana (PMFBY) is a government-sponsored crop insurance system that brings together a variety of stakeholders on a single platform. **Objectives:** • To provide insurance coverage and financial support to the farmers in the event of failure of any of the notified crops as a result of natural calamities, pests & diseases. • Farmers' income must be stabilised in order for them to continue farming. • Encourage farmers to use new, contemporary farming practises. • Ensure the flow of finance to the agricultural industry.
Gramin Bhandaran Yojana	Gramin Bhandaran Yojana or Rural Godown Scheme, is an Indian government initiative to offer subsidies to individuals or organizations which build or repair rural godowns.
	Objectives: • Create scientific storage capacity with allied facilities in rural areas. • To meet the requirements of farmers for storing farm produce, processed farm produce and agricultural inputs. • Promotion of agricultural produce grading, standardisation, and quality control in order to increase marketability. • Prevent distress sales shortly after harvest by providing pledge finance and marketing credit and enhancing the country's agricultural marketing infrastructure.
Livestock Insurance Scheme	This scheme aims to provide farmers and cattle rearers with protection mechanisms against the loss of their animals due to death, as well as to demonstrate the benefits of livestock insurance to the public and popularise it, with the ultimate goal of achieving qualitative improvement in livestock and their products. **Benefits:** • The rural insurance policy is designed to offer insurance cover to indigenous cattle owned by farmers, cooperative societies, dairy farms and the like. • Security in case of death of cattle shall be provided for the following: ■ Natural Accidents. (Flood, famine, earthquake, etc.) ■ Unpredictable circumstances. (Accidental in Origin.) ■ Surgical Operations. ■ Terrorist Act. ■ Strikes and Riots. ■ Civil Commotion Risk.
Micro Irrigation Fund (MIF)	• As part of its goal to enhance agriculture productivity and farmers' income, the government established a specific ₹ 5,000 crore budget to bring additional land area under micro-irrigation. • The fund has been set up under NABARD, which will provide this amount to states on concessional rate of interest to promote micro-irrigation, which currently has a coverage of only 10 million hectares as against the potential of 70 million hectares.
Soil Health Card Scheme	• The project was created to help state governments give Soil Health Cards to all farmers in the country. • The Soil Health Cards tell farmers on the nutrient state of their soil, as well as recommendations on the proper nutrient dose to be administered to improve soil health and fertility.

Neem Coated Urea (NCU)	• This strategy was launched to restrict urea consumption, increase nitrogen availability to crops, and minimise fertiliser application costs. • NCU delays the release of fertiliser and makes it more effective in reaching the crop. • The entire quantity of domestically manufactured and imported urea is now neem coated. • It reduces the cost of cultivation and improves soil health management.
Rainfed Area Development Programme (RADP)	Rainfed Area Development Programme (RADP) was implemented as a sub-scheme under Rashtriya Krishi Vikas Yojana (RKVY). **Aims:** • To improve the quality of life of farmers, particularly small and marginal farmers, by providing a comprehensive package of activities designed to maximise farm profits. • Increasing agricultural productivity in rainfed areas in a sustainable way through the use of farming system-based techniques. • Through diverse and composite agricultural methods, the negative impact of crop failure due to drought, flood, or uneven rainfall distribution is reduced. • Restoration of confidence in rainfed agriculture by creating sustained employment opportunities through improved on-farm technologies and cultivation practices. • Enhancement of farmer's income and livelihood support for reduction of poverty in rainfed areas.
National Watershed Development Project for Rainfed Areas (NWDPRA)	In 1990-91, the National Watershed Development Project for Rainfed Areas (NWDPRA) initiative was started, based on the dual themes of integrated watershed management and sustainable agricultural methods. **Aims:** • Natural resource conservation, development, and management that is long-term. • Sustainable enhancement of agricultural production and productivity. • Restoration of ecological balance in the degraded and fragile rainfed eco-systems by greening these areas through appropriate mix of trees, shrubs and grasses. ■ Reduction in regional disparity between irrigated and rainfed areas and; ■ Creation of sustained employment opportunities for the rural community including the landless.
Farm Bills	**Farmers' Produce Trade and Commerce (Promotion and Facilitation) Act, 2020** • Expands the scope of farmer's produce trading regions from specific places to "any place of production, collection, or aggregation". • Allows for electronic trade and e-commerce of farmers' planned product. • State governments are prohibited from imposing any market charge, cess, or levy on farmers, traders, or electronic trading platforms for the exchange of farmer's produce done in a "outside trade area". **Farmers (Empowerment and Protection) Agreement on Price Assurance and Farm Services Act, 2020** • Provides a legal framework for farmers to enter into pre-arranged contracts with buyers including mention of pricing. • Defines a dispute resolution mechanism. **Essential Commodities (Amendment) Act, 2020** • Removes cereals, pulses, potatoes, onions, edible oilseeds, and oils from the list of essential commodities; removes stock holding limits on agricultural items produced by horticulture techniques except in "extraordinary circumstances," and requires that any stock limit on agricultural produce be imposed only if there is a sharp price increase.

Cropping Pattern

- Cropping Pattern is defined as the proportion of land planted to various crops at any given moment. It is a dynamic idea since it varies across time and space.
- Rainfall, climate, temperature, soil type, and technology all influence cropping patterns in India.

Types of Cropping Seasons

- **Rabi:** Rabi crops are sown in winter from October to December and harvested in summer from April to June. Some of the important rabi crops are wheat, barley, peas, gram and mustard.
- **Kharif:** The Kharif crop is the summer crop or monsoon crop in India. Kharif crops are usually sown with the beginning of the first rains in July, during the south-west monsoon season. Major Kharif crops of India include Millets (Bajra & Jowar), Cotton, Soybean, Sugarcane, Turmeric, Paddy (Rice), Maize, Moong (Pulses), Groundnut, Red Chillies, etc.
- **Zaid:** This crop is grown in some parts of the country from March to June. Prominent examples are Muskmelon, Watermelon, bitter gourd, pumpkin, ridged gourd etc.

Factors Influencing Cropping Pattern

- **Geographical Factors**
- **Relief:** Most crops (Wheat, Cotton) require plain areas where vast stretches of land is available for cultivation and agricultural operations are easier as compared to hilly areas. Crops like tea and coffee require a large amount of water but stagnant water is harmful for their roots. They prefer hilly regions where rain water can easily drain out.
- **Soil:** Rice on clayey soil and Wheat on Loamy soil, Coarse grains on inferior soil, Fertility of soil is major determinant of crop productivity and hence cropping pattern. Ganga Brahmaputra delta=jute, Darjeeling=tea.
- **Temperature:** Each crop requires a specific temperature for its growth. Some crops require high temp and they are Kharif (Rice), some require low temp they are Rabi (Wheat). Hence temperature is very much responsible for determining cropping patterns.
- **Rainfall:** Rainfall is another determinant of cropping pattern, in many areas land use depends exclusively on rainfall.
- **Economic Factors**
- **Irrigation:** Irrigation assumes greater significance in arid and semi-arid areas, even in heavy rainfall areas it is used for higher yield. In semi-arid areas of UP, Punjab, Haryana, wheat is a traditional crop. With increase in irrigation these areas have become major rice producing areas and cropping patterns have undergone major change.
- **Size of Land Holdings:** In Smallholdings, priority of farmers is to grow food crops for the family and large holdings can go for cash crops and help crop diversification.
- **Sale price of crops and Income of farmers:** Sale price of rice is better than wheat so farmers in NW shifted. In certain areas farmers are not able to get remunerative prices then they shift to cash crop. MSP offered for some cereals like rice and wheat has changed cropping pattern tilting towards these crops.
- **Insurance:** Variation in monsoon causes heavy losses to farmers. Insurance can help farmers to pursue agriculture without fear and the most appropriate cropping pattern is adopted.
- **Investment:** To change cropping patterns, huge investment is required. Groundnut replaced cotton in Madhya Pradesh because of easy availability of seeds.
- **Political Factors**
- Govt. policies can influence cropping pattern to great extent. Export policy, Tax structure, transport, irrigation, agri credit, loan etc. Govt. can encourage any crop by providing subsidies on seeds, fertilizers, electricity. Increase in production of foodgrains and decrease in production of tobacco, poppy, indigo are largely due to govt policies. If a transport facility is available farmers can go for vegetables and horticulture.
- Changes are observed in cropping patterns in accordance with the minimum support price offered.
- **Historical Factors**
- Certain crops are grown by necessity and then that cropping pattern is maintained.

Cropping System

Cropping system refers to the crops, crop sequences and management techniques used on a particular agricultural field over a period of years. It includes all spatial and temporal aspects of managing an agricultural system.

Types of Cropping System

- **Mono-Cropping:**
- Mono-cropping refers to growing of only one crop on a piece of land year after year. It may be due to climatological and socio-economic conditions or due to specialisation of a farmer in growing a particular crop, eg.- in canal irrigated areas, under a waterlogged condition, rice crop is grown as it is not possible to grow any other crop.
- **Multiple-cropping:**
- Growing two or more crops on the same piece of land in one calendar year is known as multiple-cropping.
- It is the intensification of cropping in time and space dimensions, i.e., more number of crops within a year and more number of crops on the same piece of land any given period.
- It includes intercropping, mixed-cropping and sequence cropping.
- Double-cropping is a case where the land is occupied by two crops, which are grown in a year in sequence.

Types of Multiple Cropping

- Inter Cropping
- Mixed Cropping
- Row Intercropping
- Sequence Cropping
- Relay Cropping
- Ratoon Cropping (Ratooning)

Inter Cropping

- Growing two or more crops simultaneously on the same piece of land with definite row arrangement or in a fixed ratio.
- Inter-cropping was originally practiced as an insurance against crop failure under rained conditions. At present the main objective of inter-cropping is higher productivity per unit area in addition to stability in production. Inter-cropping system utilizes resources efficiently and their productivity is increased.
- Example- Maize + Cowpea, Potato + Mustard, Groundnut + Redgram.

Mixed Cropping

- Cultivation of two or more than two crops simultaneously on the same land without definite row pattern or fixed ratio. Sowing seeds is generally by broadcasting method.
- It is a common practice in most of the dryland tracts in India.
- The objective is to meet the family requirement of cereals, pulses and Vegetables, it is subsistence farming.
- Example- wheat, gram and mustard are grown as mixed rabi crops in dry regions of Northern India.

Sequence Cropping

- Defined as growing of two or more crops in quick succession on the same piece of land in a farming year. Crop intensification is only in time dimension and there is no intercrop competition.
- Double, triple and quadruple cropping: Growing two, three and four crops, respectively, on the same land in a year in sequence.
- Example- Double cropping: Rice: cotton; Triple cropping: Rice: rice: pulses; Quadruple cropping: Tomato: ridge gourd: Amaranth greens: baby corn.

Relay Cropping

- Growing two or more crops simultaneously during the part of the life cycle of each.
- A second crop is planted after the first crop has reached its reproductive stage of growth, but before it is ready for harvest. Often simply referred to as relay cropping.
- Example- Redgram- base crop 180 days.
- Groundnut/onion/coriander- 1st set of intercrops.
- Samai/ thinai/panivaragu- 2nd set of intercrops.

Ratoon Cropping

- Ratooning is the practise of growing crops with regrowth originating from roots or stalks after harvest.
- Ratooning is a crop harvesting procedure that leaves the roots and lower sections of the plant uncut to produce the ratoon or stubble crop.
- Because the production of the ratoon crop declines with each cycle, this approach cannot be employed indefinitely. Ratooning is most commonly utilised with crops that are known to produce a consistent yield for three years under most conditions.
- Example- Sugarcane, Banana, Pineapple.

Multilevel Cropping

- It is a pattern of cropping where short duration quick growing fruits and vegetables are grown in between the horticulture crops to utilize leisure periods of growth and development of the principal crop.
- This is the practice of growing different crops of varying height, rooting pattern and duration.

Green Revolution

Introduction

- The Green Revolution was an initiative launched by Norman Borlaug in the 1960s. Globally, he is renowned as the "Father of the Green Revolution".
- It led to his receiving the Nobel Peace Prize in 1970 for his efforts in creating wheat High Yielding Varieties (HYVs).
- In India, the Green Revolution was mainly led by M. S. Swaminathan.
- Beginning in the mid-twentieth century, the introduction of new, high-yielding variety seeds into emerging nations resulted in a significant rise in food grain output (particularly wheat and rice).
- Its first spectacular achievements were in Mexico and the Indian subcontinent.
- The Green Revolution, spreading over the period from 1967-68 to 1977-78, changed India's status from a food-deficient country to one of the world's leading agricultural nations.

Pillars of Green Revolution

High Yielding Varieties of Seeds

- Their main characteristics are increased responsiveness to chemical fertilizers, short maturity period, resistance to wind damage, large leaf size to increase photosynthesis.

Irrigation

- Irrigation is a precondition for successful introduction of HYV seeds even in areas of Heavy rainfall.
- The success of the Green Revolution lies in the availability of water at the right time and in the right quantity.

Use of Fertilizers

- HYV seeds need a heavy dose of irrigation and fertilizers to give high yields.
- Multiple cropping is possible with a trio of HYV seeds, irrigation and chemical fertilizers.

Land Reforms

- The Indian agricultural system was plagued by ills of absentee landlordism, tenancy. Land reform were therefore needed to break shackles of zamindari systems prevalent since British raj.

Industry and Infrastructure

Infrastructure

Infrastructure is the set of fundamental facilities and systems that support the sustainable functionality of households and firms.

- It is composed of public and private physical structures such as roads, railways, bridges, tunnels, water supply, sewers, electrical grids and telecommunications (including internet connectivity and broadband access).

Basic Industries

Basic industries are industries which supply their products to manufacture other goods. Examples: Iron and steel, copper, aluminium, chemical etc.

Capital Goods Industries	Goods that are used in producing other goods e.g. textile machinery, conveyor belts, mining equipment etc.
Heavy Industries	Producing large and heavy products e.g. Ship building, bulldozers, industrial machinery, electric transformers etc.

Energy

Generation Mix :

- Coal 1163 TWh (73%);
- Hydro 151 TWh (10%);
- Natural Gas 73.6 TWh (5%);
- Wind 64.3 TWh (4%);
- Biofuels & Waste 45.4 TWh (2.9%);
- Solar 39.7 TWh (2.5%);
- Nuclear 37.8 TWh (2.4%); and
- Oil 7.8 TWh (0.5%).

COAL

- Top five largest coal reserves: USA (22.31%) > Russia (15.51%) > Australia (14.01%) > China (13.15%) > India (9.45%)
- As per more recent data (2022-23), coal accounts for 46-55% of India's total primary energy supply and roughly 70-75% of the country's electricity generation.

India is the second largest coal importer, despite having the world's fifth largest coal reserves and being the second largest producer.

Coal Reserves in India

- Coal sector, which has dominant use in three core sectors i.e. power, steel and cement.

India has the 5th largest reserves of coal globally and holds about 344 billion of the world's, some 850 billion of proven reserves.

Indian coal is classified in 2 categories, i.e.,

- coking coal and
- non-cooking coal.

This is a usage based classification, as coking coal is essential for the Iron and steel industry.

More streamlined classification is on the basis of carbon content and stage of formation.

Type	Note	Carbon%
Peat	Highest moisture content, smoke pollution. Most inferior in energy.	40-60
Lignite / Brown Coal	Important states: TN (Neyveli), Gujarat, Rajasthan.	40-60
Bituminous	Upon heating, it releases a liquid called Bitumin. Important states: Chattisgarh, Jharkhand, WB, MP, Odisha.	60-80
Anthracite	Burns with short blue flame, lowest moisture content, highest energy.	80-90

Coal Sector Reforms

Objective – 4 fold – to Increase

- Investment,
- Production,
- Employment and
- Boost to Make in India initiative

Mineral Laws (Amendment) Act, 2020

It amends the:

- Coal Mines (Special Provisions) Act, 2015 [CMSP Act]
- Mines and Minerals (Development and Regulation) Act, 1957 [MMDR Act].

Provisions

- Allocation of coal blocks for composite prospecting license-cum-mining lease.
  It will help in increasing of the inventory of coal, lignite blocks for allocation.
- Provision for requirement of Approval from Centre – Done away.
  In cases where the allocation or reservation of coal/ lignite block has been made by the Central Government itself.
- Provided flexibility to the Central Government. in deciding the end-use of Schedule II and III coal mines under the CMSP Act.

Government introduced a slew of reforms such as:

- Easing participation norms for bidders – More competition.
- Eliminating end-use restrictions.
- Shifting from rupee per Tonne model to revenue-sharing model.
- Government has introduced a more equitable system of sharing revenues, moving away from fixed rates to an ad-valorem system.

So when the prices go up, the miner shares more with the government and if they decrease, he/she shares less. This is equitable for both the parties.

- Permitting 100 per cent foreign direct investment in the coal sector – foreign players.
- The eligibility criteria has been done away with and no coal mining experience is required to take part in the auction process.
- Simplified the process of the mining plan approval process from 90 days to 30 days.
- Other relevant measures include:
  - Promoting coal gasification through rebate in revenue share, and
  - An investment of ₹ 50,000 crore to create transportation infrastructure for evacuating one billion tonnes of coal from state-run Coal India's mines.

SHAKTI Coal Policy (2017)

- Scheme for Harnessing and Allocating Koyala (Coal) Transparently in India (SHAKTI).
- Nodal Agency: Coal Ministry.
- Previously, it was discretion of the government that which thermal power plant company will get how much coal from Coal India.
- Shakti Policy replaces that discretion with an online centralised bidding process.
- Coal Mitra App by Power Ministry to help companies in buying / selling coal.
- UTTAM App by coal ministry to monitor coal quality coming from a particular mine.

Petroleum and Natural Gas

- Gas-based economy implies gas as the main commercial energy source in the energy mix of an economy.
- The Indian government is intending to move towards a gas-based economy by increasing the share of natural gas in India's energy basket from the current 6-7% to 15% by 2022.
- Government had planned a $60-billion investment for creating gas infrastructure in the country till 2024 and that gas's share in the energy mix is expected to rise to 15% by 2030.

H-CNG

- The blending of hydrogen with CNG provides a blended gas termed as H-CNG. It can be used in place of gasoline, diesel fuel and propane (C3H8)/LPG and its combustion produces fewer undesirable gases.

Background

- The Bureau of Indian Standards (BIS) has also developed specifications (IS 17314:2019) of Hydrogen enriched Compressed Natural Gas (H-CNG) for automotive purposes as a fuel.
- The Ministry of Road Transport and Highways has allowed use of H-CNG (18% mix of hydrogen) in CNG engines.
- A notification for amendments to the Central Motor Vehicles Rules 1989, for inclusion of H-CNG as an automotive fuel has already been published.

Energy: Electricity

- Electricity is a key element in modern day life. Right from running irrigation pumps to charging mobile phones, electricity is a prerequisite for agricultural growth and digital connectivity.
- Greater access to energy improves both economic growth and human development of a country.
- India is the third largest consumer of energy in the world after the USA and China. However, India is not endowed with abundant energy resources. It must, therefore, meet its development needs by using all available domestic resources of coal, uranium, oil, hydro and other renewable resources and supplementing domestic production by imports.

Deen Dayal Gram Jyoti Yojana (2015)	• **Nodal Agency:** Rural Electrification Corporation-REC (2015) (Ministry of Power) • Central Sector Scheme, i.e., 100% funded by the Union. • In India, there is a broad lack of rural lighting which led to more use of kerosene lamps. This results in increased pollution, import bill, subsidy bill and health hazards. • So, UPA launched Rajiv Gandhi Grameen Vidyutikaran Yojana (RGGVY) which was restructured as DDUGJY by the present government. • **Target:** 24×7 uninterrupted 'metered' electricity supply to each rural household by 2022, in following way: ▪ Separate feeder lines for rural households vs agricultural use. ▪ Strengthen sub-transmission and distribution network to reduce power losses. ▪ Install electricity meters.
PM Sahaj Bijli Har Ghar Yojana (SAUBHAGYA)	• **Nodal Agency:** Rural Electrification Corporation-REC (2017) (Ministry of Power) • Central Sector Scheme. 100% funded by Union. (100% in the sense that the State government is not required to contribute money, although for the remainder of the project. • **Target:** To give electricity connections to all remaining un-electrified households in rural and urban areas. Scheme also aims to provide 24*7 power supply for all by 2019. • Based on SECC-2011 data, govt. will identify beneficiaries, give them free electricity connection with meters. • If a household in a remote area is not possible to join with grid connected electricity lines, then solar cells, DC battery pack, LED lights will be given. • REC gives 75-90% of project cost as grants to DISCOMs (public and private), state electricity departments etc. • Grant percentage depends on whether General or Special Category state, & how much progress achieved. • As of march 2019: All the States have reported 100% electrification of all households except few households in Naxal affected region of Chhattisgarh.

Health Sector

- According to some estimations, the Indian healthcare sector will be worth $ 638 billion by 2025.
- Hospitals, medical tourism, health insurance, medical equipment, telemedicine, outsourcing, clinical trials and medical gadgets are all part of India's healthcare industry.

Education Sector

- In India, the education sector is growing rapidly, due to significant private individuals collaborating with the government to improve it.
- The government is also considering a number of measures to improve India's educational quality.

Road Sector

- India has the world's second-largest road network, with a total length of 6.6 million kilometres (comprising national & state highways and urban & rural roads).
- Every year, highways carry around 85-87 percent of people and 60-70 percent of freight traffic. Short-distance travel is better served by road transit.
- Roads are classified as National Highways for the purposes of construction and maintenance (NH).
  - National Highways (NH),
  - State Highways (SH)
  - Major District Roads, and
  - Rural Roads
- The government is unquestionably making great progress in the road sector. However, in this sector, talent development and research are most needed. The improvement of roads will boost the economy of the country.

Ports

- Port infrastructure is essential to every country's success. India's coastline is approximately 7,500 kilometers long.
- Ports handle roughly 90 percent of India's external trade by volume and 70% by value.
- The maritime route is used to import crude petroleum, iron ore, coal and other critical goods.
- On India's coast, there are 13 major seaports (12 government-owned and one private) and 205 minor ports.

Logistics

- The presence of a robust logistics-related infrastructure and an effective logistics management system promotes the seamless transfer of commodities from point of origin to point of consumption, assisting an economy's growth.
- The development of the logistics sector is also extremely important for the Indian economy, as it will boost exports, create jobs and give the country a prominent position in the global supply chain.

Industry

- Industry or the secondary sector of the economy is another important area of economic activity. After independence, the government of India emphasized the role of industrialization in the country's economic development in the long run.
- India's vision of a USD 5 Trillion Economy will significantly depend on the growth of the Industrial sector. There are eight industrial sectors that are considered the core in India.

Pre-Independence

Most of the products were handicrafts and were exported in large numbers before the British era started.
The first charcoal fired iron making was attempted in Tamil Nadu in 1830.
India's present-day largest conglomerate Ta ta Group started by Jamsetji Ta ta in 1868.
Slow growth of Indian industry due to regressive policies of the time.
Indian industry grew in the two world war periods in an effort to support the British in the wars.

1948-91

Focus of Indian Government on basic and heavy industries with the start of five-year plans.
A comprehensive Industrial Policy resolution announced in 1956. Iron and steel, heavy engineering, lignite projects, and fertilisers formed the basis of industrial planning.
Focus shifted to agro-industries as a result of many factors while license raj grew in the country and public sector enterprises grew more inefficient. The industries lost their competitiveness.

Post 1991 reforms

Indian markets were opened to global competition with the LPG reforms and gave way to private sector entrepreneurs as license raj came to an end.
Services became the engines of growth while the industrial production saw volatility in growth rates in this period.
MSMEs in the country were given a push through government's policy measures.

2014-22

Make in India campaign was launched to attract manufacturers and FDI.
Government is aiming to establish India as global manufacturing hub through various policy measures and incentives to specific manufacturing sectors.
In FY21, there were 39,539 new business registrations in the manufacturing sector, a 50% increase from 26,406 in Fy20.
Electronics, vehicle, and solar panel production account for around 80% of total manufacturing expenditure, with semiconductors/electronics value chain accounting for 50% of total expenditure in February 2022.

Index of Industrial Production (IIP)

- It is an indicator that measures the changes in the volume of production of industrial products during a given period. Base Year- 2022-2023.
- It is compiled and published monthly by the National Statistical Office, Ministry of Statistics and Programme Implementation.
- It is a composite indicator that measures the growth rate of industry groups classified under:
  - **Broad sectors:** Mining, Manufacturing and Electricity.
  - **Use-Based Sectors:** Basic Goods, Capital Goods and Intermediate Goods.
- **Index of Eight Core Industries (ICI):** This is an index of the eight most fundamental industrial sectors of the Indian economy and comprises 40.27% of the weight in IIP.
  - The monthly Index of Eight Core Industries (ICI) measures collective and individual performance of production in eight core industries.
  - The eight core sector industries in decreasing order of their weightage:
    - Refinery Products> Electricity> Steel> Coal> Crude Oil> Natural Gas> Cement> Fertilizers.

Government Initiatives for Growth of the Industrial Sector in India:

- **Production-Linked Incentive (PLI)** – To scale up domestic manufacturing capability.
- **PM Gati Shakti** – National Master Plan – Multimodal connectivity infrastructure project.
- **Bharatmala Project** –To Improve connectivity in North East India.
- **Start-up India** – To catalyse Startup culture in India.
- **Make in India 2.0** – To transform India into a global design and manufacturing hub.
- **Atmanirbhar Bharat Campaign** – To cut down import dependence.
- **Disinvestment Plans** –To support India's economic recovery.
- **Special Economic Zones** – To create additional economic activity and boost the export of goods and services.
- **MSME Innovative Scheme** – To promote the complete value chain from developing ideas into innovation through incubation and design interventions.

Unit-5: External Sector

Balance of Payments (BOP)

Introduction

Balance of Payments (BoP) is a account of transactions between people of a country and the rest of the world in commodities, services and assets over a specific time period, generally a year.

Balance of Payments Formula

Balance of Payment = Balance of Current Account + Balance of Capital Account + Balance of Financial Account.

Purposes of Calculation of BoP

- Describes a country's financial and economic situation.
- It may be used to determine if a country's currency is appreciating or declining.
- Aids the government in making budgetary and trade policy decisions.
- Provides critical information for analysing and comprehending a country's economic relations with foreign countries.

Components of a Balance of Payments

- **Current Account:** Deals with inflow and outflow of goods and services between countries.
- **Capital Account:** Deals with foreign exchange reserves, investments, loans & borrowings.
- **Financial Account:** Deals investments in real estates, business ventures, Foreign Direct Investments (FDI).

Current Account

- It is a record of goods and service trade as well as cash exchanges.
- The current account is made up of three key components: product trade, service trade, and transfer payments.
- Trade-in items include both exports and imports.
- Transactions involving trade-in services include both factor income and non-factor revenue.
- Transfer payments are receipts that people of a country receive 'for free', without supplying any products or services in exchange.
- They may be presented by the government or by individual citizens who live overseas.
- **Current Account Balance:** A current account is in balance when its receipts match its payments.
- A country with a current account surplus is a lender to other countries.
- A current account deficit shows that the country is a foreign borrower.
- The current account balance is made up of two parts: the trade balance and the invisible balance.
- **Balance of Trade (BoT):** It is the difference between a country's exports and imports of goods during a specified time period.
- In the balance of trade, exports are recorded as credit items, while imports are recorded as debit items.
- A trade surplus or excess balance of commerce happens when a country sells more items than it imports.
- A trade imbalance, also known as a balance of trade deficit, happens when a country buys more products than it exports.
- Balance of Invisibles (BoI): This term also refers to net invisible.
- It is defined as the difference between a country's exports and imports over a given time period.
- Invisibles include services, transfers and income movements between countries.
- Income from services trade is composed of both factor and non-factor income.
- Income from elements of production is defined as the net international earnings on factors of production (such as labour, land, and capital).
- Net sales of service items such as shipping, banking, tourism, and software creation generate non-factor revenue.

Capital Account

- It records all international asset transfers.
- An asset is any of the several forms of wealth that may be retained, such as cash, stocks, bonds, or government debt.
- Investment, foreign borrowings, and external help are the three key components of a capital account.
- Asset purchase is reported as a negative item on the capital account.
- If an Indian acquires a UK automobile company, the acquisition is recorded as a debit item in the capital account (as foreign exchange is flowing out of India).
- A credit item on the capital account is the sale of assets, such as shares in an Indian company to a Chinese consumer.
- Balance on Capital Account: The capital account is balanced when capital inflows (such as loans from abroad, the sale of assets or shares in foreign companies) equal capital outflows (such as loan repayment, the purchase of assets or shares in other nations).
- When capital inflows exceed capital withdrawals, a capital account surplus is created.
- Capital account deficits occur when capital inflows exceed capital outflows.

Surplus and Deficits in Balance of Payments

- A country with a current account deficit (spending more than it receives from exports) must fund it through asset sales or foreign borrowing.
- As a result, any current account deficit must be offset by a capital account surplus, or a net inflow of capital.

IMPORTANT POINT

If a country's current account is in deficit (it spends more abroad than it earns from exports), it must finance the imbalance via foreign borrowing or asset sales. As a result, any current account deficit must be compensated for by net capital inflows. A country is said to be in a balance of payments equilibrium when the total of its current account and non-reserve capital account equals zero, implying that the current account balance is wholly supported through international lending without the need for reserves.

External Sector

Introduction

- All economic transactions in a country that take place in foreign currency are classified as external, including imports, exports, external debt, foreign investment, capital account, current account, balance of payment, and so on.
- It is significant from a policy standpoint since developments occurring in nations throughout the world are also tied to India.

Forex Reserves

Foreign exchange reserves are the foreign currencies held by a country's central bank. They are also called foreign currency reserves or foreign reserves.

India is the fourth largest in the world in foreign exchange reserves as per the IMF, trailing only China, Japan, and Switzerland.

Forex Reserves Consist of	• Bank Deposits • Gold ■ The RBI utilises its gold reserves as a backup to create currency and deal with unanticipated balance-of-payment issues. ■ Special Drawing Rights (SDRs) are international reserve assets established by the IMF in 1969. ■ SDR is an international reserve asset, created by the IMF in 1969. ■ Value of the SDR is based on a basket of five currencies- Dollar, Euro, Renminbi, Yen and Pound Sterling. ■ It is neither a currency nor a claim on the IMF. Rather, it is a potential claim on the freely usable currencies of IMF members.

	• Reserve Tranche Position (RTP) ▪ The reserve tranche part of the quota can be accessed at any time by the member nation, although the remainder of the member's quota is normally unavailable. ▪ If money is lent to the IMF's General Resource Account in excess of the quota, it forms part of the Reserve Tranche. • Foreign Currency Assets (FCA) ▪ Foreign currency assets are the currencies of various countries kept in foreign exchange reserves. For example, reserves kept in US dollars, euros, Japanese yen, and other currencies. • Government Securities
Foreign Exchange Reserves as of May 29, 2026	• $682.3 billion

Exchange Rate

- Exchange rate is Price at which one currency is converted into or exchanged for another currency.
- It is closely tied to monetary policy and is typically influenced by many of the same issues.
- Exchange rate regimes are typically classified into two types: fixed and variable.

> **Foreign Exchange:** It refers to money denominated in a currency other than the domestic currency.
> **Exchange Rate:** Foreign exchange, like every other commodity, has a price. The exchange rate is the value of one currency in relation to another. For example, if the exchange rate between the rupee and the US dollar (USD) is ₹ 65, this means that ₹ 65 is required to purchase 1 Dollar.

Fixed Exchange Rate

- Complete intervention of Authority (government or central bank) in determination of the currency exchange rate.

Floating Exchange Rate

- Market forces (demand and supply) determine the value of currency.
- No role of authority.

Managed Floating Exchange Rate System

- The controlled floating (semi fixed exchange rate) exchange rate system exists between the two extreme exchange rate regimes. It combines fixed and variable exchange rate systems.
- The currency rate is given a precise objective under this system, and a central bank controls the rate from drifting too much from a target band or value.
- The exchange rate is the principal aim of economic policymaking under this regime (interest rates are regulated to achieve the target).
- Governments attempt to affect the exchange rate directly by buying or selling foreign currencies or indirectly through monetary policy (e.g. by changing interest rates on foreign currency bank accounts).
- Most of the countries have shifted to this system of exchange rate determination.

> **Relationship of Exchange Rate and Exports/Imports**
> When a country, such as India, is heavily reliant on imports, more foreign money departs the country than enters. This exerts downward pressure on the exchange rate and may lead the local currency to depreciate. When the local currency depreciates, imported items become more expensive. But depreciation will benefit the exporters as they will get more revenue in rupees when they exchange the dollars they got by exporting their products. The reverse case happens in the case of appreciation.

Important Terms

Nominal Effective Exchange Rate (NEER)	Real Effective Exchange Rate (REER)
• The nominal effective exchange rate (NEER) is the unadjusted weighted average rate at which one country's currency is exchanged for a basket of foreign currencies.	• The weighted average of a country's currency compared to an index or basket of other major currencies, adjusted for the impacts of inflation, is known as the real effective exchange rate (REER).
• NEER is a measure of a country's international competitiveness in the foreign exchange market.	• REER is determined from NEER after correcting it for price change.
• NEER = Domestic currency exchange rate in terms of SDR/Foreign currency exchange rate in terms of SDR.	• REER = NEER × (Domestic Price Index/ Foreign Price Index)

Currency Convertibility

Currency convertibility is the ease with which the currency of a country can be freely converted into any other foreign currency or gold at market determined exchange rate.

Partial Convertibility

- Portion allowed by the government which can be converted into foreign currency with least restrictions.
- Union Budget for 1992-93, introduced it on current account under Liberalized Exchange Rate Management System (LERMS).
- Also known as Dual exchange system.
- Presently partial convertibility still operational on capital account.

Full Convertibility

- Freedom to convert domestic currency into any foreign currency and vice versa without any regulatory intervention.
- Dual exchange rate system got automatically abolished and LERMS was now based upon the open market exchange.
- In 1994, the Government of India declared full convertibility of Rupee on Current account.

Tarapore Committee I (1997) and II (2006)

- Constituted by the RBI for suggesting a roadmap on full convertibility of Rupee on Capital Account.

Advantages of capital account convertibility

- Availability of large funds.
- Reduction in cost of capital.
- Greater financial competitiveness.
- Increase in FII/FPI flow.

Foreign Exchange Market

- The foreign exchange market, sometimes known as the forex market, is a marketplace where worldwide foreign currencies are traded and acquired at the same time.

Par value system till 1971: Government fixes external value	Pegged regime (1972-1992): Rupee was pegged to US dollar	Partial convertibility (1992-93): Under the Liberalised Exchange Rate Management System (LERMS)	Market based exchange rate Regime since 1993

LERMS (Liberalized Exchange Rate Mechanism System)

- It became operational in 1993.
- India's currency was decoupled from the fixed currency system, ushering in the age of floating exchange rates.

Economic Reforms

Introduction

The 1991 Economic Reforms in India refer to the opening of the country's economy to the rest of the world in order to increase the role of the private sector and foreign investment.

Economic Reforms of 1991 brought in LPG Reforms in India.

- The lifting of governmental restrictions on private person activity is referred to as liberalisation.
- The movement of a business, industry, or service from public to private ownership and administration is referred to as privatisation.
- Globalization is the flow of products, services, capital and labor across international borders.

New Economic Policy 1991

- Economic policy refers to government economic activity. It encompasses taxation, state budgets, the supply of money, interest rates, labour market, national ownership and numerous other economic areas of the government.
- India began its new economic policy in 1991, under the leadership of P. V. Narasimha Rao. The first time the whole economy has been opened up using this method.
- This administration reduced import tariffs, freed up the private sector and reduced the Indian rupee to encourage exports under the New Economic Policy P. V. Narasimha Rao. Also known is the LPG growth model.

Major Reforms Carried Out in 1991

Fiscal Stabilisation

- The effectiveness of economic reforms depends on the achievement of fiscal stabilization.
- To ensure the success of the reforms, the Central Government's budget deficit, which had reached 8.4% in the fiscal year 1990-1991, had to be lowered.
- The following steps were taken to reduce the budget deficit.
  - Export subsidies were phased off in 1991-1992, while fertiliser subsidies were modified in 1992-1993.
  - Budget assistance to loss-making public-sector units in the form of government loans to cover their losses was gradually phased out.
  - Some development expenditure, such as spending on social and economic infrastructure, was reformed.

Industrial Policy

- As a result of the reform plan, the most fundamental changes in industrial policy have occurred. There is no longer a requirement for the government to approve new investments or large expansions of existing capacity, as there was previously under industrial licencing (Licence Raj).
  - Only a tiny number of firms are needed to get licences these days, owing to environmental and pollution concerns. In addition, the MRTP Act was repealed.
  - The list of industries that were solely for the public sector to operate was drastically reduced and many crucial sectors were made available to the private sector, including power generation, hydrocarbons (oil and gas exploration, production and refining), air transportation, telecommunications and others.

De-licensing of items reserved for the MSME Sector

- Since 1991, the Ministry of Commerce and Industry has been gradually de-licensing the products specified for the MSME sector through a proactive approach.

Foreign Investment

- Prior to 1991, India's foreign investment policy was severely restricted and frequently considered as unfriendly.
- The new policy actively encouraged foreign investment in a number of ways. Permission is automatically granted for foreign equity investments of up to 51 percent in a long list of 34 industries; for investments of more than 51 percent, government approval is necessary.

Trade and Exchange Rate Policy

- Prior to 1991, the Reserve Bank of India (RBI) set an official exchange rate at which the Indian Rupee was convertible into foreign currencies. In July 1991, the value of the rupee fell by about 24%. (for alignment of the exchange rate with the market rate). In 1993, India switched to a market-based exchange rate system (managed float/floating rate).

Tax Reforms

- The highest marginal rate of personal income tax in June 1991 was 56%. This was reduced to 40%.
- Corporate income tax for publicly traded companies was reduced from 51.75% to 46%.
- The average amount of customs tax dropped from 200% to merely 65%.

Public Sector Reforms

- The government started a restricted process of disinvesting its ownership and equity in public sector enterprises instead of going through full privatization, keeping 51% of the equity and management control.

Financial Sector Reforms

- New private banks were permitted to participate in the banking industry, and several new banking licences were issued.
- Trading practises in capital markets are transparent and strictly regulated. In order to oversee the major players in the capital markets and regulate stock exchanges, an independent statutory entity called SEBI was created in 1988.
- The capital market was opened up to portfolio investments, and Indian companies were allowed to join global financial markets by issuing stock or shares outside via Global Depository Receipts (GDR).

What International Events Have Been Linked To Indian Reforms?

- To address its Balance of Payments (BoP) issues, India borrowed huge sums from the International Monetary Fund (IMF).
- The Asian financial crisis of 1997-1999 drove India to its knees.
- The worldwide recession and dot-com bust of 2001, as well as the enormous global uncertainty that surrounded the invasion of Iraq in 2003.
- From 2003 to 2008, China was at the forefront of the global economic boom.
- The Soviet Union was collapsing at the time, proving that more socialism could not be the solution to India's issues.
- Deng Xiaoping's market-friendly reforms have transformed China.
- The Gulf nation's flow of foreign cash was halted as a result of the 1990-91 Iraq conflict.

Impact of Economic Reforms of 1991

Positive Impact	• India's GDP growth rate has accelerated. According to the IMF, India's GDP growth rate was only 1.1 percent in 1990-91, but after 1991 reforms, it increased generally upward, reaching 7.5 percent in 2015-16. • India has established itself as a lucrative foreign investment destination since 1991, with FDI equity inflows totaling US$ 58.84 billion in 2025-26. Per capita income increased as employment increased. • The unemployment rate was high in 1991, but when India implemented a new LPG strategy, more jobs were created as new international firms arrived in India and many new entrepreneurs established businesses as a result of liberalisation.
Negative Impact	• Agriculture employed 72 percent of the people and contributed 29.02 percent of GDP in 1991. • Agriculture's share of GDP has dropped dramatically to 18%. Farmers' per capita income has decreased as a result and rural indebtedness has increased. • As the Indian economy has been more open to international competition, more multinational corporations (MNCs) are competing with local firms and enterprises that are struggling owing to financial limitations, a lack of sophisticated technology and inefficient manufacturing. • Globalisation has also resulted in environmental degradation from industrial pollutants and the disappearance of natural cover. It has an effect on people's health as well. • The country's economic inequities have grown as a result of LPG policy. Greater economic growth comes at the expense of people's earnings, which may be cut as a result of job losses.

International Organization, Reports and Indices

- An international organisation (an intergovernmental organisation) is one that is founded by a treaty or other document controlled by international law and has its own international legal personality, such as the United Nations, World Health Organisation, or NATO.
- International organisations are largely made up of member nations, although other entities, such as other international organisations, may also be included. Entities (including nations) may also be granted observer status.

- United Nations Monetary and Financial Conference, commonly known as Bretton Woods conference, was held in Bretton Woods, New Hampshire, USA to regulate the international monetary and financial order after the conclusion of World War II (1939-45).
- In total, 44 countries took part, including India.The decisions reached at the conference culminated in the establishment of the International Bank for Reconstruction and Development (IBRD), also known as the World Bank, and the International Monetary Fund (IMF).
- It proposed 3 international institutions:

Bretton Woods Conference (1944)	International Bank for Reconstruction and Development (IBRD), commonly known as World Bank.
	International Monetary Fund (IMF)
	International Trade Organisation (ITO) – (Proposed)

Bretton Woods Institutions – World Bank, (Washington, 1945)

- Initially, the World Bank concentrated on rebuilding war-torn European countries. After the 1950s, the emphasis shifted to poor Asian and African countries.
- WB collaborates with national governments, the business sector, civil society organisations, regional development banks, think tanks, and other international institutions on a wide range of topics, including climate change, conflict, and food security, as well as education, agriculture, finance, and trade.
- The World Bank is a vital source of financial and technical assistance to developing countries around the world. This is not only a bank in the ordinary sense but a unique partnership to reduce poverty and support development.

- The World Bank, comprised of IBRD and IDA, offers loans to governments for capital programmes.

World Bank Group
• International Bank for Reconstruction and Development • International Development Association • International Finance Corporation • Multilateral Investment Guarantee Agency • International Centre for Settlement of Investment Disputes

International Bank for Reconstruction and Development (IBRD)	Known colloquially as the World Bank. Provides interest-bearing development financing. **Voting power –** Depends on the share capital provided by a country. USA highest, followed by various European giants.
International Development Association (IDA)	Aids the poorest nations with interest-free long-term loans (sometimes known as "concessional loans" or "soft loans"). **Voting power –** Depends on the share capital provided by a country. USA highest, followed by various European giants.
International Finance Corporation (IFC)	Supports enterprises of developing countries. Known for its Masala Bonds. **Voting power –** Depends on the share capital provided by a country. USA highest, followed by various European giants.
Multilateral Investment Guarantee Agency (MIGA)	Insurance protects (foreign) investors against non-commercial risk (such as political instability, regime change, and so on). This helps 3rd world nations attract foreign investment. Voting power – Depends on the share capital provided by a country. USA highest, followed by various European giants.
International Centre for the Settlement of Investment Disputes (ICSID)	Aids in the resolution of disputes involving foreign investment and international corporations in third-world countries. India has signed but not ratified the ICSID Convention, and is therefore not a Contracting State. **Voting power –** It is a "dispute settlement" body, so the concept of 'each country's voting power' does not apply to it.

Non-Bretton Woods – Multilateral Development Banks

A multilateral development bank (MDB) is an entity established by a group of countries to offer development finance and expert advice.

Multilateral Development Banks

- BRICS Bank
- AIIB

BRICS Bank and AIIB

BRICS Bank New Development Bank (NDB)	**AIIB:** Asian Infrastructure Investment Bank
Started in 6th BRICS Summit in Fortaleza (2014) members signed treaty	Started in 2015-16
Members – Brazil, Russia, India, China South Africa ,Bangladesh, Egypt, United Arab Emirates (UAE), Uruguay, Colombia and Uzbekistan.	Members – China, India, UK, Switzerland etc. more than 109 approved members as of 2024.
Voting power – Each member is given equal 20% voting power.	Voting power – Based on share capital provided. China about 27%, India about 7%. Asian countries control about 75% voting.
HQ- Shanghai, China	HQ – Beijing, China
$1 billion COVID-19 loan to India (2020-April).	$750 million COVID-19 loan to India (2020-June).

Other Multilateral Development Banks

- African Development Bank
- Asian Development Bank (ADB)
- Bank for International Settlements
- European Bank for Reconstruction & Development (EBRD)

BIS: Bank for International Settlements	• 1930: Setup in BASEL, Switzerland. • Made up of 63 countries' Central Banks. • Its committee on banking supervision set norms in 1988 (I), 2004 (II), 2011(III) to ensure global financial stability.
African Development Bank	• 1964: Setup in Abidjan in Ivory Coast. • India is a member, also gets loans.
Asian Development Bank (ADB)	• 1966: Setup in Manila, Philippines. • India is a member and also gets loans.
European Bank for Reconstruction & Development (EBRD)	• 1991: Setup in London. • In 2018, India became a member (shareholder). India will not be eligible for EBRD loans, but it can launch collaborative loan proposals for Asian, African, and European states as part of its soft diplomacy. (Usually India does it to win friendship with poor nations, so they vote in favour of India during Kashmir – Arunachal etc. resolutions in UN General Assembly).

Bretton Woods Institutions: IMF, Washington (1945)

- IMF was conceived at a UN conference in Bretton Woods in July 1944.
- The International Monetary Fund (IMF) is a non-profit organisation with 189 member nations, each of which has representation on the IMF's executive board proportionate to its financial importance, ensuring that the most powerful countries in the global economy have the greatest voting power.

- The International Monetary Fund (IMF) aids in global currency exchange stability and combats balance-of-payments crises.
- Acts as a reservoir of all member countries' currencies, from which a borrower nation can borrow the currency of other nations via the Special Drawing Rights (SDR) system.
- As a result, it aims to offer a structured process for foreign exchange transactions in order to encourage investment and balanced global economic commerce.
- IMF important decisions need to be passed with an 85% majority. The USA has 16.52% voting power so it can effectively block/veto it.
- India has 2.6% voting rights.

Functions of IMF	**Provides Financial Assistance:** To member countries with balance of payments problems.
	IMF Surveillance: It is in charge of overseeing the international monetary system as well as monitoring the economic and financial policies of its 189 member countries.
	Capacity Development: Provides technical assistance and training to central banks, finance ministries, tax authorities and other economic institutions.

Facilities of IMF to Lend Money

Stand-by agreement	Offers financing of a short – term balance of payments, usually between 12 to 18 months.
The extended fund facility (EFF)	It is a medium-term agreement under which countries can borrow a particular amount of money for three to four years.
Poverty reduction and growth facility (PRGF)	It strives to alleviate poverty in the poorest member nations while also providing the groundwork for economic progress. Loans are made available at extremely cheap interest rates.
Emergency Fund	The IMF also offers emergency funds to collapsed economies, as it did for Korea during the 1997 financial crisis in Asia.

Chief of IMF

- **2019:** Christine Lagarde (France) resigned to become the president of the European Central Bank (ECB, headquartered in Frankfurt, Germany).
- Kristalina Georgieva (Bulgarian economist and former World Bank CEO) becomes the IMF's second female chief after Christine Lagarde. She was reappointed to a second five-year term that began on October 1, 2024.
- IMF' Chief Economist, Gita Gopinath, an Indian-American economist, became the first woman to be the Chief Economist of IMF (2019-Jan). (Previously Raghuram Rajan has also served in this position).

GATT → WTO (GENEVA)

- The World Trade Organization (WTO) came into existence in 1995.
- The World Trade Organisation (WTO), one of the most recent international organisations, is the successor of the General Agreement on Tariffs and Trade (GATT), which was founded in the aftermath of World War II.
- It has 166 member countries.
- In 1948, the General Agreement on Tariffs and Trade (GATT) was established.
- The General deal on Tariffs and Trade was the first multilateral free trade deal signed on a global scale.
- Uruguay Round of GATT negotiations decided to set up a permanent institution which can encourage international trade not only in goods, but also in services and Intellectual Property Rights (IPR).
- WTO started functioning from 1st Jan 1995 at Geneva, Switzerland.
- India is a founding member.

General Agreement on Tariffs and Trade (GATT)	• It all began with trade in goods. • GATT was the platform for negotiating reduced customs tax rates and other trade obstacles from 1947 to 1994; the language of the General Agreement set out essential norms, including nondiscrimination. • Since 1995, the modified GATT has served as the WTO's umbrella agreement for goods trade.
General Agreement on Trade in Services (GATS)	• The General Agreement on Trade in Services (GATS) requires most-favoured-nation Treatment, market access commitments and national treatment. • GATS was agreed upon at the conclusion of the Uruguay Round discussions, with all Member Countries, including developing countries, participating. • The GATS applies to a wide range of service industries, including finance, transport & shipping, communications, construction, and distribution.

World Trade Organization

Ministerial Conference	• Supreme Decision-Making body. • Usually meets once every two years, deliberates on trade agreements. • One country = one vote. (unlike IMF & World Bank, where the money power → shareholding → determines the voting power) • The Ministerial Conference has the authority to make decisions on all issues arising from any multilateral trade agreement. • It brings together all WTO members, who are all nations or customs unions. • Appoints a Director General to oversee administrative matters. Dr. Ngozi Okonjo-Iweala is currently in office.
General Council	• Day to day decision making body at Geneva.

	• Has representatives from each member country. • Implements the decision of ministerial conferences. • General council has two bodies, with separate chairpersons: ▪ **Dispute settlement body:** a Appellate Body. ▪ **Trade policy review body:** a Below general council, there are committees on individual agreements and annexes e.g. Anti-dumping, Subsidies & countervailing measures (SCM) etc.
Goals of WTO	• The WTO's global system eliminates trade obstacles via negotiation and operates on the nondiscrimination principle. • The WTO's system deals with these in two ways: ▪ One is by talking: countries negotiate rules that are acceptable to all. ▪ The other is by settling disputes about whether countries are playing by those agreed rules. • The WTO can encourage good governance. Transparency—shared information and knowledge—levels the playing field. • The WTO can cut the cost of doing business internationally. • The WTO can stimulate economic growth and employment.

WTO and Notable Agreements

Objective	Agreement(s)
Reduce the tariff barriers	General Agreement on Tariffs and Trade (GATT) for goods
	General Agreement on Trade in Services (GATS)
Reduce the non-tariff barriers	For non-food: Agreement on Technical Barriers to Trade (TBT) e.g. talcum powder should not have more than x% of asbestos.
	For food: Agreement on Sanitary and Phytosanitary Measures (SPS) e.g. 'x' food item must not have more than y% pesticides residue.
Reduce non-tariff barriers Subsidies	For non-food a Subsidies and Countervailing Measures (SCM) For food a Agreement on Agriculture (AoA) – It tries to manage agricultural subsidies using its 'box' mechanism: • Subsidies that are classified in Green & Blue box category – are allowed (e.g. Research, Cattle-Vaccination). • Amber box category subsidies will be subjected to quantitative limits (e.g. Fertilizer, Electricity, Diesel, MSP).

Miscellaneous measures to encourage global trade	Trade-Related Aspects of Intellectual Property Rights **(TRIPS)**
	Trade-Related Investment Measures on Foreigners. **(TRIMs)**
	Plurilateral agreements: They are not signed by all WTO members e.g. Agreements on aircrafts, dairy product, bovine meat, Information Technology Agreement (ITA).

TRIPS & TRIMS

Trade-Related Aspects of Intellectual Property Rights (TRIPS)

- The Agreement on Trade-Related Aspects of Intellectual Property Rights (TRIPS) is an international legal agreement between all the member nations of the World Trade Organization (WTO).
- It establishes minimal requirements for national governments to regulate numerous types of intellectual property (IP) as they apply to nationals of other WTO member states.
- TRIPS was negotiated at the end of the Uruguay Round of the General Agreement on Tariffs and Trade (GATT) in 1994 and is administered by the WTO.

Trade Related Investment Measures (TRIMS)

- The WTO defines TRIMs as investment measures that discriminate against foreign investment and hence breach the core WTO principle of National Treatment.
- These measures include – local content requirement, domestic employment, technology transfer requirement etc.
- The goal of TRIMs is to guarantee that investment is treated fairly in all member nations.
- Members are obligated under the TRIMs Agreement to notify the WTO Council for Trade in Goods of any existing TRIMs that are inconsistent with the agreement.

Other Notable Groupings Related to Economy

Indian Subcontinent

- ASEAN
- BIMSTEC
- Shanghai Cooperation Organization
- SAARC
- Mekong- Ganga Cooperation

SAARC (1985)	South Asian Association for Regional Cooperation. • HQ: Kathmandu, Nepal (1985) • Afghanistan, Bangladesh, Bhutan, India, Nepal, Maldives, Pakistan, and Sri Lanka are the eight member countries. • **2016:** Summit @Islamabad cancelled after India and others boycotted due to Uri attack. • The chairman of the SAARC Standing Committee is Mr. Amrit Bahadur Rai, the Foreign Secretary of Nepal.

BIMSTEC (1997)	Bay of Bengal Initiative for Multi-Sectoral Technical and Economic Cooperation (BIMSTEC) ● Dhaka, Bangladesh (1997) ● 7 members: Nepal, India, Bangladesh, Myanmar, Sri Lanka, Thailand, and Bhutan. ● Summits every four years. ● The 6th BIMSTEC Summit was hosted by Thailand in Bangkok on April 4, 2025.
Mekong-Ganga Cooperation	● India + five of the ASEAN countries, namely, Cambodia, Laos, Myanmar, Thailand and Vietnam. ● Objective – Tourism, culture, education, transportation, and communication all benefit from collaboration. ● Mekong river starts from China, flows through Myanmar, Laos, Thailand, Vietnam, Cambodia, drains in the South China Sea.
ASEAN	● Association of Southeast Asian Nations. ● Formed in 1967 by Bangkok declaration. ● HQ: Jakarta, Indonesia ● 11 Members: Brunei, Cambodia, Indonesia, Laos, Malaysia, Myanmar, Philippines, Singapore, Thailand, Timor Leste and Vietnam. ● **2018:** Their leaders were invited to India to commemorate the 25th anniversary of the ASEAN-India Dialogue Relationship. The topic of the Delhi Declaration is "Shared Values, Common Destiny". ● Their 10 leaders also graced our 26th January 2018 Republic Day parade as chief guests. 2019 celebrated as ASEAN-India Tourism Year. ● 47th ASEAN Summit and Related Summits, held in Kuala Lumpur, Malaysia, from October 26 to 28, 2025. During this summit, world leaders formally admitted Timor-Leste as the 11th full member of the bloc
Shanghai Cooperation Organization (SCO)	● 2001 → HQ: Beijing, China. ● Regional Anti-Terrorist Structure (RATS) at Tashkent, Uzbekistan. ● 6 founding members: Russia, China, Kazakhstan, Kyrgyzstan, Tajikistan and Uzbekistan. ● 3 new members: India, Pakistan and Iran. ● Newest Members: Belarus (joined in 2024) ● 2017: SCO summit at Astana, Kazakhstan → India, Pakistan formally given membership. ● The 25th Shanghai Cooperation Organization (SCO) Summit was held in Tianjin, China, from August 31 to September 1, 2025. Hosted by China, the leaders of the 10 member nations convened to discuss counter-terrorism, sustainable development, regional security, and plans to establish an SCO Development Bank.

List of Reports and Indices

Reports	Organization
Ease of Doing Business	World Bank
World Development Reports	
Remittance Report	
Universal Health Coverage Index	
Ease of Living Index	
Global Economic Prospect (GEP) Report	
Global Financial Stability Report	IMF
World Economic Outlook	
World Trade Outlook Indicator	World Trade Organisation (WTO)
Global Information Technology Report	World Economic Forum (WEF)
Global Gender Gap Index	
Global Competitiveness Report	
Human Capital Index	
World Power Language Index	
Travel and Tourism Competitiveness Report	
Global Environment Performance Index	
Inclusive Development Index	
Enabling Trade Report	
Global Education Monitoring Report	United Nations Educational, Scientific and Cultural Organisation (UNESCO)
Gender Parity Index	
The State of the World's Children Reports	United Nations Children's Emergency Fund (UNICEF)
Global Report on Trafficking in Persons	United Nations Office on Drugs and Crime (UNODC)
World Wildlife Crime Report	
World Drug Report	
World Investment Report	United Nations Conference on Trade and Development (UNCTAD
The Least Developed Countries Report	
The Technology and Innovation Report	
The Trade & Development Report	
The Information Economy Report	

State of World Population Report	United Nations Population Fund (UNFPA)
World Economic Situation and Prospectus Report	UN Department for Economic and Social Affairs (UN-DESA)
World Happiness Report	UN-Sustainable Development Solutions Network (SDSN)
World of Work Report	International Labour Organisation (ILO)
Global Wage Report	
World Employment and Social Outlook	
World Social Protection Report	
Gender Inequality Index	United Nations Environment Programme (UNEP)
Emission Gap Report	
The Rise of Environmental Crime Report	UNEP & INTERPOL
World State of Forest Report	Food and Agriculture Organisation (FAO)
World Tuberculosis Report	World Health Organisation (WHO)
Ambient Air pollution Report	
World Health Statistics	
CORSIA (Carbon Offsetting and Reduction Scheme for International Aviation)	International Civil Aviation Organisation (ICAO)
World Energy Outlook (WEO)	International Atomic Energy Agency (IAEA)
Southeast Asia Energy Outlook	
Corruption Perception Index	Transparency International
The Energy Report & Living Planet Report	World Wide Fund for Nature (WWF)
World Press Freedom Index	Reporters Without Borders
Global Hunger Index Report	International Food Policy Research Institute (IFPRI)
An Economy for the 99%	Oxfam
Climate Change Performance Index	German Watch
Global Peace Index	Institute of Economics & Peace (IEP)
Global Ecological Footprint	Global Footprint Network

Important Terms in Economy

- **Per Capita Income:** Average national income per head of population. It is obtained by dividing the National Income by population size.
- **Gross Domestic Product:** Total monetary value of the goods and services produced by that country over a specific period of time, normally a year.
- **GNP:** Total money value of final goods and services produced in a country during a particular year (one year) including depreciation and net exports.
- **NNP:** Total money value of final goods and services produced in a country during a particular year (one year) excluding depreciation including net exports.
- **NNP at Factor cost:** The total of income payment made to factors of production.
- **Personal Income:** Total income received by the individuals of a country before payment of direct taxes.
- **Economic Growth:** Transformation of an economy from a state of under development to a state of development which is measured by Gross Domestic Product.
- **Nationalisation:** The process of transforming private assets ownership into government ownership.
- **Human Development Index:** It is a composite statistic of life expectancy education and per capita income indicators.
- **Foreign Direct Investment:** An investment in a business by an investor from another country.
- **SLR:** Statutory Liquidity Ratio refers to the amount that the commercial banks require to maintain in the form of cash or gold or government approved securities before providing credit to the customers.
- **SEZ:** It is an area in which business and trade laws are different from rest of the country mainly aiming at increasing trade, investment and job creation.
- **Globalization:** Globalization stands for the consolidation of the various economies of the world.
- **Unemployment:** When there are people, who are willing to work and able to work but cannot find suitable jobs.
- **Open Unemployment:** Unemployed persons are identified as they remain without work.
- **Seasonal Unemployment:** Employment occurs only in a particular season and workers remain unemployed in the remaining period of a year.
- **Full employment:** Persons who are willing to work and able to work must have employment or a job.
- **Poverty:** Condition where the basic needs of the people like food, clothing and shelter are not being met.
- **Liberalization:** Liberalization refers to the relaxation of the government restriction usually in the area of social and economic policies.
- **Value:** Power of a commodity to command other commodities in an exchange.
- **Price:** Value of a commodity expressed in terms of money.
- **Consumption:** The use of goods and services for satisfying one's wants.
- **Macroeconomics:** The branch of economics that studies the behaviour and performance of an economy as a whole.
- **Microeconomics:** The part of economics concerned with single factors and the effects of individual decisions.
- **Economic System:** The manner in which individuals and institutions are connected together to carry out economic activities in a particular area.
- **Capitalism:** The system where the means of production are privately owned and market determines the economic activities.
- **Socialism:** A way of organizing a society in which major economic activities are owned and controlled by the government rather than by individual people and companies.

- **Mixedism:** An ideology that mixes or combines the principles of Capitalism (Private Role) and Socialism (Nation Role) in an economy.
- **Money:** An asset that is generally acceptable as a medium of exchange.
- **Supply of Money:** It refers to the amount of money which is in circulation in an economy at any given time
- **Inflation:** An increase in average level of prices.
- **Deflation:** A fall in average level of prices, the opposite of inflation
- **Disinflation:** Process of reversing inflation without generating adverse effects.
- **Stagflation:** The co-existence of a high rate of unemployment and inflation.
- **Credit Creation:** It means the multiplication of loans and advances. Commercial banks receive deposits from the public and use these deposits to give loans.
- **Bank Rate:** It is the rate at which the Central Bank of a country is prepared to re-discount the first-class securities.
- **Statutory Liquidity Ratio (SLR):** It is the amount which a bank has to maintain in the form of cash, gold or approved securities.
- **Cash Reserve Ratio (CRR):** Banks are required to hold a certain proportion of their deposits in the form of cash with RBI. This is known as CRR.
- **Monetary Policy:** It is the macro-economic policy laid down by the Central Bank towards the management of money supply and interest rate.
- **Capital Market:** It is a financial market in which long-term debt or equity backed securities are bought and sold.
- **Demonetisation:** It is the act of stripping a currency unit of its status as legal tender. It occurs whenever there is a change of national currency.
- **Balance of Trade:** The balance between the values of goods exchanged between two countries. It is a trade in merchandise items or visible items only.
- **Balance of Payments:** The balance between the values of goods and services exchanged between two countries. It is a trade in both visible and non-visible items.
- **Devaluation:** It means official reduction in the value of a currency in terms of gold or other currencies.
- **Purchasing power:** Purchasing power is the value of a currency expressed in terms of the amount of goods or services that one unit of money can buy.
- **Foreign Exchange:** The currency of another country.
- **Exchange Rate:** The rate at which one currency is exchanged for another currency.
- **Fixed Exchange Rates:** An exchange rate that is held within a narrow band by the monetary authorities.
- **Flexible Exchange Rates:** Flexible exchange rates are freely determined in an open market primarily by private dealings, and they, like other market prices, vary from day by day.
- **Foreign Direct Investment:** The investment made by a multinational enterprise in a foreign country and an investment in a foreign country that involves some degree of control and participation in management.
- **Special Drawing Rights:** International monetary reserve currency created by the International Monetary Fund (IMF) that operates as a supplement to the existing money reserves of member countries.
- **Free Trade Area:** A region encompassing a trade bloc whose member countries have signed a free-trade agreement (FTA). Such agreements involve cooperation between at least two countries to reduce trade barriers.
- **Proportional Tax:** Tax is imposed at the same rate irrespective of tax base.
- **Progressive Tax:** The rate of tax increases with the increase in tax base (income).
- **Regressive Tax:** High rate of tax is levied on the poor and low rate is levied to the rich.
- **Internal public debt:** A loan taken by the Government from the citizens or from different institutions with in the country.
- **External public debt:** A loan is taken from abroad or from an international organisation
- **Fiscal Policy:** Policy related with the revenue and expenditure process of the Government
- **Public expenditure:** The expenditure incurred by public authorities like central, state and local governments to satisfy the collective social wants of the people is known as public expenditure.
- **Budget:** It is an annual financial statement which shows the income and expenditure of the Government.
- **Balanced budget:** The government may spend an amount equal to the revenue it collects. This is known as a balanced budget.
- **Deficit Budget:** The gap between Government anticipated revenue and the targeted expenditure.
- **Surplus budget:** The budget is a surplus budget when the estimated revenues of the year are greater than anticipated expenditures.
- **Zero based budgeting:** Zero-based budgeting is a budgeting that allocates funding based on efficiency and necessity rather than on budget history. It is a method of budgeting in which all expenses must be justified and approved for each new period.
- **Call money/ Notice money:** The money that is lent for one day in this market is known as call money and, if it exceeds one day, is referred to as notice money. Notice Money refers to the borrowing and lending of funds for 2-14 days.
- **Direct Tax:** Direct tax is referred to as the tax, levied on person's income and wealth and is paid directly to the government.
- **Indirect Tax:** Indirect Tax is referred to as the tax, levied on a person who consumes the goods and services and is paid indirectly to the government.
- **Laissez-faire:** Laissez-faire economics is a theory that restricts government intervention in the economy.
- **Tobin Tax:** Tax on international flow of short-term capital currency transactions. Burden of tax is inversely proportional to the length of transaction.

Important One Liners

- The Banking Regulation Act was passed in India in 1949.
- Adam Smith is called the father of modern Economics.
- The SLR is determined by the RBI. SLR stands for Statutory Liquidity Ratio.
- The base financial year for the calculation of the all-India Index of Industrial Production (IIP) is 2022-23 since May 2026.
- The agricultural sector is the largest employer in the Indian economy. However, this sector accounts for only about 17% of India's GDP.
- An economic condition when there is one buyer and many sellers is called Monopsony.
- A fiscal deficit occurs when a government's total expenditures exceed the total revenue that it generates, excluding money from borrowings.
- An increase in price will decrease consumer surplus.
- A situation where the expenditure of the government exceeds its revenue is called Budget Deficit.
- Theory of opportunity cost is given by Gottfried Haberler.
- When the output is equal to zero, the variable cost is zero. A variable cost is a corporate expense that changes in proportion to production output.
- A substantial increase in capital expenditure or revenue deficit leads to Fiscal Deficit.
- The Khadi and village Industries Commission Act was passed in the year 1956.
- The Micro, Small and Medium Enterprises Development Act was passed in the year 2006.
- Union Budget of India is presented by the Finance Minister of India in Lok Sabha of the Parliament.
- Micro-economics is also called Price theory.
- Hire and Fire is a policy of capitalist economy.
- A closed economy is one that has no trading activity with outside economies.
- Gender Budget Statement (GBS) was first introduced in the Indian Budget in 2005-06.
- The symbol of Indian rupee has been prepared by Udaya Kumar.
- Economic survey is prepared by the Ministry of Finance.
- The two main indicators of inflation in India are the wholesale price index and the consumer price index.
- The national income estimation is the responsibility of National Statistical Office (NSO).
- The new GDP series calculates GDP based on Market price.
- First Five-Year Plan was based on the Harrod–Domar model.
- Indian income tax is Direct and progressive.
- Software industry is not affected by seasonal unemployment.
- RTGS full form is Real Time Gross Settlement.
- Foreign direct investment is full form of FDI.
- Rate of growth of an economy is measured in terms of National income.
- France was the first country to implement the GST in 1954.
- DD is called a banker cheque.
- Balance Sheet show the assets and liabilities which includes real account and personal account.
- 'Capital and growth' written by John Richard Hicks.
- GDP is an indicator of the financial health of a country.
- Prime Minister Narendra Modi launched GST into operation on the midnight of 1 July 2017.
- New Economic Policy of India was announced in the year 1991.
- One Rupee note bears the signature of the Finance Secretary of India.
- Third five year plan is also known as "Gadgil Yojana".
- In India, Fiscal Policy is formulated by the Ministry of Finance.
- Export-Import bank of India was established in 1982.
- Small Industries Development Bank of India (SIDBI), set up on April 2, 1990.
- The central banking functions in India are performed by the Reserve Bank of India.
- Income inequality is the major determinant of poverty both in developed and non-developed countries.
- GATT was the earlier name of the WTO.
- A Golden Handshake Scheme is associated with voluntary retirement.
- The International Monetary Fund (IMF) is an organization of 189 countries.
- The objective of self-reliance and zero net foreign aid was declared in the Fourth Five year plan.
- Brent Index is associated with the price levels of light Crude oil.
- On July 12, 1982, the ARDC was merged into NABARD.
- The second Five Year plan was based on Mahalanobis model.
- Short-term finance is usually for a period ranging up to 12 months.
- 'Planned Economy for India' was a book written by M. Visvesvaraya.

❑❑❑

Unit and Dimensions

- **Physical Quantities:** The quantities that can be defined and measured are called physical quantities.

Measurement of Physical Quantities

Measurement is the systematic process of comparing an unknown quantity with a standard reference quantity. The result of measuring a physical quantity is expressed in terms of the following two parameters:

- Magnitude is a measure indicating how many times the chosen unit is present in a given quantity. For instance, in 15 Newtons of force, "15" represents the magnitude, and Newton is the unit measuring the force.

Fundamental Derived Quantities

- **Fundamental Quantities:** The physical quantities that do not depend on any other physical quantities for their measurement is called fundamental quantities. For example, mass, length, time and temperature are fundamental quantities.
- **Derived Quantities:** The physical quantities that are derived from the fundamental quantities are called derived quantities. For example, area, volume, density, force, velocity, acceleration, etc.

Systems of Units

The following system of units are in common use:

- **Centimetre-Gram-Second System (CGS):** In this system the units of length are centimetre, mass is gram and that of time is second.
- **Foot-Pound-Second (FPS) System:** In this system the units of length, mass and time are foot, pound and second respectively.
- **Metre-Kilogram-Second (MKS) System:** In this system, the units of length, mass and time are metre, kilogram and second respectively.
- **International System of Units (SI System):** This system is an extended version of the MKS system. Replace withb: SI defines seven base quantities.
- **Comment:** Supplementary units (radian and steradian) were abolished as a separate class in 1995.

Fundamental Quality		S.I. Unit	
Name	Symbol	Name	Symbol
Mass	m	Kilogram	kg
Length	l	Metre	m
Time	t	Second	s
Current	I	Ampere	A
Temperature	T	Kelvin	K
Amount of Substance	n	Mole	mol
Luminous Intensity	I_v	Candela	cd

Definition of Units

- **Metre:** One metre is the distance travelled by light in 1/299,792,458 of a second in vacuum.
- **Kilogram (kg):** The kilogram is the SI unit of mass. It is defined by fixing the numerical value of the Planck constant, h, to exactly $6.62607015 \times 10^{-34}$ joule-second (J·s).
- This follows modern SI standards while maintaining standard textbook language.
- **Second:** One second is the time taken by a caesium atom (Cs-133) to complete 9,192,631,770 vibrations.

Some Important Units

- **Light Year:** A light year is the distance travelled by light in vacuum in one year.

$$1 \text{ light year} = 9.46 \times 10^{15} \text{ m} = 9.46 \times 10^{12} \text{ km}$$

- **Astronomical Unit (AU):** It is equal to the mean distance between the earth and the sun.

$$1 \text{ AU} = 1.496 \times 10^{11} \text{ m}$$

- **Parsec (Parallactic Second):** It is the largest unit of distance.

$$1 \text{ Parsec} = 3.26 \text{ light year} = 3.08 \times 10^{16} \text{ m}$$

- **Fathom:** The depth of the ocean measured in fathoms.

$$1 \text{ Fathom} = 6 \text{ feet} = 1.828 \text{ m}$$

- **Nautical Mile:** It is used to measure distance in the seas and oceans.

$$1 \text{ nautical mile} = 1852 \text{ m}$$

Derived Quantity		S.I. Unit	
Name	Symbol	Name	Symbol
Displacement	d	metre	m
Area	A	metre squared	m^2
Volume	V	metre cubed	m^3
Speed	s	metre/second	m/s
Velocity	v	metre/second	m/s
Acceleration	a	metre/second^2	m/s^2
Force	F	newton	$N = kg\ m/s^2$
Energy	E	joule	J = N m
Density	ρ	kilogram/metre cubed	kg/m^3
Moment	T	newton metre	N m
Power	P	watt	W = N m/s
Work	W	joule	J = N m
Momentum	p	kilogram metre/second	kg m/s = N s
Pressure	P	pascal	$Pa = N/m^2$

Prefix used with SI unit

SI Prefix	SI Symbol	SI unit Conversion Factor (Standard Form)	Factor (Power)	Factor Language
yotta	Y	1 yottametre = 1 000 000 000 000 000 000 000 000 metres	10^{24}	septillion
zetta	Z	1 zettametre = 1 000 000 000 000 000 000 000 metres	10^{21}	sextillion
exa	E	1 exametre = 1 000 000 000 000 000 000 metres	10^{18}	quintillion
peta	P	1 petametre = 1 000 000 000 000 000 metres	10^{15}	quadrillion
tera	T	1 terametre = 1 000 000 000 000 metres	10^{12}	trillion
giga	G	1 gigametre = 1 000 000 000 metres	10^{9}	billion
mega	M	1 megametre = 1 000 000 metres	10^{6}	million
kilo	k	1 kilometre = 1 000 metres	10^{3}	thousand
hecto	h	1 hectometre = 100 metres	10^{2}	hundred
deca	da	1 decametre = 10 metres	10^{1}	ten
		1 metre = 1 metre	10^{0}	**one**
deci	d	1 decimetre = 0.1 metres	10^{-1}	tenth
centi	c	1 centimetre = 0.01 metres	10^{-2}	hundredth
milli	m	1 millimetre = 0.001 metres	10^{-3}	thousandth
micro	μ	1 micrometre = 0.000 001 metres	10^{-6}	millionth
nano	n	1 nanometre = 0.000 000 001 metres	10^{-9}	billionth
pico	p	1 picometre = 0.000 000 000 001 metres	10^{-12}	trillionth
femto	f	1 femtometre = 0.000 000 000 000 001 metres	10^{-15}	quadrillionth
atto	a	1 attometre = 0.000 000 000 000 000 001 metres	10^{-18}	quintillionth
zepto	z	1 zeptometre = 0.000 000 000 000 000 000 001 metres	10^{-21}	sextillionth
yocto	y	1 yoctometre = 0.000 000 000 000 000 000 000 001 metres	10^{-24}	septillionth

Motion

Rest and Motion

- **Rest:** If the position of an object does not change with respect to a reference point as time passes, the object is said to be at rest.
- **Motion:** A body is said to be in motion when its position changes continuously with respect to a stationary object taken as a reference point, as time passes.
- **Motion is Relative:** An object can be at rest with respect to one thing and in motion with respect to some other thing ahe the same time. So, motion is relative and not absolute.

- **Scalar Quantity:** A physical quantity which is described only by its magnitude and has no direction is called a scalar quantity. Examples include distance, mass, time, speed, and work.
- **Vector Quantity:** A physical quantity that can be described by magnitude as well as direction is called a vector quantity. Examples include displacement, velocity, and acceleration.

Distance and Displacement

- **Distance:** The length of the path travelled by a body is called distance. It is a scalar quantity.
- **Displacement:** Displacement is the shortest straight-line distance from the initial position to the final position of a body, together with its direction. It is a vector quantity.

Speed and Velocity

- Speed is the distance travelled per unit time. It is a scalar quantity.

$$\text{Speed} = \frac{\text{Distance travelled}}{\text{Time taken}}$$

- If a body travels a distance s in time t then its speed v is given by:

$$v = \frac{d}{t}$$

- The SI unit of speed is m/s or ms^{-1}
- **Uniform Speed:** A body is said to be moving with uniform speed if it covers equal distances in equal intervals of time throughout its motion. For example, a vehicle moving at a constant speed on a straight road exhibits uniform motion.
- **Non-Uniform Speed:** A body is said to be moving with non-uniform speed if it covers unequal distances in equal intervals of time. For example, the motion of a ball on a rough surface.
- **Average Speed:** The ratio of the total distance travelled by the body to the total time of journey is called its average speed. Thus,

$$\text{Average Speed} = \frac{\text{Total distance travelled}}{\text{Total time taken}}$$

- **Velocity:** Distance travelled in a given direction" is not the best definition. Velocity is based on displacement, not distance. replace with: "Velocity is the rate of change of displacement with time in a specified direction." Velocity is a vector quantity. Its S.I. unit is m/s.

$$\text{Velocity} = \frac{\text{Distance travelled in a given direction}}{\text{Time taken}}$$

Or

$$v = \frac{d}{t}$$

where, v = Velocity of the body
d = displacement
t = time taken

Acceleration

- The rate of change of its velocity with time.

$$\text{Acceleration} = \frac{\text{Change in velocity}}{\text{Time taken}}$$

- SI unit of acceleration is m/s^2. It is a vector quantity.
- **Relative velocity:** The relative velocity of a body with respect to that of another is the rate of change of displacement of one body relative to that of another.
- **Retardation:** If the velocity of an object decreases then it has a deceleration or retardation.
- For example, a train is retarded when it slows down on approaching a station because its velocity decreases.
- **Constant acceleration:** If acceleration does not change with time, it is said to be constant acceleration.

Equations of Uniformly Accelerated Motion (Along straight line)

- If a body started its motion with initial velocity u and attains final velocity v in any interval t. Let the acceleration assumed be a and the distance travelled is s, then equations of motion:

$$v = u + at$$

$$s = ut + \frac{1}{2}at^2$$

$$v^2 = u^2 + 2as$$

- For freely falling bodies, acceleration a is replaced by g. For upward motion, g is taken as negative
- In above equations if an object is thrown vertically upward, then of motion a is replaced by $(-g)$.

Projectile Motion

- Whenever a body is thrown from any horizontal surface making an angle (θ) except 90°, then its motion under gravity is a curved parabolic path which is called trajectory and its motion is known as projectile motion.
  Examples:
- The motion of a bullet shot from the gun.
- The motion of a rocket after burn-out.

Circular Motion

- When a body moves in a circle it is called circular motion.
- When a body moves in a circular path, then its direction of motion keeps changing continuously. The velocity changes (due to continuous change in direction), therefore, the motion along a circular path is said to be accelerated.
- **Uniform Circular Motion:** Uniform circular motion refers to the movement of an object in a circular path at a constant speed. Examples include the moon orbiting the Earth, Earth revolving around the Sun, and satellites in stable circular orbits around the Earth.

Centripetal Force

- A force always acts on the body towards the centre of the circular path, during circular motion called centripetal force.

Centrifugal Force

- Centrifugal force is an apparent force experienced in a rotating frame, directed away from the centre. This is imaginary force and also called as pseudo force.

Applications of Centripetal and Centrifugal Forces

- Cyclist inclined itself from vertical to obtain required centripetal force. To take a safe turn, cyclist slower down his speed and moves on a path of larger radius.
- For taking turn on a curved road, the frictional force is acting between the tyres of the vehicle and the road acts as centripetal force.
- Roads are banked at turns to provide required centripetal force for taking a turn.
- If a bucket containing water is revolved fast in a vertical plane, the water may not fall even when bucket is completely inverted because a centrifugal force equal or greater than the weight of water pushes the water to the bottom of the bucket.
- **Force:** It is an external push or pull with can change or tries to change the state of rest or of uniform motion. SI unit is newton (N) and CGS unit is dyne.

$$1\text{ N} = 10^5\text{dyne.}$$

- If sum of all the forces acting on a body is zero, then body is said to be in equilibrium.
- The force has both magnitude and direction. It is therefore a vector quantity.
- Force can be categorised as:
- **Balanced Forces:** If the resultant of all the forces acting on a body is zero.
- **Unbalanced Forces:** If the resultant of all the forces acting on a body is not zero.

Newton's Laws of Motion

- **Newton's First Law of Motion:** A body at rest will remain at rest, and a body in motion will continue in motion in a straight line with uniform speed, unless it is compelled by an external force to change its state of rest or of uniform motion.
  It has two statements in it:
- If a body is at rest, it remains at rest unless a force is applied on it.
- If a body is moving, it will continue to move with the same speed in the same direction unless a force is applied on it.

- **Inertia:** The property of an object by virtue of which it neither changes its state nor it tends to change the state is called inertia. It is an inherent property of each object. Inertia is of the following two kinds:
  - Inertia of rest
  - Inertia of motion
- **Inertia of rest:** If a body is at rest, it will remain at rest unless a non zero external force is applied on it to change its state of rest.

  Examples:
  - When a smooth card placed over the mouth of a tumbler is flicked sharply in the horizontal direction, the card flies away, but the coin kept over the card falls into the tumbler.
  - When a train suddenly starts moving forward, the passenger standing in it tends to fall backwards.
  - The dust particles come out from a carpet when it is beaten with a stick due to their inertia of rest.
- **Inertia of Motion:** A body in a state of motion, continues to be in the state of motion with the same speed in the same direction in a straight line unless an external force is applied on it to change its state.

  Examples:
  - A cyclist riding along a level road does not came to rest immediately after he stops pedalling.
  - When a running car stops suddenly, the passenger tends to lean forward.
  - When a passenger jumps out of a moving train he falls down.

Newton's first law of motion gives the definition of Inertia.

- **Momentum:** The momentum of a body is defined as the product of its mass and velocity. Thus:

$$\text{Momentum} = \text{mass} \times \text{velocity}$$

or, $$p = m \times v$$

where

$$p = \text{momentum}$$
$$m = \text{mass}$$
and $$v = \text{velocity of the body.}$$

- When an object is at rest, its velocity and momentum are both zero. Momentum, a vector quantity, is measured in kg m s^{-1} or kg·m/s. For instance, a karate player can break tiles or ice by striking swiftly, demonstrating the impact of momentum.
- **Conservation of Linear Momentum:** The linear momentum of a system of particles remains conserved if the external force acting on the system is zero.
- Rocket propulsion and engine of jet aeroplane works on principle of conservation of linear momentum. In rocket, ejecting gas exerts a forward force which helps in accelerating the rocket upward.
- **Newton's Second Law of Motion:** Force is equal to the rate of change of momentum and acts in the direction of the applied force.

$$\text{Force} \propto \frac{\text{Change in Momentum}}{\text{Time Taken}}$$

$$F \propto \frac{m\Delta v}{t}$$

Or, $$F = km \times \frac{\Delta v}{t} \text{ (where k is constant)}$$

Or, $$F = km \times \left(a = \frac{\Delta v}{t}\right)$$

- The value of k in SI units is 1 therefore

  For cosntant mass,

$$F = m \times a$$

Or, $$\text{Force} = \text{mass} \times \text{acceleration}$$

- Thus, Newton's second law gives the relationship between force and acceleration. The SI unit of force is newton.

$$1N = 1kg\ m/s^2$$
$$1N = 10^5 \text{ dyne}$$

Examples:
- While catching a ball, the cricketer withdraws his hands along the ball.
- Athletes often land on sand (or foam) after taking a high jump.
- When a glass vessel falls on a hard floor it breaks, but it does not break when it falls on a carpet.

- **Newton's Third Law of Motion:** Whenever one body exerts a force on another body, the second body exerts an equal and opposite force on the first body. The force exerted by the first body on the second body is known as action and the force exerted by the second body on the first body is known as a reaction. In other words, to every action there is an equal and the opposite reaction.

  Examples:
  - When a bullet is fired from a gun, the gun recoils.
  - A jet plane accelerates by ejecting gases in the backward direction.
  - When a person jumps out of a boat, the boat is pushed backwards with the feet. As per Newton's third law the boat pushes the person in forward direction.

Impulse

- A large force that acts on a body for a very short interval of time and produces a large change in its momentum is called an impulsive force. Its unit is newton-second.
- A fielder lowers his hand when catching a cricket ball because by lowering his hands, he increases the time of contact for stopping the ball and therefore the fielder has to apply lesser force to stop the ball. The ball will also exert lesser force on the hands of the fielder and the fielder will not get hurt.

Moment of a Force

- The turning effect of force applied on the body about an axis is due to moment of force (or torque). The moment of a force is equal to the product of the magnitude of the force and the perpendicular distance of the line of action of force from the axis of rotation. Its SI unit is N m. For example, to open or close a door, we apply a force (push or pull) normal (perpendicular) to the door at its handle, which is at the maximum distance from the hinges.
- **Equilibrium of Objects:** When a number of forces acting on a body produce no change in its state of rest or of motion, the body is said to be in equilibrium.

  The equilibrium is of two kinds:

  (i) Static Equilibrium and (ii) Dynamic Equilibrium.

- **Static Equilibrium:** When a body is in the state of rest under the influence of several forces, the body is in static equilibrium. For example, if an object lying on the table is pulled by some force to its right and by an equal force to its left, along the same line, the body does not move, as both forces are equal and opposite and they balance each other.
- **Dynamic Equilibrium:** When a body remains in the same state of motion under the influence of several forces, then the body is said to be in dynamic equilibrium. For example, an aeroplane moves at a constant height when the upward lift on it balances its weight downwards.

Friction

- Friction is a force that opposes the relative motion or the tendency of relative motion between two surfaces in contact. For example, when a ball rolls over a surface, it slows down after travelling for a certain distance. This is due to friction force which acts in a direction opposite to the direction of motion of the ball and causes deceleration.
- **Types of Friction:** There are three types of friction, namely.
- **Static Friction:** Static friction comes into play whenever the two surfaces are stationary, relative to each other, in spite of an external force being applied to the body in the direction of the plane of surfaces in contact. Here the friction balances the applied forces.
- **Sliding Friction:** When a body slides over a surface, the friction developed between the sliding body and the surface on which it is sliding is known as sliding friction.
- **Rolling Friction:** It is the frictional force which comes to play when a body rolls over the other.

Static Friction > Sliding Friction > Rolling Friction

- **Application of Friction:**
- Following are some of the application of friction
- A ball bearing is a type of rolling-element that uses balls to maintain the separation between the bearing races. The purpose of a ball bearing is to reduce rotational friction and to support loads (weight).
- It is friction which makes it possible to hold an object in our hands.
- Tyres are made of synthetic rubber because its coefficient or friction with road is larger and therefore, large force of friction acts on it, which stops sliding at turns.
- Writing with chalk on a board is possible due to friction between the surface of the board and the chalk.
- **Disadvantages of Friction**
- Friction causes the wear and tear of machine parts.
- It produces heat and more energy is required to overcome it.
- It causes loss of energy during transformation of energy from one form to another.
- **Laws of Limiting Friction**
- It depends on the nature of the surfaces in contact and their state of polish.
- It acts tangential to the two surfaces in contact and in a direction opposite to the direction of motion of the body.
- The value of limiting friction is independent of the area of the surface in contact so long as the normal reaction remains the same.
- **Methods to Reduce Friction**
- Friction can be reduced by using lubricants such as boric powder, oil, air, etc.
- It can be reduced by polishing the surface in contact.

Projectile

- When a body moves under the influence of gravity it moves along a vertical straight line, only if there is no horizontal component for the initial velocity.
  For example, a fruit falling from a tree, a ball projected vertically upwards.
  If the initial velocity has both horizontal and vertical components, the path of a particle will not be a straight line, but will be a parabola called trajectory. For example, a ball kicked horizontally from the top of a building, a missile fired from a cannon.
  The motion of a projectile is a result both the vertical and horizontal components and it follows a parabolic path.

Gravitation

Every object in the universe attracts every other object. The force of attraction between two objects because of their masses is called gravitational force of attraction.

- **Universal Law of Gravitation:** According to Newton's law of gravitation the force of attraction between two objects is directly proportional to the product of their masses and inversely proportional to the square of the distance between them.
- **Force due to Gravity:** The force with which the earth attracts a body is called the force due to gravity on the body, which acts vertically downwards at the centre of gravity of body.
- **Acceleration Due to Gravity:** The uniform acceleration produced in a freely falling body due to the earth's gravitational pull, is called acceleration due to gravity, $g = GM / R^2$ where, M = mass of the earth, R = radius of the earth.
  The value of g changes slightly from place to place but its value near the earth's surface is 9.8 m/s^2.
- Gravitational force is the weakest force in nature. Gravitational force is much weaker than electromagnetic and nuclear forces, but it dominates at astronomical scales because it is always attractive.
- Factors Affecting Acceleration due to Gravity
- **Shape of Earth:** Earth is not completely spherical its radius at equator is approximately 42 km greater than its radius at poles. The value of g is maximum at poles and minimum at equator. There is no effect of rotation of the earth at poles and maximum at equator.
- **Effect of Altitude:** g decreases with altitude.
- **Effect of Depth:** g decreases with depth and becomes zero at centre of the earth.
- **The Centre of Gravity:** It is that point of a body at which the whole weight of the body appears to act. The centre of gravity of a body can be inside the material of the body or outside it.

Mass and Weight

- **Mass:** The mass of a body is the quantity of matter it contains. It is a scalar quantity. It is constant anywhere in the universe. It is an intrinsic property of the body. Mass is measured by a physical balance or a beam balance, because the value of g is the same on both the pans. Its SI unit is kg.
- **Weight:** The weight of a body is the force with which the earth attracts it. In other words, it is a gravitational pull of the earth on a body. It is a vector quantity, its direction is downwards towards the centre of the earth.

> Weight = mass × acceleration due to gravity
> or, W = mg

Since, the value of g varies from place to place, the weight of a given body also varies from place to place. It is measured using a spring balance in newton.

Weight of an object at different places

- **Space:** Zero
- **Moon:** The weight of an object on the moon is one-sixth ($1/6^{th}$) of its weight on the earth. As mass and radius of moon is lesser than the earth, so the force of gravity at the moon is also less than that of the earth. It's value at the moon's surface is g/6.
- **Equator:** The radius of the earth is maximum at the equator, so the value of g is minimum at the equator, therefore, the weight of an object is minimum at the equator.
- **Poles:** Since the radius of earth at poles is minimum, the value of g is maximum at the poles, hence the weight of an object is maximum at the poles.
- **Altitude:** As we go up from the surface of the earth, the distance from the centre of the earth increases, hence, the value of g decreases. Therefore, the weight of the object decreases as we go up.
- **Centre of Earth:** The value of g decreases as we go down inside the earth and becomes zero at the centre of the earth. Hence, the weight of an object will be zero at the centre of the earth.

> The acceleration due to gravity does not on the mass of the body, all bodies Depend fall with the same acceleration towards the surface of the earth. For example, if a big stone and a small stone are dropped from the roof of a house simultaneously they will reach the ground at the same time.

- Weight of Body in a Lift
  - When the lift is stationary, the scale shows his actual weight.
  - When the lift accelerates downward, the scale shows less weight.
  - If the lift accelerates upward, the scale shows more weight.
  - If the cable of the lift breaks and it starts falling freely, the person experiences weightlessness.
  - If the lift is in uniform motion, there will be no change in the weight of a person.
  - While descending, if the acceleration of the lift is more than the acceleration due to gravity, then the person will collide to the roof of the lift.

Kepler's Laws of Planetary Motion

- **First Law:** The planets move in elliptical orbits around the sun, with the sun at one of the two foci of the elliptical orbit.
- **Second Law:** Each planet revolves around the sun in such a way that the line joining the planet to the sun sweeps over equal areas in equal intervals of time. A planet moves faster when it is closer to the sun, and moves slowly when it is farther from the sun.
- **Third Law:** The cube of the mean distance from the sun is directly proportional to the square of time it takes to move around the sun.

$$T^2 \propto R^3$$

- **Artificial Satellite:** The moon is a natural satellite of the earth. A man- made orbit around the earth is called an artificial satellite. They have many uses like weather forecasting, collecting and relaying information, conducting scientific experiments etc.
- **Orbit:** The fixed path which a satellite revolving around the earth is called an orbit.
- **Orbital Velocity:** The velocity of a satellite in an orbit is called orbital velocity.
- **Escape Velocity:** The velocity at which an object can escape the earth's gravity is called escape velocity.
- The escape velocity of earth is 11.2 km/s and that of moon is 2.38 km/s.

Simple Harmonic Motion

- **Periodic Motion:** A motion such as that of the earth around the sun, the movement of the hands of the clock, etc. is referred to as periodic motion. The motion of the objects repeat itself at regular intervals of time.
- **Harmonic Motion:** A to-and-fro motion, such as the swinging of the pendulum, vertical oscillations of a mass suspended from a spring, etc. is referred to harmonic motion.
- **Simple Harmonic:** Motion A harmonic motion in which the amplitude and time period of oscillation remain constant is called a simple harmonic motion (SHM).
- **Simple Pendulum:** A simple pendulum is suspended by means of a thread from a rigid support and vibrates in a vertical plane.
- The pendulum oscillates to and fro and the time taken for one complete oscillation is known as time period (T).
- The number of vibrations the pendulum bob makes in unit time is known as frequency (n) and its unit is hertz (Hz).

$$n = \frac{1}{T}$$

$$T = 2\pi\sqrt{\frac{l}{g}}$$

Where, l is effective length of pendulum and g is acceleration due to gravity.

- The time period of a simple pendulum of infinite length is 84.6 min.
- The time period of a seconds pendulum is 2s.

Frequency of Simple Pendulum in different situations

- **Summer:** Pendulum length increases, time period increases, clock becomes slow.
- **Winter:** Pendulum length decreases, time period decreases, clock becomes fast.
- **Altitude:** At higher altitude, g decreases, time period increases, clock becomes slow.
- **Moon:** Since the acceleration due to gravity on the Moon is about one-sixth of that on Earth, the time period of a pendulum becomes about $\sqrt{6}$ times greater.
- **Centre of Earth:** g is zero at the Earth's center or in a satellite, pendulum doesn't work there.

Thrust and Pressure

Thrust

- Thrust is the force exerted vertically upward by a body resting on a surface.
- It always equals the body's weight and remains constant regardless of the body's position. Thrust is a vector quantity, measured in Newtons (N).
- **Pressure:** The effect of thrust depends on the area of the surface on which it acts. The effect of thrust is less on a large area while it is more on a small area.
- The thrust on an unit area is called pressure. If a thrust F acts on area A, then

$$\text{Pressure} = \frac{\text{Thrust}}{\text{Area}}$$

or

$$P = \frac{F}{A}$$

- Pressure is a scalar quantity. SI unit of pressure is Pascal (Pa) or N/m^2. 1 Pa = 1 Nm^{-2}
- Application of Thrust and Pressure
  - A camel can run in a desert easily.
  - School bags have wide straps to reduce pressure on the shoulders.
  - An army tank weighing more than a thousand tonne rests upon a continuous chain.
  - Cutting tools have sharp edges so that even a small thrust may cause a great pressure at edges and cutting can be done more easily.
- Pressure in Fluids
  - Fluids are the substances which can flow easily . All the liquids and gases are fluids. A fluid like a solid also exerts pressure due to its weight. A fluid contained in a vessel exerts pressure at all points and in all directions.
- Pressure exerted by liquid is given by:

$$P = \rho g h$$

Where ρ is the density of a liquid, h is the height of the liquid in a beaker, and g is an acceleration due to gravity.

- Thus, pressure increases with the depth from the free surface of the liquid.

Laws of Liquid Pressure

- Inside the liquid, pressure increases with the increase in depth from its free surface.
- In a stationary liquid pressure is the same at all points on a horizontal plane.
- Pressure is the same in all directions about a point in liquid.
- Pressure at the same depth is different in different liquids.

Phenomena based on Liquid Pressure

- The scuba divers feel pain in the ears, due to increased pressure, as they go deeper in water.
- The dam is made thicker at the bottom because the pressure exerted by a liquid increase with its depth.
- Water supply tank is placed high because from great height, the pressure of water will be more in the taps of a house.
- **Pascal's Law:** Pascal's Law states that the pressure exerted anywhere in a confined liquid is transmitted equally throughout the liquid in all directions.
- Hydraulic brakes, hydraulic presses and hydraulic lifts work on Pascal's law.
- **Atmospheric Pressure:** The thrust exerted per unit area on the earth surface due to column of air, is called the atmospheric pressure on the surface of earth. One atmosphere (1 atm) is equivalent to the pressure exerted by a mercury column of height 76 cm (760 mm) at sea level.

Consequences of Atmospheric Pressure

- At high altitudes, air pressure becomes low and blood pressure becomes much more than atmospheric pressure. This may cause nose bleeding.
- It is because of atmospheric pressure that the ink rises in the tube of a fountain pen, and liquid rises in a syringe when the piston is pulled.
- One is able to have a soft drink using straw due to low air pressure in the straw.
- **Measurement of Atmospheric Pressure:** Atmospheric pressure at a place is measured by a barometer.
- A simple barometer and Fortin barometer uses mercury as the barometric liquid. The aneroid barometer has no liquid, it is light and portable and can be carried from one place to another.
- Since atmospheric pressure varies with altitude, a barometer can be used to determine altitude. An aneroid barometer calibrated to determine altitudes is called an altimeter.

Weather forecasting using a Barometer

- A sudden fall in the barometric height indicates a storm or a cyclone.
- A gradual fall in the barometric height indicates a possibility of rain.
- A gradual increase in barometric height indicates fair weather.

Upthrust in Fluids

- **Upthrust or Buoyant Force:**
  - Buoyant force, also known as upthrust, is the upward force exerted by a fluid on an immersed object. It depends on the fluid's density and demonstrates a fluid's buoyancy property.
  - When an airtight plastic bottle is placed in water, the water exerts an upward force, pushing the bottle upwards.

- **Archimedes' Principle:** When a body is partially or completely immersed in a liquid, it experiences an upthrust which is equal to the weight of the liquid displaced by it.
- Due to the upthrust, acting on the body, it apparently loses a part of its weight and the apparent loss of weight is equal to the upthrust.

Upthrust = weight of fluid displaced = apparent loss of weight of the body

For example, it requires relatively less effort to lift a boulder from the bottom of a pond as long as it is in water. But once it comes out of water a greater effort is required to lift it.

Applications of Archimedes' Principle

- It is used in determining the relative density of a substance.
- Archimedes' principle is used in designing ships and submarines.
- Lactometers used for determining purity of milk and hydrometers used for determining the density of liquids are based on Archemedes' principle.

Density and Relative Density

- **Density:** The density of a substance is mass per unit volume i.e.,

Density of a substance = Mass of the substance / Volume of the substance

It is a scalar quantity and its unit is kg/m^3.

- **Relative Density (RD):** The relative density of a substance is ratio of density of the substance to the substance to the density of water at 4°C i.e.

$$\text{R.D.} = \frac{\text{Density of substance}}{\text{Density of water at 4°C}}$$

It is a scalar quantity and it has no unit.

- **Floatation:** When a body is immersed in a fluid sink two possibilities arise. The body may in the fluid or it may float.
  - **Case I:** If the weight of the body is greater than the weight of the fluid displaced by it, a net downward force acts on the body and it sinks in the fluids.
  - **Case II:** If the weight of the body is equal to the weight of the fluid displaced by it, the net force acting on the body is zero and the body just floats in the fluids.
  - **Case III:** If the weight of the body is less than the weight of the fluids displaced by it, then a net upward force acts on the body and as a result the body moves upward and a part of the body floats above the free surface of the fluid.

Laws of Floatation

- The weight of a floating body in a fluid is equal to the weight of the fluid displaced by the body.
- The centre of gravity of the floating body and the centre of buoyancy are in the same vertical line.
- **Application of Principles of Floatation**
  - A ship floats on water because the volume of water displaced by the ship is much less than the volume of the ship.
  - A ship begins to submerge more as it sails from sea water to river water.
  - A loaded ship is submerged more while an unloaded ship is less submerged.
  - It is because of higher density of sea water that it is easier to swim in the sea.
  - A solid ball of iron will sink in water but float on mercury because density of iron is more than water but less than that of mercury.
  - The density of ice is less than the density of water. Ice floats in water with one tenth of its volume above the surface and nine-tenth below the water.
  - A submarine floats in water based on principle of floatation.
  - Laws of floatation are also applicable to hot air balloons.
- **Surface Tension:** The property of a liquid by virtue of which it tries to minimize its free surface area is called surface tension. It is also defined as the force acting perpendicularly per unit length on an imaginary line drawn at the surface of the liquid.

Surface Tension (s) = Force (F) / Length (l)

The SI unit of surface tension is N/m.

- **Adhesive and Cohesive Forces**
  - Cohesive forces act between the molecules of same type of substances where adhesive forces act between the molecules of different substances.
  - Water forms a concave meniscus in a glass tube because its adhesive force on the glass surface is stronger than its cohesive force between water molecules.
  - Conversely, mercury, with strong cohesive forces, forms a convex meniscus when poured into a narrow glass tube.
- **Applications of Surface Tension**
  - The larvae of mosquitoes float on water due to surface tension. But when oil is sprinkled on the stagnant water, its surface tension is lowered and the larvae drown in water.
  - Antiseptics like dettol have low surface tension, therefore they reach even the smallest portion of cuts in the wound.
  - Soaps and detergents can easily clean clothes because they have low surface tension which increases their wetting power and ability to reach dirt particles.
  - When a paintbrush is dipped in water, its bristles spread out and upon removal, surface tension causes the bristles to come together.
  - Liquid drops like raindrops, oil drops are spherical because of surface tension.
  - A needle can be made to float on water due to surface tension.
- **Factors affecting Surface Tension**
  - With the rise in temperature the surface tension of a liquid decreases.
  - Soluble impurities increase the surface tension.
  - Insoluble impurities decrease the surface tension.
- **Capillarity:** The phenomenon of rise or fall of a liquid in a capillary tube when it is dipped in a liquid is known as capillarity. Capillarity occurs due to surface tension of the liquid and the cohesive and the adhesive forces.

Applications of Capillarity

- Oil rises in oil lamps through the wick by capillary action.
- Roots of plants absorb water from the ground through capillary action.
- The ink rises into the blotting paper through capillary action.
- If one end of a sugar cube is dipped in water, the other end of the cube gets quickly wet due to capillary action.
- **Viscosity:** When a layer of a liquid slips or tends to slip on another layer in contact, the motion between the two layers is opposed. This property of a liquid to oppose relative motion between the layers is called viscosity.
- The less the viscosity of a liquid, more is the mobility of the liquid. Viscosity of a liquid decreases as its temperature is increased. The viscosity of liquids except water increases with the increase in pressure. The viscosity of water decreases with increase in pressure.
- **Stoke's Law:** The viscous force F acting on an object falling through a fluid of coefficient of viscosity n depends on its size r (in case of a ball r is its radius) and its velocity v.

$$F = 6\pi\eta rv$$

Streamlined and Turbulent Flow

- **Streamlined Flow:** When a liquid flows in such a way that each liquid particle when passed through the same point follows exactly the same path as followed by the proceeding particles, then the flow is said to be streamlined and the path is called streamline.
- **Turbulent Flow:** When the motion of the particles of the fluid are disorderly, velocity is more than critical value, the disordered motion of the fluid is called turbulent flow.
- **Bernoulli's Theorem:**
  - When a fluid moves without friction, its total energy (kinetic, potential, and pressure energy) remains constant. As fluid velocity increases, pressure decreases. This phenomenon explains why two suspended ping-pong balls move closer when a high-speed air current passes between them.
  - During storms, roofs can be blown off due to decreased pressure caused by high-speed winds passing over the roof. Venturimeter aspirator pumps also operate based on this principle, known as Bernoulli's theorem.

Elasticity

- **Elasticity:** The property of a body by virtue of which it regains its original removal of configuration after the deforming force is called elasticity.
- **Plasticity:** The property of a body by the virtue of which it does not regain its original configuration after the removal of deforming force, is called plasticity.
- **Stress:** The internal restoring force acting per unit area of cross section of a deformed body is called stress.
- **Strain:** The fractional change in configuration i.e. length, volume and shape is called strain.
- **Hooke's Law:** Within the limit of elasticity the strain produced in a body is directly proportional to stress applied to it.

$$\text{Strain} \propto \text{Stress}$$
$$\text{Strain} = E \times \text{Stress}$$
$$\text{Strain / Stress} = E, \text{ where E is called modulus of elasticity}$$

- Young's Modulus (Y) of Elasticity Young's modulus is a measure of stiffness of a given material. It is known as the modulus of elasticity. It is defined as the ratio of normal stress to longitudinal strain. The SI unit of Y is Nm^2. Greater is the value of Y for a material, larger is its elasticity.

Work, Energy and Power

- **Work:** Work is said to be done when a net force acting on the body displaces the body in the direction of the force. The work done on a body is proportional to the net force acting on the body and the displacement, produced by the force on the body.

$$\text{Work (W)} = \text{Force (F)} \times \text{Displacement (d)}$$

The SI unit of work is Nm or Joule. It is a scalar quantity.

Work Done in Special Conditions

- When the net force is perpendicular to the displacement, the work done is always equal to zero.
- Work done is equal to zero, if $s = 0$ or $F = 0$.

  For example, a man may get completely exhausted while pushing a stationary wall, but since there is no displacement (the wall does not move), the work done by the man on the wall is zero. Also, a person standing still with a load on his head may get tired, but does no work in this case.

  Note: The centripetal force acts on a body perpendicular to the direction of motion. Therefore, work done by or against centripetal force in circular motion is zero.
- Power Power is defined as the rate at which work is done.

  If a force does work W in time t, the average power P delivered by the force is:

$$\text{Power (P)} = \text{Work (W) / Time (t)}$$

The unit of power is watt (W) or Joule / second (J/s). Other commonly used units of power are kilowatt and horsepower.

$$1 \text{ Horsepower (hp)} = 746 \text{ watts}$$

The electric bulbs are rated as 100W, 60W etc, which gives its power. A 100W bulb consumes 100 Joules of electric energy per second.

- **Energy:** The capacity of an object to do work is called energy of an object. Since energy is measured in terms of the work done by a body, the unit of energy is same as that of work. SI unit of energy is Joule (J) Others Units
- **Kinetic Energy:** The energy of a body due to its motion is called kinetic energy. The kinetic energy of a moving body is measured by the amount of work it can do before coming to rest.

$$\text{Kinetic Energy} = \frac{1}{2}mv^2$$

where, m = mass of the body
v = velocity of the body.

Example, a bullet with a high velocity possess kinetic energy, due to which it penetrates the object it strikes.

Observations

- If the mass of the body is doubled, its kinetic energy also gets doubled and if the mass of a body is halved its kinetic energy also gets halved.
- If the velocity of a body is doubled, its kinetic energy becomes four times and if the velocity of a body is halved then its kinetic energy becomes one-fourth.
- **Potential Energy:** It is defined as the energy possessed by a body by the virtue of its position or state.

Potential Energy = mgh
Where, m = mass of the body
g = acceleration due to gravity
h = height at which body is present.

- **The Law of Conservation of Energy:** Energy can neither be created nor destroyed but it can be converted from one form to another.

Transformation of Energy

- Electric heater = Electric energy → Heat energy
- Electric bulb = Electric energy → Light energy
- Electric iron = Electric energy → Heat energy
- Loudspeaker = Electric energy → Sound energy
- Solar cell = Light energy → Electrical energy
- Dynamo = Mechanical energy → Electric energy
- Electric motor = Electrical energy → Mechanical energy
- Microphone = Sound energy → Electrical energy
- Speaker = electrical energy → Sound energy
- **Einstein's Mass-Energy Relation:** According to this relation, the mass can be transformed into energy and vice-versa.

  When Δm mass is disappeared, then produced energy

  $$E = \Delta mc^2$$

  where, c = speed of light in vacuum.

Wave, Motion and Sound

- **Wave:** A wave is a disturbance produced at a point in a medium or a field and is transmitted to other parts of the medium or field without the actual translatory motion of the particles. The transfer of energy in the form of waves is known as wave motion.

  For example, ripples or circular waves on the surface of water, which are created when a stone is dropped in a calm pool of water. Sound waves, light waves, radio waves and TV waves are other example of waves.

Terms Associated with Waves

- **Crest:** It is the point of maximum displacement of a particle in upward direction.
- **Trough:** It is the point of maximum displacement of a particle in downward direction.
- **Amplitude (A):** It is the maximum displacement of the particles either upwards or downwards.
- **Wave Length (λ):** It is the distance between any two successive crests or troughs.
- **Time Period (T):** It is the time taken by a particle to complete one oscillation or vibration.
- **Frequency (n):** It is the number of oscillations or vibrations made by a particle in one second. The SI Unit of frequency is hertz.
- **Velocity of a Wave (v):** It is the speed with which the wave propagates in the medium.
- **Classification of Waves:** Waves are broadly of two types:
  - Mechanical Wave
  - Non-mechanical Wave
- **Mechanical Wave:** The waves which required material medium (solid, liquid or gas) for their propagation are called mechanical wave or elastic wave. Mechanical waves are of two types.
  - **Longitudinal Waves:** If the particle of a medium moves along the direction of motion of the wave, the wave is called a longitudinal wave. Longitudinal waves move in spring in the form of compressions (regions where waves are very close to each other) and rarefactions (regions where they are far apart). These waves can propagate in solids, liquids and gases. Sound waves are an example of longitudinal waves.
  - **Transverse:** If the particles of a medium move perpendicular to the direction of motion of the wave, the wave is called transverse wave. The displacement of the vibrating particles is in the form of crests and troughs. Transverse waves propagate only in solids. Example, Electromagnetic wave.
- **Non-mechanical waves or electromagnetic waves:**
  - Non-mechanical waves, also known as electromagnetic waves, propagate without the need for a medium, including through vacuum, at a speed of 3×10^8 m/s.
  - Examples include light and heat; these waves are transverse and not deflected by electric and magnetic fields.
  - Electromagnetic waves consist of photons and have a wavelength range from $1/10^{14}$ m to 10^4 m.
  - They propagate at the velocity of light, are neutral, and carry energy and momentum.
  - Waves such as cathode rays, canal rays, alpha (α) rays, beta (β) rays, sound waves, and ultrasonic waves are not electromagnetic.
- **Sound:** Sound is a form of energy which causes sensation in our ears. It is produced by bodies, which vibrate. It is a form of longitudinal wave.

  When sound propagates speed and wavelength changes but frequency remains constant.

  It is of three types:
  - Infrasonic waves < 20 Hz
  - Audible waves 20 to 20,000 Hz
  - Ultrasonic waves >20,000 Hz
- **Propagation of Sound:** Sound is produced by vibrating objects.

  The matter or substance through which sound is transmitted is called medium. It can be solid, liquid or gas.

Characteristics of Sound

- A sound wave can be described by its amplitude, frequency, wavelength, and speed.
- **Frequency:** When sound is propagated through a medium, the density of the medium oscillates between a maximum and minimum value. The change in density from maximum value to minimum value and again to maximum value is one complete oscillation. The number of such oscillations per unit time is called frequency of sound wave. SI unit of frequency is hertz (Hz).
- **Pitch:** The pitch (shrillness) of a sound depends on its frequency. The faster the vibration of the source, the higher is the frequency and the higher is the pitch. The pitch of a woman's voice is higher than that of a man.
- **Amplitude:** The magnitude of the maximum disturbance in the medium on either side of the mean valve is called the amplitude of the wave.
- **Loudness of Sound:** The loudness or softness of a sound is determined by its amplitude. When a sound wave travels, energy is transferred from one part of the medium to another. This energy depends on the amplitude of the wave. The larger the amplitude the greater is the energy that passes through any place per unit time and louder is the sound.Unit of loudness is called decibel (dB).
- **Quality (timbre) of sound:** The quality of sound is that characteristic that helps to distinguish one sound from another having the same pitch and loudness. The sound of a particular frequency is called a tone.
- **Intensity of Sound:** The amount of sound energy passing each second through the unit area is called the intensity of sound. It is not the same as loudness.
- **Speed:** The speed of sound is defined as the distance which a point on a wave travels per unit time. The speed of sound in air is 331 m/s at 0°C and 344 m/s at 22°C.

  The velocity of sound depends on the elasticity and density of the medium. The velocity of sound is maximum in solids, then in liquids and least in gases.
- **Sonic Boom:** When a body moves with a speed greater than the speed of sound in air, it is said to be travelling at supersonic speed. For example, jet aircraft, bullets, etc. travel at supersonic speed. When such a sound producing source moves it produces shock waves, which has a very sharp and loud sound called sonic boom.

Range of Hearing

- The human ear can hear sound in a frequency range of about 20 Hz to 20,000 Hz. We cannot hear sounds of different animals have different ranges of audible frequencies. A dog can hear frequencies up to 50 KHz, and a bat upto about 100 KHz. Dolphins can hear sound of even higher frequencies. Elephants and whales produce sound of frequencies less than 20 Hz. Rhinoceros communicate using infrasounds of frequency around 5Hz.

Factors Affecting Speed of Sound in Air

- **Temperature:** The speed of sound in air increase by 0.61 m/s for 1°C rise in temperature.
- **Density:** The speed of sound is inversely proportional to the square root of density of the gas.
- **Humidity:** The speed of sound in air increases with increase in humidity in air.

Factors Not Affecting Speed of Sound in Air

- **Pressure:** The speed of sound in air is independent of pressure.
- **Amplitude:** The speed of sound does not depend on the amplitude of the sound wave.
- **Wave length (or Frequency):** The speed of sound does not depend on the wavelength (or frequency) of the sound wave.
- **Reflection of Sound:** The returning back of the sound wave on striking a surface such as wall, metal sheet etc is called reflection of sound wave.
- **Echo:** An echo is the reflected sound heard after the original sound stops, bouncing off distant obstacles like cliffs or walls. It becomes distinct if it arrives 0.1 second after the original sound (our ear retains sound for 0.1s). For clear echoes, the reflecting surface should be at least 17.2 meters away from the listener.
- **Refraction of Sound:** When sound waves move through successive layers of air having different temperature, it travels faster in warm air than in cold air. This causes the bending of sound waves, which is known as refraction of sound. It is due to refraction that sound can be heard over long distances during night than in day.
- **Resonance:** Any vibrating object has a natural frequency. When the frequency of an externally applied force on a body is equal to its natural frequency, the body begins to vibrate with an increased amplitude. This phenomenon is called resonance.
- **Doppler Effect:** The phenomenon of apparent change in the frequency of sound whenever there is a relative motion between the source of sound and observer, is called Doppler Effect.

  Example, when a train approaches a station while blowing the horn, the frequency of sound appears to increase and appears to be lower than its actual frequency when the train moves away from the observer.

Heat

- **Heat:** Heat is the internal energy of molecules constituting the body. It flows from a hot body to a cold body. Heat is a form of energy. When some quantity of heat is supplied to a body, its molecular motion increases which results in the increase of kinetic energy of its molecules. The SI unit of heat is Joule (J).

  1 calorie = 4.2 joule.
- **Temperature:** The degrees of hotness and coldness is measured by a physical quantity called temperature. When a body is heated, its temperature rises. Thus, heat is a cause and temperature is an effect, Temperature determines the direction of flow of heat. The SI unit of

temperature is Kelvin (K). Other commonly used units are degree Celsius (°C) and degree Fahrenheit (°F).

Scale of Temperature

- **Celsius scale of temperature**
  Freezing point is 0°C
  Boiling point of water is 100°C
- **Fahrenheit scale of temperature**
  Ice point or freezing of water = 32° F
  Boiling point of water = 212° F
- **Kelvin or absolute scale of temperature** (K = °C + 273.15)
  Ice point of water = 273 K
  Boiling point of water = 373 K
- **Reaumur scale of temperature**
  Ice point of water is 0°R,
  Boiling point of water = 80°R

Relation between Different Scales of Temperature

C/100 = F – 32/180 = R/80 = K – 273/ 100

Note: At temperature – 40°C = – 40°F, Celsius scale is equal to Fahrenheit.

- **Absolute Zero:** It is that temperature at which the volume of the gas becomes zero if pressure is constant. The value of absolute zero is -273.15°C.
- **Thermal Expansion:** The expansion of a substance on heating is called the thermal expansion of that substance. Solids, liquids and gases expand on heating and contract on cooling.
- **Thermal Expansion of Solids:** When a solid is heated it expands in all directions. The increase in length is called linear expansion, the increase in area is called superficial expansion and the increase in volume is called cubical expansion.
- **Anomalous Expansion of Water:** When water is heated from 0°C to 4°C it contracts and on further heating, it expands. This is called anomalous expansion of water. The density of water is maximum at 4°C.

Consequences of Anomalous Expansion of Water

- In cold countries and hill stations the water pipes generally burst in winter due to expansion of water.
- Aquatic animals can survive in frozen water bodies though the surface is frozen, the water below the surface is at 4°C and hence in liquid state.
- In extreme cold, vegetables and fruits get damaged as the water pressure can burst them open.
- **Transmission of Heat:** Heat transmission takes place by three different processes namely conduction, convection and radiation.

- **Conduction:** In this process, heat energy flows from one molecule to another molecule of a solid without their actual movement.
  Example, when one end of an iron rod is heated the other end becomes hot.
- **Convection:** The transmission of heat due to movement of molecules from one place to another place is called convection. In fluids heat energy flow by this process.
  Applications of Convection Current
- Ocean water in tropical regions becomes hot and moves towards cold polar regions, giving rise to warm ocean currents.
- The sea breeze and land breeze are formed due to convection currents.
- The unequal heating of the earth sets up convection current in the air leading to formation of wind.

- **Radiation:** In this process of heat transmission, a material medium may or may not be present between a hot and a cold body. The heat energy exchanged between the two bodies is called radiant heat or thermal radiation. The thermal radiation are electromagnetic wave and can travel through vacuum. They do not heat the medium through which they pass.

Application of Radiation

- The cooking utensils are blackened at the bottom so that heat is absorbed rapidly.
- To keep tea hot for a long time, teapots are kept shining as shining surfaces are bad radiators.
- The base of an electric iron is highly polished so that it does not lose heat by radiation.

Newton's Law of Cooling

- The rate with which a hot body loses heat is directly proportional to the difference between its temperature and the surrounding temperature.
  Example, if we take hot water and fresh water and put it in a refrigerator, then rate of cooling of hot water will be faster than the fresh water. Hot water takes less time in cooling from 80°C to 70°C than in cooling from 30°C to 20°C.

Latent Heat

- Latent Heat Heat energy absorbed or liberated in change of state is not externally manifested by any rise or fall in temperatures called latent heat. Latent heat when expressed for unit mass of substance, is called the specific latent heat.

Specific Heat

- The amount of heat required to raise the temperature of unit mass (m) of a substance through 1°C, is called its specific heat.
  It is denoted by s and its unit is cal/g/°C or Joule/g/°C. The specific heat of water is 4200 J/kg/°C which is high compared with most other substances. Therefore, water is used as coolant in radiator in vehicle and hot water is used for the fermentation.

Color Theory: A Comprehensive Guide

Overview

- **Color theory:** Fusion of art and science for harmonious color combinations.
- **Isaac Newton's color wheel (1666):** Basis for understanding color relationships.

Color Wheel Basics

- **12 main colors:** Red, Blue, Yellow, Green, Orange, Purple, Amber, Vermillion, Magenta, Violet, Teal, Chartreuse.
- Categorized into primary, secondary, and tertiary colors.

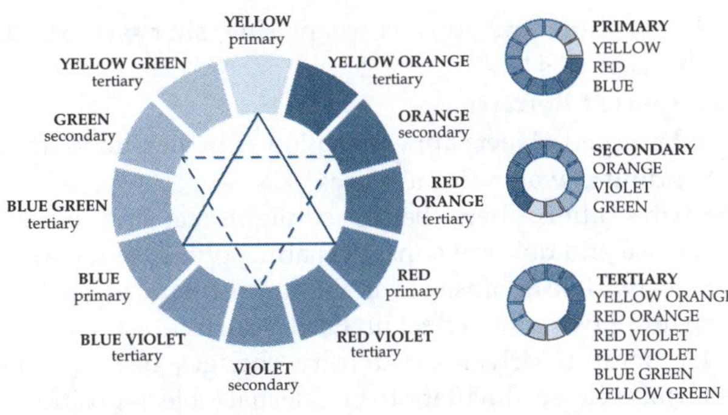

Figure: Color Wheel

Primary Colors

- **Definition:** Foundational hues; cannot be produced by mixing other colors.
- **Types:** Red, Yellow, Blue.
- **Concept:** Evolution in different fields (philosophy, art history, science).
- **Purpose:** Starting point for creating all other colors.

Secondary Colors

- **Definition:** Result from mixing two primary colors (Purple, Orange, Green).
- **Concept:** Positioned between primary colors on the wheel.
- **Purpose:** Accent colors, complementing primary colors.

Tertiary Colors

- **Definition:** Emerge from combining a secondary color with a primary color (Amber, Vermillion, Magenta, Violet, Teal, Chartreuse).
- **Concept:** Occupy space between primary and secondary colors.
- **Purpose:** Complementary colors to accentuate main color.

Complementary Colors

- **Definition:** Opposite on the wheel, create striking contrast (Red-Green, Purple-Yellow, Orange-Blue).
- **Concept:** Intensify each other when paired.
- **Purpose:** Attract attention, essential for aesthetically pleasing design.

Conclusion

- Understanding primary, secondary, tertiary, and complementary colors is key to effective color usage in design.
- Guide provides insights for creating visually appealing and harmonious designs.

Light

- Light is a form of energy which enables vision. Though light is invisible, it makes objects around us visible.

Properties of Light

- Light is an electromagnetic wave.
- Light does not need any material medium to travel i.e. it can travel through a vacuum too.
- Light travels at a speed of 3×10^8 m/s in vacuum.

Source of Light

- **Luminous Bodies:** The bodies which give light on their own are called luminous bodies. for example, the Sun, the stars, etc.
- **Non-Luminous Bodies:** The bodies which do not give out light on their own, but are made visible due to reflection of light are called non-luminous bodies. for example, walls, chairs, earth, moon, etc.

Convergent and Divergent Beam

- **Convergent Beam:** If the light rays converge and meet at a point then the beam of light is called a convergent beam.
- **Divergent Beam:** If two or more rays appear to spread out from a point then such a collection of rays is called a divergent beam.
- **Shadow:** When an opaque object is placed between a source of light and the wall in a dark room, a dark patch is formed on the wall, which is known as a shadow.
  A shadow consists of two regions- umbra and penumbra. Umbra is the region of total darkness and penumbra is the region of partial darkness.
- **Reflection of Light:** The return of light into the same medium after striking a surface is called reflection.

Basic Terms Related to Reflection

- **Incident Ray:** The light ray striking a reflecting surface.
- **Reflected Ray:** The light ray obtained after reflection from the surface.
- **Point of Incidence:** The point at which the incident ray strikes the reflecting surface.
- **Normal:** The perpendicular drawn to the surface at the point of incidence.
- **Angle of reflection:** The angle between the reflected ray and normal.
- **Angle of incidence:** The angle between the incident ray and normal.

Laws of Reflection

- The angle of incidence is equal to the angle of reflection.
- The incident ray, the reflected ray and the normal to the surface at the point incidences lie in the same plane.

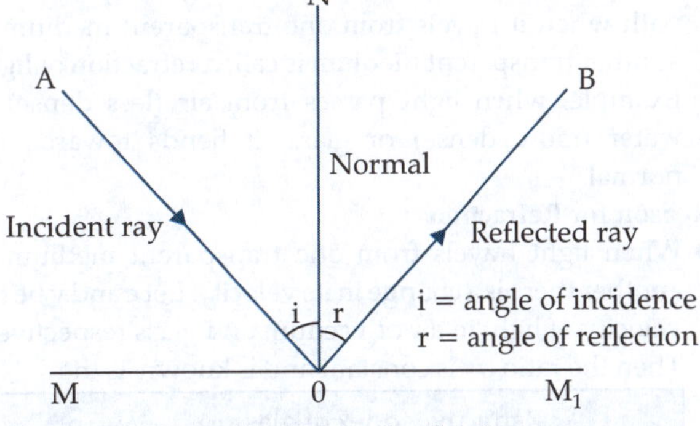

Figure: Laws of reflection

Plane Mirror

- The mirror whose reflecting surface is plane is called plane mirror.

Image formed by a Plane Mirror

- The image is of the same size as the object.

- The image is as far behind the mirror as the object is in front of the mirror.
- Image formed by plane is virtual.
- Image is erect but laterally inverted.

Uses of Plane Mirrors

- They are primarily used as looking glasses.
- They are used as reflectors in solar cookers.
- They are used in making kaleidoscopes.

Spherical Mirror

Spherical mirrors are a part of hollow glass spheres. These are of two types:

- **Convex Mirror:** If a portion of a hollow sphere is silvered or polished on the inner side, the outer side or the bulging side becomes the reflecting surface and is referred to as a convex mirror.

  Uses of Convex Mirror

  - It is a diverging mirror, so it is used as a rear view mirror in vehicles because they provide a wide field of view and a driver can see the entire traffic behind.
  - Convex mirrors are also placed in some ATM centres at a certain height above the machine as a security measure.
- **Concave Mirror:** If the bulging or the outer side of the mirror is silvered then the inner side becomes the reflecting surface and this mirror is referred to as a concave mirror. When the object is placed between the pole and focus, a concave mirror forms a virtual, erect and magnified image. For other positions it may form real and inverted images. Also, they have a wider field of view as they are curved outwards.

  Uses of Concave Mirror

  - Concave mirrors are used to produce magnified virtual images. So these can be used as shaving mirrors.
  - Concave mirrors are commonly used in torches, search-lights and vehicles headlights to get powerful parallel beams of light.
  - They are used by dentists and ENT specialists to view interior portions of a body.
  - Concave mirrors are used in solar devices to reflect light rays.

Refraction

- The phenomenon of deviation of light rays from its path when it travels from one transparent medium to another transparent medium is called refraction of light. Example, when light passes from air (less dense) to water (more dense) or glass, it bends towards the normal.

Reason for Refraction

- When light travels from one transparent medium to another there is a change in its velocity. Let c and v be the velocity of light in air or vacuum and glass respectively. Then the ratio c/v is constant and is known as the

$$\text{Refractive index of glass}(\mu) = c / v$$

Laws of Refraction

- The incident ray, the refracted and ray the normal to the interface at the point of incidence, all lie in the same plane.
- For a given pair of media and for a given colour, the ratio of the sine of the angle of incidence to the sine of the angle of refraction is constant. sin i / sin r = constant. This is Snell's law.

Examples of Refraction

- Submerged objects appear shallower in air due to light bending at water-air interface.
- Earth's atmosphere bends sunlight, causing earlier sunrise and delayed sunset via atmospheric refraction.
- Stars twinkle because of variable atmospheric refraction, creating twinkling effect on Earth's surface.
- Temperature-driven air density changes near Earth's surface cause fluctuation in celestial object positions, resembling twinkling.
- Astronomers adjust for atmospheric refraction to ensure accuracy in celestial measurements and navigation.

Critical Angle and Total Internal Reflection

- **Critical Angle:** Critical angle (c) is the angle of incidence in the denser medium corresponding to which the angle of refraction in the rarer medium is 90°.

$$\text{Refractive index of a denser medium } \mu = 1 / \sin c$$

- **Total Internal Reflection (TIR):** When a ray of light travelling in a denser medium is incident at the surface of a rarer medium such that the angle of incidence is greater than the critical angle for the pair of media, the ray is totally reflected back into the denser medium. This phenomenon is called total internal reflection.

Conditions for TIR

- The light must travel from a denser to a rarer medium.
- The angle of incidence must be greater than the critical angle for the pair of media.

Applications

- Glittering of Diamond
- Mirage
- In optical fibres.

Lenses

Lens is an optical device made of glass which is bounded by two refracting surfaces.

There are two types of lens:

- **Convex lens:** A convex lens is thick at the centre but thinner at the edges. When the light rays are incident on the convex lens, the emergent rays meet at a point. Hence a converging lens is a converging lens.
- **Concave Lens:** A concave lens is thin in the middle but thicker at edges. The incident rays after refraction diverge from each other. Hence a concave lens is a diverging lens.
- **Power of a Lens:** The power of a lens is defined as the reciprocal of its focal length.

$$P = 1 / f$$

If focal length (f) is measured in metres, it will be in metre[1]. The unit in power metre[1] is also called dioptre (D). The power of a concave lens is negative, while the power of a convex lens is positive.

Dispersion

- The splitting of light into its component colors is called dispersion.
- **Prism:** A prism is a solid with five faces, three rectangular and two triangular faces. When a narrow beam of

sunlight falls on the face of a prism, a band of colours resembling those of a rainbow are observed on the other side of the prism. The order of colours from the base of the prism is violet, indigo, blue, green, yellow, orange and red in the increasing order of their wavelengths and is abbreviated as VIBGYOR.

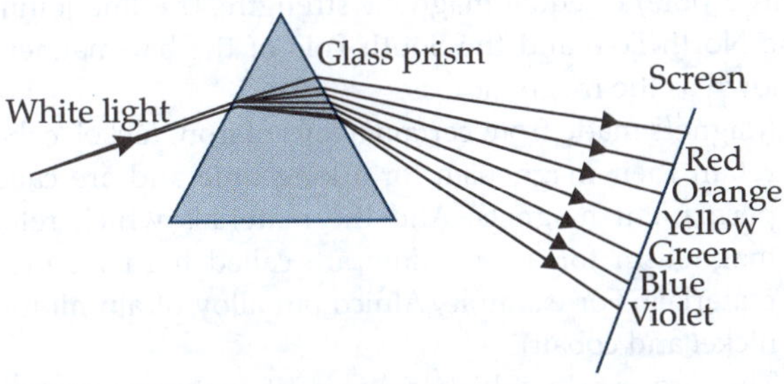

Figure: Refraction through prism

- The red light bends the least whereas the violet the most.
- **Rainbow:** The rainbow is an arch of seven colours visible in the sky which is produced by the dispersion of sun's light by raindrops in the atmosphere. A rainbow is always formed in a direction opposite to that of a sun.
- The droplets act like prisms. In each droplet there is dispersion as well as total internal reflection. The formation of a rainbow in the sky shows that white sunlight consists of a mixture of seven coloured lights.

Scattering of Light

- Scattering means to throw light in various random directions. Light is scattered when it falls on various types of suspended particles in its path.

Consequences of Scattering

- Blue Colour of Sky
- Red Colour of sun at sunrise and sunset
- In the absence of atmosphere, the sky would appear black because there would be no scattering of light.

Total Internal Reflection

- Total internal reflection is a phenomenon that occurs when light travels from a more optically dense medium to a less optically dense one, such as glass to air or water to air.

Examples of Total Internal Reflection:

- **Mirage:** Hotter air is less dense, and has smaller refractive index than the cooler air. On hot summer days, the air near the ground becomes hotter than the air at higher levels noticed that while moving in a bus or a car during a hot summer day, a distant patch of road, especially on a highway, appears to be wet.
- **Diamonds:** Their brilliance is mainly due to the total internal reflection of light inside them.
- Optical fibers utilize total internal reflection, ensuring minimal light signal loss as it undergoes repeated reflections along the fiber's length.

Human Eye

- The human eye works on the refraction of light through a natural convex lens which enables us to see things around us.
- The main parts of the human eye are- iris, pupil, ciliary muscles, eye lens.
- **Power of Accommodation:** A normal eye can see the distant objects as well as nearby objects clearly due to its power of accommodation. A normal eye can focus objects from infinity up to its near point, which is about 25 cm from the eye.

Defects of Vision

Myopia (Short Sightedness): A person suffering from myopia is not able to see distant objects clearly.

- **Reasons:**
  - Eyeball becomes elongated i.e. longer than the normal eye due to which the distance between the retina and the lens increases.
  - The curvatures of the lens or cornea are such that the eye-lens has a shorter focal length and hence image forms short of the retina.
- **Correction:** It is corrected by using a concave lens in front of the eye. Due to this a parallel beam is made divergent before it enters the eye.

Hypermetropia (Far-sightedness): In this defect of vision a person cannot see nearby objects clearly although they can see distant objects clearly.

- **Reasons:**
  - The eyeball becomes shorter than normal due to which the distance between the retina and the lens decreases.
  - If the eye-lens has a focal length that is larger than the normal due to abnormal curvatures of the cornea or the eye lens, it leads to hypermetropia.
- **Correction:** It is corrected by using spectacles containing convex lens.
- **Presbyopia:** Presbyopia is that defect of vision due to which an old person cannot see nearby objects clearly due to the loss of power of accommodation of the eye. Corrected by the same way as hypermetropia by using spectacles having convex lenses.
- **Astigmatism:** In this defect of vision, a person cannot focus on horizontal and vertical lines at the same distance at the same time. This defect can be removed by using suitable cylindrical lenses.

Optical Instruments: A Comprehensive Exploration

Introduction

- Optical instruments enhance images, from basic magnifying glasses to complex lenses.
- This article explores their significance, types, and applications in research and daily life.

What are Optical Instruments?

- Process light for improved object images and light analysis.
- Historical use by Galileo in telescopes for magnification.
- Utilize basic optical phenomena: refraction and reflection.

Optical Magnification

- Net magnification power: ratio of visual angle subtended by the image to the object.
- Involves combining convex and concave lenses for desired magnification effects.

Importance of Optical Instruments

- Inseparable from modern life and research.
- Human visual system as a natural optical instrument.
- Optical fibers for communication signals using total internal reflection.
- Applications in cameras, microscopes, telescopes contribute to understanding light characteristics.

Types of Optical Instruments

- **Camera**
  - Captures and records images through aperture and lens.
  - Allows focus adjustment by changing lens position.
- **Microscope**
  - Light microscope magnifies small objects.
  - Compound microscope uses eyepieces and objective lenses for detailed observation.

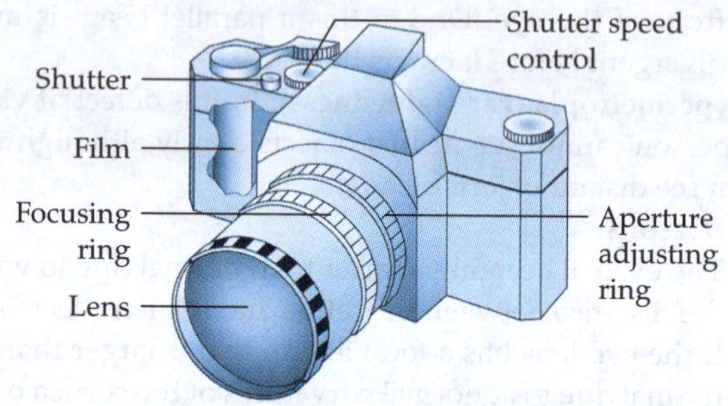

Figure: Structure of a Camera

- **Telescopes**
  - Magnify distant objects like stars and planets.
  - Utilize convex lenses for image magnification.
- **Periscopes**
  - Observational device for non-direct line of sight.
  - Consists of two parallel plane mirrors at a 45° angle.

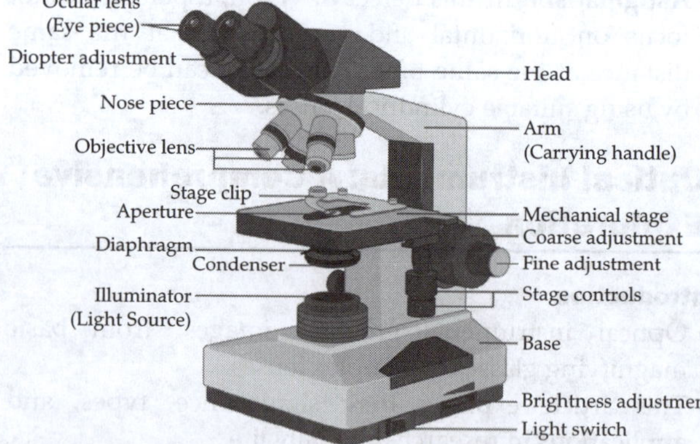

Figure: Microscope Part

- **Kaleidoscope**
  - Optical instrument creating symmetrical patterns.
  - Multiple mirrors reflect objects to generate intricate designs.

Conclusion

- Optics, the study of light, enhanced by optical instruments.
- From magnification to communication systems, optical instruments significantly contribute to our understanding and interaction with the world.

Magnetism

Magnets: Certain rocks behave as natural magnets, they orient themselves in north-south direction. These natural magnets contain magnetite (Fe_3O_4), a magnetic compound. A bar magnet has two magnetic poles (N pole and S pole) of equal magnetic strength. The line joining the North Pole and the South Pole of the bar magnet is known as the magnetic axis.

- Magnets made from certain alloys of iron, nickel, cobalt retain their magnetism for a long time and are called permanent magnets. And the materials which retain magnetism for a long time are called hard magnetic materials. For example, Alnico (an alloy of aluminium, nickel and cobalt).
- The process in which a piece of magnetic material acquires the magnetic properties temporarily in presence of another magnet near it is called magnetic induction.

Properties of Magnet

- **Attractive property:** A magnet can attract small pieces of magnetic substances like iron, steel, cobalt, nickel etc. The attraction is maximum at poles. Unlike poles attract and like poles repel.
- **Directive property:** A magnet, when suspended freely, aligns itself approximately along geographical N-S line.
- **Magnetic poles exist in pairs:** If a magnet is cut into two equal parts transverse to its length, then N and S-poles of the magnet do not get separated.
- **Magnetic Field:** The space around a magnet in which the needle of a compass rests in a direction other than the geographic north-south direction, is called the magnetic field of the magnet.
  Magnetic lines of force is an imaginary line drawn in magnetic field at which a magnetic north pole will move, if it is free to do so.
- The magnetic flux linked with a surface is equal to the total number of magnetic lines of force passing through that surface normally. Its unit is weber.
- Earth acts as a magnet, causing suspended magnets to align north-south.
- Earth's south magnetic pole is near the geographical north, attracting the north pole of the suspended magnet.
- Conversely, Earth's north magnetic pole is near the geographical south, attracting the south pole of the suspended magnet.
- Earth's magnetic field is inclined at an angle of about 15°
- **Magnetic Effect of Current:** A current flowing in a wire always gives rise to a magnetic field around it. The magnetic effect of current is also called electromagnetism.
- **Electromagnets:** A magnet formed temporarily due to the magnetic field of a current is called an electromagnet. The cores of electromagnets use soft magnetic material like soft iron. This is to ensure that the electromagnet loses its magnetism once the current is switched off.
  An electric bell is one of the most commonly used application of an electromagnet.

Magnetic Substances

- There are three types of magnetic substances Paramagnetic, Diamagnetic and Ferromagnetic.
- **Paramagnetic Substances:** Those substances which are feebly magnetised in the direction of magnetic field when placed in a strong magnetic field, are called paramagnetic substances. For examples—Aluminium, platinum, chromium, manganese, solutions of salts of iron, nickel, oxygen etc.
- These substances are attracted towards strong magnetic field in a non-uniform magnetic field.
- The magnetism of these substances decreases with increase in temperature.
- **Diamagnetic Substances:** Those substances which are feebly magnetised in the opposite direction of magnetic field when placed in strong magnetic field are called diamagnetic substances. For examples— Gold, silver, zinc, copper, mercury, water, alcohol, air, hydrogen etc.
- These substances are attracted towards weak magnetic field in a non-uniform magnetic field.
- The magnetism produced in these substances does not change with increase or decrease in temperature.

Ferromagnetic Substances

- Substances which are strongly magnetised in the direction of magnetic field when placed in it, are called ferromagnetic substances. For example - Iron, nickel, cobalt etc.
- The magnetism produced in these substances decreases with increase in temperature and at a particular temperature, called Curie temperature.
- At the Curie temperature, a ferromagnetic substance loses its ferromagnetism and behaves as a paramagnetic substance.
- Magnetic Resonance Imaging (MRI) An electric current always produces a magnetic field. Even weak ion currents that travel in the body produce magnetic fields. These fields are very weak. Heart and brain are two organs which produce magnetic fields significantly. The magnetic field inside the body forms the basis of obtaining the images of different body parts. This is done using a technique called MRI.

Electromagnetic Induction (EMI)

- Whenever the magnetic flux linked with an electric circuit changes, an emf is induced in the circuit. This phenomenon is called electromagnetic induction.
- **Faraday's Laws of Electromagnetic Induction (EMI):** Whenever the magnetic flux linked with a circuit changes, an induced emf is produced in it. The induced emf loses as long as the change in magnetic flux continues.
- **Lenz's Law:** The direction of induced emf or induced current is always in such a way that it opposes the cause due to which it is produced.
- **Eddy Current:** If a piece of metal is placed in a varying magnetic field or rotated with high speed in a uniform magnetic field, then induced current set up in the piece is like whirlpool of air, called eddy current, also known as foucault's current.
- **Application of eddyys current**
  - Eddy currents are used in dead beat galvanometer, induction furnaces, induction motor, speedometers of automobiles etc.
  - Eddy currents are used in diathermy for deep heat treatment of the human body.
- **Self and Mutual Induction:** The phenomenon of production of induced emf in a circuit due to change in current flowing in its own, is called self induction. It's unit of self induction is Henry (H).

  The phenomenon of production of induced emf in a circuit due to change in magnetic flux in its neighbouring circuit, is called mutual induction. Its unit is Henry (H).
- **Alternating Current**
  - An electric current whose magnitude and direction changes continuously is called alternating current. The frequency of alternating current in India is 50 Hz.
  - An AC ammeter and AC voltmeter read root mean square value of alternating current and alternating voltage respectively.

AC Motor

Introduction

- Converts AC into mechanical power.
- Stator and rotor are crucial components.
- Invented by Nikola Tesla in 1887.

Construction of an AC Motor

- Alternating current drives the motor.
- **Components:** Stator, Rotor, Motor Shaft, Bearings, Enclosure.

Stator

- Stationary part delivering a rotating magnetic field.
- **Stator Core:** Thin metal sheets reduce energy loss.
- **Stator Windings:** Coils of insulated wires stacked together.

Rotor

- Central component fixed to the shaft.
- **Common Type:** Squirrel cage rotor.

Motor Shaft

- Rotor pressed onto a steel shaft.
- Extends outside the motor casing for external connections.

Bearings

- Hold the motor shaft, minimizing friction.
- Enhances motor efficiency.

Enclosure

- Protects internal parts from environmental elements.
- Consists of a frame and two end brackets.

Classification of AC Motor

- Two main types based on operation:
  - Synchronous Motor
  - Induction Motor

Synchronous Motor

- Runs at synchronous speed.
- Electromagnet in the rotating magnetic field locks with the field.
- Fixed speeds, calculated using synchronous speed formula.

Induction Motor

- Most commonly used motor.
- Divided into Squirrel Cage Motor and Slip Ring Motor based on rotor construction.
- Operates at speeds slower than synchronous speed.

Working Principles

Synchronous Motor

- Works with two electrical inputs: AC for stator and DC for rotor.
- Rotor and stator poles experience repulsive and attractive forces, leading to rotation.

Induction Motor

- Stator winding fed with AC supply, creating a rotating magnetic field.
- Relative speed induces emf in rotor conductors, causing rotor rotation.

Applications of AC Motors

- **Longevity:** Few moving parts, durable for years.
- **Efficiency:** Excellent performance without overheating.
- **Quiet Operation:** Ideal for noise-sensitive environments.
- Availability: Wide range of sizes and power outputs.

Conclusion

- AC motors play a crucial role in power conversion, with applications ranging from industrial to household use.

DC Motor Overview

Introduction

- Converts DC electrical energy into mechanical energy.
- Operates using direct current.

Different Parts of a DC Motor

- Composed of:
  - Armature or Rotor
  - Field Coil or Stator
  - Commutator and Brushes

Armature or Rotor

- Cylinder of magnetic laminations.
- Rotates on its axis, separated from the field coil by an air gap.

Field Coil or Stator

- Non-moving part with winding to produce a magnetic field.
- Cylindrical cavity between its poles.

Commutator and Brushes

- **Commutator:** Cylindrical structure made of copper segments.
- **Brushes:** Made with graphite and carbon structure, conducting electric current.

DC Motor Working

- Magnetic field created in the air gap when the field coil is energized.
- Torque generated due to opposing forces on rotor conductors.
- Rotor rotates in the direction of the magnetic field, converting electrical energy to mechanical energy.

Types of DC Motor

- Classified based on field winding connections:
  - Self Excited DC Motor
  - Separately Excited DC Motor

Self Excited DC Motor

- Further classified into Shunt, Series, and Compound DC motors.

Separately Excited DC Motor

- Field coils energized from an external DC supply.

Classified on the basis of presence and absence of brushes:

- Brushed DC motors
- Brushless DC motors
- Brushless DC motors do not have a commutator and use electronic servomechanism.
- Brushed DC motors feature a commutator for current reversal.

Applications of DC Motor

- **Shunt DC Motors:**
  - Centrifugal and reciprocating pumps.
  - Lathe machines, blowers, fans, drilling machines.
- **Series DC Motors:**
  - Conveyors, hoists, elevators, cranes.
  - Electric locomotives.
- **Cumulative Compound DC Motors:**
  - Shears, heavy planers, rolling mills.
  - Elevators.

Conclusion

- DC motors play a crucial role in various applications, with different types suited for specific purposes. The conversion of electrical energy to mechanical energy makes them indispensable in numerous industries.

Difference Between AC Motor and DC Motor

AC Motor

- Operates on alternating current.
- The stator produces a rotating magnetic field.
- No commutator is needed.
- Suitable for high-power applications.
- Commonly used in industrial and household appliances.
- Maintenance is relatively easier.

DC Motor

- Operates on direct current.
- The stator provides a constant magnetic field.
- Requires a commutator for current reversal.
- Suitable for low to moderate power applications.
- Found in applications like electric vehicles and small appliances.
- Maintenance may involve commutator and brush inspection/replacement.

Power Source:

- AC motors use an alternating current power source.
- DC motors use a direct current power source.

Construction:

- AC motors have a simpler construction without a commutator.
- DC motors have a commutator and brushes for current reversal.

Starting and Stopping:

- AC motors typically start and stop smoothly.

- DC motors may have a jerky start, and rapid stopping can cause issues with the commutator.

Speed Control:

- AC motors have limited speed control options.
- DC motors offer better speed control capabilities.

Applications:

- AC motors are common in appliances, industrial machinery, and HVAC systems.
- DC motors are used in electric vehicles, small household appliances, and some industrial applications.

Efficiency:

- AC motors are generally more efficient for high-power applications.
- DC motors can be more efficient for low to moderate power applications.

Maintenance:

- AC motors often require less maintenance.
- DC motors may require more maintenance due to the commutator and brushes.

Cost:

- AC motors are typically more cost-effective for high-power applications.
- DC motors may be more cost-effective for specific applications requiring precise speed control.

Conversion:

- AC motors can be easily transformed to different voltage levels using transformers.
- DC motors require additional components for voltage conversion.

Power Transmission:

- AC power is suitable for long-distance power transmission.
- DC power transmission is less efficient for long distances.

Size and Weight:

- AC motors are generally bulkier and heavier.
- DC motors can be more compact and lighter, making them suitable for portable applications.

Electricity

Static Electricity

- **Frictional Charging:** When objects like glass or ebonite rods are rubbed with silk or fur, friction generates an attractive force, leading to the object's surface becoming charged.
- **Static Electricity:** The charged surface on the rod due to rubbing is known as static electricity or electrostatics, emphasizing the stationary nature of the charges.
- **Cloud Charge Separation:** In clouds, positive charges gather near the upper edges, while negative charges accumulate the near lower edges due to natural processes.
- **Lightning Formation:** When accumulated charges reach a critical point, air, a poor conductor, can't resist their flow. Negative and positive charges meet, producing streaks of light and sound, seen as lightning—a process called electric discharge.
- **Lightning Conductors:** It is a device used to protect buildings from the effects of lightning. A metallic rod is installed on the top of the building. One end of the rod is kept out in the air and the other is buried deep in the ground. The rod provides an easy route for the transfer of electric charge to the ground.

Types of Materials

- **Insulators:** The substances that do not allow the current to flow through them are called insulators. They do not have free electrons.
  Example - Cotton, rubber, plastic, wood, glass, leather, etc.
- **Conductors:** The substances that allow the current to flow through them easily are called conductors. They have a large number of free electrons. All metals such as copper, silver, aluminium, iron, steel, etc. are conductors. Human body is also a conductor.
- **Superconductors:** It is a substance of zero resistance at a very low temperature. Example, mercury below 4.2K, lead below 7.25 K are superconductors.
- **Semiconductors:** Certain substances have electrical resistivity between those of conductors and insulators. These materials are called semiconductors. Examples - silicon, and germanium.
- **Electric Cell:** In an electric cell, chemical energy changes into the electrical energy when it sends current in a circuit. The terminal with higher potential is called the positive terminal and the one with lower potential is called the negative terminal.
- **The cells are of two kinds:**
  - **Primary Cells:** These cells provide current as a result of irreversible chemical reaction. Such cells are discarded after use and cannot be recharged. Examples of primary cells are simple voltaic cells, Daniel cell, Leclanche cell, dry cell etc.
  - **Secondary Cells or Accumulators:** In this type of cell, chemical reaction is reversible and so they can be recharged after use. These cells are also called storage cells. Example, Lead accumulators, Li-H battery.

Electric Current and Basic Electrical Concepts

- **Electric Current:** A flow of charge is called an electric current. The direction of current flow is opposite to the direction of flow of negative charges.

Current (I) = Charge (Q) / Time (t)

- The S.I. unit of current is coulomb / second. This unit is called ampere whose symbol is A.
- **Potential Difference:** The potential difference between two points is equal to work done in moving a unit positive charge from one point to the other. It is expressed in volts.
- **Electromotive Force (EMF):** When current is not being drawn from a cell, the potential difference that exists between the terminals of the cell is called its electromotive force. Its unit is also volt. It is essential to maintain a continuous flow of current in a circuit.
  - **Ammeter:** An ammeter is an instrument used to measure the magnitude of current flowing in a circuit. It is joined in series in a circuit.
  - **Voltmeter:** It is used to measure the potential difference between two points of a circuit. It has a high resistance.

- **Galvanometer:** It is used to detect the presence of very weak current in an electric circuit or to know only the direction of flow of current in a circuit. It is connected to a circuit in series.
- **Electrical Resistance:** The obstruction offered to the flow of Current by the wire (conductor) is called its resistance.
- **Ohm's Law:** The current flowing in a conductor is directly proportional to the potential difference across its ends, provided the physical conditions and the temperature of conductor remains constant.

$$I \propto V$$
$$\text{or,} \quad V/I = \text{Constant}$$
$$\text{or,} \quad V = IR \text{ (putting constant equal to R)}$$

- The unit of resistance is ohm (Ω).
- **Resistivity:** The resistance (R) of a wire is directly proportional to its length (l) and area of the cross section(A) of the wire.

$$R \propto l/A$$
$$\text{or,} \quad R = \rho l/A$$
$$\text{or,} \quad R = \rho l/\pi r^2$$

- Here, ρ is a constant and is called the resistivity of the material of the wire.
- The resistivity of a metal increases with the increase in its temperature, while for a semiconductor it decreases with the increase in temperature.
- **Commercial Unit of Electrical Energy:** The commercial unit of electrical energy is expressed in kilo-watt hour.

$$1 \text{ kWh} = 3.6 \times 10^6 \text{ J}$$

Domestic Wiring System

- **Fuse:** A fuse is a safety device that protects a circuit by melting and breaking the circuit when excessive current flows. It is a short piece of wire having a high resistance and a material of low melting point, so that it may easily melt due to overheating when the current in excess to the prescribed limit passes through it. A fuse wire is made from an alloy of lead and tin.
- MCB stands for miniature circuit breaker. It is used for individual circuits. If a heavy current flows in the line, the MCB falls down to switch off the circuit.
- **Switch:** A switch is an on-off device for current in a circuit.
- **Earthing:** The earth wire is used for earthing the metal casings of electrical appliances and is a safeguard against shocks.
- Electrical Devices
- **Transformer:** A transformer is an electrical device that converts alternating current (AC) from one voltage level to another.
- **Types:** There are two main types of transformers:
- **Step-Up Transformers:** Increase low voltage to high voltage.
- **Step-Down Transformers:** Decrease high voltage to low voltage.
- **Operation:** In India, transformers normally operate on AC supply of frequency 50 Hz.
- **Dynamo (Electric Generator):** It is an electrical device which converts mechanical energy into electrical energy.
- **Microphone:** It is an acoustical device which converts sound energy into electrical energy. This electrical energy is converted into sound energy by a loudspeaker or a telephone receiver.

Modern Physics

Radioactivity

- The phenomenon of radioactivity was discovered by Henry Becquerel in 1896. Radioactivity is a nuclear phenomenon. It is a process of spontaneous emission of α or β or γ radiations from the nuclei of atoms during their decay.
- **Radioactive Substances:** Radioactive substances are materials whose nuclei undergo spontaneous disintegration accompanied by the emission of radiation.

Nucleus Emission

- **Alpha Emission:** The atomic number decreases by 2 units and the mass number decreases by 4 units.
- **Beta Emission:** The mass number does not change, but atomic number is increased by 1.
- **Gamma Emission:** There is no change in the mass number and atomic number of the nucleus in gamma emission.

Uses of Radioactivity

- The salts of weak radioactive isotopes such as radio-iron, radio-iodine are used for diagnosis of brain tumours, blood clots.
- γ-rays emitted by radio-isotopes are used to sterilise bandages, dressings, syringes, etc.
- Gamma radiation obtained from cobalt-60 is used to treat cancer.
- U-235 is used as fuel in nuclear reactors.
- The age of rocks is estimated by study of the rate of decay of carbon (C). The process is called carbon dating.
- **Nuclear Fission:** The division of a nucleus into two approximately equal parts is called nuclear fission accompanied by the release of energy.
- The atomic bomb operates on the principle of nuclear fission.
- **Nuclear Reactor:** It is the furnace in which energy is generated by controlled nuclear fission.
- **Fuel:** $^{92}U_{235}$, $^{4}Pu_{239}$ undergo fission by a neutron.
- **Moderator:** The material like heavy water, graphite and beryllium oxide which can retard and control fast moving neutrons is called moderator.
- **Control Rods:** The rods of material like cadmium, which can control the rate of chain reaction are called control rods.
- Controlled chain reaction is a slow process and needs only one neutron for further fission. Atomic reactors work on the principle of controlled chain reaction.
- Uncontrolled chain reaction is fast and needs more than one neutron for further fission. Atom bombs are based on uncontrolled chain reactions.

- **Nuclear Fusion:** It is the process of combining or fusing two lighter nuclei into a stable and heavier nucleus with the liberation of energy.
- Hydrogen bombs are based on nuclear fusion. The energy released during nuclear fusion is known as thermonuclear energy.
- **Semiconductors:** Semiconductors are those materials whose electrical conductivity, at room temperature, lies in between that of insulator and conductor.
  Examples: Germanium and silicon. Pure germanium and silicon in their natural state are called intrinsic semiconductors. Addition of suitable impurities to intrinsic semiconductors in order to increase their conductivities is known as doping. Doped semiconductors are known as extrinsic semiconductors.

Types of Semiconductors

- **N-type Semiconductor:** Germanium and silicon, the intrinsic semiconductors are tetravalent. When impurities of some pentavalent elements like P, As, Sb, Bi, etc. are mixed in a controlled manner, N-type semiconductors are produced. The impurity atoms donate one electron. Hence, the semiconductor is called donor type semiconductor.
- P-type Semiconductors are created by intentionally adding trivalent elements like B, In, Ga, etc., in a controlled manner.
- These impurity atoms can accept only one electron. Due to this property, semiconductors with such impurities are known as acceptor-type semiconductors.
- **Transistor:** A transistor is a device which is obtained by growing a thin layer of one type semiconductor in between two thick layers of the other similar type semiconductors. It is of two types:
  - **N-P-N Transistor:** If the central thin layer is of P-type and outer thick layers are of N-type semiconductor, the transistor is of N-P-N configuration.
  - **P-N-P Transistor:** If the central thin layer is of N-type and outer thick layers are of P-type semiconductor, the the transistor is of P-N-P configuration.

□□□

Chemistry

Matter

- Matter Anything that can occupy space and has mass and offers resistance is called matter. It is made up of very tiny particles and these particles are so small that we cannot see them with naked eyes. For example, water, sugar, iron, wood, milk, air etc.

Characteristics of Matter

- Matter is made of very tiny particles.
- Particles of matter are moving continuously.
- Particles of matter have spaces between them.
- Particles of matter attract each other.

States of Matter

Matters exist in three different states - solid, liquid and gas.

- **Solid State:** In the solids, particles are closely packed. There is a strong force of attraction between particles of a solid which holds them together in a fixed position. They cannot move from one place to another. Examples sugar, sand, iron, wood, etc.
- **Liquid State:** In liquids, the particles are close together but they are not as close as in solids. The spaces between the particles of a liquid are slightly more than that in a solid, but they are still very small. The liquids have no fixed shape but have a fixed volume. They take up the shape of the container in which they are kept. Liquid flow and change shape, so they are not rigid and can be called fluid. Examples, water, milk, oil, kerosene, petrol and alcohol.
- **Gaseous State:** In gases, the particles are much farther apart from one another as compared to solids and liquids. The force of attraction between particles of a gas is negligible. So the particles of a gas are free to move in any direction. Examples are air, oxygen, hydrogen, carbon dioxide and steam.

Plasma

- It is considered as the fourth state of matter. It consists of particles with extremely high kinetic energy (KE). Plasma is produced in the sun and in stars due to high temperature and it makes them glow.

Bose-Einstein Condensate (BEC)

- It is the fifth state of matter. BEC is formed by cooling of a gas of extremely low density to super low temperatures.

Substance / Chemical Substance

- A "substance" is a kind of matter that can not be separated into other kinds of matter by any physical process. Examples, gold, silver, iron, sodium chloride, calcium carbonate etc.

Pure Substance

- It is one that is a single substance and has a uniform composition. Such a substance always have the same texture and taste. Examples, water, salt, sugar etc.

Characteristics of Pure Substances

- They are mostly homogeneous in nature containing only one type of atom or molecule.
- These substances mainly have a constant or uniform composition throughout.
- The substances have fixed boiling and melting points.

Types of pure substances

- Element
- Compound

Classification of Matter Based on Chemical Constitution

- **Elements:** Element are substances which cannot be split into two or more simpler substances by usual chemical methods of applying heat, light or electric energy. An element is a pure substance consisting of only one type of atom. Examples, copper, iron, gold, etc.
- Elements are divided into three categories:
  - metals,
  - non-metals
  - metalloids

Metals

- A metal is an element that is malleable and ductile and conducts electricity. For example iron, aluminium copper, silver, gold, chromium, sodium, etc. are metals. Mercury is the only metal which is liquid at room temperature.

Properties of Metals

- They can be hammered into thin sheets.
- They are ductile drawn into wires.
- They have lustre or shine.
- They conduct heat and electricity.
- They make a ringing sound when hit.

Non Metals

- A non-metal is an element that is neither malleable nor ductile and does not conduct electricity. For example, carbon, sulphur, phosphorus, hydrogen, oxygen, fluorine, chlorine, bromine, argon, etc. are non-metals.

Properties of Non-Metals

- They display a variety of colours.
- They are poor conductors of heat and electricity.
- They are not lustrous, sonorous or malleable.

Metalloids

- Some elements have intermediate properties between those of metals and non-metals, they are called metalloids. For example, boron, silicon, germanium, antimony, bismuth, arsenic, etc.

Compounds

- A compounds is a substance made up of two or more elements chemically combined in a fixed proportion by mass. Example, water (H_2O) is a compound made up of two elements hydrogen and oxygen chemically combined in a fixed proportion of 1:8 by mass.

Properties of Compounds

- A compound cannot be separated into its constituent elements by mechanical or chemical methods.
- The properties of compound differ entirely from those of its constituent elements.

Mixture

- A mixture is a substance which consists of two or more elements or compounds.
- not chemically combined together. For example, air is a mixture of gases like oxygen, nitrogen, carbon dioxide, argon, and water vapour, etc.

  Mixture are of 2 types:

- **Homogenous Mixtures:** Those mixtures in which the substances are completely mixed together and are indistinguishable are called homogeneous mixtures. For example sugar solution, salt solution, copper sulphate solution, alcohol, etc.

Properties of Compound

- Those mixtures in which substances remain separate and one substance is spread throughout the other substances as small particles, droplets or bubbles, are called heterogeneous mixtures. For example, sugar and sand mixture, gun powder, polluted air, milk, ink, paint, glass, coal, soil, wood, blood, starch solution.

Separation of the Components of a Mixture

- Insoluble solid in solvent - Sedimentation followed by filtration. In case of a fine solid centrifugation is used instead of filtration.
- Solution of solid in liquid - Evaporation, crystallization, distillation.
- Miscible mixture of liquids - Fractional distillation.
- Immiscible mixture of liquids - Separating funnel.
- Mixture of two solids one of which is sublime - Sublimation.
- Mixture of substances in solution - Chromatography.

Solution

- A solution is a homogenous mixture of two or more substances. It has a solvent and a solute as its components. For example, a solution of sugar in water is a solution of solid in liquid. Aerated drinks are gas in liquid solutions. These contain carbon dioxide (gas) as a solute and water (liquid) as a solvent.
- **Saturated Solution:** A solution in which no more solute can be dissolved at the same temperature is called Saturated solution.
- **Unsaturated Solution:** It is a solution in which more solute can be dissolved at the same temperature.
- **Super-saturated Solution:** It is a solution which contains more mass of the dissolved solute than the saturated solution at the same temperature and pressure.
- **Suspension:** Suspension is a heterogeneous mixture in which the solute particles do not dissolve but remain suspended throughout the bulk of the medium. For example, sand particles in water, chalk particles in water, milk of magnesia (magnesium hydroxide in water).
- **Colloids:** It is a type of solution in which the particle size of the solute is bigger than that of a true solution, but smaller than that of a suspension. Colloidal solutions are heterogeneous. Examples, fog, clouds, milk, face cream, shaving cream, butter, foam.
- **Emulsion:** Emulsions are liquid-liquid colloids. Emulsions are of two types:
  - Water in oil
  - Oil in water
- Emulsifiers are those substances that help in forming stable emulsions of oil and water, for example, milk, cod-liver oil, cold creams, moisturising cream, vanishing creams, paints, etc.

Structure of the Atom

- The atomic structure refers to the structure of an atom which comprises a nucleus (centre) in which the protons (positively charged) and neutrons (neutral) are present. The negatively charged particles called electrons revolve around the centre of the nucleus.

Atoms and Molecules

- **Atom:** It is the smallest particle of an element which can take part in a chemical reaction. Atoms of most elements do not exist freely. They exist in a combined state as molecules or ions. The atoms of only noble gases (like helium, neon, argon, krypton etc.) have free existence. Atomic radius is measured in nanometres.
- **Molecule:** It is an electrically neutral group of two or more atoms chemically bonded together. It is the smallest particle of an element that is capable of independent existence and shows all the properties of that substance. Atoms of the same element or of different elements can join together to form molecules.

Mole Concept

A mole is defined as the amount of a substance that contains as many atoms, molecules, ions, electrons or other elementary particles, as there are atoms in exactly 12 g of carbon - 12. Mole is a link between the mass of atoms and the number of atoms. It represents 6.022×10^{23} particles of the substance. For example 1 mole of oxygen (O) atoms = 6.022×10^{23} oxygen atoms. 1 mole of oxygen molecules (O_2) = 6.022×10^{23} oxygen molecules.

Subatomic Particles

- There are three subatomic particles electrons, protons and neutrons.
- **Electrons:** They are negatively charged particle found in the atoms of all the elements. The electrons are located outside the nucleus of an atom. They revolve rapidly round the nucleus in fixed circular paths known as energy levels or shells. The electron was discovered by J. J. Thompson. Electrons were discovered from cathode rays experiments.
  The absolute charge = 1.758820×10^{11} Ckg^{-1}
- The charge of an electron was measured by R. Millikan in Oil drop experiment.
- **Protons:** They are discovered by Eugene Goldstein. The proton is a positively charged particle found in the atoms of all the elements. The protons are located in the nucleus of the atom. Since an atom as a whole is electrically neutral, therefore, the number of electrons outside the nucleus is equal to the number of protons inside the nucleus. Protons were discovered by the anode rays experiments.
- The absolute charge on the electron to be 1.6×10^{-19}C.
- **Neutrons:** Neutrons were discovered by James Chadwick by the bombardment of the element beryllium with a - particles.
- Neutrons have no charge. They are present in the nucleus of all atoms except hydrogen.
- The neutrons along with protons constitute the nucleus of an atom, and they are collectively known as nucleons. The mass of a neutron is taken as one unit each.

- **Atomic nucleus:** It was discovered by E Rutherford by the gold foil experiment.
  - The mass of an atom is the sum of the masses of protons and neutrons present in the nucleus.
- **Atomic Number:** The number of protons in one atom of an element is known as the atomic number of that element.
  Example, one atom of oxygen has 8 protons in it, so the atomic number of oxygen is 8.
  - The atomic number of an element is denoted by the letter Z.
- **Mass Number:** Total number of protons and neutrons present in one atom of an element is known as its mass number. Mass number is denoted by letter A,
  Example, carbon has 6 neutrons and 6 protons in its nucleus, therefore its mass The number is 6+6=12 U.
- **Arrangement of Electrons in the Atom:** The electrons are arranged according to their potential energy in different energy levels or shells. The energy levels of electrons are represented by the letter K, L, M, N, O and P.
  - 1st energy level is K shell
  - 2nd energy level is L shell
  - 3rd energy level is M shell
  - 4th energy level is N shell and so on.
- **Isotopes:** The isotopes are the atoms of the same elements having the same atomic number but different mass numbers. Neutral isotopes of an element have the same number of protons and electrons and therefore exhibit nearly identical chemical properties.
- **Radioactive Isotopes:** Radioactive isotopes are unstable isotopes whose nuclei undergo spontaneous decay because of an unstable ...
  Example, Carbon - 14, Arsenic - 74, Sodium - 24, Iodine - 131 etc.
- **Application of Radioactive Isotopes**
  - U-235 isotope is used as a fuel in nuclear reactors.
  - Cobalt (Co-60) is used in the treatment of many types of cancer.
  - Sodium (Na-24) is used to diagnose the presence of blood clots.
  - Iodine (I-131) is used to determine activity of the thyroid gland.
  - Isotopes are used to locate cracks in metal castings.
  - Arsenic (As-74) is used to detect the presence of tumours.
- **Isobars:** Isobars are atoms of different elements having different atomic numbers but the same mass number. Isobars have different numbers of protons in their nuclei but the total number of nucleons (protons + neutrons) in them is the same.
- **Isotones:** Isotones are atoms of different elements with the same number of neutrons. For example, carbon-14 and nitrogen-15 are isotones, sharing 7 neutrons despite being different elements, carbon and nitrogen.
- **Isoelectronics:** It refers to two atoms, ions or molecules that have the same electronic structure and same number of valence electrons.
- **Mass defect:** The mass defect is the difference between the rest mass of a nucleus and the sum of the rest masses of its constituent nucleons.
- **Ions:** Mass defect refers to the difference between the total mass of individual nucleons in an atomic nucleus and its actual mass.
- It's essential in nuclear reactions, like fusion, where the mass is converted into energy. For example, in a helium nucleus, the mass defect leads to the release of energy in stars.
  They are of two types: cations and anions.
- **Cation:** When an atom loses an electron, it becomes positively charged and the ions so formed are known as cations.
- **Anion:** A negatively charged ion is known as an anion. It is formed by the gain of one or more electrons.

Periodic Classificaton of Elements

- **Periodic Table:** The periodic table is a chart in which elements with similar properties are arranged in a group and the elements having similar properties are repeated after certain intervals into periods.
- **Group:** The arrangement of elements in vertical columns are called groups.
- **Periods:** The horizontal rows in periodic tables are called periods.
- **Mendeleev's Periodic Table:**
  - States that elements' physical and chemical properties are periodic functions of their atomic masses.
  - Implies elements with similar properties recur at regular intervals when arranged by increasing atomic masses.
  - Developed when 63 elements were known.
  - Classified elements into seven periods and eight groups.
  - Laid the groundwork for the modern periodic table.
- **Modern Periodic Table:** It states that "the physical and chemical properties of the elements are periodic function of their atomic numbers".
- There are 7 periods and 18 groups in the modern periodic table.

The modern periodic table is divided into four blocks.

- **s - block elements:** Elements belonging to group 1 and 2. The elements of group 1 are called alkali metals and of group 2 are called alkaline earth metals.
- **p - block element:** Elements of group 13 to 18.
- **d-block elements:** Elements belonging to group 3 to 12. They are also called transition elements.
- **f- block elements:** Elements at the bottom of the periodic table. The f-block elements with atomic numbers 57 to 71 are called lanthanides series (because their first element is Lanthanum) and with atomic numbers 89 to 103 are called actinide series (because their first element is Actinium).

Trends in Periodic Table

- **Valency:** On moving from left to right in each short period, the valency of elements increases from 1 to 4 and then decreases to 0. In a group the valency does not change.
- **Atomic Size:** Atomic size refers to the radius of an atom. On moving left to right in a period, the atomic radius of elements decreases. Group In a group from top to bottom the atomic size increases.
- **Metallic Character:** The metallic character of elements gradually decreases from left to right (but non-metallic character increases). Therefore, the typical metals are

on the extreme left whereas typical non- metals are on the extreme right of the periodic table. Group Down the group the metallic character increases.

- **Ionisation Energy:** The energy required to remove an electron from a neutral isolated gaseous atom and convert it into a positively charged gaseous ion is called ionisation energy. Period It increases as one moves from left to right across a period. It decreases as one moves down a group.
- **Electron Affinity:** It is defined as the energy given out when an extra electron is added to a neutral isolated atom.
- **Electronegativity:** The tendency of an atom in a molecule to attract the shared pair of electrons towards itself is called electronegativity.
- **Period:** It increases from left to right in a period.
- **Group:** It decreases down a group.

Chemical Bonding

- **Octet Rule:** Every atom wants stability i.e. they want to achieve the electronic arrangement of an inert gas i.e. octet in the outermost shell. Helium has two electrons (duplet) and all other inert gases like neon, argon, krypton, xenon and radon have eight electrons (octet) in their outermost shell.
- **Types of Chemical Bonds**
  There are five types of chemical bonds:
- Electrovalent (or Ionic) Bonds
- Covalent Bonds
- Coordinate Bonds
- Hydrogen bond
- Van der Waal's forces
- **Electrovalent (Ionic) Bond:** The chemical bond formed between two atoms by the transfer of one or more valence electrons from one atom to the other is known as an electrovalent or ionic bond.
- These bonds are formed between metals and non-metals.
- These conduct electricity when dissolved in water and insoluble in water. These are insoluble in organic solvents like alcohol etc.

Examples: Magnesium chloride ($MgCl_2$), Calcium oxide (CaO), Potassium bromide (KBr), Calcium chloride ($CaCl_2$), Caesium fluoride (CsF) (Caesium fluoride is the most ionic compound).

- **Covalent Bond**
- Covalent bonds involve an equal contribution of electrons from each atom.
- Covalent compounds are often liquids or gases at room temperature.
- These compounds have low melting and boiling points.
- They do not conduct electricity.
- Covalent compounds are insoluble in water but can dissolve in organic solvents.
  Covalent bonds are of the following three types:
- **Single Covalent Bond:** It is formed by sharing one pair of electrons between the atoms, each atom contributing one electron.
- **Double Covalent Bond:** It is formed by sharing of two pairs of electrons between two atoms.
- **Triple Covalent Bond:** It is formed by sharing of three pairs of electrons.

Examples: Methane (CH_4), Ethane (C_2H_6), Butane (C_4H_{10}), Ethylene (C_2H_4), Acetylene (C_2H_2), Water (H_2O), Ammonia (NH_3), Carbon dioxide (CO_2), Hydrogen chloride (HCl), Carbon tetrachloride (CCl_4).

- **Coordinate Bond:** The bond formed between two atoms by sharing a pair of electrons; provided entirely by one of the combining atoms but shared by both, is called a coordinate bond or dative bond.
- **Lone Pair of Electrons:** A pair of electrons which is not shared with any other atom is known as the lone pair of electrons but it is provided to the other atom for the formation of coordinate bonds

Examples: Ammonium ion (NH_4^+), Hydronium ion (H_3O^+)

- **Hydrogen Bond:** The electrostatic force of attraction between the hydrogen atom (which is covalently bonded to a highly electronegative atom) and any other electronegative atom which is present in the same or different molecules, is known as hydrogen bond.
  Hydrogen bonding is generally strongest in solids, weaker in liquids, and weakest in gases.
- **Intermolecular H-bonding:** It occurs between different molecules of a compound and results in increasing solubility in water and high boiling point.
  Example, HF, water (H_2O) molecule.
- **Intramolecular H-bonding (e.g., *o*-nitrophenol):** It occurs within different parts of a same molecule. It results in decreasing solubility in water and low boiling point.
- **Van der Waals' Forces:** The ability of lizard which can hang on a glass surface using only one toe to climb on sheer surfaces had been attributed to the Van der Waals' forces between these surfaces and their foot-pads.

Acid, Bases and Salts

- **Acid:** An acid is a compound that produces hydrogen ions, H^+(aq), in solution, leading to their acidic properties. According to the Bronsted-Lowry theory, an acid is any species capable of donating a proton to another species.
- **Characteristics:** Acids have a sour taste. They change the color of blue litmus paper to red.
- **Strong Acids:** Examples include hydrochloric acid, sulfuric acid, nitric acid, etc.
- **Weak Acids:** Examples include acetic acid, formic acid, carbonic acid, etc.

Natural source	Acid	Natural Source	Acid
Vinegar	Acetic acid	Sour milk (curd)	Lactic acid
Orange	Citric acid	Lemon	Citric acid
Tamarind	Tartaric acid	Ant sting	Methanoic acid
Tomato	Oxalic acid	Nettle sting	Methanoic acid

- **Base:** Base is a substance that gives OH-ions when dissolved in water. Bases are usually metal hydroxides (MOH).
- According to Bronsted-Lowry theory, - a base is a proton acceptor.
- Bases are bitter in taste and change the colour of the red litmus to blue.
- **Examples of Strong Base:** Sodium hydroxide: NaOH (caustic soda), Potassium hydroxide: KOH(caustic potash), Calcium hydroxide: $Ca(OH)_2$ etc.
- **Examples of Weak Base:** Magnesium hydroxide: $Mg(OH)_2$, Ammonium hydroxide: NH_4OH etc.

Some Common Bases

- Sodium hydroxide (caustic soda) → In manufacture of soap, refining of petroleum.
- Potassium hydroxide (caustic potash) → In alkaline storage batteries, shops, etc
- Ammonium hydroxide → In removing grease stains from clothes.
- Calcium hydroxide (slaked lime) → In manufacture of bleaching powder,softening of hard water, for white wash, etc.
- Magnesium hydroxide → As an antacid to remove acidity from the stomach.

- Carbon dioxide gas does not support combustion. So, it can extinguish a burning substance like a burning candle.
- Sodium hydrogen carbonate is used as baking soda in cooking food, for making baking powders, as an antacid to cure indigestion and in soda - acid fire extinguishers.
- **Neutralisation:** A neutralisation reaction may be defined as a reaction between an acid and a base producing salt and water.

$$NaOH + HCl \rightarrow NaCl + H_2O$$

- **Salt:** It is an ionic compound that can be formed by the neutralization reaction of an acid and a base.

  For example, Sodium hydrogen sulphate ($NaHSO_4$), Potassium sulphate (K_2SO_4), Sodium sulphate (Na_2SO_4) Calcium sulphate ($CaSO_4$), Sodium chloride (NaCl), etc.
- **Types of Salt:**
- **Acidic Salt:** The salt formed by partial neutralization of a diprotic or a polyprotic acid is known as an acidic salt. These salts have ionizable H+ ion along with another cation. For example, $NaHSO_4$, KH_2PO_4 etc.
- **Basic or Alkali Salt:** The salt formed by the partial neutralization of a strong base by a weak acid is known as a basic salt. For example, White lead ($2PbCO_3 \cdot Pb(OH)_2$).
- **Double salt:** Salts that contain more than one cation or anion are known as double salt. They are obtained by the combination of two different salts crystallized in the same ionic lattice. For example, Potassium sodium tartrate ($KNaC_4H_4O_6.4H_2O$) also known as Rochelle salt.
- **Mixed Salts:** The salt that consists of a fixed proportion of two salts, often sharing either a common cation or common anion is known as mixed salt. For example, $CaOCl_2$

- **Application of Salts**
- Sodium chloride (NaCl) is used in the manufacture of chlorine, caustic soda, washing soda and baking soda.
- Ammonium salts are used as fertilizers.
- Potassium nitrate (KNO_3) is used in the manufacture of gun powder and fire works.
- Silver bromide is used in photography.
- Potassium Chlorate is used in the match industry.
- Aluminium sulphate is used in preparing alums.

The pH Scale

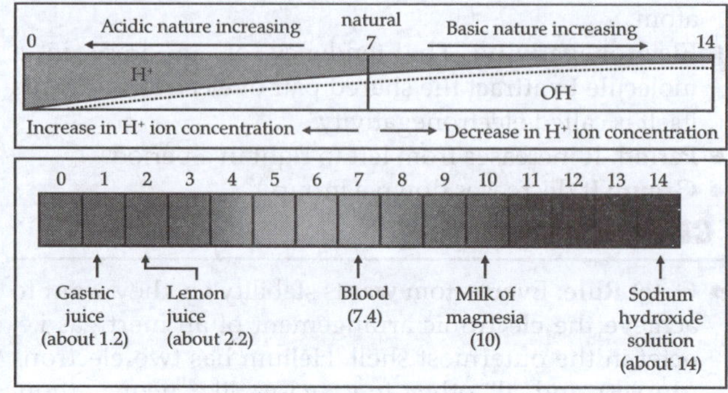

- Optimizing Soil pH for Ideal Crop Growth:
- Maintaining an optimal pH level is crucial for the growth of food crops, typically falling between 7 to 7.8. To address imbalances:
- **Acidic Soil (pH Below 7):** Add lime or slaked lime to neutralize excess acidity, enhancing soil quality for crops.
- **Alkaline Soil (pH Above 7.8):** Introduce gypsum or suitable substances to neutralize excess alkali, effectively balancing the soil pH for optimal crop cultivation.
- **Stomach:** The medium in our stomach is highly acidic and has pH around 1.2. Our stomach produces hydrochloric acid which helps in digestion of food. Magnesium hydroxide (Milk of magnesia) , which is a mild base and an antacid which neutralises the excess acid.
- Tooth decay starts when the pH of the mouth is lower than 5.5.
- **Acid Rain:** When pH of rain water is less than 5.6, it is called acid rain.
- **Blood pH:** For proper functioning our body needs to maintain blood pH between 7.35 and 7.45. Values of blood pH greater than 7.8 or less than 6.8 often results in death.

  Note: The atmosphere of venus is made up of thick white and yellowish clouds of sulphuric acid.
- **Indicators:** An indicator is a dye that changes colour when it is put into an acid or a base. The three common indicators to test for acids and bases are Litmus, Methyl Orange and Phenolphthalein.
- Litmus is an indicator which is extracted from lichens, a plant belonging to the division Thallophyta. It has a purple colour in distilled water. When added to an acidic solution, litmus turns red and when added to a basic solution, it turns blue.

- The solutions which do not change the colour of either red or blue litmus are known as neutral solutions. These substances are neither acidic nor basic.

Indicators	Colour Change (ACID)	Colour Change (BASE)
Litmus	Red	Blue
Turmeric	Yellow	Red
Methyl Orange	Red	Yellow
Phenolphthalein	Colourless	Pink

- An acid turns blue litmus red.
- A base (or alkali) turns red litmus blue.
- **Efflorescence:** It is a property of some substances to lose wholly or partly their water of crystallisation when their crystals are exposed to dry air even for a short time. They become powdery.
  Examples: washing soda, epsom salt and blue vitriol.
- **Deliquescence:** Many substances have the property to absorb moisture when exposed to the atmosphere at ordinary temperature. They become wet and ultimately dissolve in absorbed water to form a solution. Such substances are called deliquescent substances and this property is called deliquescence.
  Examples: sodium hydroxide (NaOH), potassium hydroxide (KOH), ferric chloride ($FeCl_2$).
- **Hygroscopy:** Certain substances absorb moisture from the atmosphere without dissolving in it. Such substances are called hygroscopic substances and the phenomenon is called hygroscopy.
  Examples: phosphorous pentoxide (P_2O_5), quick lime (CaO), silica gel, concentrated sulphuric acid (H_2SO_4)

Oxidation and Reduction

- **Oxidation:** Oxidation may be defined as gain of oxygen, loss of hydrogen, or loss of electrons.
- **Oxidising agents:** Substances which give oxygen for oxidation and substance which removes hydrogen.

Oxidising agent:

- Acceptors of electrons.
- It is a substance which removes the electron from an atom.
- It brings oxidation.
- **Reduction:** Reactions which involve loss of oxygen or gain of hydrogen.
- **Reducing agents:** Substances which gives hydrogen for reduction and a substance which removes oxygen.

Reducing agent

- Donors of electrons.
- It is a substance which adds electrons to an atom.
- It brings about reduction.
- **Redox reaction:** The reaction in which oxidation and reduction both take place simultaneously.
  Photosynthesis in plants digestion of food in animals; dry and wet batteries and corrosion of metals are diverse examples of oxidation and reduction reactions.

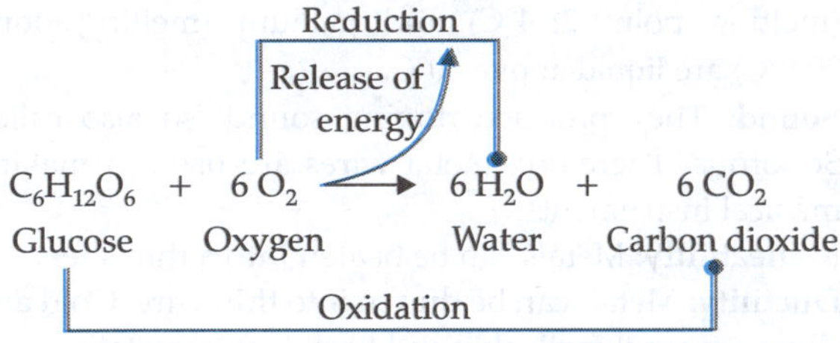

- Corrosion is the process in which metals are decayed gradually by the action of air, moisture or a chemical on their surfaces. Oxidation of metals by the oxygen present in air is the main cause of rusting.
- **Rusting:** The corrosion of iron is called rusting. During this process, when iron or items made of iron are exposed to moist air, a reddish brown powder (rust) is deposited on its surface.

Prevention Methods:

- Painting iron objects.
- Greasing and oiling iron objects.
- Galvanization i.e. by depositing a layer of zinc on the surface of iron objects.

> - Items of copper or brass are left open in air, a greenish layer is deposited on the surface. The carbon dioxide present in the atmosphere reacts with copper to form copper carbonate.
> - Silver develops black coating due to corrosion.

- **Rancidity:** The condition produced by aerial oxidation of fats and oil in food marked by an unpleasant smell and taste is called rancidity. Butter, ghee, boiled rice, etc. become rancid after prolonged exposure to air.

Prevention of Rancidity

- Anti-oxidants such as BHA (Butylated Hydroxy Anisole) and BHT (Butylated Hydroxy Toluene) are used to prevent rancidity.
- Food materials may be kept at a very low temperature.
- Food may be preserved in airtight containers.
- Chips (example, potato chips) sold in the market come in packets filled with nitrogen gas.

Metals and Non-metals

Metals

- Metals are the elements that conduct heat and electricity and are malleable and ductile. For example, Iron, Aluminium, Copper etc.
- Almost all the metal oxides are basic in nature but zinc oxide and aluminium oxide are amphoteric.

Physical Properties of Metals

- **Conduction:** Metals are good conductors of heat and electricity. Therefore, electric wires are made of metals like copper and aluminium. Silver is the best conductor of heat followed by copper.
- **Hardness:** Most of the metals are hard except alkali metals such as sodium, potassium, lithium, etc. Alkali metals are very soft metals that can be cut by using a knife.
- **Strength:** Most metals possess high tensile strength, although alkali metals such as sodium and potassium are relatively soft.
- **State:** Metals are Solid at room temperature except mercury (melting point 39°C) which is liquid, caesium

(melting point 28.4°C) and gallium (melting point 29.8°C) are liquid above 30°C.

- **Sound:** They produce ringing sound, so also called Sonorous. Therefore, metal wires are used in making musical instruments.
- **Malleability:** Metals can be beaten into a thin sheet.
- **Ductility:** Metals can be drawn into thin wire. Gold and silver are most malleable and best ductile metals.
- **Melting and Boiling Point:** Metals generally have high melting and boiling points except sodium and potassium.
- **Density:** Most metals have relatively high densities, though some metals such as lithium, sodium and potassium have low densities.
- **Colour:** Most of the metals are grey in colour except gold and copper.
- **Lustre:** Generally Shiny in appearance.

Applications

- Chromium is used for making rust free stainless steel.
- Zinc is used for galvanisation of iron objects. Zinc sulphide is used in the preparation of X-ray screens. Zinc oxide is known as philosopher's wool. Zinc sulphate ($ZnSO_4$. $7H_2O$) is white vitriol.
- Copper and aluminium are used for making electric wires.
- Mercury is used in thermometers.
- Zirconium is used for making bullet proof alloy steels.It is used for making core of nuclear reactors and for making pumps, valves and heat exchangers.
- Silver foils are used to decorate sweets.
- Lead is used in car batteries. Lead is mainly found in the form of sulphide ore called galena (PbS). Red lead (minium or sindhur) is Pb_3O_4 used for making protective paint for iron and in match industry.
- Lithium, sodium, potassium, rubidium and caesium are alkali metals. Alkali metals are stored under kerosene or liquid paraffins to protect them from action of air.
- Metallic sodium is prepared by the electrolysis of molten mixture of 40% sodium chloride and 60% calcium chloride in a Down's cell.
- Sodium bicarbonate ($NaHCO_3$), baking soda is used in effervescent drinks and fruit salts in fire extinguishers and it is also used in the form of sesquicarbonate. It is used for wool washing.
- Sodium carbonate (Na_2CO_3. $10H_2O$) washing soda is used in the manufacturing of glass, soap, washing powder and for softening hard water.
- Mixture of sodium carbonate and potassium carbonate is known as fusion mixture.
- Sodium sulphate (Na_2SO_4. $10H_2O$) is Glauber's salt. It is used as purgative.
- Sodium thiosulphate ($Na_2S_2O_3$. $5H_2O$) or Hypo. It is used in the photography as a fixing agent.
- Potassium super oxide (KO_2) used in space capsules, submarines and breathing masks as it produces oxygen and removes carbon dioxide and carbon monoxide.
- Potassium cyanide (KCN) is used in the extraction of silver, gold and as a germicide in agriculture. KCN is more poisonous than sodium cyanide.
- Potassium hydroxide (KOH) is known as caustic potash used in the preparation of soft soap. Its aqueous solution is known as potash lye.
- Potassium carbonate (K_2CO_3) is potash or pearl ash.
- De-icing of Roads after snowfall - De-icing in the process of removing ice from a surface by using salts on the surface. Now-a-days, liquid $CaCl_2$ and $MgCl_2$ are also used for this purpose.
- Calcium oxide (CaO) is also called quick lime. It is used in the manufacturing of glass, calcium chloride, cement, bleaching power, calcium carbide, slaked lime, in the extraction of iron and as a drying agent for ammonia and alcohol.
- Calcium hydroxide, slaked lime [$Ca(OH)_2$] is used in the manufacturing of caustic soda, sodalime and for softening of hard water.
- Calcium sulphate, gypsum ($CaSO_4$. $2H_2O$) loses a part of its water of crystallization when heated upto 120°C to from [$CaSO_4$]$_{½}$. H_2O which is known as plaster of Paris.
- Plaster of Paris is a white powder, which sets into hard mass on wetting with water and it is used in making statues, toys, etc., in medical applications of setting fractured bones in right positions and in dentistry.

Some Metals and Their Properties

- **Boron:** It is a semimetal (metalloids). In the nature, it occurs in combined state as borax.
- Boron and boron carbide rods are used to control the nuclear reactions. Boron carbide (B_4C) is hardest, known as an artificial substance after diamond and is known as Norbia. Orthoboric acid (H_3BO_3) is used as an antiseptic and eye wash under the name boric lotion.
- **Aluminium:** It is a third most abundant element of Earth's crust. It isextracted from bauxite (Al_2O_3. $2H_2O$). Aluminium powder is used in fireworks, flash light powder, thermite welding.
- Ammonal (a mixture of aluminium powder and ammonium nitrate) is used as an explosive.
- Ruby and sapphire are essentially Al_2O_3. Ruby is red due to the presence of Cr and sapphire is blue due to Fe and Ti. Emerald is green, it contains V/Cr and aluminium silicates (Al_2SiO_3).
- **Tin:** Cassiterite (SnO_2) or tin stone is an important ore of Tin. In cold countries, white tin is converted to grey tin (powder), the process is known as tin disease or tin plague. Tin plating is done to prevent the rusting of iron. Tin amalgam is used in making mirrors. Pentahydrate of stannic chloride ($SnCl_4$. $5H_2O$), is called butter of tin used as mordant in dyeing.
- **Vanadium:** Vanadium pentoxide (V_2O_5) is a very good catalyst for manufacturing of sulphuric acid by contact process.
- **Tungsten:** Tungsten filaments are used in electric bulbs. Calcium tungstate is used in X-ray tube.
- **Iron:** It is extracted from its haematite ore.
- Cast iron It is the most impure form of iron and contains 2.5–4% carbon.
- Wrought iron or Malleable iron is the most purest form of iron and contains minimum amount of carbon (0.12–0.5%)
- Iron (II) is present in haemoglobin (blood).

- Mild steel contain 0.25%–0.5% carbon while hard steels contains 0.5%–1.5% carbon. Soft steels contain carbon upto 0.25%.
- Stainless steel is an alloy of iron (Fe), chromium (Cr) and nickel (Ni).
- Ferric chloride ($FeCl_3$) is used as stypic to stop bleeding from a cut. Ferrous sulphate ($FeSO_4$) is used in making blue black ink.
- Copper, Silver and Gold (Cu, Ag and Au) these are called coinage metals.
- Silver is used as amalgam for filling teeth and in silvering mirrors.
- Silver bromide (AgBr) is used in photography.
- $AgNO_3$ is called lunarcaustic used in preparing marking inks and hair dyes.
- $CuSO_4$. $5H_2O$ is called blue vitriol or nila thotha and $CuFeS_2$ is called fool's gold.
- **Non-Metals:** Non-metals are elements that do not conduct heat and electricity, and are neither malleable nor ductile. They are brittle. For example, Carbon, sulphur, Phosphorus etc.

Physical Properties of Non-metals

- **Conduction:** Non-metals are bad conductors of heat and electricity except Graphite which is an allotrope of carbon.
- **Hardness:** They are generally soft except diamond which is the hardest naturally occurring substance.
- **State:** Non-metals may be solid, liquid or gas. Generally, they are brittle.
- **Sound:** They do not produce a typical sound on being hit and hence are non sonorous.
- **Malleability and Ductility:** They do not exhibit these properties.
- **Melting and boiling point:** Non-metals generally have low melting and boiling points.
- **Density:** Most of the non-metals have low density.
- **Colour:** Non-metals are in many colours.
- **Lustre:** They are Dull in appearance except diamond and iodine.

Applications

- Hydrogen is used in the hydrogenation of vegetable oils to make vegetable ghee.
- Nitrogen is used in the manufacture of ammonia, nitric acid and fertilisers.
- Sulphur is used in the vulcanization of rubber. It is also used as a fungicide and in the preparation of sulphuric acid and gunpowder.
- Fluorine is used in fluoride toothpastes.
- Inert gases like neon are used in sign tubes for advertising.
- Graphite (carbon) is used for making electrodes in dry cells and electrolytic cells.
- Compounds of nitrogen like Trinitrotoluene (TNT) and nitroglycerine are used as explosives.
- Due to its inertness, nitrogen is used to preserve food materials.

Allotropy

Allotropy is the property of an element by the virtue of which it can exist in different structural forms which have the same chemical properties but different physical properties. The various forms of an element are called allotropes.

Non-metals exhibit allotropy.

Carbon - diamond, graphite, fullerenes

Sulphur - monoclinic, rhombic, plastic

Phosphorus - red, yellow, violet, scarlet, black

Minerals and Ores

- **Minerals:** Metal bearing substances, found in the earth's crust, are called minerals. Example, NaCl, KCl, $MgCO_3$, ZnS, etc.
- **Ores:** The minerals from which metals can be obtained on a commercial scale are called ores. For example, bauxite is an ore of aluminium and cinnabar that of mercury.

Metallurgy

Terms related to Metallurgical Process:

- **Dressing of ore:** The removal of impurities associated with the ore is called dressing or enrichment of the ore.
- **Calcination:** The process of heating a metal - rich ore to a high temperature to convert the metal into its oxide in the absence of air is called calcination.
- **Roasting:** Heating the concentrated ore in the presence of air to remove volatile impurities is called roasting.
- **Flux:** A substance added in the furnace during smelting to remove the gangue.

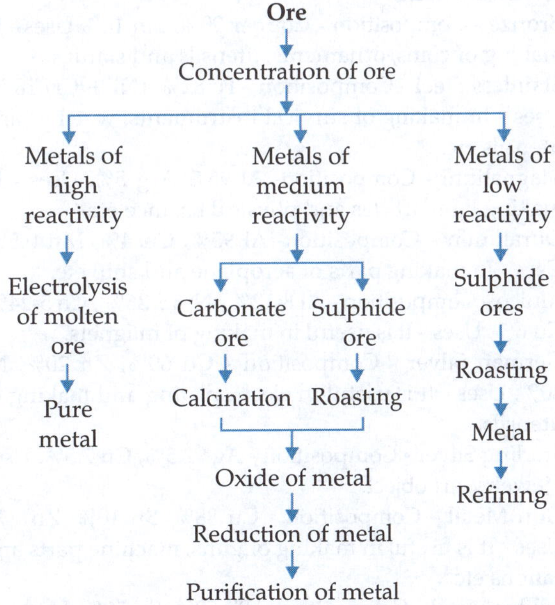

- **Gangue:** Rocky and earthly impurities present in ores are called gangue.
- **Slag:** A substance formed when flux reacted with gangue is called a slag.

$$SiO_2 + CaCO_3 \rightarrow CaSiO_2 + CO_2$$

- **Smelting:** The process of obtaining the metal by reducing its oxide ore with coke is known as smelting.

- **Methods of Concentration of Ore**
- **Froth Floatation:** Finally ground sulphide ore + water + pine oil + air blast. Ore particles come up with froth and float on the surface. The Rocky matter settles to the bottom. For example, zinc blende is concentrated by this method.
- **Electromagnetic Separation:** Magnetic ores are separated by this process like iron ores.
- **Gravity Separation:** Heavier ores are separated.
- **Refining of metals**
- **Distillation:** Easily volatile metals like zinc, cadmium and mercury are removed by this method.
- **Liquation:** Easily fusible metals like lead and tin may be removed.
- **Oxidation:** Easily impurities like copper and tin may be removed by passing air blast through molten impure metals.
- **Electrolytic Refining:** Metals like Cu, Al, Zn, Ag and Au may be refined using the impure metals as anodes, pure metals strip as cathode and metal salt solution as electrolyte.

Alloys

- It is a homogeneous mixture of two or more metals, or a metal and a non-metal.
- It is prepared by first melting the primary metal, and then, dissolving the other elements in it, in definite proportions. It is then cooled to room temperature.
- Electrical conductivity and melting point of an alloy is less than pure metals.
- Brass - Composition- zinc 30%, copper 70%. Uses - In making of utensils, pipes and radiator statues etc.
- Yellow Brass - Composition - Cu 67%, Zn 33% Uses - Hardware items
- Bronze - Composition - Copper 90%, Tin 10% Uses - In making of coins, ornaments, utensils and statues.
- Stainless Steel - Composition - Fe 82%, (Ni + Cr) 18 %. Uses - In making of surgical instruments, watches and utensils etc.
- Magnalium - Composition- Al 95%, Mg 5%. Uses - In making light articles and physical balance etc.
- Duralumin - Composition- Al 95%, Cu 4%, Mn 0.5%. Uses - In making parts of aeroplane and ship etc.
- Alnico - Composition - Al 8-12% , Ni 15-26% , Co 5-24%, Cu 6%. Uses - It is useful in making of magnets.
- German Silver - Composition - Cu 60%, Zn 20%, Ni 20%. Uses - It is useful in electroplating and making of utensils.
- Sterling Silver - Composition - Ag 92.5%, Cu 7.5%. Uses - jewelry, art object.
- Gun Metal - Composition - Cu 88%, Sn 10%, Zn 2%. Uses - It is useful in making of guns, machine parts and canons etc
- Solder Metal - Composition - Pb 50%, Sn 50%. Uses - It is mainly useful to join electric wires.
- Bell Metal - Composition - Cu - 77%, Sn - 23%. Uses- casting of bells.
- Coin Metal - Composition - Cu 75%, Ni 25%. Uses - U.S. coins.
- Wood's Metal - Composition - Bi 50%, Pb 25%, Sn 12.5%, Cd 12.5% Uses - fuse plugs, automatic sprinklers.
- Monel - Composition - Ni 67%, and copper, with small amounts of manganese, carbon, and silicon. Uses - It is resistant to corrosion and acids and thus used for making valves, pumps, shafts, fittings, fasteners, and heat exchangers.
- Plumber's Solder - Composition - Pb 67%, Sn 33%. Uses- soldering joints.

Characteristics of alloys

- Alloys are stronger than metals from which they are made.
- Alloys are harder than the constituent metals.
- Alloys are more resistant to corrosion.
- They have lower electrical conductivity than pure metals.
- Alloys have lower melting points than the constituent metals.

Some Common Metals, Ores, Chemical composition

- **Iron, Fe**

Ores

- Hematite, Fe_2O_3
- Magnetite, Fe_2O_4
- Limonite, $2Fe_2O_3.3H_2O$
- Siderite, $FeCO_2$
- Iron Pyrite, FeS_2

Varieties of Iron

- Pig iron and cast iron produced in the blast furnace is pig iron. It has a high percentage of carbon. Pig iron is melted, mixed with steel scrap and allowed to cool in moulds to give cast iron.
- **Wrought iron:** It is almost a pure form of iron which contains only 0.12% to 0.25% of carbon. It is used in making chains, wires, anchors and cores of electromagnets.
- **Steel:** It is an alloy of iron and carbon.
- **Aluminium, Al**

Ores

- Cryolite, NA_3AlF_6
- Corundum, Al_2O_3
- Bauxite, $Al_2O_3.2H_2O$

Extraction of Aluminium from Bauxite

- Preparation of alumina - Bayer process
- Electrolyte reduction - Hall-Heroult of alumina process
- Electrolytic refining of aluminium - Hope's method
- **Copper, Cu**

Ores

- Copper pyrite, $CuFeS_2$
- Cuprite, Cu_2O
- Malachite, $Cu_2CO_3(OH)_2$

Uses

- Since copper is a good conductor of heat and electricity, it is used in making electrical wires, cables, etc.
- Compounds of copper like cupric sulphate are used as a fungicide and germicide.
- **Sulphur, S**

Ores

- Cinnabar, HgS
- Zinc blende, ZnS
- Copper pyrites, $CuFeS_2$
- Galena, PbS
- Stibnite, SbS_2
- Sulphur is extracted by Frasch process.

- The process of hardening rubber by heating it with sulphur is called vulcanisation.
- **Amalgam:** An amalgam is an alloy of mercury and one or more metals. Most metals form amalgams except iron and platinum. Therefore, amalgams can be stored in iron bottles.

Notes:

- Pure gold, known as 24 carat gold, is very soft.
- It is not suitable for making jewellery.
- It is alloyed with either silver or copper to make it hard.
- Generally, in India, 22 carat gold is used for making ornaments. It means that 22 parts of pure gold are alloyed with 2 parts of either copper or silver.
- The Iron pillar near the Qutub Minar in Delhi was built more than 1600 years ago and it still stands to prevent it from rusting.

Carbon and its Compounds

- **Carbon:** Carbon is a versatile element. It is non-metal. Carbon forms a large number of compounds which are called organic compounds (except the oxides of carbon carbonates, hydrogen carbonates and carbides). Carbon exists in both elemental form and in combined form with other elements.
- **Allotropes of Carbon:** Allotropes is the property of some elements to exist in two or more different physical states despite similar chemical properties.

Three main Allotropes of Carbon:

- **Diamond:** In this form, an atom is bonded to four other carbon atoms forming three-dimensional structures.
- It is considered the hardest substance and an insulator.
- It is used for drilling rocks and cutting and making jewellery.

Uses of Diamond

- Used in cutting instruments like glass cutters, saw for cutting marbles and in rock drilling equipment.
- It is used in making jewellery.
- Diamond 'dies' are used for drawing thin and long metallic wires.
- A sharp diamond edged knife (called keratome) is used by eye-surgeons to remove cataract from the eye.
- **Graphite:** In this form, each carbon atom is bonded to three other carbon atoms. It is a good conductor of electricity and used as a lubricant.

Uses of Graphite

- Powdered graphite is used as a lubricant for the moving parts of machinery.
- Graphite is a good conductor of electricity, thus, it is used in making electrodes in dry cells and electric arcs.
- It is also used in pencil 'lead', which is made of graphite and clay, not metallic lead.
- Graphite tiles are used in most spacecraft as they can bear very high temperatures.
- **Buckminsterfullerene:** It is often referred to as a buckyball, is a molecule composed entirely of carbon atoms. It is a form of fullerene, a hollow sphere, ellipsoid, tube, or other various shapes made entirely of carbon atoms.
- **Uses of Fullerenes:**
- Fullerenes are used in artificial photosynthesis, cosmetics, surface coatings etc.

Organic Compounds

- The compounds of carbon are known as organic compounds. They occur in all living things like plants and animals.

  Functional group: It is an atom or a group of atoms which determines the characteristic properties of a particular compound.

Some Important Carbon Compounds

- **Methane (CH_4):** It is also called marsh gas and is formed by the decomposition of vegetable matter in the absence of air. Methane is a major constituent of gobar gas, sewage gas and biogas produced by decomposition of dung, excreta and plant wastes, respectively.

Uses

- It is employed as domestic fuel.
- Carbon black, obtained from methane, is used as a filler in the rubber industry.
- It is used in the preparation of useful compounds like ethyne (acetylene), formaldehyde, methanol and carbon tetrachloride.
- **Ethanol or Ethyl Alcohol (CH_3CH_2OH):** Ethanol, also known as ethyl alcohol, is a clear, colorless liquid used as a solvent, fuel, and in alcoholic beverages.

Uses

- Ethanol is a good solvent for gums and resins.
- It is also used in thermometers and as preservatives for biological specimens, due to its low freezing point.
- It is an important raw material in the manufacture of chloroform, iodoform, ether, acetic acid, etc.
- Ethyl alcohol is used in alcoholic beverages.
- It is also used as a fuel in the form of power alcohol and as an antifreeze in automobile radiators.

Synthetic Fibres and Plastics

- The fibres which are made by human beings by chemical means are called synthetic or man-made fibres. Many such small units combine to form a large subunit called polymer.

> Polymers also occur in nature. Cotton is a polymer of cellulose. Cellulose is made up of a large number of glucose units.

Types of Synthetic Fibres

- **Rayon:** Rayon is a synthetic fibre which is obtained by chemical treatment of wood pulp (cellulose). It is also called artificial silk. Rayon is mixed with cotton to make bed sheets or mixed with wool to make carpets.
- **Nylon:** Nylon was made without any natural raw material (plant or animal). It was prepared from coal, water and air. It was the first fully synthetic fibre. It is strong, elastic, light, lustrous and easy to wash.
- It is used to make socks, ropes, car seat belts, sleeping bags, curtains, etc. It is also used for making parachutes and ropes for rock climbing.
- **Polyester:** Polyesters are actually made up of repeating units of a chemical called an ester. This fibre remains crisp and is easy to wash, so it is used in making dress material. Terylene is a popular polyester.
- **Acrylic:** It is another synthetic fibre which is used in making clothes resembling wool. These are cheap and available in a variety of colours.
- **Plastics:** Plastic is a polymer which may have a linear or cross-linked arrangement.

- Polythene (Poly+ethene) is an example of plastic which is used for making polythene bags.
- **Thermoplastics:** Such plastics which get deformed easily on heating and can be bent easily are known as thermoplastics. For example, polythene and PVC.
- **Thermosetting Plastics:** Plastics which when moulded once, cannot be softened by heating are called thermosetting plastics. For example, bakelite and melamine.
- **Bakelite (Phenol formaldehyde resins):** It is used for making electrical switches and utensils.
- **Melamine:** It resists fire and is used for making floor tiles and kitchenware.
- **Coal and Petroleum:** A fuel is a material that has energy stored inside it. When the fuel is burned, the energy is released mainly as heat and some light. Most of the fuels are either carbon or carbon compounds, such as, coal, coke, charcoal, kerosene, petrol, diesel, LPG, CNG, etc.
- **Natural Gas:** It consists mainly of methane (about 85%), ethane, propane and butane. It can be used as a fuel in homes and factories. Compressed Natural Gas (CNG). It is used as an alternative to petrol as automobile fuel.
- **Liquefied Petroleum Gas (LPG):** Petroleum gas is stored as a liquid under pressure. It is called Liquefied Petroleum Gas (LPG). Petroleum gas is a mixture of propane and butane. It burns readily, producing a lot of heat. To help detect any leakage of gas from the cylinder a strong smelling substance like ethyl mercaptan is added to the gas.

Soaps and Detergents

- **Soaps:** A soap is the sodium salt or potassium salt of a long chain carboxylic acid or glycerol, which has cleansing properties in water. Sodium palmitate, sodium stearate, sodium oleate are some examples of soap.
- **Detergents:** Detergents are the sodium salt of a long chain benzene sulphonic acid (or the sodium salt of a long chain alkyl hydrogen sulphate) which have cleansing properties in water. Detergents have a stronger cleansing action than soaps, and they are also more soluble than soaps.

Graphene

- Graphene is a form of carbon comprising a single layer of atoms arranged in a honeycomb shaped lattice, the thinnest substance in existence. Andre Geim and Novoselov have been awarded the Nobel Prize for isolating graphene. Graphene has applications in the energy, construction, health, and electronics sectors.

Chemistry in Everyday Life

- **Common Salt (NaCl):** It is chemically known as sodium chloride (NaCl). It occurs as mineral rock salt and in natural brines and salt water.

Uses

- It is used universally as a preservative and as an essential ingredient of food.
- It helps to maintain electrolyte balance in our body.
- It is also used in the manufacture of soap.

- **Sodium Hydroxide (NaOH):** Sodium hydroxide is also called caustic soda.

Uses

- It is used to prepare soaps and detergents.
- It is used in the manufacture of paper and artificial fibres.

- **Washing Soda, (Na_2CO_3. $10H_2O$):** Washing soda is chemically known as sodium carbonate.

Uses

- It is used as a cleansing agent for domestic purposes.
- It is used in softening hard water.
- It is used in the manufacture of glass.
- It is also used in the photography, textile and paper industries.

- **Baking Soda, ($NaHCO_3$):** Baking soda is sodium hydrogen carbonate or sodium bicarbonate.

Uses

- It is used in the manufacture of baking powder (a mixture of potassium, hydrogen-tartrate and sodium bicarbonate). During the preparation of bread, CO_2 is evolved, which causes the bread to swell.
- It is used in medicine as soda bicarb which acts as an antacid.
- It also used fire extinguishers.

Bleaching Powder ($CaOCl_2$): Bleaching powder is commercially called chloride of lime or chlorinated lime. It is prepared by passing chlorine over slaked lime at 313 K.

$Ca(OH)_2$	+	Cl_2	→	$CaOCl_2$	+	H_2O
Calcium hydroxide (Slaked lime)		Chlorine		Calcium Oxychloride (Bleaching Powder)		Water

Uses

- It is used as a bleaching agent in paper and textile industries and to bleach cotton clothes.
- It is also used as a disinfectant to make water free from germs.
- It is used to make chloroform.

- **Plaster of Paris ($CaSO_4.1/2\ H_2O$):** It is prepared by heating gypsum ($CaSO_4.2H_2O$) at about 393 K.

Uses

- It is used in making toys, cosmetics and casts of statues.
- It is used as a cast for setting broken bones.
- It is also used in laboratories for sealing gaps to make airtight arrangements.
- It is also used in making moulds in pottery.

- **Lime (CaO):** It is chemically known as calcium oxide or quicklime.

Uses

- It is used for making mortar and for white washing.
- It is used for making desiccating agents to dry ammonia.
- It is used for making cement, glass, calcium carbide, etc.
- It reacts with water to produce slaked lime, $Ca(OH)_2$.

- **Hard Water and Soft Water:** The water which lathers easily on shaking with soap solution is called soft water, for example, rain water, while the water which does not produce lather with soap solution readily is called hard water, for example, sea water.

- **Cause of Hardness of Water:** The hardness of water is due to the presence of soluble salts of calcium, magnesium and other heavy metals in it.
- **Heavy Water, D_2O:** It is chemically Deuterium Oxide (D_2O). One part of D_2O is present in 6000 parts of H_2O. It is used in nuclear reactors as a moderator.
- **Cement:** Cement is a mixture of calcium silicates and aluminates with a small amount of gypsum. The main components of cement are-tricalcium silicate, dicalcium silicate and tricalcium aluminate.
- **Portland Cement:** Its a mixture of lime, magnesium oxide, silica, ferric oxide, alumina and sulphur trioxide. Limestone, clay and gypsum are the raw materials for the manufacture of cement.
- **Mortar:** It is a mixture of cement, sand and water. It is used for plastering walls and binding bricks and stones.
- **Concrete:** It is a mixture of cement, sand gravel or small pieces of stone and water. It is used for the construction of floors.

Glass

Glass is a hard and brittle material which is a supercooled liquid of silicates. Raw materials used in the formation of glass are sodium carbonate, calcium carbonate, and sand.

Types of Glass

- **Soda:** Lime Glass It is the common glass used in windows and bottles.
- **Pyrex Glass:** It is borosilicate glass. It is used in making cooking utensils, pharmaceutical containers and laboratory apparatus.
- **Photochromic Glass:** It contains a dispersion of silver chloride or silver iodide. On exposure to sunlight the glass darkens.
- **Crown Glass:** It is used in making lenses for spectacles.
- **Crookes Glass:** It contains cerium oxide which cuts UV rays.It is used for making lenses for spectacles.
- **Soft Glass:** It is a mixture of sodium or calcium silicates. It is used in making window glass, mirrors and common glass wares etc.
- **Hard Glass:** It is a mixture of potassium and calcium silicates. It is more resistant to the action of acids for making hard glass apparatus.
- **Flint Glass:** It is mainly a mixture of sodium, potassium and lead silicates. It is used in making bulbs and optical instruments.

Polymerization

- Polymers are defined as the high molecular mass macromolecules, which consist of repeating structural units derived from the corresponding monomers.
- Polymers occur in nature also. Cotton, for example, is a polymer called cellulose. Cellulose is made up of a large number of glucose units.
- Few important polymers are:

Polythene

- **Low density polythene:** It is done by polymerisation of ethene under high pressure in the presence of traces of dioxygen or a peroxide initiator (catalyst).
- **High density Polythene:** It is done by polymerisation of ethene in the presence of a catalyst such as triethylaluminium and titanium tetrachloride (Ziegler-Natta catalyst).
- **Polytetrafluoroethene (Teflon):** Teflon is manufactured by heating tetrafluoroethene with a free radical or persulphate catalyst at high pressures.
- **Polyacrylonitrile:** Polymer of acrylonitrile in presence of a peroxide catalyst.

Rubber

- **Natural Rubber:** Its a polymer of isoprene i.e. it is polyisoprene. It is soft and elastic. It is obtained from latex, an exudate from the bark of a rubber tree. When rubber is heated with sulphur it is called vulcanisation of rubber. It makes rubber hard, elastic and strong.
- **Synthetic Rubber**
- **Buna-S:** It is used in making automobile tyres and footwear.
- **Buna-N:** It is used in making tank linings and hose-pipes.
- **Neoprene:** It is used in making conveyor belts and printing rollers.
- **Thiokol:** It is used as a rocket fuel.

> **Zeolite:** Zeolites are aluminosilicates which are used as catalysts in petrochemical industries for cracking of hydrocarbons.

Chemicals in Agriculture

Fertilizers

- Urea is the best fertilizer as it leaves only carbon dioxide after ammonia, has been assimilated by plants.
- It contains about 46% nitrogen and is generally considered neutral in its direct effect on soil pH.
- Mixture of $Ca(CN)_2$ and C is known as nitrolim. Commerically, calcium nitrate is known as Norwegian saltpetre.
- The mixture of nitrogenous, phosphatic and potash fertilizers in suitable amounts, is referred as NPK fertilizers.

Pesticides

- Pesticides are the chemicals which are applied to crops, for example, DDT and malathion.

Difethialone

- Vitamin K has been suggested and +successfully used, as antidote for pets or humans accide accidentally or intentionally exposed to anticoagulant poisons.

Drugs

- **Antiseptics:** Those chemical substances which prevent the growth of microorganisms or kill them. For example, dettol, picric acid, cresol, resorcinol, etc.
- **Antipyretics:** Those chemicals that are used for bringing down the temperature of humans during high fevers. For example - aspirin, paracetamol.
- **Tranquillisers:** Those chemical substances which are used for the cure of mental diseases. For example, barbituric acid.
- **Analgesics:** These are the chemical substances which are used for relieving pain. For example, aspirin, analgin.
- **Anaesthetics:** These are the drugs which produce loss of sensation. e.g. nitrous oxide, xylocains and cyclopropane.
- Sedatives calm anxiety without causing drowsiness.

- **Hypnotics:** There drugs produce sleep and are habit forming.
- **Antihistamines:** These are chemical substances which diminish or abolish the main action of histamine released in the body and hence prevent allergic reactions such as hay fever, mild asthma, nasal discharge, etc.
- Hallucinogens are used for mental illness. For example, LSD i.e. Lysergic Acid Diethylamide.
- **Antimalarials:** These chemical substances are used for the treatment of malaria. For example, chloroquine, quinine, paraquine, primaquine, etc.
- **Antidepressants:** They induce a feeling of well-being and confidence in a person of depressed mood. For example Prozac.
- **Dyes:** Dyes are coloured substances which can be applied in solution or dispersion to a substrate such as textile fibers (cotton, wool, silk, nylon etc.). A dye has two parts:
  - Chromophores which impart colour to a compound, and.
  - Auxochromes which themselves do not absorb light but deepen the colour when introduced into the coloured compounds.
- Dyes are of two kinds:
  - **Natural Dyes:** These are obtained from the plants such as alizarin, indigo, logwood.
  - **Synthetic Dye:** These are prepared in the laboratory such as martius yellow, malachite green, congo red, aniline, etc. The first synthetic dye was mauveine.

Organic Compound and their Applications

- **Medicine:** Aspirin (acetylsalicylic acid) relieves pain; caffeine stimulates; ethanol is a solvent in medications.
- **Cosmetics:** Parabens preserve products; glycerin moisturizes; retinol (vitamin A) reduces wrinkles.
- **Polymers:** Polyethylene is used in plastic bags; PVC (polyvinyl chloride) makes pipes; nylon is in textiles.
- **Dyes:** Alizarin gives red color; indigo provides blue; anthraquinone dyes fabrics.
- **Fuels:** Gasoline fuels vehicles; biodiesel is derived from plant oils; methane is a natural gas.
- **Flavors and Fragrances:** Vanillin flavors food; citronellal gives lemon scent; menthol produces cooling sensation.
- **Insecticides:** Pyrethroids repel insects; neonicotinoids kill pests; diethyltoluamide (DEET) repels mosquitoes.
- **Food Additives:** Sorbic acid preserves food; citric acid enhances flavor; aspartame sweetens beverages.
- **Cleaning Products:** Ethanol is a disinfectant; surfactants like sodium lauryl sulfate aid in cleaning.
- **Pharmaceuticals:** Ibuprofen treats pain; penicillin is an antibiotic; statins lower cholesterol.
- **Explosives:** Nitroglycerin is used in dynamite; TNT (trinitrotoluene) is a powerful explosive.
- **Plastics:** Polypropylene forms containers; polystyrene is used in packaging; PET (polyethylene terephthalate) makes bottles.
- **Perfumes:** Aldehydes add floral notes; musk compounds provide base notes in perfumes.
- **Fertilizers:** Urea provides nitrogen; potassium chloride is a potassium source in fertilizers.
- **Solvents:** Acetone is a nail polish remover; benzene is a solvent in chemical processes.
- **Artificial Flavorings:** Ethyl acetate adds fruity flavor; vanillin imparts vanilla taste; limonene provides citrus aroma.
- **Preservatives:** Sodium nitrite preserves processed meats; sulfur dioxide keeps dried fruits fresh.
- **Insect Pheromones:** Methyl (E,Z)-2,4-decadienoate attracts certain insects for pest control.
- **Fire Retardants:** Brominated flame retardants prevent fires in electronics and textiles.
- **Adhesives:** Cyanoacrylate (super glue) bonds quickly; epoxy resins provide strong adhesion.
- **Plasticizers:** Phthalates make plastics flexible; adipates are used in PVC products.
- **Antifreeze:** Ethylene glycol prevents freezing in car radiators; propylene glycol is used in food-grade antifreeze.
- **Antibacterials:** Triclosan is found in some soaps; quaternary ammonium compounds disinfect surfaces.

Food Additives

- **Preservatives:** Chemicals like sodium benzoate extend shelf life by inhibiting microbial growth.
- **Flavor Enhancers:** Substances like monosodium glutamate (MSG) intensify taste.
- **Colorants:** Synthetic dyes like tartrazine provide food products with specific colors.
- **Sweeteners:** Artificial sweeteners such as saccharin and aspartame add sweetness with little or no caloric value.
- **Emulsifiers:** Compounds like lecithin stabilize mixtures of substances like oil and water.

Explosives

- Explosives are the substances that contain a great amount of stored energy that can produce an explosion. For example, nitroglycerine (Noble's oil), nitrocellulose, TNT (Trinitrotoluene), RDX (Research and Development Explosive) dynamite, etc. are some explosives.

Hydrocarbons

- Hydrocarbons are organic compounds consisting of hydrogen and carbon atoms. Types include alkanes (saturated), alkenes (with double bonds), alkynes (with triple bonds), and aromatics (ring structures).
- **Saturated hydrocarbons:** They contain only single bonds.
- These are also called alkanes or paraffins and have general formula C_nH_{2n+2}.
- Methane is the first member of.this group.
- **Unsaturated hydrocarbons:** These have atleast one double (=) or triple (≡) bond and are called alkenes and alkynes respectively.
  They have general formula C_nH_{2n} for alkene and C_nH_{2n-2} for alkynes.
- **Aromatic hydrocarbons:** They have ring structure with alternate double bonds and (4n + 2) πe –(Huckel's rule example, benzene).

Some Important Hydrocarbons and their Uses

- **Methane (CH_4)**
- It is also known as marsh gas or damp fire.
- Natural gas contains mainly 90% methane along with ethane, propane, butane etc. Rice agriculture is a big source of atmospheric methane.
- Methane is the cause of occurrence of the explosions in mines.
- Methane is used as a fuel gas in making carbon black.
- **Biogas:** It is produced during decay of biomass in the absence of oxygen. Methane (75%) is the main constituent of biogas).
- **Ethane (C_2H_6):** Natural gas contains approx. 10% ethane. Its hexachloro derivative C_2Cl_6 is used as an artificial camphor.
- **Butane (C_4H_{10}):** It is the main constituent of LPG (liquefied petroleum gas).
- **Ethylene ($CH_2 = CH_2$)**
- It is used as an anesthetic for the preservation and artificial ripening of green fruits.
- It was used for the manufacturing of mustard gas (poisonous gas) In World war l(1914-18).
- **Benzene (C_6C_6):** It is the simplest aromatic hydrocarbon. It was discovered by Faraday in 1825. It is also used as a motor fuel under the name benzol.
- **Toluene ($C_6H_5CH_3$)**
- It is used as a commercial solvent in the manufacturing of explosive (TNT), drugs (chloramines-T) and dyestuffs.
- It is used in the manufacturing of saccharin and printing inks.
- It is used as antifreeze.
- **Naphthalene ($C_{10}H_8$):** It is used for preventing moths in clothes, as an insecticide.

Halogen Derivatives of Hydrocarbons

- **Chloroform ($CHCl_3$)**
- It was discovered by Sir James Young Simpson.
- Chloroform is stored in closed dark coloured bottles completely filled because it is oxidized by air in the presence of sunlight to an extremely poisonous gas phosgene ($COCl_2$).
- It reacts with conc. HNO_3 and form chloropicrin (CCl_3NO_2).
- Chloropicrin is an insecticide.
- The major use of chloroform today is in the production of the Freon refrigerant, R-22.
- **Iodoform (CHI_3):** It is used as an antiseptic due to liberation of free iodine.
- **Carbon tetrachloride (CCl_4):** It is used as a fire extinguishers under the name pyrene.
- **Dichloro diphenyl trichloro ethane (DDT)**
- It was the first chlorinated organic insecticides.
- It was originally prepared in 1873.

Alcohols

- **Methyl alcohol (CH_3OH)**
- Methyl alcohol or Methanol is also known as wood spirit or wood naphtha.
- Methyl alcohol is poisonous in nature and when taken out internally it can cause blindness and even death.
- This alcohol is used for denaturing alcohol (methylated spirit is denatured ethyl alcohol).
- **Ethyl alcohol (C_2H_5OH):** It is simply known as alcohol, spirit of wine or grain alcohol.
- **Glycerol ($CH_2OH. CHOH. CH_2OH$)**
- It is trihydric alcohol known as glycerine.
- It is sweet in taste and very hygroscopic in nature.
- It is used in the manufacturing of cosmetics and transparent soaps.
- **Phenol (C_6H_5OH):** It is commonly known as carbolic acid or benzenol.
- **Methyl isocyanate (CH_3NCO):** This gas leakage was responsible for Bhopal gas tragedy.
- **Fuels**
- Producer gas is a mixture of carbon monoxide and nitrogen.
- Coal gas is a mixture of hydrogen, methane, carbon monoxide, ethane, acetylene, carbon dioxide, nitrogen and oxygen.
- Water gas in mixture of carbon monoxide and hydrogen.
- Oil gas and petrol gas is a mixture of methane (CH_4), ethylene and acetylene etc., and is obtained by cracking of kerosene.
- LPG (Liquefied Petroleum Gas) is the mixtures of hydrocarbons such as propane, propene, n-butane, isobutene and various butane with small amount of ethane. The major sources of LPG are natural gas.
- CNG (Compressed Natural Gas) is highly compressed from of natural gas. CNG has a high octane rating, usually around 120–130.
- Gasohol is a mixture of ethyl alcohol (10%) and petrol (90%).
- **Rocket Fuel**
- The fuel used in rockets is called rocket propellant.
- Liquid propellants are alcohol, liquid hydrogen, liquid ammonia (NH_3), kerosene oil etc.
- Solid propellants are polybutadiene and acrylic acid used along with oxidizers such as aluminium per chlorate, nitrate or chlorate.

Biology

Unit-1: Introduction

- **Biology** is the science of life or living matter in all its forms and phenomena, especially with reference to origin, growth, reproduction, structure, and behavior is called biology (Greek: bios = life; logos = study).
- The term Biology was first used in 1802 by Lamarck (France) and Treviranus (Germany).
- Aristotle (384-322 BC) was the first person to study the animals in details.

Divisions of Biology

- **Botany:** It is the study of different aspects of plants. Theophrastus is known as father of Botany.
- **Zoology:** It is the study of various aspects of animals. Aristotle is called Father of Biology as well as Zoology.

Branches of Biology

- **Based on Special Group of Organisms**

Branch	Study / Area
Bacteriology	Bacteria
Virology	Virus
Mycology	Fungi
Entomology	Insects
Ichthyology	Fishes
Ophiology	Snakes
Myrmecology	Ants
Ornithology	Birds
Arachnology	Spider
Phycology	Algae
Herpetology	Reptiles and amphibians

- **Applied Biology**

Branch	Study / Area
Agriculture	Raising crops
Marine biology	Life in the sea
Veterinary science	Treatment and surgery of animals
Horticulture	Growing fruits, vegetables, flowers, etc.
Sericulture	Production of silk by silkworms
Pisciculture	Fish
Apiculture	Bee keeping
Bioinformatics	Study and analysis of biological information
Exobiology	Studying life elsewhere from earth

- **Taxonomic Hierarchy:** It is the sequence of arrangements of taxonomic categories in a descending order during the classification of an organism. Kingdom is the highest and species is the lowest category in this hierarchy. Species is the basic unit of taxonomy.

Unit-2: Cytology

The cell

- A cell is defined as the basic unit of life that is responsible for all life processes. Cells are the structural, functional and biological units for all living beings. They are known as building blocks of life.
- All organisms are made up of cells. They can be made up of a single cell (unicellular) or many cells (multicellular).
- Anton Van Leeuwenhoek was the first person to describe and see a live cell.
- Nucleus was later discovered by Robert Brown.
- Cells are microscopic in nature.
- Cells provide structure and support to the body of an organism.

Components of The Cell

Plasma membrane

- It encloses a cell and separates its contents from the surrounding.
- It is flexible and made up of phospholipids and proteins.
- It is selectively permeable and regulates the transport of molecules in and out of the cell.

Cytoplasm

- It is a semifluid liquid which fills the interior of the cell.
- It also contains various organelles and micro and macro molecules which help in the functioning of the cell.
- In eukaryotic cells, cytoplasm refers to the region between the nucleus and the plasma membrane.
- Cytosol is the part of the cytoplasm that contains organic molecules and ions in solution.

Nucleoid or Nucleus

- Each cell contains DNA (deoxyribonucleic acid).
- In prokaryotes, most of the genetic material lies in a single circular molecule of DNA.
- Resides near the centre of the cell in an area called the nucleoid which contains the genetic material.
- The nucleus is composed of RNA and proteins.

Ribosomes

- A complex molecule made up of ribosomal RNA molecules and proteins forming a factory of protein synthesis in cells.

Cell organelles

- Specialized structures that perform various jobs inside cells.
- They perform specific functions that keep the cell alive.

Mitochondria

- A double membrane bound structure with outer and inner membrane.

- It is the site of aerobic respiration and produces cellular energy in the form of ATP (adenosine triphosphate) hence called power houses of the cell.

Endo-Membrane System

- Endomembrane system comprises endoplasmic reticulum (ER), Golgi complex, lysosomes and vacuoles.
- **Endoplasmic reticulum (ER):** It is a network of membranes inside a cell which helps in the movement of proteins and molecules.

Types of Endoplasmic Reticulum (ER):

Rough endoplasmic reticulum (ER)	Smooth endoplasmic reticulum (ER)
It has ribosomes attached to its surface. It is an active site for protein synthesis.	In the absence of ribosomes, they appear smooth. It is a major site for synthesis of lipids.

- **Golgi apparatus:** It helps process and package proteins and lipid molecules. Also known as Golgi body.
- **Lysosomes:** A membrane bound cell organelle that contains various hydrolytic enzymes which help in destruction and breakdown of various worn-out cell parts of the cell, thus helping in detoxification of the cell. They also destroy pathogens and play a role in immunity. They are also called suicide bags of the cell as they help in self-destruction of the cells.
- **Vacuoles:** A membrane bound space found in the cytoplasm. It contains water, sap and excretory products. It is bounded by a single membrane named tonoplast.

Plastids

- Found in plant cells and in euglenoids.
- They impart specific colors to the plants though specific pigments.
- On the basis of type of pigments plastids can be classified into chloroplasts, chromoplasts and leucoplasts.

Stem cells

- They are undifferentiated or partially differentiated cells in multicellular animals that can specialize into many types of cells and multiply endlessly to produce additional stems.

Classification of Cells

- On the basis of complexity cells can be classified into Eukaryotic cells and Prokaryotic cells.

Prokaryotic cell	Eukaryotic cell
Size of cell is 0.2-2.0 μm in diameter	Size of cell is 10-100 μm in diameter
Nucleus is absent	Nucleus is present
Absence of membrane enclosed organelles	Presence of membrane enclosed organelles
Cell wall is usually present	Cell wall is existing only in plant cells and fungi
Only one chromosome present	More than one chromosome present
Smaller ribosomes	Larger ribosomes
Example: bacteria and archaea	Example: plants and animals

- On the basis of components eukaryotes are divided into plant cells and animal cells.

Plant cell	Animal cell
Larger than animal cells	Smaller than plant cells
Cell wall is present	Cell wall is absent
Plasmodesmata present	Plasmodesmata absent
Chloroplast present	Chloroplast absent
Vacuole large and permanent	Vacuole small and temporary
Centrioles absent	Centrioles present
Tonoplast present around vacuole	Tonoplast absent
Lysosomes are rare	Lysosomes present

Cell Division

- **Meiosis:** The procedure where a single cell divides twice to produce four cells comprising half the original amount of genetic information.

Phases of cell cycle

The cell cycle is divided into two basic stages:

- **Interphase (Resting phase) comprises of:**
- **G1 Phase (gap 1):** The cell is metabolically active and grows continuously during this phase.
- **S phase (synthesis):** The DNA replication or synthesis occurs during this phase.
- **G2 Phase (gap 2):** Protein synthesis takes place in this phase.
- **Quiescent Stage (G0):** The cells don't undergo any further division, exits the G1 phase and enters the inactive stage.
- **M Phase (Mitosis phase):** Mitosis is the process in which a single cell divides into two identical daughter cells. M Phase involves four stages:
- Prophase
- Metaphase
- Anaphase
- Telophase

Unit-3: Classification of organisms

Classification of Organisms

- Aristotle was the first one to attempt a more scientific basis of classification. He used simple morphological characters to categorize plants into trees, shrubs and herbs. He also divided animals into two groups into ones having red blood and ones not having red blood. This technique of classifying organisms is known as Taxonomy.

Taxonomy Category:

There are seven main taxonomy ranks:

- **Kingdom:** It is the highest level of classification with subcategories.
- **Phylum:** It is the classification of living organisms to find some kind of physical similarities among organisms within the kingdom.

- **Class:** It is a rank used in the biological taxonomy of all organisms. Each class is split into orders.
- **Order:** It is a group of organisms sharing a similar set of characters.
- **Family:** A taxonomic group containing one or more genus sharing a common set of characters.
- **Genus:** It is a condensed group of related species having similar characters in common.
- **Species:** It is the basic unit of classification.

R. H. Whittaker proposed a Five Kingdom Classification. The main characteristics used by him include cell structure, body organization, mode of nutrition, reproduction and phylogenetic relationships. The kingdoms defined by him were named:

- Monera • Protista • Fungi • Plantae • Animalia

Characters	Five Kingdoms				
	Monera	Protista	Fungi	Plantae	Animalia
Cell type	Prokaryotic	Eukaryotic	Eukaryotic	Eukaryotic	Eukaryotic
Cell wall	Non cellulosic (Polysaccharide + amino acid)	Present in some	Present with chitin	Present (cellulose)	Absent
Nuclear membrane	Absent	Present	Present	Present	Present
Body organization	Cellular	Cellular	Multicellular/loose tissue	Tissue/organ	Tissue/organ/ organ system
Mode of nutrition	Autotrophic (chemosynthetic and photosynthetic) and heterotrophic (saprophytic/ parasitic)	Autotrophic (photosynthetic) and heterotrophic	Heterotrophic (saprophytic/ parasitic)	Autotrophic (photosynthetic)	Heterotrophic (holozoic/ saprophytic etc.)

Kingdom Monera

- Bacteria are sole members of the Kingdom Monera. They are the most abundant micro-organisms. Bacteria occur almost everywhere. Bacteria are grouped under four categories based on their shape:
  - The spherical Coccus
  - The rod-shaped Bacillus
  - The comma shaped Vibrium
  - The spiral Spirillum
- **Archaebacteria:** These bacteria are special since they live in some of the harshest habitats such as extreme salty areas, hot springs, and marshy areas. Archaebacteria differ from other bacteria in having a dissimilar cell wall structure and this feature is responsible for their existence in extreme conditions.
- **Eubacteria:** There are thousands of eubacteria. They are categorized by the presence of a rigid cell wall, and if motile, they have a flagellum.
- **Cyanobacteria:** Also referred to as blue green algae. They have chlorophyll similar to green plants and are photosynthetic autotrophs. They are unicellular, colonial or filamentous, freshwater/marine or terrestrial algae.
- **Chemosynthetic Autotrophic Bacteria:** Oxidize various inorganic substances such as nitrates, nitrites, and ammonia and use the released energy for their ATP production.
- **Heterotrophic Bacteria:** Most abundant in nature. The majority are important decomposers. They are used in creation of curd from milk, production of antibiotics, fixing nitrogen in legume roots, etc. Some are pathogens triggering damage to human beings, crops, farm animals and pets. Cholera, typhoid, tetanus, citrus canker are well known diseases caused by diverse bacteria.
- **Mycoplasma:** Organisms that completely lack a cell wall. They are the minutest living cells known and can survive without oxygen.

Kingdom Protista

All single celled eukaryotes are positioned under Protista, but the limitations of this kingdom are not well defined.

- **Chrysophytes:** This group comprises diatoms and golden algae. They are found in freshwater as well as in marine surroundings. They are miniscule and float passively in water currents. Most of them are photosynthetic.
- **Dinoflagellates:** These organisms are typically marine and photosynthetic. They seem yellow, green, brown, blue or red depending on the main pigments existing in their cells. The cell wall has stiff cellulose plates on the extra surface. Most of them have two flagella; one lies longitudinally and the other diagonally in a furrow amongst the wall plates.
- **Euglenoids:** Majority of them are freshwater organisms found in stagnant water. As an alternative of a cell wall, they have a protein rich layer called pellicle which makes their body flexible. They have two flagella a short and a long one. Though they are photosynthetic in the presence of sunlight, but behave like heterotrophs in the absence of sunlight.
- **Slime Moulds:** They are saprophytic protists. The body travels along decaying twigs and leaves engulfing

organic material. They form an aggregation called plasmodium which may grow and spread over several feet, under suitable conditions. During hostile conditions, the plasmodium distinguishes and forms fruiting bodies bearing spores at their tips.

- **Protozoans:** They are heterotrophs and live as per predators or parasites. They are supposed to be primitive relatives of animals.

- **Amoeboid protozoans:** These organisms live in freshwater, sea water or moist soil. They passage and capture their prey by putting out pseudopodia as in *Amoeba*.
- **Flagellated protozoans:** They are either free living or parasitic. They have flagella. The parasitic forms cause diseases such as sleeping illness. Example, *Trypanosoma*.
- **Ciliated protozoans:** These are aquatic, actively moving organisms because of the presence of thousands of cilia. They have a cavity that unlocks to the outside of the cell surface. Example, *Paramoecium*.
- **Sporozoans:** This includes diverse organisms that have a infectious spore like stage in their life cycle. The most notorious is *Plasmodium* which causes malaria.

Kingdom Fungi

- The fungi constitute a exclusive kingdom of heterotrophic organisms. They show a great variety in morphology and habitat. Most fungi are heterotrophic and absorb solvable organic matter from dead substances and hence are named saprophytes.
- Parasites depend on living plants and animals.
- Reproduction in fungi can happen by vegetative means – fragmentation, fission and budding. Asexual reproduction is by spores termed conidia or sporangiospores or zoospores and sexual reproduction is by oospores, ascospores and basidiospores. The numerous spores are produced in distinct structures termed fruiting bodies.

- **Phycomycetes:** Found in aquatic habitats and on decaying wood in moist and damp places or as obligate parasites on plants. The mycelium is aseptate and coenocytic. Asexual reproduction happens by zoospores or by aplanospores. Some examples are *Mucor* and *Rhizopus*.
- **Ascomycetes:** Generally known as sac-fungi, the ascomycetes are typically multicellular, eg Penicillium or rarely unicellular, example, yeast. They are saprophytic, decomposers, parasitic or coprophilous. Mycelium is branched and septate. The asexual spores are conidia produced exogenously on the special mycelium termed conidiosphores. Conidia on germination produce mycelium. Some examples are *Aspergillus* and *Penicilium*.
- **Basidiomycetes:** Commonly known forms of basidiomycetes are mushrooms, bracket fungi or puffballs. They grow in soil, on logs and tree stumps and in living plant bodies as parasites, eg rusts and smuts. The mycelium is branched and septate. The asexual spores are generally not found, but vegetative reproduction by fragmentation is commonly brought about by fusion of two vegetative or somatic cells of different stains or genotypes. Some examples are Mushrooms, Rust and Smut fungus.
- **Deuteromycetes:** Frequently known as imperfect fungi since only the asexual or vegetative phases of these fungi are known. When the sexual forms of these fungi were discovered, they were moved into classes they truly belong to. Some adherents are saprophytes or parasites while a large amount of them are decomposers of litter and support in mineral cycling. Some examples are *Alternaria*, *Collectotrichum* and *Trichoderma*.

Kingdom Plantae

- They are non-motile.
- They make their own foods and are called autotrophs.
- They reproduce both sexually and asexually by vegetative propagation.
- They contain photosynthetic pigments called chlorophyll.

Classification is based on the following criteria:

- **Plant Body:** Presence or absence of a well-defined plant body.
- **Vascular System:** Presence or absence of a vascular system for the transportation of water and other substances.
- **Seed Formation:** Presence or absence of flowers and seeds and if the seeds are naked or inside a fruit.

The plant kingdom has been divided into five sub groups:

- **Thallophyte:** Thallophytes lack well differentiated body structure and the plant body is thallus like. It includes plants with primitive and simple body structures. Example, green algae, red algae, brown algae.
- **Bryophyta:** They don't have vascular tissues and the plant body has root like, stem like and leaf like structures. They are named as amphibians of the plant kingdom because they need water for sexual reproduction. They are present in moist and shady places Example mosses, hornworts and liverworts.
- **Pteridophyte:** They have well differentiated body into root, stem and leaves. They have a vascular system for the transmission of water and other substances. Example, *Selaginella*, *Equisetum*, *Pteris*, etc.
- **Gymnosperms:** They have well differentiated body and vascular tissues. The seeds are not enclosed within a fruit. Examples, *Cycas*, *Pinus*, *Ephedra*, etc.
- **Angiosperms:** They are seed bearing vascular plants having a well differentiated body. The seeds are enclosed within fruits. They are further divided into monocotyledons and dicotyledons. Examples, mango, tomato, rose, onion, wheat, maize, etc.

Plant kingdom can also be separated into two groups:

- **Cryptograms:** Non flowering and non-seed-bearing plants. Example thallophyte, bryophyte, pteridophyte.
- **Phanerogams:** Flowering and seed-bearing plants. Example, gymnosperms, angiosperms.

Kingdom Animalia

Kingdom animalia includes all the animals. Animals are multicellular eukaryotes. The members of animal kingdom exhibit a heterotrophic mode of nutrition.

The different types of phyla of animal kingdom are:

Phylum Porifera

- Porifera means organisms with holes commonly known as sponges.
- They are non-motile, multicellular organisms with a hard core.

- They have a porous body.
- They do not have a well-developed organ or organ system.
- They include marine habitat. Example, *Spongilla*, *Sycon*.

Phylum Coelenterata
- They have a hollow body cavity.
- The body is differentiated into two ends.
- The body is made up of two layers of cells inner and outer linings.
- They live in colonies and solitary.
- Example, *Hydra*, Jellyfish.

Phylum Platyhelminthes
- Commonly known as flatworms.
- They do not have a true internal cavity or coelom.
- They are either free living or parasitic.
- Examples, *Tapeworm*, *Planaria*.

Phylum Nematoda
- They have a cylindrical body.
- They are bilaterally symmetrical and triploblastic.
- They are parasitic and cause diseases such as elephantiasis, ascariasis.
- Examples, *Ascaris*, *Wuchereria*.

Phylum Annelida
- They are commonly known as segmented or ringed worms.
- Their body is differentiated into head and tail.
- They are bilaterally symmetrical and triploblastic.
- They have a true body cavity.
- Example, Earthworm, Leech.

Phylum Arthropoda
- They have jointed legs, exoskeleton and a segmented body.
- They have well differentiated organ and organ system.
- They are bilaterally symmetrical.
- They have an open circulatory system but don't have differentiated blood vessels.
- Example, Spiders, Mosquitos, and Butterflies.

Phylum Mollusca
- They are bilaterally symmetrical and triploblastic.
- They have a well-developed organ and organ system.
- They have an open circulatory system.
- A muscular foot is usually present.
- They have a less segmented body.
- Example, Snails, Octopus.

Phylum Echinodermata
- They have radial symmetry and are triploblastic.
- They have a hard calcium carbonate skeleton structure.
- They have true coelom.
- They are free living marine animals.
- Example, Sea urchins, Starfish.

Phylum Hermichordata
- Their body is soft and fragile and divided into proboscis.
- The epidermis is single layered.
- They have an open circulatory system.
- They respire through gills.
- They have separate sexes and external fertilization is seen.

Phylum Chordata
- They are bilaterally symmetrical and triploblastic with an organ system level of classification.
- They have a closed circulatory system.
- They possess a notochord and a nerve cord.
- It can be divided into the following sub phyla:
  - Urochordata
  - Cephalochordate
  - Vertebrata

Class Cyclostomata
- They have sucking and circular mouth without jaws.
- They don't have scales or paired fins.
- Example, Petromyzon (Lamprey) and Myxine (Hagfish).

Class Chondrichthyes
- They are marine animals with streamlined bodies and have cartilaginous endoskeleton.
- They have tough skin having minute placoid scales.
- They have a two chambered heart.
- Notochord is persistent throughout life.
- Example, Scoliodon (Dog fish) pristis (Saw fish).

Class Osteichtyes
- It includes both freshwater and marine fishes with ebony and endoskeleton.
- They have a two chambered heart.
- They are cold blooded animals.

  Examples: *Marine – Exocoetus* (Flying fish), *Hippocampus* (Sea horse)
- Freshwater – *Labeo* (Rohu), Catla

Class Amphibia
- They can live in both aquatic and terrestrial habitats.
- They mostly have two pairs of limbs.
- The eyes have eyelids.
- Respiration is done through gills, lungs and through skin.
- They have a three chambered heart.
- They are cold blooded animals.
- Example, *Bufo* (Toad), *Rana* (Frog), *Hyla* (Tree frog).

Class Reptilia:
- They are creeping or crawling animals.
- They are mostly terrestrial animals and their body is covered by dry and cornified skin, epidermal scales or scutes.
- They don't have external ear openings.
- They usually have a three chambered heart but crocodile has four chambered heart.
- Example, *Chelone* (turtle), *Testudo* (tortoise), *Chameleon* (Tree lizard), Snakes.

Class Aves
- They have feathers and most of them can fly.
- They have beaks.
- Their forelimbs are modified into limbs.
- The hind limbs generally have scales and are modified for walking, swimming, or clasping the tree branches.
- Heart is four chambered.
- They are warm blooded animals.
- They have a fully ossified endoskeleton and hollow long bones with air cavities.

- Example, *Corvus* (Crow), *Columba* (Pigeon), *Struthio* (Ostrich).

Class Mamaliga

- They are found in a variety of habitats- polar ice caps, deserts, mountains, forests, grasslands and dark caves.
- They have adapted to fly or live in water.
- They have milk producing glands by which young ones are nourished.
- They have a four chambered heart and different types of teeth.
- Example, *Panthera Leo* (Lion), *Pteropus* (Flying fox), *Balaenoptera* (Blue whale).

Unit-4: Botany

- **Botany**
- Botany is a branch of Biology focused on the study of plants. Scientists specializing in this field are called botanists, plant scientists, or phytologists.
- **Scope of Botany:** Traditionally, botany also includes the study of fungi (by mycologists) and algae (by phycologists). These three groups of organisms continue to be of interest to the International Botanical Congress.
- **Applied Sciences:** The principles and discoveries of botany serve as the foundation for applied sciences such as agriculture, horticulture, and forestry.

History

- Theophrastus: "Father of Botany", classified plants in "Enquiry into Plants" based on various factors.
- Robert Hooke's 1665 compound microscope advanced plant anatomy studies.
- Chlorophyll discovery enhanced understanding of photosynthesis.
- Gregor Johann Mendel's pea plant experiments revealed genetic inheritance in plants.

Branches of Botany

- **Plant Pathology:** It is the study of organisms and environmental conditions that are responsible for causing diseases in plants, the mechanisms by which the disease occurs, and the methods of controlling plant diseases.
- **Plant Ecology:** Plant ecology studies the distribution of plants, how do the environmental factors affect plants and the interaction between plants and other organisms.
- **Palaeobotany:** This is the branch of botany that deals with the recovery and identification of plant fossils, thereby, studying the evolutionary history of plants.
- **Archaeobotany:** It is the branch of Botany in which the scientist's study as to how were the plants used by the people in the past. Understanding a plant also helps in understanding the medicinal and spiritual significances of a plant in the past.
- **Forensic Botany:** Forensic botany is the use of plants and parts of plants such as pollens, seeds, leaves, etc. to examine criminal or non-criminal cases, legal disputes or questions, to determine the cause of death or former location.

Unit-5: Microorganisms

- A microorganism or a microbe is a microscopic organism of microscopic size, which may occur in its single celled form or as a colony of cells.
- The different types of microorganisms are:

Bacteria

- They are unicellular microscopic, prokaryotic microorganisms that contain no true nucleus. They are of different types depending on their shapes and sizes. Example, spherical-shaped bacteria are recognized as cocci; rod-shaped bacteria are recognized as bacilli; spiral-shaped, spirilla, etc.
- They reproduce through binary fission, transfer of genetic material occurs through transformation, transduction and conjugation, and through sporulation.
- Bacteria play an important role in human survival.
- They break down nutrients in the digestive system into simpler forms. Example, *Rhizobium*.

Fungi

- Fungi can be unicellular or multicellular with the cell wall made of chitin.
- They are heterotrophic and cannot synthesize their own food.
- They comprise membrane-bound organelles. Yeasts, moulds, mushrooms are some of the significant fungi.
- They decompose dead plants and animals, extracting nutrients from them. Example, Yeast.

Viruses

- Viruses are a kind of microorganisms, which reproduce inside the host cell. The host can be a human, a bacterium or an animal.
- A virus cannot reproduce without a host i.e. they grow and multiply in their hosts.
- The virus size ranges from 14 to 400 nm, making it the smallest of the infective agents.

Protists

- They are unicellular, microscopic organisms that are neither plants nor animals.
- They may be autotrophic or heterotrophic.
- They reproduce mainly through binary fission or budding.
- This group includes plant-like protists such as diatoms, dinoflagellates, animal-like protists such as *Amoeba*, and fungus-like such as Slime moulds.

Archaea

- These are unicellular prokaryotic organisms having a structure similar to bacteria.
- Their cell wall is different from bacteria and contains unique lipids that enable them to survive in extreme conditions.
- They are also found in human gut and skin.

Unit-6: Animal tissues

The different types of animal tissues based on the functions they perform are:

- **Function:** Body's protective covering.
- **Examples:** Skin, mouth lining, blood vessels, lung alveoli, kidney tubules.

Epithelial Tissue

- Epithelial tissues are found extensively throughout the body, providing coverage to external surfaces, lining internal body cavities and hollow organs, and constituting the predominant tissue type in glands.
- **Types:**
- **Simple Epithelium:** Single layer, lines cavities (e.g., intestines).
- **Compound Epithelium:** Multiple layers, skin's outer layer (epidermis).

Classification of Epithelia

- **Squamous Epithelium:** It is made up of a single thin layer of flattened cells with irregular boundaries. They are found in the walls of blood vessels and air sacs of lungs and are involved in purposes like creating a diffusion boundary.
- **Stratified Squamous Epithelium:** They are arranged in many layers to prevent wear and tear. The skin which protects the body is made up of squamous epithelium.
- **Ciliated Columnar Epithelium:** It is composed of a single layer of tall and slender cells. Their nuclei are located at the base. They are mainly existent in the inner surface of hollow organs like bronchioles and fallopian tubes.
- **Glandular Epithelium:** They are also called gland cells as they can secrete substances at the epithelial surface.
- **Cuboidal Epithelium:** It is composed of a single layer of cube like cells. This is commonly found in ducts of glands and tubular parts of nephrons in kidneys and its main functions are secretion and absorption.

Connective tissue

- They are most abundant and widely distributed in the body of complex animals. Their special function is linking and supporting other tissues/organs of the body. They range from soft connective tissues to specific types which include cartilage, bone, adipose and blood. The fibers provide strength, elasticity and flexibility to the tissue. These cells also secrete modified polysaccharides, which accumulate between cells and fibers and act as matrix.

Connective tissues are divided into three types:

- **Loose Connective Tissue:** Loosely arranged cells and fibers in a semi-fluid substance, providing support. Contains fibroblasts, macrophages, and mast cells. Adipose tissue is a type found beneath the skin.
- **Dense Connective Tissue:** Fibers and fibroblasts densely packed. Examples: tendons (muscles to bones) and ligaments (bone to bone).
- **Specialized Connective Tissue:** Includes cartilage (pliable, resists compression), bones (hard, rich in calcium and collagen, provides structure and support), and blood (fluid tissue with plasma, red and white blood cells, and platelets, facilitating substance transport).

Muscular tissue

- Muscles are of three types, skeletal, smooth, and cardiac. Muscle fibers contract (shorten) in answer to stimulation, then relax (lengthen) and return to their uncontracted state in a synchronized fashion. Muscles comprise special proteins named contractile proteins, which contract and relax to cause movement.
- **Skeletal muscle tissue:** They are also called voluntary muscles. These muscles are also named skeletal muscles as they are typically attached to bones and help in body movement. Skeletal muscle tissue is carefully attached to skeletal bones.
- **Smooth Muscle Tissue:** They are also called involuntary muscles. They can be found in the iris of the eye, in ureters and in the bronchi of the lungs. The cells are long with sharp ends (spindle-shaped) and uninucleate (having a single nucleus). They are also called unstriated muscles.
- **Cardiac Muscle Tissue:** The muscles of the heart show rhythmic contraction and relaxation throughout life. These involuntary muscles are called cardiac muscles. It is a contractile tissue present only in the heart.

Nervous tissue

- **Neural Tissue Control:** Neural tissue regulates the body's responsiveness to changing conditions.
- **Components of Neural Tissue:** Neural tissue comprises the brain, spinal cord, and nerves.
- **Cell Types:** Cells in neural tissue are called neurons or nerve cells.
- **Neuron Structure:** Neurons have a cell body with a nucleus and cytoplasm. They feature long, hair-like parts: An axon and many short, branched dendrites.
- Neurons can be exceptionally long, up to a meter in length.
- **Formation of Nerves:** Nerves are formed by numerous nerve fibers bound together by connective tissue.

Unit-7: Integumentary system

The integumentary system includes a set of organs forming the outermost layer of the body. It includes skin, glands, nails and hair.

Human Integumentary system

- **The Skin:** Tt is the largest and heaviest organ of the body consisting of numerous layers each with a different function.
- **Epidermis:** Tt is the outermost layer of the skin. It is thin and continuously sheds dead skin cells.
- **Dermis:** It is the middle layer of the skin consisting of sweat glands, blood vessels, nerves and hair follicles.
- **Subcutaneous layer:** It is the innermost layer of skin comprising connective tissue and fat that connects the skin to the muscles beneath it. It provides insulation and cushion.
- **Glands:** Cells that function as unit to discharge a substance such sweat or oil are called glands. The body has two different type of glands. The endocrine glands lack a duct system so they immediately release their

substances into the blood. The exocrine glands has ducts which help them to discharge chemicals into the epithelial surface.

- **Apocrine sweat glands:** Odorous perspiration is produced by these glands. These are present in the genital region and armpits.
- **Eccrine sweat glands:** It cools the body and excretes waste by water secretion. They are primary, coiling, tube like glands found all over the body producing little to no oily and odorless perspiration.
- **Sebaceous glands:** These glands release sebum and oily material which protects the skin.
- **Ciliary glands:** They are modified apocrine sweat glands which are found in the eyelids. They lubricate the eye and keep it clean.
- **Ceruminous glands:** These are modified apocrine glands which are responsible for producing ear wax.
- **Mammary glands:** They are present in the front of the chest including two mammary glands. The glands produce milk to nourish newborns.

- **Hair:** They are thin thread like structures which are generally pigmented, which give them color and are made of a protein called Keratin. They cover our whole body excluding for the palms of the hands and soles of the feet. They protect us against UV rays, wounds and extreme temperatures.
- **Nails:** They are hard bony structures on the upper surface of the fingers and toes. They are made of a protein called Keratin.

Unit-8: The Musculoskeletal System

- The musculoskeletal system comprises bones, muscles, tendons, and ligaments, enabling body movement, support, and protection of internal organs.
- Skeletal system constitutes hard internal living or non-living parts that form the support framework of the body. Basic functions of the skeletal system to provide shape to the body, supporting framework, protection to delicate and vital organs, mineral and fat storage, attachment of muscles and making the body an integrated unit.

Endoskeleton of Man

- Originally the human skeleton consists of 270 bones, which are fused to become 206. Out of these, 6 bones occur as ear ossicles. The 206 bones are divided into axial and appendicular skeletons.
- **Facts:**

Longest bone	Femur
Strongest bone	Mandible (lower jaw)
Smallest bone	Stapes (in middle ear)
Cells found in bones	Osteoblasts

Joints: A bone joint is the junction of two bones. The study of such joints is known as arthrology. Joints are of following types.

- **Fixed or Immovable:** Joints No movement occurs in the bones of such joints. Example, bones of the skull.
- **Semi Movable Joints:** Such joints allow little movement of bones. Example, Joints between centra of 2 vertebra.
- **Movable or Synovial Joints:** These are perfect joints and allow free movements in one or more directions. These are of following types:
  - **Pivot Joints:** One of the two bones is fixed and bears a peg-like process over which the other bone rotates. Such joints are found between atlas and axis vertebrae and between radius and ulna.
  - **Ball and Socket Joints:** The of one bone fitting with the socket of the other bone and allowing free movements in all planes. Examples: shoulder joint and hip joint.
  - **Hinge Joints:** It allows the movement only in one plane. Example - elbow joint and knee joint.
  - **Gliding Joints:** These joints permits sliding of one bone over the other. For example, joints between radio-ulna and carpals.

Muscles

Skeletal Muscle

- Skeletal muscles are also called striated muscles. These are mostly attached to bones and take part in moving them. They bring about voluntary movements under conscious control of the brain. Therefore, they are called voluntary muscles.
- Muscle contraction mechanism explained by A.F. Huxley's sliding filament theory.
- Actin filaments slide inward on myosin filaments in the A-band during muscle contraction.
- Myofibrils, proteinaceous fibrils, act as the muscle's contractile elements.
- Sarcomeres are the specific contractile units within myofibrils.
- Muscle contraction converts chemical energy into mechanical energy.
- Energy for muscle contraction is supplied by ATP.
- **Tendon:** Tendons are thin and strong thread-like structures which connect muscles to bones.
- **Ligament:** These are tissues that connect a bone to another bone.
- **Fatigue:** It is the inability of a muscle to contract due to depletion of its chemicals and lactic acid accumulation.
- **Facts**

• Gout Accumulation of uric acid crystals in joints leading to painful movements.
• Osteoporosis It is the loss of bone density due to excessive absorption of calcium and phosphorus from the above.
• Gluteus maximus is the largest muscle.
• Stapedius of the stapes is the smallest muscle.
• Massetors of the jaw are the Strongest muscle.
• Muscle contraction of the shortest duration occurs in eye-lids.

Unit-9: Digestive System

The digestive system of humans includes the alimentary canal and glands associated with digestion.

- **Alimentary Canal:** The human alimentary canal which runs from mouth to anus is about 8 to 10 metre in length. It has the following parts.

Mouth

- The mouth consists of an oral cavity, through which food is ingested. It is bounded by lips and cheeks. It contains gums, teeth, a tongue, and openings of salivary glands.
- **Teeth:** In humans, teeth develop during life in two successive sets, a condition known as diphyodont. The first set of teeth are called deciduous teeth or milk teeth or lacteal teeth, whereas the second set is called permanent teeth. The milk teeth fall after the age of 6-7 years after which the permanent teeth arise.
- The teeth are implanted in individual pits called alveoli or theca. Such teeth are called thecodont. The human teeth are of four types; hence it is also called heterodont.

Incisors, i	Cutting and biting
Premolars, pm	Crushing, grinding, chewing
Canines, c	Piercing, tearing, offence and defense
Molar, m	Crushing, grinding, chewing

Dental Formula

- The dental formula for adult humans is: 2-1-2-3 / 2-1-2-3. This indicates the arrangement of teeth in each half of the upper and lower jaws, with numbers representing incisors, canines, premolars, and molars from the middle outward.
- A human tooth has three parts - root, neck and crown. Enamel is the outermost the covering of the teeth is considered the hardest part of the body. The layer below The enamel is called dentine.

Tounge

- It is a muscular and protrusible organ present on the floor of the mouth cavity. In humans, the anterior end of the tongue feels a sweet taste, the posterior part feels a bitter taste, sides feel a sour taste and a small part behind the anterior end feels salty taste.

Salivary Glands

- There are three pairs of salivary glands which open into the mouth cavity. These are parotid glands, submaxillary glands and sublingual glands. These glands secrete saliva containing digestive enzyme salivary amylase or ptyalin, which helps in digestion of carbohydrate (starch). The pH of saliva is slightly acidic i.e 6.3 to 6.8. Daily secretion of saliva is 1.5 liters.

Oesophagus

- It is a narrow thin tube 25 cm long. No digestive glands are present. It only conveys the fluid and food through peristalsis.

Stomach

- It is a thick muscular J - shaped organ which is placed behind the diaphragm on the left side. It helps in mechanical churning and chemical digestion of food.
- Gastric juice in stomach contains:
- Hydrochloric acid (HCl),
- Pepsinogen
- Mucus and other enzymes
- Functions of Hydrochloric acid (HCl):
- It kills microorganisms.
- It lowers the stomach pH to between 1.5 and 2.5.
- It converts inactive pepsinogen to active pepsin.
- Pepsin is an enzyme that starts protein digestion and controls the hydrolysis of proteins into peptides. Chyme, the mix of acid and food in the stomach, leaves the stomach and enters the small intestine.

Small Intestine

- It is the largest (3m long) part of alimentary canal that lies coiled in abdomen. It has 3 parts: duodenum, jejunum and ileum. It completes the digestion and absorbs digestion products.
- Maltose, sucrose, and lactose are the main carbohydrates present in the small intestine; They are absorbed by the microvilli.
- Fat digestion is usually completed by the time the food reaches the ileum (lower third of the small intestine).
- Bile salts are in turn absorbed in the ileum and are recycled by the liver.

Large Intestine

- It is about 1.5 m long. Its diameter is always larger than the small intestine, hence it is so named. It is divisible into 3 parts: caecum, colon and rectum.

Digestive Glands

- **Pancreas** Pancreas is situated between the stomach and duodenum. It secretes pancreatic juice. Pancreatic juice and bile are poured in the duodenum through a common bile duct. The pancreatic juice contains 98% water, and rest is enzymes and salts.
- It produces several important hormones:
- Including insulin,
- Glucogen,
- Somatostatin, and
- Pancreatic polypeptide which circulate in the blood.
- The important enzymes secreted by pancreas are :
- **Trypsin and Chymotrypsin:** It acts on protein.
- **Pancreatic amylase:** It acts on carbohydrates.
- **Lipase (Steapsin):** It acts on fats.
- **Nuclease:** It acts on nucleic acids.
- These enzymes help to further break down the carbohydrates, proteins, and lipids in the chyme.
- Liver is the largest gland in the body. It is an exocrine gland. A gall bladder is situated on the right lobe of the liver. The liver produces and sends bile to the small intestine via the hepatic duct. Bile contains cholesterol, phospholipids, bilirubin and a mix of salts.

Functions of Liver

- Storage of fat (lipogenesis).
- Synthesis of urea.

- Erythropoiesis (formation of RBC) mainly during foetal life.
- It secretes bile.
- It synthesizes Vitamin A from carotenoids and stores vitamin A, D, E and B12.
- It produces anticoagulant heparin which prevents coagulation of blood in arteries and veins.
- Excess quantity of carbohydrates converted (glucose) is to glycogen (glycogenesis) and is stored therein.
- Maximum iron storage in the body.
- Kupffer cells in the liver remove bacteria, worn out blood elements and foreign particles.
- Liver is the site of detoxification of different toxic substances.

Bile Juice

- Bile juice is secreted from the liver and is stored in gallbladder. It is greenish yellow in color, alkaline and has a pH between 7.6 to 8.6. It contains bile salts (sodium glycolate and sodium taurocholate) and bile pigments (bilirubin and biliverdin).

Role of Bile in Digestion

- It helps in emulsification of fats where bile salts break large fat droplets into smaller ones.
- It increases the alkalinity to make the medium stable for enzymatic action.
- It helps in the elimination of heavy metals such as Cu, Hg, Zn, etc.

Physiology of Digestion

- The process of digestion involves five steps: ingestion, digestion, absorption, assimilation and egestion.

Ingestion

- It is the intake of food through the mouth.

Digestion

- **Digestion in Mouth cavity** the food is masticated in the buccal cavity with the help of teeth. During this process food is broken down into small pieces, which increases its surface area. During this time salivary glands, secrete saliva which contains salivary amylase which acts on starch.
- **Oesophagus** Food passes through the oesophagus and reaches the stomach. During the swallowing of food, the epiglottis covers the respiratory tract which prevents the food from passing into it.
- **Digestion in Stomach:** Before the food reaches the stomach, gastrin hormone stimulates gastric glands to secrete gastric juice. Gastric juice consists:
  - **Hydrochloric acid (HCl):** It is secreted by oxyntic or parietal cells. It inactivates the action of ptyalin, makes the food acidic and kills the microorganisms. It also stimulates the enzymes for its action. Oxyntic cells also secrete intrinsic factor which helps in the absorption of Vitamin B12.
  - **Pepsin:** It is a proteolytic enzyme.
  - **Rennin:** It helps in the curdling of milk.
- The food which now leaves the stomach is called chyme and moves to the small intestine.

> **Lactose Intolerance**
>
> In some human's secretion of lactase decreases or ceases with age. This condition is called lactose intolerance. Lactose intolerant persons fail to digest lactose of milk.

Digestion in Small Intestine

As the chyme reaches duodenum, the pancreatic juice from pancreas, bile from liver and intestinal juice from intestinal glands, acts upon it.

- **Bile:** Bile has no enzymes. Bile removes the acidic nature of food and makes it alkaline, so that pancreatic juice can act upon it. Bile helps in emulsification of fats so that steapsin can act on it.
- **Cholecystokinin:** It is a hormone secreted by the I-cells of the upper small intestine. This hormone stimulates gallbladder to secrete bile.
- **Pancreatic Juice:** The wall of duodenum secretes a hormone secretin, which stimulates pancreas to secret pancreatic juice. It contains many enzymes.
- **Intestinal Juice:** Intestinal juice or succus entericus is secreted by the Brunner's gland and crypts of Lieberkuhn. It contains many enzymes:
  - **Erepsin:** Acts on remaining peptones and breaks them into amino acids.
  - **Maltose:** Acts on maltose and changes it to glucose.
  - **Invertase:** It converts sucrose into glucose and fructose.
  - **Lactose:** It converts lactose into glucose and galactose.
- **Absorption:** Small intestine is the main absorptive organ. The internal folds of intestinal wall and microvilli enhance the absorption. The end products of carbohydrates (glucose) and proteins (amino acids) are absorbed from the intestine into the blood. Whereas glycerol and fatty acids are absorbed by lacteals.
- **Assimilation:** It is an anabolic process by which absorbed nutrients enters into the cells and are involved in metabolic processes to resynthesize the complex biomolecules like proteins, carbohydrates, lipids, etc.
- **Egestion:** It is the elimination of faecal matter which is formed by undigested food along with water and excess of digestive enzymes. It is finally expelled out through the anus.

Nutritional Requirements

- Nutritional requirements can be given with food. Food is a substance which when taken and assimilated in body tissues, provides material for energy, growth, etc. Food consists of macromolecules such as carbohydrates, fats, proteins, vitamins, minerals, etc. If all of them are present in proper proportion, then the food is called a balanced diet.
- **Components of Food:** On the basis of their functions, there are three components of food:
  - **Energy providing component:** Carbohydrates, Fats
  - **Body building component:** Proteins
  - **Protective component:** Vitamins, Minerals

Carbohydrates

- Carbohydrates are organic compounds with the formula $(CH_2O)_n$, providing energy to living cells and comprising sugars, starches, and fibers.

Types of Carbohydrates

- **Monosaccharides:** These are simple sugars with 3 to 7 carbon atoms. Examples, glucose, fructose, galactose, ribose, deoxyribose, etc.
- **Disaccharides:** These are formed by condensation of two molecules of monosaccharides. Examples:
  - Sucrose (table sugar) = glucose + fructose
  - Lactose (milk sugar) = glucose + galactose
  - Maltose (malt sugar) = glucose + glucose
- **Polysaccharides:** These are formed by the condensation of more than ten monosaccharides. Examples are cellulose, chitin, starch, glycogen, etc.

Function of Carbohydrates

- Primary energy source of the body.
- Starch and glycogen serve as reserve fuel.
- Ribose and deoxyribose sugars are components of nucleic acids.
- Glucose is stored in the liver and muscle in the form of glycogen when the rate of production is high.
- Cellulose and hemicellulose are the main component of cell walls of plants.

Fats

- Fats, also known as lipids, serve as energy storage molecules and consist of triglycerides, composed of glycerol and fatty acids. They are used as stored food to be used in production of energy. Fat is stored in adipose tissues of animals.
- There are two basic sources of fats:
  - **Animal Fat:** Milk, milk products, eggs and fish oil.
  - **Plant Fat:** Groundnut, coconut, mustard, sunflower, etc. Fats obtained from animals are in solid form and that obtained from plants is in liquid form known as oil.
- **Functions of Fats**
  - Lipids are also a major energy source.
  - They are stored in the liver, and fat bodies.
  - Derived fats participate in synthesis of fat-soluble vitamins A, D, E and K.
  - Fats act as shock absorbers for eyeballs, gonads, kidneys, etc.

Proteins

- First coined by Berzelius.
- Comprises 75% of the human body, serving diverse roles.
- Essential functions include enzymatic activities, oxygen transport, immunity (antibodies), and hormonal regulation.
- Structural Units: Proteins are polymers made of 20 different amino acids.
- Abundant sources include milk, eggs, fish, meat, pulses, and cereals in the human diet.
- Protein-energy malnutrition (PEM) may cause conditions such as marasmus and kwashiorkor in children.
- **Functions of Proteins**
  - **Transport proteins:** Hemoglobin, albumin.
  - **Hormones:** Insulin, growth hormone.
  - **Contractile proteins:** Actin, myosin.
  - **Protective proteins:** Fibrin, immunoglobulins, interferon.
  - **Enzymes:** Hexokinase, pepsin
  - **Structural proteins:** Collagen, elastin, keratin.

Vitamins

- N. I. Lunin discovered vitamins. The term vitamin was first used by Funk.
- Vitamins are complex organic compounds needed daily in minute quantities and act as growth and metabolic substances. They regulate various metabolic processes. Based on solubility, vitamins are of two kinds.
  - **Fat soluble vitamins:** Vitamin A, vitamin D, vitamin E and vitamin K.
  - **Water soluble vitamins:** B complex and C.
- **Vitamin A (Retinol):**
  - **Function:** Essential for vision, immune system support, and proper organ function.
  - **Sources:** Carrots (*Daucus carota*), sweet potatoes (*Ipomoea batatas*), spinach (*Spinacia oleracea*), kale (*Brassica oleracea* var. acephala), eggs, dairy products.
- **Vitamin B Complex:**
  - **Vitamin B1 (Thiamine):**
    - **Function:** Supports energy metabolism and normal nerve function.
    - **Sources:** Whole grains, legumes, nuts, pork, beef.
  - **Vitamin B2 (Riboflavin):**
    - **Function:** Important for energy production, cell growth, metabolism.
    - **Sources:** Dairy products, green leafy vegetables, eggs, nuts.
  - **Vitamin B3 (Niacin):**
    - **Function:** Essential for DNA repair, supports skin health.
    - **Sources:** Meat, fish, mushrooms, whole grains, legumes.
  - **Vitamin B5 (Pantothenic Acid):**
    - **Function:** Involved in fatty acid synthesis, energy production.
    - **Sources:** Meat, broccoli, avocados, whole grains, mushrooms.
  - **Vitamin B6 (Pyridoxine):**
    - **Function:** Aids in brain development, immune function, hemoglobin production.
    - **Sources:** Meat, fish, potatoes, bananas, fortified cereals.
  - **Vitamin B7 (Biotin):**
    - **Function:** Supports metabolism, healthy skin, nails, and hair.
    - **Sources:** Nuts, sweet potatoes, eggs, spinach, broccoli.
  - **Vitamin B9 (Folate/Folic Acid):**
    - **Function:** Essential for cell division, DNA synthesis, prevents neural tube defects during pregnancy.
    - **Sources:** Leafy greens, legumes, citrus fruits, avocado, fortified grains.
  - **Vitamin B12 (Cyanocobalamin):**
    - **Function:** Important for red blood cell formation, nerve function, DNA synthesis.

➢ **Sources:** Meat, fish, dairy products, fortified foods.

- **Vitamin C (Ascorbic Acid):**
- **Function:** Acts as an antioxidant, supports the immune system, aids in collagen synthesis.
- **Sources:** Citrus fruits, strawberries, broccoli, bell peppers, tomatoes.
- **Vitamin D (Calciferol):**
- **Function:** Facilitates calcium absorption, crucial for bone health and immune system support.
- **Sources:** Sunlight, fatty fish (Salmonidae), fortified dairy products.
- **Vitamin E (Tocopherol):**
- **Function:** Acts as an antioxidant, protects cells from damage, supports immune function.
- **Sources:** Nuts, seeds, spinach, broccoli, vegetable oils.
- **Vitamin K (Phylloquinone):**
- **Function:** Essential for blood clotting, aids in bone health.
- **Sources:** Leafy greens (such as kale, spinach), broccoli (*Brassica oleracea*), Brussels sprouts (*Brassica oleracea*).

Minerals

- are inorganic chemical elements which perform a wide range of functions Depending on their necessity and amount for normal functioning of metabolic process, these are divided into:
- **Macro elements:** Daily requirement is more than 100 mg. Examples- Calcium, Phosphorus, Magnesium, Sodium, Potassium, Chlorine and Sulphur.
- **Microelements:** Daily requirement in trace amounts less than 100 mg. Examples- Iron, Zinc, Manganese, Molybdenum, Selenium, Cobalt, Fluorine, Iodine, etc.
- **Water** usually forms about 65-75% of the whole human body. It is the most stable solvent in which the majority of the chemical compounds are dissolved.

Functions:

- It helps in transport of food matter and other products.
- It acts as a temperature stabilizer.
- It removes excess body heat through sweating.

Roughage

- Cellulose constitutes roughage in our food. It is indigestible portion of the diet. Fruits, vegetables and outer coats of seeds and grains are rich in roughage. The roughage enables the food to move easily through the intestine.

Test for Starch: When a few drops of iodine solution is poured on a food item, its color changes to blue-black. This indicates that the food item contains starch.
Test for Protein: By adding two drops of copper sulphate and ten drops of caustic soda to the food item, the color changes to violet. A violet color indicates the presence of proteins in food items.
Test for Fats: When a food item is wrapped in a piece of paper, an oily patch appears on the paper. This displays the presence of fats in the food items.

Unit-10: The Respiratory System

- Respiration is a catabolic process that involves exchange of environmental oxygen and body's carbon dioxide through a liquid medium to utilize oxygen for oxidation of glucose in the mitochondria to produce energy. The term respiration is often confused with breathing.
- Breathing is a physical procedure where as respiration is a biochemical procedure. Breathing is a process of periodic filling of lungs with atmospheric air and then emptying it.

Respiratory System

- This system consists of a conducting portion and a respiratory portion.
- **Nasal Cavity:** The cavity of the nose is called nasal cavity, which is divided into two parts by nasal septum. Each part is called the nasal chamber. It warms the air as it passes over. Its mucous secretion entraps harmful particles. An extra function of the nose is to smell.
- **Pharynx:** From the nasal cavity air enters the pharynx. It serves as a common passage for both air and food. The opening into the trachea is a glottis. Just on the tip of the trachea is present a larynx or voice box. Larynx is more bulging in males than in females. It has a prominence which is called Adam's apple.
- **Trachea:** It is a 12 cm long tube with C-shaped rings of cartilage in its walls. The rings make the wall non collapsible. The trachea branches into two bronchi (bronchus), one going to each lung and these branches within the lungs into many smaller bronchioles. These further branch into alveolar ducts and finally into alveoli or air sacs.
- **Lungs:** The lungs are a pair of spongy and elastic organs. The left lung has two lobes and the right lung has three lobes. The left lung is somewhat smaller to accommodate the heart in between. The lungs are covered by a pleural membrane.
- **Process of Respiration:** The energy for metabolic process obtained from oxidation of carbohydrates.

$$C_6H_{12}O_6 + 6O_2 \rightarrow 6CO_2 + 6H_2O + \text{Energy}$$

- The method of respiration is completed in four steps:
- Breathing or ventilation
- Exchange of gases or external respiration
- Transport of gases
- Cellular respiration
- **Breathing or Ventilation:** There are two phases of each breathing inspiration and Movement expiration.
- **Inspiration:** It is an active process, where external intercostal muscles contract and internal intercostal muscles relax. At the same time the diaphragm muscles contract, which compresses the diaphragm. Both actions increase the volume of the thorax. As a result, the pressure in the thorax and hence the lungs become less in comparison atmospheric pressure, therefore. Air enters the lungs.
- **Expiration:** It is a passive process, where external intercostal muscles relax and internal intercostal muscles contract. At the same time diaphragm relaxes

and becomes dome shaped. These events reduce the thoracic cavity and raise its pressure above the atmosphere. As an outcome, air is forced out of the lungs.

- **Exchange the Gases:** The exchange of gases between the alveoli and blood in lungs, and between the blood and the tissue is a result of difference in partial pressure of respiratory gases. Gases move from regions of high partial pressure towards low partial pressure.
- **Transport of Gases:** Blood carries oxygen from respiratory organs to the tissue's cells for oxidation and CO_2 from tissue cells to respiratory organs for elimination.
- **Transport of oxygen:** About 97% of oxygen is carried by RBC. Four Fe^{2+} ions (ferrous ions) of each hemoglobin can bind with 4 molecules of O_2 and is carried as oxyhemoglobin.
- Transport of CO_2 the blood transports CO_2 in three ways:
  - CO, reacts with hemoglobin to form carbaminohemoglobin. About 23 % of CO_2 is transported by this method.
  - In dissolved state in plasma. This accounts for about 7% of CO_2 transport.
  - In the form of bicarbonates - About 70% of CO_2 is transported in the form of bicarbonates.
- **Cellular Respiration:** The glucose formed during the process of digestion is transported to the cells by blood. It undergoes oxidation with the help of enzymes and produces energy in the form of ATP (Adenosine Triphosphate).
- **Anaerobic Respiration:** It happens in the absence of oxygen and is also called fermentation. In this, glucose is metabolized into lactic acid in anaerobic conditions.

$$C_2H_{12}O_6 \rightarrow 2\,C_2H_5OH + 2CO_2 + \text{Energy}$$

- **Aerobic Respiration:** It occurs in the presence of oxygen. The oxygen completely oxidized the food into carbon dioxide and water, releasing large amounts of energy.

$$C_6H_{12}O_6 + 6O_2 \rightarrow 6CO_2 + 6H_2O + \text{Energy}$$

- **Notes**

Cough: It is a reflex action stimulus that takes place from trachea and lungs.

Sneezing: Reflex action stimulated by olfactory epithelium of the nasal chamber.

Hiccupping: It is a noisy inspiration caused by muscular spasm of diaphragm at irregular levels.

Yawning: It is a continued inspiration due to low oxygen tension in blood.

Emphysema: A situation of short breath due to breakdown of alveolar walls as it happens due to smoking.

Asthma: Difficulty breathing due to spasm in bronchial muscles and narrowing of bronchi.

Thalassemia: It is a genetic disease where globin protein is not formed and hence blood is unable to transport oxygen.

- One cycle of inspiration and expiration is completed in 5 seconds.
- One gram hemoglobin carries 1.34 ml of oxygen.

Unit-11: The Circulatory System

- The circulatory system is responsible for circulating body fluids, transporting various substances to different parts of the body.
- Humans have a closed circulatory system, meaning blood circulates within vessels and the heart.

Blood

- Blood is a connective tissue. A healthy person has 5 to 6 litres of blood. Female comprises half litre of blood less in contrast to male. The pH of blood is 7.4 (slightly basic). The red colour of blood is due to hemoglobin present in it.
- The study of blood is called Hematology.

Blood Composition:

- Blood is composed of two main components:
  - **Plasma:**
    - Plasma is the fluid part, constituting 50-60% of blood.
    - It is a light yellow-colored alkaline liquid primarily consisting of: Water: 90-92%, Proteins: 7-8% and Inorganic Salts: 1%.
  - **Cellular Elements:**
    - Red Blood Cells (RBC), White Blood Cells (WBC), and Platelets make up 40-45% of blood volume.

Cellular Elements of Blood

Red Blood Cells (Erythrocytes)

- These are minute biconcave disc-like structures Nucleus is absent in RBC (except camels and llamas).
- In adults, RBC is synthesized in the marrow of long bones (in embryos RBC is produced in the liver and spleen).
- The average life of an RBC is about 120 days.
- An adult human male has about 5 million RBC per cubic mm of blood and females has about 4.5 million.
- RBC contains hemoglobin, which provides red color to the blood. Hemoglobin has an iron containing part (haeme) and a protein (globin). It combines readily with oxygen to form an unstable oxyhemoglobin, which dissociates in the tissues to release oxygen.
- When the RBC count is below normal it is known as anemia.

Carbon monoxide (CO) has a very strong affinity for hemoglobin, forming a stable compound carboxyhemoglobin. This reduces the capacity of blood to transport oxygen, which sometimes leads to death.

White Blood Cells (Leucocytes)

- WBC is larger than RBC. They differ from RBC in three ways - they have nuclei, they have no haemoglobin, so they are colourless and they are capable of amoeboid movement.
- Their number is about 5000 to 8000 per mm^3 of blood.
- WBC are formed in red bone marrow and lymph glands. They have an average life of 2 - 6 days.
- WBC engulfs bacteria and is important in defending our body against infection. The lymphocytes produce antibodies which kill or neutralise the germs. The HIV virus of AIDS affects the lymphocytes.
- When the number of WBC increases manifold, it results in leukaemia (which is also known as blood cancer).

Blood Platelets (Thrombocytes)

- Platelets are much smaller than RBC. They are irregularly shaped and colourless. They are formed in red bone marrow and are disposed off in the spleen. Their life duration is about 3 to 5 days. Their normal count is 1.5 lakh to 4 lakh per mm^3 of blood. But their count declines rapidly in dengue and chikungunya.
- Platelets are responsible for clotting of blood.

Blood Clotting

- When a blood vessel is cut, the platelets disintegrate and release thromboplastin (or thrombokinase). It reacts with prothrombin in presence of calcium to form thrombin.
- Thrombin changes fibrinogen, a protein to form fibrin. Fibrin are tiny threads, which trap blood cells and form clots which prevents outflow of blood. After a while the network shrinks which is in the form a clear liquid, called serum.

Functions of Blood

- The blood transports oxygen, carbon dioxide, digested food products, excretory products and hormones.
- It also fights infection and regulates temperature.
- Blood forms a clot whenever there is a cut in a blood vessel.
- Blood helps to maintain homeostasis of the body.

Blood Groups

- The concept of blood groups was given by Karl Landsteiner of Vienna. RBCs of humans have specific proteins called glycoproteins on their surface. These proteins are known as antigens. The plasma, on the other hand, has its complementary known as antibodies.
- If a person with blood group A gives his blood to A or AB, then the blood will not agglutinate. When a person with blood group A donates his blood to a person having blood group O or B, then the blood will form clumps (i.e. it will agglutinate).
- **ABO System:** O negative blood group is called universal donor because it can be given to persons with all types of blood types i.e., O, A, B and AB for red blood cell transfusion. Whereas, AB positive blood group is a universal recipient because the person can receive blood from all types i.e., from AB, A, B and O.
- **Blood Transfusion:** It is a mechanism by which blood from a healthy person is injected into a patient's body who is undergoing an operation or a treatment for injury is known as the blood transfusion.

Circulation of Blood

Heart

- The heart is a cone - shaped muscular organ located under the breastbone in the thoracic cavity, between the lungs.
- Heart is four chambered with two frontal auricles and two latter ventricles. The right atrium and right ventricle together make up the "right heart" The left atrium and left ventricle make up the "left heart".
- A wall of muscle termed the septum separates the two sides of the heart.
- **Valves of the Heart:** It prevent back flow, keeping the blood flowing in one direction through the heart.
- Tricuspid valve is positioned between the right auricle and the right ventricle.
- Bicuspid (or mitral) valve is present between the left auricle and left ventricle.
- Three semilunar valves are present between the right ventricle and the pulmonary artery.
- Aortic semilunar valves are located between the left ventricle and aorta.

Blood Vessels: The blood vessels are of two types:

- **Arteries:** They carry oxygenated blood from the heart to different parts of the body. It does not have valves. Pulmonary artery is the solitary artery which transports deoxygenated blood from the right ventricle to the lungs.
- **Veins:** They carry deoxygenated blood from tissues to the heart. They contain valves which prevent back flow of the blood. Pulmonary veins transport oxygenated blood from lungs to the left atrium.

Types of Blood Circulation

- **Pulmonary Circulation:** The movement of blood from heart to lungs and back to heart.
- **Systemic Circulation:** It is Movement of blood between heart and different part of the body except lungs.
- In the pulmonary circuit, deoxygenated blood leaves the right ventricle of the heart via the pulmonary artery and journeys to the lungs, then proceeds as oxygenated blood to the left atrium of the heart via the pulmonary vein.
- In the systemic circuit, oxygenated blood leaves the body via the left ventricle to the aorta, and from there enters the arteries and capillaries where it supplies the body's tissues with oxygen. Deoxygenated blood returns via veins to the vena cava, re-entering the heart's right atrium.

Heart attack vs Cardiac arrest

- In The cardiovascular system circulates blood from the heart to the lungs and around the body via blood vessels. Obstruction of any artery can cause a heart attack, or injury to the muscle of the heart. The heart contains electrical "pacemaker" cells, which cause it to contract — producing a heartbeat.
- A heart attack is different from cardiac arrest, which is an abrupt loss of heart function that usually occurs as a consequence of electrical disturbances of the heart rhythm.

● **Important points**

- **Myocardial Infarction:** It is the death of a part of heart muscle following cessation of blood supply to it. It is an acute heart attack.
- **Rheumatic Heart Disease (RHD):** Defect in the heart valve due to infection caused by bacteria streptococcus.
- The Largest artery in humans is the aorta and largest vein in inferior vena cava.
- **TMT or Treadmill Test** is used to check the effectiveness of the heart.
- **Jarvic - 7:** It is an artificial heart which is designed to function like a natural heart.
- World's first heart transplant was done by Dr. Christian Barnard of South Africa in 1967.

● **Blood Pressure:**

■ Blood pressure is the force exerted by blood against the walls of blood vessels.

■ **Measurement:** A Sphygmomanometer is the device used for measuring blood pressure. Normal blood pressure is typically recorded as 120/80 mm Hg.

● **Electrocardiogram (ECG):** It is the graphical recordings of electrical changes that accompany cardiac cycle. Defects in cardiac structure and function are recorded in the ECG. It is represented by 5 waves i.e., P, Q, R, S, and T.

Unit-12: The Excretory System

Excretion

● It is the removal of waste products from the body of an organism. Based on the type of excretory product, there are three types of animals:

■ **Ammonotelic:** These organisms secrete ammonia which is very toxic. Examples, protozoans and fishes.

■ **Ureotelic:** They secrete urea. Examples are amphibians and mammals.

■ **Uricotelic:** The excretory product is uric acid. Examples, reptiles, birds.

Excretory Organs

● Kidney is the primary excretory organ in humans. Components of this system in vertebrates comprise the kidneys, liver, lungs, and skin.

● **Kidney:** The human excretory system comprises of a pair of kidneys, ureters, a urinary bladder and a urethra.

● **Kidneys:** Each kidney is a bean-shaped organ about 10 cm long and 5 cm wide. The left kidney occurs at a slightly higher level than the right one. Kidneys are mesodermal in origin.

● **Ureters:** From each kidney arises ureter which opens in a common urinary bladder. It acts as a passage for urine from kidneys to urinary bladder.

● **Urinary Bladder:** It stores the urine temporarily.

● **Urethra:** It is a muscular tube that connects the urinary bladder and the external opening of the urinary tract.

● **Structure of Kidneys:** Each kidney is covered by a thin fibrous capsule of connective tissue. The Inner kidney is divided into two regions - outer cortex and inner medulla. Each kidney has about 1 million nephrons. Nephron is the structural and practical unit of kidney.

● **Process of Excretion:** The process excretion has two parts:

■ Creation of urea in the liver by urea cycle or ornithine cycle.

■ Formation of urine.

● **Urine Formation:** It involves three steps:

■ **Ultrafiltration:** It is a passive process that takes place from glomerulus into Bowman's capsule. The efferent arteriole is narrower as compared to afferent arteriole and a high pressure develops in the glomerulus which enables a large amount of filtrate into the Bowman's capsule.

Glomerular Filtration at Rate: It is the filtered blood incoming into the Bowman's capsule. In a normal adult it is 120 ml per minute and around 180 litres per day. An adult man normally passes 1 to 1.8 litres of urine in 24 hours.

■ **Reabsorption:** It is the process by which useful constituents of the glomerular filtrate are returned into the blood stream.

■ **Tubular Secretion:** It is the supporting mechanism for filtration and reabsorption.

➢ **Urine:** It is a transparent yellowish fluid with a slightly acidic pH of 6.0. A pigment know as urochrome causes the yellow color of urine. Urine contains 95% water, 2.6% urea, uric acid, salts, etc.

➢ Antidiuretic Hormone (ADH) or vasopressin causes reabsorption of water in the kidneys. Absence of ADH reduces reabsorption causing increased urination, a condition which is known as diabetes insipidus.

Diseases of Urinary Tract

- Glycosuria Presence of glucose in urine due to diabetes mellitus.
- Uraemia The concentration of urea in blood is increased.
- Haematuria Presence of blood in urine.
- Diuresis Excretion volume of urine is increased.
- Anuria Failure of kidney to form urine.

Unit-13: Nervous System

Nervous system is a system of highly specialized nerve cells, nerve fibers, and organs, that coordinate and control the activities of different parts of the body. Neurons are the structural and functional units of the nervous system.

Parts of Nervous System

The nervous system of humans is divided into three parts:

● **Central Nervous System (CNS):** The CNS controls all the body functions. It is composed of two main organs: brain and spinal cord. The brain is covered by three connective tissue membranes which are known as meninges.

■ **Brain** is situated inside the cranium, the bones of which protect it from injuries. The cranial capacity is about 1650 ml and average weight is 1.5 kg. The brain is divided into three main sections:

➢ Forebrain,

➢ Midbrain and

➢ Hindbrain.

- **Spinal Cord:** It is an elongated cylindrical structure which lies in the neural canal and is continued with the medulla oblongata through foramen magnum of the skull. It conducts impulses to and from the brain and controls most of the reflex activities.
- **Peripheral Nervous System:** It is formed of a number of long, thin nerves which arise from the brain and spinal cord. The nerves arising from the brain are called cranial nerves. There are 12 pairs (24) cranial nerves. The nerves arising from the spinal cord are called spinal nerves which are 31 pairs. This nervous system connects the central nervous system to various receptors in the body and establishes an effective communication channel in the body.
- **Autonomic Nervous system:** The autonomic nervous system is entirely involuntary and automatic. It is composed of two parts: the sympathetic system and the parasympathetic system.
- **Function of Sympathetic nervous system:** It helps to regulate the action of heart, the secretion of endocrine glands, the arterial blood supply, the action of the smooth muscles of the stomach and the intestines and the activity of other internal organs.
- **Functions of Parasympathetic nervous system:** It opposes the action of the sympathetic system. The major nerve of this system is the vagus nerve. The whole autonomic nervous system serves as a system of checks and balances. For example, the sympathetic system acts to speed up heart action, but stimulation of vagus nerve slows down the heart rate.
- **Fact File**

Fact File
• Parkinson's disease is a defect of the brain, which is caused by the degeneration of brain neurons.
• Alzheimer is an old age disease, characterized by dementia.
• Traditionally, IQ was calculated as mental age divided by chronological age multiplied by 100.
• Electroencephalograph (EEG) is an electrical instrument to record the electrical activity of the brain.
• Epilepsy Happens when electrical activity in the brain is not normal.

Unit-14: The Endocrine System

Three types of glands are present in the human body:

- **Exocrine Glands:** These glands have ducts for discharging their secretions. Examples: liver, gastric glands, intestinal glands, etc.
- **Endocrine Glands:** These glands lack ducts and discharge their secretion directly into the blood. They are therefore called ductless glands. Examples: parathyroid, adrenal, pituitary, thymus, etc.
- **Heterocrine Glands:** These glands contain both exocrine and endocrine tissues. For example, pancreas. These are also called mixed glands.

Endocrine Glands	Exocrine Glands
Endocrine glands do not have ducts.	Exocrine glands have ducts.
They release hormones.	They release sweat, enzymes, mucus, sebum.
Secretory products are released. directly into the bloodstream, eventually reaching the target organ.	Secretory products are released to an internal organ or the external surface through a duct.
Examples - Thyroid glands, parathyroid glands, pituitary glands, adrenal glands.	Examples- Salivary glands, liver, Brunner's glands, oesophageal glands.

- Hormones are chemical messengers secreted by endocrine glands directly into the blood and are carried by the blood to their target organs where they stimulate or inhibit specific physiological responses. The term hormone was coined by Starling.

Endocrine Glands

- **Pituitary Glands:** Pituitary gland is a small pea shaped gland situated at the base of the brain in a cavity called Sella turcica of sphenoid bone. It is the smallest endocrine gland. It is also known as the master gland because it controls practically all other endocrine glands.
  Some important hormones released by pituitary glands are:
- **Growth Hormone (GH) (Somatotropin):** It is essential for normal growth of the human body. Its deficiency in childhood results in gigantism and a sudden over secretion in an adult result in acromegaly.
- **Thyroid Stimulating Hormone (TSH):** It activates thyroid gland to secrete thyroxine.
- **Adrenocorticotropic Hormone (ACTH):** It regulates the activity of adrenal cortex.
- **Gonadotropic Hormone (GTH):** It regulates the activity of testes and ovaries.
- **Oxytocin:** It is called the birth hormone because it stimulates uterine contraction during child birth. After child birth, it facilitates release of milk (lactation) from mammary glands.
- **Thyroid Gland:** It is the largest endocrine gland, located in the neck between the trachea and larynx, it is an H-shaped gland. It is a thyroxine hormone, which contains iodine.
  Thyroxine: stimulates oxygen consumption and increases metabolic rate. It regulates tissue growth and development. It also increases oxidation of glucose in tissues.
  Hypersecretion of Thyroxine
- Toxic Goiter Heart beat increases, blood pressure increases and rate of respiration also increases.
- **Exophthalmic Goiter:** The eyes appear as if they are coming out of their sockets.

- **Parathyroid Gland:** Parathyroid gland is embedded at the back surface of the thyroid gland.
- Parathormone (PTH): It is also called Collip's hormone. It regulates the amount of calcium and phosphate ions in the blood. Its hypersecretion causes tetany.
- **Adrenal Gland:** Adrenal glands yellowish glands located on the superior side of the kidney. It is divided into two regions -outer cortex and inner medulla.
- **Adrenal Cortex:** It secretes following hormones:
- **Glucocorticoids:** It includes three main hormones cortisol, corticosterone and cortisone. These hormones play an important role in carbohydrate, fat and protein metabolism. Its hypersecretion results in Cushing syndrome.
- **Mineralocorticoids:** Its hormone is aldosterone, salt - retaining hormone. It promotes reabsorption of sodium ions and excretion of potassium ions in urine. Hyposecretion of both mineralocorticoid and glucocorticoid leads to Addison's disease.
- **Sex Corticoids:** These hormones regulate the development of sex organs, secondary sexual characters and promote growth and protein metabolism.
- **Adrenal Medulla:** It secretes two hormones:
- **Epinephrine (Adrenaline):** It increases blood pressure, BMR.
- **Nor Epinephrine (Nor - adrenaline):** It produces greater constriction of blood vessels in muscles. Hormones released from adrenal glands are also known as fight or flight hormones.
- **Pancreas:** It is a heterocrine gland as it has both exocrine and endocrine tissues. The hormone secreting cells of pancreas are called islets of Langerhans. Hormones secreting cells present in islets of Langerhans are:
- α cells - Glucagon
- β cells - Insulin
- γ cells - Somatostatin

Insulin: It stimulates glycogenesis (conversion to glycogen) in muscles and liver and maintains normal glucose. Its hypersecretion causes diabetes mellitus.

Glucagon: It is secreted whenever there is a decreased level of plasma glucose.

- **Gonads**
- **Testes (male gonad):** It secretes testosterone for growth and development of male secondary sex organs. It also stimulates spermatogenesis.
- **Ovary (female gonad):** It secretes three types of female hormones:
- **Estrogen:** It stimulates growth and development of female secondary sex organs and female secondary sexual characteristics.
- **Progesterone:** It is responsible for maintenance of pregnancy.
- **Relaxin:** It relaxes the uterine muscles and ligaments of pelvic girdle for easy birth of the child.

Unit-15: Genetics and Evolution

- Genetics is a ranch of biology that deals with the study of heredity and its biological process. Gregor Johann Mendel is recognized as the 'Father of modern genetics. Variation is the volume of dissimilarity that exists between children and their parents.
- Some of the major reasons of variation are:
- Genetic/Chromosomal rearrangement
- Mutation due to the influence of ecosystem.
- Crossing over
- Mendel tested on a pea plant and considered 7 main contrasting traits in the plants.
- **Monohybrid cross:** Mendel took two pea plants of contradictory traits (one short and one tall) and crossed them. He found the first-generation offspring were tall and called F1 progeny. Then he crossed F1 progeny and obtained both tall and short plants in the ratio 3:1.
- **Dihybrid cross:** Mendel considered two traits. He crossed wrinkled green seed and round yellow seeds and observed that all the first progeny were round and yellow. This means that the dominant traits were the round shape and yellow color. Then he self-pollinated the F1 progeny and obtained 4 different traits round yellow, round green, wrinkled yellow and wrinkled green seeds in the ratio 9:3:3:1.

Mendel's Laws

- **Law of Dominance:** According to this law hybrid offspring will only inherit the dominant trait in the phenotype. The alleles that are suppressed are called the recessive traits while alleles hat determine the trait are known as dominant traits.
- **Law of Segregation:** According to this law during the production of gametes two copies of each hereditary factor segregate so that offspring acquire one factor from each parent.
- **Law of Independent Assortment:** According to this law a pair of traits segregates independently of another pair during gamete formation. As the individual hereditary factors assort independently, different traits get equal opportunity to occur together.

Evolution

- The theory of evolution by natural selection was proposed by Charles Darwin in the mid-19th century. In his book 'On the origin of species', he theorized that evolution by natural selection was first demonstrated by observing that more offspring are produced that can possibly survive.
- Evolution means 'change over time'. Natural selection is the procedure through which change happens.
- All organisms are born with small variations but nature selects which of these variations are to be reproduced, therefore eliminating the rest of the variations.
- Example, if the climate becomes warmer or colder those who cannot deal with extreme temperatures will perish.
- Evolution impacts every phase of the form and behaviour of organisms, with the most prominent being specific behavioral and physical adaptations. These adaptations increase fitness by adding activities such as finding food, avoiding predators or attracting mates.
- Evolution has no long-term goal and doesn't necessarily produce greater complexity.

□□□

Computer

Introduction of Computer

- The word *'Computer'* comes from the Latin word *'Computare' meaning to compute*. Computer is defined as:
- A computer is an automatic man made machine which stores, reads and processes data to produce meaningful information as output.
- A computer accepts data from an input device and processes it into useful information which it displays on its output device. It works very fast and accurately but its capacity is limited.

Components of Computer

- Computers are made from components that perform simple and well-defined functions. Primarily, a computer system has the following components:

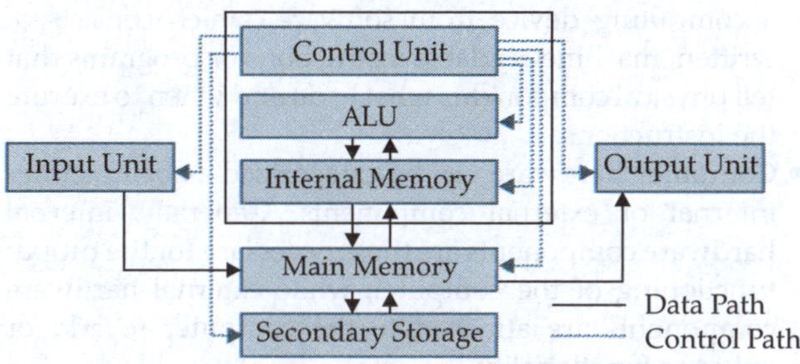

Components of Computer

Input Devices

- Input device is peripheral (piece of computer hardware) equipment to provide data and control signals to an information processing system such as a computer or other information appliance.
- Input device translate data from that humans understand to one that the computer can work with. Most common are keyboard and mouse.

Keyboard, Numeric Keypad, Pointing Device, Remote Control, Joystick, Touch Screen, Scanner, Graphics Tablet, Microphone, Digital Camera, Webcams, Light Pens

Central Processing Unit (CPU)

- Processing is the manipulation of information inside the computer in an area called the Central Processing Unit (CPU).
- All processing work of the computer is performed by the CPU.
- It is also termed as the brain of a computer.
- It controls all the parts of the computer system.
- CPU is further classified into three components:

Arithmetic Logic Unit

- The arithmetic logic unit is a part of the execution unit, a core component of all CPUs. ALU performs all arithmetic and logic operations. It consists of a number of small locations, termed as registers.
- It has two parts:
- **Arithmetic Section**: All complex arithmetic expressions are performed by repetitive combinations of these operations.
- **Logic Section**: It performs all logic operations like comparing, selecting and merging data.

Control Unit

- A control unit is the part of a CPU that directs its operation. It gives commands to transfer data from the input device to memory and from memory to the arithmetic logic unit. It transfers the results from memory to the output unit.

Memory

- **RAM (Random Access Memory)** : RAM is where all active programs and data are stored so that they are readily available and easily accessed by the CPU.
- **ROM (Read only Memory)**: Since ROM is logical, it follows that data stored on it cannot be changed. ROM is nonvolatile which means that it can keep its contents even without a power source.

Output Devices

- Output is the result of processing. The output may be viewed on a computer monitor, heard through speakers, print materials through a printer, etc.

Generation of Computer

- Generation is computer terminology in the world of electronics and technology. This word refers to the transformation that a computer undergoes. Previously, the word generation was used to distinguish between various hardware technologies. However, generation can now refer to both software and hardware, which together comprise the overall computer system.

The First Generation of Computers

Year	1940-56
Switching Device	Vacuum Tubes/ Electronic Valves
Storage Device	Acoustic delay lines and later magnetic drum. 1 KB memory.
Speed	333 Microseconds
Operating System	Mainly Batch
Language	Machine and assembly languages. Simple monitors.
Application	Mostly scientific; later simple business systems.

The Second Generation of Computers

Year	1956–1963
Switching Device	Transistors
Storage Device	Magnetic core, main memory, tape and disk peripheral memory. 100 KB main memory.
Speed	10 Microseconds
Operating System	Multiprogramming, time sharing.
Language	High Level languages, Fortran, Cobol, Algol, Batch operating systems.
Application	Extensive business applications. Engineering design optimization scientific research.

The Third Generation of Computers

Year	1964–1971
Switching Device	Integrated Circuits
Storage Device	High Speed magnetic cores. Large disks 100MB. 1MB main memory.
Speed	100 Nanoseconds
Operating System	Real time, time sharing
Language	Fortran IV, Cobol 68 PI/I. Time Sharing operating systems.
Application	Data base management systems, Online systems.

The Fourth Generation of Computers

Year	1971-1997
Switching Device	Large Scale Integrated Circuits. Micro- Processors (LSI)
Storage Device	Semiconductor memory, Winchester disk. 10 MB main memory. 1000 MB disks.
Speed	300 Nanoseconds
Operating System	Time sharing. Networks
Language	Fortran 77, Pascal, ADA, Cobol –74
Application	Personal computers, Distributed systems. Integrated CAD/CAM. Real time control. Graphics oriented systems.

The Fifth Generation of Computers (Present and the future)

- Artificial Intelligence, which employs the parallel processing approach and Ultra- Large Scale Integration (ULSI), is one of the key electrical components utilised in today's computers.
- The fifth generation of computers is capable of comprehending natural human language.
- The speeds are really fast and the sizes are also small.
- The fifth-generation computers are portable and have a huge storage capacity.
- Keyboards, displays, touchscreen pens, printers, light scanners, and other input/output devices are examples. Laptops, desktop computers, tablets, cellphones, and other similar devices are examples.

Facts Related to Computer

- **Data:** The word data has been derived from the Latin word "datum" (**Means facts**). It is a collection of facts and figures which are not in directly usable form.
- **Processing:** The act of performing some actions to convert data into useful form.
- **Information**: It is the processed data or final result which is indirectly usable form, and conveys some meaningful results.
- **Instructions**: It is a type of action to be taken on data.

Hardware

- The term hardware distinguishes the tangible aspects of a computing device from software, which consists of written, machine-readable instructions or programs that tell physical components what to do and when to execute the instructions.
- Computer hardware can be categorized as being either internal or external components. Generally, internal hardware components are those necessary for the proper functioning of the computer, while external hardware components are attached to the computer to add or enhance functionality.

Internal Computer Hardware

- Internal components Collectively process or store the instructions delivered by the program or operating system (OS).

- Motherboard
- CPU
- RAM
- Hard Disk
- Solid State Drive
- Optical Drive
- Heat Sink
- Network Interface Card

External Hardware Components

- External hardware components, also called peripheral components, are those items that are often externally connected to the computer to control either input or output functions.

- Mouse
- Touchpad
- Keyboard
- Microphone
- Camera
- USB flash Drive
- Memory Card

Computer Memory

- Because a computer cannot execute simple tasks without memory, memory is the most important component of a computer. Computer performance is mostly determined by memory and CPU. Memory is internal storage media of computer that has several names such as majorly categorized into two types:

- Main memory/ Primary Memory
- Secondary Memory

Primary Memory

- Primary memory is computer memory that is accessed first or directly by a processor or computer. It enables a processor to access running execution apps and services stored in a specified memory address. Primary memory can also be referred to as primary storage or main memory.

- RAM (Volatile Memory).
- ROM (Non-Volatile Memory).

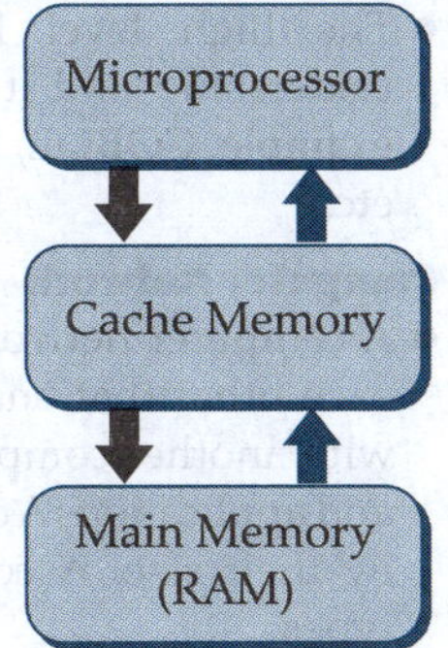

Random Access Memory (RAM)

- It is a temporary recollection. It indicates that it does not keep data or instructions permanently. It is read/write memory that saves data while the computer is running. When you turn on your computer and complete a job, the data and instructions from your hard disc are saved in RAM.

Read Only Memory (ROM)

- It is a type of non-volatile memory. It does not lose any of the data or programmes that were written on it at the time of production. As a result, it is a permanent memory that holds all of the critical data and instructions required to accomplish important operations such as the boot process.

Register Memory

- Register memory is the computer's smallest and quickest memory. It is stored in registers within the CPU. A register temporarily stores frequently used data, instructions, and memory addresses so that the CPU may access them fast.

Cache Memory

- It is compact but quicker than main memory. The CPU can access it faster than primary memory. It stores the CPU's commonly used data and programmes. So if the CPU finds the required data or instructions in cache memory it doesn't need to access the primary memory (RAM). Thus, it speeds up the system performance.

Secondary Memory:

- Secondary memory of the computer refers to storage devices in or linked to the computer. Because it is non-volatile, it retains data even after the computer is shut off.
- The CPU cannot access secondary memory directly.
- The secondary memory data must first be moved to primary memory before the CPU may access it.
- Common secondary storage devices are the hard disk and optical disks. The hard disk has enormous storage capacity compared to main memory.
- There are three main types of secondary storage in a computer system:
- **Solid state storage devices (such as USB memory sticks):** Because data is stored electrically on silicon chips called cells, solid state storage is also quicker than traditional hard disc drives. The binary data is stored within the cells by keeping an electrical current in a transistor with a on / off state.
- **Optical storage devices (such as CD, DVD and Blu-ray discs):** A laser is used in optical devices to scan the surface of a rotating disc comprised of metal and plastic. The disc surface is separated into tracks, each with several flat sections and hollows. The flat portions are referred to as lands, while the hollows are referred to as pits.
- **Magnetic storage devices (such as hard disk drives):** Magnetic devices, such as hard disc drives, magnetise tiny individual parts of a metal rotating disc using magnetic fields. Each little piece corresponds to one bit. A magnetised segment is a binary '1' while a demagnetized section is a binary '0'.

Hard drive

- It is a non-removable storage device containing magnetic disks or platters rotating at high speeds. The hard drives store data in segments of concentric circles. It may spin at 5,400 to 15,000 RPM.

Optical disk

- An electronic data storage medium that can be written to and read using a low-powered laser beam.

Floppy Disk

- Floppy disk is composed of a thin, flexible magnetic disk sealed in a square plastic carrier. Floppy disks were widely used to distribute software, transfer files, and create backup copies of data. To read and write data from a floppy disk, a computer system must have a floppy disk drive (FDD).

Magnetic Tape

- Magnetic tape used in recording sound, pictures, or computer data.

Flash memory

- A kind of memory that retains data in the absence of a power supply.

Software

- "Software is a set of programs (sequence of instructions) that allows the users to perform a well-defined function or some specified task".
- In simpler terms, software tells a computer how to function. It's a catch-all phrase for apps, scripts, and programmes that operate on PCs, mobile phones, tablets, and other smart devices. In contrast to software, hardware refers to the actual components of a computer that do the job.

Types of Software

The two major types of computer software are:

- **Application Software**
- Application software is software that helps an end user complete tasks such as doing research, taking notes, setting an alarm, designing graphics or keeping an account log.
- **Word processors:** Applications used for documentation. Examples include Microsoft Word, Google Docs and AppleWorks.
- **Spreadsheet software:** Software used to compute quantitative data. Examples include Microsoft Excel, Google Sheets, and Quattro Pro.
- **Database software**: Software used to create and manage a database to organize data. This is also known as database management software (DBMS). Examples include MySQL, Clipper and FileMaker.
- **Multimedia software:** Tools that are able play, create or record images, audio or video files. It's used for video editing, animation, graphics and image editing. Examples include Adobe Photoshop and Picasa.

- **Internet browsers:** Software used to access and view websites. Examples include Google Chrome, Mozilla Firefox and Microsoft Edge.
- **Email programs:** Software used for emailing. Examples include Outlook and Gmail.
- **Application suites:** A collection of related programs sold as a package. Microsoft Office is the most widely used application suite.

- **System Software**

- System software helps the user, hardware and application software to interact and function with each other. System software acts as a mediator or middle layer between the user and the hardware.
- **Boot:** Loads the OS into the computer's main memory or RAM.
- **Assembler:** Takes basic instructions and converts them into a pattern of bits that the processor can use to perform basic operations.
- **Basic Input/Output System (BIOS):** The built-in firmware that determines what a computer can do without accessing programs from a disk.
- **Device driver:** Controls a certain sort of computer-attached device, such as a keyboard or mouse.

Two other types of computer software include:

- **Programming Software**

- Programming software is a program that is used to write, develop, test and debug other software, including application and system software.
- Assigns data storage.
- Enlists source code as well as program details.
- Offers diagnostic reports
- Rectifies system errors during runtime.

- **Driver Software:** Driver software operates and controls devices and peripherals plugged into a computer, enabling a device to perform the designated task.

- BIOS Driver
- Display Driver
- Motherboard Driver
- ROM Driver
- USB Driver
- VGA Driver

Programming Languages

- The computer system is simply a machine and hence it cannot perform any work; therefore, in order to make it functional different languages are developed, which are known as programming languages or simply computer languages. Languages comes with its own set of vocabulary and rules, better known as syntax. Following are the major categories of Programming Languages:

- Machine Language
- Assembly Language
- High Level Language
- System Language
- Scripting Language

Machine Language or Code

- This is the language that is written for the computer hardware. Such language is effected directly by the central processing unit (CPU) of a computer system.

Assembly Language

- It is a language of an encoding of machine code that makes simpler and readable.

High Level Language

- The high level language is simple and easy to understand and it is similar to English language. For example, COBOL, FORTRAN, BASIC, C, C++, Python, etc.

Computer Network

- A computer network is a group of computers linked to each other that enables the computer to communicate with another computer and share their resources, data, and applications A computer network can be categorized by their size. A computer network is mainly of four types:

- LAN(Local Area Network)
- PAN(Personal Area Network)
- MAN(Metropolitan Area Network)
- WAN(Wide Area Network)

LAN (Local Area Network)

- Local Area Network is a group of computers connected to each other in a small area such as building, office.

PAN (Personal Area Network)

- Personal Area Network is a network arranged within an individual person, typically within a range of 10 meters.

MAN (Metropolitan Area Network)

- A metropolitan area network is a network that covers a larger geographic area by interconnecting a different LAN to form a larger network. Government agencies use MAN to connect to the citizens and private industries.

WAN (Wide Area Network)

- A Wide Area Network is a network that extends over a large geographical area such as states or countries.

Input Device

Keyboard

- A keyboard is for putting information including letters, words and numbers into your computer. You press the individual buttons on the keyboard when you type. Nowadays a USB keyboard is also available which is edited into USB port of computer system and a wireless keyboard which has no need to add into the computer system.

The keyboard has 5 different types of Keys:

- **Alphabet Keys:** The keyboard has 26 alphabet keys which are used to type sentences or words on a computer system in both capital and small letters.
- **Numeric Keys:** The number keys across the top of the keyboard are also found on the right of the keyboard. A numeric keypad refers to a section of a computer keyboard with numbered keys from 0 to 9 (called numeric keys) like a calculator. It enables you to enter numbers quickly.

- **Function Keys:** The function keys are used to perform specific tasks. They are labeled as F1, F2, F3, and so on, up to F12. The functionality of these keys differs from program to program.
- **Cursor Keys:** When you open a document or click in a box to type, you will see a vertical flashing line. This is the cursor, it shows you where you are about to start typing on a page or screen.
- **Special Keys:** Some of the special keys present on a keyboard are:
  - **Caps Lock Key:** The 'caps lock' key allows you to write in capital letters. To turn it on, press it once and type. To turn it off, press it again.
  - **Num Lock Key:** This is a short form for numeric lock or number lock. This key is used to enable and disable the numeric keypad.
  - **Shift Key:** The 'shift key' is a keyboard modifier key that allows users to type a single capital letter and change the top number keys to a symbol.
  - **Enter Key:** This key submits information you type on the display screen. Before you press the Enter key, you can change the information. Pressing the Enter key submits the information to the system. The Enter key often is labeled with the word "Enter". Sometimes the key that returns you to the beginning of the next line also submits information. The return key often is labeled with a bent arrow.
  - **Space Bar Key:** The 'space bar' puts a space between words. Press it once to put it in a space.
  - **Tab Key:** The 'tab' key puts a bigger space between words. Press it once to put it in a space.
  - **Escape Key (Esc):** The Escape key originates from command line-based operating systems like DOS and UNIX.
  - **Backspace Key:** It is just like an eraser. It is used to erase the numbers and letters on the left of the cursor.
  - **Delete Key:** Delete means to erase. Delete key is used to erase letters and numbers. It erases the letters and numbers one by one to the right of the cursor.
  - **Control Key:** The Control key is one of the combination keys on a computer's keyboard, similar to the Shift key. The user must press it down in combination with other keys. By doing so, certain commands are activated and actions are performed. The Control key thus serves as a shortcut for various commands.
  - **Scroll Lock Key:** Sometimes abbreviated as ScLk, ScrLk or Slk, the Scroll Lock key is found on a computer keyboard, often located close to the pause key.
  - **Pause Key:** A pause key is a keyboard button found on all Windows computers that, when pressed, temporarily suspends the computer's current activity.
  - **Modifier Key:** A modifier key is a key on a computer's keyboard that's only used in conjunction with another key. Modifier keys are used with other keys to perform computer keyboard shortcuts and other commands. For example, in many text editor programs pressing the Ctrl+A selects all text.
- **Mouse:** The mouse is a portable input device used to move the cursor or pointer across the screen. It is designed to be used on a flat surface and generally has left and right button and a scroll wheel between them. Laptop computers include a touchpad that functions as a mouse. It allows you to move the cursor or pointer by moving your finger across the touchpad. Some mice include built-in functionality such as additional buttons for performing multiple functions.

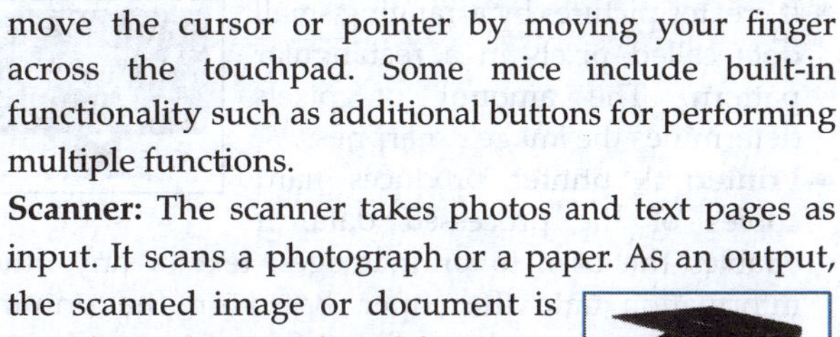

- **Scanner:** The scanner takes photos and text pages as input. It scans a photograph or a paper. As an output, the scanned image or document is transformed into a digital format or file and presented on the screen.

- **Joystick:** A joystick, like a mouse, is a pointing input device. It consists of a stick with a spherical base. The base is inserted into a socket, allowing the stick to move freely. The movement of the stick on the screen controls the cursor or pointer.
- **Light Pen:** A light pen is a type of computer input device that resembles a pen. The light pen's tip has a light sensitive detector that allows the user to point to and select things on the display screen. Its light sensitive tip identifies the position of the item and provides the relevant signals to the CPU.
- **Microphone:** A microphone is a type of computer input device that is used to input sound. It detects sound vibrations and turns them into audio signals, which it then transfers to a recording media. The auditory impulses are translated into digital data, which is then saved in the computer.
- **Magnetic Ink Character Recognition (MICR):** The MICR computer input device is intended to read magnetic ink-printed text. MICR is a character recognition system that uses magnetised ink that is sensitive to magnetic fields. It is commonly used in banks to process checks and other organisations where security is a top priority.
- **Optical Character Reader (OCR):** OCR computer input device is designed to convert the scanned images of handwritten, typed or printed text into digital text. It is widely used in offices and libraries to convert documents and books into electronic files.
- **Bar Code Readers:** A bar code reader is a device that reads bar coded data (information in the form of light and dark lines). Bar coded data is commonly used in branding things, numbering books and so on. It might be a portable scanner or an integrated scanner in a fixed scanner.
- **Optical Mark Reader (OMR):** OMR is a form of optical scanner that recognises the type of mark created by a pen or pencil. It is used when one of several possibilities must be chosen and noted.

Output device

- **Monitor:** Monitors, also known as Visual Display Units (VDU), are the primary output device of a computer.
- It creates pictures by arranging small dots called pixels in a rectangular pattern. The amount of pixels determines the image's sharpness.

- **Printer:** A printer produces hard copies of the processed data. It enables the user, to print images, text or any other information onto the paper. Based on the printing mechanism, the printers are of two types: Impact Printers and Non-impact Printers.

■ **Impact Printers:** They are of two types:

➢ Character Printers
 (i) Dot Matrix printers
 (ii) Daisy Wheel printers

➢ Line printers
 (i) Drum printers
 (ii) Chain printers

■ **Non-impact Printers:** They are of two types:

➢ Laser printers

➢ Inkjet printers

- **Projector:** It is an output device that enables the user to project the output onto a large surface such as a big screen or wall. Projector can be connected to a computer and similar devices to project their output onto a screen. It uses light and lenses to produce magnified texts, images, and videos. So, it is an ideal output device to give presentations or to teach a large number of people, etc.

Abbreviations associated with Computer

- AAC – Advanced Audio Coding
- AI – Artificial Intelligence
- ARPANET – Advanced Research Projects Agency Network
- ALU – Arithmetic Logic Unit
- ALGOL – Algorithmic Language
- AOL – America Outline
- API – Application Program Interface
- APT – Automatically Programmed Tooling
- ARP – Address Resolution Protocol
- ASP – Active Server Pages
- ATM – Asynchronous Transfer Mode
- AUI – Attachment Unit Interface
- AT – Advanced Technology
- ASCII – American Standard Code for Information Interchange
- AVI – Audio Video Interleave
- BCC – Blind Carbon Copy
- BASIC – Beginner's All-Purpose Symbolic Instruction Code
- Bps – Bytes Per Second
- BCD – Binary Coded Decimal
- B HTML – Broadcast Hypertext Markup Language
- BIU – Bus Interface Unit
- BMP – Bitmap
- B2C – Business to Consumer
- B2B – Business to Business
- CUI – Character User Interface
- CSS – Cascading Style Sheets
- CPI – Clock/Cycle Per Instruction
- CC – Carbon Copy
- CAI – Computer-Aided Instruction
- CDMA – Code Division Multiple Access
- CRT – Cathode Ray Tube
- COBOL – Common Business Oriented Language
- CISC – Complex Instructions Set Computers
- CADD – Computer-Aided Design in Drafting
- CAD – Computer-Aided Design
- CD – Compact Disk
- CD RW – Compact Disk Rewritable
- CMD – Command
- CD ROM – Compact Disk Read Only Memory
- CROM – Computerised Range of Motion
- CAM – Computer-Aided Manufacturing
- DAT – Digital Audio Tape
- DNA – Distributed Network Architecture
- DDR – Double Data Rate
- DPI – Dots Per Inch
- DDR-SDRAM – Double Data Rate-Synchronous Dynamic Random Access Memory
- DML – Data Manipulation Language
- DOS – Disk Operating System
- DOC – Date Optimising Computer
- DHTML – Dynamics Hypertext Markup Language
- Doc – Document
- DVD – Digital Versatile Disk
- DVI -Digital Visual Interface
- DDL – Data Definition Language
- D-RAM – Dynamic Random Access Memory
- DBMS – Database Management System
- DVDR – Digital Versatile Disk Recordable
- DVDRW – Digital Versatile Disk Rewritable
- DVR – Digital Video Recorder
- DARPANET – Defence Advanced Research Project Agency Network
- E-Commerce – Electronic Commerce
- EDGE – Enhanced Data Rate for GSM Evolution
- EDI – Electronic Data Interchange
- EDP – Electronic Data Processing
- FS – File System
- FTP – File Transfer Protocol
- FORTRAN – Formula Translation
- FDD – Floppy Disk Drive
- FDC – Floppy Disk Controller
- ENIAC – Electronic Numerical Integrator and Calculator
- EDSAC – Electronic Delay Storage Automatic Calculator
- EDVAC – Electronic Discrete Variable Automatic Computers
- EB – EXAByte
- EiB – EXBIByte
- EROM – Erasable Read-Only Memory
- EPROM – Erasable Programmable Read-Only Memory
- EEPROM – Electrically Erasable Programmable Read-Only Memory
- E-Mail – Electronic Mail
- EFS – Encrypted File System
- FAT – File Allocation Table

- FPS -Frames Per Second
- FLOPS – Floating Point Operations for Second
- FM – Frequency Modulation
- GB – Gigabyte
- GiB – Gibibyte
- GIGO – Garbage in Garbage Out
- GHz – Gigahertz
- GIF – Graphics Interchangeable Format
- GDI – Graphical Device Into
- GPRS – General Packet Radio Service
- GUI – Graphical User Interface
- GBPS – Gigabytes/Gigabits Per Second
- 3GP – 3rd Generation Project
- 3GPP – 3rd Generation Partnership Project
- GML – Geography Markup Language
- GSM – Global System For Mobile Communication
- IBM – International Business Machines
- IC – Integrated Circuit
- IO – Input Output
- IOP – Input Output Processor
- IPV6 – Internet Protocol Version 6
- IPV4 – Internet Protocol Version 4
- IP – Internet Protocol
- INFO – Information
- HDMI – High Definition Multimedia Interface
- HTTPS – Hypertext Transfer Protocol Secure
- HD – Hard Disk
- HDD – Hard Disk Drive
- HPC – Handheld Personal Computer
- HP – Hewlett Packard/Horsepower
- INTEL – Integrated Electronics
- IMAP – Internet Message Access Protocol
- ISO – International Organisation for Standardisation
- HSDPA – High-Speed Downlink Packet Access
- ICT – Information Communication Technology
- IT – Information Technology
- MIPS – Million Instructions Per Second
- MHz – Megahertz
- MBPS – Megabits/Megabytes per Second
- MB – Motherboard/Megabyte
- MAN – Metropolitan Area Network
- LLL – Low-Level Language
- Kbps – Kilobits/Kilobytes per Second
- KBD – Keyboard
- KB – Kilobyte
- JSP – Java Server Page
- JS – JavaScript
- JPEG – Joint Photographic Expert Group
- JAD – Job Application Descriptor/Development
- J2EE – Java 2 Platform Enterprise Edition
- JAR – Java Archive
- MIME – Multipurpose Internet Mail Extensions
- MICR – Magnetic Ink Character Recognition
- MPEG – Motion Picture Experts Group
- Mp3 – MPEG Audio Layer 3
- Mp4 – MPEG-4 AVC
- NAT – Network Address Translation
- NIC – Network Interface Card
- NIIT – National Institute of Information Technology
- NTP – Network Time Protocol
- NTFS – New Technology File System
- OMR – Optical Mark Reader/Recognition
- OOP – Object-Oriented Programming
- OpenGL – Open Graphics Library
- OSI – Open Systems Interconnection
- PHP – Hypertext Preprocessor
- PB – Petabyte
- PiB – Pebibyte
- PNG – Portable Network Graphics
- PNP – Plug and Play
- PDA – Personal Digital
- PDU – Protocol Data Unit/Power Distribution Unit
- PAN – Personal Area Network
- PROM – Programmable Read-Only Memory
- PCI – Peripheral Component Interconnect
- POST – Power on Self Test
- PSU – Power Supply Unit
- PING – Packet Internet/Internetwork Groper
- RDBMS – Relational Database Management System
- RIP – Routing Information to Protocol
- RPM – Revolutions Per Minute
- SMPS – Switch Mode Power Supply
- SMTP – Simple Mail Transfer Protocol
- SRAM – Static Random Access Memory
- SIM – Subscriber Identity Module
- SAM – Software Asset Management/Sequential Access Method
- SNAP – Subnetwork Access Protocol
- SNOBOL – String Oriented Symbolic Language
- SIU – Serial Interface Unit
- SW – Software
- SMS – Short Message Services
- SQL – Structured Query
- TB – Terabyte
- TiB – Tebibyte
- TCP – Transmission Control Protocol
- TBPS – Terabytes Per Second
- TAPI – Telephony Application Programming Interface
- TXT – Text
- UNIVAC – Universal Automatic Computer
- UHF – Ultra High Frequency
- UMTS – Universal Mobile Telecommunication System
- VAN – Value Added Network
- UPS – Uninterruptible Power Supply
- UI – User Interface
- VDU – Visual Display Unit
- VIRUS – Vital Information Resource Under Siege
- VCD – Video Compact Disk
- VHF – Very High Frequency
- VOIP – Voice Over Internet Protocol
- VRAM – Video Random Access Memory
- VPN – Virtual Private Network
- WAN – Wide Area Network
- WAP – Wireless Application Protocol
- WORM – Write Once Read Many
- WWW – World Wide Web
- WBMP – Wireless Bitmap Image
- WLAN – Wireless Local Area Network
- WMV – Windows Media Video
- WML – Wireless Markup Language
- WMA – Windows Media Audio
- WINS – Windows Internet Name Service
- XT – Extended Technology
- XMF – Extensible Music File

- XML – Extensible Markup Language
- XMS – Extended Memory Specification
- XHTML – Extensible Hypertext Markup Language
- XSL – Extensible Style Language
- Yahoo – Yet Another Hierarchical Officious Oracle
- YB – Yottabyte
- YiB – Yobibyte
- ZiB – Zebibyte
- ZB – Zettabyte

Computer Short Forms Related to Internet and Network

- DNS – Domain Name Server
- FTP – File Transport Protocol
- HTML – HyperText Markup Language
- HTTP – Hypertext Transfer Protocol
- IP – Internet Protocol
- ISP – Internet Service Provider
- LAN – Local Area Network
- PPP – Point to Point Protocol
- SEO – Search Engine Optimisation
- URL -Uniform Resource Locator
- USB – Universal Serial Bus
- VR – Virtual Reality
- VRML – Virtual Reality Modeling Language

Basic Computer Keyboard Shortcut Keys A to Z

Shortcuts	Uses of Shortcut Keys
Alt + F	File menu options in the current program
Alt + E	Edits options in the current program
F1	Universal help (for any sort of program)
Ctrl + A	Selects all text
Ctrl + X	Cuts the selected item
Ctrl + Del	Selected item
Ctrl + C	Copy the selected item
Ctrl + Ins	Copy the selected item
Ctrl + V	Paste the selected item
Shift + Ins	Paste the selected item
Home	Takes the user to the start of the current line
Ctrl + Home	Go to the beginning of the document
End	Go to the end of the current line
Ctrl + End	Go to the end of a document
Shift + Home	Highlight from the prevailing position to the start of the line
Shift + End	Highlight from the prevailing position to end of the line
Ctrl + (Left arrow)	Move one term to the left at a time
Ctrl + (Right arrow)	Move one term to the right at a time

Computer Shortcut Keys for Microsoft Windows

Shortcut Keys	Uses of Shortcut Keys
Ctrl + Plus Key	Adjust the widths of all columns automatically, in Windows Explorer
Alt + Enter	Open the properties window for the selected icon or program
Alt + Print Screen	Take a screenshot of the current page
Ctrl + Alt + Del	Reboot/Windows task manager
Ctrl + Esc	These keys allow you to activate the start menu
F4	In Windows Explorer, F4 activates the address bar.
F5	Refresh the contents of your windows system
F3	Find anything from your system's desktop
Alt + Esc	Switch between desktop applications on the taskbar
F2	Rename the selected icon
Alt + Shift + Tab	It allows you to switch back between ongoing applications
Alt + Tab	Switch between open applications/ programs.
Shift + Delete	When you press the Shift and Delete keys together, your program or files will be deleted permanently.
Alt + F4	It is used to close the ongoing program
Ctrl + F4	It's used to swiftly close a document or a file that's currently open.

Computer Shortcut Keys for MS Excel

Shortcut Keys	Uses of Shortcut Keys
Alt + Shift + F1	When you wanna insert new worksheet use these keys together
Shift + F3	With the help of these keys, you can open the MS-Excel formula window
Shift + F5	When you press these keys together it will open the search box
F11	The F11 key is used to create a chart in MS-Excel
Ctrl + Shift +;	With the help of these keys, you can enter the current time
Ctrl +;	Use these keys together to enter the current date
Ctrl + K	When you want to Insert a link, you can use these keys together
Ctrl + F	Used to find and highlight specific words, phrases, or characters

Ctrl + G	Use these keys together to open go-to options
Ctrl + B	When you press these keys together it will bold highlighted selection.
F2	When you want to edit the selected cell using this key
F5	With the help of this key, you can go to a specific cell
F7	With the help of this key, you can check the spell of selected text
Ctrl + I	These commands are used to Italicize highlighted selection.
Ctrl + Space	Use these keys together to select the entire column
Shift + Space	Use these keys together to select the entire row
Ctrl + W	Use these keys together to close the document
Ctrl + H	Use these keys to open find and replace options
Ctrl + U	With help of these keys, you can underline highlighted text.
Ctrl + Y	With help of these keys, you can Redo.
Ctrl + Z	With the help of these keys, you can undo the last deleted action
Ctrl + F9	Use these keys to minimize a current window in MS-Excel
Ctrl + F10	Use these keys to maximize the currently selected window in MS-Excel
Ctrl + Tab	With the help of these keys, you can move between two or more open MS-Excel files
Alt + =	With the help of these keys, you can initiate the formula to add all of the above cells
Ctrl + ' (apostrophe)	To copy formula from the cell above
Ctrl + D	To fill down
Ctrl + (Right arrow)	With the help of these keys, you can jump on to the next section of text
Ctrl + O	Use these keys to open options in MS-Excel
Ctrl + N	Use these keys together to open the document in MS-Excel
Ctrl + P	Use these keys together to open the print dialogue box in MS-Excel

Computer Shortcut Keys for MS Word

Shortcut Keys	Uses of Shortcut Keys
Ctrl + B	Bold highlighted selection
Ctrl + C	Copy selected text
Ctrl + X	Cut selected text
Ctrl + N	Open new/blank document
Ctrl + O	Open options
Ctrl + P	Open the print window
Ctrl + F	Open find box
Ctrl + I	Italicize highlighted selection
Ctrl + K	Insert link
Ctrl + U	Underline highlighted selection
Ctrl + V	Paste
Ctrl + G	Opens Go To dialog.
Ctrl + H	Find and replace options
Ctrl + J	Justify paragraph alignment
Ctrl + L	Align selected text or line to the left
Ctrl + Q	Align selected paragraph to the left
Ctrl + E	Align selected text or line to the center
Ctrl + R	Align selected text or line to the right
Ctrl + M	Indent the paragraph
Ctrl + T	Hanging indent
Ctrl + D	Font options
Ctrl + Shift + F	Change the font
Ctrl + Shift + >	Increase selected font +1pts up to 12pt and then increase font +2pts.
Ctrl +]	Increase selected font +1
Ctrl + [	Decrease selected font -1
Ctrl + Shift + *	View or hide non printing characters
Ctrl + (Left arrow)	Move one word to the left
Ctrl + (Right arrow)	Move one word to the right
Ctrl + (Up arrow)	Move to the beginning of the line or paragraph
Ctrl + (Down arrow)	Move to the end of the paragraph
Ctrl + Del	Delete the word to the right of the cursor
Ctrl + Backspace	Delete the word to the left of the cursor
Ctrl + End	Move the cursor to the end of the document

Ctrl + Home	Move the cursor to the beginning of the document
Ctrl + Space bar	Reset highlighted text to the default font
Ctrl + 1	Single-space lines
Ctrl + 2	Double-space lines
Ctrl + 5	1.5-line spacing
Ctrl + Alt + 1	Change text to heading 1
Ctrl + Alt + 2	Change text to heading 2
Ctrl + Alt + 3	Change text to heading 3
Shift + F3	Change case of selected text
Shift + Insert	Paste
F4	Repeat the last action performed (Word 2000+)
F7	Spell check selected text and/or document
Shift + F7	Runs a Thesaurus check on the selected word
F12	Save as
Ctrl + S	Save
Shift + F12	Save
Alt + Shift + D	Insert the current date
Alt + Shift + T	Insert the current time
Ctrl + W	Close document
Ctrl+=	Set chosen text as a subscript
Ctrl+Shift++	Inserts a new column or row
Ctrl+Shift+=	Creates superscript text

Computer Shortcut Keys for PowerPoint

Shortcuts Keys	Uses of Shortcut Keys
Ctrl+Shift+<	Reduce the font size of the selected text by one size.
Ctrl + G	Group things together
Ctrl+M	Create a new slide just after your chosen slide.
Ctrl + D	Create a duplicate of your current slide.
Esc	Exit the ongoing slideshow and it will redirect you to the earlier live view.
Ctrl+K	When you want to enter a hyperlink use these keys together.
Ctrl+Shift+>	These commands are used to maximize the font size of the selected text by one size.
F5	With the help of F5, you can start the presentation from the initial slide.
Ctrl+N	Creates a new blank presentation.

Memory unit

Unit	Description
Bit (Binary Digit)	A binary digit is logical 0 and 1 representing a passive or an active state of a component in an electric circuit.
Nibble	A group of 4 bits is called nibble.
Byte	A group of 8 bits is called byte. A byte is the smallest unit, which can represent a data item or a character.
Kilobyte (KB)	1 KB = 1024 Bytes
Megabyte (MB)	1 MB = 1024 KB
Gigabyte (GB)	1 GB = 1024 MB
Terabyte (TB)	1 TB = 1024 GB
Petabyte (PB)	1 PB = 1024 TB
Exabyte	1 EB = 1024 PB
Zettabyte	1 ZB = 1024 EB
Yottabyte	1 YB = 1024 ZB

Definitions and terminologies of Computer

- Application: An application is a set of codes designed to allow specific tasks to happen. Microsoft Windows and Internet Explorer are common examples.
- **Access time:** The performance of a hard drive or other storage device - how long it takes to locate a file.
- **Active program or window:** The application or window at the front (foreground) on the monitor.
- **ALGOL:** It was the first language with a formal grammar. ALGOL was created by a committee for scientific use in 1958. Its major contribution is being the root of the tree that has led to such languages as Pascal, C, C+ + and Java.
- **Algorithm:** In computing, an algorithm is a procedure for accomplishing some tasks which, given an initial state, will terminate in a defined end-state.
- **ASCII (pronounced ask key):** American Standard Code for Information Interchange. a commonly used data format for exchanging information between computers or programs.
- **Amplifier:** A device that takes in a weak electric signal and sends out a strong one. It is used to boost electrical Signals in many electronic devices such as radios, televisions and telephone.
- **Analog Computer:** A computer that operates on data which is in the form of continuous variable physical quantities.
- **Android:** It is a Linux based operating system designed Primarily for touchscreen mobile devices such as smartphones and tablets computer.
- **Antivirus Software:** Antivirus software consists of computer programs that attempt to identify threat and eliminate computer virus and other malicious software (Malware).
- **API:** API refers to Application Programming Interface. It's the platform used by a program to access different services on the computer system.
- **Application Software:** Application software is a subclass of computer software that employs the

capabilities of a computer directly to a task that the user wishes to perform. e.g., word document, spreadsheet, etc.

- **Archive:** It provides backup storage.
- **Artificial Intelligence:** Fifth generation computing devices, based on artificial intelligence, are still in development, though there are some applications, such as voice recognition, that are being used today.
- **Array:** An array is similar data saved on a computer system in a sequential form. Assembler: A program that translates mnemonic statement into executable instruction. Attribute: The characteristics of an entity are called its attributes.
- **BIOS:** BIOS stands for Basic Input/Output System. It gives the computer a platform to run the software using a floppy disk or a hard disk. BIOS is responsible for booting a PC.
- **Bit:** Bit is Binary Digit. It refers to a digit number, either a 0 or a 1. The binary digit is used to represent computerized data.
- **Backup:** A copy of a file or disk you make for archiving purposes.
- **Backspace:** Backspace key is used on the keyboard to delete the text. Backspace will delete the text to the left of cursor.
- **Bandwidth:** The maximum amount of data that can travel in a communication path in a given time, measured in bits per second (bps).
- **Bitmap:** A method of storing a graphic image as a set of bits in a computer memory. To display the image on the screen, the computer converts the bits into pixels.
- **Blog:** It is a discussion or informational site published on the world wide web.
- **Bluetooth:** A protocol that permits a wireless exchange of information between computers. cell phones and other electronic devices within a radius about 30 feet,
- **Booting:** Booting is a bootstrapping process which starts the operating system when a computer is switched on.
- **Botnet:** It is a collection of internet connected programs communicating with other similar programs in order to perform tasks.
- **Boot Sequence:** A boot sequence is the set of operations the computer performs when it is switched on which loads an operating system.
- **Browser:** A special software that enables users to read/ view web pages and jump from one web page to another.
- **Buffering:** The process of storing data in a memory device, allowing the devices to change the data rates, perform error checking and error retransmission.
- **Bug:** A software bug is an error, flaw, failure, or fault in a computer program or system that produces an incorrect or unexpected result.
- **Boolean:** An expression, the value of which is either true or false.
- **BUS:** A bus is a set of wires that enables flow of data from one location of the computer to another.
- **CGI:** CGI stands for Common Gateway Interface. It defines how an auxiliary program and a Web server would communicate.
- **Client:** A client is a program that asks for information from other processes or programs. Outlook Express is a great example of a client.
- **CD-ROM:** An acronym for Compact Disc Read-Only Memory.
- **Client – Server:** A common form of distributed system in which software is split between server tasks and client tasks. A client sends requests to a server, according to some protocol, asking for information or action, and the server responds.
- **Clipboard:** A portion of memory where the Mac temporarily stores information. Called a Copy Buffer in many PC applications because it is used to hold information which is to be moved, as in word processing where text is "cut" and then "pasted".
- **Clock Rate (MHz):** The instruction processing speed of a computer measured in millions of cycles per second (i.e.,200 MHz).
- **Compiler:** A program the converts programming code into a form that can be used by a computer.
- **Compression:** A technique that reduces the size of a saved file by elimination or encoding redundancies (i.e., JPEG, MPEG, LZW, etc.)
- **Chip:** A tiny wafer of silicon containing miniature electric circuits that can store millions of bits of information.
- **Client-Server:** Client-server is a network architecture which separates the client from the server. Each instance of the client software can send requests to a server or application server.
- **Cookie:** A packet of information that travels between a browser and the web server
- **Compiler:** A compiler is a computer program that -translates a series of instructions written in one computer language (called the source language) into another computer language (also called the object or target language).
- **Cracker:** The preferred term used to refer to a computer criminal who penetrates a computer to steal information or damage the program in some way
- **Crash:** a system malfunction in which the computer stops working and has to be restarted.
- **Cursor:** The pointer, usually arrow or cross shaped, which is controlled by the mouse.
- **CMOS:** CMOS is an abbreviation for Complementary Metal-Oxide-Semiconductor. It is the battery powered chip that is situated on the Motherboard that retains system information such as date and time.
- **Defragment:** (also - optimize) to concatenate fragments of data into contiguous blocks in memory or on a hard drive.
- **Dialog box:** An on-screen message box that appears when the computer requires additional information before completing a command.

- **Digitise:** To convert linear, or analogue, data into digital data that can be used by the computer. Disk - a spinning platter made of magnetic or optically etched material on which data can be stored. Disk drive: The machinery that writes the data from a disk and/or writes data to a disk.
- **Disk window:** The window that displays the contents or directory of a disk. Document - a file you create, as opposed to the application which created it. DOS - acronym for Disk Operating System - used in IBM PCs.
- **Download:** To transfer data from one computer to another. (If you are on the receiving end, you are downloading. If you are on the sending end, you are uploading).
- **Drag:** To move the mouse while its button is being depressed.
- **Driver:** A file on a computer that tells it how to communicate with an add-on piece of equipment (like a printer).
- **DTP:** Desk Top Publisher (ing) is a term that describes a program that enables users to create, design, and print items such as business cards, birthday cards, letterheads, calendars, invitations, and so on.
- **Editing:** The process of changing information by inserting, deleting, replacing, rearranging and reformation.
- **E-mail:** Electronic mail, abbreviated e-mail is a method of composing, sending, storing and receiving messages over electronic communication systems.
- **Encapsulation:** It is a mechanism that associates the code and the data it manipulates into a single unit and keeps them safe from external interference.
- **Encryption:** In cryptography, encryption is the process of encoding messages (or information) in such a way that hackers cannot read it, but the authorised users can access it.
- **Folder:** An electronic subdirectory that contains files.
- **Font:** A typeface that contains the characters of an alphabet or some other letter forms. Fragmentation - The breaking up of a file into many separate locations in memory or on a disk. Freeze - a system error, which causes the cursor to lock in place
- **Front End:** It is an interface through which a program can be accessed by common users.
- **Gateway:** A device that is used to join together two networks having different base protocols.
- **Hyperlink:** An image or portion of text on a web page that is linked to another web page.
- **Highlight:** To select by clicking once on an icon or by highlighting text in a document.
- **Hit rate:** The fraction of all memory reads which are satisfied from the cache.
- **Hz:** Abbreviation for hertz, the number of cycles per second, used to measure clock speed
- **Icon:** Icon is a small visual display of an application which can be activated by clicking on it.
- **IDE:** It stands for Integrated Development Environment. IDE is a programming system that combines several tools of programming to provide an integrated platform for programming. For instance, Visual Basic provides an IDE.
- **Peripheral:** An add-on component to your computer.
- **Pop-up menu:** Any menu that does not appear at the top of the screen in the menu bar. (May pop up or down)
- **Power PC:** A processing chip designed by Apple, IBM and Motorola (RISC based).
- **Power Mac:** A family of Macs built around the PowerPC chip.
- **Scroll bar:** A bar at the bottom or right side of a window that contains the scroll box and allows scrolling.
- **Scroll box:** The box in a scroll bar that is used to navigate through a window.
- **SCSI:** Acronym for Small Computer System Interface.
- **Serial port:** A port that allows data to be transmitted in a series (one after the other), such as the printer and modem ports on a Mac.
- **WWW:** WWW stands for World Wide Web. It's a term used to define the Internet.
- **WAN:** WAN is an acronym for Wide Area Network. Such a network spans over an area larger than a LAN.
- **WORM:** Acronym for Write Once-Read Many; an optical disk that can only be written to once (like a CD-ROM).
- **Zoom box:** a small square in the upper right corner of a window which, when clicked, will expand the window to fill the whole screen.
- **ZIP:** ZIP is an acronym for Zone Information Protocol. ZIP application enables transfer of data using compression of files.

❑❑❑

Miscellaneous

First in the World

First in the World	Description
Radio Telescope Satellite that was launched into space	HALCA (Japan)
Country to use Glass	Egypt and Mesopotamia
Country to make Map	The Greeks
Spaceship landed on Mars	Viking-I (July 1976)
Multipurpose River Valley Project	Tennessee River Valley Project (USA)
Space Shuttle Launched	Columbia (April 1981)
Rocket to go near the Sun	Helius 'B'
Country to make written Constitution	USA
Country to start Underground Metro Rail	Britain
Unmanned Mission on the Moon	LUNA-9
Spacecraft to carry man on the Moon	Apollo - 11
Country to do Artificial Satellite Experiment	Russia (Then USSR)
Country in the world to give Voting Right to Women	New Zealand
Country in the world to appoint Lokpal	Sweden
Country to impose Carbon Tax	New Zealand

First in the World (Male)

Achievement	First
Asian to Head the International Cricket Council	Jagmohan Dalmiya
Man to climb Mount Everest without Oxygen	Reinhold Messner and Peter Habeler
Man in the world to climb Mount Everest	Sir Edmund Hillary and Sherpa Tenzing Norgay (29th May, 1953)
Secretary of the United Nations	Trygve Lie (Norway)
Person to go on both the Poles (North and South)	Ranulph Fiennes
Man to reach the North Pole	Robert Peary
Man to reach the South Pole	Roald Amundsen
Person to give information about planets	Nicolaus Copernicus
Man to compile an Encyclopedia	Aspheosis (Athens)
Man to go into Space	Major Yuri Gagarin from USSR in 1961
Man to walk in Space	Alexei Leonov (Russia)

First in the World (Female)

Achievement	First
Woman President of a Country	Maria Estela Peron (Argentina)
Woman Cosmonaut in Space	Valentina Tereshkova from USSR
Woman Prime Minister	Sirimavo Bandaranaike (Sri Lanka)
Woman to have a Spacewalk	Svetlana Savitskaya
Woman to climb Mount Everest	Junko Tabei (Japan)
Woman to cross the Strait of Gibraltar	Mercedes Gleitze (Britain)
Woman Space Tourist	Anousheh Ansari (Irani-American)
Female Amputee to Climb Mount Everest	Arunima Sinha
Woman CFO and MD of World Bank	Anshula Kant
Woman Chief Economist for IMF	Gita Gopinath
Astronaut to complete all-female Spacewalk	Christina Koch and Jessica Meir
Woman to lead World Trade Organisation	Ngozi Okonjo-Iweala

Largest, Biggest, Smallest, Longest, & Highest in the World

Geographical Feature	First
Largest Airport (by size)	King Fahd International Airport (Dammam, Saudi Arabia)
Highest Airport	Daocheng Yading Airport, Sichuan (China)
Tallest Building	Burj Khalifa, Dubai, United Arab Emirates (828 m)
Largest Bay	The Bay of Bengal
Longest Big-ship Canal	Suez Canal (linking Red Sea and Mediterranean Sea)
Busiest Canal (Ship)	Kiel Canal
Largest Epic	The Mahabharata
Largest Diamond	The Cullinan (South Africa)
Largest Island	Greenland

Largest Mosque	Masjid al-Haram, Mecca
Largest Delta	Sundarbans, India
Largest Desert	Sahara, Africa
Largest Lake	Caspian Sea
Deepest Lake	Baikal (Siberia)
Highest Lake	Titicaca (Bolivia and Peru)
Largest Coral Formation	Great Barrier Reef (Australia)
Largest Continent	Asia
Smallest Continent	Australia
Largest Country (by population)	India
Largest Country (by area)	Russia
Tallest Minar (Free standing)	Great Hassan II Mosque, Casablanca, Morocco
Largest City (by population)	Tokyo
Highest Town	Wen Chuan (Tibet, China)
Longest Bridge (Railway)	Danyang-Kunshan Grand Bridge (China)
Largest Dam (Concrete)	The Three Gorges Dam (China)
Highest Dam	Jinping-I Dam, across River Yarlong, China
Highest Straight Dam	Bhakra Nangal Dam
Highest Capital City	La Paz (Bolivia)
Highest Asian Desert	Gobi, Mongolia
Largest Democracy	India
Biggest Bell	The Tsar Bell, Moscow
Longest Wall	Great Wall of China
Largest Volcano	Mauna Loa (Hawaii Islands)
Highest Mountain Peak	Mount Everest (Nepal)
Highest Mountain Range	Himalayas
Longest Mountain Range	Andes Central (South America)
Highest Volcano	Ojos del Salado, Andes, Argentina-Chile (6893 m)
Highest Waterfall	Salto Angel Falls (Venezuela)
Biggest Museum	British Museum (London)
Longest Gulf	Gulf of Mexico
Deepest and Biggest Ocean	The Pacific
Largest Peninsula	Arabia
Largest Palace	Imperial Palace (Gugong), Beijing (China)
Largest Park	Northeast Greenland National Park, Greenland
Largest Archipelago	Malay Archipelago
Coldest Place	Eastern Antarctic Plateau, Antarctica. (98°C)
Driest Place	McMurdo Dry Valleys, Antarctica
Hottest Place	Death Valley, California, USA, recorded temperature 134°F (56.7°C)
Largest Platform (Railway)	Gorakhpur (Uttar Pradesh)
Largest Plateau	Tibetan Plateau
Largest River Basin	Amazon Basin
World's Rainiest Spot	Mawsynram (Meghalaya)
Largest Gorge	Grand Canyon on the Colorado River, USA
Largest Port	Shanghai (China)
Busiest Port	Shanghai (China)
Longest Railway	Trans-Siberian Railway
Longest River	Nile (6650 km)
Longest River Dam	Hirakud Dam, Odisha, India
Largest Sea-Bird	Wandering Albatross
Largest Sea	Philippine Sea
Tallest Statue	Statue of Unity, Gujarat (India)
Tallest Tower	Tokyo Skytree (Japan)
Longest Swimming Course	English Channel (between London and Edinburgh)
Longest Passenger Train	Rhaetian Railway Passenger Train, Switzerland
Longest Tunnel (Railway)	Gotthard Base Tunnel
Longest and Largest Canal/ Tunnel	The Rove Tunnel (France)
Lightest Gas	Hydrogen
Lightest Metal	Lithium
Highest Melting Point (Metal)	Tungsten (3422°C)
Hardest man made Substance	Graphene
Fastest Bird	The Peregrine Falcon
Longest Poisonous Snake	King Cobra
Largest Temple	Angkor Wat (Cambodia)
Largest Diamond Mine	Aikhal Diamond Mine, Yakutia, Russia
Tallest Structure	Burj Khalifa (Dubai)

Countries (Capitals and Currencies)

Country	Capital	Currency
Afghanistan	Kabul	Afghan Afghani
Albania	Tirana	Lek
Algeria	Algiers	Algerian Dinar
Angola	Luanda	Kwanza
Argentina	Buenos Aires	Peso
Australia	Canberra	Australian Dollar
Austria	Vienna	Euro
Bangladesh	Dhaka	Taka
Belarus	Minsk	Belarusian Ruble
Belgium	Brussels	Euro
Bhutan	Thimphu	Ngultrum
Brazil	Brasilia	Brazilian Real
Cambodia	Phnom Penh	Riel
Canada	Ottawa	Canadian Dollar
Chile	Santiago	Chilean Peso
China	Beijing	Yuan, Renminbi
Colombia	Bogota	Colombian Peso
Denmark	Copenhagen	Danish Krone
Egypt	Cairo	Egyptian Pound
France	Paris	Euro
Germany	Berlin	Euro
Greece	Athens	Euro
Hungary	Budapest	Forint
India	New Delhi	Rupee
Indonesia	Jakarta	Rupiah
Iran	Tehran	Rial
Iraq	Baghdad	Iraqi Dinar
Ireland	Dublin	Euro
Israel	Jerusalem	Shekel
Italy	Rome	Euro
Japan	Tokyo	Yen
Kazakhstan	Astana	Tenge
Kenya	Nairobi	Shilling
North Korea	Pyongyang	Won
Kuwait	Kuwait City	Kuwait Dinar
South Korea	Seoul	Won
Libya	Tripoli	Libyan Dinar
Malaysia	Kuala Lumpur	Ringgit
Maldives	Male	Rufiyaa
Mauritius	Port Louis	Rupee
Mongolia	Ulaanbaatar	Tugrik
Montenegro	Podgorica	Euro
Myanmar	Naypyidaw	Kyat
Namibia	Windhoek	Namibian Dollar
Nepal	Kathmandu	Nepalese Rupee
Netherlands	Amsterdam	Euro
New Zealand	Wellington	New Zealand Dollar
Nigeria	Abuja	Naira
Norway	Oslo	Norwegian Krone
Pakistan	Islamabad	Rupee
Philippines	Manila	Philippine Peso
Poland	Warsaw	Zloty
Portugal	Lisbon	Euro
Qatar	Doha	Qatari Riyal
Russia	Moscow	Ruble
Saudi Arabia	Riyadh	Saudi Riyal
Somalia	Mogadishu	Somali Shilling
Singapore	Singapore	Singapore Dollar
South Africa	Pretoria	Rand
Spain	Madrid	Euro
Sri Lanka	Sri Jayawardenepura Kotte	Sri Lankan Rupee
Sudan	Khartoum	Sudanese Pound
South Sudan	Juba	South Sudanese Pound
Sweden	Stockholm	Krona
Switzerland	Bern	Swiss Franc
Taiwan	Taipei	New Taiwan Dollar
Thailand	Bangkok	Baht
Turkey	Ankara	Lira
Uganda	Kampala	Ugandan Shilling
Ukraine	Kyiv	Hryvnia
UK	London	Pound Sterling
US	Washington DC	US Dollar
Venezuela	Caracas	Bolivar
Zimbabwe	Harare	Zimbabwe Gold (ZiG)/US Dollar

Geographical Epithets

Nickname	Location
Blue Mountains	Nilgiri Hills, India
The City Beautiful	Chandigarh, India
City of Golden Gate	San Francisco, USA
City of Magnificent Buildings	Washington, D.C., USA

City of Palaces and City of Joy	Kolkata, India
City of Seven Hills	Rome, Italy
Cockpit of Europe	Belgium
Continent of Birds	South America
Dark Continent	Africa
Forbidden City	Beijing
Gift of the Nile	Egypt
Granite City	Aberdeen, Scotland
Holy Land	Palestine
Island Continent	Australia
Island of Cloves	Zanzibar, Tanzania
Isle of Pearls	Bahrain
Key to the Mediterranean	Gibraltar
Land of Golden Fleece	Australia
Land of Maple Leaf	Canada
Land of Morning Calm	South Korea
Land of the Midnight Sun	Norway
Land of the Rising Sun	Japan
Land of the Thunderbolt	Bhutan
Land of Thousand Lakes	Finland
Land of White Elephant	Thailand
Mistress of Eastern Sea	Sri Lanka
Pearl of the Antilles	Cuba
Roof of the World	Pamirs, Central Asia
Spice Garden of India	Kerala, India
Sugar Bowl of the World	Cuba

Discoveries

Discovery	Discoverer
America	Christopher Columbus
New Foundland	John Cabot
Sea Route to India via Cape of Good Hope	Vasco Da Gama
Hudson Bay	Henry Hudson
Solar System	Copernicus
Circumnavigation of World	Magellan
South Pole	Roald Amundsen
Brazil	Pedro Alvares Cabral
North Pole	Robert Peary
Tasmania Island	Abel Tasman
China	Marco Polo
Cape of Good Hope	Bartolomeu Dias

Official Books of Major Countries

Book	Country
Blue Book	British Government
Green Book	Italy and Iran
Grey Book	Japan and Belgium
Orange Book	Netherlands
White Book	China, Germany, Portugal
White Paper	Britain and India
Yellow Book	France

Important Monuments of Some Famous Countries

Monument	Country
Imperial Palace (Tokyo)	Japan
Leaning Tower of Pisa	Italy
Eiffel Tower (Paris)	France
Pyramid (Giza)	Egypt
Great Wall of China	China
Opera House (Sydney)	Australia
Kremlin Palace (Moscow)	Russia
Statue of Liberty (New York)	USA
Kinderdijk	Netherlands
Taj Mahal (Agra)	India

The Seven Wonders of the World

Ancient World Wonders	Modern World Wonders	The New Wonder
The Colossus of Rhodes	The Channel Tunnel	Pyramid at Chichen Itza, Mexico
The Great Pyramid of Giza	CN Tower	The Christ Redeemer, Brazil
The Hanging Gardens of Babylon	The Empire State Building	The Great Wall of China
The Mausoleum at Halicarnassus	The Golden Gate Bridge	Machu Picchu, Peru
The Statue of Zeus at Olympia	Itaipu Dam	Petra, Jordan
The Lighthouse of Alexandria	North Sea Protection Works	Roman Colosseum, Italy
The Temple of Artemis at Ephesus	Panama Canal	The Taj Mahal, India

Intelligence/Detective Agencies of the World

Detective Agency	Country
Ministry of State Security (MSS)	China
Australian Security and Intelligence Organisation (ASIO)	Australia
Federal Security Service (FSB) and Foreign Intelligence Service (SVR)	Russia
National Intelligence Agency	South Africa
MI (Military Intelligence)-5 and 6, Joint Intelligence Organisation	United Kingdom
Inter Services Intelligence (ISI)	Pakistan
Federal Bureau of Investigation (FBI) and Central Intelligence Agency (CIA)	United States of America (USA)
Intelligence Bureau (IB) and Research and Analysis Wing (RAW)	India
The General Intelligence Service or MOSSAD	Israel
Mukhabarat	Egypt
SAVAK (Sazamane Etelaatva Amniate Kechvar)	Iran
The Cabinet Intelligence and Research Office or Naicho	Japan
General Security Directorate	Iraq
DGSE (Direction Generale de la Securite Exterieur)	France

Important Symbols or Signs

Symbol	Meaning
Red Cross	Symbol of medical aid and hospital
Red Flag	Symbol of revolution and danger
Black Flag	Symbol of protest
Yellow Flag	Flown on ships/vehicles carrying patients suffering from infectious diseases
Flag flown at half mast	Symbol of national mourning
Flag flown upside down	Symbol of distress
White Flag	Symbol of truce
Black strip on face/ arm	Sign of mourning or protest
A blindfolded woman holding a balanced scale	Symbol of justice
Pigeon or Dove	Symbol of peace
Pen	Symbol of knowledge
Lotus	Symbol of culture and civilization
Wheel (Chakra)	Symbol of progress
One skull on two bones crossing each other diagonally	Sign of danger
Olive Branch	Symbol of peace

Languages Spoken in the World

Rank	Language	Approx. Total Speakers (2025)
1	English	~1.5 billion
2	Mandarin Chinese	~1.2 billion
3	Hindi	~610 million
4	Spanish	~560 million
5	French	~320 million
6	Modern Standard Arabic	~310 million
7	Bengali	~280 million
8	Portuguese	~270 million
9	Russian	~255 million
10	Urdu	~235 million

Major Newspapers of the World

Newspaper	Country
The Sydney Morning Herald	Australia
The Hindustan Times	India
The Age	Australia
Mainichi Daily News	Japan
Globe and Mail	Canada
The New Zealand Herald	New Zealand
The Gazette	Canada
The Press	New Zealand
The Times	United Kingdom
Die Welt	Germany
The Scotsman	United Kingdom
The Times of India	India
The Guardian	United Kingdom
The Hindu	India
The Herald	United Kingdom
The Tribune	India
The Courier	United Kingdom
The Statesman	India
Washington Post	United States of America

Parliaments of the World

Country	Name	Country	Name
Afghanistan	The National Assembly (Mili Shura)	Maldives	People's Majlis
Australia	Federal Parliament	Japan	National Diet
Bangladesh	Jatiya Shangsad	Nepal	Snghiya Sansad (Federal Parliament)
Bhutan	Tshogdu	Pakistan	Majlis-e-Shura
Canada	Parliament	Russia	The Federal Assembly
China	National People's Congress	Spain	Cortes Generales
Egypt	People's Assembly	Sweden	Riksdag
France	French Parliament	South Africa	Parliament
Germany	Bundestag	Mauritius	National Assembly
Britain	Parliament	USA	Congress

Top 5 Largest and Smallest Countries

Largest Country (Area-wise)	Largest Country (Population-wise)	Smallest Country (Area-wise)	Smallest Country (Population-wise)
Russia	India	Vatican City	Vatican City
Canada	China	Monaco	Tuvalu
China	USA	Nauru	Nauru
United States	Indonesia	Tuvalu	Palau
Brazil	Pakistan	San Marino	San Marino

Religions of the World

Religion	Member	Percentage
Christianity	2.4 billion	31.2%
Islam	1.8 billion	24.1%
Hinduism	1.2 billion	15.1%
Buddhism	0.5 billion	6.9%
Sikhism	25 million	0.29%
Jewish	14.5 million	0.23%

National Emblems of Major Countries

Country	Emblem	Country	Emblem
Australia	Kangaroo	Italy	The star, the cog-wheel, and olive and oak branches
Bangladesh	Water Lily	Japan	Chrysanthemum
United States of America	The bald eagle	New Zealand	Kiwi, Silver Fern
Belgium	Lion	Netherlands	Lion
France	Lily	Canada	Maple Leaf Tartan
Chile	Candor and Huemul	Norway	Lion
Iran	Four curves and a sword	Pakistan	Crescent and Star
Germany	Black eagle		
India	Lioned Capital	United Kingdom	Coat of Arms with various symbols

First in India

Category	First in India
Newspaper	Bengal Gazette (James Hickey)
Vernacular Daily	Samachar Darpan (Bengali)
Hindi Newspaper	Udant Martand (Pt. Jugal Kishore Shukla)
Telegraph Line	Diamond Harbour to Kolkata
International Telephone Service	Mumbai to London (1881)
Silent Movie	Raja Harish Chandra (Dadasaheb Phalke 1913)
Talkie Movie	Alam Ara (Ardeshir Irani-1931)
Aircraft Carrier Warship	INS Vikrant
Satellite	Aryabhatta (19th April, 1975)
Satellite dedicated exclusively for Education purposes	EDUSAT
Dedicated multi wavelength space observatory	Astrosat
Successful indigenous launch vehicle	SLV-3
Nuclear Reactor	Apsara (1956)

Lunar Mission	Chandrayaan-I (October, 2008)
Mars Mission	Mars Orbiter Mission (5th November, 2013)
Hydroelectric Project	Sidrapong, Darjeeling (1897)
Asian Games	Delhi (1951)
Census	1872
Regular Decadal Census	1881 Onwards
Biosphere Reserve	Nilgiri National Park
First National Park	Hailey National Park (Jim Corbett), 1936
First asymmetrical cable stayed bridge	Signature Bridge (New Delhi)
E-court	Ahmedabad Court
Technology Park	Technopark, Thiruvananthapuram
Cloned Animal	Samrupa
Rail University	Vadodara
Jnanpith Award	G. Sankara Kurup
Posthumous Bharat Ratna Recipient	Lal Bahadur Shastri
Padma Bhushan for Cricket	C. K. Nayudu
Indian Civil Service (ICS)	Satyendra Nath Tagore (1869)
English Channel Swimmer	Mihir Sen (1958)
Chief of Defence Staff	Bipin Rawat
First Indian Pilot	J. R. D. Tata

First in India (Male)

Achievement	First Indian Male
Governor-General of India	William Bentinck (1833)
Indian Governor-General of Free India	C. Rajagopalachari
Commander-in-Chief of Free India	General K. M. Cariappa
Field Marshal of India	General Sam Manekshaw
Indian in Space	Rakesh Sharma
Everest Climber without Oxygen	Sherpa Phu Dorjee
Managing Director of World Bank	Gautam Kaji
Judge in the International Court of Justice	Dr. Nagendra Singh
Nobel Prize in Physics	C. V. Raman (1930)
Nobel Prize in Literature	Rabindranath Tagore (1913)
Nobel Prize in Economics	Dr. Amartya Sen (1998)
Nobel Prize in Medicine (Physiology)	Dr. Har Gobind Khorana (1968)
Bharat Ratna Recipients	Dr. S. Radhakrishnan, C. Rajagopalachari, Dr. C. V. Raman (1954)

First in India (Female)

Achievement	First Indian Female
Chairperson of Indian National Congress	Sarojini Naidu (1925)
Everest Climber	Bachendri Pal (1984)
Cabinet Minister	Rajkumari Amrit Kaur (1947)
Chairman of the UN General Assembly	Vijaya Lakshmi Pandit
President of India	Pratibha Patil
Speaker of Lok Sabha	Meira Kumar (2009)
Deputy Chairman of Rajya Sabha	Violet Alva (1962-66)
Prime Minister of India	Indira Gandhi
Antarctic Explorer	Aditi Pant, Sudipta Sengupta
IAS Officer	Anna Rajam Malhotra (1950)
Defence Minister	Nirmala Sitharaman
Bharat Ratna Recipient	Indira Gandhi
Nobel Prize Winner	Mother Teresa (1979)
Century in World Cup Cricket	Thirush Kamini
Olympic Silver Medalist (Badminton)	P. V. Sindhu
Member of International Olympic Committee	Nita Ambani
Olympic Bronze Medalist (Wrestling)	Sakshi Malik
Female Fighter Pilot	Avani Chaturvedi (2018)
Female Naval Pilot	Shubhangi Swaroop, Shivangi and Divya Sharma (2018)
Female ICC Match Referee	G. S. Lakshmi
Female Astronaut	Kalpana Chawla

Biggest, Highest, Largest, Longest, and Smallest etc. in India

Category	Name	Location
Longest River	The Ganga (2525 km)	India
Longest Canal	Indira Gandhi Canal (Rajasthan Canal) (649 km)	Rajasthan, India
Longest Dam	Hirakud Dam (26 km)	Odisha, India
Longest Sea Beach	Marina Beach (13 km)	Chennai, India
Highest Lake	Gurudongmar Lake	Sikkim, India
Largest Saline Water Lake	Chilka Lake	Odisha, India
Biggest River Islands	Majuli, Brahmaputra River	Assam, India
Largest Fresh Water Lake	Wular Lake	Jammu and Kashmir, India
Highest Dam	Tehri Dam (260 m)	Uttarakhand, India
Highest Waterfall	Kunchikal Falls (455 m)	Karnataka, India
Deepest River Valley	Bhagirathi and Alaknanda	India
Longest River Bridge	Bhupen Hazarika Setu, Assam	Assam, India
Biggest Cantilever Bridge	Rabindra Setu or Howrah Bridge	Kolkata, India
State with Longest Coastline	Gujarat	India
Longest River without Delta	Narmada	India
Longest Sea Bridge	Bandra-Worli Sea Link (5.6 km)	India
Largest Artificial Lake	Gobind Ballabh Pant Sagar	Uttar Pradesh
Longest River of Southern India	Godavari	India
Longest Railway Platform	Gorakhpur	Uttar Pradesh, India
Longest National Highway	NH-44 (Srinagar to Kanyakumari)	India
Longest Corridor	Corridor of Ramnathswami Temple	Tamil Nadu, India
Highest Road	Road at Khardungla	Leh-Manali Sector, India
Highest Airport	Leh Airport	Ladakh, India
Largest Desert	Thar	Rajasthan, India
Largest Delta	Sunderbans	Paschim Bengal, India
State with Maximum Forest Area	Madhya Pradesh	India
Largest Zoo	Arignar Anna Zoological Park (Vandalur Zoo)	Chennai, Tamil Nadu
Biggest Stadium	Narendra Modi Stadium (Motera Stadium)	Ahmedabad, Gujarat
Highest Award	Bharat Ratna	India
Highest Gallantry Award	Param Vir Chakra	India
Largest Gurudwara	Golden Temple	Amritsar, India
Largest Cave Temple	Kailash Temple (Ellora)	Maharashtra, India
Highest Peak	Kangchenjunga	India/Nepal Border
Largest Mosque	Taj-ul-Masjid	Bhopal, Madhya Pradesh
Longest Road Tunnel	Chenani Nashri Tunnel (Syama Prasad Mookerjee Road Tunnel)	Jammu and Kashmir, India
Largest Auditorium	Sri Shanmukhanand Hall	Mumbai, India
Largest Animal Fair	Sonepur	Bihar, India
Largest Cave	Amarnath	Jammu and Kashmir, India
Highest Gate Way	Buland Darwaza, Fatehpur Sikri	Uttar Pradesh, India
Tallest Statue	Statue of Unity	Gujarat, India
Largest Public Sector Bank	State Bank of India	India
Most Populous City	Delhi	Delhi, India
Biggest Church	Saint Cathedral at Old Goa	Goa, India
Highest Battlefield	Siachen Glacier	India/Pakistan Border

Books and Authors

Author Name	Book Name
Alexandre Dumas	The Three Musketeers
Amartya Sen	Identity and Violence: The Illusion of Destiny

Amartya Sen	The Argumentative Indian
Amartya Sen	Development as Freedom
Amitav Ghose	River of Smoke, Sea of Poppies, The Circle of Reason, The Great Derangement: Climate Change and the Unthinkable
Amrita Pritam	Death of a City, Pinjar
Anita Desai	Clear Light of the Day
Aristotle	Politics
Arun Shourie	A Secular Agenda
Arundhati Roy	The Algebra of Infinite Justice, Greater Common Good, The God of Small Things
Ashwaghosha	Buddha Charitham
Aung San Suu Kyi	Freedom from Fear
Barrett Lee, Marina Chapman	The Girl with No Name
Barack Obama	Dreams from My Father, A Promised Land
Bankim Chandra Chatterji	Anand Math, Durgeshnandini
Benazir Bhutto	Pakistan the Gathering Storm
Javier Moro	The Red Saree
Chandrashekar	Meri Jail Diary
Chetan Bhagat	Revolution 2020, What Young India Wants, Half Girl Friend, One Night at the Call Centre, Making India Awesome, One Indian Girl
Charles Dickens	David Copperfield
Chitra Subramaniam	India is for Sale
Dr C. Rangarajan	Indian Economy: Essays on Money and Finance
Dalai Lama	Freedom in Exile, Ethics for the New Millennium
Dante Alighieri	The Divine Comedy
Eleanor Catton	The Luminaries
E. M. Forster	A Passage to India
Gen V. P. Malik	Kargil: From Surprise to Victory
Gunter Grass	The Tin Drum
Herbert George Wells	The Time Machine
Indira Gandhi	My Truth
Jai Shankar Prasad	Ajatshatru
Jawaharlal Nehru	Discovery of India, Glimpses of World History
Jayaprakash Narayan	Prison Diary
K. Natwar Singh	Walking with Lions, Curtain Raisers
Kapil Dev	Straight from the Heart
Karl Marx	Das Kapital, Communist Manifesto
Khushwant Singh	Train to Pakistan
Kiran Bedi	I Dare, As I See
Kuldeep Mathur	Too Old to be Bold
L. K. Advani	A Prisoner's Scrap
Mahatma Gandhi	My Experiments with Truth
Malala Yousafzai	We Are Displaced
Mark Tully	The Heart of India
Mulk Raj Anand	Untouchable
Narendra Modi	Exam Warriors
Pranab Mukherjee	The Coalition Years, The Presidential Years
Premchand	Godan
Ramchandra Guha	Gandhi, Makers of Modern India
R. K. Narayan	The Guide
Ruskin Bond	A Garland of Memories, Death under the Deodars
Sarojini Naidu	Golden Threshold, The Broken Wings
Shashi Tharoor	An Era of Darkness, Paradoxical Prime Minister
Sir Richard Burton	The Arabian Nights
Sri Aurobindo Ghosh	Essays on the Gita
Stephen Hawking	A Brief History of Time
Taslima Nasreen	All About Women
Thomas Pynchon	Against the Day
Ved Vyas	Bhagwad Gita
V. S. Naipaul	India: A Wounded Civilisation, Letters between a Father and Son, Half a Life, An Area of Darkness, Magic Seeds
Vikram Chandra	Love and Longing in Mumbai
Vimal Kumar	Sachin: Cricketer of the Century
Vikram Seth	An Equal Music
Yuvraj Singh	The Test of My Life
Vijay Lokapally	Driven: The Virat Kohli Story

International Decades

Decade	Time Period
UN Decade for Desert and Fight against Desertification	2010-2020
UN Decade of Sustainable Energy for All	2014-2024
International Decade for People of African Descent	2015-2024
UN Decade of Action on Nutrition	2016-2025
International Decade for Action "Water for Sustainable Development"	2018-2028
UN Decade of Family Planning	2019-2028
UN Decade of Healthy Ageing	2021-2030
International Decade of Indigenous Language	2022-2032

International Years

Year	Theme
2009	International Year of Astronomy
2010	International Year of Biodiversity
2011	International Year of Forests
2012	International Year of Cooperatives
2013	International Year of Water Cooperation
2014	International Year of Family Farming
2015	International Year of Light and Light-based Technologies
2016	International Year of Pulses
2017	International Year of Sustainable Tourism for Development
2019	International Year of Indigenous Languages
2020	International Year of Plant Health
2021	International Year for Elimination of Child Labour
2023	International Year of Millets

Important Dates and Days

Month	Date(s)	Event/Day
January	1	Global Family Day
January	9	NRI Day (Pravasi Bharatiya Divas)
January	12	National Youth Day (Or Swami Vivekanand Jayanti)
January	15	Indian Army Day
January	25	National Tourism Day, Voter's Day
January	26	Indian Republic Day, International Customs Day
January	28	Data Protection Day
January	30	Martyr's Day (Mahatma Gandhi's Martyrdom), World Leprosy Eradication Day
February	4	World Cancer Day
February	13	World Radio Day
February	20	World Day of Social Justice
February	24	Central Excise Day
February	28	National Science Day
March	8	International Women's Day
March	15	World Consumer Rights Day
March	21	World Forestry Day, International Day for the Elimination of Racial Discrimination
March	22	World Water Day
March	23	World Meteorological Day
March	24	World TB Day
April	4	International Day for Mine Awareness
April	5	National Maritime Day
April	7	World Health Day
April	18	World Heritage Day
April	21	Civil Services Day
April	22	World Earth Day
May	1	International Labour Day (May Day)
May	3	World Press Freedom Day
May	8	World Red Cross Day
May	17	World Telecommunications Day
May	21	Anti-Terrorism Day
June	5	World Environment Day
June	7	World Food Safety Day
June	8	World Oceans Day
June	12	World Day against Child Labour
June	21	International Yoga Day
July	1	National Doctor's Day
July	7	International day of Cooperatives
July	11	World Population Day
July	12	International Malala Day
August	6	Hiroshima Day
August	10	World Bio-Fuel Day
August	12	International Youth Day
August	20	Sadbhavna Divas
August	29	National Sports Day (Dhyanchand's Birthday)

September	5	Teachers' Day (Dr. Radhakrishnan's Birthday)
September	14	Hindi Day, World First Aid Day
September	16	World Ozone Day
September	21	International Day of Peace
September	26	International Day for Elimination of Nuclear Weapons
September	27	World Tourism Day
October	2	International Non-Violence Day, Lal Bahadur Shastri, and Mahatma Gandhi's Birthday
October	1st Monday	World Habitat Day
October	5	World Teacher's Day
October	8	Indian Air Force Day
October	16	World Food Day
October	24	United Nations Day
October	31	National Integrity Day
November	9	National Legal Services Day
November	11	National Education Day (India)
November	14	World Diabetes Day, Children's Day
November	20	Universal Children's Day (UN)
November	26	World Environment Protection Day
November	25	Good Governance Day
December	1	World AIDS Day
December	3	International Day of Persons with Disabilities
December	4	Indian Navy Day
December	7	Armed Forces Flag Day
December	10	Human Rights Day
December	16	Vijay Diwas
December	25	Good Governance Day
December	26	Veer Baal Diwas

Abbreviations

Abbreviation	Full Form
ABM	Anti Ballistic Missiles
ADB	Asian Development Bank
AERE	Atomic Energy Research Establishment
AFSPA	Armed Forces Special Power Act
AGOC	Asian Games Organising Committee
AIDS	Acquired Immuno Deficiency Syndrome
AIIMS	All India Institute of Medical Sciences
ALH	Advanced Light Helicopter
APPLE	Ariane Passenger Payload Experiment
AMRUT	Atal Mission for Rejuvenation and Urban Transformation
APEC	Asia-Pacific Economic Cooperation
ASAT	Anti-Satellite Weapon
ASEAN	Association of Southeast Asian Nations
ASCII	American Standard Code for Information Interchange
ASLV	Augmented Satellite Launch Vehicle
ASI	Archaeological Survey of India
ATM	Automated Teller Machine
ATS	Anti-Terrorism Squad
AU	African Union
AVES	Acute Viral Encephalitic Syndrome
BCSBI	Banking Codes and Standard Board of India
BARC	Bhabha Atomic Research Centre
BBC	British Broadcasting Corporation
BCG	Bacillus Calmette Guerin (Anti-Tuberculosis Vaccine)
BCCI	Board of Control for Cricket in India
BENELUX	Belgium, Netherlands, Luxembourg
BIMSTEC	Bay of Bengal Initiative for Multisectoral Technical and Economic Cooperation
BIS	Bureau of Indian Standards
BMD	Ballistic Missile Defence System
BPO	Business Process Outsourcing
BRO	Border Roads Organisation
CAA	Citizenship Amendment Act
CABE	Central Advisory Board of Education
CAG	Comptroller and Auditor General
CAPES	Computer-Aided Paperless Examination System
CAZRI	Central Arid Zone Research Institute
CBI	Central Bureau of Investigation
CECA	Comprehensive Economic Cooperation Agreement
CFC	Chlorofluoro Carbon
CID	Criminal Investigation Department
CISF	Central Industrial Security Force
CITES	Convention on International Trade in Endangered Species
CNG	Compressed Natural Gas
COFEPOSA	Conservation of Foreign Exchange and Prevention of Smuggling Act
CPCB	Central Pollution Control Board
CPRI	Central Power Research Institute
CRR	Cash Reserve Ratio
CSIR	Council of Scientific and Industrial Research

DAVP	Directorate of Advertising and Visual Publicity
DDT	Dichloro-Diphenyl Trichloroethane (insecticide)
DNA	De-oxyribonucleic Acid
DPSA	Deep Penetration Strike Aircraft
DPT	Diphteria, Pertussis and Tetanus
DRDO	Defence Research and Development Organisation
DTH	Direct-to-Home (Broadcasting)
DVD	Digital Versatile Disk
ECG	Electro cardiogram
EEG	Electro-Encephalography
EET	Eastern European Time
ESCAP	Economic and Social Commission for Asia and the Pacific
EVM	Electronic Voting Machine
FDI	Foreign Direct Investment
FII	Foreign Institutional Investor
FBI	Federal Bureau of Investigation
FERA	Foreign Exchange Regulations Act
FICCI	Federation of Indian Chambers of Commerce and Industry
FDR	Fixed Deposit Receipt
FLAG	Fibre Optic Link Around the Globe
GAIN	Global Alliance for Improved Nutrition
GANDHI	Green Action for National Dandi Heritage Initiative
GATS	General Agreement on Trade in Services
GATT	General Agreement on Tariffs and Trade
GEF	Global Environment Fund
GMPS	Global Mobile Personal Communications System
GNSS	Global Navigation Satellite System
GPS	Global Positioning System
GSLV	Geosynchronous Satellite Launch Vehicle
HAC	Hindustan Aluminium Corporation
HAL	Hindustan Aeronautics Limited
HIV	Human Immunodeficiency Virus
HTML	Hypertext Markup Language
HTTP	Hypertext Transfer Protocol
HYV	High Yielding Variety
IAAI	International Airport Authority of India

IAEA	International Atomic Energy Agency
IBRD	International Bank for Reconstruction and Development
ICAO	International Civil Aviation Organisation
ICAR	Indian Council of Agricultural Research
ICMR	Indian Council of Medical Research
ICRC	International Committee of the Red Cross
IDBI	Industrial Development Bank of India
IMA	Indian Military Academy
IMO	International Maritime Organisation
INMAS	Institute of Nuclear Medicines and Allied Sciences
INSAS	Indian Small Arms System
INSAT	Indian National Satellite
INTERPOL	International Police Organisation
IPCC	Intergovernmental Panel on Climate Change
IRBM	Intermediate Range Ballistic Missile
IRSS	Indian Remote Sensing Satellite
ISCS	Integrated Smart Card System
ISRO	Indian Space Research Organisation
ITU	International Telecommunication Union
JNNURM	Jawaharlal Nehru National Urban Renewal Mission
LCA	Light Combat Aircraft
LOC	Line of Control
LAC	Line of Actual Control
LTA	Light Transport Aircraft
MAT	Minimum Alternative Tax
METSAT	Meteorological Satellite
MNP	Mobile Number Portability
MMS	Multimedia Messaging Service
MODEM	Modulator-Demodulator
MRI	Magnetic Resonance Imaging
MRTS	Mass Rapid Transit System
MSP	Minimum Support Price
MTCR	Missile Technology Control Regime
NAA	National Airport Authority
NABARD	National Bank for Agriculture and Rural Development
NADA	National Anti-Doping Agency
NASA	National Aeronautics and Space Administration

NEERI	National Environment Engineering Research Institute
NATA	Natural Aptitude Test for Architecture
NCEP	National Committee on Environmental Planning
NCERT	National Council of Educational Research and Training
NeGP	National e-governance Plan
NEP	National Education Policy
NEPA	National Environment Protection Authority
NHDP	National Highways Development Project
NHRC	National Human Rights Commission
NITI Aayog	National Institution for Transforming India
NRC	National Register of Citizens
OCI	Overseas Citizenship of India
OAS	Organisation of American States
ODS	Ozone Depletion Substances
OIC	Organisation of Islamic Countries
OPEC	Organisation of the Petroleum Exporting Countries
OSCE	Organisation for Security and Cooperation in Europe
PURA	Providing Urban Amenities in Rural Areas
PATA	Pacific Asia Travel Association
POTA	Prevention of Terrorism Act
PPE	Personal Protective Equipment
PSLV	Polar Satellite Launch Vehicle
QIB	Qualified Institutional Buyer
QIP	Qualified Institutional Placement
RAF	Rapid Action Force
RBI	Reserve Bank of India
RCC	Reinforced Concrete Cement
RDSS	Radio Determination Satellite Service
RTGS	Real Time Gross Settlement System
RTE	Right to Education
RTI	Right to Information
SAARC	South Asian Association for Regional Cooperation
SAFTA	South Asian Free Trade Area
SAIL	Steel Authority of India Limited
SAPTA	SAARC Preferential Trading Agreement
SATNAV	Satellite Navigation
SALT	Strategic Arms Limitation Talks
SAVE	SAARC Audio Visual Exchange
SCO	Shanghai Cooperation Organisation
SEBI	Securities and Exchange Board of India
SIDBI	Small Industries Development Bank of India
SPIN	Software Process Improvement Networks
STARS	Satellite Tracking and Ranging Station
START	Strategic Arms Reduction Treaty
SWIFT	Society for Worldwide Interbank Financial Telecommunications
TADA	Terrorist and Disruptive Activities (Prevention) Act
TAPS	Tarapur Atomic Power Station
TIN	Tax Identification Number
TRAI	Telecom Regulatory Authority of India
TRIPS	Trade Related Intellectual Property Rights
TVOA	Tourist Visa on Arrival
UNCTAD	United Nations Conference on Trade and Development
UNDP	United Nations Development Programme
UNEP	United Nations Environment Programme
UNFPA	United Nations Fund for Population Activities
UPS	Uninterruptible Power Supply
VAT	Value Added Tax
VoIP	Voice over Internet Protocol
VPN	Virtual Private Network
VSAT	Very Small Aperture Terminals
WADA	World Anti-Doping Agency
WAP	Wireless Application Protocol
WAVE	Wireless Access for Virtual Enterprise
WFP	World Food Programme
WFTU	World Federation of Trade Unions
WHO	World Health Organisation
WLL	Wireless in Local Loop
WWW	World Wide Web
XML	Extensible Markup Language
YWCA	Young Women's Christian Association
ZSI	Zoological Survey of India
ZUPO	Zimbabwe United People Organisation

AWARDS & HONOURS

International

Nobel Prize

- The most prestigious award in the world, established in 1900 under the will of Alfred Bernhard Nobel.
- Presented annually on 10th December, the death anniversary of the founder.
- Given in the fields of Peace, Literature, Physics, Chemistry, Physiology or Medicine (from 1901), and Economics (from 1969).

Winner	Field	Year
Abhijit Banerjee	Economics	2019
Kailash Satyarthi	Peace	2014
Venkatraman Ramakrishnan	Chemistry	2009
Amartya Sen	Economics	1998
Subrahmanyan Chandrasekhar	Physics	1983
Mother Teresa	Peace	1979
Hargobind Khorana	Medicine	1968
C. V. Raman	Physics	1930
Rabindranath Tagore	Literature	1913

Grammy Awards

- Awarded for outstanding achievements in the music industry by the National Academy for Recording Arts and Sciences, America.
- Started in 1959.

Pulitzer Prize

- Instituted in 1917 and named after US publisher Joseph Pulitzer.
- Conferred annually in the United States for accomplishments in journalism, literature, and music.

Magsaysay Awards

- Instituted in 1957, named after Ramon Magsaysay, the former President of the Philippines.
- Awarded annually on 31st August, the birth anniversary of Magsaysay.
- Given for outstanding contributions in public service, community leadership, journalism, literature and creative arts, and international understanding.

Man Booker Prize

- Highest literary award in the world, established in 1968.
- Set up by the Booker Company and the British Publishers Association.
- Similar to the Pulitzer Prize of the USA.

Right Livelihood Award

- Established in 1980, also known as the "Alternative Nobel Prize".
- Given to individuals working on practical and exemplary solutions to urgent global challenges.

Oscar Awards

- Instituted in 1929, awarded annually by the Academy of Motion Pictures, Arts and Sciences, USA.
- Recognizes outstanding contributions in various fields of filmmaking.
- Notable Indian achievements: Mother India (1957), Salaam Bombay (1988), Lagaan (2001).
- Bhanu Athaiya was the first Indian to win an Oscar Award in 1982 for costume design in the movie Gandhi.
- A. R. Rahman won two Oscars in 2009 for his work in Slumdog Millionaire.

UN Human Rights Award

- Instituted in 1966, awarded every five years for individual contributions to the establishment of human rights.

National

Bharat Ratna

- India's highest civilian award established in 1954.
- Award designed in the shape of a peepal leaf with Bharat Ratna inscribed in Devanagari script and a Sun Figure.

Winners

Winner	Year
Karpoori Thakur	2024
Lal Krishna Advani	2024
Chaudhary Charan Singh	2024
P. V. Narasimha Rao	2024
M. S. Swaminathan	2024
Pranab Mukherjee	2019
Bhupen Hazarika	2019
Nanaji Deshmukh	2019
Madan Mohan Malaviya	2015
Atal Bihari Vajpayee	2015
Sachin Tendulkar	2014
C. N. R. Rao	2014
Pandit Bhimsen Joshi	2008
Lata Dinanath Mangeshkar	2001
Ustad Bismillah Khan	2001
Prof Amartya Sen	1999
Lokpriya Gopinath Bordoloi	1999
Loknayak Jayprakash Narayan	1999
Pandit Ravi Shankar	1999
Chidambaram Subramaniam	1998
Madurai Shanmukhavadivu Subbulakshmi	1998
Dr. Abul Pakir Jainulabdeen Abdul Kalam	1997
Aruna Asaf Ali	1997
Gulzari Lal Nanda	1997
Jehangir Ratanji Dadabhai Tata	1992
Maulana Abul Kalam Azad	1992
Satyajit Ray	1992
Morarji Ranchhodji Desai	1991
Rajiv Gandhi	1991

Sardar Vallabhbhai Patel	1991
Dr. Bhimrao Ramji Ambedakr	1990
Dr. Nelson Rolihlahla Mandela	1990
Marudur Gopalan Ramachandran	1988
Khan Abdul Ghaffar Khan	1987
Acharya Vinoba Bhave	1983
Mother Teresa (Agnes Gonxha Bojaxhiu)	1980
Kumaraswamy Kamraj	1976
Varahagiri Venkata Giri	1975
Indira Gandhi	1971
Lal Bahadur Shastri	1966
Dr. Pandurang Vaman Kane	1963
Dr. Zakir Hussain	1963
Dr. Rajendra Prasad	1962
Dr. Bidhan Chandra Roy	1961
Purushottam Das Tandon	1961
Dr. Dhonde Keshav Karve	1958
Pt Govind Ballabh Pant	1957
Dr. Bhagwan Das	1955
Jawaharlal Nehru	1955
Dr. MokshagundamVivesvaraya	1955
Chakravarti Rajagopalachari	1954
Dr. Chandrasekhara Venkata Raman	1954
Dr. Sarvapalli Radhakrishnan	1954

Republic Day Awards

Padma Awards

- Instituted in 1954, announced annually on Republic Day.
- Given in three categories: Padma Vibhushan (2nd highest), Padma Bhushan (3rd highest), and Padma Shri (4th highest).
- These awards are not given to government employees except doctors and scientists.

Gallantry Awards

- **Param Vir Chakra:** Highest decoration for valor in the presence of the enemy.
- **Mahavir Chakra:** Second-highest gallantry award for conspicuous gallantry in the presence of the enemy.
- **Vir Chakra:** Awarded for gallantry in the presence of the enemy.
- **Ashok Chakra:** Highest military award during peacetime.
- **Kirti Chakra:** Award for conspicuous gallantry.
- **Shaurya Chakra:** Award for gallantry during peacetime.

Sports Awards

Rajiv Gandhi Khel Ratna Award

- Instituted in 1991-92, highest sports award in India.
- Renamed as Major Dhyan Chand Khel Ratna Award in 2021.

Arjuna Award

- Instituted in 1961, recognizes outstanding achievement in national sports.

Dronacharya Award

- Instituted in 1985, recognizes excellence in sports coaching.

Dhyanchand Award

- Instituted in 2002, given to sports -persons who have contributed to sports even after retirement.

Indian Cinema Awards

Dadasaheb Phalke Award

- Presented first in 1969.
- Highest national film award named after Dadasaheb Phalke, the Father of Indian Cinema.
- Awarded for outstanding contribution to the growth and development of Indian cinema.

Other National Awards

Bharatiya Jnanpith Award

- Instituted in 1961, given for the best literary writing by an Indian citizen in a language listed in the Eighth Schedule of the Indian Constitution.

Gandhi Peace Prize

- Established in 1994, awarded for outstanding work in international peace, disarmament, and development.

Indira Gandhi Prize for Peace, Disarmament and Development

- Instituted in 1985, awarded to individuals who have done outstanding work in international peace, disarmament, and development.

Borlaug Award

- Instituted in 1973, honors outstanding agricultural scientists.

Sahitya Akademi Award

- Established in 1954.
- Awarded for outstanding literary work.

Indian Defence

Indian Defence Training Institutions

Training Institution	Place	Established
Rashtriya Indian Military College (RIMC)	Dehradun	1922
Army Cadet College (ACC)	Dehradun	1929
Indian Military Academy (IMA)	Dehradun	1932
National Defence Academy (NDA)	Khadakwasla, Pune	1954
High Altitude Warfare School (HAWS)	Gulmarg	1948
National Defence College (NDC)	New Delhi	1960
Officers Training Academy (OTA)	Chennai	1963

Counter Insurgency and Jungle Warfare School	Vairengte (Mizoram)	1970
College of Defence Management	Secunderabad	1970
College of Combat/Army War College	Mhow (Madhya Pradesh)	1971
Army School of Physical Training (ASPT)	Pune	1978
Army Air Defence College (AADC)	Gopalpur (Odisha)	1989
Officers Training Academy Gaya	Gaya	2011 (later redesignated as the Junior Leaders Academy (JLA) in 2021).

Ranks of Commissioned Officers

Army	Air Force	Navy
Field Marshal	Marshal of the Air Force	Admiral of the Fleet
General	Air Chief Marshal	Admiral
Lt. General	Air Marshal	Vice Admiral
Major General	Air Vice Marshal	Rear Admiral
Brigadier	Air Commodore	Commodore
Colonel	Group Captain	Captain
Lt. Colonel	Wing Commander	Commander
Major	Squadron Leader	Lt. Commander
Captain	Flight Lieutenant	Lieutenant
Lieutenant	Flying Officer	Sub-Lieutenant

NOTE: The Chief of Defence Staff (CDS) is the head and permanent Chairman of the Chiefs of Staff Committee of the Indian Defence Forces. The Chief of Defence Staff is the highest-ranking (4-Star) uniformed officer on active duty in the Indian military and chief military adviser to the Minister of Defence. He also heads the Department of Military Affairs.

Paramilitary, Reserve Forces, and other Agencies

Indo-Tibetan Border Police (ITBP)
- Established in 1962 after the Chinese attack.
- Primarily deployed in the Northern borders to monitor and prevent smuggling and illegal immigration.

National Security Guards (NSG)
- Established in 1986 to counter militancy in the country.
- Highly trained force specialized in dealing with militants effectively.

Central Industrial Security Force (CISF)
- Established in 1969 based on the recommendations of Justice B. Mukherji.
- Objective is to provide security to industrial complexes under the Central Government.

Assam Rifles
- Established in 1835, it is the oldest paramilitary force in the country.
- Main objective is to maintain vigilance of international borders in the North East region and conduct counter-insurgency operations in Arunachal Pradesh, Manipur, Mizoram, and Nagaland.

Border Security Force (BSF)
- Established in 1965.
- Tasked with the responsibility of guarding the international borders to prevent intrusion into the country.

National Cadet Corps (NCC)
- Established in 1948.
- Aims to stimulate interest among the youth in the defense of the country and build a reserve manpower for the armed forces.

Central Reserve Police Force (CRPF)
- Established in 1939.
- Assists the State/Union Territory Police in maintaining law and order.
- The 88th Battalion of CRPF, known as the 'Mahila Battalion', is the world's first paramilitary force comprising entirely of women.

Territorial Army (TA)
- Established in 1949.
- Voluntary, part-time force composed of civilians between the ages of 18 and 42 who wish to assist in the defense of the country.

Home Guard
- Established in 1946.
- Assists the police in maintaining security, supporting defense forces, and helping local authorities in case of emergencies.

Indian Coast Guard
- Established in 1977.
- Objective is to protect maritime and other national interests in India's maritime zones.

Intelligence Bureau (IB)
- Established in 1887.
- Objective is to collect secret information related to the country's security.
- Originally known as Central Special Branch (CSB) in 1887, it was renamed IB in 1947.

Central Bureau of Investigation (CBI)
- Established in 1963.
- Objective is to investigate cases of misconduct by public servants, cheating, embezzlement, and fraud.
- Also entrusted with the investigation of international crime cases in collaboration with INTERPOL.

National Crime Records Bureau (NCRB)
- Established in 1986.
- Objective is to collect crime statistics at the national level and information on inter-state and international criminals to assist investigation agencies.

Rapid Action Force (RAF)
- Established in 1991.
- Operated under the command of CRPF.
- 10 battalions of CRPF have been reoriented to tackle communal riots in the country.

Nuclear and Space Research Centers in India

Research Centre	Place
Indian Rare Earths Limited	Mumbai
Uranium Corporation of India Limited	Jadugoda (Jharkhand)
Atomic Energy Commission (AEC)	Mumbai
Electronics Corporation of India Limited	Hyderabad
Bhabha Atomic Research Centre (BARC)	Trombay (Mumbai)
Radio Astronomy Centre	Ootacamund (Tamil Nadu)
Tata Institute of Fundamental Research	Mumbai
Saha Institute of Nuclear Physics	Kolkata
Centre of Earth Sciences Studies	Thiruvananthapuram (Kerala)
Physical Research Laboratory	Ahmedabad
Space Commission	Bengaluru
Vikram Sarabhai Space Centre	Thiruvananthapuram
Indian Space Research Organisation (ISRO)	Bengaluru
Space Application Centre	Ahmedabad
Thumba Equatorial Rocket Launching Station	Thumba (Kerala)
Second Satellite Launch Port (Planned)	Thoothukudi (Tamil Nadu)

Sports

Olympics

- The Olympics games were initiated in 776 BC on Mount Olympia to honor the Greek God, Zeus.
- The modern Olympic Games started in Athens, Greece on 6th April 1896, thanks to the efforts of French nobleman Baron Pierre de Coubertin.
- The Olympic Games are held every four years.
- The Olympic Flag consists of five interwoven rings as the Olympic Emblem.
- The rings are arranged in a 3-2 pattern on a white background, with the blue ring on the extreme left, followed by yellow, black, green, and red, representing Europe, Asia, Africa, Oceania and Americas respectively.
- The official Olympic Motto is "Citius, Altius, Fortius", which is Latin for "Swifter, Higher, Stronger".
- The 2024 Summer Olympics will be held in Paris, France.

Commonwealth Games

- The first Commonwealth Games took place in 1930 in Hamilton, Canada.
- The games have been conducted every four years since 1930, except for 1942 and 1946 due to World War II.
- The Commonwealth Games Federation (CGF) is responsible for the direction and control of the Commonwealth Games.
- The Commonwealth of Nations currently consists of 56 member countries.
- The 21st Commonwealth Games were held on the Gold Coast, Queensland, Australia in 2018, with Australia winning the most gold medals.
- The most recent 22nd Commonwealth Games, was held in Birmingham from 28 July to 8 August 2022.

Asian Games

- The Asian Games, also known as the Asiad, are a multi-sport event held every four years among athletes from across Asia.
- The games are regulated by the Olympic Council of Asia (OCA) under the supervision of the International Olympic Committee (IOC).
- The first Asian Games were held in 1951 in New Delhi, India.
- The 18th Asian Games were held in Jakarta, Indonesia in 2018, where India finished in eighth position.
- The 19th Asian Games was held from 23 September to 8 October 2023 in Hangzhou, China.

Cricket World Cup

- The first Cricket World Cup was organized in England in 1975, and a separate women's Cricket World Cup has been held every four years since 1973.
- The 13th ICC Cricket World Cup 2023 was held in India from 5 October to 19 November.
- T20 Cricket World Cups have also been held since 2007.

Hockey World Cup

- The first Men's Hockey World Cup was organized in Barcelona, Spain in 1971, while the Women's Hockey World Cup has been held since 1974.
- The 15th Men's Hockey World Cup was held in Bhubaneswar and Rourkela, India in 2023.

Football World Cup

- The Football World Cup is organized by FIFA (Federation of International Football Association).
- The first Football World Cup was organized in Uruguay in 1930.
- The 20th FIFA World Cup was held in Brazil, with Germany emerging as the champion by defeating Argentina 1-0 in the final.
- The 2022 Football World Cup was held in Qatar, and the upcoming 2026 World Cup is scheduled to take place in Canada, Mexico and United State of America collectively.

Cricket World Cup Winners

Year	Host	Winner	Runner-Up
1975	England	West Indies	Australia
1979	England	West Indies	England
1983	England	India	West Indies
1987	India	Australia	England
1992	Australia	Pakistan	England
1996	Pakistan	Sri Lanka	Australia
1999	England	Australia	Pakistan
2003	South Africa	Australia	India
2007	West Indies	Australia	Sri Lanka
2011	India	India	Sri Lanka
2015	Australia and New Zealand	Australia	New Zealand

2019	England	England	New Zealand
2023	India	Australia	India

T20 Cricket World Cup Winners

Year	Host	Winner	Runner-Up
2007	South Africa	India	Pakistan
2009	England	Pakistan	Sri Lanka
2010	West Indies	England	Australia
2012	Sri Lanka	West Indies	Sri Lanka
2014	Bangladesh	Sri Lanka	India
2016	India	West Indies	England
2021	India	Australia	New Zealand
2024	West Indies & United States	India	South Africa
2026	India & Sri Lanka	India	New Zealand

NOTE: The 2024 T20 Cricket World Cup is scheduled to held in West Indies and USA.

United Nations Organization

The United Nations (UN)

- The United Nations was established on 24th October 1945, following World War II, with the aim of maintaining global peace.
- The original membership of 51 nations has grown to 193 members, with the most recent addition being South Sudan.
- The United Nations Headquarters is located in New York City, and it also has offices in Nairobi, Geneva, and Vienna.
- The General Assembly serves as the main platform for discussions and policy-making within the United Nations.
- The Security Council is responsible for maintaining international peace and security, consisting of 15 members, including five permanent members (China, France, Russia, United Kingdom and United States) and 10 non-permanent members elected for two-year terms.
- The Economic and Social Council focuses on coordinating and reviewing policies related to economic, social, and environmental issues.
- The International Court of Justice, based in The Hague, Netherlands, is the primary judicial organ of the United Nations.
- Trygve Lie of Norway served as the first Secretary-General of the UN, and Antonio Guterres is the current Secretary-General, succeeding Ban Ki-moon.

Non-permanent members of the United Nations Security Council (UNSC)

Country	Term Ends
India, Ireland, Kenya, Mexico, and Norway	2022
Albania, Brazil, Gabon, Ghana, and United Arab Emirates	2023
Ecuador, Japan, Malta, Mozambique, and Switzerland	2024
Algeria, Guyana, Republic of Korea, Sierra Leone, and Slovenia	2025
Denmark, Greece, Pakistan, Panama, and Somalia	2026

Important UN Agencies

Name	Established	Headquarter	Purpose
International Telecommunication Union (ITU)	1865	Geneva	Sets international regulations for telecommunication and space communications.
International Labour Organisation (ILO)	1919	Geneva	Improves working conditions and living standards for workers.
International Monetary Fund (IMF)	1944	Washington, DC	Promotes international monetary cooperation.
United Nations Children's Fund (UNICEF)	1946	New York	Promotes children's welfare worldwide.
Food and Agricultural Organisation (FAO)	1945	Rome	Improves living conditions of rural populations.
United Nations Educational, Scientific and Cultural Organisation (UNESCO)	1945	Paris	Promotes collaboration among nations in education, science, and culture.
World Health Organisation (WHO)	1948	Geneva	Aims for the highest level of health for all people.
International Atomic Energy Agency (IAEA)	1957	Vienna	Promotes peaceful uses of atomic energy.
International Development Association (IDA)	1960	Washington, DC	Affiliated with the World Bank, aims to help underdeveloped countries raise living standards.

United Nations Development Programme (UNDP)	1965	New York	Assists developing countries in increasing the wealth-producing capabilities of their resources.
United Nations Environmental Programme (UNEP)	1972	Nairobi	Promotes international cooperation in environmental matters.
United Nations Office on Drugs and Crime (UNODC)	1997	Vienna	Prevents illicit trafficking and abuse of drugs, and focuses on crime prevention.
UN Women	2010	New York	Promotes gender equality and women empowerment.
World Food Programme	1961	Rome	Aims to eradicate hunger and malnutrition.
United Nations High Commissioner for Refugees	1950	Geneva	
United Nations Conference on Trade and Development	1964	Geneva	
United Nations Industrial Development Organization	1966	Vienna	
International Civil Aviation Organization	1944	Montreal	
Universal Postal Union	1874	Bern	

Other International Organizations and Groups

Name	Established	Headquarter	Objective
The Commonwealth	1926	London	An association of sovereign and independent states formerly part of the British empire.
Asia Pacific Economic Cooperation (APEC)	1989	Singapore	Promotes trade and investment in the Pacific basin.
Asian Development Bank (ADB)	1966	Manila	Promotes regional economic cooperation.
Association of South-East Asian Nations (ASEAN)	1967	Jakarta	Enhances regional cooperation in Southeast Asia.
Commonwealth of Independent States (CIS)	1991	Minsk	Coordinates inter-commonwealth relations and provides a mechanism for the dissolution of the USSR.
Group of 7 (G-7)	1975	-	Promotes cooperation among major non-communist economic powers.
Group of 15 (G-15)	1989	Geneva	Promotes economic cooperation among developing nations.
International Olympic Committee (IOC)	1894	Lausanne	Promotes Olympic ideals and administers Olympic games.
International Organisation for Standardisation (ISO)	1947	Geneva	Promotes the development of international standards.
Non-Aligned Movement (NAM)	1961	-	Political cooperation separate from the influence of both the USA and USSR during the Cold War era.
European Union (EU)	1993	Brussels	Aims to create a united Europe with strong economic and political bonds.
North Atlantic Treaty Organisation (NATO)	1949	Brussels	Ensures mutual defense and cooperation among member states.
Organisation of Petroleum Exporting Countries (OPEC)	1960	Vienna	Sets world oil prices and pursues member interests in trade and development.
South Asian Association for Regional Cooperation (SAARC)	1985	Kathmandu	Promotes economic, social, and cultural cooperation among member countries.
Amnesty International (AI)	1961	London	Monitors and advocates for human rights worldwide.
World Wildlife Fund (WWF) for Nature	1961	Gland	Works to save wildlife from extinction.
Shanghai Cooperation Organisation (SCO)	2001	Beijing	Strengthens relations and cooperation among member countries in various fields such as security and economics.
Gulf Cooperation Council (GCC)	1981	Riyadh	Promotes cooperation among states bordering the Persian Gulf.

Bay of Bengal Initiative for Multi-Sectoral Technical and Economic Cooperation (BIMSTEC)	1997	Dhaka	Promotes multi-sectoral cooperation among member countries in the Bay of Bengal region.
World Trade Organisation (WTO)	1995	Geneva	Establishes rules for world trade to reduce tariffs.
Organisation for Economic Cooperation and Development (OECD)	1961	Paris	Stimulates economic progress and world trade.

Indian Railways

History and Important Facts of Railways

- The first train in India was inaugurated on 16th April 1853, running between Mumbai and Thane.
- The second train in India started operating in 1854, connecting Howrah and Hoogly.
- The Indian Railway Board was established in 1905, with its headquarters located in New Delhi.
- Indian Railways was nationalized in 1950.
- Indian Railways holds the first position among Asian nations and is the fourth largest railway network in the world.
- The first electric train in India, "Deccan Queen", was introduced in 1929 on the Mumbai-Pune route.
- Indian Railways is the largest public sector enterprise in the country.
- It has the second largest electrified system globally, following Russia.
- The fastest train in India is the Train 18 or Vande Bharat Express, which was flagged off by Prime Minister Narendra Modi on 15th February 2019 from the New Delhi railway station.
- Vande Bharat Express covers the Delhi-Varanasi route in 9 hours and 45 minutes, with stoppages at Kanpur and Prayagraj.
- The maximum speed of Vande Bharat Express is 160 km/hour.
- The train was indigenously produced at the Integral Coach Factory, Chennai, within 18 months.
- The total track length covered by Indian Railways is 121,407 km.
- There are 7,325 passenger railway stations in India.
- The largest railway yard of Indian Railways is the Deen Dayal Upadhyaya Yard.
- The longest railway platform in India is at Hubballi Railway Station, Karnataka, measuring approximately 1,507 meters.
- The highest freight revenue generating station in India, after Mumbai, is Dhanbad, known as the Coal Capital of India.
- The longest route train in India is the "Vivek Express" which runs from Dibrugarh in Assam to Kanyakumari in Tamil Nadu.
- The second longest train in the country is the "Himsagar Express" that runs from Jammu Tawi to Kanyakumari, covering a total route of 3726 kilometers and passing through ten states.
- The first metro rail in India was introduced on 24th October 1984, between Dumdum and Belgachhia railway stations in Kolkata, West Bengal.
- Currently, 13 states in India have functional metro rail facilities.
- The longest railway tunnel in India is located in the Pir Panjal Range of the Himalayas in Jammu and Kashmir, spanning 11 km.
- The first railway bridge in India was the Dapoorie Viaduct on the Mumbai-Thane route in Thane, Maharashtra.
- The first mile-long railway tunnel in India is the Parsik Tunnel.
- The world's longest railway route is the Trans-Siberian Railways.
- India's first computerized railway reservation system started in New Delhi in 1986.
- The Railway Staff College is located in Baroda (Vadodara).

Facts About Railway Tracks

- According to the distance between railway lines, there are three systems operating in the country:
  - Broad Gauge - Distance: 1.676 meters
  - Meter Gauge - Distance: 1.00 meter
  - Narrow Gauge - Distance: 0.762 or 0.610 meters

Railway Manufacturing Units

Manufacturing Unit	Location	Product
Chittaranjan Locomotive Works (CLW)	Chittaranjan, West Bengal	Electric engines
Diesel Locomotive Works (DLW)	Varanasi, Uttar Pradesh	Diesel engines
Integral Coach Factory (ICF)	Perambur, Tamil Nadu	Rail coaches
Wheel and Axle Plant	Yelahanka, Karnataka	Wheels and axles
Diesel Component Works	Patiala, Punjab	Components of diesel engines
Rail Coach Factory	Kapurthala, Punjab	Railway coaches
Konkan Rail Project (Konkan Railway)	Maharashtra, Goa, Karnataka, Kerala	Joint venture project

❑❑❑